THE SOCIAL PSYCHOLOGY OF AGGRESSION

Thoroughly revised and updated, this third edition offers a comprehensive and up-to-date overview of the social psychology of aggression, covering all the relevant major theories, individual differences, situational factors, and applied contexts.

Understanding the causes, forms, and consequences of aggression and violence is critical for dealing with these harmful forms of social behaviour. Addressing a range of sub-topics, the first part deals with the definition and measurement of aggression, presents major theories, examines the development of aggression and discusses individual and gender differences in aggressive behaviour. It covers the role of situational factors in eliciting aggression and the impact of exposure to violence in the media. The second part examines specific forms and manifestations of aggression, including chapters on aggression in everyday contexts and in the family, sexual aggression, intergroup aggression, and terrorism. The new edition also includes additional coverage of gender differences, gun violence, and terrorism, to reflect the latest research developments in the field.

Also discussing strategies for reducing and preventing aggression, this book is essential reading for students and researchers in psychology and related disciplines, as well as practitioners and policy makers.

Barbara Krahé is Professor of Social Psychology at the University of Potsdam, Germany. She was awarded the German Psychology Prize for her work on aggression in 2015 and has served as President of the International Society for Research on Aggression.

THE SOCIAL PSYCHOLOGY OF AGGRESSION

Third Edition

BARBARA KRAHÉ

Routledge
Taylor & Francis Group

LONDON AND NEW YORK

Third edition published 2021
by Routledge
2 Park Square, Milton Park, Abingdon, Oxon OX14 4RN

and by Routledge
52 Vanderbilt Avenue, New York, NY 10017

Routledge is an imprint of the Taylor & Francis Group, an informa business

First edition published by Psychology Press 2001
Second edition published by Psychology Press 2013

British Library Cataloguing-in-Publication Data
A catalogue record for this book is available from the British Library

Library of Congress Cataloging-in-Publication Data
A catalog record has been requested for this book

ISBN: 978-1-138-60850-4 (hbk)
ISBN: 978-1-138-60852-8 (pbk)
ISBN: 978-0-429-46649-6 (ebk)

Typeset in Giovanni Book, Bookman and Helvetica Neue
by Newgen Publishing UK

For Arthur, Rosa, and Hassanatou

CONTENTS

Preface to the Third Edition

In the two decades since the first edition of this book was published, the world has changed dramatically, and many of these changes are related to aggression. Millions of people have had to flee from their homes and livelihoods as a result of violent conflict, terrorist attacks have caused an unprecedented number of deaths, mass shootings have shocked the world, and hate speech in digital media has almost become commonplace. At the same time, great progress has been made across many areas of psychological research in studying aggressive behaviour in its different forms and promoting the understanding of its causes and consequences. Thus, the time has come for an updated review of what we know about aggressive behaviour based on the current state of knowledge in social psychology.

For this third edition, all chapters were thoroughly revised, with lots of new content added, and readers will note that the reference list consists predominantly of sources that came out in the last ten years, after work on the second edition had been completed. Preference was given to meta-analyses and systematic reviews over a discussion of individual studies. The chapter structure has remained largely unchanged, with a few exceptions: Research on the development of aggression and on individual differences in aggression, formerly discussed in one chapter, is now presented in two separate and extended chapters (Chapters 3 and 4). A new section on the availability of firearms has been added to the discussion of situational factors promoting aggression in Chapter 5. An updated selection of key texts for further reading is offered at the end of each chapter, followed by a list of "tasks to do" to prompt readers to go beyond the contents presented in the text and embark on their own investigations of key aspects of aggression related to life in their part of the world.

ACKNOWLEDGEMENTS

In working on this third edition, I received most valuable support from a number of people. I am indebted to my colleagues Eduardo Vasquez and Ralf Wölfer for their constructive comments and suggestions on how to improve the structure and contents. I am also very grateful to Eleanor Taylor, Alex Howard, Lauren Ellis, and Jane Fieldsend at Routledge for their efficient and cooperative handling of the manuscript, which made the production stage a smooth and enjoyable experience.

Closer to home, I would like to thank the current members of my group at Potsdam, Robert Busching, Johannes Lutz, Juliette Marchewka, Marika Skowronski, and Paulina Tomaszewska, and former members Anja Berger, Steffen Bieneck, Janis Jung, Fabian Kirsch, Ingrid Möller, Helena Rohlf, Isabell Schuster, and Lylla D'Abreu Winzer, for their collaborative input to the studies from our lab, many of which are cited in the different chapters. I am even more grateful to them for being such a fabulous team and for all the inspiring discussions about aggression and other challenging research topics we have had over many years. The help of Ariane Scheffner in preparing the manuscript is also gratefully acknowledged.

The biggest thank you goes to my family for their constant encouragement, support, and pleasant distractions, during and well beyond the current project.

I dedicate the third edition to three special young people in my life, wishing that the research presented in this book may help to create a non-aggressive, peaceful world in which they can grow up in happiness and security.

INTRODUCTION

The latest report on the "Global Burden of Armed Violence" issued by the Geneva Declaration on Armed Violence and Development estimated that between 2007 and 2012, 377,000 people died each year around the world as the result of intentional homicide. In addition, 70,000 deaths occurred as a direct result of armed conflict (Geneva Declaration on Armed Violence and Development, 2015). These figures are assumed to be conservative estimates because many countries do not have reliable incidence reporting systems and are likely to underreport violent deaths. The number of fatalities from violent action, shocking as it is, represents only the tip of the iceberg as far as the scale of aggression worldwide is concerned. Another global report, the "Global Status Report on Violence Prevention" published by the World Health Organization (2014), presented data on the prevalence of various forms of non-fatal interpersonal violence and concluded that "women, children and elderly people bear the burden of the non-fatal consequences of physical, sexual and psychological abuse" (p. 13). In 2020, the Global Status Report on Preventing Violence against Children estimated that one in two children between the ages of 2 and 17 years worldwide experience violence each year, which includes physical and psychological abuse by caregivers, exposure to intimate partner violence in their family, sexual abuse, bullying by peers, and homicide (World Health Organization, 2020).

Although the focus of the research presented in this volume will be on the social and psychological costs, it is important to recognise that aggression and violence also incur heavy material costs for societies in different domains, such as losses in gross domestic product or overall work productivity, and expenses for health care and criminal justice systems. Hoeffler (2017) presented a calculation of the material cost of violence for societies in different world regions for the year 2013, applying different measures of cost. One metric by which costs can be compared across regions and across forms of violence is the percentage of costs incurred by violence relative to the gross domestic product, which indicates a region's or country's productivity. Her analysis found that the worldwide costs of violence by that measure were 0.20% for collective violence (including civil and international war, refugee populations, and terrorism), 5.18% for intimate partner violence, and 4.21% for non-fatal child abuse within the family. These findings show that, contrary to what might be expected, everyday forms of aggression in the family are much more costly for societies than large-scale political violence that receives a far greater amount of attention (see Chapter 8 for a discussion of psychological research on aggression in the family).

The analysis in this book takes a broad perspective on aggression that extends beyond severe forms of physical violence and considers all forms of social behaviour that are carried out with the intention to harm another person or group of persons (see Chapter 1 for definitions and different forms of aggression). Given the complexity of human aggression and its underlying causes, it is clear that no single discipline can offer a comprehensive understanding of its manifestations, causes, and consequences. Therefore, it should be stated at the outset what issues are at the focus of the *social psychological* perspective on aggression adopted in this volume, and what aspects fall within the realm of other fields.

From a social psychological point of view, aggression is a social problem in interactions between individuals and groups, resulting from the joint influence of the personal characteristics of the actors and the situational and societal conditions in which their behaviour takes place. Accordingly, when considering *manifestations* of aggression, the focus will be on aggressive behaviour that occurs in social relationships between individuals and/or groups and is prompted by certain features of more stable social environments or specific situational circumstance. This focus means that other forms of aggression, such as self-destructive behaviour, psychopathological or criminal forms of aggression, or the destruction of material objects, will not be included in the discussion. Similarly, in terms of *explaining* the occurrence of aggressive behaviour, the focus will be on individual differences that emerge in the course of development and interact with situational states as well as more stable factors in the social environment. Other causal influences, such as hormonal processes, are considered only insofar as they influence a person's readiness to engage in aggressive social interactions. Finally, our examination of the *consequences* of aggression will focus on the psychological functioning of both victims and perpetrators in the context of their social relationships, excluding such issues as the forensic or psychiatric treatment of aggressive offenders and therapeutic help for targets of aggressive behaviour in coping with their victimisation.

In addition to stating what will, and will not, be covered in the chapters to follow, the present volume should be positioned in the existing social psychological literature on aggression. Readers looking for a concise summary of the main issues and findings of aggression research will find a chapter on aggression in every textbook of social psychology. Those seeking in-depth analyses of particular topics will find excellent collections of specialised papers in handbooks and edited volumes, such as those by Bushman (2017), Ireland, Birch, and Ireland (2018), and Sturmey (2017). The present volume takes an intermediate position between these two levels of specificity. It aims to provide an up-to-date and critical overview of aggression research from a social psychological perspective, so as to inform readers about the central concepts, issues, and findings in the study of aggression. Furthermore, it is intended to create a knowledge base from which the more specialised literature can be approached.

Aggression research has made enormous progress in the last decade, both in quantity and quality. The majority of studies covered in this third edition have been published after work on the second edition was completed, resulting in a thorough update and extension of the reference list. This is not to say that the older sources have become obsolete. Instead, it is a reflection of the fact that the older studies have informed new research that built on their findings and developed them further. For example, interventions to reduce gang violence or sexual aggression were made more effective based on systematic evaluations that revealed the strengths and limitations of earlier programmes. Wherever possible, systematic reviews and meta-analyses were included to facilitate a full picture of the current state of knowledge on a particular issue. In addition, a focus was laid on new experimental and longitudinal studies to gain a better understanding of the causes of aggressive behaviour and the efficacy of interventions.

Stepping back to look at the 20 years since the first edition came out, the impression is that few of the findings and conclusions suggested by the evidence that was available then need to be reversed or revised in a substantial way in the light of new evidence that was accumulated in the meantime. But with improved research designs and statistical tools, we can have greater confidence in the soundness in the findings. At the same time, psychological research has responded in a flexible way to new forms of aggression or the identification of neglected areas of research, for example by studying aggression in the context of social media or recognising the need for improved interventions addressing sexual aggression.

A PREVIEW OF THE CHAPTERS

The dual role of social psychological aggression research as a basic and an applied field of study is reflected in the chapters of the present volume. In the first part, basic issues of definition, measurement, and explanation will be discussed, which are of general significance to the understanding of aggressive behaviour irrespective of its specific manifestations. In the second part, this body of knowledge will be applied to the analysis of specific forms and contexts of aggressive behaviour.

Chapter 1 sets the stage by presenting definitions and characteristic features of aggressive behaviour and introducing the main methodologies for measuring aggression. The advantages and limitations of studying aggression in the realistic contexts of naturally occurring situations or in the artificially created, but better controlled settings of the psychological laboratory play an important part in this discussion.

Chapter 2 presents an overview of theories explaining aggressive behaviour, dividing them into approaches that stress the biological foundations of aggressive behaviour and those that explain aggression as the result of psychological processes. It will become clear that the different theories encompass a broad spectrum of conceptualisations of the causes of aggressive behaviour and the processes that lead to aggression. The General Aggression Model (Anderson & Bushman, 2018) will be presented as a framework that integrates personal and situational input variables, internal psychological processes, and social consequences of aggression into a comprehensive theoretical model.

Chapter 3 is concerned with the development of aggressive behaviour, starting in infancy and following trajectories of development through childhood and adolescence. Research will be discussed which shows that aggressive behaviour tends to decline from early childhood to adolescence in line with children's cognitive development and self-regulation capacities, but that some children do not follow this age-normative pattern. Emotional and cognitive processes as well as influences in the child's social environment will be discussed to explain individual differences in the development of aggressive behaviour.

Individual differences in adulthood in the tendency to engage in aggressive behaviour will be examined in *Chapter 4*. Everyday experience tells us that people vary considerably in their tendency to show aggressive behaviour. Some respond with aggression to the slightest provocation that does not seem to bother others at all. Individual differences in aggression in adulthood show a high stability over the life course, and we will examine psychological constructs that may explain these differences, such as trait anger, narcissism, and lack of self-control. Furthermore, gender differences in aggression will be discussed. Traditionally, it has been assumed that men are more aggressive than women, and this assumption is supported, at least for physical aggression. The focus on male aggression has meant that women's aggressive behaviour has been largely neglected by researchers in the past. However, recent years have seen an increasing interest in female aggression, stimulated in part by the introduction of the concept of relational aggression and by the controversy about women as perpetrators of intimate partner violence.

In *Chapter 5*, situational factors will be examined which facilitate aggressive behaviour and can explain why individuals are more likely to act aggressively in some situations than in others. The discussion includes a large body of research examining the disinhibiting effects of alcohol, the experience of social exclusion as a precipitator of aggression, the role of aggressive cues that enhance the salience of aggression as a potential response, the availability of firearms, and the role of environmental stressors, such as heat and crowding. Throughout this chapter it will be shown that no matter how powerful situational factors are as determinants of behaviour, they do not affect individuals in a uniform way. Therefore, for a proper assessment of the determinants of aggression, the impact of situational factors needs to be considered in interaction with individual difference variables.

Chapter 6 focuses on the effects of violent media contents on aggressive behaviour in viewers. This chapter addresses an issue that has attracted intense controversy, particularly in public debate and in confrontation between social scientists and the user community as well as the media industry. Three aspects will be at the focus of the analysis: (a) the strength of the evidence addressing the general question of whether exposure to violent media contents leads to increased aggression in viewers, in particular children and adolescents, both in the short term and over time; (b) the psychological processes by which violent media stimuli may increase users' aggression, both after a single exposure and as a result of habitual use of violent media over time; and (c) the role of pornography, especially violent pornography, in promoting aggression generally, and sexual aggression in particular.

The first six chapters present basic concepts and psychological processes that play a role in explaining who is likely to show aggressive behaviour under what circumstances. The research covered in these chapters highlights the interaction between individual dispositions and situational influences, both in the development of aggressive behaviour over time and in the emergence of aggression in a particular context. In combination, this research lays the foundations for a more detailed examination of specific forms of aggression in different domains of life, which is offered in the second part of the book.

Chapter 7 examines different forms of aggression that are common in everyday life in the public sphere. Bullying in school and at the workplace are forms of aggression that are characterised by an imbalance of power between perpetrators and victims and typically take place over extended periods of time. Both forms of aggression can have severe negative consequences for the victims, and there is evidence that the victims of bullying in school are at higher risk of being victimised again in the workplace. Aggressive driving is another form of aggression that is common in everyday life, not least because road traffic presents many frustrations. Finally, this chapter reviews research on aggression and violence in the context of the sports world, as shown by competitors as well as spectators.

Chapter 8 covers a broad literature dealing with aggression in the family. It examines the prevalence, risk factors, and outcomes of children's exposure to aggression in their families, including physical abuse, sexual abuse, psychological abuse, and witnessing violence between parents and other family members. Research studying violence against intimate partners will be presented with a focus on gender differences in perpetration and victimisation, and evidence on abuse of elders in the family will be reviewed as an increasingly recognised social problem. Unlike aggressive behaviour in the public domain, these forms of aggression occur in the confined sphere of the home, making it easier for perpetrators to conceal their aggression and more difficult for their victims to attract attention to their plight. At the same time, they are particularly traumatising because the victims are harmed by the very people whom they love and trust.

A similar point can be made for sexual aggression, which is the topic of *Chapter 9*. The majority of sexual assaults involve individuals who know each other, often in the context of intimate relationships. We will review a large body of evidence on the prevalence of sexual aggression in heterosexual and same-sex relationships. Explanations and risk factors for sexual aggression at the societal and the individual level will be discussed, as well as factors associated with increased vulnerability to sexual victimisation. Following a review of research on the consequences of sexual assault for the victims, the final section explores a recent and controversial issue on the agenda of sexual aggression research, namely women's sexual aggression against men.

The following two chapters move the perspective from interpersonal aggression between two or more individuals to intergroup aggression involving the real or imagined presence of different social groups. *Chapter 10* examines the problem of aggression and violence between social groups. Following a discussion of two influential social psychological explanations of intergroup conflict, the *theory of realistic group conflict* and *social identity theory*, it presents research on gang violence and on hate crimes involving aggression towards targets selected on the basis of their ethnic group membership, religious affiliation, or sexual orientation. It also reviews evidence on the conditions under which people behave aggressively when they are part of a crowd.

Chapter 11 addresses terrorist violence as a special form of intergroup conflict that has plagued the world for many years with little sign of abatement. Psychological research is presented that seeks to explain why people are attracted to terrorism to the point of sacrificing their own life, but also why out of a large number of disenchanted individuals, only a few end up committing terrorist acts of violence. It will also be asked why terrorists find support for their violent actions in their communities, and how the experience or fear of terrorist violence affects people's attitudes, behaviours, and psychological well-being.

Chapter 12 discusses strategies aimed at controlling and preventing aggressive behaviour. Compared to the extensive knowledge based on causes of aggression, the evidence about effective ways of controlling and preventing aggression is slim, and the demand for strategies based on sound theoretical models and empirical evidence remains high. The chapter will begin by looking at general strategies that are potentially applicable to many forms of aggressive behaviour, for example observational learning or punishment. These include societal-level interventions, such as the deterrent function of capital punishment and the potential effectiveness of tighter gun-control legislation. and measures targeting the individual aggressors in an attempt to change their emotions, cognitions, and behaviour. This review will be followed by an examination of measures custom-tailored to deal with specific forms of aggression, such as gang violence, domestic violence, and sexual aggression.

Finally, *Chapter 13* presents some concluding thoughts and a brief outlook to a future interdisciplinary agenda for the study of aggression and violence.

Each chapter ends with a summary of the main topics and conclusions and lists sources for further reading. In addition, specific tasks are suggested to encourage readers to embark on a more active search for information and independent thinking about some of the issues raised in the chapters. Because of the nature of aggression as inherently harmful and distressing, much of the research covered in this book makes grim reading. Nevertheless, I hope that readers will enjoy diving into this prolific field of research and feel better equipped to join the professional and societal discourse about what social psychology has to offer in understanding aggressive behaviour.

Chapter 1

AGGRESSION AS SOCIAL BEHAVIOUR: DEFINITION AND MEASUREMENT

aggression: any form of behaviour intended to harm or injure another living being who is motivated to avoid such treatment.

The word *aggression* derives from the Latin verb "aggredi", which means "to approach" or "to go to" and has found its way from Latin into a wide range of different languages. From the early 18th century onward, this broad and neutral meaning has been narrowed into a more circumscribed definition of "attack", with negative connotations of approaching others in an unfriendly, hostile, or harmful way. Beyond this basic definition, the term leaves much room for interpretation. How exactly do we decide if a certain behaviour is aggressive or not, what are the different forms in which aggressive behaviour appears, is all aggressive behaviour negative, or is there something like a "healthy" level of aggression that enables people to stand up for themselves in different domains of life?

When you raise these questions with your friends or colleagues, you will discover great diversity in how people use the term aggression to interpret their own and others' behaviour. For instance, is it aggression to spread rumours about an unfriendly colleague or is this just common workplace behaviour? Is it aggression to smack a child that has ignored a parent's command or is it just part of normal child-rearing practices? Is there such a thing as sexual aggression in marriage or do husbands have the right to overcome their wives' refusal to have sex with them?

These examples show that the meaning of "aggression" is socially constructed, which means it is defined on the basis of a shared understanding in a society in a given historical period. In the course of this book, we will see that physical punishment was considered a legitimate way of disciplining children until fairly recently, and is still seen and practised as such by parents in many societies across the world. Similarly, questioning a husband's right to force his wife to have sex with him at his convenience, and calling such behaviour marital rape, is a relatively recent development in the Western world, and is by no means universally shared around the globe.

To set the stage for the research to be presented in this book, it is critical to be clear from the start what exactly psychologists mean when they study aggressive behaviour. We need to establish a consensus about the basic criteria for deciding whether or not a given behaviour should be classified as aggressive, and to think about ways of categorising different forms of aggression to come to grips with the multiple ways in which aggressive behaviour may present itself.

Once it is clear how the object of study is defined, the next step is to ask how aggression can be measured. It should go without saying that the findings generated by empirical research always need to be interpreted against the background of the methods by which they were obtained. However, in the public debate about aggression, conclusions about causes and consequences of aggression are typically discussed without much attention to their methodological foundations. Therefore, it seems appropriate that a review of the scholarly literature on aggression should start by looking at the definitions and methodological strategies adopted in this field.

WHAT IS AGGRESSION?

The term "aggression" is as firmly established in ordinary language as it is in the vocabulary of social psychologists. Unfortunately, just because people use the same term, they do not necessarily agree about its meaning, and this is clearly true for aggression. For example, when prompted for their definition of aggression, laypersons often mention "good" or "healthy" aggression in addition to "bad" aggression. For social psychologists, as we will see below, there is no positive meaning of aggression. They see aggression as a negative form of social behaviour that causes problems between individuals, groups, and societies.

Beyond the basic consensus about conceptualising aggression as a form of negative or antisocial behaviour, more precise definitions are needed to specify the criteria by which a behaviour is categorised as "aggressive". A classic definition was proposed by Buss (1961) who characterised aggression as "a response that delivers noxious stimuli to another organism" (p. 1). However, this purely behaviourist definition is too broad in some ways and too narrow in others. It is too broad because it includes many forms of behaviour that should not be categorised as aggression, such as the accidental infliction of harm. At the same time, it is too narrow because it excludes all non-behavioural processes, such as thoughts and feelings, and – most importantly for a behavioural definition – it excludes behaviours that are intended to cause harm but, for whatever reason, fail to achieve their objective.

These limitations are addressed in the definition proposed by Baron and Richardson (1994). They suggested that the term "aggression" should be used to describe *"any form of behavior directed toward the goal of harming or injuring another living being who is motivated to avoid such treatment"*

(p. 7, emphasis in original). This definition is widely accepted (Parrott & Giancola, 2007), and it is also adopted for the present volume. Broadly speaking, "harm" denotes any form of treatment that is not wanted by the target persons, such as causing them physical injury, hurting their feelings, damaging their social relationships by spreading rumours about them, or taking away or destroying their cherished possessions. In terms of distinguishing aggression from other forms of social behaviour, the definition offered by Baron and Richardson (1994) has three important implications:

(1) Aggressive behaviour is characterised by its underlying motivation (to harm another living being), *not* by its consequences (whether or not harm actually occurs). This means that a behaviour is regarded as aggressive if it was guided by the intention to harm, even if no actual harm was caused to the target. According to this criterion, a gunshot that misses its target represents an aggressive act even though not a hair on the target's head may have been harmed. Focusing on the person's intention to harm also allows non-action to be classified as aggressive, such as the deliberate withholding of care or the refusal to help a person in need.

(2) Defining aggressive behaviour through the intention to harm implies the actor's *anticipation* that a specific action will produce a harmful outcome. If one person's actions lead to harm or injury of another, but the actor could not have foreseen those adverse effects, the actions do not qualify as aggressive behaviour. They may be due to carelessness or incompetence, but are excluded from the definition of aggression.

(3) Finally, defining aggression as harmful treatment that the target would want to *avoid* means that actions which may cause harm but are performed with the target's consent do not represent instances of aggression, such as injury inflicted in the context of sadomasochistic sexual practices.

It is important to add that, of course, individuals may act aggressively against themselves up to the point of taking their own life. However, self-inflicted harm does not fall within the above definition, as it does not involve harming "another person who is motivated to avoid such treatment". Therefore, self-harm is outside the social psychological perspective on aggression, which focusses on aggression as a form of social behaviour between individuals and groups.

Aggressive behaviour can appear in a great variety of forms. Rather than presenting a long and necessarily incomplete list of specific examples of aggressive behaviour, it is useful to look for broader dimensions by which aggressive behaviour may be described. Important aspects of a typology for mapping the many faces of aggressive behaviour are presented in Table 1.1.

TABLE 1.1 Aspects of a typology of aggressive behaviour

Defining aspect	Example
Response modality	
verbal	Shouting or swearing at someone
physical	Hitting or shooting someone
postural	Making threatening gestures
relational	Giving someone "the silent treatment"
Immediacy	
direct	Punching someone in the face
indirect	Spreading rumours about someone behind their back
Response quality	
active	Making another person engage in unwanted sexual acts
passive	Withholding important information from a colleague at work
Visibility	
overt	Humiliating someone in front of others
covert	Sending threatening anonymous messages to a classmate
Instigation	
proactive/unprovoked	Grabbing a toy from another child
reactive/retaliative	Yelling at someone after having been physically attacked
Goal direction	
hostile	Hitting someone out of anger or frustration
instrumental	Taking a hostage to secure a ransom
Type of harm	
physical	Broken bones
psychological/emotional	Undermining self-esteem or sense of safety
Duration of effects	
transient	Minor bruises
lasting	Long-term inability to form relationships
Social units involved	
individuals	Intimate partner violence
groups and societies	Riots and wars

relational aggression: behaviour intended to harm the target person through damaging their social relationships.

physical aggression: behaviour intended to cause physical harm to another person.

indirect aggression: aggression delivered behind the target person's back by damaging their social relationships, for example through spreading rumours.

As with any typology, some forms of aggression may fit into more than one category. This is true, for example, for *relational aggression*, which is often treated as a response modality that is distinguished from *physical aggression*, but it is also seen as a form of *indirect aggression* because it involves acting against other people behind their back (Archer & Coyne, 2005). Furthermore, the different aspects are not mutually exclusive.

Indeed, they need to be considered in conjunction to properly understand specific forms of aggression. For example, aggression can be driven by primarily hostile rather than instrumental motives, expressed overtly, in physical terms, and reactively as a response to a preceding provocation.

Although most of the aspects in Table 1.1 are self-explanatory, some of them require further comment. One such aspect is the distinction between *direct* and *indirect aggression* (Richardson, 2014). Direct aggression involves a face-to-face confrontation between the aggressor and the target, whereas indirect aggression is aimed at harming other people behind their back by spreading rumours about them or otherwise damaging their peer relationships (Björkqvist, Lagerspetz, & Österman, 1992). The term *relational aggression* is also used by some authors instead of indirect aggression to denote aggression aimed at harming the target person's social relationships (Crick & Grotpeter, 1995). Because indirect/relational aggression can be inflicted covertly, without the target being aware of the aggressor's identity, it represents an alternative strategy for harming another person when the costs of engaging in direct forms of aggression would be high (see also Chapter 4 for a detailed discussion of direct and indirect aggression in the context of gender differences).

The distinction between hostile and instrumental aggression refers to the psychological *function* of the aggressive behaviour for the actor. The primary motive for aggressive behaviour may be either the desire to harm another person as an expression of negative feelings, as in *hostile aggression*, or the aim of achieving an intended goal by means of the aggressive act, as in *instrumental aggression*. The two types of motivation for aggressive behaviour frequently coexist. Nevertheless, we shall see when discussing theories of aggressive behaviour that it makes sense to look at them separately, because different psychological processes may be involved (however, for a critical analysis of the instrumental/hostile distinction see Bushman & Anderson, 2001).

direct aggression: aggressive behaviour directed immediately at the target, such as hitting or shouting abuse.

hostile aggression: aggressive behaviour motivated by the desire to express anger and hostile feelings.

instrumental aggression: aggressive behaviour performed to reach a particular goal, as a means to an end.

An additional feature to be considered when defining aggression refers to the normative appraisal of the behaviour in question. Is aggression always to be condemned or are some forms of aggression accepted by social consensus? Whether or not the aspect of *norm violation* should be included among the defining features of aggression is controversial, which is why it was not listed in Table 1.1. Disciplinary measures used by parents and acts of physical self-defence are examples of behaviours that satisfy the criteria of intention, anticipation, and the target's desire to avoid them. Accordingly, they should be classified as aggressive. Yet they are covered by social norms that make them acceptable. Therefore, some authors have argued that behaviour should only be considered aggressive if it involves the violation of a social norm. However, as Berkowitz (1993) has pointed out, defining aggression in terms of norm-violating or socially unacceptable behaviour is problematic, as the normative evaluation of a behaviour often differs depending on the perspectives of the parties involved. For example, some people and cultures regard corporal punishment as an acceptable and effective child-rearing practice, while others consider it to be an unacceptable form of aggression.

A similar point can be made with regard to the distinction between *legitimate* and *illegitimate* aggression. Capital punishment, for example, satisfies all elements in the definition by Baron and Richardson (1994). Actions are carried out with the intention and anticipation of inflicting harm on the convicted person, who is motivated to avoid such treatment. However, these actions are legitimised in the laws of many countries. Is it therefore appropriate to regard them as aggression, provided that the legal procedures are properly conducted? Although many people will reject this idea, others may have a different view. In the absence of explicit legal regulations, the question of legitimacy becomes even more difficult. Are violent acts committed by separatist movements or oppressed minorities legitimate or illegitimate forms of aggression? It is obvious that the answer to this question will depend to a large extent on the position a person takes in the underlying controversy, as poignantly captured, for example, in the phrase "one person's terrorist is another person's freedom fighter". Therefore, although issues of norm violation and legitimacy are highly relevant, for example, when analysing dynamics of intergroup conflicts or justifications for aggressive behaviour, they are problematic to accommodate as critical features in a basic definition of aggression.

Before turning from the definition to the measurement of aggressive behaviour, we should briefly look at the meanings of three related terms, namely antisocial behaviour, coercion, and violence. *Antisocial behaviour* denotes behaviour that violates social norms of appropriate conduct (DeWall & Anderson, 2011). It is a broader construct than aggression in that it includes behaviours that are not intended to harm other people, such as vandalism or lying. *Coercion* is defined by Tedeschi and Felson (1994) as "an action taken with the intention of imposing harm on another person or forcing compliance" (p. 168). Defined in this way, coercion can be seen as a form of instrumental aggression. Coercive action can take the form of

antisocial behaviour: behaviour that violates social norms about appropriate conduct.

threats, punishments, or bodily force, and it is directed as much at gaining compliance as at causing harm. Coercion is seen as a form of social influence, which highlights the social nature of this type of behaviour and brings it conceptually closer to processes of communication and interaction not previously examined in the context of aggression.

In contrast to antisocial behaviour and coercion, which are broader constructs than aggression, the term *violence* is more narrow in meaning and is restricted to behaviours carried out with the intention to cause serious harm that involve the use or threat of *physical force*, such as hitting someone over the head, or – in the ultimate form – taking another person's life. Thus, not all instances of aggression involve violence (e.g., shouting at someone would be described as aggressive, but not violent), but all acts of violence qualify as aggression. Violence is defined by social psychologists as "the infliction of intense force upon persons or property for the purposes of destruction, punishment, or control" (Geen, 1995, p. 669) or as "physically damaging assaults which are not socially legitimised in any way" (Archer & Browne, 1989, p. 11). These definitions by psychologists are in line with the definition proposed by the World Health Organization. It describes violence as

> the intentional use of physical force or power, threatened or actual, against oneself, another person, or against a group or community, that either results in or has a high likelihood of resulting in injury, death, psychological harm, maldevelopment or deprivation.
>
> (Krug, Dahlberg, Mercy, Zwi, & Lozano, 2002, p. 49)

violence: behaviours carried out with the intention to cause serious harm that involve the use or threat of physical force.

A functional typology of violence has been presented by Mattaini, McGowan, and Williams (1996), who identified six potential functions of violent behaviour: (1) change of, or escape from, aversive situations; (2) positive reinforcement (i.e., attainment of a particular goal); (3) release of negative affective arousal; (4) resolution of conflict; (5) gaining of respect; and (6) attack on a culturally defined "enemy" (i.e., a member of a devalued outgroup).

A special form of violence has been termed structural violence and denotes societal conditions that entail harmful consequences for certain social groups. Structural violence is seen as a feature of social systems that leads to social inequality and injustice – for example, by institutionalising a power hierarchy between men and women, which leaves women largely unprotected against male sexual coercion (Lubek, 1995). In the present analysis, the focus will be on violence between individuals and social groups, but issues of structural violence will also be touched upon in several places in the course of our discussion.

HOW TO MEASURE AGGRESSION

Measuring aggressive behaviour according to the standards of systematic empirical research poses particular challenges for researchers due to its potentially harmful nature. When studying prosocial behaviour, for example, researchers can create experimental situations in which research participants may give help to others. By contrast, designing experiments in which research participants may inflict harm on another person, become targets of other participants' aggressive behaviour, or are exposed to treatments expected to increase the likelihood that they will show aggressive behaviour is problematic from an ethical point of view.

With regard to studying aggression in real life outside the laboratory, other problems arise. With the exception of unusual circumstances, such as war or civil unrest, acts of severe aggression are relatively rare in everyday life, which makes them hard to measure in natural contexts. Therefore, the methodological toolbox available to aggression researchers is quite limited, and they often have to resort to artificial contexts to reconcile experimental rigour and ethical feasibility. Table 1.2 presents an overview of the different methods used by social psychologists to study aggressive behaviour as well as aggressive thoughts and feelings.

Existing measures of aggression may be broadly classified into two categories: measures relying on direct observation and measures relying on reports of aggressive behaviours that the researchers have not been able to observe directly. Observational methods enable researchers to gain first-hand evidence of aggressive behaviour in a given situation, either in the laboratory or in the field. Measures based on reporting provide them with second-hand accounts of aggressive behaviour that can cover longer periods of time and a wider spectrum of situations. The approaches in each group have both strengths and limitations, as will become evident in the following discussion.

Observing aggressive behaviour in natural contexts

Observing aggression "in the field" (i.e., under natural conditions) is a good strategy because information can be collected in an unobtrusive way without people realising that their behaviour is being observed and

TABLE 1.2 Summary of methods for studying aggression	
(1) *Observing behaviour in natural contexts*	Naturalistic observation
	Field experiments
(2) *Observing behaviour in the laboratory*	Teacher–learner paradigm
	Essay evaluation paradigm
	Competitive reaction time task
	Hot sauce paradigm
	Tangram help/hurt task
(3) *Collecting reports of aggressive behaviour, thoughts, and feelings*	Self-reports of aggressive behaviour
	Parent or teacher reports
	Peer nominations
	Measures of anger and hostility
	Implicit Association Test
	Projective techniques
(4) *Using official records*	Crime statistics
	Archival data

recorded. With a behaviour such as aggression that everybody knows to be socially undesirable, this is a particular advantage because it avoids the problem of measurement *reactivity* (i.e., people's tendency to change their usual patterns of behaviour because they are aware that they are under observation). At the same time, the fact that people are not made aware that they are being observed – and therefore have no chance to opt out – poses particularly strict ethical constraints on this type of method. Observational measures in natural contexts mainly come in two forms: *naturalistic observation* in which the researcher records behaviour as it unfolds naturally without manipulating the situation in any way, and *field experiments* that involve a systematic, yet unobtrusive manipulation of certain variables to observe the effects of that manipulation on the likelihood of aggressive behaviour.

Naturalistic observation. One aim of observation in natural contexts is to obtain a picture of the various forms of aggression in a particular setting, and the frequency with which they occur (Lampe, Mulder, Colins, & Vermeiren, 2017). It is a suitable method in settings in which the spontaneous occurrence of aggressive behaviour is sufficiently high to generate

naturalistic observation: recording the natural occurrence of aggressive behaviour in everyday situations.

field experiment: manipulating conditions in everyday situations to observe the effects of the manipulation on the likelihood of aggressive behaviour.

enough counts of behaviour per time unit of observation such as on a school playground during break time.

For example, Graham & Wells (2001) conducted an observational study in 12 bars in Ontario, Canada, to record the frequency of aggressive incidents among young adults. Aggressive incidents were defined as involving "personal violation (verbal insults, unwanted physical contact), behavior that was offensive according to the norms of the place, or a dispute in which the participants had personal investment" (p. 197). Trained observers were positioned in different parts of the bar and recorded each aggressive incident. They observed, for example, that 77.8% of the incidents involved men only, 3.4% of them involved women only, and the remaining incidents involved both men and women. In a third of all incidents, severe physical aggression (e.g., kicking, punching, brawling) occurred.

Naturalistic observation is particularly useful in studies with young children, who are not yet able to provide self-report data or participate in structured laboratory experiments. In a study by Ostrov and Keating (2004), trained observers watched preschool children during a free-play situation and recorded their behaviour as physical aggression (e.g., hitting, pushing, punching), *verbal aggression* (e.g., antagonistic teasing, calling mean names), or relational aggression (e.g., excluding from playgroup, ignoring a peer). Frequency counts of behaviours in each category were summed up to yield physical, verbal, and relational aggressiveness scores for each child.

verbal aggression: use of verbal means, such as insults, to cause harm to another person.

In this type of research, the natural flow of behaviour is first recorded, then broken down into more fine-grained units of analysis, and finally assigned to the pre-defined categories. Questions of when and where to sample behaviour and how to define the basic units of analysis are central to this methodological approach (e.g., Wehby & Symons, 1996).

Moreover, it is important to check how reliably the units can be assigned to the different categories by examining the correspondence achieved by independent coders. As noted in the comprehensive review by Lampe et al. (2017), existing observational studies demonstrate the feasibility of coding natural occurrences of different forms of aggressive behaviour with sufficient agreement between coders.

Field experiments. Another line of research using observation in natural contexts is directed at exploiting inconspicuous everyday situations to examine the link between certain antecedent conditions and subsequent aggressive responses. Unlike naturalistic observation, where researchers do not interfere with the situation itself, field experiments involve the unobtrusive variation of one or more variables in order to assess their impact on aggressive behaviour as the dependent variable. For example, to test the prediction that de-individuation (not being personally identifiable; see Chapter 10) would lower the threshold for aggression, Rehm, Steinleitner, and Lilli (1987) asked a group of fifth-grade students to dress in identical T-shirts for their sports lessons, ostensibly so that a new teacher would find it easier to tell them apart from members of the opposing team, who wore their own clothes. The number of aggressive acts during the ensuing handball game was recorded by two independent observers who were unaware of the experimental hypotheses. Students who were wearing the uniform T-shirts committed more aggressive acts than students who were wearing their own clothes, supporting the prediction that anonymity increases the likelihood of aggressive behaviour.

As another example of a field experiment, Baron (1976) studied behaviour in a common traffic situation to test the hypothesis that drivers would show more aggressive behaviour when they were frustrated. *Frustration* was manipulated by the time that a confederate took to move his car when the traffic lights turned green. The dependent variable was drivers' aggressive behaviour, defined in terms of latency and duration of horn honking. In support of his prediction, Baron showed that the drivers, who were unaware that they were taking part in an experimental study, honked faster and longer when the confederate took longer to move his car. In a different context, a field experiment by Harris (1974), designed to test the frustration-aggression hypothesis (see Chapter 2), showed that people waiting in a queue responded more aggressively if a confederate jumped in close to the head of the queue (high frustration) than when he jumped in closer to the end of the queue (low frustration).

Despite their advantages in terms of facilitating the analysis of naturally occurring behaviour uncontaminated by social desirability concerns, such field experiments suffer from the problem that many additional variables may operate that are not under the experimenter's control. Suppose, for example, that the queue-jumping approach was to be used to study the aggressive responses of people waiting for a bus. There would be a problem if, in some of the trials, the bus for which people were waiting was already 15 minutes late at the time of the experimental intervention, creating an additional and powerful source of frustration that might contaminate

frustration: external interference with the goal-directed behaviour of the person.

the effects of the queue-jumping manipulation. In addition, a key feature of experimental research, namely the random allocation of participants to experimental conditions, is often not possible in natural contexts without making people aware that they are part of an experiment.

Observing aggressive behaviour in the laboratory

The lack of control over so-called "third variables" that might interfere with the experimental variations and problems with the assignment of respondents to experimental treatments are the main reasons why the vast majority of observational studies on aggressive behaviour have been conducted as *laboratory experiments*. In this setting, situations can be created by the investigator to meet three essential criteria:

(1) respondents are exposed to an experimental manipulation aimed at influencing their aggressive response tendencies
(2) they can be randomly assigned to the experimental and control conditions, and
(3) many factors which might influence participants' behaviour over and above the experimental treatment can be controlled.

Experimental studies of aggression need to resort to paradigms in which participants can show behaviour *intended* to harm another person without actually allowing real harm to be inflicted on anyone. Several experimental paradigms have been developed to address this challenge by creating situations in which participants are given the opportunity to deliver a range of different aversive stimuli to another person without actually causing them any harm (Ritter & Eslea, 2005). Each paradigm uses a somewhat different cover story to disguise the true purpose of the measure.

(1) The *teacher–learner paradigm*. This paradigm uses the set-up of an alleged learning experiment in which one person adopts the role of a teacher and presents a word-association learning task to another person, the learner. Assignment to the two roles is rigged so that the participant always ends up as the teacher, and the learner is a confederate of the experimenter. In the first round, the participant presents pairs of words to the learner. In the second round, only the first word of each pair is presented, and the learner has to correctly remember the second word of the pair. The teacher is instructed to punish errors made by the learner at a predefined rate through administering aversive stimuli. The participant's choice of punishment intensity represents the measure of aggressive behaviour. In the original version of this paradigm, punishments are delivered in the form of electric shocks, the strength of which is determined by the teacher. This procedure, which is probably better known from the famous study of obedience by Milgram (1974) than from the context of aggression research, was pioneered by Buss (1961). He developed an "aggression machine" that

teacher–learner paradigm: measure of aggressive behaviour in the lab whereby participants in the role of teachers assign aversive stimuli to an alleged learner.

enabled respondents to choose the *intensity* and the *duration* of electric shocks which they thought would be delivered to the learner whenever he made a mistake (no shocks were actually delivered, but respondents received mild shocks in a trial run to convince them that the device was genuine). In later studies, electric shocks were replaced by other aversive stimuli, such as loud noise (e.g., Edguer & Janisse, 1994) or air blasts to the throat (Verona & Sullivan, 2008), and the intensity and duration chosen by the participant were used as measures of aggressive behaviour. The teacher–learner paradigm provides an experimental framework in which the effects of a variety of independent variables on aggression may be studied (Baron & Richardson, 1994). Differences in aggressive responding may be examined, for example, as a function of respondents' group membership (male vs. female; prisoners vs. students) or situational manipulations (different degrees of frustration or physiological arousal).

proactive aggression: also called unprovoked aggression; aggressive behaviour shown without a prior provocation.

However, a criticism of the teacher–learner paradigm has been that if they accept the cover story, participants may be motivated by prosocial concerns to help the alleged learner to improve his task performance, rather than showing aggressive behaviour. In addition, it can only measure *proactive/ unprovoked aggression*, as the learner has no opportunity to retaliate. These problems are addressed, at least to some extent, in other paradigms.

essay evaluation paradigm: measure of aggressive behaviour in the lab whereby participants assign negative feedback on an alleged co-participant's essay.

(2) The *essay evaluation paradigm*. In this paradigm, the aggressive behaviour consists of delivering negative evaluations of an essay purportedly written by the target person. This paradigm has been used to investigate aggressive behaviour in response to preceding frustrations or provocations and was first introduced by Berkowitz (1962). Participants are told that they are to provide a written solution to a problem-solving task, which will then be evaluated by a fellow participant, who is in fact a confederate of the experimenter. They are also informed that the evaluation will be expressed in terms of the number of electric shocks delivered by the evaluator, with one shock indicating the best possible and ten shocks indicating the worst possible evaluation. Irrespective of the quality of their solution, participants then receive either few or many shocks, depending on whether they are in the provocation or control condition. In the second and main phase of the experiment, the roles are reversed, and the participant gets the chance to evaluate the solution provided by the other person. The number of shocks administered indicates the strength of the aggressive response. Typically, more shocks are administered to a target person who is seen responsible for a negative evaluation of the actor in the first round of the experiment, supporting the hypothesis that provocation leads to aggression. The essay evaluation paradigm has been modified by later studies that replaced electric shocks with other aversive stimuli, such as the level of negative verbal feedback in the essay evaluation (e.g., Krahé & Bieneck, 2012). Vasquez, Denson, Pedersen, Stenstrom, and Miller (2005) adapted the paradigm to use feedback about participants' performance on an anagram task rather than an essay. They used the length of time for which participants made

the target persons submerge their hands in unpleasantly cold water as a measure of aggression. Beyond addressing the role of anger or provocation, this experimental set-up allows researchers to examine additional variables moderating the effects on aggression. A case in point is Berkowitz and LePage's (1967) well-known study on the so-called "weapons effect", which will be examined in more detail in Chapter 2. They showed that when participants had been angered, they were more aggressive towards the person who was the source of the anger when an aggression-related cue (such as a revolver) was present than in the presence of a neutral object (such as a badminton racket).

(3) The *competitive reaction time task* (CRTT). Using a different cover story, this widely used paradigm leads participants to believe that they are engaging in a competitive reaction time task against another participant. It is also referred to as the Taylor Aggression Paradigm (TAP), as it was first introduced by Taylor (1967). When a visual cue appears on a screen, both participants have to press a button, and the person who presses the button first is the winner of that trial. Before each trial, participants have to set the intensity of the aversive stimulus delivered to the other person in case they win, which represents the measure of aggressive behaviour. In the original version, electric shocks were used as aversive stimuli. Because success and failure of the naive participants are in fact predetermined by the experimenter, each genuine participant receives, as well as delivers, a set number of shocks in the course of the task. In order to make sure that participants perceive the shocks to be aversive but not painful, each participant's threshold of unpleasantness is established in a pilot phase. As the task is programmed so that the genuine participants always win the first trial, the intensity they set for the first trial yields a measure of proactive or unprovoked aggression. After the first trial that they lost and in which they received a shock from their alleged opponent, participants' subsequent intensity levels reflect the strength of their *reactive or retaliative aggression*. Rather than delivering electric shocks, recent studies have used other aversive stimuli, such as unpleasantly loud noise (Bartholow & Anderson, 2002), and measured the intensity and duration chosen by the participant as a measure of aggressive behaviour. Yet other studies have replaced the electric shocks with points deducted from an opponent so as to reduce the other person's reward (e.g., Stadler, Rohrmann, Steuber, & Poustka, 2006). An extension of the CRTT in which participants are led to believe that they compete against two opponents with different levels of provocation was developed by Beyer, Buades-Rotger, Claes, and Krämer (2017).

As noted by Giancola and Parrott (2008), there is ample evidence for the validity of the CRTT as a measure of aggressive behaviour. Several studies have shown that the extent to which participants deliver aversive stimuli was significantly correlated with trait measures of aggression (see, however, Ferguson & Rueda, 2009, for disconfirming evidence) and also

competitive reaction time task (CRTT): measure of aggressive behaviour in the lab in which participants assign aversive stimuli to an alleged opponent if they are faster in responding to a signal detection task.

reactive aggression: also called retaliative aggression; aggressive behaviour shown in response to a provocation.

differentiated between individuals with and without a history of violence. In their own study, Giancola and Parrott (2008) showed that the intensity of electric shocks was more closely related to trait measures of physical aggression than to trait measures of verbal aggression, anger, or hostility, as one would expect from a measure intended to inflict physical harm. A criticism raised about the standard format of the CRTT refers to the absence of a non-aggressive response option. Participants can only choose to deliver more or less aversive shocks or noise blasts, the procedure does not allow them to refrain from delivering aversive stimuli altogether. To address this criticism, modifications have been proposed to include non-aggressive response options (Bushman, 2002; Reidy, Shirk, Sloan, & Zeichner, 2009).

Further suggestions for standardising the procedure of the CRTT have been proposed by Elson, Mohseni, Breuer, Scharkow, and Quandt (2014). In a recent comprehensive review, Warburton and Bushman (2019) concluded that the CRTT is a valid and flexible tool for assessing aggressive behaviour in the laboratory. In addition, Hyatt, Chester, Zeichner, and Miller (2019) found that different versions of the CRTT yielded similar results, underlining the robustness of this measure. Finally, Chester (2019) presented a multilevel approach that makes it possible to analyse patterns of stability and change in an individual's aggressive behaviour over the 25 trials of the CRTT in relation to the aggressive behaviour of the real or alleged opponent.

hot sauce paradigm: measure of aggressive behaviour in the lab whereby participants assign a certain quantity of aversively hot sauce to an alleged co-participant who does not like spicy food.

(4) The *hot sauce paradigm*. This paradigm for measuring aggression also consists of delivering unpleasant stimuli to a target person. Participants are asked to set the amount of hot spicy sauce to be consumed by a target person who allegedly dislikes this kind of food (Lieberman, Solomon, Greenberg, & McGregor, 1999; McGregor et al., 1998). Participants are first made to taste the sauce themselves before being asked to allocate a portion to a person who they believe strongly dislikes spicy food. The selected quantity of sauce is measured and constitutes the measure of aggressive behaviour (see Figure 1.1). Using this method, Ayduk, Gyurak, and Luerssen (2008) found that participants allocated more hot sauce to a target person who had rejected them as a potential partner in the experiment than to a target person who had chosen them as a partner. Meier and Hinsz (2004) showed that participants allocated more hot sauce to a target person when they were in a group than acting individually and gave more hot sauce to each target when targets were in a group rather than encountered as individuals.

Other studies extended the method by giving their participants a choice of sauces that differed in their degree of hotness (Barlett, Branch, Rodeheffer, & Harris, 2009; Santos, Briñol, Petty, Gandarillas, & Mateos, 2019). Using a combined index of the hotness of the sauce selected and the quantity assigned to the target person, Barlett et al. (2009) were able

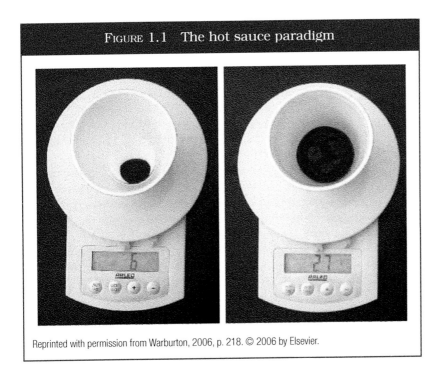

FIGURE 1.1 The hot sauce paradigm

Reprinted with permission from Warburton, 2006, p. 218. © 2006 by Elsevier.

to show that participants who had played a violent video game subsequently showed more aggressive behaviour than those who had played a non-violent video game. The hot sauce measure yields an easily quantifiable index of aggressive behaviour. Moreover, it is ethically feasible because it does not lead to any harmful effects other than, perhaps, temporary discomfort in the participants as a result of having to test a small quantity of the sauce themselves.

(5) *The Tangram help/hurt task.* In this recent addition to the toolkit of laboratory measures of aggressive behaviour, participants are asked to select Tangram puzzles differing in the level of difficulty for another participant. The more difficult puzzles they select, the more they undermine the alleged other participant's chances of completing the puzzles successfully and win a prize, reflecting an intention to harm by which their behaviour qualifies as aggressive (Saleem, Anderson, & Barlett, 2015; Saleem, Barlett, Anderson, & Hawkins, 2017). The task also yields a measure of prosocial behaviour through the number of easy puzzles assigned to the partner. The task can be modified to the assignment of other tasks of varying difficulty, such as anagrams or number sequences (Lutz, 2016; Lutz & Krahé, 2018).

Each of the paradigms discussed so far uses deception (concealing the true purpose of the experiment) to make participants believe that they are

Tangram help/ hurt task: measure of aggressive behaviour in the lab whereby participants assign easy (help) or difficult (hurt) Tangram puzzles to a co-participant. Tangram puzzles consist of a set of polygonal pieces that need to be put together without overlap.

harming another person. In addition to obtaining ethical approval for the chosen procedures beforehand, it is important to stress that participants in these experiments have to be carefully debriefed to explain the true purpose of the experiment, and to reassure them that they did not inflict any real harm on another person. If these conditions are met, a recent study suggests, the ill effects of taking part in laboratory studies on aggressive behaviour can be considered minimal, and the paradigms typically used in these studies are safe measures of aggressive behaviour (Parrott, Miller, & Hudepohl, 2015).

The use of behavioural observation is not limited to the assessment of aggressive behaviour but can also be extended to the assessment of anger as an affective antecedent of aggression. This is especially important in studies with young children, who are not yet able to provide valid self-reports of anger intensity and anger regulation strategies. Rohlf and Krahé (2015) developed a paradigm in which children were angered by asking them to build a tower of bricks that kept collapsing because some bricks were rounded at the bottom (see Chapter 3, for a detailed description). Children's maladaptive anger regulation strategies (e.g., venting their anger by throwing the bricks around) were recorded and related to teacher ratings of aggressive behaviour. An age-adapted version of the task was developed to study the same children three years later (Kirsch, Busching, Rohlf, & Krahé, 2019).

Critique of laboratory measures of aggressive behaviour. Although the experimental procedures discussed in this section have generated a strong body of knowledge on aggressive behaviour, their use has not been uncontroversial (e.g., Giancola & Chermack, 1998; Tedeschi & Quigley, 1996). The main challenge refers to their validity – that is, the extent to which they (a) represent the underlying theoretical construct of aggression (construct validity), and (b) can explain aggressive behaviour occurring outside the laboratory in the "real world" (external validity). In terms of construct validity, the criticism has been raised that the different approaches are potentially susceptible to alternative interpretations of what is taken to be aggressive behaviour. In the teacher–learner paradigm, participants may choose high levels of shock because they want to help the learner to do well in the supposed learning task. In the essay evaluation paradigm, high shock intensities may similarly reflect compliance with the cover story, namely to provide critical feedback on a person's problem-solving abilities. In the competitive reaction time task, participants' responses may be motivated by competitiveness rather than by aggression. As far as external validity is concerned, critics have pointed out that the artificial and impoverished nature of many laboratory settings is a far cry from those contexts in which aggression occurs as a social problem in the real world. Thus, it has been questioned that evidence gained from laboratory studies can contribute to a better understanding of aggression as it occurs in natural contexts. Without being able to review the controversy in detail (see Anderson, Bushman, & Groom, 1997; Berkowitz, 1993; Ritter & Eslea, 2005; Tedeschi & Quigley,

1996, for comprehensive discussions), two main lines of reasoning have been advanced in defence of the use of laboratory experiments for the study of aggression:

(1) Experimental procedures for measuring aggressive behaviour can be said to have high construct validity (i.e., to measure the same underlying construct) if they meet the following requirements. First, a person's responses should be correlated across different indicators of aggression, such as duration and intensity of shocks versus negative verbal feedback or amount of hot sauce chosen. This means that if Person A delivers more intensive electric shocks than Person B, then Person A should also give more negative feedback or allocate more hot sauce compared with Person B. Secondly, the different measures of aggression should be triggered by the same antecedent conditions. This means that if the induction of negative affect is found to elicit higher shock intensities compared with a control condition, it should equally result in higher amounts of hot sauce or more intense noise blasts being administered to a target person. Integrating results from over 100 published studies, Carlson, Marcus-Newhall, and Miller (1989) examined these aspects of construct validity, and concluded that "critics have gone too far in rejecting outright the thesis that specific aggression measures typically index a common behavioral disposition." (p. 386).

(2) The second criticism refers to a lack of external validity (i.e., the correspondence of laboratory measures with a person's aggressive behaviour in the real world). This criticism was tackled by Anderson & Bushman (1997; see also Bushman & Anderson, 1998). They conducted a meta-analysis including 53 studies of laboratory and real-world aggression to explore the correspondence between the two sources of data across a range of independent variables. *Meta-analysis* is a statistical procedure in which the results from a number of individual studies are converted to a common metric and then integrated into a quantitative index of effect size. The effect size indicates the magnitude of the difference between two variables, such as aggressive behaviour measured in the laboratory versus the real world, across the entire range of studies (Glass, McGaw, & Smith, 1981). More specifically, Anderson and Bushman (1997) looked for converging evidence concerning the role of individual difference variables (sex, trait aggressiveness, and type A personality; see Chapter 4) and situational variables (provocation, alcohol, anonymity, temperature, and media violence; see Chapters 5 and 6) as determinants of aggressive behaviour. With the exception of temperature, for which the laboratory evidence was inconsistent both in itself and with field research, they found substantial convergence across the two data sources. In both laboratory and field research, aggression was found to increase as a function of provocation, alcohol consumption, anonymity, and exposure to violent media content. Aggression was also found to be higher in both settings for men (physical aggression only) and for individuals with high trait aggressiveness and type A personality. It is worth noting, however, that the magnitude

meta-analysis: quantitative review integrating the findings from individual studies into a common metric of effect size.

of the effects varied across the two approaches. For example, the effect of violent media use was found to be higher in laboratory experiments than in field studies, whereas the link between measures of aggressiveness as a personality trait and behavioural measures of aggression was stronger in field studies than in the laboratory. As Bushman and Anderson (1998) pointed out, these differences are conceptually plausible. They argue that the stronger effect size for the impact of trait aggressiveness on aggressive behaviour found in field studies was to be expected, because laboratory studies mostly involve relatively homogeneous samples of college students, whereas variability in trait aggressiveness is greater among the largely unselected samples observed in many field studies. In contrast, the effect of media violence on aggressive behaviour was expected to be stronger in the laboratory, because the time interval between exposure to media violence and measurement of subsequent aggression is typically shorter in laboratory experiments, and extraneous influences that might undermine the impact of the media stimuli can be controlled more effectively in the laboratory. Further contributing to the cross-validation of laboratory methods and other measures of aggressive behaviour, a study by King and Russell (2019) demonstrated that the CRTT as a lab analogue of aggressive behaviour correlated significantly with self-reports of different forms of aggressive behaviour, such as violence against an intimate partner and alcohol-related aggression.

In conclusion, these analyses show that the unquestionable advantage of laboratory experiments (i.e., their ability to test causal hypotheses in a controlled context) is not necessarily undermined by a lack of external validity (for a similar appraisal, see Berkowitz, 1993). Therefore, laboratory studies are of prime importance for testing cause–effect hypotheses and illuminating conceptual links between instigating variables, aggressive behaviour, and its consequences. On the other hand, they do not allow researchers to study severe manifestations of aggressive behaviour, which would be unethical to elicit deliberately. Therefore, there is clearly a need for additional methodological tools for studying these forms of aggressive behaviour.

Collecting reports of aggressive behaviour

Measuring aggressive behaviour through direct observation of research participants' aggressive behaviour in natural contexts or in the laboratory is not always feasible. As noted above, the harmful and potentially dangerous nature of aggressive acts prevents researchers from creating conditions under which such behaviours might be observed, and severe forms of aggression and violence are too rare to lend themselves to systematic observation in the real world. Moreover, many aggressive acts occur without prior warning or only come to light after they have been performed. This is typically the case for acts of violence, such as physical assault, rape, or homicide. In these cases, researchers have to rely on reports of aggressive behaviour rather than gaining first-hand evidence of its occurrence. In other contexts, research questions refer to internal variables, such as aggressive thoughts and fantasies, which – unlike overt behaviour – are not open to observation. An overview of different strategies for collecting reports about aggression is presented in the third part of Table 1.2. Most of these methods are common techniques of data collection that can be applied to the measurement of aggression in a wide range of contexts.

Self-reports of aggressive behaviour. In this widely-used approach, participants are asked to provide reports of their own aggressive behaviour. The reports can either refer to general patterns of behaviour that reflect trait aggression, such as how characteristic particular aggressive behaviours are for the person, or they can refer to the frequency of specific behaviours shown in the past, such as how many times in the last year the person has spread rumours about a colleague at work.

Probably the best-known general measure of dispositional or trait aggression relying on self-reports is the *Aggression Questionnaire* (AQ) developed by Buss and Perry (1992). Based on the earlier Buss-Durkee Hostility Inventory (Buss & Durkee, 1957), the AQ measures the habitual tendency to engage in physical aggression and verbal aggression. In addition, it contains two scales measuring individual differences in anger and hostility, seen as important affective correlates of aggressive behaviour. Box 1.1 shows the full set of all 29 items of the AQ, together with mean scores for men and women in the original study by Buss and Perry (1992). You can assess your trait aggression by completing the items in Box 1.1 and comparing your mean score on each scale with the original sample.

Aggression Questionnaire (AQ): self-report instrument to measure stable individual differences in trait aggressiveness.

The AQ has been translated into many other languages (e.g., German, Herzberg, 2003; Spanish, Santisteban, Alvarado, & Recio, 2007; or Japanese, Nakano, 2001), and has undergone some extensions and modifications. For example, Buss and Warren (2000) added a scale measuring relational aggression, with items such as "I sometimes spread gossip about people I don't like" and "When someone really irritates me, I might give him or her the silent treatment". Other authors developed more parsimonious short forms of the AQ with fewer items (Bryant & Smith, 2001; Webster et al., 2015). In its different forms, the AQ remains one of the most widely used instruments for measuring trait aggression (McKay, Perry, & Harvey, 2016).

Other self-report measures have been developed to specifically measure individual differences in indirect and relational aggression. The Richardson Conflict Response Questionnaire (RCRQ; Richardson & Green, 2003) contains ten items that measure direct verbal and physical aggression (e.g., "threw something at them", "yelled or screamed at them") and ten items that measure indirect, relational aggression (e.g., "gossiped about the person behind their back") as behaviours that individuals show when they are angry.

Another aspect of indirect aggression is captured in the Displaced Aggression Questionnaire (DAQ) by Denson, Pedersen, and Miller (2006). The DAQ was designed to measure individual differences in the tendency

Box 1.1   Items from the Aggression Questionnaire (AQ) by Buss and Perry (1992)

Where do you stand on trait aggression?

Response scale:

1	2	3	4	5
Extremely uncharacteristic of me				Extremely characteristic of me

Physical Aggression

- Once in a while I can't control the urge to strike another person.
- Given enough provocation, I may hit another person.
- If somebody hits me, I hit back.
- I get into fights a little more than the average person.
- If I have to resort to violence to protect my rights, I will.
- There are people who pushed me so far we came to blows.
- I can think of no good reason for ever hitting a person.*
- I have threatened people I know.
- I have become so mad that I have broken things.

Verbal Aggression

- I tell my friends openly when I disagree with them.
- I often find myself disagreeing with people.
- When people annoy me, I may tell them what I think of them.
- I can't help getting into arguments when people disagree with me.
- My friends say that I'm somewhat argumentative.

Anger

- I flare up quickly but get over it quickly.
- When frustrated, I let my irritation show.
- I sometimes feel like a powder keg ready to explode.
- I am an even-tempered person.*
- Some of my friends think I'm a hothead.
- Sometimes I fly off the handle for no good reason.
- I have trouble controlling my temper.

Hostility

- I am sometimes eaten up with jealousy.
- At times I feel I have gotten a raw deal out of life.

- Other people always seem to get the breaks.
- I wonder why sometimes I feel so bitter about things.
- I know that "friends" talk about me behind my back.
- I am suspicious of overly friendly strangers.
- I sometimes feel that people are laughing at me behind my back.
- When people are especially nice, I wonder what they want.

Please give each item a number from 1 to 5 depending on how characteristic it is of you.

Reverse the coding on the items marked with * so that high scores always mean high aggressiveness. Then compute the mean of the items for each scale.

In the Buss and Perry (1992) study, men had significantly higher scores on Physical Aggression, Verbal Aggression, and Hostility, but not on Anger. The sex difference was largest on the Physical Aggression scale.

You can compare your mean score on each scale with the following mean scores derived from Buss and Perry (1992, Table 3), based on U.S. college students:

Scale	Men (n = 612)	Women (n = 641)
Physical aggression	2.70	1.98
Verbal aggression	3.04	2.70
Anger	2.42	2.38
Hostility	2.66	2.52

Reprinted with permission from Buss & Perry, 1992;
© 1992 by the American Psychological Association.

to engage in displaced aggression. Displaced aggression is said to occur when people shift their aggressive response to a provocation or frustration away from the original source onto an innocent target (see Chapter 2 for a more detailed discussion). The DAQ was developed to capture stable individual differences in the tendency to displace aggression and consists of three subscales, addressing Angry Rumination (e.g., "I often find myself thinking over and over about things that have made me angry"), Revenge Planning ("I have long living fantasies of revenge after the conflict is over"), and Displaced Aggression at the behavioural level ("I take my anger out on innocent others").

Whereas these questionnaire measures are designed to collect self-reports of people's aggressive behaviour in general and across situations, recent research has provided a first test of an experience-sampling measure of situational aggression, the Aggression-ES-Scale (Borah, Murray, Eisner, & Jugl, 2018). In this approach, participants receive prompts via smartphones to report on their current thoughts, feelings, and behaviours, and the method has been used successfully in a range of contexts (e.g., Eatough, Shockley, & Yu, 2016). In the first test of their new method, participants in the study by Borah et al. (2018) received five prompts per day over a period of eight days and indicated at each prompt whether and in what intensity they had shown each of 12 specific forms of aggressive behaviour in the last 30 minutes. They were also asked to report to what extent they had just experienced eight different provocations. This new approach has the potential to provide time-locked information about an individual's aggressive behaviour and about situational dynamics, for instance the reciprocity of provocation and aggression.

Each of the measures discussed so far was designed to assess aggressive behaviour in a wide range of contexts. In addition, self-report measures are available that are custom-tailored to specific manifestations of aggressive behaviour in different domains, such as sexual aggression, aggressive driving, or school bullying. In the area of sexual aggression, one of the most widely used instruments is the *Sexual Experiences Survey* (SES) by Koss et al. (2007; 2008). The SES can be used to obtain self-reports of sexual aggression and, in a parallel format, self-reports of sexual victimisation. In the original version, which was developed in the 1980s (Koss, Gidycz, & Wisniewski, 1987; Koss & Oros, 1982), the scales were phrased to assess men's sexual aggression perpetration and women's sexual victimisation. In the revised version by Koss et al. (2007), the items are worded in a gender-neutral manner, so that both men and women can be asked about their experiences as perpetrators as well as victims of sexual aggression. It presents a list of different sexual acts, combined with a list of different coercive strategies, and respondents are asked to indicate how many times since the age of 14 or in the last year they engaged in or experienced each specific combination. An example of the format of the SES is presented in Box 1.2.

Building on the SES, other self-report scales to assess sexual aggression and victimisation have been developed that include further aspects. One example is the Sexual Aggression and Victimization Scale (SAV-S), which is a gender-inclusive instrument that tailors the questions to the sexual experience background of participants (heterosexual and/or same-sex contacts) and breaks down self-reports by the relationship between perpetrator and victim (Krahé et al., 2015; Krahé et al., 2016; Krahé & Berger, 2013). A discussion of research based on these methods will be presented in Chapter 9.

Instruments for collecting parallel reports from aggressors and victims have also been developed in other domains. For example, Forrest, Eatough, and Shevlin (2005) developed the Indirect Aggression Scales (IAS) that contained the same set of items from the aggressor perspective (e.g., "criticised another person in public") and from the target perspective ("someone criticised me in public"). Another prominent example are the *Conflict Tactics Scales* (CTS), designed to elicit reports of intimate

---

Sexual Experiences Survey (SES): self-report measure to assess the perpetration of, and victimization by, sexual aggression.

Conflict Tactics Scales (CTS): instrument for measuring intimate partner violence by collecting self-reports of perpetration and/or victimization.

Box 1.2   Example items from the Short Form of the Sexual Experiences Survey (Koss et al., 2007)

Item 2 of the Short Form Perpetration (SES-SFP)

	How many times in the past 12 months?	How many times since age 14?
I had oral sex with someone or had someone perform oral sex on me without their consent by:	0 1 2 3+	0 1 2 3+
a. Telling lies, threatening to end the relationship, threatening to spread rumors about them, making promises about the future I knew were untrue, or continually verbally pressuring them after they said they didn't want to.	☐ ☐ ☐ ☐	☐ ☐ ☐ ☐
b. Showing displeasure, criticizing their sexuality or attractiveness, getting angry but not using physical force after they said they didn't want to.	☐ ☐ ☐ ☐	☐ ☐ ☐ ☐
c. Taking advantage when they were too drunk or out of it to stop what was happening.	☐ ☐ ☐ ☐	☐ ☐ ☐ ☐
d. Threatening to physically harm them or someone close to them.	☐ ☐ ☐ ☐	☐ ☐ ☐ ☐
e. Using force, for example holding them down with my body weight, pinning their arms, or having a weapon.	☐ ☐ ☐ ☐	☐ ☐ ☐ ☐

Item 2 of the Short Form Victimization (SES-SFV)

	How many times in the past 12 months?	How many times since age 14?
Someone had oral sex with me or made me have oral sex with them without my consent by:	0 1 2 3+	0 1 2 3+
a. Telling lies, threatening to end the relationship, threatening to spread rumors about me, making promises I knew were untrue, or continually verbally pressuring me after I said I didn't want to.	☐ ☐ ☐ ☐	☐ ☐ ☐ ☐
b. Showing displeasure, criticizing my sexuality or attractiveness, getting angry but not using physical force, after I said I didn't want to.	☐ ☐ ☐ ☐	☐ ☐ ☐ ☐

Item 2 of the Short Form Victimization (SES-SFV)

c.   Taking advantage of me when I was too drunk or
     out of it to stop what was happening.   □ □ □ □   □ □ □ □

d.   Threatening to physically harm me or someone
     close to me.   □ □ □ □   □ □ □ □

e.   Using force, for example holding me down with
     their body weight, pinning my arms, or having □ □ □ □   □ □ □ □
     a weapon.

See Koss et al., 2007, for the full item list.
Reprinted with permission.

partner aggression from both the aggressor and the target perspective
(Straus, 1979). In the latest version, the Conflict Tactics Scales 2 (CTS2),
respondents are asked to indicate which of a list of behaviours representing
psychological aggression, physical assault, and sexual coercion they have
shown against their partner in the past year (Straus, Hamby, Boney-McCoy,
& Sugarman, 1996). In addition, they are asked to indicate, for the same set
of behaviours, how many times their partner showed the respective behaviour towards them. This enables researchers to examine the agreement
between couples about the behaviour shown by each of the partners and
to see whether intimate partner aggression is mutual or only shown by
one partner in a relationship. A similar set of scales addressing aggression
in parent–child interactions was developed by Straus, Hamby, Finkelhor,
Moore, and Runyan (1998). In a comprehensive review, the CTS was
found to be a robust and reliable measure (Jones, Browne, & Chou, 2017),
although its reliance on lists of behaviours without considering the context
in which they are shown has attracted criticism. Research based on the CTS
and the controversy surrounding it will be reviewed in Chapter 8.

One problem with the use of self-reports is that aggression is a socially
undesirable behaviour, and respondents are aware that they are being asked
to report behaviour that makes them appear in a negative light. This renders
self-report measures susceptible to response distortions in the direction of
social desirability, resulting in an under-reporting of aggressive behaviour.
Applying a polygraph, which is a kind of "lie detector" that infers from the
magnitude of test persons' psychophysiological responses whether or not
they respond truthfully, a recent study by Poltavski, van Eck, Winger, and
Honts (2018) examined socially desirable response biases to items from
prominent self-report measures. They included a 12-item short form of
the Aggression Questionnaire by Buss and Perry (1992) plus six additional
items from the Buss-Durkee (1957) Hostility Inventory assessing indirect
aggression and the Reactive-Proactive Questionnaire by Raine et al. (2006).

Skin conductance, breathing time, and blood pressure were selected as critical responses and correlated to the self-reported answers to the questionnaire items. The magnitude of physiological responses correlated negatively with two self-report scores, anger and indirect aggression, which means that the lower the self-report, the stronger the physiological responses. This discrepancy may be seen as evidence for the underreporting of aggressive behaviour. No significant correlations were found for the remaining aggression measures. The relevance of this approach to studying social desirability response bias is twofold: first, it provides empirical evidence of a mismatch between self-reports and physiological responses to items assessing anger and aggression, and second it enables researchers to identify individual items and scales in self-report measures that are particularly affected by these discrepancies. This information may be valuable for designing questionnaire measures that are less susceptible to socially desirable responding.

Despite the known limitations of self-reports, it is often inevitable to ask people to report on their aggressive behaviour, as there are no other reliable sources one could consult instead. However, in some contexts it is feasible to rely on information from third parties who can provide information about the aggressive behaviour of research participants.

Parent or teacher reports of aggressive behaviour. In studies measuring aggression in childhood and adolescence, parents and teachers may be recruited as informants. They have first-hand knowledge of a target person's aggressive behaviour, and can provide behavioural ratings that can then be examined for their convergence with each other and with the person's self-reports. Parent ratings of aggression are particularly useful for studying aggression in young children. An example is provided by Tremblay et al. (1999), who asked parents to rate their children on a list of 11 items addressing physical aggression, such as "bites", "kicks", and "takes away things from others". Similarly, teachers can provide ratings of a child's aggressive behaviour. For example, the teacher form of the Preschool Social Behavior Scale (PSBS-T) developed by Crick, Casas, and Mosher (1997) consists of 16 items on which preschool teachers are asked to rate the children in their class in terms of relational aggression (e.g., "Tells others not to play with or be a peer's friend") and overt aggression (e.g., "Hurts other children by pinching them"). In a study with adolescents, self-reported use of violent media was related to teacher reports of the participant's aggressive behaviour in school to examine the link between media violence use and aggression (Krahé & Möller, 2011).

Peer nominations. Whereas parents and teachers are typically asked to rate research participants on a number of items describing aggressive behaviour, peers are asked to nominate (i.e., select from their group) individual children who fit certain behavioural descriptors. For example, students in a class may be asked to nominate classmates who "attack others without reason", "say nasty things to other children even if they had done nothing wrong", or "take other children's possessions" (Kokko, Pulkkinen,

peer nominations: method for measuring aggressive behaviour by asking other people (e.g., classmates) to rate the aggressiveness of an individual.

Huesmann, Dubow, & Boxer, 2009). The more nominations participants receive, the higher their aggression score. Peer nominations have also been used to measure indirect forms of aggression. For example, in the Direct-Indirect-Aggression Scale (DIAS) by Björkqvist et al. (1992), participants are asked to nominate a peer "who says unpleasant thing's behind the person's back". Using this approach, Kokko et al. (2009) demonstrated significant correlations of $r = .43$ between peer-nominated aggression at age 8 years and peer-nominated aggression at age 19 years for both boys and girls in an American sample. In the same study, a correlation between peer-nominated aggression at age 8 years and peer-nominated aggression at age 14 years of $r = .38$ for girls and $r = .35$ for boys was found in a Finnish sample. These correlations are impressive, given that different peers provided the ratings at the two measurements.

Measures of aggressive affect: anger and hostility. In addition to eliciting reports of aggression at the behavioural level, researchers are often interested in studying the affective concomitants of aggressive behaviour, most notably *anger* and *hostility*. Standardised scales have been developed to capture individual differences in the disposition to experience affective states that are relevant to aggressive behaviour. As shown in Box 1.1, Buss and Perry's (1992) "Aggression Questionnaire" contains two such scales, measuring dispositional anger and hostility. Another pertinent measure of anger is the *State-Trait-Anger Expression Inventory* (STAXI) developed by Spielberger (1996). The STAXI addresses five facets of anger and the way it is characteristically expressed. The State–Anger scale asks participants to describe how they feel at a particular moment in time (e.g., "I feel angry", "I feel irritated"). The Trait–Anger scale addresses the habitual tendency to experience these affective states. The Anger/In and Anger/Out scales refer to individual differences in the tendency to direct anger towards others in the social environment as opposed to directing it towards the self, and the Anger/Control scale measures the extent to which people try to keep their anger under control (Forgays, Forgays, & Spielberger, 1997). The STAXI is available in many languages and has been established as a reliable and valid measure of anger in a variety of domains (for a review, see Eckhardt, Norlander, & Deffenbacher, 2004).

Measure of aggressive cognitions: the Implicit Association Test (IAT). Given the undesirable nature of aggression, self-reports of aggressive thoughts and feelings may be susceptible to the problem of systematic under-reporting similar to aggressive behaviour. Therefore, measures of aggressive cognitions have been developed that cannot be easily distorted in the direction of social desirability. Several studies have adapted the Implicit Association Test (IAT), first developed as a measure of attitudes (Greenwald, McGhee, & Schwartz, 1998), for the measurement of aggressive cognitions and aggression-related self-construals (for a review, see Richetin & Richardson, 2008). The IAT is designed to tap into aggressive cognitions in an unobtrusive way by examining the speed with which aggression-related stimuli are recognised. It is based on the assumption that the strength of the association

State-Trait-Anger Expression Inventory (STAXI): measure of individual differences in anger expression (state and trait scales).

Implicit association test (IAT): reaction-time measure to assess the speed with which a person can activate aggressive cognitions.

between a target category (e.g., self vs. other) and an attribute category (e.g., aggressive vs. non-aggressive) can be inferred from the speed with which participants can recognise particular combinations of the target and the attribute category. Participants are presented with a list of words that refer to either the target category (e.g., I, ME vs. THEM, YOU) or the attribute category (e.g., AMBUSH, CHOKE vs. HELP, COMFORT; see Richetin, Richardson, & Mason, 2010). For each word, they are asked to indicate as fast as they can whether it refers to the category in question (e.g., press the left key if it is a word related to "me" and press the right key if it is a word related to "other") or whether it refers to the attribute category in question (e.g., press the right key if it is an aggressive word, press the left key if it is a non-aggressive word). If participants respond faster to aggression-related words when they share the same key with the "me" words than when they share the same key with the "other" words, this is regarded as an indication that "me" and "aggression" are closely related in the person's self-concept.

Scores on the Aggression IAT are interpreted as a measure of stable dispositions towards aggression, and they have been used to predict aggressive behaviour in specific situations. There is evidence that the Aggression IAT may capture both relatively stable individual differences in aggressiveness and situation-specific variability in aggressive behaviour (Lemmer, Gollwitzer, & Banse, 2015). Richetin et al. (2010) found that participants' implicit aggression scores on the IAT predicted their negative behaviour towards a target person, but only after a preceding provocation by the same person. A study by Gollwitzer, Banse, Eisenbach, and Naumann (2007) showed that IAT scores may be useful as unobtrusive outcome measures for evaluating the efficacy of interventions designed to reduce aggression. Other studies have shown that the IAT can also detect changes in aggression-related self-concept as a result of situational influences. In research on exposure to media violence, it has been found that playing a violent video game for brief periods of time leads to shorter reaction times for aggressive words associated with the self than playing a non-violent game (Bluemke, Friedrich, & Zumbach, 2010; Uhlmann & Swanson, 2004).

Projective techniques. Another approach for exploring the affective and cognitive correlates of aggressive behaviour involves the use of projective techniques in which participants are presented with ambiguous stimulus material and asked to generate a verbal or written response. Their responses are then scored for aggressive content by trained raters. The best-known projective technique for the measurement of aggression is the Picture Frustration Test (PFT) by Rosenzweig (1945). It consists of a set of cartoon drawings, each depicting a situation that involves some mild to moderate form of everyday frustration. An example is shown in Figure 1.2.

projective techniques: measures of aggressive dispositions in which participants project their aggressive thoughts, feelings, and behavioural intentions onto ambiguous stimulus material.

The person who caused the frustration (e.g., the driver responsible for splattering the pedestrian) makes a comment that is designed to attenuate or add to the initial frustration. The participant suggests a verbal response from the perspective of the frustrated person in the cartoon, and responses across all cartoons are coded for aggressive content (Rosenzweig, 1976). For

FIGURE 1.2   Example from the Rosenzweig Picture Frustration Test (PFT)

Reprinted with permission from Rosenzweig, 1945, p. 4; ©1945 by Wiley.

example, responses are categorised as "extraggression" if they are directed at the social environment, or as "intraggression" if they are directed towards the self, a distinction similar to the STAXI scales of Anger/in and Anger/out. A children's version of the PFT is also available, and an example situation is "A girl on a swing is telling another girl that she is planning to keep the swing all afternoon" (Rosenzweig, Fleming, & Rosenzweig, 1948).

Apart from the time-consuming task of coding free-response statements into a manageable set of categories, the reliability of such codings (i.e., their consistency across independent raters and across repeated codings by the same rater) has been difficult to achieve (Rosenzweig, Ludwig, & Adelman, 1975). Moreover, responses to the PFT have been found to be affected by social desirability concerns.

Another well-known projective test is the Rorschach inkblot test, which has been used to measure aggression since the 1940s (see the review by Kivisto & Swan, 2013). Participants' associations in response to the inkblots are coded in terms of aggressive content (e.g., "an explosion"), aggressive potential (a response that an aggressive act is about to occur), aggressive past (a response that an aggressive act has occurred or the object has been the target of aggression), and sado-masochism (a response in which devalued, aggressive, or morbid content is accompanied by pleasurable affect). Despite generally good inter-rater agreement and some evidence of criterion validity in past studies, Kivisto and Swann (2013) found little evidence that scores on the Rorschach tests were correlated with lab-based or self-report measures of aggressive behaviour.

Taken together, these problems with the PFT and the Rorschach test may explain why projective techniques are not widely used in the social psychological analysis of aggression.

Using official records

Rather than asking individuals to provide reports about their own behaviour or rate the aggressive behaviour of their children, pupils, or peers, researchers can derive information about aggressive behaviour from publicly available databases. These data sources are not compiled for research purposes, and therefore researchers are limited to whatever information has been recorded. Typically, they do not yield information about individuals, but about aggressive behaviour at the macro level of communities and societies. Such information may nevertheless be useful for answering research questions about the scale of different forms of aggressive behaviour and the link between rates of aggression and other variables.

Crime statistics. Official records of reported crime are compiled by most countries, and these figures can be used by aggression researchers who want to study criminal forms of aggression. For example, the Uniform Crime Reporting (UCR) Program in the USA, which was started in 1929, presents detailed information about the rates of different forms of criminal violence, broken down by a range of demographic characteristics, such as perpetrator and victim sex or age, and also by geographic location (see www.fbi.gov/about-us/cjis/ucr/ucr). For 2017, it tells us that 17,284 cases of murder were reported to the police, which corresponds to a rate of 5.3 cases per 100,000 inhabitants (https://ucr.fbi.gov/crime-in-the-u.s/2017/crime-in-the-u.s.-2017/topic-pages/murder). This figure compares with 23,438 cases or a rate of 9.4 per 100,000 inhabitants for the year 1990, which indicates that homicide rates have decreased in this period. For Germany, the national crime statistic reports a rate of 2.9 cases of murder per 100,000 inhabitants in 2017 (Bundeskriminalamt, 2017). These records can be used, for example, to test hypotheses about gender differences in the likelihood of perpetration and victimisation and about differences in violent crime rates in different times or cultures. Crime statistics can also be used to examine changes in crime rate in covariation with legal measures to address research questions about aggression. For example, they can help to answer the question of whether murder rates go

official records: data collected for purposes other than research providing information about aggressive and violent behaviour (e.g., crime statistics, newspaper reports).

up when the death penalty is abolished, or whether the tightening of gun control legislation is followed by a decrease in the number of gun-related homicides. We shall come back to crime statistics when we discuss these questions in later chapters.

A possibly less obvious candidate for the use of official records to study aggression is the analysis of meteorological data that provide information on average annual temperatures and comparisons between geographic regions. Meteorological records have been used as an important source for studying the link between temperature and aggression. Historical analyses revealed that riots were more frequent in hotter regions and during hotter periods of the year, and this observation was followed by systematic analyses relating temperature scores and violent crime rates within and across different regions to further explore the link. By relating crime statistics to weather records, Anderson and his colleagues found, for example, that the incidence rates of serious and deadly assault were higher in years with a higher average temperature, whereas robbery figures remained unaffected by temperature (Anderson et al., 1997; for a more detailed discussion of this research, see Chapter 5).

Finally, newspaper reports have been used as another form of archival records by aggression researchers. For example, Mullen (1986) referred to this data source in his analysis of violent behaviour by lynch mobs. Based on newspaper reports of 60 lynchings in the USA between 1899 and 1946, Mullen demonstrated that the larger the mob relative to the number of victims, the more savage the lynch mobs were in their atrocities. Mullen used these data to argue that the larger the mob, the more difficult it is for members to retain self-focused attention that is important for inhibiting violent behaviour. We will return to this issue in our discussion of intergroup aggression in Chapter 10.

Archival records are a useful addition to the toolbox of aggression researchers because they provide data at the aggregate level of societies based on large samples. At the same time, they have obvious limitations, for example that researchers have to take the data as they are in the data base. Moreover, the analyses facilitated by these data are mostly correlational and do not lend themselves to the testing of causal hypotheses. However, the advent of modern statistical methods for multilevel analysis opens up promising directions for analysing the interplay between variables at the individual level and societal-level variables contained in archival data bases. Such multilevel designs have been used to examine the role of country-level variables, such as different indicators of gender equality at the national level, in explaining differences in the rate of violence against women (e.g., Heise & Kotsadam, 2015).

SUMMARY

- This chapter was designed to lay the ground for understanding and critically evaluating the research findings to be discussed in the course of this volume. A definition of aggression was presented that focuses on three aspects, namely *harmful consequences, intention and expectancy of inflicting harm,* and *desire by the target person to avoid the harmful treatment.* Dimensions for classifying aggressive acts were discussed to provide a framework for the systematic description of different forms of aggressive behaviour.

- A variety of methods are available for the social psychological analysis of aggression. Systematic observations of aggressive behaviour in natural contexts works well if the behaviour has a sufficiently high frequency of occurrence, for example to record aggressive behaviour between young children. Field experiments involve a manipulation of the naturally occurring situation, but random assignment of participants to the manipulated conditions is usually not feasible, undermining the ability of this design to identify causal effects.

- Ethical constraints prevent researchers from setting up situations in which participants are given the opportunity to harm another person. Therefore, experimental analogues have been developed that facilitate the study of behaviours intended to harm another person without causing any actual harm. Evidence was presented which shows that findings obtained in artificially created laboratory tasks correspond in many areas to findings obtained from studies conducted in the real world.

- When first-hand observation is not possible, a range of methods are available for collecting reports of aggressive behaviour. These include self-reports, parent or teacher reports, peer nominations, and projective techniques. Archival records, such as crime statistics and even weather data, provide an additional data source that can be used to establish the rates of different violent offences and to examine covariations of aggression and a range of other variables.

TASKS TO DO

(1) Plan the design of an experiment using the *competitive reaction time* paradigm to study the effect of frustration on aggression.
(2) Find out how you score on the Aggression Questionnaire presented in Box 1.1, and compare your score with the Buss and Perry sample at the bottom of the box.
(3) Visit the official crime statistics database in your country, find out the most recent annual figure for homicide rates, and compare this rate with the figures recorded 10 and 20 years earlier.

SUGGESTED READING

Anderson, C. A., & Bushman, B. J. (1997). External validity of "trivial" experiments: The case of laboratory aggression. *Review of General Psychology, 1*, 19–41.

Richardson, D. S. (2014). Everyday aggression takes many forms. *Current Directions in Psychological Science, 23,* 220–224.

Warburton, W. A., & Bushman, B. J. (2019). The competitive reaction time task: The development and scientific utility of a flexible laboratory aggression paradigm. *Aggressive Behavior, 45,* 389–398.

Chapter 2

THEORIES OF AGGRESSION: WHY DO HUMANS SHOW AGGRESSIVE BEHAVIOUR?

Aggressive behaviour causes harm and suffering to individuals and groups on a large scale, and incurs enormous social and material costs for societies. Therefore, it is critical to understand and explain *why* people engage in aggressive behaviour, not least because identifying the factors that instigate aggressive behaviour is a first step towards prevention. In this chapter, the most important theories will be presented and discussed in terms of their contribution to understanding the origins and causes of aggressive behaviour. The purpose of this discussion is twofold: first, to highlight the diversity of approaches that have been offered to explain aggressive behaviour, and secondly, to build up a stock of theoretical constructs pertaining to different aspects of aggressive behaviour that can help to understand specific forms of aggression addressed in the following chapters.

Before we enter into the discussion of different theories in detail, Table 2.1 presents an overview of the major theories that seek to explain aggression as a form of social behaviour. For each theory, the table presents its core assumptions about what causes aggression and a summary statement about its empirical support, which, of course, will be substantiated in more detail in the course of this chapter.

Theories of aggression may be broadly categorised into two groups: *biological theories*, which look for the roots of aggressive behaviour in biological processes and mechanisms, and *psychological theories*, which refer to mental processes to explain aggressive behaviour. The approaches in the top half of Table 2.1 are based on biological concepts and principles, whereas the approaches in the bottom half of the table address psychological processes. Rather than seeing them as competing or even mutually exclusive, biological and psychological explanations complement each other, stressing different aspects of aggression as a complex form of social behaviour. The next sections will introduce each of the approaches in turn,

TABLE 2.1 Major theories of aggression: an overview

	Aggression conceptualised as …	Main data base	Empirical evidence
Biological approaches			
Ethology	… an internal energy released by external cues; steam-boiler model	Animal studies	No support as a model for human aggression, but still popular in lay discourse
Sociobiology	… a product of evolution through natural selection	Animal studies and correlational studies in humans	Support for correlational, but not causal links
Behaviour genetics	… transmitted as part of genetic make-up	Twin and adoption studies	Support for the predictive value of genetic similarity
Hormonal explanations	… influenced by sex hormones and cortisol	Comparisons of violent and nonviolent individuals	Some empirical support
Psychological approaches			
Freudian psychoanalysis	… a destructive instinct	Case studies	No quantitative empirical evaluation, but important source for the F-A-hypothesis
Frustration-aggression (F-A) hypothesis	… a likely response to frustration, likelihood enhanced by aggressive cues	Experimental studies	Supported by empirical evidence
Cognitive neo-associationist model and excitation transfer theory	… a result of affect elicited by aversive stimulation that is interpreted as anger	Experimental studies	Supported by empirical evidence
Social learning theory	… a result of reinforcement, either direct or indirect (observed)	Experimental and observational studies	Supported by empirical evidence
Social information processing models	… a result of social information processing, enactment of learned scripts	Experimental and longitudinal studies	Supported by empirical evidence
I^3 theory	… a result of the balance between promoting and inhibitory factors in the situation	Experimental studies	Supported by empirical evidence
General Aggression Model (GAM): A meta-theory of aggression	… a result of personal and situational input variables eliciting affective, cognitive, and physiological responses	Correlational, experimental, and longitudinal studies	Integrating findings from different psychological approaches

paying special attention to the answers they provide to two closely related questions:

(1) Is aggression an innate quality of human nature?
(2) How is aggression shaped in the process of socialisation, and is it possible for aggressive behaviour to be avoided or controlled?

BIOLOGICAL EXPLANATIONS

In this section, we look at four lines of research that refer to biological principles in explaining human aggression, namely the *ethological* approach, the *sociobiological* approach, the *behaviour genetic approach*, and the study of *hormonal influences* on aggression. This discussion is necessarily selective and cannot do justice to the impressive breadth of research on the role of biological factors in explaining aggression (Bedrosian & Nelson, 2018), for example on the role of the brain in understanding aggression (Bartholow (2017) and conclusions from animal studies for understanding pathological violence (deBoer, 2017).

The ethological view: Aggression as an internal energy

Among the biological approaches to aggression, one of the earliest contributions came from the field of ethology, which is concerned with the comparative study of animal and human behaviour. In his famous book *On Aggression*, Konrad Lorenz (1966) offered a model of aggression that dealt specifically with the issue of how aggressive energy is produced and released in both animals and humans. His core assumption was that the organism continuously builds up aggressive energy. Whether and when this energy will be released and lead to an aggressive response depends on two factors: (a) the level of aggressive energy inside the organism at any one time, and (b) the strength of external stimuli capable of triggering an aggressive response. In his *hydraulic model*, also known as the *steam-boiler model*, Lorenz assumed that aggressive energy is produced continuously inside the organism until it is released by an external cue, such as the appearance of a rival in competition for a mating partner. If the energy rises above a certain level without being released by an external stimulus, it will overflow, leading to spontaneous aggression. According to this model, aggressive behaviour is the inevitable consequence of the continuous production of aggressive energy. Even if it were possible to remove all instigating stimuli, this would not get rid of aggressive behaviour. As Lorenz (1966) put it, such an attempt would be "as judicious as trying to counteract the increasing pressure in a continuously heated boiler by screwing down the safety valve more tightly" (p. 269).

steam-boiler model: part of Konrad Lorenz's theory of aggression, assuming that aggressive energy is produced continuously within the organism and will burst out spontaneously unless released by an external stimulus.

Although Lorenz regarded aggression as a permanent and inevitable feature of human nature, he saw the possibility of releasing aggressive energy
in a controlled and socially accepted way, e.g., through sports activities.
In this way, he thought it would be possible to keep levels of aggressive
energy below the critical threshold above which spontaneous outbursts of
violence and other highly destructive forms of aggression would occur. As
Lorenz believed, "the main function of sports today lies in the cathartic discharge of aggressive urge" (1966, pp. 271–272).

When applying this model based on animal studies to human aggression,
it has to be explained why the inhibition against killing members of their
own species, widely observed among animals, clearly does not generalise
to humans. Lorenz (1966) argued that strong inhibitions against intra-
species killing were not needed in the early history of mankind, when
fists and teeth were the only (relatively innocuous) weapons for attacking
one another. With the development of ever more sophisticated and lethal
weapons, the fact that there is no innate inhibition to counterbalance the
potential for destroying one's own species could give rise to uncontrolled
levels of aggression and violence.

The application of Lorenz's findings from animal studies to human
aggression were soon considered problematic (Lore & Schultz, 1993). An
important criticism is directed at the implication that once the internal

reservoir of aggressive energy has been used up by an aggressive act, it is impossible to trigger another aggressive response for as long as it takes the organism to rebuild a sufficient energy level. Sadly, there is ample evidence from school shootings and other instances of multiple killings that humans can perform several aggressive behaviours in quick succession, and that one aggressive act often serves to precipitate rather than suppress further aggressive acts. Neither of these observations is compatible with the depletion effect assumed by the steam-boiler model. Furthermore, Lorenz's belief in the cathartic release of aggressive energy through sports activities is contradicted both by a large literature on sports aggression (Russell, 2008, and Chapter 7 of this volume) and by research debunking the catharsis hypothesis (Gentile, 2013, and Chapter 12 of this volume). Given that there is little support for Lorenz's ethological model as an explanation of human aggression, you may wonder why it has been presented here at all. The reason is that it still remains widely popular in everyday discourse when people suggest explanations, and indeed cures, for aggression. Enabling readers to participate in this discourse well-equipped with critical arguments to challenge popular myths about aggression is one of the goals of the present volume.

The sociobiological view: Aggression as a product of natural selection

Sociobiology is concerned with analysing the biological foundation of social behaviour on the basis of the evolutionary principle of *natural selection*. This approach also offers an explanation of aggression in both humans and animals, focusing on the long-term, "ultimate" mechanisms that shape and promote aggression through the generations. Rooted in Darwin's (1859) theory on "the origin of species", evolutionary theory is based on the idea that in order for a behaviour to be genetically transmitted within a species, it has to be *adaptive*. Behaviours are adaptive to the extent that they increase the chances of survival of the species as a whole in the environment in which it lives.

> **sociobiology:** discipline devoted to the study of the evolutionary basis of social behaviour.

Concise presentations of the evolutionary thinking about social behaviour have been provided by Daly and Wilson (1994) and Buss and Shackelford (1997). Applying the principle of evolution through natural selection to the study of aggression, aggressive behaviour directed at fighting off attackers as well as rivals in mate selection is seen as adaptive in the sense of enhancing the reproductive success of the aggressor (Archer, 1995). Because they are better able to control access to female mating partners, the more aggressive members of a species are more successful in passing their genes on to the next generation, thus favouring the natural selection of aggressive behaviour. Their genetic make-up slowly spreads at the expense of less aggressive, and therefore less reproductively successful, members. However, aggression may be a potentially costly and maladaptive behaviour in certain cases. For example, attacking an opponent of superior fighting power entails the risk of being killed. Therefore, the functional mechanism seen as driving the evolution of aggressive behaviour is a cost–benefit calculus (Archer, 2009; Georgiev, Klimczuk, Traficonte, & Maestripieri, 2013). As it would be maladaptive to engage in aggressive behaviour when the risk of being overpowered and potentially killed by the opponent is high, it is functional from the point of view of reproductive success to withdraw from confrontations that involve an opponent of superior strength and fighting power.

Evidence cited to support the sociobiological account of aggression mainly comes from animal studies, which have been used to generate and test hypotheses about aggressive behaviour in humans. For example, the observation that members of some species respond to cues indicating fighting power, such as opponent size, and refrain from attacking a stronger opponent, has led to the hypothesis that size and physical strength might be correlated with aggression in humans. Studies showing a positive correlation between height and physical aggression in boys and men support this line of reasoning. For example, Archer and Thanzami (2007) found significant correlations between physical aggression scores on the Aggression Questionnaire (see Chapter 1) and body weight ($r = .25$) as well as height ($r = .34$) in a sample of young men.

Arguably the most controversial contribution of the sociobiological approach in the aggression domain refers to its explanation of sexual aggression (Malamuth & Heilmann, 1998; L. Miller, 2014). From an evolutionary point of view, sexual aggression is an optional, if high-risk mating strategy for those men who have limited opportunities for reproduction through consensual sexual relationships (Thornhill & Thornhill, 1991). This view implies that the potential for rape is part of the evolutionary inheritance of all males. It also implies that reproduction is the main function of rape, not in the rapist's conscious awareness, but in terms of the evolutionary significance of his behaviour. To substantiate their arguments, proponents of the sociobiological explanation of rape refer to two main sources of data: (a) evidence from animal studies of forcible mating behaviours in different species (Brown, 2000); and (b) crime statistics, showing that the vast majority of rape victims are young women at the peak of their reproductive capacity and that men of low socio-economic status (indicating reduced reproductive opportunities by non-aggressive means) account for a disproportionate percentage of convicted rapists. Both data sources have been fundamentally challenged by critics of the sociobiological approach (Travis, 2003), and the controversy is far from being settled. We will return to the arguments of both sides of this debate in more detail in Chapter 9.

In summary, sociobiologists view aggression as a form of behaviour that has evolved in animals as well as humans because of its potential to enhance an individual's reproductive success, thereby facilitating the selective transmission of aggressive genes to future generations. The fact that aggression is universally observed in human societies is seen as corroborating the evolutionary account, although differences between cultures in the level of aggression have been acknowledged (Ferguson & Beaver, 2009).

The evidence presented in support of the evolutionary account is largely correlational – for example, the covariation of physical strength and physical aggression – precluding statements about cause–effect relationships. Furthermore, alternative hypotheses may be advanced for many of the findings. For instance, the greater tendency of taller and stronger men to engage in physical aggression may be the result of learning through reinforcement in the individual's socialisation history. Although evolutionary and socialisation hypotheses are often discussed as incompatible, integrations between the two approaches have been suggested, such as the "confluence model" of rape (Malamuth, 1998; Malamuth & Hald, 2017) discussed in Chapter 9. By drawing attention to the roots of aggressive behaviour in the ancient genetic heritage of the human species and explaining how it may be passed on through the generations, the evolutionary approach has made an important contribution to the theoretical debate about the causes of aggression.

Behaviour genetics: Is aggression hereditary?

The sociobiological argument that aggression has evolved because it is instrumental in enhancing the reproductive success of individuals and species rests on the assumption that aggressive behaviour is transmitted through individuals' genetic make-up. This assumption is central to the field of *behaviour genetics*, which is directed at exploring the role of genetic similarity in explaining similarities in personal characteristics and behaviour. Specifically, behaviour geneticists have sought to demonstrate that genetically related individuals are more similar in terms of their aggressive tendencies than individuals who are not genetically related.

behaviour genetics: field of study devoted to the genetic basis of social behaviour.

Because most children are raised by their biological parents, to whom they are also genetically related, the effects of "nature" and "nurture" normally coincide in individual development. Therefore, to separate the influences of family environment and heritability, special methods are needed. *Adoption studies* are capable of separating the influence of genetic and environmental factors by comparing individuals with their biological parents (shared genes) and with their adoptive parents (shared environment). If children are more similar in their aggressive behaviour to their biological parents than to their adoptive parents, this is an indication that shared genes are more influential than shared environment. Conversely, if adopted children are more similar in aggression to their adopted parents than to their biological parents, this suggests a stronger role of environmental compared with genetic factors. A second methodological approach is provided by *twin studies* that compare identical and fraternal twins in terms of how similar they are in their aggressive behaviour. Identical twins share 100% of their genetic make-up, whereas fraternal twins have only 50% of their genes in common. Therefore, evidence that identical twins are

adoption studies: study design whereby the similarity between children and their biological parents is compared to the similarity with their adoptive parents to compare shared genes against shared environment.

twin studies: study design comparing identical and fraternal twins in how similar they are in their aggressive behaviour.

more similar than fraternal twins in showing aggressive behaviour would indicate that aggression is to some extent genetically transmitted.

Evidence from both twin and adoption studies was reviewed by Miles and Carey (1997). They conducted a meta-analysis of 22 studies in which ratings of aggressive or antisocial behaviour had been obtained either from the respondents themselves or, in the case of young children, from their parents. Two further studies were included in which actual aggressive behaviour had been observed. The authors concluded from their findings that shared genetic make-up plays a large role in similarities in self-ratings as well as parent ratings of aggressiveness, explaining up to 50% of the variance. Taking into account the different age groups included in the meta-analysis, they further suggest that the relative importance of genetic and environmental influences in shaping aggression may change in the course of development. Shared genes were found to be more powerful than shared environmental influences in explaining similarities in aggression in adulthood, whereas the reverse pattern was found for children and adolescents. However, an important qualification of these conclusions comes from the two studies that used behavioural observation as measures of aggression. In these studies, the impact of shared environment was substantially greater than that of genetic similarity. A later meta-analysis by Rhee and Waldman (2002), including 51 twin and adoption studies, also found substantial effects of genetic similarity, explaining 41% of the variance, but environmental influences were even stronger, accounting for 59%.

DiLalla and Gottesman (1991) also found in their study of antisocial behaviour that genetic similarity was more influential on questionnaire measures than on behavioural indicators, such as criminal convictions. At the same time, they concluded from their review of adoption studies that genetic factors and environmental factors may have an additive effect. Individuals whose biological as well as adoptive parents were criminal had the highest likelihood of becoming criminal themselves, followed by individuals whose biological parents, but not adoptive parents, had criminal records. The risk of the latter group becoming criminal was found by several studies to be substantially higher than that of the group whose adoptive parents were criminal but whose biological parents were not, suggesting that genes are relatively more influential than shared environment. A meta-analysis by Burt (2009) comparing physical aggression and rule breaking as distinct aspects of antisocial behaviour concluded that genetic similarity played a greater role, and environmental factors played a lesser role, in aggressive as compared with rule-breaking behaviour. That genetic factors differ in the extent to which they can explain variability in aggressive behaviour was also concluded in a recent review of twin studies, which found higher heritability for physical and proactive aggression than for reactive aggression (Waltes, Chiocchetti, & Freitag, 2016).

On balance, the available evidence suggests that genetic make-up must be regarded as an important source of individual variation in aggression.

A precise assessment of the magnitude of its impact relative to environmental influences is difficult, hampered by various methodological problems that have been noted throughout the literature (Tedeschi & Felson, 1994). For example, studies analysing genetic vs. environmental influences on criminality often failed to distinguish between violent and non-violent crimes. This distinction is crucial if the aim is to determine the heritability of aggressive behaviour in particular, rather than antisocial or deviant behaviour in general (Burt, 2009). Furthermore, studies combining both self-report and observation are needed to resolve the issue of why the two types of measures produce diverging evidence on the strength of genetic influences.

With regard to the question of whether or not aggression is an inevitable part of human nature and individual character, research showing the impact of genetic factors has sometimes been construed as suggesting a deterministic, and thus pessimistic, view – if individuals carry the aggressive genes, they will grow up to be aggressive. However, such a view is rejected by behaviour geneticists. They stress that individuals' genetic make-up may predispose them towards becoming an aggressive person, but environmental factors play a crucial role in determining whether or not that predisposition will actually be expressed in aggressive behaviour. As noted by Van Goozen, Fairchild, Snoek, and Harold (2007), a genetic disposition towards aggressive behaviour may become manifested in behaviour in a negative family environment, or it may be suppressed in a positive environment. As children inherit the genetic disposition towards aggression from their parents, they are likely to grow up in a more aggression-prone family environment (Moffitt, 1993). To complicate matters further, children with a genetic disposition towards aggression may elicit negative responses from their social environment through their aggressive behaviour, also pointing to the interactive influences of nature and nurture.

The critical role of environmental factors is also demonstrated by evidence from the field of *epigenetics*. This research has shown that adverse experiences affecting individuals at sensitive periods of life, especially in prenatal development and early infancy, may trigger changes in the function of genes that lead to cognitive and emotional deficits involved in aggressive behaviour (Palumbo, Mariotti, Iofrida, & Pellegrini, 2018; Waltes et al., 2016). These findings show that genetic (inherited) and environmental (acquired) factors mutually influence each other, which may explain why individual differences in aggressive behaviour are highly stable over time. We will return to the issue of stability in more detail in Chapter 4.

epigenetics: field of study showing that adverse experiences may change a person's genes related to aggressive behaviour.

Hormones and aggression

Another line of biological research on aggression is concerned with the role of hormonal and other physiological processes in explaining variations in aggressive behaviour (Archer & Carré, 2017; Van Goozen, 2005). An obvious candidate for examination is the male sex hormone testosterone, both to

hormones: higher levels of testosterone and lower levels of cortisol have been linked to aggression, but they need to be considered in combination with environmental influences.

account for individual differences among men in their aggressive tendencies, and to explain the widely demonstrated gender differences in physical aggression (see Chapter 4). Testosterone is related to the activation of fight impulses and the inhibition of flight or avoidance behaviour, thereby increasing the likelihood of an aggressive response. A meta-analysis of 18 studies conducted by Archer, Birring, and Wu (1998) found that highly aggressive men had higher levels of testosterone than non-aggressive men. A later meta-analysis confirmed the significant association between testosterone and aggression in both men and women (Archer, Graham-Kevan, & Davies, 2005). However, the correlations are weaker than those found in animal studies (Van Goozen, 2005).

Rather than assuming a general link between testosterone and aggression, the "challenge hypothesis" argues that testosterone levels vary depending on whether they are adaptive from an evolutionary point of view (Archer, 2006). High testosterone levels are adaptive in relation to the challenge of sexual competition (i.e., selecting a mate and fighting off rivals), whereas low testosterone levels are adaptive in relation to the challenge of parental investment (i.e., forming relationships and caring for offspring). This pattern is proposed to hold for both men and women.

With regard to situational variations in testosterone levels, Klinesmith, Kasser, and McAndrew (2006) conducted an interesting experimental study. They asked male participants to handle a gun or a children's toy for 15 minutes and measured testosterone levels before and after. Men who had handled the gun showed a significant increase in testosterone levels, whereas those who had handled the toy did not. Those who had handled the gun also showed more aggressive behaviour in a subsequent phase, as measured by the hot sauce paradigm (see Chapter 1), and this effect could be at least partly explained by the increase in testosterone levels. Studying fluctuating testosterone levels in women, a recent study found that reactive aggression was higher when testosterone levels were also high (Probst, Golle, Lory, & Lobmaier, 2018).

Cortisol has been examined as another hormonal correlate of aggression, as it is related to the experience and management of stress. Low cortisol levels have been linked to fearlessness, risk taking, and insensitivity to punishment. Longitudinal studies have shown that low levels of resting cortisol in boys predict aggressive behaviour over time (McBurnett, Lahey, Rathouz, & Loeber, 2000; Shoal, Giancola, & Kirillova, 2003). Psychological underreactivity, as indicated by low cortisol levels, seems to be a characteristic feature of aggressive and antisocial behaviour, due to its disinhibiting function (for a review, see Van Goozen et al., 2007). By way of explanation, it has been argued that individuals with low levels of cortisol are less susceptible to fear of punishment, which would prevent them from engaging in aggressive behaviour (Raine, 1996).

dual hormone hypothesis: postulates that it is the combination of high testosterone and low cortisol that promotes aggressive behaviour.

Building on the two strands of research, the *dual hormone hypothesis* proposes that it is the combination of high testosterone and low cortisol levels (i.e., a high testosterone–cortisol ratio) that predicts high levels of aggression (Terburg, Morgan, & van Honk, 2009). In this combination, the aggression-stimulating effect of high testosterone levels is not counterbalanced by the inhibitory effect of cortisol, resulting in unmitigated aggressive behaviour. While the dual hormone hypothesis has received support for men, evidence for women has been inconclusive so far (Denson, O'Dean, Blake, & Beames, 2018). In addition to testosterone and cortisol, other hormones, such as higher oxytocin and lower serotonin, have been discussed as correlates of aggression (see Denson et al., 2018; Duke, Bègue, Bell, & Eisenlohr-Moul, 2013; Montoya, Terburg, Bos, & van Honk, 2012; Narvaes & Martins de Almeida, 2014), along with other biological processes, such as low resting heart rate (Portnoy & Farrington, 2015) and increased heart rate variability (Puhalla, Kulper, Fahlgren, & McCloskey, 2019). Although a detailed discussion is beyond the scope of this chapter, these are promising lines of research for a better understanding of the biological basis of aggressive behaviour.

Although the research discussed in this section shows that dispositional and situational differences in testosterone and cortisol may be related to aggressive behaviour, it is clear that hormones do not shape aggressive behaviour in a deterministic fashion. They work together with a wide range of factors in the social environment that may reinforce or attenuate the impact of biological influences on aggression.

PSYCHOLOGICAL EXPLANATIONS

The theoretical approaches considered so far have referred to biological processes in explaining aggression. We shall now turn to contributions that focus on the psychological mechanisms involved in aggressive behaviour. It is worth noting, though, that the earliest line of theoretical development in this tradition, namely Freud's psychoanalytic account of aggression, also started off from a biological construct by conceptualising aggressive behaviour as the expression of a genetically rooted *instinct*.

Freudian psychoanalysis: Aggression as a destructive instinct

In his *dual instinct theory*, Freud (1920) proposed that individual behaviour is driven by two basic forces that are part and parcel of human nature: the life instinct (*Eros*) and the death instinct (*Thanatos*). Whereas Eros drives the person towards pleasure seeking and wish fulfilment, Thanatos is directed at self-destruction. Due to their antagonistic nature, the two instincts are a source of sustained intrapsychic conflict that can be resolved by diverting the destructive force away from the individual on to others. Thus, acting aggressively towards another person is seen as a mechanism for releasing destructive energy in a way that protects the intrapsychic stability of the actor. In his notion of *catharsis*, Freud acknowledged the possibility of releasing destructive energy through non-aggressive expressive behaviour (e.g., sarcastic jokes), but with only temporary effects. According to this view, aggression is an inevitable feature of human behaviour beyond the control of the individual. It is interesting to note that Freud revised his earlier model, focusing on Eros only, and added a destructive force after witnessing the violence of World War I (Ekstein, 1949; for a review of psychoanalytic thinking on aggression following Freud; see also Jaffe & Straus, 1982).

Empirical evidence in support of Freud's theorising is scarce and largely based on case studies without the stringent operationalisations required in modern-day quantitative studies. Nonetheless, his ideas have played a significant role in promoting the understanding of aggression insofar as they inspired the influential frustration–aggression hypothesis, which will be considered next.

The frustration–aggression hypothesis and the role of aggressive cues

frustration–aggression hypothesis: assumes that frustration – that is, blockage of a goal-directed activity – increases the likelihood of aggressive behaviour.

aggressive cues: situational cues with an aggressive meaning that increase the accessibility of aggressive cognitions.

Instinct-related explanations of aggression have met with a critical reception, not least because of a shortage of empirical evidence to support them (see Baron & Richardson, 1994). However, the idea that there is a force within the organism which, in conjunction with external events, leads to aggressive behaviour has been central to an influential line of research that postulated an aggressive *drive* as motivating aggressive behaviour. Unlike an instinct, a drive is not an ever present, continuously increasing source of energy, but is activated only if the organism finds itself deprived of the means of satisfying a vital need. A drive, then, serves as a goal-directed, energising force directed at terminating a state of deprivation.

In the *frustration–aggression hypothesis* (Dollard, Doob, Miller, Mowrer, & Sears, 1939), aggression is seen as triggered by frustration. Frustration is defined as an external interference with the goal-directed behaviour of the person. The experience of frustration activates the desire to restore the path to goal attainment, and aggressive behaviour results from the drive to remove the source of the interference. For example, in the field experiment by Harris (1974) discussed in Chapter 1, a person waiting in a queue is pursuing a goal-directed activity, such as buying a train ticket at a busy ticket office. If someone else jumps the queue and cuts in just in front, the person's goal-directed activity is blocked (i.e., frustrated). This releases aggressive energy to restore the goal-directed activity (e.g., by pushing the person aside).

In the first version of the frustration–aggression hypothesis, Dollard et al. (1939) assumed that frustration would always trigger aggression, and that aggression would always be attributable to a preceding frustration. However, it quickly became clear that not every frustration leads to an aggressive response. Alternatively, frustrated individuals may withdraw from the situation or become upset rather than angry. Moreover, not every aggressive act is the result of a preceding frustration. Acts of instrumental aggression carried out to achieve a particular goal, such as robbing a bank to resolve a desperate financial situation, do not necessarily entail a previous frustration. Therefore, the earlier assumption of a deterministic relationship between frustration and aggression was changed into a probabilistic version by N. E. Miller (1941), one of the authors of the original theory. He stated that "frustration produces instigations to a number of different types of response, one of which is an instigation to some form of aggression" (p. 338). In this revised view, aggression is not the only but merely one possible response to frustration. To the extent that the aggressive act reduces the strength of the underlying drive, it becomes self-reinforcing – there is an increasing likelihood that an aggressive response will be shown following subsequent frustrations.

Displaced aggression. Whether or not frustration will result in an aggressive response depends on the influence of moderating variables. Fear of punishment for overt aggression or unavailability of the frustrator are factors that may inhibit aggression following a frustration. These moderators also explain why aggression may be "displaced" away from the frustrator on to a more easily accessible or less intimidating target. The concept of *displaced aggression* plays a role in understanding aggression not only in response to frustration, but particularly in response to provocation. Frustration and provocation are related, but distinguishable constructs. Whereas frustration focuses on goal blockage, *provocation* refers to an interpersonal encounter. However, the two concepts converge, for example, when the provocation takes the form of exposing another person to frustrating events, such as insoluble tasks or failure in a competition. Therefore, research on displaced aggression after a provocation is also relevant to understanding the frustration–aggression link. A meta-analysis of

displaced aggression: tendency to react to frustration with an aggressive response directed not at the original source of the frustration but at an unrelated, more easily accessible target.

provocation: anger-eliciting interpersonal encounter.

40 studies by Marcus-Newhall, Pedersen, Carlson, and Miller (2000) found consistent evidence for the displacement of aggression from the source of the frustration or provocation onto a less powerful or more accessible target.

Subsequent research into "triggered displaced aggression" has provided further insights into the psychological processes involved in the path from frustration or provocation to aggression (N. E. Miller, Pedersen, Earleywine, & Pollock, 2003). Triggered displaced aggression describes the outcome of a sequence of events which starts with the experience of a frustration or provocation that activates the desire to retaliate. If this desire cannot be acted out, a relatively mild subsequent provocation, the "trigger", may elicit a disproportionately strong aggressive response (Pedersen, Gonzales, & Miller, 2000). For example, a man who is told off at work by his boss, against whom he cannot retaliate because the boss is too powerful, may react with an outburst of verbal abuse in response to a mildly teasing comment from his wife when he gets home. The same comment might have been dismissed as a joke in the absence of the prior provocation. Experimental research has shown that participants who were first exposed to a provocation without being able to retaliate and then encountered a mildly provoking trigger showed much stronger aggressive responses than participants who were exposed to the same trigger without being previously provoked (Vasquez, Denson, Pedersen, Stenstrom, & Miller, 2005).

To explain displaced triggered aggression, two processes have been proposed (N. E. Miller et al., 2003). The first is the elicitation of negative arousal by the initial provocation that is still present when the trigger is encountered, and is intensified by the trigger. The second process refers to rumination about the initial provocation that is maintained because the person is unable to deliver an aggressive response to the source of the frustration. The anger elicited by the original provocation is kept on the back burner and is caused to flare up again by the trigger. As both arousal and rumination subside over time, triggered displaced aggression is likely to occur primarily when the trigger is encountered shortly after the initial provocation. However, Miller et al. (2003) discussed a number of situational and personal variables that may lead to displaced triggered aggression even over extended periods of time, such as the importance of the goal that is impeded, or the dispositional tendency to engage in ruminative thinking (for a discussion of research on rumination and aggression, see Chapter 4). A recent series of studies has shown that displaced aggression may serve an instrumental function as a means to restore a sense of competence after a goal-directed action has been blocked by a frustration and may be reduced if the person can restore competence and self-efficacy by other, non-aggressive behaviours (Leander & Chartrand, 2017).

Aggressive cues. If aggression is seen as just one of different possible responses to frustration, the question arises as to when people are likely to choose aggressive behaviour rather than alternative responses when they are experiencing a frustration. One answer to this question comes from research into the role of aggressive cues that are present in the situation. Aggressive cues can be any stimuli with an aggressive meaning that increase the salience of aggressive thoughts, such as the presence of weapons, or being reminded of the names of famous boxing champions. It is assumed that if aggression-related cues are present, individuals are more likely to select an aggressive response when angered or provoked.

In a much-cited study, Berkowitz and LePage (1967) demonstrated that angered participants subsequently showed more aggressive behaviour in the presence of aggressive cues than in the presence of neutral cues. Half of their participants were angered by receiving negative feedback in a problem-solving task from an alleged co-participant (who was in fact a confederate of the experimenter); the other half received positive feedback. Both groups were then given the opportunity to evaluate the other person's performance on the task by administering electric shocks (ranging from one shock, indicating a very positive evaluation, to a maximum of ten shocks, indicating a very negative evaluation). The number of electric shocks delivered represented the measure of aggressive behaviour. To manipulate the role of aggressive cues, the setting was created such that participants saw:

(1) a 38 mm calibre revolver and a 12 gauge shotgun allegedly left behind by the other student in the experiment (associated weapons condition), or
(2) the same weapons allegedly left behind by a third student in an earlier experiment (unassociated weapon condition), or
(3) two badminton rackets and shuttlecocks (neutral objects condition), or
(4) no objects at all (control condition).

Figure 2.1 presents the number of shocks administered in the different conditions.

After receiving negative feedback, participants delivered significantly more shocks in the presence of a weapon than in the presence of a neutral object or in the no-object control condition. Whether the weapon was associated or unassociated with the person who was the source of the negative evaluation made no difference. Significantly fewer shocks were delivered by the non-angered participants, and the availability of aggressive cues had no effect on the aggressive behaviour in this group.

Although subsequent studies did not always replicate the effect, with some failing to find a *weapons effect* and others finding an effect in the non-angered participants as well, overall support for the role of aggression-related cues in facilitating aggressive behaviour is impressive. From their meta-analysis of 57 studies, Carlson, Marcus-Newhall, and Miller (1990) concluded that "aggression-related cues present in experimental settings act to increase aggressive responding" (p. 632). In an experimental study of aggressive driving behaviour, Ellison-Potter, Bell, and Deffenbacher (2001) showed that participants who drove past billboards bearing aggressive messages while steering through a course in a driving simulator committed

weapons effect: finding that individuals who were previously angered showed more aggressive behaviour in the presence of weapons than in the presence of neutral objects.

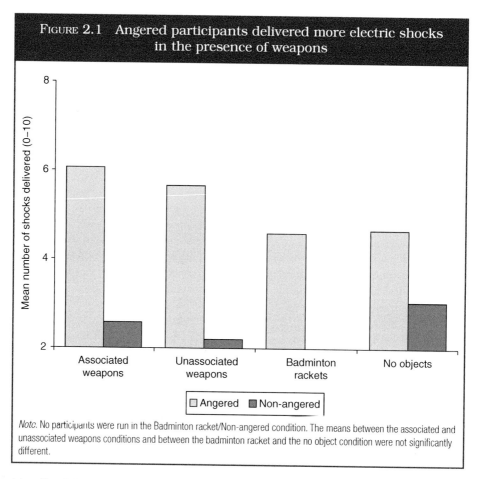

FIGURE 2.1   Angered participants delivered more electric shocks in the presence of weapons

Note. No participants were run in the Badminton racket/Non-angered condition. The means between the associated and unassociated weapons conditions and between the badminton racket and the no object condition were not significantly different.

Adapted from Berkowitz & LePage, 1967, Table 2.

more acts of aggressive driving (speeding, driving through red lights, and killing pedestrians) than participants exposed to non-aggressive billboard messages (for more research on aggressive driving, see Chapter 7). By way of explaining the underlying processes, cognitive priming has been offered as the key mechanism. Being exposed to aggressive cues enhances the accessibility of aggressive cognitions that in turn facilitate aggressive behaviour. We shall come back to the role of aggressive cues as situational primes in more detail in Chapter 5.

To summarise, starting off as a drive model, the frustration–aggression hypothesis has been developed into a more complex approach, stressing the cognitive appraisal of situational cues as a crucial mediator between an anger-eliciting event and an aggressive response. This line of thinking was developed further by Berkowitz (1989) in his cognitive neo-associationist model to be discussed next.

Cognitive neo-associationism: The role of anger

In trying to explain why frustration leads to aggression in some circumstances but not in others, Berkowitz (1989, 1993, 2008) proposed that negative affect in the form of *anger* and its cognitive appraisal are important mediators between frustration and aggression. Frustration leads to aggression only when it arouses negative affective states. Some frustrations may be perceived as challenges, such as struggling to play the piano well, and remain unrelated to aggression, and other frustrations may be perceived as accidental, such as being slowed down by an elderly pedestrian when rushing to catch a bus. Although they may elicit anger, the anger response is likely to be weaker in these situations than if the frustration was considered to be deliberate, such as another driver cutting in to take the last empty space in a crowded car park. Viewed in this way, frustrations can be seen as just one example of a more general category of aversive events that elicit negative affect. Other types of aversive stimulation, such as fear, physical pain, or psychological discomfort, can equally instigate aggression through their capacity to make the person angry (Berkowitz, 1997, 1998; Groves, 2018). *Anger* is defined as "a syndrome of relatively specific feelings, cognitions, and physiological reactions linked associatively with an urge to injure some target" (Berkowitz & Harmon-Jones, 2004, p. 108). The process that leads from the exposure to an aversive stimulus to the experience of anger according to Berkowitz's model is presented in Figure 2.2.

Berkowitz proposed that unpleasant stimuli give rise to unspecific negative feelings that evoke two immediate reactions – *fight* and *flight*. In a swift and automatic appraisal process that occurs with little or no conscious awareness, the fight impulse is associated with aggression-related thoughts, memories, and behavioural responses, whereas the flight impulse is associated with escape-related responses. These responses serve to quickly channel the initially undifferentiated negative affect into the more specific emotional states of (rudimentary) anger or (rudimentary) fear. In a subsequent more elaborate and controlled appraisal process, the person *interprets* these basic or rudimentary feelings. They are considered in relation to the situational input, and the person enters into a more specific and consolidated emotional state of anger *or* fear. The final emotional state is "a collection of particular feelings, expressive motor-reactions, thoughts and memories that are associated with each other" (Berkowitz, 1993, p. 59). It should be noted that pitting "fight" against "flight" shows parallels with the "dual-hormone hypothesis" discussed earlier into the antagonistic role of testosterone and cortisol as instigators and inhibitors of aggression, respectively, but in the present context the focus is on cognitive rather than physiological processes.

Although the model stops at the level of emotional responses, it is assumed that when the evaluation gives rise to feelings of anger, irritation, or annoyance, an aggressive response becomes likely. For example, when a child is hit by a stone thrown by a classmate, he will immediately

cognitive neo-associationism: explanation of aggressive behaviour as the result of negative affect that is subjected to cognitive processing and activates a network of aggression-related thoughts and feelings.

anger: a syndrome of relatively specific feelings, cognitions, and physiological reactions linked associatively with an urge to injure some target.

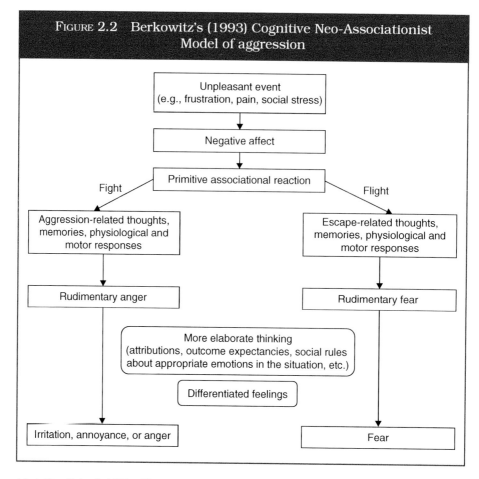

FIGURE 2.2   Berkowitz's (1993) Cognitive Neo-Associationist Model of aggression

Adapted from Berkowitz, 1993, p. 57.

experience pain associated with negative affect, probably a combination of anger, inducing the urge to fight, and fear, inducing the urge to run away. Depending on the context and the child's past experience, either the anger or the fear response will prevail and guide his further analysis of the situation. Before deciding how to respond, the child will engage in a more careful appraisal process, including an assessment of his classmate's motives. If he concludes that his classmate threw the stone on purpose, the immediate feeling of anger will be consolidated, and retaliation (i.e., aggression) will be contemplated as an appropriate response.

Because all the components of the emotional experience are associated with each other, the activation of one component is assumed to trigger other components relative to the strength of their association, hence the term "associationism". For example, activating memories of past aversive events can give rise to aggressive thoughts and feelings, which may then increase the likelihood of aggressive behaviour in a new situation or towards a target that is completely unrelated to the initial aversive event.

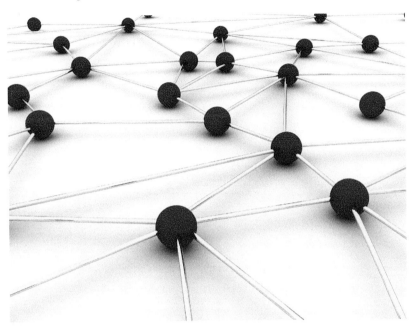

From the above discussion, it is clear that, according to Berkowitz, aggression is only one of several possible responses to aversive stimulation, depending on a chain of processes involving feelings and cognitive appraisals. This implies that aggression is not an inevitable feature of human behaviour, but rather a potential one, which is facilitated or suppressed by the emotional experience elicited by the aversive event and its subsequent cognitive processing.

Excitation transfer theory: Anger and the attribution of arousal

excitation transfer theory: transfer of neutral physiological arousal onto arousal resulting from frustration, thus augmenting negative affect and increasing the strength of an aggressive response.

The cognitive appraisal of physiological arousal is also at the core of another influential theory of aggression, the excitation transfer model proposed by Zillmann (1979). Like the cognitive neo-associationist model, excitation transfer theory highlights the role of negative arousal as a powerful stimulant of aggression. Building on Schachter's (1964) two-factor theory of emotion, Zillmann (1979) proposed that the intensity of an anger experience is a function of two components: (a) the strength of the physiological arousal generated by an aversive event, and (b) the way in which the arousal is explained and labelled. For example, every motorist is familiar with the sudden increase in physiological arousal that occurs after a narrow escape from a dangerous traffic situation, such as stopping one's car inches away from a pedestrian who stepped out into the road from behind a parked car.

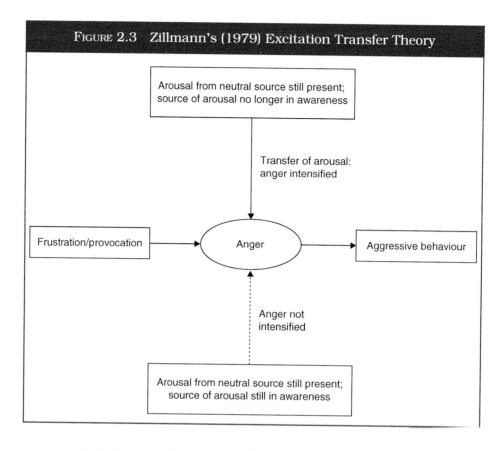

FIGURE 2.3   Zillmann's (1979) Excitation Transfer Theory

Whether or not this arousal will be interpreted as anger depends largely on the appraisal of the situation. If the pedestrian is an adult, then the driver's arousal is likely to be experienced as anger about the other person's carelessness. However, if that person is a young child, feelings of relief are likely to prevail over feelings of anger. Thus, the interpretation of physiological arousal elicited by an aversive event is crucial for the link between the aversive event and a potential aggressive response. The associations proposed by the excitation transfer model are shown in Figure 2.3.

Zillmann argued that the effects of frustration as a trigger for aggressive behaviour can be augmented by physiological arousal from a neutral source, unrelated to anger, through a process of misattribution. If physiological arousal from a neutral activity, such as climbing up a flight of stairs or riding a bike, is still present when the person encounters an anger-eliciting situation, such as being verbally attacked, the earlier neutral arousal (*excitation*) is *transferred* on to the anger-related arousal and falsely attributed as anger. As a result, the strength of the subsequent aggressive response is increased. However, this misattribution will only occur if the person is no longer aware of the source of the neutral arousal. This in turn means that excitation transfer can only take place within a relatively narrow time

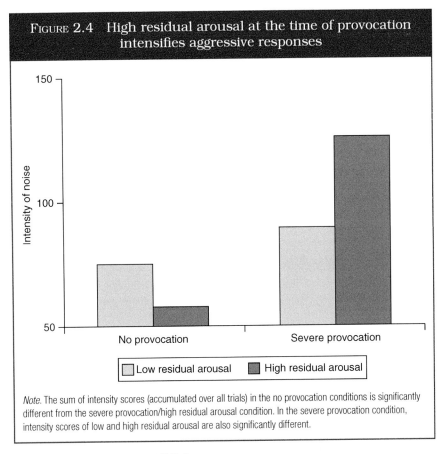

FIGURE 2.4   High residual arousal at the time of provocation intensifies aggressive responses

Note. The sum of intensity scores (accumulated over all trials) in the no provocation conditions is significantly different from the severe provocation/high residual arousal condition. In the severe provocation condition, intensity scores of low and high residual arousal are also significantly different.

Adapted from Zillmann & Bryant, 1974, Table 2.

window, in which arousal from the neutral source is still sufficiently high, yet the actor is no longer aware of its origin.

To support the excitation transfer model, Zillmann and Bryant (1974) conducted an experiment in which the participants had to perform either a physically non-arousing task (threading discs on a wire) or an arousing task (pedalling a bike ergometer for 1 minute). Two minutes later they received a provocation from another person in the form of an aversive noise, another six minutes later, they were given the opportunity to administer aversive noise blasts to the person who had provoked them with the noise, using an intensity scale from 1 to 10. The findings are shown in Figure 2.4.

As predicted by the model, participants in the bike condition, who were still aroused from the physical exercise at the time of the provocation, administered louder noise blasts than did participants in the disc-threading condition, who did not feel any neutral arousal that might have augmented the anger elicited by the provocation.

The excitation transfer model deals with the combined effects of physiological arousal and its cognitive appraisal on the emotional experience of anger. By influencing attributions of physiological arousal, aggressive response tendencies can be strengthened, as shown by Zillmann and Bryant (1974). By the same token, misattributions of arousal may be used to weaken aggressive response tendencies. If people are led to believe that their arousal was caused by a pill rather than by the provocation they experienced from another person, they perceive themselves as less angry and react less aggressively than those who are not offered a neutral explanation for their arousal (Younger & Doob, 1978). Therefore, this approach also supports the view of aggression as a potential, but by no means inevitable, manifestation of human behaviour.

The social cognitive approach: Aggressive scripts and social information processing

aggressive scripts: cognitive representations of when and how to show aggressive behaviour.

social information processing (SIP) approach: theory about social–cognitive processes that pave the way to aggressive behaviour.

The importance of cognitive processes in the formation of an aggressive response has been stressed throughout the preceding sections. The way in which people think about an aversive event and the emotional reaction they experience as a consequence is critical in determining the level of anger as well as the likelihood and strength of an aggressive response. The social cognitive approach further extends this perspective by studying individual differences in aggression as a function of differences in social information processing. In particular, two issues have been explored by this research: (a) the development of cognitive schemata that guide the enactment of aggressive behaviour; and (b) characteristic ways of processing social information that distinguish between aggressive and non-aggressive individuals.

Cognitive schemata referring to situations and events are called "scripts". Scripts consist of knowledge structures that describe "appropriate sequences of events in a particular context" (Schank & Abelson, 1977, p. 41). These knowledge structures are acquired through first-hand experience with the respective situation or through observation (e.g., in the media). In his social cognitive approach, Huesmann (1998, 2017) proposed that social behaviour in general, and aggressive behaviour in particular, is controlled by behavioural experiences acquired in the process of early socialisation. From these experiences, scripts develop as abstract cognitive representations, containing the characteristic features of a situation in which aggressive behaviour may be shown, expectations about the behaviour of other people involved, and beliefs about the consequences of engaging in aggressive behaviour.

For example, if children have repeatedly responded (or seen others responding) to conflict situations by showing aggressive behaviour and thereby settled the conflict to their advantage, they develop a generalised cognitive representation in which aggression and success are closely linked. When they encounter a conflict situation, this representation is likely to be activated, leading them to engage in further aggressive behaviour. Aggressive scripts also contain normative beliefs about whether or not an aggressive response is appropriate under the given circumstances. For example, children may develop the normative belief that it is OK to hit back if attacked by a peer in a fight, but not if one is hit by a parent as a disciplinary measure. In a study by Huesmann and Guerra (1997), a significant correlation was found between the endorsement of normative beliefs approving aggressive behaviour and actual aggressive behaviour. Failure to learn the normative restrictions imposed on showing aggressive behaviour will lead to the repeated display of inappropriate aggression that may form the basis for long-term adjustment problems (Eron, 1987).

Whether or not an aggressive script is activated and guides the person towards responding in an aggressive fashion depends to a significant extent on the initial cognitive processing of the information that precedes the behavioural act. Following the perception of another person's behaviour, the individual looks for an interpretation of that behaviour. Several studies have shown that individuals with a history of aggressive behaviour selectively prefer interpretations that attribute the other's behaviour to hostile intentions, especially when that behaviour is ambiguous (Geen, 1998). This "hostile attribution bias" may then activate an aggressive script and increase the probability that an aggressive reaction will be selected from the individual's response repertoire (for a more detailed discussion of the hostile attribution bias, see Chapter 4).

The role of scripts as cognitive blueprints for aggressive behaviour has been demonstrated in different domains. For example, Vandello and

Cohen (2003) showed that cultural scripts about male honour predicted the acceptance of physical violence by a man betrayed by his female partner, and also predicted a more positive view of victimised women remaining with their abusive partners rather than leaving the relationship. Similarly, the more strongly certain known risk factors for sexual aggression, such as drinking alcohol in a sexual encounter, are rooted in individuals' script for consensual sexual interactions, the more they were inclined to accept sexual aggression as normative and to engage in sexually aggressive behaviour (Krahé, Bieneck, & Scheinberger-Olwig, 2007).

Another influential model of the role of social information processing in aggression has been proposed by Dodge (2011; Fontaine & Dodge, 2009). His *social information processing (SIP)* model sees the development of social behaviour as a transactional process in which individuals are both influenced by their social environment and actively shape that environment. With regard to aggression, or more broadly antisocial behaviour, the SIP model specifies a sequence of social-cognitive processes that pave the way to aggressive behaviour. The first step, *encoding of cues*, involves the perception and encoding of the social stimulus, such as receiving a derogatory comment from a peer. In the second step, *interpretation of cues*, attributions are made about intent and causality (e.g., Did this person mean to be nasty to me or was he just generally in a bad mood?). In the third step, *clarification of goals*, individuals engage in a process of identifying and prioritising their interests in the situation (e.g., to remain friends with the other person or to save face by retaliating). Depending on the goals that are identified, possible responses are generated in the fourth step (*response access or construction*), such as dismissing the remark as funny or responding with an angry comment. In the fifth and final step, the sequence ends with the selection of a response that is then enacted in the situation (*response selection*). It is clear from this five-step model that the individual may leave the pathway to aggression at any of the stages, depending on the appraisal processes and their outcomes. In support of the SIP model, Fontaine and Dodge (2009) presented evidence to show that antisocial youths (a) encode fewer social cues, (b) are more likely to attribute another person's ambiguous behaviour to hostile intentions, (c) are more likely to activate goals that are harmful to social relationships, (d) generate more aggressive and fewer non-aggressive behavioural options, and (e) evaluate aggressive responses more favourably.

The script model and the SIP model both stress the role of the cognitive appraisal of aggressive cues and of potential responses, based on past behaviour and generalised knowledge structures. The development of aggressive scripts as well as the emergence of patterns of information processing conducive to aggressive responding are shaped by an individual's experiences in the course of socialisation. These experiences give rise to the learning of aggressive behaviour, which will be examined next.

Learning to be aggressive: The role of reinforcement and observation

Like all forms of social behaviour, aggression is, to a significant degree, acquired through learning processes (Bandura, 1983). The role of genetic dispositions notwithstanding, it is clear that social experiences shape an individual's propensity to engage in aggressive behaviour. Learning is defined as behaviour change through experience, and two mechanisms in particular are involved in the learning of aggressive behaviour: (a) *learning through reinforcement*, which means that aggressive behaviour is rewarded by success or praise or inhibited by negative consequences, and (b) *observational learning*, which involves watching others being rewarded or punished for their aggressive behaviour.

When individuals are rewarded for aggressive behaviour, either by achieving a desired goal through the aggressive act or by winning social approval for showing aggressive behaviour, they are more likely to show that behaviour on future occasions. Children who are praised by their parents for "standing up for themselves" after being provoked, or who succeed in getting hold of a desired toy by grabbing it from another child, learn that aggressive behaviour pays off, and they are encouraged by the positive effects of their behaviour to perform similar aggressive acts in the future. *Observational learning* refers to learning by imitation. Watching others engage in aggressive behaviour also increases the likelihood of aggressive behaviour in the observer, particularly if the models are attractive and/or similar to the observer, and if they are seen being rewarded for their aggression.

observational learning: learning aggressive behaviour by observing and imitating the aggressive behaviour of others.

The effects of observational learning were shown in a classic study by Bandura, Ross, and Ross (1961). They pioneered the *Bobo doll paradigm*, in which children were shown adult models behaving in either an aggressive or a non-aggressive way towards a large inflatable clown figure called Bobo. When the children were subsequently given the opportunity to play with the doll, those who had watched the aggressive model showed more aggressive behaviour towards Bobo, such as hitting it with a hammer, than those who had watched the non-aggressive model. These findings suggest that observing an aggressive model may lead to the *acquisition* of the observed behaviour even if the model is not reinforced for his or her behaviour.

Bobo doll paradigm: using a large inflatable doll (Bobo) to show that adults' aggressive behaviour towards the doll leads to imitation by children who observed their behaviour.

In predicting whether or not the learned behaviour will actually be *performed*, the perceived consequences of the model's as well as the observer's behaviour do play an important role. Bandura, Ross, and Ross (1963) showed in a later study that an aggressive model elicited more imitative aggression when he was praised for his aggressive behaviour than when he was punished (i.e., beaten up by the target of the aggression). Thus, the more positive the consequences of the aggressive behaviour are for the model, the greater is the likelihood of imitation by the observer.

The model's behaviour as well as its consequences serve as external stimuli that elicit aggressive reactions in the observer. The observers' normative standards with regard to the adequacy of the model's behaviour and their self-efficacy beliefs (i.e., the conviction that they are capable of performing the behaviour with the intended effects) serve as internal mechanisms that regulate aggressive behaviour. Repeated experiences of *direct reinforcement* of aggressive behaviour or repeated exposure to models who successfully engage in aggression accumulate over time to promote the acquisition of aggressive scripts and create a dispositional tendency for showing aggressive behaviour (Huesmann & Kirwil, 2007).

direct reinforcement: experience of positive consequences of aggressive behaviour (e.g., status gain among peers) that increases the probability of future aggressive acts.

Both direct reinforcement and observation play a role in explaining aggression in a variety of domains, as will be seen in the next chapters. The social learning perspective has been a particularly prominent theoretical approach for conceptualising the effects of media violence on aggressive behaviour. Exposure to violent media models can be regarded as a paradigmatic case of observational learning, as will be discussed in Chapter 6. Moreover, witnessing violence between parents in childhood has been shown to be a risk factor for later aggressive behaviour (see Chapter 8).

I³ theory: theory that explains aggression by the interplay of three factors: instigation, impellance, and inhibition.

I³ theory: Aggressive behaviour as a function of promoting vs. inhibitory forces

A final explanation of aggressive behaviour is provided by I³ theory (Finkel & Hall, 2018; Slotter & Finkel, 2011). This theory, pronounced "I-cubed", is a general theory seeking to explain why and when certain behaviours occur, which has also been applied to the understanding of aggressive behaviour (Finkel, 2014). According to I³ theory, interpersonal behaviour is the result of the interplay of three factors. All three start with the letter "I", hence the name I³ theory. The first factor, "Instigation", denotes the situational triggers of an aggressive behaviour. These triggers have a strong normative component, which means that they are more likely to lead to an aggressive response if they are preceded by the violation of a social norm, such as a provocation or an insult. The second factor, "Impellance", refers to the intensity or strength of the aggressive response. Impelling factors may lie within the person, such as individual differences in trait aggression, or in the situation, such as the availability of a weapon. Instigation and impellance interact such that the same instigator may lead to a different response depending on how strongly the actor feels impelled to respond aggressively. For example, an individual may respond more aggressively to an insult from a subordinate than to an insult from his or her boss, or an individual high on trait aggression may respond more aggressively than a more even-tempered person to the same provocation. Whereas both instigation and impellance drive the individual towards aggressive behaviour, the third factor, "Inhibition" describes the forces that weaken the tendency to act aggressively. Inhibiting factors can also be related to the person, such as individual differences in self-control, or to the situation, such as impaired restraint due to alcohol intoxication. The interactive effects of all three forces yield complex predictions as to the likelihood and intensity of aggressive behaviour in a given situation. Aggressive behaviour should be most likely and most intense when a strong instigating stimulus meets with strong impellance and weak inhibition.

A major field of application of I³ theory has been the study of intimate partner violence (Birkley & Eckhardt, 2019), especially with regard to the role of alcohol as a disinhibiting factor for aggression in conflict situations. Using the noise blast paradigm described in Chapter 1, a laboratory experiment studied couples who were asked to think about an unresolved issue in their relationship (Watkins, DiLillo, & Maldonado, 2015). Members of the couple were more likely to administer aversive noise blasts to their partner when intoxicated, especially when they were instructed to ruminate. The positive association between the tendency to ruminate about the relationship conflict (to turn it round in their head again and again) and aggressive behaviour toward the partner was augmented by alcohol.

A special feature of I³ theory is its explicit consideration of inhibitory processes that reduce the likelihood and strength of an aggressive response by weakening the impact of instigating and impelling factors. In line with this view, which amounts to a three-way interaction between the three types of forces, Li, Nie, Boardley, Dou, and Situ (2015) showed that individuals with a strong acceptance of aggression as normative reacted more aggressively to a provocation only when their self-control resources had been depleted by a distracting task. Another study revealed that the association between trait aggressiveness and aggressive responses to provocation was eliminated when participants received an explicit warning that aggression would lead to negative consequences, demonstrating that aggression may be reduced by strengthening attention to inhibitory cues (Sherrill, Magliano, Rosenbaum, Bell, & Wallace, 2016). We will return to the constructs of rumination and self-regulation when discussing individual differences in aggression in Chapter 4.

Putting it all together: The General Aggression Model (GAM)

The different approaches reviewed in this chapter reflect the multiplicity of theories designed to understand aggressive behaviour. The biological approaches concentrated on the role of individual differences based on genetic and hormonal influences, whereas the psychological approaches highlighted the interplay of affective states, cognitive processes, and learning experiences in the course of socialisation for the implementation of aggressive responses.

General Aggression Model (GAM): integrative theoretical framework explaining how personal and situational input variables lead to aggressive behaviour via cognitive appraisal, negative affect, and physiological arousal.

A comprehensive model that integrates aspects of many of the theories discussed so far is the *General Aggression Model* (GAM) developed by Anderson and his co-workers (Anderson & Bushman, 2018). The GAM represents a "meta-theory" that aims to explain how aggressive behaviour emerges both in the course of development and in specific situations. Therefore, it addresses both long-term processes that give rise to individual differences in aggressive behaviour and short-term processes that influence an individual's decision whether or not to engage in aggressive behaviour under a given set of circumstances. Both parts of the model are shown in Figure 2.5.

The top part of Figure 2.5 conceptualises the emergence of aggression as a personality trait as the result of biological factors, incorporating theorising and research on the role of genetic dispositions or hormones, and environmental influences, incorporating theories and evidence on social learning. These variables operate both individually and in interaction to yield stable differences between people in their propensity for aggressive behaviour. The feedback loop from social encounters to personality differences reflects the idea that from their experience with specific situations, individuals develop aggressive scripts as generalised knowledge structures and characteristic styles of social information processing that shape their behavioural responses across situations. Each aggressive episode is seen as a social learning trial in which aggression-related knowledge structures are rehearsed and reinforced. The more often a person engages in aggressive behaviour without negative consequences, the lower the threshold becomes for choosing to act aggressively in the future, the more readily aggressive scripts are accessed, and the more rapidly aggressive cognitions are activated. In combination, these processes work to firmly establish aggression in individuals' behavioural repertoires, eventually making it part of their personality (Anderson & Carnagey, 2004).

Individual differences in the form of aggression as a trait affect the odds that a person will engage in aggressive behaviour in a particular situation, as shown in the bottom part of the model, including the likelihood of entering situations in which aggressive behaviour may be precipitated. The GAM assumes that the starting point of an aggressive interaction lies in individual dispositions, such as trait anger, and external stimuli, such as aggressive cues, that meet in a particular situation and evoke an interrelated set of internal processes in the actor. They elicit an internal state that is characterised by specific cognitions, feelings, and arousal symptoms. For example, someone who is easy to anger may only need a small provocation from a stranger to enter into a state of fury, characterised by aggressive thoughts ("This person is an idiot"), negative feelings ("This person makes me mad"), and bodily symptoms ("I can feel my blood pressure rising"). This internal state in turn gives rise to a fast automatic appraisal of the situation (e.g., "This person's behaviour is outrageous"). In the subsequent

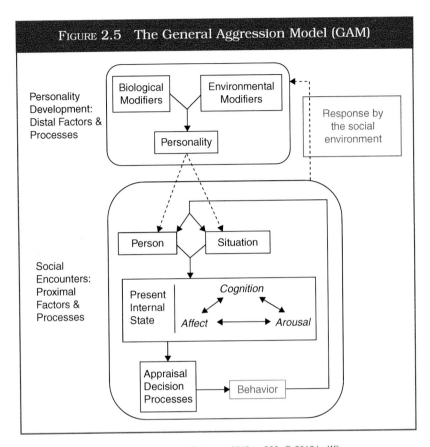

FIGURE 2.5   The General Aggression Model (GAM)

Reprinted with permission from Anderson & Bushman, 2018, p. 389; © 2018 by Wiley.

reappraisal stage, the initial evaluation of the situation is considered in a more controlled and elaborate way, leading to the selection and enactment of a behavioural response. Depending on the reappraisal, this response will either be aggressive ("This person annoyed me on purpose and therefore, I will retaliate in kind") or non-aggressive ("Let's try to calm down"). The behavioural decision may trigger a response from the target that marks the beginning of a new episode and may further escalate or de-escalate the conflict.

The GAM incorporates ideas and findings from several of the theoretical approaches discussed in the course of this chapter, such as the neo-associationist model of anger in response to aversive stimuli or the role of aggressive scripts. It provides a structure that helps us to understand the complex processes through which particular input variables, such as violent media stimuli or biographical experiences of abuse, can lead to aggressive behaviour as the critical outcome variable. The GAM has also been found useful as a theoretical framework for conceptualising different forms of violent behaviour and for designing violence prevention programmes (DeWall & Anderson, 2011; Gilbert & Daffern, 2011).

To conclude this review of theoretical approaches to understanding aggression, one important point of comparison relates to their implications for the controllability and prevention of aggressive behaviour. The early instinct-related views entail a pessimistic view because they conceptualise aggression as an inevitable part of human nature. However, there is now a consensus that a deterministic view of aggression is not appropriate. Even though evolutionary principles may be applied to understanding aggressive behaviour, and genetic make-up as well as physiological processes can explain variability in aggressive behaviour, it is clear that individual learning, thinking, and feeling play a major role in shaping social behaviour, including aggression. As Berkowitz (1993, p. 387) pointed out, "people have a *capacity* for aggression and violence, but not a biological urge to attack and destroy others that is continually building up inside them." This view is supported by theories that emphasise the mediating role of cognitions and learning as well as decision-making processes. By highlighting how aggressive behaviour is acquired, these approaches also generate knowledge about strengthening the inhibitory forces against aggression, and they acknowledge the individual's freedom to decide against acting aggressively in favour of alternative courses of action.

SUMMARY

- Theoretical explanations of aggressive behaviour include both biological and psychological lines of thinking and research.
- Biological models refer to evolutionary and genetic principles and the role of hormones in explaining aggression. The ethological perspective regards the manifestation of overt aggression as a function of an internal aggressive energy that is released by aggression-related external cues, but it cannot conclusively explain aggressive behaviour in humans. The sociobiological approach postulates that aggression has developed as an adaptive form of social behaviour in the process of evolution. Evidence from the field of behaviour genetics suggests that the propensity to act aggressively is at least partly influenced by genetic dispositions. Finally, there is some evidence that hormones, such as testosterone and cortisol, are involved in regulating aggressive behaviour and explaining individual differences in the propensity to engage in aggression.
- Early psychological models also assumed aggression to be an innate response tendency. Freud's view of aggression as an expression of the antagonism of Eros and Thanatos inspired the frustration–aggression hypothesis, which sees aggression as driven by the desire to overcome frustration.

- Subsequent psychological approaches widened the frustration–aggression hypothesis into a more general model of negative affect, and highlighted the role of cognitive factors, learning experiences, and decision-making processes in eliciting aggressive responses. According to cognitive neo-associationism and excitation transfer theory, negative affect (caused by a range of aversive stimuli, such as frustration, pain, or noise) is a powerful trigger of selective information processing that enhances the probability of aggressive behaviour.
- Social–cognitive approaches refer to the role of aggressive scripts (i.e., generalised knowledge structures of how and when aggressive behaviour may be enacted) and sequential appraisal processes that lead to the choice of an aggressive response. From the perspective of learning theory, aggression becomes part of an individual's repertoire through direct reinforcement as well as observational learning and imitation of aggressive models. The I^3 model conceptualises aggressive behaviour in specific situations as an interaction between the promoting factors of instigation and impellance and the weakening factor of inhibition.
- The General Aggression Model integrates assumptions about the affective, cognitive, and arousal-based antecedents of aggressive behaviour from different models into a comprehensive meta-theory. The psychological explanations of aggression share the assumption that aggressive behaviour is not inevitable but depends on the operation of a variety of promoting and inhibiting factors located both within the person and in the environment.

TASKS TO DO

(1) Watch the original video of Bandura's Bobo doll experiment on YouTube (www.youtube.com/watch?v=jWsxfoJEwQQ).
(2) Sit down for ten minutes and think back to situations that made you angry in the course of the last week. Write down how you responded in these situations, and then analyse your responses with reference to one or two of the theories discussed in this chapter.
(3) Ask five people you know, who are not psychologists, how they would explain aggression. Compare their answers with the theories discussed in this chapter. How much difference or overlap do you see?

SUGGESTED READING

Anderson, C. A., & Bushman, B. J. (2018). Media violence and the General Aggression Model. *Journal of Social Issues, 74*, 386–413.
Archer, J., & Carré, J. (2017). Testosterone and aggression. In B. J. Bushman (Ed.), *Aggression and violence: A social psychological perspective* (pp. 90–104). New York: Routledge.

Berkowitz, L., & LePage, A. (1967). Weapons as aggression-eliciting stimuli. *Journal of Personality and Social Psychology, 7,* 202–207.

Huesmann, L. R. (2017). An integrative theoretical understanding of aggression. In B. J. Bushman (Ed.), *Aggression and violence: A social psychological perspective* (pp. 3–21). New York: Routledge.

Chapter 3

DEVELOPMENT OF AGGRESSIVE BEHAVIOUR IN CHILDHOOD AND ADOLESCENCE

Aggression is to a certain extent an age-normative behaviour in childhood and adolescence (Loeber & Hay, 1997). Young children have problems controlling emotions that give rise to aggressive behaviour, such as anger, and they have yet to learn the normative constraints against acting out aggressive impulses. Typical developmental trajectories in childhood show a nonlinear pattern: aggressive behaviour is common in early childhood up until pre-school age, then decreases in middle childhood, increases again in adolescence before becoming less prevalent in adulthood (Petersen, Bates, Dodge, Lansford, & Pettit, 2015; Teymoori et al., 2018). Thus, from a general developmental perspective, aggression is a transient phenomenon in the life course. However, there are children and adolescents who deviate from this normal course of development by showing high and persistent levels of aggressive behaviour that are not considered age-normative (Hay, 2017). In addition to the burden that high levels of aggressive behaviour place on the individuals concerned and their social environment, the costs for societies are high. A study by Rivenbark et al. (2018) calculated that children with life-course persistent conduct problems were disproportionately more likely to be convicted for a criminal offence and also accounted for a disproportionate rate of emergency department visits, injury claims, and welfare-benefit months in adulthood.

When trying to understand the developmental dynamics of aggression, the following questions are of key importance and will guide our discussion (Loeber & Hay, 1997):

(1) When does aggressive behaviour first appear and what forms does it take in childhood and adolescence?
(2) How stable are early manifestations of aggressive behaviour as children get older?

(3) Does the development of aggressive behaviour follow a pattern of escalation, whereby milder forms of aggression predict more severe aggressive behaviours?

(4) What are the emotional and cognitive antecedents of aggressive behaviour?

(5) What is the role of the social environment in the formation and persistence of aggressive behaviour patterns?

EMERGENCE AND MANIFESTATIONS OF AGGRESSION IN CHILDHOOD AND ADOLESCENCE

The first precursors of individual differences in aggression emerge very early in life. At about three months of age, a child is able to recognise anger in adults' facial expressions. This is followed by the expression of anger by the child in response to frustration in the second half of the first year. Young children still lack the ability to foresee the consequences of their actions, and are therefore unable to intentionally inflict harm on others, as required by our definition of aggressive behaviour (see Chapter 1). Nonetheless, it is possible to identify certain early affective and behavioural indicators that are predictive of individual differences in aggression later on. For example, the Cardiff Infant Contentiousness Scale (Hay et al., 2010) was developed to address six aspects of the use of physical force in social interactions and the expression of anger in babies: *doesn't want to let go of toys, pulls hair, hits out at other people, bites, has angry moods,* and *has temper tantrums.* Reports elicited from parents and other informants when the children were between 5 and 8 months of age predicted the use of physical force against peers observed in a free play situation in the laboratory when the children were between 11 and 15 months old (Hay et al., 2010). In a later study, Hay et al. (2018) found that the more anger and physical force children had displayed as infants, the more likely they were to engage in violent actions within a video game when they were assessed again at the age of seven years.

Aggression in conflicts with peers and adults becomes more frequent during the second and third years of life in the form of temper tantrums and the intentional use of physical force (Tremblay et al., 1999), although overt physical aggression tends to decline after about 30 months of age (Alink et al., 2006). At the same time, indirect and relational forms of aggression begin to emerge, in line with children's improvement of verbal skills and understanding of social relationships (Vaillancourt, 2005). In the early school years, gender differences in aggression become apparent. Boys show higher levels of physical aggression than do girls, who are more likely to engage in indirect and relational forms of aggression (see the detailed discussion of gender differences in Chapter 4). Although the two forms of aggression were substantially correlated, a meta-analysis by

Card, Stucky, Sawalani, and Little (2008) found that direct aggression was uniquely related to externalising problems, such as attentional deficits and delinquency, whereas indirect aggression was uniquely associated with internalising problems, such as depression and anxiety. These differential associations were confirmed in a ten-year longitudinal study of an all-male sample from adolescence to adulthood (Fite, Raine, Stouthamer-Loeber, Loeber, & Pardini, 2010).

An important change in the pattern of aggressive behaviour from childhood to adolescence is that aggression and violence tend to become more socially organised, and peer groups become more important as socialising agents (Dishion, 2015). Juvenile gangs assemble adolescents who share aggressive norms and mutually reinforce their aggressive behaviour patterns. Gangs account for a high proportion of juvenile aggression and are attractive to highly aggressive individuals because they provide a like-minded group of peers. Although gang violence is still largely seen as a male phenomenon, reports of girl gangs engaging in serious aggression are becoming increasingly frequent (see also Chapter 10). However, there does seem to be a gender difference in that girls' aggressive behaviours are replaced by non-aggressive strategies of conflict resolution to a greater extent, whereas boys' tendencies to use aggression to resolve social conflicts more frequently persist into adolescence and early adulthood.

STABILITY OF AGGRESSIVE BEHAVIOUR AND PATTERNS OF CHANGE

An important question is whether children with aggression levels that are higher than normative for their age group remain highly aggressive in subsequent periods of development. Longitudinal studies have produced evidence that aggressive behaviour is indeed relatively stable over time (Tremblay, Vitaro, & Côté, 2018). Based on data from 16 studies exploring the stability of male aggressiveness, Olweus (1979) estimated stability coefficients of $r = .76$ over a one-year period, $r = .69$ over a period of five years, and $r = .60$ over a ten-year period. These figures suggest that aggression is almost as stable as intelligence, even over extended periods of time.

Several long-term studies have shown that aggression in childhood is linked to aggressive behaviour in later life. Following a sample of boys over five measurements from 12 to 24 years of age, Barker et al. (2007) found two stable developmental trajectories. For the majority of their sample (87%), low levels of aggression were found at each point over the 12-year period. At the same time, a highly aggressive subgroup at age 12 (13%) showed continuously high levels of aggression over time, with a peak at the age of 18 years. Boys in the high aggression trajectory performed significantly worse than did the non-aggressive group on a series of cognitive tests, indicating a link between cognitive deficits and aggression. In a Finnish study, the stability of peer nominations of aggression obtained at the ages of 8 and 14 years was $r = .35$ for boys and $r = .38$ for girls, and the link between peer-nominated aggression at 14 years and aggression in adulthood (a composite measure of self-reports obtained at the ages of 36 and 42 years) in the same participants was $r = .33$ for men and $r = .29$ for women (Kokko, Pulkkinen, Huesmann, Dubow, & Boxer, 2009).

In a study that covered a period of 30 years, Temcheff et al. (2008) found significant links between peer-nominated aggression in childhood and self-reports of aggression towards children and spouses in adulthood. The link was mediated by low educational attainment in adolescence, and the authors discuss the possibility that educational achievement may act as a protective factor to buffer the risk of aggressive children carrying their dispositions into adulthood. Further extending the study period, a 40-year longitudinal study by Huesmann, Dubow, and Boxer (2009) demonstrated significant links between physical aggression in childhood, adolescence, and adulthood. In their Columbia County Longitudinal Study, the authors obtained peer nominations of aggression at age 8 and used a combined index of self-reported severe physical aggression and aggressive personality as a measure of aggression at the ages of 19, 30, and 48 years. The correlations between the aggression measures over time for male and female participants are presented in Table 3.1.

Table 3.1 not only reveals a very consistent pattern of significant correlations for both gender groups, it also shows that the stability is higher in adulthood than in the transition from childhood to age 19. For example, the correlation between aggression at age 30 and aggression at age 48 was $r = .56$ for both men and women. Another way of looking at the issue of stability used by Huesmann et al. (2009) was to identify the proportion of participants who remained consistently high (above the median) or low (below the median) in aggression over the 40 years of the study. This analysis showed that 37% of participants who were low in aggression at

TABLE 3.1 Pairwise correlations of aggression over time in the Columbia County Longitudinal Study

Aggression at	Age 8	Age 19	Age 30	Age 48
Age 8	–	.23***	.15*	.13*
Age 19	.37***	–	.44***	.45***
Age 30	.35***	.61***	–	.56***
Age 48	.29***	.41***	.56***	–

Note: correlations for $n = 420$ females above the diagonal, correlations for $n = 436$ males below the diagonal. * $p < .05$; ** $p < .001$.

Reprinted with permission from Huesmann et al., 2009, Table I, p. 143; © 2009 by Wiley.

the age of 8 years remained low in the three subsequent waves, and 35% of participants who scored above the median when they were 8 years old remained in the high aggression group throughout the study.

An important message that emerges from these findings is that aggression at a young age is not a problem that children can be expected to outgrow as they get older. To explain the stability of aggression in the course of development, two interlocking processes have been proposed (Caspi, Elder, & Bem, 1987). Through the first process, *cumulative continuity*, aggression is maintained because of its own consequences that accumulate over time. For example, highly aggressive children often experience academic failure, which may increase anger and hostility and thereby consolidate aggressive behaviour (Jung, Krahé, Bondü, Esser, & Wyschkon, 2018; Patterson, DeBaryshe, & Ramsey, 1989). According to the second process, *interactional continuity*, aggression is maintained through the responses it elicits from others. For example, highly aggressive children are socially rejected by non-aggressive peers, which may lead them to selectively associate with other aggressive peers, creating an environment in which aggression is socially accepted (Martino, Ellickson, Klein, McCaffrey, & Edelen, 2008).

However, even though high stability coefficients were found for aggressive behaviour from childhood into adolescence and early adulthood, it is important to recognise that there is also the possibility of changes in aggression over time. For example, an individual who was non-aggressive as a child may become an aggressive adolescent (i.e., show late onset of aggression). Alternatively, an aggressive child may become less aggressive over time (i.e., show a desisting pattern of aggressive behaviour). There is evidence to support both patterns of change. For example, Kingston and Prior (1995) measured aggression in a group of Australian children on three occasions between the ages of 2–3 and 7–8 years, and identified three distinct groups. The first and largest group, comprising 55% of the boys and 41% of the girls, was the stable group that showed similar levels of aggression at the age of 2 and at the age of 8 years. The second group, consisting of 31% of the boys and 24% of the girls, showed a decrease in aggression from age 2 to age 8 years. The final group consisted of children with low levels of aggression at 2 years whose level of aggressive behaviour went up from the age of 5 years. These children showed an increase in aggression. Each of the latter two groups displayed variability in their aggressive behaviour over time, albeit in different directions. In a study following adolescents from Grades 7 to 11, Martino et al. (2008) found that almost half of their sample showed an increase (23%) or a decrease (22%) in aggression over the four-year period, compared with 37% whose level of aggression remained consistently low and 17% who remained consistently high.

Overall, there is evidence of a continuous decline in aggression as a function of age (Broidy et al., 2003; Loeber & Stouthamer-Loeber, 1998), so desistance may reflect the age-normative pattern of development with regard to aggressive behaviour. However, it is equally clear that a substantial proportion of aggressive children do not show a decline but exhibit an increase or escalation of aggressive behaviour in adolescence and adulthood. *Short-term escalation* denotes a rapid increase in individuals who only start to become aggressive relatively late. *Long-term escalation* refers to a gradual increase in the severity of aggressive actions from childhood to adolescence. At a group level, evidence of long-term escalation comes from studies that have explored the cumulative onset curves for different forms of aggression varying in severity. An example of this approach is provided in Figure 3.1. It presents Loeber and Hay's (1997) analysis of the age at

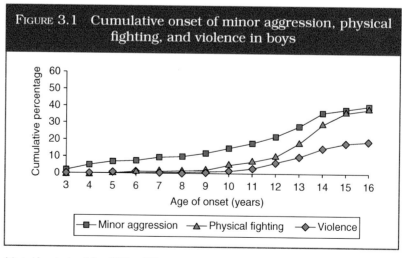

FIGURE 3.1   Cumulative onset of minor aggression, physical fighting, and violence in boys

Adapted from Loeber & Hay, 1997, p. 379.

which minor aggression, physical fighting, and severe violence became apparent in boys' behaviour.

Figure 3.1 indicates that comparatively minor forms of aggression (annoying others, bullying) showed the earliest onset, followed by physical fighting. Despite its later onset, physical fighting showed a steeper increase than minor aggression, and by the age of 15 years, the two curves reached similar prevalence levels. The latest and slowest-rising onset was observed for violence (strong-arming, assault, and forced sex). As would be expected, its prevalence at age 16, although standing at almost 20%, was substantially lower than the prevalence rates for the two less violent forms of aggression.

In addition to describing different patterns of development, it is crucial to identify their correlates at the level of the person and the social environment. Moffitt's (1993; 2007) work on the distinction between *adolescence-limited* and *life-course persistent* aggressive and antisocial behaviour exemplifies this approach (Jolliffe, Farrington, Piquero, MacLeod, & van de Weijer, 2017). Moffitt argues that life-course persistent antisocial behaviour is associated with specific risk factors and manifestations that distinguish this developmental pattern from adolescence-limited antisocial behaviour. Table 3.2 summarises some of the differences between the two developmental trajectories.

The life-course persistent antisocial behaviour pattern is assumed to start in early childhood, originating from a combination of neuropsychological deficits and adverse social conditions. Individuals with a life-course persistent pattern of antisocial behaviour typically show early cognitive and affective deficits and are often born into a high-risk family environment. As noted by Moffitt (2007), "Over the first two decades of development, transactions between the individual and the environment gradually

TABLE 3.2 Two prototypes of antisocial behaviour over the life course

Life-course persistent antisocial behaviour	Adolescence-limited antisocial behaviour
• Originates in early childhood	• Emerges in puberty as a virtually normative pattern of behaviour
• Early neurodevelopmental risk factors	• Psychological discomfort during the "maturity gap"
• Cognitive deficits	• Desire for autonomy
• Difficult temperament	• Desistance from antisocial behaviour when adopting adult roles
• Hyperactivity	• Social mimicry of antisocial models
• Exacerbated by high-risk social environment	• Associated with nonviolent delinquent offences in adulthood
• Inadequate parenting	
• Family conflict	
• Rejection by peers	
• Associated with violent crime in adulthood	

Based on Moffitt, 2007.

construct a disordered personality with hallmark features of physical aggression and antisocial behavior persisting to midlife" (p. 50).

By contrast, individuals with an adolescence-limited pattern typically do not show developmental abnormalities in early childhood, and come from normal family backgrounds. They are described as "otherwise ordinary healthy youngsters" who take up aggressive and antisocial behaviour in adolescence out of discomfort about experiencing a "maturity gap" (i.e., the feeling that their biological maturation is not matched by social maturation because they are denied access to adult role behaviour and entitlement). Engaging in aggressive and antisocial behaviour to demonstrate autonomy in relation to parents and hasten social maturation is seen by these adolescents as a normative pattern of behaviour, which is given up once they grow into adult social roles. Rather than being driven by neuropsychological deficits and adverse family conditions, adolescence-limited aggression results from social mimicry (i.e., the imitation of, and attraction to, antisocial peers) (Moffitt, 2007).

Support for the distinction between the two developmental prototypes comes from several large-scale longitudinal studies reviewed by Moffitt (2007), including the famous "Dunedin Study", of which she is a co-author. In this ongoing study, which started in Dunedin, New Zealand, in 1972, more than 1,000 children were first studied at 3 years of age and were then followed every 2–3 years up to the age of 45 years, as per the latest wave. The study has accumulated an extremely rich set of data from the different developmental stages, including adult mental health and personality measures, criminal offending, and work-related and economic measures (Moffitt, Caspi, Harrington, & Milne, 2002)

However, other authors have cautioned against regarding adolescence-limited antisocial behaviour as a kind of "benign" form of aggression. When they compared adolescence-limited aggressive individuals with continuously non-aggressive individuals, Roisman, Monahan, Campbell, Steinberg, and Cauffman (2010) found that adolescence-limited individuals differed significantly from continuously non-aggressive individuals on a number of childhood risk factors, such as showing a more difficult temperament in early childhood and experiencing less maternal sensitivity in infancy and childhood. The authors concluded that although the individual and environmental risk factors of adolescence-limited aggressive youths may be less extreme than those of the early-onset, life-course persistent individuals, they "clearly experience risks during their preadolescent years that have been reliably linked with later antisocial behavior" (Roisman et al., 2010, p. 309).

In conclusion, the longitudinal studies reviewed in this section showed that there is evidence for both stability and change in aggressive behaviour in the course of childhood and adolescent development. With regard to stability, Moffitt (1993) argued that only a small group of highly aggressive children fall into the life-course persistent group and account for the observed stability of aggressive behaviour. However, as shown by other studies (Barker et al., 2007; Huesmann et al., 2009; Roisman et al., 2010), such stability is also due to a comparatively large group of individuals who show little aggression throughout the different developmental stages. At the same time, there is evidence for both escalation and decline of aggression in individual biographies. To understand these different trajectories, it is necessary to take a closer look at the emotional and cognitive processes involved in the instigation and regulation of aggressive behaviour.

EMOTIONAL AND COGNITIVE PROCESSES ASSOCIATED WITH THE DEVELOPMENT OF AGGRESSIVE BEHAVIOUR

To understand why some children are more aggressive than others and continue to be so in the course of development, both affective and cognitive processes have been examined. The psychological theories of aggression reviewed in Chapter 2 explain how hostile affect, such as anger, and hostile information processing pave the way to aggressive behaviour, not only in a given situation, but also over time. Children with deficits in emotion regulation and impulse control are more likely to develop and sustain aggressive behaviour patterns. These children are often perceived as having a difficult temperament, and find it hard to constrain their aggressive impulses in an age-appropriate way (Pepler, 2018; Van Goozen, 2015).

To assess deficits in anger regulation as risk factors for the development of aggressive behaviour, Rohlf and colleagues developed an observational measure in which elementary school children were exposed to an anger-eliciting situation to record their affective responses (Kirsch, Busching,

FIGURE 3.2   An observational measure of anger regulation in childhood

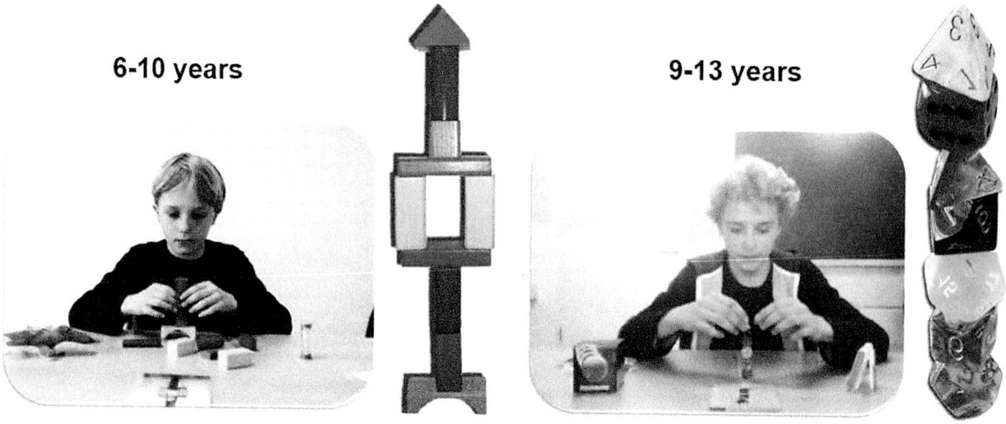

6-10 years   9-13 years

Based on Kirsch et al., 2019; Rolf & Krahé, 2015, photos used with permission.

Rohlf, & Krahé, 2019; Rohlf & Krahé, 2015). The children were told that they would be able to win an attractive prize if they managed to build a tower of bricks in a given period of time. The bricks were manipulated so that the tower kept collapsing. Three years later, the same children were tested again with an age-adapted task of a similar nature, asking them to make a tower out of seven dice. Because one of the dice was pyramid-shaped, the tower was impossible to build despite the (manipulated) image provided. The task is illustrated in Figure 3.2.

Children's behavioural strategies for regulating their anger when they failed to build the tower were observed, distinguishing between maladaptive (e.g., venting the anger, verbal and visual focus on the frustrating stimulus) and adaptive (solution orientation) strategies. Maladaptive anger regulation significantly correlated with teacher ratings obtained ten months later of how frequently the child had shown physical and relational aggression in the past six months and to what degree the aggressive behaviour was reactive, that is shown in response to a provocation (Rohlf, Busching, & Krahé, 2017). Extending the longitudinal analysis to a total of three years, the path from maladaptive anger regulation to teacher-rated aggressive behaviour was still significant (Kirsch et al., 2019). By then, children were old enough to provide reliable and valid self-reports of aggressive behaviour, and these reports also correlated significantly with maladaptive anger regulation observed three years earlier. Moreover, maladaptive anger regulation was a significant prospective predictor of problems with peers, as assessed through self-, parent-, and teacher ratings.

Individual differences in experiencing and handling anger are thought to be more closely related to reactive aggression (i.e., aggression shown in response to a provocation) than to proactive or unprovoked aggression (Hubbard, McAuliffe, Morrow, & Romano, 2010). For example, children who showed more anger, as established through physiological data and observations of anger expression, when losing in a game were also rated by their teachers to be more reactively aggressive, but not more proactively aggressive (Hubbard et al., 2002).

Being able to regulate anger in an adaptive way can be seen as a facet of *self-control*, defined as the capacity to stop, override, or alter unwanted behaviours. Lower habitual self-control has been linked consistently to a greater tendency to show aggressive behaviour (see Chapter 4). Recent longitudinal evidence shows that the basis for individual differences in self-control is laid in early childhood. A study following participants from infancy to adolescence showed that high maternal sensitivity and a stable home environment assessed when the children were between 6 and 15 months of age predicted higher levels of children's self-control at the age of four-and-a-half years, and higher self-control predicted lower levels of overt reactive and relational aggression up to the age of 15 years (Vazsonyi & Javakhishvili, 2019).

Self-control requires a set of cognitive abilities, grouped under the heading of *executive function*, that are involved in the regulation of aggressive and antisocial behaviour (Ogilvie, Stewart, Chan, & Shum, 2011). *Executive function* (EF) comprises cognitive activities that govern goal-directed action and planning of behaviour, and enable adaptive responses to novel, complex, or ambiguous situations. It is important for self-regulation, including anger regulation, and consists of four main components: inhibition, working memory updating, shifting, and planning (Karr et al., 2018). Rohlf, Holl, Kirsch, Krahé, and Elsner (2018) investigated the relationship between executive function and different types of aggression in a three-wave longitudinal study over three years with primary school children aged 6 to 11 years at the start of the study. The lower children scored on the measures of EF at the start of the study, the higher their aggression was rated by their teachers one and three years later, controlling for initial levels of aggressive behaviour. This was true for both physical and relational aggression. With regard to the different functions of aggressive behaviour, deficits in EF were related to increased reactive aggression over time, but did not predict proactive aggression. This ties in with the idea of proactive aggression as "cold-blooded", planned aggression for which affect control is less critical than for reactive aggression, which is more strongly based on anger and therefore may be more affected by deficits in EF (Rathert, Fite, Gaertner, & Vitulano, 2011). Moreover, a longitudinal study showed that early onset of chronic anger predicted more antisocial behaviour problems in adulthood as compared with a later onset, especially among boys, but that good cognitive control in adolescence buffered these negative outcomes (Hawes et al., 2016).

A second basic ability relevant for understanding the development of aggressive behaviour is *Theory of Mind* (ToM). ToM refers to the ability to

self-control: capacity to stop, override, or alter unwanted behaviours.

executive function: cognitive activities that govern goal-directed action and planning of behaviour, and enable adaptive responses to novel, complex, or ambiguous situations.

theory of mind: ability to form a mental representation of the internal states of other people.

form a mental representation of the internal states of other people and is differentiated into two facets: cognitive ToM, describing the ability to make inferences regarding others' beliefs, intentions, or desires, and affective ToM, referring to the ability to infer others' emotions (Derksen, Hunsche, Giroux, Connolly, & Bernstein, 2018). Numerous studies have examined the relation between ToM and aggressive behaviour in children (Wellman, Cross, & Watson, 2001). Holl, Kirsch, Rohlf, Krahé, and Elsner (2018) conducted a three-wave analysis of the reciprocal relations of ToM with physical and relational aggression. Lower ToM prospectively predicted both forms of aggression as rated by the children's class teachers. These results are in line with the predictions derived from the SIP model (Dodge, 2011), described in Chapter 2, that deficits in ToM may lead to biased or deficient social information processing, which in turn may lead to more aggressive behaviour. As noted by Lemerise and Arsenio (2000), emotional responses and processes of emotion regulation play a role at each stage in the SIP model, as the way in which social information is interpreted at one stage elicits affective responses that shape the processing of information at the subsequent stages. For example, if another person's behaviour is interpreted as malicious at the second stage of the model ("interpretation of cues"; see Chapter 2), this is likely to elicit anger. If the person is overwhelmed by the feeling of anger, this will stand in the way of a balanced appraisal of the possible courses of action and precipitate the activation of the intention to strike back in the third step in the model, the clarification of goals (see Smeijers, Benbouriche, & Garofalo, 2020 for a review).

Among more specific cognitive precursors to aggression, aggression-related attitudes were found to play an important role. For example, Erdley and Asher (1998) found that children who saw aggression as a legitimate form of social behaviour showed higher levels of aggressive behaviour (as evidenced by peer ratings and the children's own responses to ambiguous interactions described in hypothetical scenarios). The difference in aggressive behaviour as a function of legitimacy beliefs was found for both boys and girls, but levels of aggression were generally lower for girls than for boys (see Chapter 4 for a discussion of gender differences). Beliefs about the legitimacy of aggression can be seen as part of individuals' aggressive scripts, developed on the basis of direct and vicarious learning experiences (Huesmann, 1998; see also Chapter 2).

Another feature of the scripts of children who show high levels of aggression is the perception of hostile intent in others. Children with a *hostile attribution bias* habitually interpret their peers' behaviour in the light of a pre-existing knowledge structure that sees potentially harmful behaviour by others as an expression of their hostile intentions. Dodge (2006) argued that, in young children, equating (hostile) intent with (negative) outcome is a common reaction when they experience harm from others. In the course of socialisation, children learn to acquire a benign attributional style – that is, they learn to consider the possibility that the other person's actions were not intended to be harmful. According to this view, a learning

hostile attribution bias/ hostile attributional style: tendency to attribute hostile intentions to a person who has caused harm when it is unclear whether or not the harm was caused accidentally or on purpose.

process is required to make benign attributions, and children who maintain a hostile attributional style beyond early childhood show deficits in this learning process. Every time they attribute behaviours of others to hostile intentions and react with an aggressive response, the link between the perception of hostile intent and aggression is reinforced, a cycle which may account for the long-term stability of aggressive behaviour.

A meta-analysis including 41 studies with over 6,000 participants confirmed the link between hostile attributional style and aggression in children (Orobio de Castro, Veerman, Koops, Bosch, & Monshouwer, 2002). A more recent systematic review of 27 studies with children and adolescents concluded that the hostile attribution bias is related to both physical and relational aggression. Regarding the functions of aggression, hostile attribution bias was significantly related to reactive aggression, but not to proactive aggression when reactive aggression was partialled out (Martinelli, Ackermann, Bernhard, Freitag, & Schwenck, 2018). Little evidence of gender differences in the associations between hostile attribution bias and aggression was found in this review.

The connection between hostile knowledge structures and aggression over time was demonstrated in a longitudinal study by Burks, Laird, Dodge, Pettit, and Bates (1999). They obtained mother and teacher ratings of aggressive behaviour in kindergarten and Grade 8. In Grade 8, they also assessed children's attributions of hostile intent in response to hypothetical conflict scenarios and their hostile knowledge structures (i.e., the salience of hostility-related thoughts). In support of their hypotheses, Burks et al. (1999) found that children who had hostile knowledge structures were more likely to attribute hostility in a specific social encounter, and were also rated as more aggressive by their mother and teacher. In addition, they found that the link between early aggression and aggressive behaviour in Grade 8 was mediated by hostile knowledge structures.

A construct related to the hostile attribution bias is justice sensitivity, which refers to the dispositional tendency to perceive events and experiences as unjust. Victim sensitivity characterises a cognitive structure in which individuals habitually see themselves treated unjustly by others and respond with anger and the desire to retaliate. By contrast, perpetrator sensitivity refers to the perception of one's own actions as causing injustice to others. A study by Bondü and Krahé (2015) showed that victim sensitivity was positively correlated with parent- and teacher-rated aggression among children and adolescents, with consistent associations for both physical and relational and both proactive and reactive aggression. Perpetrator sensitivity showed a negative correlation with aggressive behaviour, indicating that being aware of the possibility that one's own actions cause injustice to others may reduce the use of aggressive behaviour.

The propensity towards hostile attributions may be socially shared, and thus reinforced, among peers. A study of adolescents by Halligan and Philips (2010) found significant correlations within peer groups in their members' tendency to attribute hostile intent, and the link was particularly close in reciprocal friendships. This shows that the stability of hostile attributional styles is also promoted through associations with like-minded peers.

In combination, the research discussed in this section has demonstrated that individual differences in aggression emerge as a result of both affective and cognitive variables. Inability to regulate anger in a socially acceptable way and schematic, habitual ways of information processing that promote aggression as an adequate response in social interactions are intrapersonal risk factors for the development of aggression.

INFLUENCES OF THE SOCIAL ENVIRONMENT ON THE DEVELOPMENT OF AGGRESSION

A variety of adverse influences in the social environment have been examined as risk factors for the development of aggressive behaviour. These include proximal risk factors in the family and peer group (Pepler, 2018) as well as more distal risk factors, such as high levels of neighbourhood violence (Chang, Wang, & Tsai, 2016) or exposure to violent media contents (see Chapter 6). Therefore, a comprehensive analysis of the developmental risk factors for aggression needs to include such interpersonal and environmental factors and examine how they operate and interact with intrapersonal risk factors (Dishion, 2015). In the current section, we will focus on two proximal risk factors: family and peer relationships.

The family is the most important social context for young children's development, critically shaping the way they feel, think, and act. The effects of the family environment on the development of aggression have be analysed in a broad body of research (Labella & Masten, 2017). A well-established family risk factor for the development of aggressive behaviour is harsh parental discipline (Farrington, Ttofi, & Coid, 2009). This finding is unsurprising from a social learning perspective, because children whose parents use harsh punishment come to believe that aggression is an acceptable form of conflict resolution. When parents respond to the child's non-compliance with coercion, they trigger further oppositional behaviour that, in turn, leads to more coercive behaviour by the parents. This coercive cycle becomes a stable feature of the parent–child relationship, consolidating the child's aggressive behaviour over time (Dishion, 2015).

The bidirectional influence between parents and children was also demonstrated in a three-wave longitudinal study by Krahé, Bondü, Höse, and Esser (2015). The more aggressive children and adolescents were at Time 1, as rated by themselves, their parents and their teachers, the more parenting stress the parents reported at Time 2, and the more aggressive their children were at Time 3. The mediating role of parenting stress was demonstrated by a significant indirect path from initial aggression to later aggression via parenting stress. Witnessing and experiencing violence in the family are related risk factors for aggressive behaviour, contributing to the transgenerational transmission of violence within families, as we will discuss in more detail in Chapter 8. Moreover, economic pressure may trigger and exacerbate negative parental behaviour by increasing hostility in parents that is directed against the children, as shown in a three-year longitudinal study by Williams, Conger, and Blozis (2007).

Peer relationships constitute the second powerful source of social influence on the development of aggression. Aggressive children are rejected by their peers from an early age, and rejection is associated with subsequent increases in aggression (Godleski, Kamper, Ostrov, Hart, & Blakely-McClure, 2015; Rohlf, Busching, & Krahé, 2017). Consistent with this pattern, Rohlf et al. (2017) showed that children who respond to anger-eliciting situations in a maladaptive way, such as acting out their anger by throwing objects around, are likely to be rejected by their peers, and social rejection predicts an increase in aggressive behaviour. As a result of being marginalised by their non-aggressive peers, aggressive children tend to associate with other aggressive peers, entering social systems that further promote aggressive norms (Halligan & Philips, 2010) and aggressive and antisocial behaviour (Jung et al., 2018; Patterson et al., 1989). Thus, they become immersed in a social context where social acceptance depends on the willingness to engage in further aggression.

In addition to reacting to the aggressive behaviour of individuals with social rejection or approval, peers are a direct source of influence on the development of individuals' aggressive behaviour. A fruitful line of thinking to conceptualise the effect of aggressive peer groups on the individual is captured by the metaphor of aggression as a *"contagious disease"* (Dishion, 2015; Huesmann, 2017). Past research on the peer contagion of aggression focussed on either self-selected peer groups or on groups preselected for having a high level of aggression (see Jung, Busching, & Krahé, 2019, for a review). By contrast, studies examining contagion effect in classroom communities, to which students are assigned by the school administration, are able to minimise self-selection effects and can exploit the greater variability in aggressive behaviour compared with groups preselected for high levels of aggression. In a two-wave study with elementary-school children, Rohlf, Krahé, and Busching (2016) investigated the effect of classroom aggression on both physical and relational aggression. They found that the higher the level of both forms of aggressive behaviour were in their class community, the more aggressive individual class member were ten months later, controlling for the temporal stability of aggression as well as participants' gender and age. Similar results were found in a study with adolescents that investigated the contagion of peer aggression in the broader context of antisocial behaviours, such as delinquency, vandalism, or substance abuse, which often co-occur with aggressive behaviour (Busching & Krahé, 2018). In a sample of almost 17,000 male and female adolescents distributed across approximately 1,300 classrooms at two points in time one year apart, the higher the average level of antisocial behaviour in a classroom was at Time 1, the more antisocial behaviour individual class members showed at Time 2. Other findings support the idea that the contagious effect of aggression not only spreads within a group but also permeates other, interconnected ecosystems: Individuals who are surrounded by aggressive friends are at risk of introducing aggression into other spheres of their life and affecting individuals that had no direct contact with the original source of the aggressive behaviour (Greitemeyer, 2018).

In line with the idea of aggression as a contagious disease, studies have examined the differential susceptibility of individuals to the influence of aggressive peers. As with diseases, exposure to peer aggression should particularly affect those individuals who enter the group with a low level of aggression, that is those who have not yet "caught the disease", whereas those already infected should be comparatively less affected by the aggressive behaviour around them. This line of reasoning was supported in a series of studies using multilevel modelling to study the interaction between classroom levels of aggression and individual levels of aggression over time (Jung et al., 2019). Multilevel modelling offers a statistical approach for addressing the question whether exposure to an aggressive peer environment has the same effect on all individuals or varies in relation to the level of aggression the individuals bring to the environment. The finding that children's aggressive behaviour increases over time if the level of aggression in their class as a whole is high represents a main effect of the classroom level of aggression. If this classroom level affects individual class members differently depending on how aggressive they were when they entered the class, this reflects a cross-level interaction between the classroom level and the individual level of analysis.

Consistent with the idea of contagion, Rohlf et al. (2016) found a significant cross-level interaction between individuals' relational aggression and the level of relational aggression among their class members. Elementary-school children who showed low initial levels of relational aggression scored significantly higher on relational aggression 10 months later if they were in classrooms with a high level of relational aggression. By contrast, students with initially high levels of relational aggression were unaffected by the level of relational aggression in their classroom, which means that they remained at a high level even in classes in which the overall level of aggression was low. Similarly, Busching and Krahé (2018) analysed cross-level interactions between individual and classroom antisocial behaviour in an adolescent sample. In line with their hypotheses, initially non-antisocial participants showed more antisocial behaviour one year later the higher the level of classroom antisocial behaviour had been in their class at the beginning of the study. By contrast, participants with initially high levels of antisocial behaviour were largely unaffected by their peers' level of antisocial behaviour.

These findings indicate that being part of an aggressive environment "infects" initially "healthy" class members, whose aggression levels move towards the class level over the course of time, whereas it has little effect on those who have already "caught" the aggressive behaviour. To understand how this contagious effect is generated, it is helpful to consider the normative beliefs about aggression in classrooms with a higher level of aggressive behaviour. Busching and Krahé (2015) found a significant cross-level interaction between class-level normative beliefs and individual physical aggression. Individuals with low levels of aggressive behaviour at the start of the study showed more physical aggression 12 months later if they had been in a class with a high tolerance of aggression than if they had been surrounded by classmates with a low tolerance of aggression. By contrast, individuals with initially high levels of physical aggression were more aggressive ten months later regardless of their peers' tolerance of physical aggression. This finding is consistent with the learning of aggressive scripts discussed earlier (Huesmann, 1998), which not only involves the acquisition of aggressive behaviour but also the learning of group-specific social norms promoting or suppressing aggression. In addition, by looking at cross-level interactions in the path from aggression to social rejection over time, Rohlf et al. (2016) were able to show that aggressive students become less socially rejected over time if they are in a class with a high collective level of aggression. No effect of class level on social rejection of initially non-aggressive students was found. This finding suggests that aggressive behaviour becomes normalised in aggressive classrooms, changing the normative and social context in the direction of making aggressive behaviour more acceptable. As a result, aggressive children meet with less social rejection.

The reported studies also examined the role of gender as a possible moderator of class-level effects and cross-level interactions. Although significant moderator effects of gender were identified, the results did not yield a consistent pattern. In the younger sample studied by Rohlf et al. (2016), class members were more affected by the collective levels of relational aggression of their same-sex than their opposite-sex peers. In their adolescent sample, Busching and Krahé (2015) found that the aggression level of girls in a class had a greater impact on both male and female class members than the aggression levels of boys in predicting increases in aggressive behaviour over a period of three years. To the extent that boys become more interested in being accepted as dating partners by girls, they may move in the direction of the girls' collective norms and aggressive behaviour. However, more research is needed to clarify the role of gendered patterns of aggressive behaviour as a class-level influence on individual aggression.

This chapter has traced the emergence of individual differences in aggression from early childhood to adolescence, but development does not stop there. Adults differ as much as children and adolescents in their aggressive response tendencies. The next chapter will therefore address the relationship between personality and aggression in adulthood. It will also summarise the large literature on the role of gender as another variable related to individual differences in aggressive behaviour.

SUMMARY

- Aggressive behaviour emerges in early childhood, with boys generally displaying higher levels of aggression than girls from preschool age onwards. In age-normative patterns of development, aggression declines as children get older, giving way to non-aggressive strategies of conflict resolution. However, if aggressive behaviour persists into adolescence, it becomes more harmful in its consequences and is more often socially organised in the form of gangs and group violence.
- Individual differences in aggression show considerable stability from childhood to adolescence and into young adulthood. Nonetheless, some children who start off with a high level of aggression show a declining trajectory as they grow older, and others show a late onset of aggression in adolescence without a previous history of aggressive behaviour.
- Intrapersonal risk factors for the development of aggression include both affective and cognitive variables. Maladaptive anger regulation, deficits in executive function and theory of mind and the habitual tendency to attribute hostile intentions to others were found in longitudinal studies to predict higher aggression levels over time.
- Among the risk factors in the social environment, exposure to harsh parental discipline, social rejection by peers and the selective affiliation with aggressive peer groups contribute to the development and stabilisation of aggressive behaviour.
- In line with the idea of aggression as a "contagious disease", research has shown that being exposed to an aggressive classroom community of peers leads to an increase of aggressive behaviour over time. This is true especially for those individuals who enter these classrooms with a low level of aggression, who "catch" aggressive behaviour from their peers and show an increase in aggressive behaviour over time.

TASKS TO DO

(1) Visit the website of the Dunedin Study (http://dunedinstudy.otago.ac.nz) to find out more about the findings of this exciting study that has been following the same group of people from birth for over 40 years and succeeded in retaining almost 95% of the initial participants in the sample over this period.
(2) Think back to the time when you were three or four years of age and remember how you reacted in situations in which you experienced anger. Talk to someone who knew you at the time to find out how they remember you in those situations.
(3) Corporal punishment is still seen by many parents as an effective and acceptable form of disciplining children, and Pope Francis made the headlines in 2015 by stating that it is ok for parents to spank their children to discipline them – "as long as their dignity is maintained"

(www.bbc.com/news/world-europe-31163219). Find a recent survey in your country on the number of parents who report that they used physical punishment against a child in the last year and check what the legal situation is in your country regarding the use of physical punishment.

SUGGESTED READING

Dishion, T. J. (2015). A developmental model of aggression and violence: Microsocial and macrosocial dynamics within an ecological framework. In M. Lewis & K. D. Rudolph (Eds.), *Handbook of developmental psychopathology* (pp. 449–465). New York: Springer.

Jung, J., Busching, R., & Krahé, B. (2019). Catching aggression from one's peers: A longitudinal and multilevel analysis. *Social and Personality Psychology Compass, 13,* e12433.

Kirsch, F., Busching, R., Rohlf, H., & Krahé, B. (2019). Using behavioral observation for the longitudinal study of anger regulation in middle childhood. *Applied Developmental Science, 25,* 105–118.

Rivenbark, J. G., Odgers, C. L., Caspi, A., Harrington, H., Hogan, S., Houts, R. M., ... Moffitt, T. E. (2018). The high societal costs of childhood conduct problems: Evidence from administrative records up to age 38 in a longitudinal birth cohort. *Journal of Child Psychology and Psychiatry, and Allied Disciplines, 59,* 703–710.

Chapter 4

Personality and Gender Differences in Adulthood

It is clear from everyday observation that people differ in predictable ways in their tendency to show aggressive behaviour. Some go mad at the slightest provocation, others are almost impossible to fall out with, and there is a broad spectrum in between. In this chapter, we will take a closer look at variables associated with individual differences in aggressive behaviour in adulthood. The first part of the chapter reviews the evidence on personality variables that can help to clarify some of the processes underlying differences in the general tendency to show aggressive behaviour. This discussion will focus on research with a primary focus on individual differences in aggression. Studies considering personality variables as moderators of particular forms of aggression, such as intimate partner violence or aggressive driving, will be reviewed in their respective contexts. The second part of the chapter is devoted to the topic of gender differences in aggressive behaviour. In this part, the stereotypical belief that men are more aggressive than women will be put to the test of systematic empirical investigation, leading to a more complex picture of when and why men and women may differ in aggressive behaviour.

PERSONALITY CONSTRUCTS RELATED TO AGGRESSION

According to the General Aggression Model (GAM) presented in Chapter 2, personality variables play an important role in explaining aggressive behaviour. Personality variables are conceptualised as "traits" that are relatively stable over time and can help to explain why not all people behave equally aggressively in the same situation. In this section, personality traits will be discussed that have been linked to individual differences in aggressive

TABLE 4.1 Personality variables associated with individual differences in aggression	
Associated with higher aggression	**Associated with lower aggression**
• Trait aggression, anger and hostility • Irritability and emotional susceptibility • Rumination • Hostile attributional style • Narcissism	• Dissipation • Perspective-taking and empathy • Self-control

behaviour through shaping both affective and cognitive processes. In addition, the role of stable differences in self-esteem and self-regulation will be examined in relation to their effects on aggressive behaviour. Evidence of significant associations between personality constructs and aggressive behaviour in everyday situations (Jones, Miller, & Lynam, 2011) and in controlled laboratory experiments will be discussed (Hyatt, Zeichner, & Miller, 2019). Consistent with our social psychological perspective, we will focus on constructs that play a role in explaining stable differences in aggression in everyday interactions, excluding constructs that are primarily relevant for explaining severe forms of aggression and violence in the context of psychopathology and criminal offending. A summary of the main personality constructs and their relationship with aggression is presented in Table 4.1.

Trait aggressiveness, anger, and hostility

Stable individual differences in the tendency to engage in aggressive behaviour are captured in the construct of "trait aggression", which is typically measured by self-report instruments. One prominent measure, the Buss-Perry Aggression Questionnaire (AQ) was introduced in Chapter 1, and its validity and reliability have been demonstrated in many studies (Kalmoe, 2015). Validating the construct of trait aggression, a large body of research has shown that people scoring higher on measures of trait aggression are more likely to show aggressive behaviour in specific situations than individuals with lower trait aggression (Bettencourt, Talley, Benjamin, & Valentine, 2006; Krahé et al., 2011). Moreover, as conceptualised by the General Aggression Model (see Chapter 2), *trait aggressiveness* has been shown to moderate the influence of situational factors eliciting aggressive behaviour. For example, exposure to violent film clips led to more aggressive behaviour in individuals scoring high vs. low in trait aggression (Bushman, 1995).

trait aggressiveness: denotes stable differences between individuals in the liklelihood and intensity of aggressive behaviour.

As reflected in measures such as the AQ, trait aggression is a multidimensional construct composed of both behavioural aspects (physical and verbal aggression) and affective and cognitive components (anger and hostility). As shown in Chapter 2, anger and hostility are considered by several theoretical accounts of aggression as key components of trait aggressiveness. Anger involves physiological arousal and preparation for aggression and represents the emotional or affective component of trait aggression. Hostility consists of feelings of ill will and injustice and represents the cognitive component (see also the section on hostile attributional style below). There is ample evidence that individuals who are habitually prone to anger and hostility show more aggressive behaviour in situations that elicit these affective and cognitive responses (Veenstra, Bushman, & Koole, 2018).

A prominent instrument for measuring both the trait and the state component of anger is the State-Trait-Anger Expression Inventory (STAXI) by Spielberger (1996), which has been validated in many studies (Lievaart, Franken, & Hovens, 2016). In a meta-analysis by Bettencourt et al. (2006), trait anger was established as a significant predictor of aggressive behaviour following a provocation. A study by Tafrate, Kassinove, and Dundin (2002) found that individuals who scored high on trait anger experienced more anger episodes that lasted for longer periods of time and were more likely to involve verbal aggression on their part than those who scored low on trait anger (see also Chapter 3 for developmental pathways into trait aggression).

Irritability and emotional susceptibility

Irritability refers to the habitual "tendency to react impulsively, controversially, or rudely at the slightest provocation or disagreement" (Caprara, Perugini, & Barbaranelli, 1994, p. 125; Toohey & DiGiuseppe, 2017). Habitually irritable people, as identified by the Caprara Irritability Scale (Caprara et al., 1985), which consists of items such as "I think I am rather touchy", were found to show increased levels of aggression compared with non-irritable individuals. The difference was particularly pronounced in response to a frustration. Similarly, irritability augmented the differences in aggressive behaviour observed in response to exposure to aggressive

irritability: habitual tendency to react impulsively, controversially, or rudely at the slightest provocation or disagreement.

cues (Caprara et al., 1994). In a study by Giancola (2002), highly irritable participants selected more painful electric shocks for an alleged coparticipant as a measure of aggressive behaviour (see Chapter 1). Drinking alcohol increased aggressive behaviour in highly irritable but not in less irritable participants, although this pattern was only found for the male participants. The meta-analysis by Bettencourt et al. (2006) confirmed the link between trait irritability and situational aggression across a broader range of studies.

Emotional susceptibility is defined as an individual's tendency "to experience feelings of discomfort, helplessness, inadequacy, and vulnerability" (Caprara et al., 1994, p. 125). Like irritability, it is presumed to indicate a generally increased readiness (or lower threshold) for aggressive behaviour. The findings reported by Caprara and his colleagues for emotional susceptibility largely parallel the effects they found for irritability. Emotionally susceptible participants showed more aggressive behaviour, particularly following prior frustration. In addition, they showed a larger increase in aggression following physical exercise, lending support to Zillmann's "excitation transfer model" (see Chapter 2). The meta-analysis by Bettencourt et al. (2006) also found that individual differences in emotional susceptibility predicted aggressive behaviour, particularly following provocation. The two constructs of irritability and emotional susceptibility may thus explain individual differences in affective or hostile aggression.

Rumination and dissipation

Rumination and dissipation are two constructs referring to cognitive processes linked to individual differences in aggression. They represent the opposite poles of a continuum that describes the extent to which people are preoccupied with angry thoughts following an aggression-eliciting stimulus. *Anger rumination* is defined as "perseverative thinking about a personally meaningful anger-inducing event" (Denson, 2013, p. 103). Low ruminators/high dissipators quickly get over a provocative or hostile encounter without investing much time and effort in thinking about the experience. By contrast, ruminators have a tendency to mull over the aggression-eliciting situation for extended periods of time and are more likely to plan and engage in retaliation. In order for ruminative vs. dissipative tendencies to show an effect, sufficient time must be allowed between the hostile or provoking stimulus event and the aggressive response. The more time elapses, an aggressive reaction will become less likely in dissipators, but more likely in ruminators. People holding the meta-cognitive belief about themselves that they are prone to habitually ruminate over anger-eliciting events scored higher on measures of anger and displaced aggression, and the link was mediated by increased anger rumination (Salguero, García-Sancho, Ramos-Cejudo, & Kannis-Dymand, 2020). Although some people may be generally more prone to rumination than others in all areas of life, the contents of the ruminative thoughts are

anger rumination: perseverative thinking about a personally meaningful anger-inducing event.

important for the link with aggression. Peled and Moretti (2010) showed that only the tendency to ruminate about anger was linked to aggression, whereas the tendency to ruminate about feelings of sadness was associated with depression. Similarly, Bettencourt et al. (2006) found in their meta-analysis that trait rumination was associated with observed aggressive behaviour only in the context of provocation. Later studies showed that participants were more likely to show aggressive behaviour after a frustration (Hennessy, 2017) or when intoxicated (Borders & Giancola, 2011) the higher they scored on a measure of anger rumination. These findings highlight once more the interaction between the person (here: the tendency to ruminate) and the situation (here: the elicitation of anger) in explaining aggressive behaviour.

Although dissipation/rumination is conceptualised as a stable individual difference variable, it is possible to demonstrate the role of rumination or dissipation by inducing the two modes in experimental situations. In a study in which participants were either instructed to ruminate about a provocation or distracted from thinking about it, those in the rumination condition reported significantly higher levels of anger after a 25-minute interval, and also showed more aggressive behaviour after a minor triggering event (Bushman, Bonacci, Pedersen, Vasquez, & Miller, 2005). Further clarifying the path from rumination to aggression, a series of studies by Denson, Pedersen, Friese, Hahm, and Roberts (2011) showed that rumination leads to a reduction in self-control, which in turn lowers the threshold for aggressive behaviour. We shall return to the link between low self-control and aggression later in this chapter.

Hostile attributional style and perspective taking

Hostile attributional style, defined as a person's habitual tendency to interpret the ambiguous behaviour of others as an expression of their hostile intent, has already been discussed in Chapter 3 in relation to the development of aggressive behaviour in childhood and adolescence. It also features as a personality correlate of aggression in adults. Attributional style not only affects the way in which people interpret actions directed at them individually, but also shapes their social perceptions in general. As Dill, Anderson, Anderson, and Deuser (1997, p. 275) graphically described it, these people "tend to view the world through blood-red tinted glasses". Attributional style is a cognitive disposition, and does not depend on the experience of affective arousal (i.e., anger) as a result of being personally affected by others' apparently hostile actions. However, this cognitive disposition may go hand in hand with affect-based dispositions towards aggression. Dill et al. (1997) showed that irritability and trait aggressiveness predicted the extent to which participants attributed aggressive thoughts to the actor in a scenario describing an ambiguous social interaction. In a systematic review of 25 studies, Klein Tuente, Bogaerts, and Veling (2019) found small to medium-size correlations between hostile attributional style and self-reported aggression in adults, with no evidence for gender differences. The finding that the association was closer for reactive than for proactive aggression is consistent with the conceptualisation of hostile attributional style as a cognitive schema about the intentions of others, to which the perceiver then shows a behavioural response in the form of aggression.

The hostile attributional style can be seen as part of a person's aggressive script that is shaped through social experience, as described in Chapter 2. The more often an aggressive script is rehearsed, the more easily hostile schemata can be accessed, promoting the tendency to interpret the behaviour of others as an expression of hostile intent (Huesmann, 1998). Thus, aggressive behaviour and hostile attributions are mutually reinforcing. Takarangi, Polaschek, Hignett, and Garry (2008) demonstrated that distorted memory plays an important part in this process. They gave participants word lists containing neutral and violence-related terms and asked them to recall which of the words had been presented in an earlier phase of the experiment. Highly aggressive participants were significantly more likely to falsely remember violent words as having been included in the earlier list. A parallel, but weaker effect was found for a situational manipulation in which participants were primed by reading a word list referring to insults (e.g., "idiot," "loser," "incompetent"), or were given a list of neutral words. Those who had seen the insult-related words were more likely to falsely remember having seen violent words than those who had received the neutral words. Hostile attributional style is seen as an important variable contributing to individual differences in trait anger, as noted by Wilkowski and Robinson (2008). However, these authors argue that angry individuals are not only prone to fast and automatic hostile interpretations of situational cues, they are also less likely to engage in more effortful cognitive processes that might correct the initial hostile attributions. The failure to revise spontaneous hostile attributions through more elaborate information processing was also stressed by Dodge (2006) in his developmental account of the hostile attribution bias discussed in Chapter 3.

Whereas the hostile attribution bias enhances aggressive behaviour, *perspective taking* is a cognitive variable associated with the inhibition of aggressive responses. Perspective taking refers to a person's ability to orient him- or herself non-egocentrically to the perspective of another person (Richardson, Green, & Lago, 1998). In the developmental literature, deficits in children's ability to develop a mental representation of the internal state of others (called "theory of mind"), have been linked to aggressive behaviour (Holl, Kirsch, Rohlf, Krahé, & Elsner, 2018), as discussed in Chapter 3. The role of perspective taking in inhibiting aggressive behaviour has been established by a variety of studies (Miller & Eisenberg, 1988). For example, Richardson, Hammock, Smith, Gardner, and Signo (1994) showed that individuals who scored high on dispositional perspective taking were less likely to report aggressive behaviour and also less likely to respond in an aggressive way to a provocation. In a later study, Richardson et al. (1998) found that individuals who scored high on dispositional perspective taking were more likely to choose a non-aggressive response to a verbal attack (as opposed to an aggressive response) than low perspective-takers. This was only true, however, if the attacker's verbal insults increased in aggressiveness from the beginning to the end of the interaction. If the verbal insults decreased from high to low levels during the interaction, no effect of perspective taking emerged. The need to understand an aggressive opponent's behaviour is probably greater if the opponent's aggression becomes more extreme in the course of the interaction than if an initially aggressive opponent becomes less aggressive over time. Therefore, high perspective takers may have chosen non-aggressive (i.e., de-escalating) responses to a greater extent when the opponent showed increasing levels of aggression.

perspective taking: ability to orient oneself non-egocentrically to the perspective of another person.

THE BIG-FIVE PERSONALITY FACTORS AND HONESTY AND HUMILITY

In a comprehensive meta-analysis, Jones et al. (2011) examined the evidence linking the *"Big Five" personality factors* of openness to experience, conscientiousness, extraversion, agreeableness, and neuroticism to aggressive behaviour across a diverse range of settings. They found significant associations for all five factors, whereby neuroticism was positively and the other four factors were negatively related to aggressive behaviour. An updated meta-analysis by Vize, Miller, and Lynam (2018) confirmed these conclusions for a more differentiated set of outcome variables, distinguishing between forms (physical and relational) and functions (proactive and reactive) of aggression. Focussing specifically on the associations

"Big Five" personality factors: basic dimensions of individual differences, consisting of openness to experience, conscientiousness, extraversion, agreeableness, and neuroticism.

between the Big Five and aggressive behaviour in the laboratory, Hyatt et al. (2019) confirmed the significant, but small associations for agreeableness and openness, both of which were negatively related to aggressive behaviour. The other three factors were not systematically related to aggressive behaviour in these specific settings.

The Big Five personality factors have been broadened to include a sixth factor called *honesty-humility* (HH), which comprises the four facets of Sincerity, Fairness, Greed-Avoidance, and Modesty (Ashton & Lee, 2005). Individuals scoring low on this factor are thought to use flattery to get what they want, break the rules, are materialistic and feel a strong sense of entitlement. Several studies have found higher tendencies to engage in aggressive behaviour, assessed both via self-report and in experimental settings, in individuals scoring lower on the honesty-humility factor (Book, Visser, Volk, Holden, & D'Agatac, 2019; Dinić & Smederevac, 2019; N. M. Knight, Dahlen, Bullock-Yowell, & Madson, 2018).

Self-esteem and narcissism

In everyday discourse, it is commonly believed that aggressive individuals have low self-esteem and engage in aggressive behaviour to increase their feelings of self-worth. However, research shows the link between self-esteem and aggression to be more complicated. Reviews of the literature have found evidence for a significant association between low self-esteem and aggression (Teng, Liu, & Guo, 2015), but also identified studies that showed the reverse relationship, a curvilinear relationship or no link at all (Ostrowsky, 2010; Walker & Bright, 2009). To make sense of this conflicting evidence, a theoretical analysis is needed as to why and how low or high self-esteem should be linked to aggression. To begin with, there is agreement among researchers that having genuinely high self-esteem, reflected in objective achievements and mirrored in a positive evaluation by others, works as a protective factor against aggression. Low self-esteem has been linked to aggression via the experience of shame and humiliation that elicits anger and thereby promotes aggressive behaviour (Walker & Bright, 2009). However, other authors have argued that aggression requires risk taking and confidence of success, which people with low self-esteem do not normally have (Baumeister, Bushman, & Campbell, 2000). They suggest that it is unrealistically high ("inflated"), but fragile self-esteem that leads to aggressive behaviour and introduced the concept of *narcissism* to denote this problematic type of self-esteem. Narcissism is characterised by a grandiose view of superiority and a sense of entitlement that leads to aggression when the person is challenged by others (Baumeister et al., 2000). It is part of the "dark triad" of personality traits linked to aggression, the other two being Machiavellianism and Psychopathy, which together make up the malevolent side of personality (Muris, Merckelbach, Otgaar, & Meijer, 2017). Several self-report scales have been developed to measure individual differences in narcissism, for example the Narcissistic Personality

narcissism: personality trait denoting a grandiose view of the self and strong sense of entitlement.

Inventory (NPI, Raskin & Terry, 1988), which contains items such as "If I ruled the world it would be a much better place" (Soyer, Rovenpor, Kopelman, Mullins, & Watson, 2001).

From the perspective of narcissism, aggression is seen as serving an ego-protective function, and it is activated to restore a threatened sense of personal superiority. Therefore, narcissists are particularly prone to aggressive behaviour in response to stimuli perceived as a threat to a positive sense of self-worth, such as negative feedback or provocation. To differentiate narcissism from high self-esteem, it can be said that "an individual with high self-esteem thinks he or she is good; a narcissistic individual thinks he or she is better" (Taylor, Davis-Kean, & Malanchuk, 2007, p. 131). In line with Berkowitz's cognitive neo-associationist model of aggression (see Chapter 2), Baumeister and Boden (1998) stipulated that a threat to self-esteem precipitates aggression by eliciting anger. To the extent that the negative appraisal is perceived as unjustified, it evokes anger, which in turn increases the probability of an aggressive response. There is evidence from correlational and experimental studies that narcissism is related to aggression in a wide range of areas, including laboratory aggression, domestic violence, driving aggression, and even murder and assault (Baumeister & Boden, 1998; Lustman, Wiesenthal, & Flett, 2010; Walker & Bright, 2009). Consistent with the proposition that narcissists engage in aggression to cope with threats to their fragile self-esteem, a meta-analysis by Rasmussen (2016) found a significant link between narcissism and retaliative aggression. In a similar vein, the review by Lambe, Hamilton-Giachritsis, Garner, and Walker (2018) found that narcissism was more strongly linked to aggression following ego threat. The finding that narcissists show more aggression in response to negative feedback that was delivered in public than to negative feedback delivered in private indicates that it is the concern about negative evaluation by others that is critical in understanding the link between narcissism and aggression (Ferriday, Vartanian, & Mandel, 2011).

Although self-esteem and narcissism are related constructs, they were found to make separate contributions to the prediction of aggressive behaviour, although findings about the combined effect are inconsistent. Bushman et al. (2009) found that the combination of high self-esteem and high narcissism produced the highest levels of direct aggression in a competitive reaction time measure of aggression. In a further study, Bushman et al. (2009) replicated the findings in a realistic context, using the essay evaluation paradigm (see Chapter 1 for the two methods). Students first received either positive or negative feedback about an essay from a fellow student, and were then asked to assign a grade to the feedback that would count towards the other student's course mark. The lowest grades (indicating the highest level of aggression) were assigned by students who scored high on both self-esteem and narcissism. By contrast, a recent study by Lamarche and Seery (2019) showed that individuals with a combination of high narcissism and low self-esteem were most likely to endorse sexual coercion following reminders of rejection by close others. In the same vein, Hart, Richardson, and Breeden (2019) found a stronger association between narcissism and aggression in participants who were low as compared with high in self-esteem. Further research is needed to clarify when and why the combination of narcissism with either high or low self-esteem is linked more closely to aggressive behaviour.

Although the theoretical concept of narcissism links it primarily to provoked and direct aggression against the source of the provocation, studies have also demonstrated a link with unprovoked aggression and aggression displaced onto a third party. Reidy, Foster, and Zeichner (2010) used a competitive reaction time task to classify their participants as *unprovoked aggressors* (those who chose to deliver an aversive shock to an alleged opponent even before they received the first shock), *retaliative aggressors* (those who only delivered aversive shocks after receiving a shock from their opponent), and *non-aggressors* (those who refrained from delivering shocks altogether). They found that unprovoked aggressors scored significantly higher on a trait measure of narcissism than both the provoked aggressor and the non-aggressor groups. With regard to displaced aggression, Twenge and Campbell (2003) studied narcissists' aggressive responses after a social rejection, which should be a powerful form of ego threat. In a series of experiments, they found that narcissists not only reacted more angrily to social rejection and showed more direct aggression against the person rejecting them, but also behaved more aggressively towards a third party. Corroborating the idea that narcissists' higher aggression is contingent upon the experience of ego threat, no difference between high and low narcissists' aggressive behaviour was found following social acceptance. We shall examine social rejection as a situational trigger of aggression in more detail in Chapter 5.

Other research has identified components of narcissism that may be particularly maladaptive as far as aggression is concerned. For example, Reidy, Zeichner, Foster, and Martinez (2008) found that entitlement (e.g., "I will never be satisfied until I get all that I deserve") and exploitation (e.g., "I find it easy to manipulate people") were the two sub-dimensions of narcissism as measured by the NPI most closely related to aggressive behaviour in a competitive reaction time task, whereas other dimensions, such as vanity and self-sufficiency, were unrelated to aggression. These findings suggest that narcissism represents a construct with multiple aspects referring to an exaggerated sense of self-worth, not all of which may be related to aggression.

A second line of research has been directed at breaking down narcissism into different domains of self-esteem. For example, Widman and McNulty (2010) found that a specific measure of sexual narcissism, with components such as sexual entitlement and a grandiose sense of sexual skills, predicted men's engagement in sexual aggression better than a global measure of narcissism. In a meta-analysis that looked at differences in narcissism scores over time, Twenge, Konrath, Foster, Campbell, and Bushman (2008) found a significant generational shift over a period of 25 years, with greater endorsement of the narcissism items of the NPI in more recent studies. Given the strong evidence that links narcissism to aggression, this does look like a worrying trend. On a more positive note, Thomaes, Bushman, Orobio de Castro, Cohen, and Denissen (2009) conducted a school-based field experiment with adolescents and were able to show that a brief self-affirmation intervention in which participants were asked to write a paragraph on their most important personal values reduced aggressive behaviour in high narcissists over a 1-week period.

Lack of self-control and impulsivity

A further aspect of the self that is relevant to the understanding of individual differences in aggression is *self-control*. This construct refers to internal restraints that should inhibit the release of aggressive response tendencies. Evidence for a link between lack of self-control and aggressive and violent behaviour comes from studies of general population samples (Larson, Vaughn, Salas-Wright, & DeLisi, 2015), as well as studies of criminal offenders (Gottfredson, 2007). The fact that many criminals commit a variety of different offences, together with the observation that criminal behaviour is often accompanied by a lack of self-control in other areas (e.g., heavy smoking, excessive alcohol consumption), supports the idea of a general self-control problem underlying aggressive behaviour (Baumeister & Boden, 1998). Lower self-control was also related to physical violence against a dating partner in a study by Archer, Fernández-Fuertes, and Thanzami (2010). According to Denson's (2013) model of rumination, individuals with deficits in executive function are more prone to angry rumination because they have problems inhibiting anger-related thoughts. In line with this theorising, a recent study by Li et al. (2019) showed that better self-control is linked to lower aggression via a reduced tendency to ruminate about anger-arousing events.

Impulsivity, which is the opposite of self-control, has consistently been linked to aggression, according to the meta-analysis of 93 studies by Bresin (2019). Impulsivity is composed of four facets, namely (negative) urgency, lack of premeditation, lack of perseverance, and sensation seeking. Negative urgency describes the tendency for rash action when experiencing negative affect, lack of premeditation refers to the tendency to act without prior planning, lack of perseverance refers to the tendency to give up quickly in the face of difficulties, and sensation seeking indicates a preference for activities that provide a sense of thrill and adventure. Significant meta-analytic effects in the small to moderate range were found for each facet, with stronger associations for negative urgency and lack of premeditation than for the other two facets.

Most of the evidence on the role of impulsivity in explaining aggression is based on self-reports, but a recent study by Subramani, Parrott, Latzman, and Washburn (2019) used an experimental design. They showed that higher trait disinhibition, defined as deficient impulse control, predicted more aggressive behaviour in response to a provocation, but only when participants' attention was not distracted away from the provoking stimulus.

The evidence reviewed in this section points to a number of personal characteristics that can help to explain why individuals differ in their readiness to act aggressively even when exposed to the same situational conditions. However, as shown by the comprehensive meta-analysis conducted by Bettencourt et al. (2006), the majority of the personality variables considered in this section only predict aggression in situations that activate the respective affective or cognitive processes – for example, by presenting a provocation. This finding supports the General Aggression Model (see Chapter 2) by showing that it is the interaction of individual differences and features of the situation that shapes the aggressive response.

GENDER DIFFERENCES IN AGGRESSIVE BEHAVIOUR

Gender is another stable person characteristic that is relevant to aggression. Everyday wisdom has it that males are generally more aggressive than females, and we will see in this chapter whether this perception is substantiated by rigorous empirical research. We first discuss evidence on the emergence and development of gender differences in aggression through childhood and adolescence, followed by a review of the evidence on gender differences in adulthood. In both cases, it is important to distinguish between direct (physical and verbal) aggression and indirect (relational) aggression (see Chapter 1 for a description of these constructs).

Gender differences in aggression during childhood and adolescence

Developmental research has revealed that gender differences in aggressive behaviour emerge early in life, and that the gap between boys and girls widens as they get older, at least as far as physical aggression is concerned (Archer & Côté, 2005; Hay, 2007). A summary of the evidence on gender differences in aggressive behaviour in different developmental periods is shown in Table 4.2 (Loeber & Stouthamer-Loeber, 1998).

Table 4.2 indicates that gender differences in aggression are established from preschool age onwards, and there is evidence that they may start to emerge as early as in toddlerhood (Alink et al., 2006). The overall direction of these differences is towards higher levels of aggression in boys, with the exception of indirect aggression, for which the evidence does not suggest a consistent gender difference. Archer (2004) conducted a meta-analysis in which he used the

TABLE 4.2 Evidence for gender differences in aggression in childhood and adolescence

Developmental period	Manifestation	Gender differences
Infancy	Frustration and rage	No
Toddlerhood	Instrumental aggression	Few
Preschool	Personal (hostile) aggression Physical fighting	Yes
Elementary school	Indirect aggression	Yes
Middle and high school	Group and gang fighting Aggravated assault Sexual violence Homicide	Yes

Reprinted with permission from Loeber & Stouthamer-Loeber, 1998, p. 253; © 1998 by the American Psychological Association.

difference (*d*) between mean aggression scores for males and females as a measure of effect size that indicates the magnitude of the difference between the two gender groups. Boys were found to be more verbally aggressive than girls, and the difference increased from childhood (6–11 years of age, effect size in the male direction of *d* = 0.19) to adolescence (11–17 years of age, effect size of *d* = 0.36). In the younger age group, the gender difference was smaller for verbal aggression (*d* = 0.19) than for physical aggression (*d* = 0.26), but in the adolescent group the effect sizes for verbal and physical aggression were almost identical.

In a large-scale international study involving adolescents aged between 12 and 15 years from 63 countries, Nivette, Sutherland, Eisner, and Murray (2019) found that boys were more than twice as likely as girls to report having been involved in frequent fighting (defined as four or more fights in the previous 12 months). Rates of physical aggression varied between countries, but they did so in parallel fashion for both boys and girls. Some research using observational methods and teacher reports has found that girls are more relationally aggressive than boys from as early as preschool age onwards. By contrast, several studies using peer reports have failed to support the gender difference (Crick, Ostrov, & Kawabata, 2007). In a meta-analysis including 148 studies and a total of over 70,000 children, Card, Stucky, Sawalani, and Little (2008) found that boys scored higher than girls on direct (i.e., verbal and physical) aggression. The gender difference was negligible for relational aggression, such as harming others' social relationships behind their back (Scheithauer, Haag, Mahlke, & Ittel, 2008). Therefore, it appears that the gender gap for physical aggression is not matched by a gender gap in relational aggression, either in the same or the opposite direction.

Moreover, Loeber and Stouthamer-Loeber (1998) noted that not only the level of aggression, but also its developmental course appears to be different for boys and girls, with a greater proportion of girls starting to become aggressive in adolescence without a previous history of aggression, and girls' involvement in serious violence peaking earlier than that of boys. However, longitudinal findings showed that a high proportion of girls diagnosed with conduct disorder in adolescence also had elevated levels of aggression in childhood, and that childhood-onset aggression may be more common in girls than was previously assumed (Keenan, Wroblewski, Hipwell, Loeber, & Stouthamer-Loeber, 2010).

To explain gender differences in physical aggression and why they seem to widen between early childhood and adolescence, several possible mechanisms have been proposed (Hay, 2007). One is that the more rapid maturation by girls in infancy promotes greater self-regulation skills, which enable girls to better control their anger. Another proposed explanation is that higher rates of rough-and-tumble play among boys spill over into aggression and bring about the development of norms condoning aggression. Indeed, boys and girls were found to differ in their normative approval of aggression (Huesmann & Guerra, 1997). Importantly, pressures created by gender role expectations may affect aggressive behaviour in boys as well as girls. Gender-role norms prohibiting overt aggression in girls may serve to curb their aggression, or may lead them to restrict their aggressive behaviour to the private sphere or to less visible forms of aggression. The latter possibility will be examined more closely in the context of intimate partner violence (see Chapter 8), where the role of women as perpetrators has been intensely debated.

Gender differences in aggression in adulthood

The view that men are generally more aggressive than women is well supported by everyday observation, crime records, and lay beliefs about gender differences. Men consistently outnumber women by a wide margin as perpetrators of violent crime. Table 4.3 illustrates this claim with statistical data taken from the United States (U.S. Department of Justice, 2018) and Germany (Bundeskriminalamt, 2019).

The data in Table 4.3 are not strictly comparable across the two countries because (a) the underlying legal definitions are somewhat different, and (b) the U.S. figures refer to the number of arrests, whereas the German data refer to the number of suspects identified. Nevertheless, they serve to illustrate the point that men are similarly over-represented in statistics for violent crime in both countries. Focusing on homicide, a recent global study on homicide rates in 2017 concluded that, worldwide, 90% of homicides were committed by men. Men also accounted for over 80% of homicide victims, according to the same report (United Nations Office on Drugs and Crime, 2019). Fox and Fridel (2017) examined patterns of male and female homicide perpetration in the period from 1976 to 2015. They found that male rates showed a greater fluctuation over time than did female rates,

TABLE 4.3 Involvement of men in violent crime: data from the United States and Germany

	United States 2018	Germany 2018
Murder and nonnegligent manslaughter	87.8	87.5
Rape	96.8	99.0
Robbery	84.9	90.7
Aggravated assault	76.4	80.3

U.S. data: U.S. Department of Justice, 2018, Table 42, data refer to persons arrested; German data: Bundeskriminalamt, 2018, p. 85, data refer to persons identified as suspects. Figures represent the percentage of men of the total number of persons arrested/suspects.

TABLE 4.4 Meta-analytic evidence on gender differences in adult aggression			
Age group	**Overall**	**Physical**	**Verbal**	**Indirect/Relational**
18–21	.46 *(33)*	.66 *(44)*	.35 *(35)*	−.11 *(19)*
22–30	.29 *(7)*	.60 *(8)*	.22 *(9)*	−.01 *(7)*
> 30	−.01 *(4)*	.25 *(8)*	.26 *(7)*	

Positive *d* scores indicate higher scores for males, negative *d* scores indicate higher scores for females. Number of studies for each effect size is given in parentheses.

Adapted from Archer, 2004, Table 5.

which decreased more steadily over the four decades. Moreover, men and women differed in the means by which they killed their victims, with men being more likely to use firearms and women more likely to use "cleaner" methods, such as poisoning or strangulation.

In addition to official crime statistics, many studies have confirmed that physical aggression is predominantly shown by men. A comprehensive review of women's aggressive behaviour in different domains is provided by Denson, O'Dean, Blake, and Beames (2018). With regard to the overall differences between men and women in aggressive behaviour, several meta-analytical reviews have found that men show higher levels of physical aggression compared with women in early adulthood (Archer, 2004; Eagly & Steffen, 1986; Hyde, 1984). In the meta-analysis by Archer (2004), the largest difference in physical aggression was found for young adults (aged 18–30 years), but the difference remained significant beyond that age. The findings from Archer's analysis referring to self-reports of aggressive behaviour are presented in Table 4.4. The measure of effect size reported in Table 4.4 is *d*, a difference score, with higher values denoting a larger gender difference. Positive *d* scores indicate that males score higher than females, whereas negative *d* scores denote higher scores in females than in males.

In each age group, positive *d* scores were found for physical aggression, indicating that men scored higher on measures of physical aggression than did women. Men were also found to be significantly more verbally aggressive in each of the three age groups, but the difference was less pronounced than for physical aggression in the two younger age groups. A small gender difference in indirect, relational aggression in the female direction was found for the group of 18- to 21-year-olds. Above the age of

21, this difference was no longer apparent, indicating that in adulthood men and women become more similar in their use of relational aggression (Richardson, 2014). A more recent meta-analysis by Archer (2019) of research across different age groups found a small effect size ($d = 0.30$) for verbal aggression, a medium effect size ($d = 0.59$) for physical aggression, a large effect size ($d = 0.88$) for weapon use, and a very large effect size ($d = 1.11$) for violent crime. All differences were in the direction of higher aggression by men. The finding that effect sizes increase as aggression becomes more severe indicates that men have a greater tendency than women to escalate aggressive encounters.

Whether or not gender differences in aggression have become smaller over recent decades has been a contentious issue. Some meta-analyses of research studies comparing men's and women's levels of aggression found that earlier studies tended to show larger gender differences than more recent publications (Hyde, 1984), and this finding has been interpreted as suggesting that socialisation is more important in eliciting gender differences than biological processes. However, G. P. Knight, Fabes, and Higgins (1996) demonstrated that the earlier and later studies differed not only with regard to their publication date, but also in their use of different methodologies. Different methodologies, in turn are systematically related to different magnitudes of gender differences shown in Table 4.4. When these methodological differences were taken into account in Knight et al.'s re-examination of studies included in Hyde's (1984) meta-analysis, the "year of publication effect" disappeared.

Explaining gender differences in aggression

Three main lines of theorising have been proposed to account for the observed gender differences in aggression: the hormonal explanation, the evolutionary or sociobiological model, and the social role model.

(1) The *hormonal* explanation attributes men's higher aggressive tendencies to the male sex hormone testosterone. Studies involving subhuman species provide some support for the role of testosterone in aggression shown by male animals (Archer, 1988). However, as discussed in Chapter 2, there is less support for the role of testosterone in explaining differences in human aggression. Cross-sectional studies comparing testosterone levels in men who differed in aggressive behaviour found some evidence of a covariation of testosterone and aggression in men (Archer, 1991; Archer, Birring, & Wu, 1998; Benton, 1992). The claim that testosterone plays a crucial role in aggression would require evidence that intra-individual variations in testosterone levels are accompanied by corresponding fluctuations in physical aggression. In particular, the dramatic increases in testosterone levels during puberty should lead to parallel increases in aggressive behaviour. In a longitudinal study that followed boys from the beginning to the end of puberty, Halpern, Udry, Campbell, and Suchindran (1993) failed to demonstrate a covariation of testosterone levels and aggression. Archer's (2004) meta-analysis also found no evidence of a substantial increase in the gender gap in physical aggression that would parallel the increase in testosterone levels in boys at puberty.

Thus, there is no conclusive evidence yet for a causal path from testosterone to aggressive behaviour that might explain the increased level of physical aggression in males.

(2) The *evolutionary* or sociobiological account, discussed in Chapter 2, stresses the adaptive value of male aggression in securing access to female mating partners (Klasios, 2019). The claim is supported by the finding that it is primarily *young* men who are responsible for the higher rates of male physical aggression, as reflected in crime statistics as well as controlled studies. According to the evolutionary perspective, men's display of aggression is designed to demonstrate their status and power and thereby to enhance their success in the reproductive competition with other men. Therefore, situations that involve a threat to a man's status should be particularly likely to elicit aggression as a means of restoring power and status. Similarly, men whose status is continuously low or under threat should be more ready to engage in aggressive behaviour than high-status men. Support for this proposition was offered by Archer, Holloway, and McLoughlin (1995), who found that compared with students (a relatively high-status group), unemployed men were significantly more likely to have been involved in a fight following public humiliation or a dispute over money or property. However, it should be emphasised that the observed link is only correlational, and does not identify low status as a *cause* of proneness to fight, as the two groups are likely to differ in many other respects.

In an experimental test of the evolutionary explanation of male aggression, Ainsworth and Maner (2014) exposed both men and women to pictures of highly attractive faces of the opposite sex, designed to activate mating-related thoughts, and then measured their aggressive behaviour towards a same-sex partner using the noise-blast paradigm, a version of the competitive reaction time task. As explained in Chapter 1, this task yields a measure of unprovoked aggression (the level of noise set for the first trial) and a measure of provoked aggression (the mean noise levels selected for the second and subsequent trials in response to the levels set by the alleged opponent). A control condition saw pictures of unattractive faces of persons of the opposite sex. Men showed more provoked aggressive behaviour towards another man after seeing the attractive vs. the unattractive female faces, but there was no effect on unprovoked aggression. Women were unaffected by the experimental manipulation measures of aggressive behaviour. In a follow-up experiment, the authors showed that the effect of the mating-related prime was stronger when the target of the aggressive behaviour was perceived to be a single man, who could be seen as a mating competitor, than when he was depicted as a married man. These findings are consistent with the evolutionary explanation of male aggression as motivated by sexual competition.

To explain men's greater involvement in intergroup conflicts, such as wars, from an evolutionary perspective, Van Vugt (2011) proposed the "male warrior hypothesis." This hypothesis argues that forming coalitions with other men to procure and protect resources has favoured the evolution of a "tribal brain" that increases men's propensity to engage in intergroup conflict. In support of this view, Van Vugt cited evidence that men are more competitive in intergroup situations, more likely to discriminate against outgroups, and more eager to defend their group against external threat.

Women's tendency to prefer indirect to direct forms of aggression can also be explained in evolutionary terms (Archer & Côté, 2005; Campbell, 2013). From a cost–benefit point of view, indirect aggression carries a lower risk of physical injury in competitions with other women for access to attractive mating partners. Protecting themselves from risk of injury is seen as more important for women than for men because their children are more dependent on their continuous availability as a carer (Cross & Campbell, 2011). Consistent with this reasoning, several studies have reported positive correlations between the use of girls' indirect aggression and their dating popularity and/or number of dating partners (Pellegrini & Long, 2003). In conclusion, indirect aggression by women may be seen as a less risky form of intimidating potential rivals in the competition for attractive male partners, thereby increasing their reproductive fitness (Vaillancourt, 2005).

(3) Whereas the hormonal and evolutionary explanations focus on biological mechanisms, the *social role* model offers a psychological explanation, proposing that differences between men and women in aggressive behaviour are the product of differences in gender roles acquired in the process of socialisation (Eagly, 1987; Eagly & Wood, 1999). According to this approach, biological sex has little explanatory power in itself, but is linked to differences in aggressive behaviour via differential social roles associated with being male or female (Richardson & Hammock, 2007). The male gender role is associated with assertiveness and dominance, which facilitate aggression, whereas the female gender role is associated with characteristics such as nurturance and empathy, which prohibit the display of aggressive behaviour. The finding that women are more likely than men to experience feelings of guilt and anxiety when engaging in aggressive behaviour supports the idea that aggression is incompatible with female role prescriptions (Campbell, 2006).

It follows from this line of reasoning that gender differences in aggression should disappear if role demands inhibiting women's aggression are removed, and several studies have found this to be the case. For example, in a study by Lightdale and Prentice (1994), gender differences disappeared when participants were de-individuated (i.e., tested under conditions of anonymity). Participants had to play a video game in which they could attack their opponents by dropping

FIGURE 4.1   Gender differences in aggression as a function of individuation vs. deindividuation

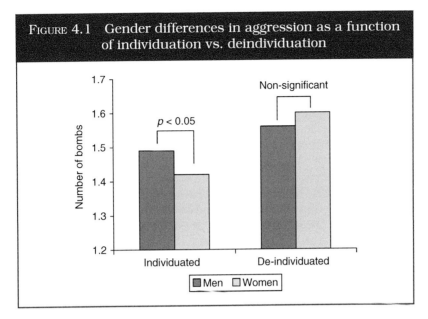

Adapted from Lightdale & Prentice, 1994, p. 41.

bombs. Figure 4.1 displays the findings for men and women under de-individuated vs. individuated conditions, using the log-transformed data reported by Lightdale and Prentice (1994, Table 3). When participants were "individuated" (i.e., when they were personally identified by large name badges), men dropped significantly more bombs on their virtual opponents than did women. However, in the de-individuated condition, where they could drop the bombs under the cloak of anonymity, women were no less aggressive than men.

The meta-analysis of 64 studies by Bettencourt and Miller (1996) further showed that gender differences in aggression are reduced when provocation is involved. Arguably, aggression in response to provocation or under conditions of anonymity is less at odds with female role prescriptions, and the decrease in gender differences under these circumstances reflects women's sensitivity to gender role norms. In the same vein, a meta-analysis by Bettencourt and Kernahan (1997) of the impact of aggressive cues on aggressive behaviour found that, in the absence of provocation, women were significantly less responsive to aggressive cues than were men. However, under conditions of provocation, both men and women showed increased levels of aggression when presented with aggressive cues.

The concept of *hegemonic masculinity*, referring to a set of gender-related beliefs that essentialise male–female differences (i.e., regard them as a biological given; Leone & Parrott, 2018), also sees gender role socialisation as a key factor in the higher tendency to show agressive behaviour by men compared with women. In the course of socialisation, boys internalise normative expectations of how they should feel, think, and act as a male in their respective society. For example, they learn that they should be dominant and stand up for themselves in conflict situations, suggesting aggression as an acceptable form of male behaviour. To the extent that they find it difficult to conform to these expectations, men are thought to experience gender role stress, either chronically or in specific situations, for example when they have to accept orders from a female boss. Engaging in aggressive behaviour, which is part of the masculine gender role, is one way in which threatened masculinity may be restored.

The impact of masculine gender-role socialisation on men's aggressive behaviour has been highlighted by research on hypermasculinity, also referred to as the "macho personality pattern" (Mosher & Sirkin, 1984). This construct seeks to explain individual differences in aggression between men. The macho personality pattern consists of three related components: (a) calloused sexual attitudes towards women, (b) the perception of violence as manly, and (c) the view of danger as exciting. Since aggression is deeply ingrained in the male gender stereotype, macho men are expected to show aggressive behaviour to a greater extent than men who do not endorse this hypermasculine role. In support of this reasoning, positive correlations were found between the endorsement of the macho personality pattern and aggression (Mosher & Sirkin, 1984). In an experimental study by Reidy, Shirk, Sloan, and Zeichner (2009), hypermasculine men were more aggressive towards a female confederate in terms of delivering electric shocks in the competitive reaction time paradigm (see Chapter 1) than men who scored lower on hypermasculinity, particularly when they were led to believe that the woman had rejected the traditional female gender role.

The social role approach explains gender differences in social behaviour as the result of the individual's adaptation to particular societal conditions and role requirements, varying over time and across societies. The evolutionary approach sees the roots of this adaptive process in the fight for survival, focusing on differences in reproductive strategies between men and women. This view leaves little room for variations in aggression across cultures and historical periods, and indeed views evidence of cross-cultural similarity in aggression as supportive of its claims. Although evolutionary and social role explanations stress different processes underlying gender differences in aggression, they are not necessarily incompatible. As has been noted by Eagly and Wood (1999), the two approaches can be fruitfully combined if they are placed along a continuum from distal to proximal influences. The evolutionary account is concerned with so-called *distal* factors that explain the long-term emergence of gender differences in the human species, whereas the socialisation approach emphasises the *proximal* influences that impinge on individuals in the course of their development. Moreover, the two approaches can be reconciled by observing the difference between intrasex aggression and intersex aggression. There is evidence that evolutionary theory is better able to explain aggressive behaviour within male sex groups, whereas social role theory is better able to explain men's aggression towards women (Wölfer & Hewstone, 2015).

SUMMARY

- Individual differences in trait aggressiveness, trait anger and hostility, irritability, emotional susceptibility, and dissipation vs. rumination following an aggression-eliciting stimulus have been linked to differences in aggressive behaviour. Moreover, hostile attributional bias (i.e., the tendency to interpret others' behaviour as hostile) was found to predict adults' aggressive behaviour. Of the Big Five personality factors, neuroticism was found to be positively correlated with aggressive behaviour, whereas extraversion, conscientiousness, agreeableness, and openness to experience showed negative correlations with aggressive behaviour.
- Research on narcissism has shown that it is not low self-esteem but unrealistically high and fragile self-esteem that makes individuals susceptible to aggressive behaviour. Individuals holding inflated and/or unstable views of themselves are more easily threatened in their self-esteem and are more likely to show aggression to restore a positive self-appraisal.
- Research on self-control and aggression has demonstrated that the failure to control aggressive impulses may explain individual differences in aggressive behaviour.
- Research on gender differences in aggression has established that men are more physically aggressive than women. Men also score higher than women on measures of verbal aggression, although the difference is smaller than for physical aggression. However, research on aggressive women suggests that women may choose indirect, relational forms of aggression to a greater extent than do men.
- There is no conclusive evidence so far on the role of the male sex hormone testosterone in explaining higher levels of male aggression. The debate on how to explain gender differences in aggression has focused on the evolutionary vs. the social role approach. The evolutionary approach attributes gender differences in aggression to differential reproductive strategies in men and women, whereas the social role approach emphasises the significance of gender-specific roles and norms to which men and women have to adapt in their social behaviour.
- Recent theorising has offered an integrative perspective in which evolutionary hypotheses refer to the distal roots of gender differences in the development of the human species, and sociocultural explanations refer to the proximal influence of socialisation processes in individual development.

TASKS TO DO

(1) Develop your own small-scale measure of the hostile attribution bias. Write down two scenarios in which one person causes harm to another, but there is ambiguity as to whether the actor did this on purpose. Then write down three items referring to the scenarios that can capture a person's hostile attributional style.

(2) Think of the most aggressive and the least aggressive person you know and write down other psychological characteristics on which the two people differ.

(3) Design an experimental study to test the hypothesis that gender differences in aggression are due to the salience of masculine and feminine gender roles.

SUGGESTED READING

Archer, J. (2019). The reality and evolutionary significance of human psychological sex differences. *Biological Reviews of the Cambridge Philosophical Society, 94*, 1381–1415.

Denson, T. F., O'Dean, S. M., Blake, K. R., & Beames, J. R. (2018). Aggression in women: Behavior, brain and hormones. *Frontiers in Behavioral Neuroscience, 12*, 81.

Hyatt, C. S., Chester, D. S., Zeichner, A., & Miller, J. D. (2020). Analytic flexibility in laboratory aggression paradigms: Relations with personality traits vary (slightly) by operationalization of aggression. *Aggressive Behavior, 45*, 377–388.

Jones, S. E., Miller, J. D., & Lynam, D. R. (2011). Personality, antisocial behavior, and aggression: A meta-analytic review. *Journal of Criminal Justice, 39*, 329–337.

Chapter 5

SITUATIONAL FACTORS PROMOTING AGGRESSIVE BEHAVIOUR

In the previous chapter, we looked at individual characteristics to answer the question of why some people are more aggressive than others in one and the same situation. In this chapter, the reverse question will be asked, namely why the same person may be more likely to act aggressively in some situations and not in others. The importance of frustration and provocation in eliciting aggressive behaviour has already been discussed in Chapter 2. In the present chapter, we discuss further variables linked to situational variations in aggressive behaviour. First, we examine the effect of alcohol intoxication on aggressive behaviour, followed by a review of the evidence on social exclusion as a trigger for aggressive behaviour. Both are proximal factors that directly impinge on the individual's thoughts and feelings. In the third section, we examine the impact of aggressive cues in the social environment. It was already mentioned in Chapter 2 that weapons are powerful aggressive cues that may precipitate aggressive behaviour by increasing the salience of aggressive thoughts. Accordingly, the fourth section looks at the availability of firearms as a risk factor for aggressive behaviour. The final section reviews evidence on the impact of heat and other more distal stressors in the physical environment on aggressive behaviour.

In each of these areas, it will become clear that situational characteristics, even if influential in themselves, interact with personal characteristics that an individual brings to the situation, and it is the interaction between the situation and the person that holds the clue to understanding aggressive behaviour. The complementary question about situational characteristics that are likely to *reduce* or *inhibit* aggression will be discussed in the context of prevention and intervention in Chapter 12.

ALCOHOL

Alcohol induces a situational state that may explain why individuals show aggression in a particular time and place and not in others. It is part of everyday wisdom that people tend to become more aggressive under the influence of alcohol, and this section examines the empirical evidence to support this proposition (Parrott & Ehrhardt, 2017). Beyond showing a link between alcohol intoxication and aggression, explanations of the mechanisms by which alcohol contributes to aggressive behaviour will be presented.

To start with a very general statement, it seems safe to conclude from the research available to date that alcohol is involved in many contexts in which aggression and violence occur. Alcohol plays an important role in the perpetration of violent crime, such as homicide (Parker & Auerhahn, 1999) and aggression in the family, including the physical and sexual abuse of children, sexual aggression, and violence against intimate partners (Barnett, Miller-Perrin, & Perrin, 2011). It features prominently in many forms of group violence, such as sports violence, rioting, and gang violence (Sønderlund et al., 2014). Alcohol is also implicated in a range of aggressive behaviour on college campuses (Wells, Mihic, Tremblay, Graham, & Demers, 2008).

However, the finding that aggressive behaviour is often shown under the influence of alcohol does not necessarily suggest that alcohol is the *cause* of an individual's aggressive actions. It may be the case that the tendency to get drunk and to show aggressive behaviour are both caused by a third variable, such as lack of impulse control, or that alcohol affects the likelihood of aggressive behaviour in an indirect way (e.g., by lowering a person's tolerance of frustration). In addition, it is possible that the aggression-promoting effects of alcohol consumption occur only in the presence of particular features of the situation, such as provocation or prior frustration.

Regarding the evidence for a link between alcohol and aggressive behaviour, three recent meta-analyses provide a comprehensive picture and a conclusive answer. Focussing on men, Crane, Godleski, Przybyla, Schlauch, and Testa (2016) found that aggression towards a female target in experimental laboratory studies was substantially higher among men who had received alcohol than among men in a no-alcohol control condition across a set of 22 studies. The effect size was higher ($d = 0.45$) when the target was an intimate partner than for female targets in general ($d = 0.32$). In a complementary meta-analysis focusing on female aggression towards male targets, Crane, Licata, Schlauch, Testa, and Easton (2017) found a significant, but smaller effect ($d = 0.17$) in the same direction across 12 studies. No separate effects for intimate partners were reported. In a meta-meta analysis (i.e., a meta-analysis integrating findings from several meta-analytic reviews rather than original studies), Duke, Smith, Oberleitner, Westphal, and McKee (2018) compiled the evidence from 18 meta-analytic studies on the alcohol–aggression link. They found an overall effect size of $d = 0.39$

and confirmed that the association was larger in male than in female samples. Overall, this evidence demonstrates a consistent and robust impact of alcohol on aggressive behaviour. The magnitude of the difference scores between intoxicated participants and controls may be interpreted as a medium-size effect. Given (a) the widespread use of alcohol and (b) the fact that no single factor can fully explain complex behaviours such as aggression, the size of the effect is meaningful both from a theoretical and an applied perspective.

Alcohol can affect aggressive behaviour through two different, but complementary routes. The first is through its *pharmacological effects*, which alter the physiological functioning of the body. The second is through its *psychological effects*, based on the knowledge of having drunk alcohol. People hold intuitive theories about the link between alcohol and aggression (e.g., that alcohol may serve as an excuse for antisocial behaviour, commonly known as "blaming the bottle"), and they have expectancies about how their feelings, thoughts, and behaviours change when they drink alcohol (Phil & Sutton, 2009). To separate the pharmacological and psychological effects of alcohol on aggression, the "balanced placebo design" is the method of choice (Bushman & Cooper, 1990). This experimental design includes four groups, as shown in Figure 5.1.

Participants in the *alcohol group* are correctly informed that they are going to receive an alcoholic drink. They will experience both physiological changes and psychological effects as a result of the alcohol intake. Participants in the *control group* are correctly informed that they will receive a non-alcoholic drink, and therefore experience neither pharmacological nor psychological effects. Participants in the *placebo group* are told they will receive an alcoholic drink, but in fact they are given a non-alcoholic drink. Thus, they may have alcohol-related expectancies, but will not experience any pharmacological changes. In the final group, called the *anti-placebo group*, participants are led to believe that they consumed a non-alcoholic drink when in fact they received an alcoholic drink. They experience

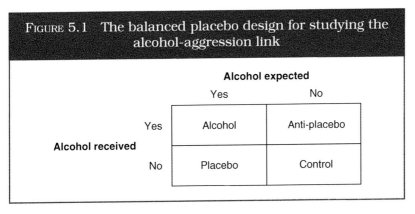

FIGURE 5.1   The balanced placebo design for studying the alcohol-aggression link

		Alcohol expected	
		Yes	No
Alcohol received	Yes	Alcohol	Anti-placebo
	No	Placebo	Control

Based on Bushman & Cooper, 1990.

pharmacological changes, but no psychological effects because they are unaware of having received alcohol.

The pharmacological effect of alcohol is most clearly discernible by comparing the control group with the anti-placebo group. Neither group thinks they have received alcohol, thereby eliminating alcohol-related expectancies, but the anti-placebo group does in fact receive an alcoholic drink. If the participants in the anti-placebo group behave more aggressively than those in the control group, the difference can be explained as a result of the physiological changes caused by the alcohol.

The psychological effects of alcohol can be assessed most conclusively by comparing the placebo group with the control group. Neither group receives alcohol, so there are no pharmacological effects. Therefore, any differences between them can be attributed to the operation of alcohol-related expectancies. By comparing the alcohol group and the control group, the combined impact of the pharmacological and psychological effects of alcohol on aggression can be established.

In a meta-analysis of 30 studies addressing the impact of alcohol on aggression in men, Bushman and Cooper (1990) found that neither the pharmacological effect on its own (the difference in aggressive behaviour between the anti-placebo group and the control group, $d = 0.06$) nor the psychological effect alone (the difference between the placebo group and the control group, $d = 0.10$) were significant. However, a significant difference of $d = 0.61$ was found between the alcohol group and the placebo group, which both thought they had consumed alcohol although only the alcohol group had actually done so. This finding suggests that the pharmacological changes induced by alcohol promote aggressive behaviour only in combination with the psychological effect (i.e., the belief that alcohol was consumed). A second, but smaller significant difference was found between the alcohol group and the control group, which differed in terms of both pharmacological and psychological effects. In this comparison, the pharmacological and expectancy effects of alcohol cannot be separated, because the alcohol group both expects and receives alcohol, whereas the control group both expects and receives a non-alcoholic drink. However, this comparison may be the most relevant one in terms of real-life significance. As Bushman and Cooper (1990) pointed out, people usually know whether or not they have consumed alcohol, which activates beliefs about how they are likely to be affected by its pharmacological effects. Unfortunately, the authors did not compare the placebo group (expectancy, but no alcohol) against the anti-placebo group (alcohol, but no expectancy) to answer the question of which of the two processes may be stronger.

The role of alcohol-related expectancies as triggers of aggression was highlighted by Subra, Muller, Bègue, Bushman, and Delmas (2010). Using a priming paradigm, they demonstrated that participants showed shorter reaction times in recognising aggression-related words after they were subliminally presented with images of alcoholic beverage bottles than following a priming with non-alcoholic beverage bottles. The priming effect of alcoholic beverage bottles was as strong as the effect elicited by images of weapons as aggression-related primes. In a second study, Subra et al. showed that participants exposed to images of alcohol bottles acted more aggressively in terms of negative evaluations of a confederate who had previously angered them than those presented with non-alcoholic beverage bottles. Again, the effect of alcohol-related primes on aggression was as strong as the effect of aggression-related primes. These findings are important because they suggest that the mere presence of alcohol-related cues may trigger cognitive associations with aggression and elicit aggressive behaviour, even when there is no anticipated or even actual consumption of alcohol.

In a naturalistic laboratory experiment, Leonard and Roberts (1998) also showed that actually consuming alcohol is not a necessary condition for eliciting aggression. They addressed the pharmacological and expectancy effects of alcohol in married couples with or without a history of the husband's physical aggression towards the wife. Husbands in one group received an alcoholic drink and were correctly informed about it (the alcohol group), while husbands in a second group were led to believe they would receive an alcoholic drink, but in fact received a non-alcoholic drink (the placebo group), and husbands in a third group both expected and received a non-alcoholic drink (the control group). All couples then engaged in a discussion about the most controversial issue in their relationship, which they had previously identified. Observations of the couples' verbal exchanges during the discussion yielded three scores for each partner: a *negativity score*, composed of negative reactions towards the partner, a *problem-solving score*, consisting of attempted solutions to the conflict, and a *positivity score*, including behaviours such as smiles and laughter. In the present context, the negativity scores are of greatest interest, as they can be seen as an indicator of aggression. To establish common levels of negativity unaffected by alcohol, couples discussed the second most controversial issue in their relationship prior to the introduction of the alcohol manipulation, so that alcohol-related effects could be established relative to this baseline. Figure 5.2 shows how the negativity scores for husbands and wives changed from baseline following the alcohol manipulation.

For the husbands in the alcohol group, a significant increase in negativity towards their partner was observed after the administration of alcohol. By contrast, the placebo group did not show an increase in their negativity scores from baseline level, and no differences were observed in the control group between baseline and drinks administration. Thus, for husbands, actually drinking alcohol was a necessary condition for increased negative reactions towards their partners. However, wives showed higher negativity when their husband was in the alcohol condition even though they had not drunk alcohol themselves. This finding is interpreted by Leonard and Roberts (1998) as an indication of the negative reciprocity in dyadic conflict. It demonstrates that alcohol intoxication by one partner in a conflict situation is sufficient to initiate an aggressive interaction and to trigger aggressive behaviour in the other partner, who did not consume

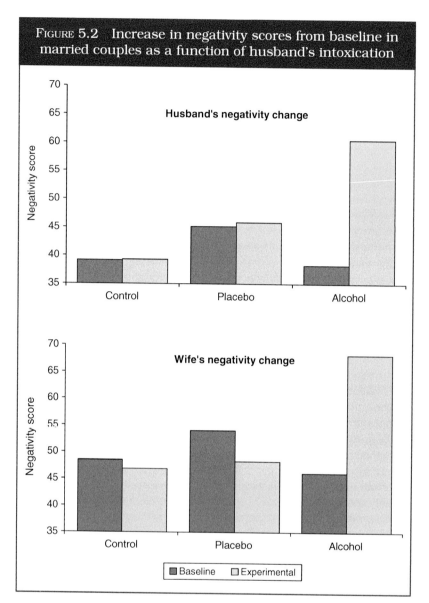

FIGURE 5.2   Increase in negativity scores from baseline in married couples as a function of husband's intoxication

Adapted from Leonard & Roberts, 1998 Table 5.

any alcohol at all (Quigley et al., 2018). The negativity scores of the wives in the placebo condition, who merely believed that their husband had received alcohol, were not affected, and no changes were observed in the wives' negativity scores in the control condition. Finally, it should be noted that couples both with and without a history of previous aggression were affected by the alcohol manipulation in the same way, disconfirming the authors' initial hypothesis that alcohol would have a stronger effect on couples with an already established pattern of dyadic aggression.

Far fewer studies are available that have examined the effects of drugs other than alcohol on aggressive behaviour (Bushman, 1993; Kretschmar & Flannery, 2007), and they mostly focus on particular domains or forms of aggression. In a longitudinal study on men's sexual aggression, Swartout and White (2010) found a significant relationship between the use of marijuana and other illicit drugs and the perpetration of sexual aggression, which remained significant after controlling for concurrent alcohol use. In a meta-analysis of 96 studies on the role of drugs other than alcohol, Moore et al. (2008) presented a fine-grained analysis of a range of drugs in relation to different forms of intimate partner aggression. They found that cocaine use in particular was significantly associated with psychological, physical, and sexual aggression against a partner. In the most recent review by Duke et al. (2018), which identified eight meta-analyses looking at illicit drugs and a further six meta-analytic studies combining alcohol and other drugs, the overall effect size was $d = 0.49$, which is similar in magnitude to the effect of alcohol. Nonetheless, there is a need for further studies, as the strength of the link between drug use and violent behaviour may vary for different drugs (Kretschmar & Flannery, 2007).

Moderators of the alcohol–aggression link

Despite the consistent support for the alcohol–aggression link, it is clear that intoxication is not linked to greater aggression in everybody and in all contexts. Therefore, it is important to identify moderators that can account for differences in the effects of alcohol on aggression. Such moderating variables can either lie in the situation, indicating that alcohol has a greater impact on aggression when certain situational variables are present at the same time, or they can lie in the person, suggesting that alcohol consumption is more or less likely to increase aggression depending on stable characteristics of the actor. We will first examine situational moderators of the impact of alcohol on aggression that have received particular attention in the literature: provocation, self-focused attention, and the presence of aggressive situational cues.

With regard to the role of *provocation*, several studies have found that alcohol consumption is more closely linked to aggression when people are provoked. Bushman (1997) reported results from a meta-analysis which showed that provocations have a greater effect on intoxicated than on sober individuals. A meta-analysis focusing on women's aggression confirmed this finding (Crane, Schlauch, Testa, & Easton, 2018).

Self-focused attention is generally thought to be impaired under the influence of alcohol (e.g., Hull, Levenson, Young, & Sher, 1983). When intoxicated, individuals are less able to concentrate on the self and to monitor their behaviour than they would be in a sober state. However, inducing self-focus in intoxicated participants who are aware of their alcohol consumption (i.e., who are in the alcohol condition of the balanced placebo design) might lead these participants to try extra hard to compensate for alcohol-related cognitive impairment. Therefore, differences between sober and intoxicated participants in aggressive behaviour should be less pronounced under high as compared with low self-awareness. This prediction was confirmed in Ito, Miller, and Pollock's (1996) meta-analysis when all 49 studies were considered simultaneously: sober and intoxicated participants behaved more similarly the higher their self-focused attention. However, when only studies that used high doses of alcohol were examined, the difference was reversed. Highly intoxicated participants and sober participants behaved more similarly when their self-focused attention was low. This finding suggests that attempts to counteract the deleterious effects of alcohol through increased self-focused attention are successful only at relatively low levels of intoxication.

The presence of *aggressive cues*, which will be discussed in more detail later in this chapter, also seems to moderate the effects of alcohol on aggression. Aggression-related cues highlight aggression as a behavioural option, but does this effect apply in the same way to sober and intoxicated individuals? Evidence suggests that intoxicated persons only respond to explicit, salient external cues (Leonard, 1989). If these cues highlight aggression, such as aggressive behaviour from a fellow participant, then an aggressive response is likely to be shown. However, if salient cues are non-aggressive, such as social pressure to set low levels of shock, then behaviour becomes less aggressive. Because sober individuals can pay attention to a greater variety of situational stimuli as well as to their personal norms, their behaviour is less affected by the salience of cues. Consistent with this reasoning, Giancola and Corman (2007) showed that when intoxicated participants working on a competitive reaction-time task were distracted, they showed less aggression compared with a non-distracted control group. The distraction task prevented them from paying full attention to the aggressive cues, the shock levels set by their opponent, thereby reducing their aggressive responses.

Among the person characteristics that affect the link between alcohol and aggression, many of the individual difference variables examined in Chapter 4 have been shown to play a role, such as trait anger, hostile rumination, and irritability. With regard to trait anger, alcohol seems to have a greater effect as a trigger of aggressive behaviour in individuals who are dispositionally anger-prone (Giancola, 2002a), and those characterised by low levels of anger control (Parrott & Giancola, 2004). Similarly, individuals with high levels of dispositional aggression scored higher on alcohol-related aggression and hostility, and the link between dispositional rumination and aggression was positively correlated with self-reported patterns of alcohol consumption (Borders, Barnwell, & Earleywine, 2007). Giancola (2002b) found a greater effect of alcohol on aggression in individuals who scored high on irritability, but this effect was limited to the men in his sample.

Another candidate for explaining individual differences in the alcohol–aggression link is weight, particularly in men. There is a stereotype of the "big, drunk, aggressive guy" that may be incorporated by heavier men as part of their identity, magnifying the effect of alcohol on aggression. Comparing an alcohol group and a placebo group, DeWall et al. (2010) found that alcohol was linked to higher levels of aggression in heavier men, but not in lighter men or in women. They concluded that "alcohol reduced the inhibition for heavy men to 'throw their weight around' and intimidate others by behaving aggressively" (DeWall, Bushman, Giancola, & Webster, 2010, p. 622). However, it should be noted that they did not control for height in their studies, so not everyone who was heavy might have been "big".

Explanations for the alcohol–aggression link

Several theoretical assumptions have been proposed to explain *how* the tendency to engage in aggressive behaviour is affected by alcohol consumption. Two main lines of theorising will be briefly described here (for reviews, see

Bègue & Subra, 2008; Parrott & Ehrhardt, 2018). The first approach focuses on the *pharmacological* effects of alcohol. It comprises several hypotheses that address different consequences of alcohol consumption. The "disinhibition hypothesis" claims that alcohol directly affects the centre of the brain which controls aggressive behaviour. According to this view, alcohol sets free aggressive impulses because it demobilises the individual's ability to suppress and avoid aggressive tendencies. However, the finding that participants who received alcohol, but were unaware of it (the anti-placebo condition of the balanced placebo design), were not found to be more aggressive than participants who neither expected nor received alcohol (the control condition) argues against the assumption of such a direct link between alcohol and aggression. The "arousal hypothesis" suggests that the stimulant effect of alcohol is responsible for its aggression-enhancing effect, and there is evidence that arousal is more closely linked to aggressive behaviour in intoxicated than in sober individuals (Giancola, Reagin, van Weenen, & Zeichner, 1998).

The second approach is concerned with the psychological mechanisms by which alcohol consumption may trigger aggressive behaviour (Parrott & Ehrhardt, 2018). It may be further subdivided into two explanations, referring to expectancy and myopia, respectively. The *expectancy hypothesis* proposes that the effects of alcohol on aggression are due at least in part to people's knowledge that they have consumed alcohol. This knowledge is associated with alcohol-related expectancies, which include cultural norms excusing or condoning aggressive behaviour under the influence of alcohol. Alcohol-related expectancies (i.e., beliefs about the effects of alcohol) were shown to be important for the pharmacological effects to occur. As noted earlier, the meta-analysis by Bushman and Cooper (1990) showed that the pharmacological effect depends on the presence of alcohol-related expectancies. Individuals who believe that alcohol causes people to engage in aggressive behaviour should be more likely to engage in aggression when intoxicated than individuals who do not subscribe to this belief. This was found to be the case in several field studies (e.g., Leonard, Collins, & Quigley, 2003), correlational studies (e.g., Barnwell, Borders, & Earleywine, 2006), and laboratory experiments (e.g., Davis, 2010).

Another explanation attributes the psychological effects of alcohol on aggression to the disruption of cognitive information processing. The *alcohol myopia model* (AMM) first introduced by Steele and Josephs (1990), suggests that alcohol has an indirect effect on aggression by reducing the attentional capacity of the individual, hampering a comprehensive appraisal of situational cues. Alcohol narrows down attention, making people "short-sighted" (myopic) with regard to the perception and processing of situational information. As a result, only the most salient cues present in a situation are attended to, and if these cues suggest aggressive rather than non-aggressive responses, aggressive behaviour is likely to be shown. Intoxicated people pay insufficient attention to inhibitory cues that might suppress aggressive behaviour. A review of the AMM by Giancola,

alcohol myopia:
Alcohol-caused reduction of attentional capacities that hampers a comprehensive appraisal of situational cues.

Josephs, Parrott, and Duke (2010) concluded that there was compelling support for the role of impaired attentional processes in explaining alcohol-related aggression. Evidence discussed earlier in this section about attention to aggressive cues as a moderator of the alcohol–aggression link is also consistent with the AMM. This model has important implications for the prevention of alcohol-related aggression, as it involves the prediction that salient anti-violence cues present in a situation should reduce aggressive behaviour. Giancola and Corman (2007) provided evidence that, when distracted so that they were unable to attend to provocation cues, intoxicated participants showed less aggressive behaviour than a sober comparison group.

In summary, several conclusions can be drawn from the literature on alcohol-related aggression. First, there is ample evidence that individuals show more aggressive behaviour when intoxicated than when sober. This evidence comes from controlled laboratory studies, including research using the balanced placebo design, as well as from studies in a variety of real-life contexts, using both self-reports and observational methods. Meta-analytic findings suggest that the effect of alcohol is stronger on men than on women. The effect is due to both the pharmacological changes induced by alcohol and alcohol-related expectancies working together to produce the aggression-enhancing effect. Second, the link between alcohol and aggression is affected by variations in the situation. Provocation, lack of self-focused attention, and the presence of aggressive cues have been identified as relevant variables accounting for differences in the effect of alcohol on aggressive responses. Third, personality variables moderate the susceptibility to aggression under the influence of alcohol. Finally, alcohol affects aggression in an indirect way. Cognitive interpretations are seen as the most promising explanations of the effects of alcohol on aggression. They emphasise that alcohol impairs a person's information-processing capacities, including attention to the normative constraints that would inhibit aggressive responses in a sober state.

SOCIAL EXCLUSION

Being accepted and liked by others serves several vital needs for humans. It gives them a sense of belonging and connectedness, helps them to maintain feelings of self-worth, and provides them with a sense of control over their social relationships. The experience of being rejected by another person or being excluded from a social group threatens these vital needs and is a powerful source of negative affect that may lead to aggressive behaviour. Several overlapping terms are used in research that addresses the impact of the experience of not belonging on aggressive behaviour (Williams, 2007a, p. 427). *Ostracism* refers to ignoring and excluding individuals or groups by other individuals or groups, *rejection* involves an explicit declaration that an individual or group is not wanted, and *social exclusion* describes the experience of being kept apart from others. Although each of these

ostracism: ignoring people or excluding them from social interactions.

constructs emphasises somewhat different aspects, they share the common core of describing experiences that undermine a person's need for social approval and connectedness. Therefore, they will be treated as synonyms for the purposes of the present discussion. A large body of research has shown that social exclusion results in feelings of sadness and anger, even when it comes from complete strangers, members of disliked groups, or an apparently randomised computer sequence (Wesselmann, Ren, & Williams, 2018; Zadro, 2011). Williams and Warburton (2003) described ostracism as a form of indirect aggression that often elicits aggressive responses, directed either against the excluding agents or against third parties.

A widely used paradigm for studying social exclusion under controlled conditions in the laboratory is the "Cyberball" game, a virtual ball-tossing game in which a person is excluded from the tossing exchanges of two or more other players (Williams, 1997; Williams, Cheung, & Choi, 2000). Another experimental strategy for studying the effects of social exclusion is the "Life Alone" paradigm developed by Twenge, Baumeister, Tice, and Stucke (2001). Participants are provided with false feedback about the projected development of their social relationships in the future. In the social exclusion condition, they are informed that based on alleged personality test scores, they will most probably end up being alone for the greater part of their future life. For example, the text of the feedback provided by Twenge et al. (2001, p. 1060) reads as follows:

> You're the type who will end up alone later in life. You may have friends and relationships now, but by your mid-20s most of these will have drifted away. You may even marry or have several marriages,

but these are likely to be short-lived and not continue into your 30s. Relationships don't last, and when you're past the age where people are constantly forming new relationships, the odds are you'll end up being alone more and more.

The paradigm also includes a social *inclusion* condition, which provides feedback about successful relationships in the future, and a negative comparison condition unrelated to social relationships in which participants are told that they are particularly likely to be accident-prone in the future. Of course, participants are carefully debriefed at the end of the experimental session to make sure that they realise the feedback was fabricated. Twenge et al. (2001) showed that participants in the social exclusion group behaved significantly more aggressively towards an experimenter (in the form of giving negative feedback relevant to his job promotion prospects) who had insulted them previously than did participants in the social inclusion or the accident-proneness conditions.

As a further method, Leary, Tambor, Terdal, and Downs (1995) designed a "Get Acquainted" paradigm to manipulate social rejection. After a brief group discussion to enable them to get acquainted, participants are asked to name two group members with whom they would like to work on the experimental task. Manipulated feedback is then provided to participants about the choices of the other group members. In the social rejection condition, they are told that no one has chosen them to work with, in the social inclusion condition they learn that everyone wants to work with them. The validity of the measure was demonstrated by the finding that participants' self-esteem was significantly reduced when they thought they had been rejected by the other group members (Leary et al., 1995).

Each of the three paradigms has generated conclusive evidence about the negative effects of social exclusion on self-esteem and feelings of control (Williams, 2007a). The experience of social exclusion has been described as a feeling of "social pain" that is no less intense than the feeling of physical pain, and brain imaging studies have revealed that being rejected in a Cyberball game activated the same areas of the brain as the infliction of physical pain (Eisenberger, Lieberman, & Williams, 2003). There are at least two common ways of reacting to this aversive experience. One is to try to restore social inclusion through ingratiation and behaving in a socially desirable way. Another is to engage in aggressive behaviour, fuelled by the experience of anger about the rejection. Williams (2007a) reviewed a large body of evidence demonstrating that socially excluded participants are more likely to engage in aggressive behaviour across a range of measures of aggression discussed in Chapter 1, such as the noise blast paradigm (Twenge et al., 2001, Experiment 4) or the hot sauce paradigm (Warburton, Williams, & Cairns, 2006).

In explaining the effects of social exclusion, Williams (2007b; see also Ren, Wesselmann, & Williams, 2018) proposed a two-stage process. The first, immediate response is seen as a *reflexive*, automatic experience of social pain experienced as a result of the exclusion. The second stage involves a more systematic appraisal and reflection of the experience. The reflexive response is largely unaffected by individual differences or contextual variables in the situation, and is followed by feelings of anger, sadness, and helplessness. A meta-analysis of 192 studies by Blackhart, Nelson, Knowles, and Baumeister (2009) found significantly less positive affect in rejected participants than in accepted or control participants, although the effect was relatively small. The reflexive, automatic effects on self-esteem are illustrated by the fact that information which should have lessened the impact of perceived exclusion is not taken into consideration at this stage. In a study by Zadro, Williams, and Richardson (2004) using the Cyberball paradigm, participants were either included (i.e., received about a third of all tosses in a three-player situation) or excluded (i.e., received no further tosses after the first two rounds). Half of the participants in the inclusion and exclusion conditions were told that they played the game with other human players, and the other half were told that they played against a computer which was programmed to toss at random. The impact of these manipulations on participants' self-esteem immediately after six minutes of playing the game is presented in Figure 5.3. As expected, when they thought they played with other human participants, the excluded participants reported significantly lower self-esteem than the included participants. The effect was equally strong among participants who thought that the tossing sequence had been determined by a computer, indicating that they had failed to consider this information.

With time to reflect on the exclusion episode, a second, reflective process sets in that involves a more *controlled* cognitive appraisal. As shown in a series of experiments by DeWall, Twenge, Gitter, and Baumeister (2009), rejected individuals generated more hostile thoughts, which in turn predicted more aggressive behavioural responses. This second phase of responding to social exclusion is influenced by stable dispositions and the features of the situation. For example, Twenge and Campbell (2003) showed that narcissists, whose self-esteem is inflated and particularly vulnerable to threat, were more aggressive after rejection than non-narcissists (for a discussion of narcissism and aggression, see Chapter 4). Similarly, a study by Ayduk, Gyurak, and Luerssen (2008) found that individuals high in rejection sensitivity, who anxiously expect and readily perceive social rejection, showed more aggressive behaviour following social rejection in a laboratory situation than those low in rejection sensitivity.

Situational variables have also been identified as moderators of the rejection–aggression link. Arguing that social rejection undermines an individual's sense of control and that aggression is a means of regaining control, Warburton et al. (2006) conducted an experiment in which participants were either excluded or included. Subsequently, they were exposed to an aversive noise blast that they could either terminate or could not control. Their findings showed that excluded participants who were given situational control over the aversive noise were not more aggressive

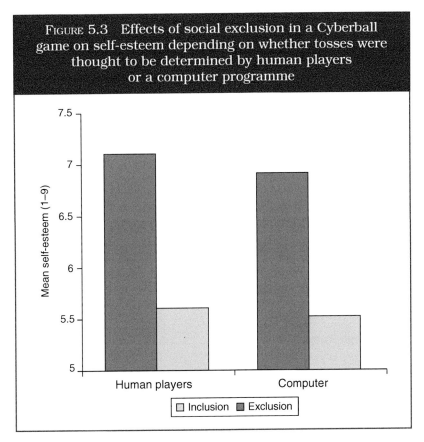

FIGURE 5.3 Effects of social exclusion in a Cyberball game on self-esteem depending on whether tosses were thought to be determined by human players or a computer programme

Adapted from Zadro, Williams, & Richardson, 2004, Table 1.

in the hot sauce paradigm than participants in the inclusion condition. By contrast, excluded participants who were denied situational control over the aversive noise assigned four times more hot sauce to the target person than any of the other groups. The critical role of control has also been demonstrated in a study by Wesselmann, Butler, Williams, and Pickett (2010). They showed that participants responded more aggressively to the experience of rejection when it occurred unexpectedly than when they had seen it coming on the basis of the experimenter's previous behaviour.

Although the present discussion has focused on single episodes of social exclusion as a situational trigger of aggressive behaviour, it is of course important to consider the effects of continuous and cumulative experiences of social exclusion over time. Many recent school shootings and also workplace killings were committed by individuals enraged by the experience of rejection in the form of being bullied at school or dismissed from their jobs (Leary, Kowalski, Smith, & Phillips, 2003). Similarly, social rejection by parents and/or peers in childhood has been linked to individual differences in aggression later in life (e.g., Hale, VanderValk, Akse, & Meeus, 2008; Lansford, Malone, Dodge, Pettit, & Bates, 2010). Taken together, the evidence discussed in this section suggests that the experience of social exclusion is both a short-term and a long-term risk factor for aggressive behaviour.

A final question in relation to the adverse effects of social exclusion on aggression refers to differences in the association as a function of culture. Based on the distinction between individualist cultures, where individual autonomy is highly valued, and collectivist cultures, where individuals define themselves through their social relationships (Hofstede, 2013), two competing hypotheses may be advanced. The first is the individuals in collectivist cultures might be more negatively affected by social rejection because they have an interdependent self-concept that is mainly defined by good relationships with others. The second is that individuals in individualist cultures should be more negatively affected because they have fewer social bonds that can potentially buffer the impact of social rejection. The review by Uskul and Over (2017) provides more conclusive evidence for the second hypothesis, arguing that entertaining an interdependent self-concept may serve a protective function against experiences of social exclusion.

AGGRESSIVE CUES

In the context of the "frustration–aggression hypothesis" discussed in Chapter 2, we saw that the presence of aggressive cues in the form of weapons and other stimuli related to aggression increases the likelihood of an aggressive response. In their experiment on the famous "weapons effect", Berkowitz and LePage (1967) demonstrated that angered participants acted more aggressively towards the source of the provocation when a firearm was present in the lab room than in the presence of a badminton racket (a neutral object) or in a no-object control condition in which no objects were present. This experiment highlighted the importance of *aggressive cues in the environment* in triggering aggressive responses, and subsequent studies demonstrated the effect of aggressive cues for a range of other stimuli, such as names and images of famous boxing champions (Carlson, Marcus-Newhall, & Miller, 1990). In addition, the meta-analysis by Carlson et al. identified an effect, albeit weaker, of aggressive cues on participants in a neutral mood state, which suggests that negative arousal may not be a necessary condition for situational cues to affect aggressive behaviour. A meta-analysis including 151 effect-size estimates from 78 independent studies confirmed that the presence of aggressive cues increases the likelihood of aggressive thoughts, hostile appraisals, and aggressive behaviour (Benjamin, Kepes, & Bushman, 2018). However, the effects are in the small range, and the measures used to assess aggressive behaviour vary substantially between studies.

Reprinted with permission from https://vliegervandam.com/; © 2019 by Vlieger & Vandam.

Bushman, Kerwin, Whitlock, and Weisenberger (2017) demonstrated the weapons effect in the context of driving behaviour. In a driving simulator, their participants had to manoeuvre a car in a simulated driving environment. They were told to reach a destination as fast as possible and experienced a series of frustrating situations during the drive (e.g., a car pulling out in front of them, progress impeded by a traffic jam). On the passenger seat, one group had a pistol and the other group a tennis racket lying there, ostensibly left behind by a previous experimenter. Speeding, defined as driving faster than 50mph, and tailgating, defined by the distance allowed to the car driving in front on the simulated road, were used as measures of aggressive behaviour. In the presence of the pistol, participants drove faster and were more likely to drive too close to the car in front than in the presence of the tennis racket (see also Chapter 7 for a discussion of research on aggressive driving).

The psychological mechanism underlying the impact of aggressive cues on aggressive cognitions and behaviour is referred to as "priming" (Todorov & Bargh, 2002). *Primes* are stimuli that activate specific mental concepts which in turn feed into subsequent judgements and behaviours. For example, media depictions of violence, words with an aggressive meaning, or names of people associated with violent crime activate a network of aggression-related thoughts. Being exposed to these stimuli facilitates the ease with which aggressive cognitions come to mind and the likelihood that aggressive behaviour will be shown.

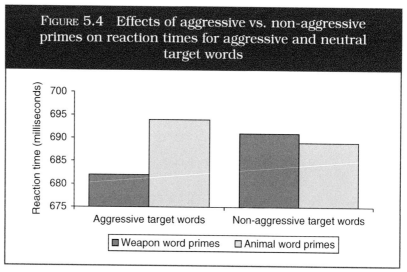

FIGURE 5.4   Effects of aggressive vs. non-aggressive primes on reaction times for aggressive and neutral target words

Adapted from Anderson, Benjamin & Bartholow, 1998, Table 2.

Using a standard reaction-time paradigm, Anderson, Benjamin, and Bartholow (1998) showed that exposure to weapon primes does indeed enhance the accessibility of aggression-related cognitions, even in individuals who were not previously angered or frustrated. They presented their participants with series of word pairs, with the first word of each pair acting as a prime. Primes were either aggression related (weapon words) or neutral (animal words). Following the silent reading of the prime word, participants were instructed to read the second (target) word of the pair out loud as fast as they could. Reaction times for reading the target word were used as the dependent variable. The target word was either aggression-related or neutral. As aggressive primes were assumed to activate aggressive thoughts, it was predicted that weapon primes would lead to shorter reaction times when reading aggressive target words compared with either neutral target words or animal primes. The findings from the study are presented in Figure 5.4.

As predicted, participants were significantly faster in reading out aggressive target words when they had been primed by a weapon word than when the prime had been an animal word. Moreover, reaction times within the aggressive-prime group were shorter for the aggressive than for the non-aggressive target words. A second study conducted by Anderson et al. (1998) using visual stimuli as primes (pictures of weapons vs. pictures of plants) confirmed these results.

If aggressive cues promote aggressive behaviour by activating a network of associated cognitions, they may also have an indirect effect by linking initially neutral thoughts to the aggressive meaning of the cue. This was shown in a study by Busching and Krahé (2013), who made their participants play a violent video game either in the context of a city environment or in the context of a ship environment. Afterwards, they used either city-related or ship-related words as primes presented before a lexical decision task in which participants had to decide as fast as possible if a string of letters was a meaningful word or not. Both aggression-related and neutral words were used in the lexical decision task. As predicted, participants who had played the violent video game in the ship environment were faster in recognising aggression-related words following the ship words as primes than following the city words, whereas participants who had played the game in a city environment were faster when primed with city-related than with ship-related words. This indicates that the initially neutral words (related to ships or cities) were charged with aggressive meaning because they had been encountered together with violent cues in the video game and subsequently served to facilitate the activation of aggressive cognitions.

Most research on the weapons effect was conducted in artificial laboratory settings. In a rare field experiment, police officers in London were randomly equipped with a Taser (a non-lethal weapon that may be used to incapacitate a violent suspect) or went on duty without a Taser (Ariel et al., 2019). The results provide further support for the weapons effect: the presence of a Taser was linked to significantly more assaulting behaviour against officers by suspects and greater use of force by the officers, compared with incidents where no Taser was present. As a practical recommendation, the authors propose that Tasers – which have been shown to be effective in reducing lethal force in police operations – should not be carried to be visible, but concealed from sight to prevent them from working as aggressive cues.

In combination, research on the weapons effect in both controlled laboratory situations and field settings has important implications for the understanding of aggression in natural, everyday contexts. Weapons and other objects or images associated with aggression are widely available in a variety of social settings. They are an integral part of children's toy boxes and video game libraries, and omnipresent in the world of film and television (for a discussion of violent media contents as aggressive cues, see Chapter 6). The more frequently such cues are encountered, the more easily aggressive cognitions and behavioural response options are activated, making them chronically accessible over time. We can conclude from the research discussed in this section that repeated exposure to aggressive cues is one of the pathways that contribute to the emergence of individual differences in the proneness to aggression.

AVAILABILITY OF FIREARMS

Easy access to a firearm is a further situational factor relevant for explaining aggressive behaviour. Although firearms are not considered the primary cause of aggressive confrontations, availability of firearms increases the risk of serious and potentially fatal injuries (Stroebe, 2013). Especially when violence is not planned and premeditated, having a gun within reach may precipitate the formation and implementation of intentions to shoot. Gun-related violence is a major problem around the world, although countries vary in the ease with which firearms may be acquired and the prevalence of gun ownership. This is illustrated in Table 5.1, which presents a list of the 25 countries with the highest rate of gun ownership from a recent international survey (Karp, 2018).

In the U.S., which features top of the list in Table 5.1, about 11,000 intentional killings involving a firearm were recorded in the first ten months of 2019, and 280 incidents of mass shootings, defined as four or more persons shot and/or killed in a single incident, happened during the same period (www.gunviolencearchive.org/). Recent incidents of mass shootings, such as the tragedy at Parkland High School in Florida in February 2018, have triggered campaigns demanding a tightening of gun laws and a reduction of the number of firearms in the hands of private individuals. To assess whether this approach would be likely to reduce aggression and violence, evidence is needed to show that *firearm availability* and aggression are, indeed, linked. The issue of tighter gun control legislation as a policy strategy for preventing violence will be discussed in Chapter 12.

firearm availability: easy access to firearms as a risk factor for violence.

TABLE 5.1	Twenty-five countries with the highest rate of gun ownership (rate per 100 residents)				
United States	120.5	Iceland	31.7	Sweden	23.1
Yemen	52.8	Bosnia and Herzegovina	31.2	Pakistan	22.3
Montenegro	39.1	Austria	30.0	Portugal	21.3
Serbia	39.1	Macedonia	29.8	France	19.6
Canada	34.7	Norway	28.8	Germany	19.6
Uruguay	34.7	Malta	28.3	Iraq	19.6
Cyprus	34.0	Switzerland	27.6	Luxembourg	18.9
Finland	32.4	New Zealand	26.3		
Lebanon	31.9	Kosovo	23.8		

Reprinted with permission from Karp, 2018, p. 4; © 2018 by the Small Arms Survey.

A large body of correlational evidence on the association between firearm availability and violence in statistical data at the level of societies has shown that a higher number of firearms in a state or country is linked to higher rates of homicides and other violent offences (Cukier, Eagen, & Decat, 2018; Stroebe, 2016). Although outside the scope of this discussion, it also should be noted that significant associations between rates of gun ownership and suicide have been documented (Knopov, Sherman, Raifman, Larson, & Siegel, 2019; Miller, Barber, & Azrael, 2016).

The problem with correlational studies of this kind is that they cannot establish the direction of causality. Higher rates of gun ownership could lead to more violence, or people might buy more guns in response to higher violence rates. To decide between these two hypotheses, quasi-experimental studies have been conducted which have looked at the link between gun ownership and violence at the individual level. These studies have compared gun-ownership rates in individuals convicted for violent crime with non-offenders from the general population and demonstrated that violent offenders were more likely to have owned a gun than the non-offender comparison groups. Although such quasi-experimental studies are faced with the challenge that the two groups are likely to differ on variables other than gun ownership, they are the closest approximation to addressing the causal influence of gun availability, given that it is impossible to conduct true experimental studies that manipulate gun ownership to observe differences in rates of serious violence or murder.

If homicides were the reason for buying guns rather than guns being the cause of homicide, the correlation would be expected for homicides generally, regardless of whether they occur between strangers or nonstrangers. However, empirical data indicate that gun ownership is more closely related to homicide between nonstrangers than between strangers (Siegel et al., 2014; Stroebe, 2016), which provides circumstantial evidence for the claim that the availability of guns precipitates violent behaviour rather than the other way round. In addition, individuals who live in households where guns are kept were found to have a substantially higher risk of being murdered than individuals in households where no guns are available (Anglemyer, Horvath, & Rutherford, 2014). This difference may be explained by the facilitating effect of guns, which means that access to guns makes conflicts more likely to end in violence and death. Having a gun at hand increases the odds that intentions to kill will be translated into action and result in death or serious injury.

In addition to increasing the odds that intentions to harm will result in severe injury or death, the widespread availability of guns may also have a causal role to play in violent behaviour. As we discussed earlier, guns are aggressive cues that were shown to augment the effect of a frustration on aggressive behaviour. Thus, they may create an intention to harm by activating aggressive cognitions, thereby increasing the likelihood of aggressive behaviour, whether with the use of a gun or by other means. This reasoning is supported by the finding that handling a toy gun led to an increase in testosterone levels in men and made them show more aggressive behaviour (Klinesmith, Kasser, & McAndrew, 2006). The finding discussed earlier that openly carrying Tasers by police officers was linked to more aggressive behaviour in interactions between police and suspects also shows that the mere exposure to weapons as aggressive cues may increase the odds of aggressive behaviour in the situation.

Offering a motivational account of the psychological functions of gun ownership, a series of studies by Leander et al. (2019), conducted in the wake of three mass shooting in the U.S., showed that gun owners were more likely to justify the use of firearms and say they would use firearms for self-protection after they had experienced failure, and this effect was mediated by a greater perception of guns as a means of empowerment in the group that experienced failure than in the control group. However, this mediated pathway was found only among those participants for whom mass shootings were salient (who perceived a high threat of becoming a victim of a mass shooting). The authors concluded that when individuals' sense of personal control and significance is threatened, for example by failure, guns become a means of restoring a sense of power when gun-related cues are salient. The link between weapons and empowerment also ties in with the finding that men are more likely to own a gun than are women (Pew Research Center, 2017). Guns are closely related to traditional notions of masculinity, which is reinforced by entertainment media (Cukier et al., 2018). We will return to this topic when we discuss the impact of violent media contents on aggression in Chapter 6.

HEAT AND OTHER ENVIRONMENTAL STRESSORS

Finally, the search for situational conditions causing or promoting violence has considered hot temperature as an environmental factor that affects human behaviour. This research is based on the so-called *heat hypothesis*, which states that uncomfortably high temperatures increase aggressive behaviour (Anderson, Bushman, & Groom, 1997). Since the late nineteenth century, scientists have observed that aggression levels vary as a function of temperature, being higher at hot than at comfortable temperatures. The finding that exposure to high temperatures promotes aggression can be explained with reference to Berkowitz's (1993) "cognitive neo-associationist model" of affective aggression described in Chapter 2. Uncomfortably high temperatures represent aversive stimuli that activate aggression-related thoughts and feelings, giving rise to aggressive behaviour. Drawing on the General Aggression Model (GAM; see Chapter 2), Anderson (2001) proposed that heat-induced discomfort may increase hostile affect and prime aggressive cognitions, both of which increase the likelihood of an aggressive response in social interactions that occur under aversively hot conditions.

heat hypothesis: hypothesis that aggression increases with higher temperatures.

geographic regions approach: method for testing the heat hypothesis by comparing violence rates in cooler and hotter climates.

time periods approach: method for testing the heat hypothesis by comparing violence rates in the same region during cooler and hotter periods.

concomitant heat approach: method for testing the heat hypothesis by manipulating room temperature and observing covariations between temperature and aggressive behaviour.

Three methodological approaches have been developed for studying the temperature–aggression link (Miles-Novelo & Anderson, 2019). The first is *the geographic regions approach*, which seeks support for the heat hypothesis by showing that aggression is more prevalent in geographic regions with hotter as compared with cooler climates. The second is the *time periods approach*, which examines variations in the level of aggression as a function of temperature changes within a region over time (seasons, months, or times of day). Both the geographic regions approach and the time periods approach rely heavily on archival data, in particular meteorological records and crime statistics, to examine the link between high temperatures and aggression (for a discussion of the use of archival data, see Chapter 1). Finally, research based on the *concomitant heat approach* manipulates temperature in the laboratory and examines differences in aggressive behaviour in relation to variations in temperature. Across different methodological approaches, the meta-analysis of 55 studies by Burke, Hsiang, and Miguel (2015) found significant positive associations between high temperature and both interpersonal and intergroup violence. With every increase of one standard deviation on the temperature scale, the relative risk of violent conflict was found to increase by 2.1% for interpersonal and 11.3% for intergroup conflict (see Chapter 10 for a discussion of intergroup conflict).

Empirical evidence for the heat hypothesis

Studies based on the *geographic regions approach* mostly compared northern and southern areas of the U.S. They showed with high consistency that, as predicted by the heat hypothesis, violent crime is more widespread in the hotter regions of the south than in the cooler regions of the north (Anderson, Anderson, Dorr, DeNeve, & Flanagan, 2000). However, this observation is merely correlational and tells us little about any causal influence of temperature on aggression. Variations in geographical location are associated with a host of other social structural variables that could be responsible, solely or in part, for observed regional differences in aggression. When controlling for a range of these variables, such as population size, ethnic composition, unemployment rate, educational background, and age composition, the link between temperature and violent crime remained significant across a range of studies (Anderson et al., 2000). However, the heat hypothesis is only one of several explanations for the higher rate of violent crime in the southern regions of the U.S. An alternative explanation was proposed by Nisbett (1993). He argued that higher rates of violent crime in the south result from a particular "Southern culture of honour", which can be traced back to the historical roots of settlement and survival in the southern part of the country. The Southern culture of honour is characterised by a greater acceptance of the use of violence, both for self-protection and in response to an insult or provocation as a way of restoring one's honour. Nisbett (1993) reported that Southerners showed greater anger in response to a provocation and were more likely to produce aggressive solutions to an interpersonal conflict following a provocation. Similarly, D. Cohen, Nisbett, Bowdle, and Schwarz (1996) showed that, following an insult, Southerners were more upset and more likely to engage in aggressive behaviour than Northerners.

A limitation of the geographic regions approach is that it examines the temperature–aggression link at a highly aggregated level (i.e., at the level of entire regions and large populations). Therefore, it does not yield insights into the link between exposure to high temperature and aggression within the individual person, as conceptualised in the heat hypothesis. On the other hand, it is a strength of geographic regions studies that they can draw on large and reliable data sets about the criterion variable (i.e., violent crime). Murder and assault rates, for example, are reported and recorded continuously over time. Therefore, geographic regions studies are able to complement evidence from other sources in evaluating the heat hypothesis

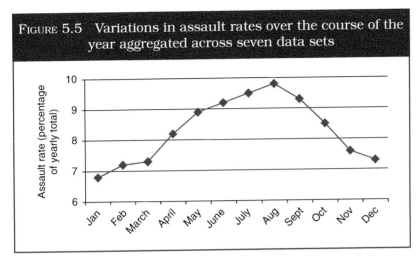

FIGURE 5.5   Variations in assault rates over the course of the year aggregated across seven data sets

(for a more detailed critique of the geographic regions approach, see also Anderson et al., 1997).

Time period studies examine variations in aggression over different periods of time within the same region and are therefore less affected by the confounding influence of socio-structural variables. This approach also supports the heat hypothesis by showing that violent crime rates are higher in the summer months than during the winter period, and in hotter than in cooler summers (Anderson, 2001; Anderson & Anderson, 1998). For example, the rates of murder, assault, and rape were found to be highest in the summer months across several studies, and the daily rates of emergency calls to police stations were found to increase as temperatures went up. Figure 5.5 illustrates the distribution of assault cases over the year course based on Anderson's (1989) aggregation of data across seven large data sets accumulated between 1883 and 1977.

As predicted by the heat hypothesis, Figure 5.5 shows a clear peak of assault rates in the summer months. Comparing years with different average temperatures and with hotter vs. cooler summers, Anderson et al. (1997) found further support for the heat hypothesis and the particular impact of heat on affective aggression: both homicide and serious assault were more prevalent in hotter years and hotter summers, but property-related crime was unaffected by variations in temperature. In addition to these studies from the U.S., support for a link between temperature oscillation and the rate of armed political conflict within tropical regions has been provided by Hsiang, Meng, and Cane (2011). They analysed rates of armed conflict in El Niño years (with higher temperatures) and in La Niña years (with lower temperatures) between 1950 and 2004, and found significantly higher rates of armed conflict in the warmer periods of the El Niño years in the regions affected by El Niño–La Niña oscillations.

Critics of the time periods approach have argued that rather than reflecting a causal effect of the aversive effects of high temperatures, the increase in violence could be explained by differences in people's routine activities (L. E. Cohen & Felson, 1979). People tend to spend more time outdoors in the summer months and in years with hotter as opposed to cooler summers. This may create more opportunities for aggressive encounters with others, leading to higher rates of violent crime. Anderson (1989) argued against this interpretation by pointing out that rates of domestic violence are also higher in the summer months, although families typically spend more time at home together in the winter months. Looking at the covariation of temperature and aggression within the context of baseball matches in which the opportunities for aggression are standardised across matches, higher temperatures interacted with in-game provocation to predict aggressive moves. When provocation was high (as defined by the number of times a team mate had been hit by a member of the opposing team), the rate of aggressive retaliation increased significantly in proportion to the temperature during the match (Larrick, Timmerman, Carton, & Abrevaya, 2011; for a discussion of aggressive behaviour in a sports context, see Chapter 7).

The third approach addressing the heat hypothesis is the *concomitant heat paradigm*. It involves manipulating temperature levels in laboratory settings and observing variations in aggressive behaviour as a function of variations in temperature. Here, intra-individual associations are observed between exposure to heat and aggressive behaviour, using very different behavioural criteria of aggression (mostly electric shocks) to the other two paradigms. The concomitant heat approach is illustrated by a study by Vrij, Van der Steen, and Koppelaar (1994), who showed a sample of police officers a virtual-reality display of a burglary that involved a face-to-face confrontation of the police officer with the suspected burglar. The participants were asked to respond to the incident as they would do in real life in their job, using laser beams as simulated weapons. During the experiment, the room temperature was systematically varied. One group was exposed to a comfortable temperature of 21°C (70°F), and the other was tested in an uncomfortably hot room at 27°C (81°F). The main dependent measures were (a) ratings of the negative affect elicited by the confrontation with the burglar, (b) perceptions of the burglar as aggressive, (c) perceived threat from the burglar, and (d) estimated likelihood to shoot. All four dependent variables showed a significant effect of room temperature, supporting the heat hypothesis. Participants tested at an uncomfortably hot room temperature perceived the suspected burglar as more aggressive, reported more negative affect, and perceived greater threat. In support of the heat hypothesis, they also indicated a higher likelihood that they would use their firearms against the suspect than participants who were tested at a comfortable room temperature. However, other laboratory studies found a curvilinear relationship between temperature and aggression, demonstrating a decrease in aggression with very high temperatures. On the basis of a meta-analysis of 11 studies, Anderson et al. (2000) concluded that the results of laboratory studies on the heat hypothesis had remained inconsistent.

Evidence supporting the temperature–aggression link has, with very few exceptions, been limited to the aggression-enhancing effects of uncomfortably *high* temperatures. No corresponding effect has been found for uncomfortably low temperatures in natural settings. The explanation offered by Anderson et al. (2000) is that people are generally better equipped to protect themselves against the cold than they are to escape from excessive heat, so they are able to reduce cold-related discomfort more easily than heat-related discomfort.

The implications of studies that support the heat hypothesis are worrying in the face of global warming. If increases in temperature are systematically related to increases in violent crime, then the continuous rise in global temperature represents a risk factor for the rise in violent crime. Miles-Novelo and Anderson (2019) have proposed both direct and indirect paths by which higher temperatures may contribute to an increase in violence. Their model is shown in Figure 5.6. The immediate impact of rising temperatures on the individual is conceptualised on the basis of the General Aggression Model as the result of an aversive state that gives rise to irritability, anger, and negative arousal. In addition, indirect effects are expected via the negative impact of rising temperatures on macrosocial changes, such as poverty as a result of bad harvests and economic instability, which are known risk factors for aggression at the individual, intergroup, and societal level. A study by Barlett et al. (2020) found a positive correlation between temperature and extreme weather events as well as a positive correlation between extreme weather events and homicide rate across the world.

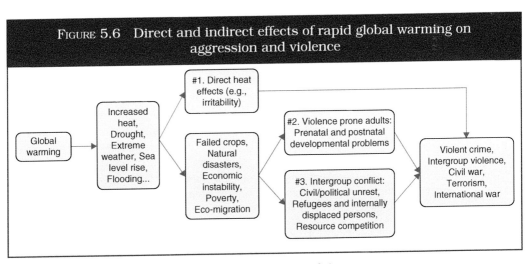

FIGURE 5.6   Direct and indirect effects of rapid global warming on aggression and violence

Moreover, scarcity of food in hotter parts of the world may increase involuntary migration, which in turn is a source of intergroup conflict. The impact of rising temperatures on intergroup aggression and violence is also at the core of the CLimate, Aggression, and Self-control in Humans Model (CLASH; van Lange, Rinderu, & Bushman, 2018). The model proposes that people in cooler climates, with large seasonal variations in temperature, need to adapt to this environmental challenge by engaging in more planning and self-control to ensure a sufficient supply of food. Both future orientation and self-control are inhibitors of aggressive behaviour, which are not required to the same extent in cultures living in hotter climates with less seasonal variation. First evidence on the association between temperature and future orientation as well as self-control in line with the proposed model is presented by van Lange et al. (2018). The authors acknowledge, however, that climate is more than just temperature and that other variables, such as national wealth, religion, or political circumstances, may have an additive or interactive effect on heat-related aggression and conflict.

Research on the heat hypothesis should alert both policy makers and the general public to the fact that the adverse effects of global warming are not restricted to our natural environment, but also pose a threat to the social functioning of human communities. At the same time, this line of research has important implications for violence prevention in the short term. As noted by Anderson et al. (2000), keeping temperatures at a comfortable level by means of air conditioning may help to bring down violence rates, and may be particularly useful in settings such as prisons, workplaces, and schools where violence is a problem.

Other stressors in the physical environment

In this concluding section, we will briefly examine the role of three further environmental stressors that promote aggressive behaviour: crowding, noise, and air pollution.

Crowding refers to the perception of spatial density as unpleasant and aversive. Note that crowding is a subjective experience, whereas density is a physical concept that is defined in terms of the number of people per space unit. This distinction is important because the same level of spatial density may give rise to feelings of crowding in some people but not in others. Similarly, the same level of spatial density may be perceived as pleasantly busy in some settings (e.g., at an open-air concert) and unpleasantly crowded in others (e.g., in a packed train compartment). Whereas density cannot be linked to aggression in a conclusive fashion, crowding has been found to increase the likelihood of aggression in a variety of settings, such as bars (Green & Plant, 2007), prisons (Lahm, 2008), and overcrowded living conditions for families (Regoeczi, 2008). Experimental evidence suggests that the aggression-enhancing effect of crowding is mediated by negative affective arousal elicited by the subjective perception of spatial constraint (Lawrence & Andrews, 2004). Furthermore, it seems that men are more likely than women to respond to crowding with aggressive behaviour (Regoeczi, 2008). This finding is consistent with the negative affect explanation, in that men have consistently been found to claim more personal space than women, and are therefore more likely to be adversely affected by restrictions of their territorial claims (e.g., Leibman, 1970; Patterson, Mullens, & Romano, 1971).

Noise is another environmental stressor linked to aggression. As an aversive stimulus, noise can trigger or reinforce aggressive behaviour. In a study by Geen and O'Neal (1969), participants were shown either a violent or a non-violent film and subsequently instructed to deliver electric shocks to another person as a punishment for errors on a learning task. While they administered the shocks, half of the participants in each group were exposed to a loud noise. It was found that the noise manipulation led to higher aggression only among those who had previously watched the violent film. Another consequence of noise is that it impairs the person's tolerance of frustration, thereby increasing aggressive behavioural tendencies following a frustration (Donnerstein & Wilson, 1976). Thus, noise operates as a reinforcer of aggressive response tendencies in individuals who are already in a state of increased readiness for aggressive behaviour. However, it does not seem to be the noise per se that facilitates aggression, but rather the fact that noise is often an uncontrollable aversive event. If the noise was perceived as controllable by the individual, its impact on aggressive behaviour was substantially reduced (Geen & McCown, 1984).

Finally, *air pollution* has been found to be a reinforcer of aggressive response tendencies in a similar way as crowding and noise. Studies examining the effect of cigarette smoke on aggression found that individuals exposed to cigarette smoke showed more hostility towards others (not only towards the person producing the smoke) as well as aggressive behaviour than a control group not exposed to smoky conditions (Jones, 1978; Zillmann, Baron, & Tamborini, 1981). The role of unpleasant smells in promoting aggression was examined in the context of the negative affect escape model (Baron & Bell, 1976). This model predicts that moderate levels of an unpleasant smell lead to an increase in aggression, while aggression levels drop again as the unpleasant smell becomes more intense. Support for this prediction was found in a study by Rotton, Frey, Barry, Milligan, and Fitzpatrick (1979). However, the comparative review of the evidence by Evans (2019) suggests that the effect of air pollution on aggression and violence is much less pronounced than the effect of high temperature.

SUMMARY

- Alcohol, social exclusion, aggression-related cues, availability of firearms, and high temperature have been identified as situational or environmental variables that have a significant influence on aggressive behaviour. More limited evidence is available on the impact of other external stressors, such as crowding, noise, and air pollution, but it

appears that these features of the physical environment also increase
or reinforce aggressive behaviour.

- The claim that people are more likely to act aggressively when under
the influence of alcohol is supported by a large body of research.
Alcohol affects aggressive behaviour through both pharmacological
and psychological effects. The pathway from alcohol consumption
to aggressive behaviour seems to be mediated by attentional deficits
and moderated by situational factors, such as provocation. Under the
influence of alcohol, individuals' attention capacity is impaired, and
they only attend to the most salient stimuli. Awareness of the normative constraints that inhibit aggressive behaviour is reduced, undermining an important mechanism in the self-regulation of aggressive
behaviour.

- There is consistent evidence that being rejected or excluded by others
precipitates aggressive behaviour. Social exclusion thwarts vital
needs for belonging, self-esteem, and control, and aggression is a
common response to this experience. Whereas the immediate social
pain experienced when excluded by others is a reflexive response that
is largely independent of personal or situational influences, individual and contextual factors affect the subsequent more controlled
processing of the exclusion experience. Chronic experience of social
exclusion has long-term effects on psychological well-being, and may
explain individual differences in aggression.

- Situational cues, such as weapons or other violence-related primes,
enhance the cognitive availability of aggression as a response option.
The "weapons effect" was strongest in individuals who were previously angered, and who were therefore already in a state of heightened
angry arousal. However, it has also been demonstrated in people
who were in an affectively neutral state. Therefore, the mere presence
of an aggression-related cue seems to increase the probability of an
aggressive response.

- Higher rates of gun ownership have been linked to higher rates of
homicide, especially against non-strangers. Men are more likely to own
guns than are women, and guns provide a sense of power that is critical
for masculine gender identity. Guns also affect aggressive behaviour
by acting as aggressive cues that increase the accessibility of aggressive
thoughts.

- The effect of temperature on aggression has been demonstrated across
different methodological paradigms. Comparing hot vs. cold regions or
hot vs. cold time periods within a region, it was found that aggression,
especially violent crime, is generally higher under conditions of high
temperature, supporting the "heat hypothesis". Experimental studies
that have explored differences in aggression as a function of variations
in temperature also provide some support for the heat hypothesis, but
the evidence is less conclusive.

- The general proposition that stressors in the physical environment cause negative affective arousal which in turn gives rise to aggressive responses is further supported by studies that have looked at crowding, noise, and poor air quality in relation to aggression. These stressors can both elicit and intensify aggressive behaviour.

TASKS TO DO

(1) Check the latest crime statistics in your country for the rates of violent crime (e.g., murder, assault) committed under the influence of alcohol.
(2) Find out more about the Cyberball paradigm as a measure of social exclusion (www1.psych.purdue.edu/~willia55/Announce/cyberball.htm).
(3) When you leave your house tomorrow, look out for aggressive cues in your environment (e.g., billboards, shop window displays, movie advertisements, etc.). Take a photo of each of them and make a list of the cues you have seen at the end of the day. If you like, you can send me the photos for my personal collection (krahe@uni-potsdam.de).

SUGGESTED READING

Ariel, B., Lawes, D., Weinborn, C., Henry, R., Chen, K., & Sabo Brants, H. (2019). The "less-than-lethal weapons effect"—Introducing TASERs to routine police operations in England and Wales: A randomized controlled trial. *Criminal Justice and Behavior, 46*, 280–300.

Miles-Novelo, A., & Anderson, C. A. (2019). Climate change and psychology: Effects of rapid global warming on violence and aggression. *Current Climate Change Reports, 5*, 36–46.

Parrott, D. J., & Ehrhardt, C. I. (2017). Effects of alcohol and other drugs. In B. J. Bushman (Ed.), *Aggression and violence: A social psychological perspective* (pp. 199–222). New York: Routledge.

Wesselmann, E. D., Ren, D., & Williams, K. D. (2017). Ostracism and aggression. In B. J. Bushman (Ed.), *Aggression and violence: A social psychological perspective* (pp. 155–168). New York: Routledge.

Chapter 6

MEDIA VIOLENCE AND AGGRESSION

In the public debate on aggression and violence, media influences are blamed by many people for the apparently increasing levels of aggression, especially among children and adolescents. A cursory and occasional sampling is sufficient to convince the everyday observer that television programmes are full of aggressive episodes, often of a highly violent nature, that are easily accessible even to young viewers. The same is true for movies, comic books, and, in particular, video games. In addition, surveys regularly show that children are exposed to violent media for substantial durations from an early age. These observations lead many people to believe that the portrayal of violence in the media affects the level of aggression in society. Some critics even argue that media consumption in general, irrespective of its aggressive content, contributes to aggression and antisocial behaviour. At the same time, the claim that violent media contents cause users to become more aggressive has been vigorously disputed, not only by users and the media industry, but also by some researchers in the field.

The present chapter will review the current state of the debate on the *link between media violence and aggression*, whereby *media violence* is defined as showing or describing behaviour by media characters intended to cause harm, especially severe physical harm, to others. The discussion is guided by the general proposition that the effects of media use on social behaviour depend on the content of the media stimuli. As we saw in Chapter 2, observational learning plays a major role in the acquisition and persistence of aggressive behaviour. For this process to happen, the observed behaviour needs to be aggressive in nature. By the same process, media depicting

media violence: media (movies, video games, music videos, etc.) showing or describing behaviour intended to cause harm, especially severe physical harm, to media characters.

media violence-aggression link: hypothesis that exposure to violent media contents makes users more aggressive.

prosocial behaviour may be a source of the learning of prosocial behaviour (Gentile et al., 2009; Halbrook, O'Donnell, & Msetfi, 2019).

An extensive literature, both in psychology and in media science, is available to address the link between media violence and aggression, focusing on television, movies, and video games as the most widely used media, but also including music (Fischer & Greitemeyer, 2006), cartoons (Zhang et al., 2019), and even texts from the Bible (Bushman, Ridge, Das, Key, & Busath, 2007). A comprehensive review of this literature, organized in the form of "frequently asked questions" is presented by Plante et al. (2020). The following summary is organised as follows: To begin with, some data are presented about the *prevalence and forms of violence* in today's media offers and about the *extent to which violent media are used*, especially by children and adolescents, who are seen as particularly vulnerable to media influences. We then address the general question of whether there is a *(causal) link* between exposure to media violence and aggression. After presenting examples of the predominant research strategies in the field, we focus on recent meta-analyses that bring together a large number of individual studies and provide the most robust evidence on the strength of the association between media violence and aggression. Based on this evidence, psychological processes explaining both *short-term effects* and *long-term effects* of exposure to violent media on aggressive thoughts, feelings, and behaviours are discussed. We then take a special look at the effects of *pornography* as a specific type of media content on aggression in general, and sexual aggression in particular. Finally, we present research on ways to *prevent or mitigate* the effects of media violence on aggression.

It is important to note that the scientific debate about media-induced aggression is *not* based on the assumption of a simple mono-causal relationship between media violence and aggression. Such an assumption would hold that exposure to media violence causes aggression regardless of other influences. Instead, it is recognised by most researchers that media violence is only one of many factors potentially leading to aggression. As will become clear in the course of our discussion, the effects of heavy use of violent media may be exacerbated by other causes of aggression (e.g., exposure to real-life violence within the family), or they may be attenuated (e.g., by teaching critical viewing skills). At the same time, heavy use of violent media may itself exacerbate the influence of other risk factors for aggressive behaviour.

PREVALENCE AND USE OF VIOLENT MEDIA CONTENTS

There are two premises to the claim that media violence produces harmful effects on viewers: (1) that violence and aggression are widely present in media programmes and (2) that these contents are used extensively in different age groups. To address the first claim, content analyses have shown that violence features prominently across a wide range of media. Analysing data from the National Television Violence Study, Wilson et al. (2002) found that programmes directed at children aged 12 years or younger contained more violence and showed more positive consequences of violence than programmes produced for older audiences. In an analysis of ten TV programmes screened in the U.K., Coyne, Robinson, and Nelson (2010) established that violent acts were committed at a rate of 42.5 acts per hour. Reality TV programmes, such as *Big Brother*, contained substantially more violence (61.5% of all violent acts counted) than non-reality programmes, such as *Eastenders*. The most common form of aggression was verbal aggression, such as yelling/arguing (38.39%), insulting (30.60%),

and name calling (9.31%). Analysing 1,162 programme hours on ten German television channels during 2002 and 2003, Grimm, Kirste, and Weiß (2005) found that 58% of all programmes contained at least one violent episode, and 33% of all violent interactions were presented as resulting from socially accepted motives.

Violent content is also rife in movies and has increased over time. In an analysis of 855 best-selling films covering 57 years, 89% of films contained violence, and there was a steady increase of violence across the study period (Bleakley, Jamieson, & Romer, 2012). Pointing out that direct physical violence is not the only form of aggression displayed in films, Coyne and Whitehead (2008) examined the prevalence of indirect aggression in 47 animated Disney films and found an average rate of more than 9 instances per hour. Indirect aggression was defined as social exclusion (e.g., malicious gossip, excluding others from the group), malicious humour (e.g., making gestures behind a person's back, playing practical jokes), guilt induction (e.g., exerting undue pressure and influencing others by making them feel guilty), and finally, indirect physical aggression (e.g., plotting and kidnapping). A content analysis of 23 best-selling animated cartoon movies for children in 2011 found an average rate of 54 acts of aggression per film (Turkmen, 2016). The most commonly depicted forms of aggressive behaviour were punching, kicking, and slapping, which correspond to everyday forms of aggression in the children's behavioural repertoire.

Content analyses of video games unanimously suggest that violent scenes are just as or even more frequent in this medium as they are on TV and in movies, A content analysis by Haninger and Thompson (2004) of 396 video games that were rated "T" (for "teens") showed that 94% of them had violent content. An analysis of popular games in Germany also concluded that many games rated by the self-regulating body of the media industry as suitable for children and adolescents contained substantial levels of violence (Höynck, Mößle, Kleimann, Pfeiffer, & Rehbein, 2007). Looking not only at the level of violence but also at the way it is presented in video games, Hartmann, Krakowiak, and Tsay-Vogel (2014) found that most games did not show the adverse consequences, provided a justification for the violent behaviour, and dehumanised the targets of violence, for example by making them all look identical or not showing their faces. Finally, analysing the popular medium of music videos, Smith and Boyson (2002) found an average rate of violent content of 15%. However, there was substantial variation by genre, with rap videos having a significantly higher percentage of violent acts (29%) than rock (12%) or rhythm and blues (9%) videos. In addition, there is growing concern about misogynous and men-hating texts in music that are hallmarks of popular artists, such as Eminem and Christina Aguilera (Adams, 2006; Fischer & Greitemeyer, 2006).

Regarding the extent to which violent media are used, surveys show that the use of media is a prominent leisure activity for children and adolescents. With regard to violent movies, Worth, Chambers, Nassau, Rakhra, and

Sargent (2008) asked a random sample of over 6,000 adolescents in the U.S. aged 10 to 14 years whether they had seen titles on a list of 40 violent movies rated "R" for violence in the U.S. and "18" ("suitable only for adults") in the U.K. Across the 40 movies, the average rate of 10- to 14-year-olds who had seen them was 12.5%, but the percentage was substantially higher for a number of specific titles. For example, the horror film *I Know What You Did Last Summer* had been seen by 44% of the sample. Extrapolating from this figure to the population as a whole, the authors concluded that the movie had been seen by more than 9 million viewers under the age of 14 years, a million of whom would have been just 10 years of age.

Arguably, video games are even more popular as entertainment media. Even in the age group of 65 years or over, 23% report playing video games (Lenhart & Macgill, 2008), and among adolescents and young adults, user rates are close to 100%. In a survey conducted in the U.S. in 2008, 97% of teenagers aged 12 to 17 years reported playing video games, 31% reported playing every day. In terms of the preferred game content, about a third of gaming teenagers reported that at least one of their three favourite games was rated "Mature", with boys outnumbering girls by three to one in this group (Lenhart et al., 2008). A representative survey of German adolescents aged 12 to 19 years found that "Grand Theft Auto", which has an age rating of 18 years in Germany, featured in the top three favourite games from age 14 onwards (Medienpädagogischer Forschungsverbund Südwest, 2017, p. 51). Another representative survey of more than 44,000 15-year-olds in Germany found that 55% of boys (compared with 9% of girls) reported playing games rated 16+ several times a month, and 48% of boys (compared with 5.2% of girls) reported regularly playing games rated 18+ (Rehbein, Kleimann, & Mößle, 2009). These figures need to be seen in the context of strict legal regulations in Germany that prohibit the sale of these games to minors.

From the evidence reviewed in this section, two points have become clear: (a) violence is prominently present across a range of different media, and (b) violent content is widely consumed not only by adults, but also by a younger, especially male, audience. Against this background, we can now turn to the question of whether exposure to media violence really leads to increased aggression in viewers.

HOW STRONG IS THE LINK BETWEEN MEDIA VIOLENCE AND AGGRESSION?

Research designs and examples

To explore the association between media violence use and aggression, three main methodologies have been used: (1) experimental studies that randomly assign participants to a violent media condition or a non-violent media condition and then observe the short-term differences in aggressive behaviour in the two groups; (2) cross-sectional studies relating self-reports of habitual violent media use to aggressive behaviour measured through observation, peer nominations, or self-reports, typically controlling for other variables potentially related to media violence use and/or aggressive behaviour; and (3) longitudinal studies that follow the same group of participants over several measurements to relate media violence use at an earlier point in time to aggressive behaviour measured later.

The *experimental approach* is illustrated by research by Carnagey and Anderson (2005), who explored the importance of reward and punishment of violent action in a video game for subsequent aggressive cognitions, affect, and behaviour. All participants played a racing game, *Carmaggedon 2*, but they were randomly assigned to three different conditions: (1) a condition in which killing competitors and pedestrians was rewarded by giving extra points, (2) a condition in which killing competitors and pedestrians was punished by deducting points, and (3) a non-violent condition in which killing pedestrians or competitors was not possible. Blood pressure and pulse were recorded as measures of arousal to make sure that the three versions did not differ in terms of their arousal quality. State hostility after the 20-minute playing period was measured as an index of aggressive affect (Experiment 1). A word completion test presenting words that could be completed to yield either an aggressive or a non-aggressive meaning was used as a measure of aggressive cognition (Experiment 2), and the duration and intensity of noise blasts administered in a competitive reaction time task (see Chapter 1) were used to measure aggressive behaviour (Experiment 3). The results are shown in Figure 6.1.

For aggressive affect, the findings revealed that both groups engaging in violent actions in the video game experienced higher levels of state hostility than the group that could not engage in violent actions. For aggressive cognition and aggressive behaviour, the participants in the reward group scored significantly higher than did those in the punishment group and those in the non-violent control group. The latter two groups did not differ significantly in either cognitions or behaviour. The finding that violence rewarded by positive consequences promotes aggressive thoughts as well as aggressive behaviour is consistent with social learning and socio-cognitive theories of aggression (see Chapter 2).

Beyond violence in films and video games, experimental research has examined violent lyrics in music as triggers of aggressive responses. In research by Fischer and Greitemeyer (2006), men who were asked to listen to songs with lyrics that disparage women (e.g., "Superman" by Eminem, and "Self-Esteem" by Offspring) recalled more negative attributes about women and behaved more aggressively towards a female experimenter than did men who listened to neutral lyrics. In a second study, women who had listened to songs with men-hating lyrics (e.g., "You Oughta Know" by Alanis Morrisette, and "Can't Hold Us Down" by Christina Aguilera) displayed more aggression towards a male confederate. In a study of violent music videos, Lennings and Warburton (2011) found that the lyrics alone, even when the visual channel was removed, increased aggression,

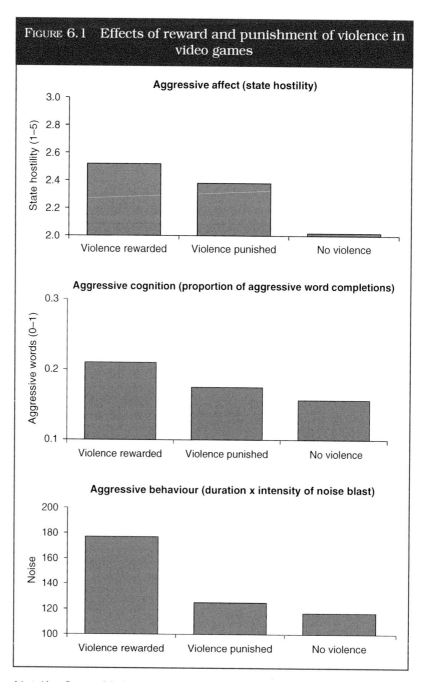

FIGURE 6.1   Effects of reward and punishment of violence in video games

Adapted from Carnagey & Anderson, 2005, Table 2.

as measured by the hot sauce paradigm (see Chapter 1), compared with a control group.

As an example of *cross-sectional studies*, Anderson et al. (2017) collected data on habitual use of violent screen media and self-reported aggression in the Buss-Perry Aggression Questionnaire (see Chapter 1) from a total of 2,154 adolescents and young adults from seven countries (Australia, China, Croatia, Germany, Japan, Romania, and the U.S.). In addition, they measured normative beliefs about aggression and empathy as potential mediators in the link between media violence use and aggression, and they included additional risk factors for aggression in six of the countries (abusive parenting, living in a violent neighbourhood, being bullied by peers, and association with delinquent peers). The links between media violence use and aggression in the seven countries are shown in Table 6.1.

In all seven countries, media violence use was significantly associated with aggressive behaviour, even though the strength of the association was in the small range and varied between countries. Looking at the pathways in the data aggregated across countries, increased media violence use predicted aggression via a greater normative acceptance of aggressive behaviour and lower empathy. When the additional risk factors were included in the analysis, media violence use not only remained a significant predictor, but turned out to be the second strongest predictor ($ß = .16$), very similar to association with delinquent peers ($ß = .17$), but higher than abusive parenting and neighbourhood crime (both $ß = .08$). However, it needs to be noted that even when controlling for such additional variables, cross-sectional studies cannot determine the direction

TABLE 6.1 Association between use of violent screen media and aggressive behaviour in seven nations: standardized regression coefficients

	Country	β
1.	Australia	0.32***
2.	China	0.34***
3.	Croatia	0.26***
4.	Germany	0.25**
5.	Japan	0.16**
6.	Romania	0.34***
7.	United States	0.35***

$** p < .01; *** p < .001$.

Adapted from Anderson et al., 2017, Table 4.

of causality in the association between violent media use and aggressive behaviour.

This limitation is overcome by *longitudinal studies* that follow the temporal pathways from media violence to aggression within the same individuals to be able to relate patterns of media violence use to patterns of aggressive behaviour. Using self-reported physical aggression as the critical outcome variable, Krahé, Busching, and Möller (2012) first sought to identify different patterns of using violent media in their adolescent sample studied over three data waves with 12-months intervals. A fourth data wave, completed after the paper by Krahé et al. (2012) had been published, is included in the analyses presented in Figure 6.2. This step yielded three distinct trajectories of media violence, as shown in the top half of Figure 6.2. The largest group were the consistently low users of violent media, which comprised 64.4% of the total sample, with a clear gender difference (89.7% of girls and 37.6% of boys fell into this group). The second largest group were the stable high users, comprising 50% of the boys and 8% of the girls. The third and smallest group were the "desisters", who showed a declining trajectory over time, which comprised 12.4% of the boys and 2.3% of the girls.

In a next step, a parallel analysis on the self-reports of aggressive behaviour was conducted, which yielded three distinct groups with stable low, stable high, and desisting trajectories of aggressive behaviour across the four data waves. In the final step, participants' membership in one of the three groups of media violence was used to predict which group they would be in on the measure of aggressive behaviour. This analysis is shown in the lower half of Figure 6.2. One can see clearly that the trajectories of aggressive behaviour covary with the trajectories of media violence use. Students who were consistently high on the use of violent media over the four data waves also fell into the stable-high group of aggressive behaviour. Students whose use of media violence declined, also showed a decline in aggressive behaviour. Beyond the use of violent media as a risk factor for aggressive behaviour, other longitudinal evidence shows that it also predicts a reduction in prosocial behaviour over time (Coyne, Warburton, Essig, & Stockdale, 2018).

Another important design used in longitudinal studies on media violence effect is the cross-lagged panel approach, in which both media violence and aggression are assessed at two or more points in time. As implied in the name, the focus of this approach is on the "crossed" (diagonal) paths from media violence at Time 1 to aggression at Time 2 and from aggression at Time 1 to media violence use at Time 2. Examining these paths enables researchers to address two alternative explanations of the relationship between media violence and aggression: (a) that viewing media violence makes viewers more aggressive (the "socialisation" hypothesis), or (b) that more aggressive individuals are more strongly attracted by violent media programmes (the "selection" hypothesis). There is no inherent contradiction between the two processes, as they can be mutually reinforcing. Indeed, the "downward spiral" model of Slater, Henry, Swaim,

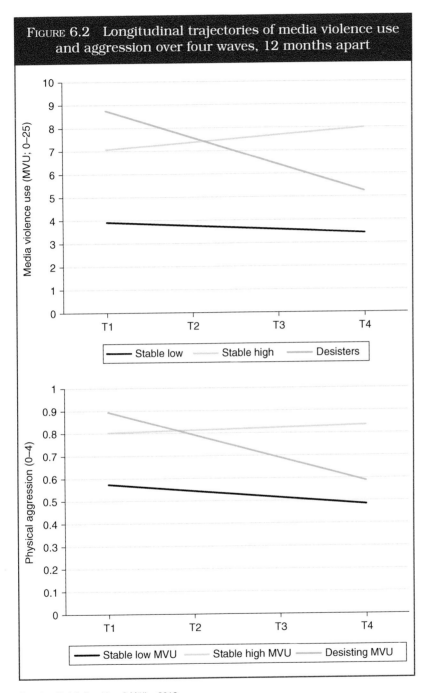

FIGURE 6.2   Longitudinal trajectories of media violence use and aggression over four waves, 12 months apart

Based on Krahé, Busching, & Möller, 2012.

and Anderson (2003) proposes that although more aggressive individuals may show a preference for violent media in the first place, the more intense use of these media may reinforce their aggressive tendencies over time.

Evidence from meta-analyses

The strongest evidence for evaluating the hypothesis that exposure to violence in the media is a risk factor for the development of aggressive behaviour comes from meta-analytic reviews that integrate the findings from many individual studies into a common metric and overall effect size. These reviews combined *different methodologies* (correlational, experimental, and longitudinal studies), *different media* (television, movies, video games, and comic books), and *different outcome variables* (aggressive cognitions, feelings, and behaviour, physiological arousal, prosocial behaviour) across samples from *different countries*. Common measures of effect size capturing the strength of the association are r (the correlation between media violence use and outcome variables), β (the prospective prediction of the link between media violence use and aggression over time), and d (the difference between exposure to violent as opposed to non-violent media, mostly used in experimental studies).

Because more recent meta-analyses typically include the studies considered in earlier meta-analyses, we will discuss the latest meta-analyses, which differ in terms of inclusiveness of media types (violent media in general vs. violent video game use), breadth of constructs (aggressive affect, cognitions, and behaviour vs. physical or relational aggression only), and methodology (across different designs vs. experimental or prospective designs only). Considering the effects of violence across a range of media types, such as TV, movies, video games, music and comic books, Bushman and Huesmann (2006) analysed 431 studies with participants of all age groups. They found an effect size of $r = .19$ for aggressive behaviour, $r = .18$ for aggressive cognition, $r = .27$ for angry feelings, and $r = .26$, for physiological arousal. Moreover, a negative association of $r = -.08$ was found between violent media use and prosocial behaviour. A subsequent meta-analysis by Bushman (2016) zoomed in on three cognitive correlates of aggressive behaviour: hostile attribution bias, which is the tendency to interpret others' behaviour as motivated by the intention to harm (see also Chapter 4), hostile perception bias, which describes the tendency to interpret other people's ambiguous behaviour as aggressive, and hostile expectation bias, defined as the tendency to believe that others will respond with aggressive behaviour in a conflict situation. For the hostile attribution bias ($r = .18$) and hostile expectation bias ($r = .26$), he found significant associations with the use of violent media, whereas the effect for hostile perception bias was nonsignificant.

Focussing specifically on violent video games, Greitemeyer and Mügge (2014) included 98 studies that used experimental, correlational, and longitudinal designs. Across their set of studies, the effect sizes were $r = .19$

for aggressive behaviour, $r = .25$ for aggressive cognition, and $r = .17$ for aggressive affect. Moreover, they also found that more violent game play was linked to less prosocial thinking ($r = -.14$), feeling ($r = -.16$), and behaviour ($r = -.11$). The meta-analysis by Prescott, Sargent, and Hull (2018) only included longitudinal studies that looked at physically aggressive behaviour. Across 24 studies that covered time spans between 3 months and 4 years, they found a significant prospective association between violent video game use and physical aggression of $ß = .11$. As in the Bushman (2016) analysis, no evidence of publication bias, which refers to the overestimation of effects in published as compared with unpublished studies, was found.

Whereas the meta-analyses discussed so far referred to physical aggression, Martins and Weaver (2019) examined the effects of exposure to aggression in the media on users' tendency to engage in relational aggression. They found an effect size of $r = .21$ for exposure to relationally aggressive media contents on relational aggression, and a smaller, but still significant effect of $r = .15$ of media depictions of physical aggression on relational aggression. These findings underline two points. The first is that a closer match between the modality in which aggression is shown between media contents and outcome produces a stronger effect, which is what one would expect on the basis of observational learning theory (see Chapter 2). The second point is that there is evidence for a carry-over effect, albeit weaker, from watching physical violence to showing relationally aggressive behaviour. Given that both physical and relational aggression are based on the intention to harm, this common motivational basis may lead to a crossover effect of different forms of media aggression on different forms of users' aggressive behaviour.

Across the meta-analyses, the magnitude of the effect sizes are quite similar, as recently corroborated in a secondary analysis of three meta-analyses by Mathur and VanderWeele (2019). Following Cohen (1988), effects in the region of ±0.10 are considered small, those in the region of ±0.30 are considered medium, and those in the region of ±0.50 or higher are considered large effects. Thus, the effect sizes obtained in the media violence meta-analyses fall into the small to medium range. However, this does not mean that they are without practical significance, as claimed by some critics (e.g., Ferguson, 2010). Rosenthal (1990) demonstrated that a correlation of $r = 0.20$ between media violence and aggression shifts the odds of someone with high media violence use showing high levels of aggressive behaviour from 50:50% (the odds if aggression was completely unrelated to media violence use) to 60:40%. This means that of 100 high users of media violence, 60% will fall into the high aggression group, compared with 40% of low media violence users, if all other things are equal in the two groups. Considering how widely violent media are available and used around the world, this difference of 20% translates into a large number of individuals who may become more aggressive as a result of using violent media. As Sparks and Sparks (2002) pointed out, if only one person in several hundred thousand viewers was inspired by a violent movie to commit a violent act, the consequences of several million people watching that movie would be dramatic.

Taken together, the meta-analytic evidence indicates that there is a link between the use of media violence and aggression. Experimental as well as longitudinal studies suggest that violent media stimuli may have a causal influence on aggression. However, as noted by Huesmann (2010), this is not to say that violent media use "determines" aggressive behaviour. Not every heavy user of violent media will be highly aggressive, just as not every drunken driver will cause a fatal accident, but the risk of aggression is increased among the high user group. Media violence may reinforce the effects of other risk factors, particularly exposure to violence in the real world (Browne & Hamilton-Giachritsis, 2005). The role of moderator variables in explaining individual differences in the susceptibility to violent media effects will be discussed later in this chapter. First, however, we will take a closer look at theoretical explanations of the underlying process that lead from media violence as the input variable to aggressive behaviour as the outcome variable. Different explanations address the short-term effects of a single episode of exposure to media violence and the long-term effects of repeated use of violent media over extended periods.

EXPLAINING THE SHORT-TERM EFFECTS OF MEDIA VIOLENCE

This section addresses the question of how exposure to media violence increases viewers' aggressive response tendencies in the period following

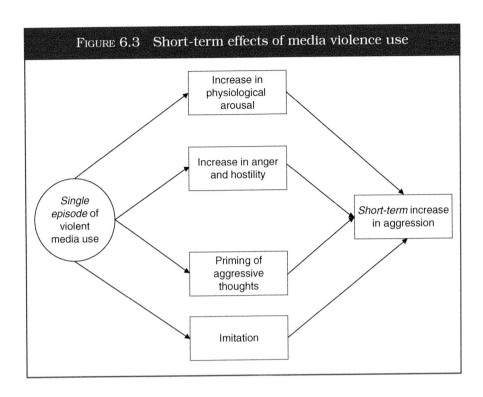

FIGURE 6.3   Short-term effects of media violence use

the presentation of the violent content. The General Aggression Model (GAM; Anderson & Bushman, 2018) introduced in Chapter 2 provides a conceptual framework which proposes that physiological arousal, aggressive affect, and aggressive cognitions pave the way for media violence as a situational input variable to elicit aggressive behaviour. The key mechanisms underlying the effects of exposure to violent media stimuli on immediate aggressive responses are presented in Figure 6.3 and will be discussed in turn.

(1) Exposure to violent media stimuli leads to an *increase in physiological* as well as *affective arousal* in the form of state anger and hostility. The meta-analyses found evidence that violent media stimuli increase physiological arousal (Greitemeyer & Mügge, 2014). This increased arousal may facilitate aggression by increasing the person's activity level and strengthening dominant responses (i.e., behaviours that are most easily activated). For example, individuals confronted with a provocation are more likely to respond aggressively if they are already in a state of increased arousal, as suggested by Zillmann's (1979) "excitation transfer model" discussed in Chapter 2. This model suggests that arousal caused by a media stimulus may be added to the arousal caused by a provocation or other adverse stimulation and mislabelled as anger if the person is no longer aware of the source of the initial arousal, thus reinforcing an aggressive response (Zillmann & Bryant, 1974).

(2) Violent media stimuli may activate *aggressive thoughts, feelings, and self-concepts*. Watching media depictions of aggressive interactions increases the ease with which users can access their own aggressive thoughts and feelings. The underlying mechanism is a priming process whereby a particular external stimulus, such as an aggressive act, guides the individual's attention to the congruent mental constructs, such as aggressive cognitions, thus lowering the threshold for using them to interpret social information (for a general discussion of priming and aggressive cues, see Chapter 5). Asking participants to list their thoughts after watching a violent or non-violent videotape, Bushman (1998) found that respondents who had watched the violent videotape produced more aggressive associations to homonyms with both an aggressive and a non-aggressive meaning (e.g., "box", "punch"). They were also faster in identifying letter strings making up aggressive words than were respondents who had been shown a non-violent videotape (see also Bushman & Anderson, 2002). Bösche (2010) replicated the faster recognition times for aggression-related words after playing a violent compared with a non-violent video game. In addition, he found faster accessibility of positively valenced words in the violent game condition, which indicates that violent entertainment is linked to positive associations.

Furthermore, there is evidence that even brief periods of media violence use may activate aggression-related aspects of players' self-concept. Playing a violent video game for 10 or 20 minutes increased the speed with which aggression-related words were associated with the self in an Implicit Association Test (IAT; see Chapter 1), compared with a non-violent control condition, eliciting a process of learning aggressive self-views (Bluemke, Friedrich, & Zumbach, 2010; Uhlmann & Swanson, 2004). No parallel effects were found on explicit self-report measures of aggression, which suggests that the effects of violent media cues operated at the automatic level. The link between violent media use and the self was highlighted further in a study by Fischer, Kastenmüller, and Greitemeyer (2010). Their participants played either a violent (boxing) game or a non-violent (bowling) game. In each condition, half of the participants could personalise their game character by modelling its physical appearance on themselves. The other half played the respective game with a non-personalised character. Participants playing the personalised violent game subsequently administered more hot sauce to another person as a measure of aggressive behaviour (see Chapter 1) than those playing the non-personalised violent game, and both groups acted more aggressively than the players of the non-violent game in either the personalised or non-personalised condition. The effects were mediated by self-activation (feeling strong, active, and motivated), which was higher in the personalised than in the non-personalised violent game conditions.

However, it seems that not only do aggressive media contents prime aggressive cognitions, but the priming of aggressive thoughts then leads to a preference for violent media contents. Langley, O'Neal, Craig, and

Yost (1992) first activated aggressive cognitions by asking participants to compose short stories using words from a list of aggressive (as opposed to non-aggressive) terms. Next, they gave them a choice of different film clips described as varying in aggressive content. Participants who had written aggression-related stories during the priming task expressed a greater preference for the violent film clips than those who had written a story based on the neutral words. These findings support the idea of a vicious cycle between media violence and aggression, in that media violence fosters aggressive cognitions just as aggressive cognitions create preferences for violent media.

(3) A further process that explains the short-term effects of exposure to violent media stimuli is *imitation*. Exposure to aggression may instigate learning processes that result in the acquisition of new behaviours. As we saw above, much of the aggression portrayed in the media is rewarded or at least unpunished. Moreover, it is often shown by attractive characters with whom viewers can identify. As social learning theory suggests, imitation is particularly likely under these circumstances (Bandura, 1983; for a more detailed discussion, see Chapter 2). The most obvious way in which aggression portrayed in the media is incorporated in the recipients' behavioural repertoire is reflected in "copycat aggression". Studies conducted as early as the 1960s showed that children imitate 1:1 the behaviours performed by adult role models (Bandura, Ross, & Ross, 1963). Direct imitation, or "copycat violence", also features with some regularity in crime reports. Deliberate as well as accidental killings were shown to have resulted from children's re-enactments of scenes they had observed in the media. Although this evidence is largely anecdotal, finding a close resemblance of a specific method of killing in a real-life murder case to a fictional murder in the media points to a possible translation of virtual reality into real life. In addition, real events that receive widespread media attention, such as hijackings, are also well documented in the literature to trigger copycat violence, including the effect of self-killings by prominent public figures on subsequent suicide rates (Arendt, 2018; Hittner, 2005; Niederkrotenthaler et al., 2009).

Individual differences and features of the violent media input as moderators of short-term effects

Violent media stimuli do not affect all people to the same extent. Several studies demonstrated that individuals differ in their susceptibility to depictions of violence in the media depending on trait aggression and trait hostility. Anderson and Carnagey (2009) showed that playing a violent video game increased the accessibility of aggressive cognitions compared with a non-violent control group only among participants who scored high on trait aggression (for similar results, see Giumetti & Markey, 2007).

However, in a study by Anderson (1997), playing a violent game increased hostile affect only among participants who scored low on trait hostility. An explanation for the latter finding may be that for individuals high on trait hostility, hostile feelings are chronically accessible, so that the violent game as a short-term aggressive prime has no additional effect on them. By contrast, people who are not habitually hostile are induced by the prime to activate aggression-related affective states.

Bushman (1995) explored the impact of media violence on aggressive behaviour shown by participants high vs. low in trait aggressiveness, who were randomly assigned to watch a violent or non-violent film clip. The noise blast paradigm was used to yield a measure of unprovoked aggression (noise selected for the first round) and a measure of provoked aggression (noise selected from the second round onwards; see Chapter 1). On the measure of unprovoked aggression, both aggressive and non-aggressive individuals were equally affected by the violent film, setting higher noise levels than participants who watched a non-violent film. However, on the measure of provoked aggression, the aggression-enhancing effect of the violent film was significantly more pronounced for the aggressive than for the non-aggressive participants.

The impact of short-term exposure to media violence is also affected by users' past experience with violent media contents. For example, Bartholow, Sestir, and Davis (2005) showed that after playing a violent video game for 20 minutes, high habitual users of violent video games were more aggressive on a competitive reaction task than were low habitual users. High users also scored lower on empathy and higher on trait hostility than did low users, and these differences partly explained the differences in aggressive behaviour (see also Anderson & Dill, 2000). Further evidence shows that the more regularly individuals use violent media, the more positive affect they experience in response to media violence. Habitual players enjoyed playing violent games more than did non-regular players (Bösche, 2010), and habitual exposure to violent media stimuli was associated with greater pleasant arousal in response to a violent film clip, but not in response to sad or funny clips (Krahé et al., 2011).

The different ways in which violence is presented also have an impact on the strength of the link between media violence use and aggression (for a review, see Barlett, Anderson, & Swing, 2009). In the study by Carnagey and Anderson (2005) discussed earlier, aggressive cognitions and behaviour were higher when the game was programmed so that violent actions were rewarded than when they were punished (see Figure 6.1). Barlett, Harris, and Bruey (2008) varied the amount of blood that was visible during the playing of a violent video game. In the condition where large amounts of blood were displayed, participants showed significantly higher arousal, state hostility, and created a higher number of aggressive words in a word completion task. Similarly, Barlett, Harris, and Baldassaro (2007) found that playing a violent video game with a controller in the shape of a realistic gun led to a larger increase in arousal from baseline than playing the same game with a standard controller. A study by Williams (2010) examined the effect of physical similarity between players and their game characters on players' physical state anger after playing a violent or a non-violent game. Participants were either instructed to create an avatar that resembled them in various physical features, such as skin colour, height, build, and hairstyle, or they were given an avatar that looked dissimilar to them. As expected, a main effect of violence level was found, with higher state anger after playing the violent game than after playing the non-violent game. However, a significant interaction was found between the violence level of the game and the physical resemblance of the main character. Participants who had played the violent game with an avatar resembling themselves were significantly angrier than those who had played the violent game with a dissimilar avatar or those who had played the non-violent game with either the similar or the dissimilar avatar. These findings are consistent with the effects reported by Fischer et al. (2010) for the comparison of personalised and non-personalised game characters. In combination, these studies suggest that the more realistically violence is presented in video games, the more likely it is to promote aggressive behaviour.

Regarding differences between passive exposure to media violence as opposed to active involvement, Polman, Orobio de Castro, and van Aken (2008) compared children who were actively playing a violent or non-violent video game with a group of children who passively observed the actions of the first group shown on a television screen. This ensured that the participants in both groups received exactly the same input and only differed in terms of active involvement. Aggressive behaviour was measured through peer nominations (see Chapter 1). The results showed that boys in the violent-active condition were more aggressive than were boys in the passive-violent condition, who had merely observed the play moves of the active group. However, they were no more aggressive than were boys in the active-non-violent condition. No effects of involvement or violence level of the game were found for girls.

With regard to the role of gender more generally, evidence was presented at the beginning of this chapter that boys are far more attracted to violent media than are girls. Whether they are differentially affected when exposed to the same level of violent content has not been established conclusively in the literature. The meta-analysis by Anderson et al. (2010) found no significant gender differences in the effect sizes for the link between media violence use and aggression, and findings from studies with all-female samples showed that women are also affected by violent media. Anderson and Murphy (2003) found higher levels of aggression in women who had played a violent compared with a non-violent game, and Fischer and Greitemeyer (2006) showed that women who had listened to men-hating lyrics acted more aggressively towards a male target person than women who had listened to neutral lyrics.

However, other studies found no effect of violent media stimuli on women (e.g., Bartholow & Anderson, 2002; Deselms & Altman, 2003;

Polman et al., 2008). Given that violent media actors are typically male, women cannot identify with aggressive media models in the same way as men, which may account for their lower preference for this type of media and, possibly, their lower levels of aggression following exposure to violent contents. This line of reasoning is supported by the finding that women playing a violent game with a female avatar showed more aggressive thoughts in a word completion task than did women playing the same game with a male avatar (Eastin, 2006). However, a later study by Yang, Huesmann, and Bushman (2014) found that both men and women showed more aggressive behaviour as measured by the hot sauce paradigm (see Chapter 1) when they played with a male as opposed to a female avatar. As aggression is linked more closely to male than female gender stereotypes, this finding suggests that female participants may have adopted the gender-stereotypic behaviour of their avatar, a phenomenon called the "Proteus effect" (Ratan, Beyea, Li, & Graciano, 2019). The question under what conditions the similarity between user and media characters or the characteristic features of the media characters lead to gender differences in media violence effects needs to be addressed in future research.

EXPLAINING THE LONG-TERM EFFECTS OF MEDIA VIOLENCE USE

Even though immediate short-term effects of media violence may give rise to instantaneous acts of aggression in specific situations, the main concern has been about the long-term effects of repeated use of violent media in promoting the readiness for aggressive behaviour. To explain the impact of habitual exposure to violent media stimuli on aggressive behaviour, several interlocking processes have been proposed (for a summary, see Huesmann & Kirwil, 2007). The most widely studied mechanisms are presented in Figure 6.4.

It should be noted that these mechanisms are not specific to violent media contents but apply in the same way to the long-term effects of exposure to violence in real life. Accordingly, many of the general theories of aggression discussed in Chapter 2 can also inform the understanding of media violence effects over time.

Observational learning plays a key role in the adoption of aggression as part of the individual's behavioural repertoire. Just as real-life models are imitated, particularly if their aggressive behaviour is followed by positive consequences, as shown by Bandura, Ross, and Ross (1961, 1963), media models are a powerful source of learning by observation. Violent media characters are typically presented as strong, powerful, often acting in pursuit of a good cause, making them appealing models to imitate. Huesmann, Moise-Titus, Podolski, and Eron (2003) found positive correlations between childhood identification with same-sex aggressive media characters and aggression measured 17 years later in both men and women. Moreover, children who perceived television violence as "real" were significantly more aggressive as young adults. A longitudinal study of Japanese children showed

FIGURE 6.4   Long-term effects of media violence use

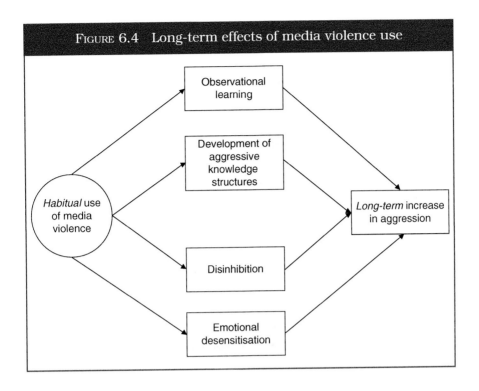

that playing video games in which violence was committed by an attractive as opposed to a less attractive actor predicted higher levels of hostility and aggression 12 months later (Shibuya, Sakamoto, Ihori, & Yukawa, 2007).

Observational learning is not limited to the imitation of specific acts of aggression, it also involves the acquisition of more general *aggressive knowledge structures*, or scripts. According to the General Aggression Model, repeated exposure to violent media promotes the learning, rehearsal, and reinforcement of beliefs and attitudes promoting aggression, hostile perceptions, and expectations as well as the acquisition of behavioural scripts (Anderson & Bushman, 2018). The more frequently people encounter violence in media depictions or engage in virtual violence in electronic games, the more likely they are to develop positive attitudes about the use of aggression in interpersonal conflicts, to see others' behaviour as hostile and antagonistic, and to access aggressive scripts when planning behavioural responses. In a study of third to fifth graders, Gentile and Gentile (2008) showed that playing violent video games predicted a higher tendency to attribute hostile intent to others five months later, which in turn was linked to higher physical aggression (for a discussion of the hostile attribution bias, see Chapter 3). Habitual violent video game play was also associated with higher trait hostility in an adolescent sample studied by Gentile, Lynch, Linder, and Walsh (2004), and trait hostility in turn was associated with the involvement in physical fights, as well as

with arguments with teachers. These links support the role of violent media use in promoting hostile schemata that lower the threshold for aggressive behaviour.

Media violence also affects aggressive behaviour through changing users' worldview. The more often individuals encounter violence in the media, the more prevalent they assume it to be in the real world. This may be explained by the increased accessibility of aggression-related cognitions in heavy users of violent media, whereby accessibility is seen as a function of the frequency and recency of exposure, and the vividness of memory representations of violence (Shrum, 1996). Demonstrating the role of vividness, it was shown that the more references people made to blood and gore in their recollections of violent scenes they had seen in movies or on TV, the higher they estimated the prevalence of crime and violence to be in the real world (Riddle, Potter, Metzger, Nabi, & Linz, 2011). Because habitual users of violent media increasingly come to see the world as a hostile and dangerous place, they are more likely to feel threatened and provoked by other people's actions and to respond with aggressive behaviour.

The role of media violence in eliciting aggressive thoughts and feelings is relevant to understanding the activation of aggressive scripts (see Chapter 2). The more violence individuals see in the media, the more often they encounter stimuli relevant to their aggressive scripts. Over time, the frequent activation of aggressive scripts will make the scripts more easily accessible, thus enhancing the likelihood that they will be used to interpret incoming stimuli. Children are particularly susceptible to this effect, because their aggressive scripts are still more malleable than those of adults (Huesmann, 1998).

A further effect of using violent media habitually that is relevant to the explanation of aggression is *disinhibition*. Exposure to violent media contents

disinhibition:
weakening the inhibitions against showing aggressive behaviour, e.g., by repeated exposure to violence in the media.

may weaken viewers' inhibitions against aggression by making aggression appear to be a common and accepted feature of social interactions. As shown earlier in this chapter, many violent acts are presented as justified without showing the suffering of victims, which undermines the perception of violence as harmful and increases the belief that aggression is a common and acceptable form of behaviour. As noted by Huesmann (1998), such normative beliefs are an integral part of aggressive scripts and are used to decide which behavioural options should be activated in a given situation. Consistent with this proposition, Huesmann and Kirwil (2007) reported longitudinal evidence that normative beliefs about aggression in adulthood were predicted by childhood preferences for violent media contents and that the normative acceptance of aggression partly mediated the link between childhood exposure to media violence and adult aggressive behaviour. Presenting aggression as justified was correlated with higher hostility and aggression assessed one year later in the Japanese study by Shibuya et al. (2007). Furthermore, in a study of German adolescents, Möller and Krahé (2009) found that the more participants played violent video games, the more accepting they were of physical aggression in interpersonal conflict situations as assessed 30 months later. Acceptance of aggression as normative was significantly associated with both physical aggression and a hostile attributional style.

Finally, habitual exposure to violent media stimuli has a lasting effect on aggression through a process of *desensitisation*. In general terms, desensitisation refers to the gradual reduction in responsiveness to an arousal-eliciting stimulus as a function of repeated exposure. In the context of media violence, desensitisation more specifically describes a process "by which initial arousal responses to violent stimuli are reduced, thereby changing an individual's 'present internal state'" (Carnagey, Anderson, & Bushman, 2007, p. 491). In particular, desensitisation to violent media stimuli is thought to reduce anxious arousal. Fear is a spontaneous and innate response of humans to violence. As with other emotional responses, repeated exposure to media violence can *decrease* physiological arousal and negative affect because violent stimuli lose their capacity to elicit strong emotions the more often the stimulus is presented (Anderson & Dill, 2000).

Several studies have demonstrated that, in the long term, habitual exposure to media violence may reduce anxious arousal in response to depictions of violence. Research has found that the more time individuals spent watching media depictions of violence, the less emotionally responsive they became to violent stimuli (e.g., Averill, Malmstrom, Koriat, & Lazarus, 1972), and the less sympathy they showed for victims of violence in the real world (e.g., Mullin & Linz, 1995). A study with adolescents by Mrug, Madan, Cook, and Wright (2015) found that adolescents who reported a high level of exposure to violence in the media showed a significant decline of blood pressure over the course of watching five violent video clips. By contrast, individuals with low or moderate levels of media violence use remained at stable blood pressure levels over the five clips.

desensitisation: process whereby the ability of a stimulus to elicit arousal becomes weaker with each consecutive presentation.

No parallel pattern was found for blood pressure levels during watching five nonviolent clips, indicating that desensitisation is specific to the violent content. In a series of studies with children aged 5 to 12, Funk and colleagues demonstrated that the habitual use of violent video games was associated with reduced empathy with others in need of help (Funk, Baldacci, Pasold, & Baumgardner, 2004; Funk, Buchman, Jenks, & Bechtoldt, 2003).

Bartholow, Bushman, and Sestir (2006) used event-related brain potential (ERP) data to compare responses by users of violent and non-violent video games to violent stimuli, and relate them to subsequent aggressive responses in a laboratory task. They found that the more violent games the participants played habitually, the less ERP activity they showed in response to violent pictures and the more aggressively they behaved in the subsequent task. No effect of habitual media violence use was found on ERP responses to negative stimuli without violence (such as pictures of accident victims or disfigured babies), again indicating that desensitisation was specific to the violent content of the media diet. A more recent ERP study found a similar pattern in the comparison of players and nonplayers of video games (Jabr, Denke, Rawls, & Lamm, 2018).

Using skin conductance level as a measure of arousal during exposure to a violent film clip, Krahé et al. (2011) found that the more participants were used to violent media, the less physiological arousal they showed while watching graphic scenes of violence, and the more pleasant arousal they reported to have experienced during the clips. Higher pleasant arousal was associated with faster recognition of aggression-related words, demonstrating the associations between affective and cognitive processes postulated by the General Aggression Model. Participants in this study were also shown sad and funny film clips, for which no association with habitual media violence was found, which demonstrates once more that the effects are specific to violent media contents.

Further evidence for the desensitising role of media influences comes from a wide range of studies into the effects of pornography on sexual aggression. Experimental studies have shown that participants exposed to violent pornography rated the impact of a subsequently presented rape scenario on the victim as significantly less severe and expressed more permissive attitudes about sexual violence than those who had not previously been exposed to the pornographic material (e.g., Linz, Donnerstein, & Adams, 1989; Mullin & Linz, 1995). The desensitising effect of violent pornography is not limited to men, but has been found to affect women as well (Krafka & Penrod, 1997). The evidence linking pornographic media contents to aggression will be reviewed in more detail in the next section.

In addition to the effects of exposure to violent media on the individual users, recent research suggests that there are also indirect effects on users' social networks. A longitudinal study by Verheijen, Burk, Stoltz, van den Berg, and Cillessen (2018) studied adolescent friendship dyads and showed that males' exposure to violent video games at Time 1 predicted their best friend's aggressive behaviour a year later (Time 2), irrespective of whether or not they had played video games together and controlling for the friend's level of violent video game play and aggression at Time 1. A study with adult participants yielded similar results (Greitemeyer, 2019). These findings provide first evidence that exposure to violence in the media may have a contagious effect on the aggressive behaviour of individuals in users' social networks.

EFFECTS OF PORNOGRAPHY

Beyond violence, pornography is a second category of media contents potentially related to aggression. *Pornography* is broadly defined as "media material used or intended to increase sexual arousal" (Allen, D'Alessio, & Brezgel, 1995, p. 259). It includes presentations of nudity, consensual sexual interactions, but also the use of coercion and violence in the context of sexual interactions. Whether pornography is "good" or "bad" for people's sexual and romantic relationship has been a topic of intense debate in many societies. A review of the history of this debate is provided by Hald, Seaman, and Linz (2014). In this section, we focus on the theorising and empirical evidence concerning the potential effects of the use of pornography in promoting not only sexual aggression but also aggressive behaviour more generally.

pornography: media material used or intended to increase sexual arousal.

Frequency of use and content analyses of violence in pornographic media

There is evidence that intentional use of pornographic media contents, at least occasionally, is widespread from early adolescence onwards (Peter & Valkenburg, 2016). For adults, the annual user statistics of the website *Pornhub* for 2018 reveal 33.5 billion visits (www.pornhub.com/insights/2018-year-in-review). The average age of users was 35.6 years, with 26% falling into the youngest user group of 18 to 26 years. The literature also shows a consistent gender difference in all age groups, with a much higher percentage of males than females reporting regular pornography use. Among *Pornhub* visitors in 2018, 29% were women, which represents an increase of 3% over the previous year.

As pornographic material has become more easily available with the advent of the internet, it is also more widely used. Analysing young adults' reported use of pornography over a 40-year period from 1973 to 2012, Price, Patterson, Regnerus, and Walley (2016) found an increase in the proportion of young male and female adults who reported having watched an X-rated movie in the past year. The increase was due in particular to the increased rate in the youngest cohorts born in the early 1980s, who grew up with the internet.

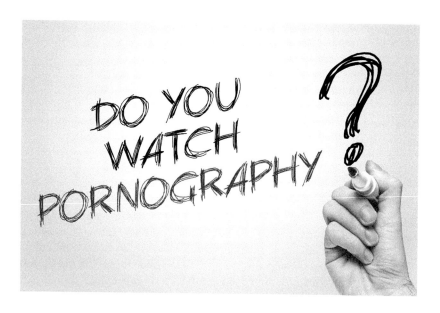

As we saw in the preceding sections, media effects strongly depend on content, so that exposure to violence promotes aggression but exposure to nonviolent media does not. Similarly, pornographic media may be expected to have an impact on aggression to the extent that they contain aggressive or violent behaviours. It should be noted that the pornography industry is a rapidly changing trade, so any content analyses of porno-graphic media can only ever be a snapshot of the predominant portrayals at the time. With this caveat in mind, content analyses revealed that vio-lence has a firm place in pornography. Analysing 50 videos at the top of the list of pornography sales and rentals in 2004 and 2005, Bridges, Wosnitzer, Scharrer, Sun, and Liberman (2010) established that aggression is an integral feature of this genre. Of a total of 304 scenes that were analysed, 88% showed acts of physical aggression, such as spanking or gagging, and 48% contained verbal aggression. Only 10% of all scenes contained positive behaviours, such as kissing or verbal compliments. Most of the aggressive behaviours were shown by a male actor towards a female target, and 95% of the targets responded either with expressions of pleasure or in a neutral way to the aggressive treatment. These findings clearly contra-dict the dismissal of violent pornography as "comparatively rare in the real world" by Ferguson and Hartley (2009, p. 323). However, the popular claim that violence has been on the increase in recent years due to users' preferences was not supported in the analysis by Shor and Seida (2019) of the online pornography website PornHub.com covering the period from 2008 to 2016. Across the total period, visible violence was presented in just under 40% of the coded videos, with little fluctuation over the years. In a further analysis of 172 videos from that website, Shor (2019) focussed on the reactions shown by female actors to aggressive male behaviour of both a physical (e.g., hitting, kicking) and sexual (e.g. forced penetration) nature, comparing teenage (under the age of 20 years) and adult (between 20 and 40 years) performers. In the clips in which such aggressive behaviour was shown, 90% of the teenage performers and more than 80% of the adult performers reacted with pleasure, a much higher rate than pleasure shown in videos that did not contain aggression. Moreover, the analysis revealed that the title of the videos featuring teenagers more often contained references to violence than the videos featuring adults, suggesting that violent behaviour towards teenagers is considered to enhance the appeal of these videos to the audience. These findings show that aggressive behaviour is not only normalised, but even presented as pleasurable in mainstream pornographic material, contributing to the formation of *sexual scripts* that link aggression to sexual pleasure.

sexual scripts: cognitive representations of sequences of actions and events in sexual encounters, serving as guidelines for sexual behaviour.

In addition to the direct impact of depictions of sexual aggression, pornographic media may have an indirect effect even in the absence of violent content by promoting stereotypes of sexual interactions that may shape users' scripts of consensual sexual interactions. Such stereotypes would be, for example, that women always say "no" at first to a sexual offer to play "hard to get", creating the belief that a rejection of a sexual offer could or even should be ignored or that initially reluctant partners become more willing if they are made to drink alcohol. A path from pornography use via scripts for consensual sex that contain such beliefs to sexual aggression victimisation and perpetration was found in several studies (D'Abreu & Krahé, 2016; Marshall, Miller, & Bouffard, 2017; Tomaszewska & Krahé, 2018; Wright, Sun, Steffen, & Tokunaga, 2015). A content analysis by Willis, Canan, Jozkowski, and Bridges (2019) showed that the importance of obtaining consent is often undermined in pornographic depictions of sexual interactions. In addition to shaping sexual scripts, there is also evidence that pornography use is related to behaviours linked to a higher risk of sexual aggression, such as drinking or engaging in casual sex (Braithwaite, Coulson, Keddington, & Fincham, 2015; Vandenbosch & van Oosten, 2018).

Evidence linking pornography use to aggression

Studies examining the link between the use of pornography and aggressive behaviour have used experimental, correlational, and longitudinal designs to address several more specific questions: (1) Is exposure to pornographic material of all kinds related to sexual as well as nonsexual aggression? (2) Is the link stronger for violent than for nonviolent pornography? (3) Is the link stronger for sexual than for nonsexual aggression? (4) Is pornography use linked to more positive attitudes about sexual aggression or other sexuality-related attitudes, such as rape myth acceptance, that may increase the risk of sexual aggression?

Is there a link between the use of pornography and sexual as well as non-sexual aggression?

A meta-analysis by Wright, Tokunaga, and Kraus (2016) analysed 22 correlational and longitudinal studies from seven countries that linked pornography use to reported acts of sexual aggression in samples from the general population. Across all 22 studies, they found a significant effect size of $r = .28$, which is moderate in size. It is similar in magnitude to the meta-analytic effect sizes presented earlier in this chapter for the link between depictions of physical aggression on viewers' aggressive behaviour. No significant differences in the effect sizes by age, gender, country, or design (cross-sectional vs. longitudinal) were found.

Additional evidence comes from experimental studies that can provide more conclusive findings about the possible causal impact of exposure to pornography on aggressive behaviour. In a study by Yao, Mahood, and Linz (2010), men were assigned to play either a sexually oriented video game or a control game without sexual content. Those who had played the sexually charged game scored significantly higher on a measure of sexual harassment and were faster at responding to words that sexually objectify women (e.g., "slut," "bitch") in a lexical decision task. Experimental evidence included in a meta-analysis by Allen et al. (1995) yielded an overall effect size of $r = .13$ for exposure to pornography on subsequent (non-sexual) aggression in the laboratory, but the effects varied depending on the level of violence in the pornographic material.

Is violent pornography more closely related to aggression than non-violent pornography?

The meta-analysis by Wright et al. (2016) found a higher effect size for studies examining the use of violent pornography than for studies that assessed general pornography use without specifying content, but the difference between the two effect sizes was only marginally significant. Donnerstein (1984) suggested that non-violent pornography may only affect individuals whose readiness for aggressive behaviour is already high (e.g., due to previous frustration, alcohol consumption, or arousal from a different source; see the discussion of excitation transfer theory in Chapter 2).

Is there a difference between violent pornography and portrayals of non-sexual violence in their effects on aggression?

This question pits the sexual against the violent aspects of pornography and addresses the role of sexual arousal in precipitating aggression. Donnerstein (1984) conducted a series of studies that compared participants' aggressive responses following the presentation of a non-aggressive pornographic film, an aggressive pornographic film, and a non-sexual aggressive film. In one of the experiments, male participants were either angered or not angered by a female confederate, were then shown one of three films, and subsequently were given the opportunity to aggress against the female confederate by means of electric shocks of varying intensity. The main results of this study are presented in Figure 6.5.

The findings in Figure 6.5 suggest that it is not so much the sexual but the aggressive content of the materials that instigates aggression. In both angered and non-angered participants, the non-sexual aggressive film led to significantly more aggression than the non-aggressive sexual film. However, aggressive and sexual content seem to add up, as the highest level of aggression was observed for the film that combined both sexual and aggressive contents.

The primary dependent variable in this study was shock intensity, which is a non-sexual aggression measure. However, Donnerstein also measured sexually aggressive responses following exposure to the films. Again, exposure to aggression, even without sexual content, was associated with a greater likelihood of aggression (willingness to use force and willingness to rape) than exposure to the non-aggressive sex film. However, it would be premature to conclude that non-violent pornography is innocuous with regard to aggression. Paik and Comstock's (1994) meta-analysis yielded a substantially higher effect size for violent and non-violent erotica combined than for non-sexual violence. This finding is consistent with Zillmann's (1998) "sexual callousness model". Zillmann suggests that the degrading portrayal of women in pornography may promote sexual callousness

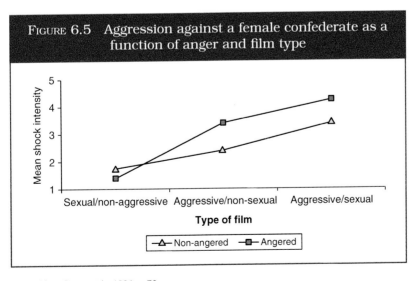

FIGURE 6.5   Aggression against a female confederate as a function of anger and film type

Adapted from Donnerstein, 1984, p. 76.

towards women that facilitates male aggression directed at female targets. His model points to the role of attitudinal variables as mediators between sexual/violent media contents and subsequent aggression, which will be addressed in the next section.

Does pornography affect attitudes that are relevant to aggression, in particular rape-supportive attitudes? This question reflects the possibility that pornographic media contents may have an indirect negative effect on aggression by promoting attitudes conducive to aggressive behaviour. As shown by the content analyses discussed above, many pornographic films contain violence against women that is seemingly enjoyed by the targets or show initially reluctant women changing their mind after forceful attempts by the man to engage in sexual contact. Such presentations may foster the view that women enjoy aggressive sexual tactics and that they are usually willing to have sex even if they initially reject a man's advances.

A review of the literature by Rodenhizer and Edwards (2019) focussing on adolescents and emerging adults found evidence that both sexually explicit material in general and sexually violent material in particular were linked to attitudes condoning both sexual violence and physical dating violence. The meta-analysis by Hald, Malamuth, and Yuen (2010) found a significant effect size of $r = .18$ across nine studies for the link between pornography use and attitudes supporting violence against women. Distinguishing between violent and non-violent pornography, they found that attitudes condoning violence against women were related significantly more closely to violent than to non-violent pornography use ($r = .24$ vs. $r = .13$).

A framework for integrating the different strands of pornography research in relation to its effect on aggression is offered by Wright's $_3$A model (Wright, 2011; Wright & Bae, 2018). The three "A"s stand for *acquisition, activation,* and *application,* and the theory draws heavily on Huesmann's theory of aggressive scripts introduced in Chapter 2. By informing users' ideas about sexuality, pornography shapes their scripts about sexual interactions, including normative beliefs about acceptable sexual conduct and expected partner behaviour. These scripts are activated in sexual situations and used as a frame of reference to interpret the situation, for example by suggesting it is OK to ignore a woman's refusal because it is not likely to be genuine. The more often pornography is used, the more easily a script is activated. The activated script is evaluated as to its suitability for enactment in the situation, for instance, in terms of the similarity of the situation to situations stored in the script or the positive consequences attached to certain behaviours based on the media portrayal. If the evaluation is positive, the script will be applied to the planning and performance of sexual behaviour. This sequence of events may explain why there is both a direct and an indirect learning effect of the use of pornography: a direct effect to the extent that the pornographic material presents aggression as normative or acceptable, and an indirect effect to the extent that even in the absence of violent content, pornography may influence sexual attitudes and behaviours associated with increased odds of showing sexual aggression. We will discuss such risk factors for sexual aggression in Chapter 9.

INTERVENTIONS TO REDUCE MEDIA VIOLENCE USE AND PROMOTE MEDIA LITERACY

It has become clear in the course of this chapter that media presentations of violence and explicit sex may affect viewers' aggressive behaviour through a number of different routes. What, then, can be done to prevent or mitigate these adverse effects? Theoretical models that explain the long-term effects of exposure to violent media as a result of observational learning, aggressive scripts, disinhibition, and desensitisation suggest that interventions should start at an early age when aggressive scripts and patterns of behaviour are not yet consolidated and therefore more amenable to change.

Compared with the large number of studies that have sought to demonstrate an effect of media violence use on aggression, effective interventions are scarce and directed mostly at children and adolescents. Existing studies have addressed one or both of two outcomes: *restricted consuming*, either in terms of the overall reduction in media exposure or the reduction of exposure to violent content, and *critical consuming*, designed to promote an understanding of the mechanisms by which violence is presented as acceptable, successful, and detached from negative consequences.

Focusing on restricted overall media use, Robinson, Wilde, Navracruz, Haydel, and Varady (2001) demonstrated the efficacy of an intervention with third and fourth graders over a period of six months. The intervention included a 10-day complete turn-off of television, videos, and video games, followed by a prescribed budget of no more than seven hours of screen time per week. Participants in the intervention group showed not only a reduction in media use compared with the control group, but also a significant decrease in peer-rated aggression as well as observed verbal aggression from baseline to post-test. However, no parallel intervention effects were apparent in parent ratings of aggression.

Byrne (2009), on the other hand, focused exclusively on the aspect of critical consuming. She compared two intervention conditions with a control group in a sample of fourth and fifth graders. In the "basic condition", students received a lesson on the negative effects of media violence, how to avoid these effects, and how to critically evaluate the aggressive behaviour of media characters, using violent clips as examples. In the "activity condition", participants were given the same instruction but were additionally required to write a paragraph about what they had learned, and were videotaped reading it aloud. No difference was found between the activity and the control conditions immediately post-intervention and at the 6-month follow-up, whereas the basic condition showed a significant *increase* in the willingness to use aggression, indicating a boomerang effect.

Using a combined approach of reducing media violence use *and* promoting critical consuming, Rosenkoetter, Rosenkoetter, Ozretich, and Acock (2004) conducted an intervention over a 12-month period with children from first to third grade. The intervention was designed to cut down the amount of violent television viewing and to reduce the identification with violent TV characters. It produced different effects for boys and girls. Girls in the intervention group scored higher than girls in the control group on knowledge about the effects of TV violence, and lower on TV violence viewing as well as identification with violent TV characters. The effect of the intervention on reducing peer-nominated aggression was significant only for boys. In a subsequent study with children from first to fourth grade, Rosenkoetter, Rosenkoetter, and Acock (2009) implemented a similar programme over a 7-month period with an immediate post-intervention measurement and an 8-month follow-up. Participants in the intervention group reported watching less violent television and expressed more critical attitudes about media violence than those in the control group, both immediately post-intervention and eight months later. The short-term effect of reduced identification with violent characters was no longer present at the follow-up. No effect of the intervention on peer-rated aggression was found, either immediately post-intervention or at the 8-month follow-up.

Both restricted consuming and critical consuming were targeted in an intervention developed by Möller, Krahé, Busching, and Krause (2012) for use with adolescents in Germany, with restricted consuming directed at violent media contents only. The intervention consisted of five weekly sessions of two school periods each, in which students worked on two modules: (1) restricted use of media violence, which involved keeping a diary of media use as a baseline and then setting targets and developing skills for reducing time spent with violent media; and (2) critical appraisal of violent media in their effect on users, which involved experiential and didactic elements demonstrating the psychological processes underlying media violence effects, as described earlier in this chapter and shown in Figures 6.3 and 6.4.

A combined experimental-longitudinal design was used to test the efficacy of the intervention. Following a baseline assessment of violent TV, movie and video game use (Time 1), 627 seventh and eighth graders were assigned to the 5-week intervention or a no-intervention control group. The main outcome measures were media violence use, nonviolent media use, and self-reported aggressive behaviour, measured about seven months post-intervention (Time 2) and at two further data waves another 12 months (Time 3) and 24 months (Time 4) later (Krahé & Busching, 2015).

Participants in the intervention group reported a significantly lower use of violent media at Time 2 than did participants in the control group, and the effect extended indirectly to Time 3 and Time 4. As expected, no effect of the intervention was found on nonviolent media use, which is consistent with the content of the intervention directed specifically at the use of violent media. Participants in the intervention group also showed less aggressive behaviour at Time 3, which was mediated by reduced exposure to violent media at Time 2. By Time 4, the indirect intervention effect via the reduction of media violence use was no longer significant. However, given that the intervention lasted no more than five weeks, seeing an effect after 18 months may be regarded as evidence of its efficacy, and the finding that an intervention effect could no longer be detected at 30 months post-intervention is not unexpected.

Beyond demonstrating that reducing exposure to violent media may successfully reduce aggressive behaviour, the combined experimental-longitudinal design of the study provided a more stringent test of the causal link between media violence use and aggressive behaviour than could be achieved by either experimental or longitudinal designs alone. While it would clearly be unethical to run a longitudinal study in which participants are assigned to a high dose of exposure to media violence over extended periods to observe increases in aggressive behaviour, it is perfectly ethical to try and experimentally reduce the exposure to media violence in order to examine a reduction of aggressive behaviour. By demonstrating the path from reduced exposure as a result of the intervention on reduced aggression, the study by Krahé and Busching (2015) provides evidence for a causal impact of media violent use on aggressive behaviour.

There is an almost total absence of systematic intervention studies designed to increase media literacy with respect to pornographic content. Vandenbosch and van Oosten (2017) related participants' self-reports about how much they learned about sexually explicit material on the Internet in their sex education classes to their tendency to view women as sex objects. Both adolescents and young adults were included in the study, and the results showed both groups were less likely to view women as sex objects the more they reported having learned about sexually explicit Internet contents. It should be noted, however, that this study did not test an intervention and was unable to assess what exactly the pornography-related content of the sex education reports contained. Given the consistent evidence of effects of pornography use on sexuality-related cognitions and behaviours, designing and evaluating theory-based porn literacy interventions, especially for adolescents, is an urgent task for future research.

A further approach to prevention seeks to reduce exposure to media violence by restricting access to violent media content by children and adolescents. Various age classification systems have been developed to designate media with violent content as unsuitable for certain age groups (for a summary of the most common rating systems in the U.S., see Bushman & Cantor, 2003; for information about the British Board of Film Classification, BBFC, film ratings in the U.K., see www.bbfc.co.uk; for the Pan European Game Information (PEGI) system, see www.pegi.info/en). However, empirical studies have revealed several problems with rating systems (for a summary, see Gentile & Anderson, 2006). First, many parents are not familiar with the ratings or do not use them to regulate their children's media access (Gentile, 2010). Second, media rated as suitable for children and adolescents often contain substantial levels of violence, and there appears to be a trend over time towards greater tolerance of violent content in media that are accessible to a young audience. An analysis of movies rated between 1950 and 2006 found a steady increase in violent content in films rated as PG-13 (designated as containing content inappropriate for children under 13 years of age) (Nalkur, Jamieson, & Romer, 2010). Third, ratings are often not matched by consumer perceptions of the same titles, especially with regard to cartoons and fantasy games and also media that contain some degree of violence, which undermines their perceived validity (Funk, Flores, Buchman, & Germann, 1999; Walsh & Gentile, 2001). Finally, and probably the most difficult to overcome, warning labels have been found to enhance the appeal of violent media to those whom they should protect. Demonstrating a "forbidden fruit" effect, Bijvank, Konijn, Bushman, and Roelofsma (2009) asked children and adolescents to rate the attractiveness of versions of the same video games that were presented with different age recommendations or with different violent content indicators taken from the PEGI system. Consistent with their predictions, the authors found that adding an age label to a video game made it more attractive to children under the indicated age, and that adding a warning label about violent content increased the attractiveness of the game, particularly to boys. These findings raise questions about the effectiveness of rating systems and highlight the challenges involved in protecting children and adolescents from exposure to violent media contents

SUMMARY

- Aggression and violence are widely present in different media types, including films, television programmes, video games, cartoons, and music lyrics. Adolescents and young adults in particular spend a lot of time using these media. Meta-analyses and review integrating the findings of experimental, cross-sectional, and longitudinal studies provide support for the proposed link between the use of violent media contents and aggression across a range of different media, although meta-analytic effect sizes are in the small to moderate range.
- Violent media contents are particularly likely to affect viewers' aggressive tendencies if the violence is presented as successful or goes unsanctioned, if it is presented as justified and not leading to any pain or harm to the victim. In addition, consistent with social learning theory, aggression shown by powerful or much admired media figures is more likely to elicit aggressive behaviour. Individual differences have been observed in response to violent media, suggesting that habitually aggressive and hostile individuals appear to be particularly affected by violence in the media.
- Violent media stimuli may affect aggressive behaviour through different mechanisms. Short-term exposure to media violence leads

to an increase in physiological arousal and aggressive affect, increases the accessibility of aggressive thoughts, and instigates the imitation of aggressive acts as observed or performed in the virtual reality.

- Habitual exposure to violence in the media creates the basis for sustained observational learning that promotes the development of aggressive knowledge structures, such as hostile expectations and attributional styles, and the formation of aggressive scripts. Through the portrayal of violence as normal and appropriate, media violence strengthens the normative acceptance of aggression that disinhibits aggressive behaviour. Finally, repeated exposure to violent media cues leads to desensitisation (i.e., reduced physiological and affective responsiveness to violent media stimuli), which is also reflected in a decrease in empathic concern for the plight of others who are in need of help.

- Pornography is widely used from adolescence onwards, and many pornographic media contain depictions of violence. Violence is often shown to be enjoyed by the targets, which normalised sexual violence against women. Both measures of general pornography use, not differentiated by content, and measures of violent pornography use are linked to aggression, with somewhat stronger effects for violent pornography. Violent content and sexual content seem to have an additive effect, as non-sexual violence triggers more aggression than sexual stimuli without violence, but violent pornography that combines sexual and aggressive cues produces a further increase in aggression. Many studies have found an effect of pornography on sexual scripts, sexual behaviours, and rape-supportive attitudes, which are established risk factors for sexual aggression.

- Intervention studies to prevent or mitigate the adverse effects of media violence are scarce. They are designed to reduce consumption and promote critical viewing through educating users about the potential risks of media violence use, but have produced mixed success. Media rating systems have been designed to protect children and adolescents from the influence of violent media. However, they are fraught with a number of problems, not least the creation of a "forbidden fruit effect", by making violent media more attractive to those whom these systems were designed to protect.

TASKS TO DO

(1) Look up the media rating systems in your country to find out what categories are used and how violence features in the criteria for assigning age labels.

(2) Go through your library of DVDs and video games and give each title a violence score on a scale ranging from 0 (not violent at all) to 4 (very violent), on the basis of how you remember the film or game. Then compare your score with the age ratings printed on the box.

(3) Pick a random 30-minute slot from your favourite TV programme or movie and count the number of violent acts you observe during this period.

SUGGESTED READING

Anderson, C. A., Bushman, B. J., Bartholow, B. D., Cantor, J., Christakis, D., Coyne, S. M., ... Ybarra, M. L. (2017). Screen violence and youth behavior. *Pediatrics, 140*(Suppl 2), S142–S147.

Hald, G. M., Seaman, C., & Linz, D. G. (2014). Sexuality and pornography. In D. L. Tolman, L. M. Diamond, J. A. Bauermeister, W. H. George, J. G. Pfaus, & L. M. Ward (Eds.), *APA handbook of sexuality and psychology* (pp. 3–35). Washington, DC: American Psychological Association.

Krahé, B. (2014). Media violence use as a risk factor for aggressive behaviour in adolescence. *European Review of Social Psychology, 25*, 71–106.

Plante, C., Anderson, C. A., Allen, J. J., Groves, C., & Gentile, D. A. (2020). *Video games: Mayhem or moral panic? FAQs and a moderate approach to media violence research.* Ames, IA: Zengen LLC Publishing.

Chapter 7

AGGRESSION IN DIFFERENT DOMAINS OF EVERYDAY LIFE

In the previous chapters, we examined research about aggression as a general construct without distinguishing between its different forms and manifestations. In the chapters to come, the focus will shift towards a closer analysis of different forms of aggressive behaviour in specific domains. We begin in the present chapter by examining common forms of aggressive behaviour in four areas of everyday life contexts: in school, at the workplace, on the roads, and in the sports world. Chapter 8 then moves to the protected realm of the family, where aggression is nonetheless a sad reality in the form of sexual, physical, and emotional abuse of children, as well as violence against partners and elders. Chapter 9 focuses on sexual aggression, most notably against women, but it will also consider the problem of male sexual victimisation. Chapter 10 turns to different forms of aggression and violence that arise from confrontations between social groups, such as gangs, ethnic groups, and mobs. Chapter 11 will review the growing literature aiming to understand terrorism as a particular form of group-based aggression, before we turn to the prevention of aggression and violence in Chapter 12.

SCHOOL BULLYING

The past 40 years have seen the emergence of a large research literature dealing with bullying in the context of schools (Smith, 2016). *Bullying* comprises forms of aggressive behaviour which are directed at victims who cannot easily defend themselves. Bullying is carried out with the intention of inflicting harm on the target person, thus meeting the core definition of aggressive behaviour (see Chapter 1). In addition, bullying is characterised by two features: (a) an imbalance of power between the aggressor and the victim, resulting, for example, from differences in physical strength or

bullying: (also known as *mobbing*) denotes aggressive behaviour directed at victims who cannot easily defend themselves, commonly in schools and at the workplace.

status in a job hierarchy, and (b) the repeated occurrence over time. Thus, a single aggressive confrontation and aggressive behaviour towards a target of equal strength or status would fall outside the definitional boundaries of bullying (Olweus, 2017).

cyberbullying:
involves the use of modern technology, such as computers, mobile phones or other electronic devices, to inflict intentional harm on others.

Bullying can take both direct forms, such as physical and verbal attacks, and sexual harassment, and indirect forms, such as relational aggression (i.e., behaviour directed at damaging the victim's peer relationships; for an explanation of the distinction between direct and indirect aggression, see Chapter 1). With the advent of modern communication technology, *cyberbullying* has appeared on the agenda as a new manifestation of bullying. *Cyberbullying* is carried out by means of modern technology, such as computers, mobile phones, or other electronic devices, to inflict intentional harm on a peer repeatedly and over time. Sending threatening emails, posting derogatory comments about a marginalised classmate on Internet platforms, or circulating photos designed to embarrass or humiliate another person of lesser popularity or status, or sharing sexual images of persons with others without their consent are all examples of cyberbullying. There has been some debate among researchers as to whether cyberbullying is a conceptually distinct construct from face-to-face bullying, but the majority opinion seems to be to regard it as just a different means of engaging in bullying behaviour (Antoniadou & Kokkinos, 2015). The overlap between the two forms, such that many victims of traditional face-to-face bullying also report being cyberbullied and vice versa, is consistent with this view (Olweus, 2017).

Different methods have been employed to study bullying (for a review, see Thomas, Connor, & Scott, 2015). First, there is a range of *self-report* instruments that ask participants to indicate the frequency with which they engaged in bullying behaviour or experienced bullying (or both) during a certain period of time, such as the last month or the last year. Self-reports can be elicited either through general questions (see, for example, the study by the World Health Organization, 2004) or through multiple items that specify different behavioural forms of bullying. A second methodological approach involves *peer nominations* in which peers are asked to name those members of their class or work group that engage in, or are made to suffer from, a range of different behaviours representing bullying (Pouwels, Lansu, & Cillessen, 2016). Bully or victim scores are assigned to individuals based on the aggregated peer nominations. In a third approach, parents and teachers can be asked to provide assessments of a child's bully and/ or victim status, and employees can be asked to nominate colleagues who bully, or are bullied by, others. Finally, direct observation can be used in certain settings, such as school breaks or office meetings, whereby trained observers record the frequency and the social context of bullying.

For all of these approaches to the measurement of bullying, it is important to provide participants with a clear definition of bullying to ensure that they respond on the basis of the same understanding of the term. A common definition, which is part of the Olweus Bully/Victim Questionnaire (Olweus, 2012), is shown in Box 7.1.

This section summarises the extant literature on the prevalence, risk factors, and consequences of bullying during childhood and adolescence and discusses evidence on the effectiveness of anti-bullying programmes. Wherever possible, we refer to meta-analytic studies, which have the advantage of integrating results from a number of individual studies, thereby yielding more solid conclusions.

Prevalence of bullying

The most extensive research programme on the causes, manifestations, and consequences of bullying has been conducted in Norway by Olweus and his colleagues (Olweus, 2017). A meta-analysis of 80 studies reporting prevalence rates for traditional bullying and cyberbullying in adolescent samples found an overall prevalence of 36% for traditional, face-to-face bullying and 15% for cyberbullying (Modecki, Minchin, Harbaugh, Guerra, & Runions, 2014). Corresponding rates for self-reported engagement in bullying behaviour were 35% for traditional and 16% for cyberbullying. The two forms of bullying were correlated for both perpetration ($r = .47$) and victimisation ($r = .40$), indicating that many adolescents engage in, or experience, both traditional and cyberbullying (Brosowski, Wachs, Scheithauer, & Vazsonyi, 2018).

Another meta-analysis confirmed this overlap (Kowalski, Giumetti, Schroeder, & Lattanner, 2014). They included 137 unique data sets that contained 736 independent effect sizes and found further support for the overlap between traditional and cyberbullying of $r = .45$ for perpetration and $r = .40$ for victimisation. However, they also showed that traditional

Box 7.1   Definitions of bullying presented to research participants

Traditional bullying:

We say a student is being bullied when another student, or several other students:

- say mean and hurtful things or make fun of him or her or call him or her mean and hurtful names
- completely ignore or exclude him or her from their group of friends or leave him or her out of things on purpose
- hit, kick, push, shove around, or lock him or her inside a room
- tell lies or spread false rumours about him or her or send mean notes and try to make other students dislike him or her
- and other hurtful things like that.

When we talk about bullying, these things may happen repeatedly, and it is difficult for the student being bullied to defend himself or herself. We also call it bullying when a student is teased repeatedly in a mean and hurtful way.

But we don't call it bullying when the teasing is done in a friendly and playful way. Also, it is not bullying when two students of about the same strength or power argue or fight.

Cyberbullying:

Here are some questions about being bullied electronically. When we say "bullied electronically", we mean

- bullied through e-mail, instant messaging, in a chat room, on a website, or through a text message sent to a cell phone.

Based on Olweus, 2012.

and cyberbullying were associated with some distinct risk factors and psychological outcomes, which we will discuss later in this section. Focusing on the role of gender in cyberbullying perpetration, the meta-analysis by Barlett and Coyne (2014) found that girls were somewhat more likely to report cyberbullying behaviour under the age of 11, but boys were more likely to engage in cyberbullying from mid-adolescence onwards.

Although traditional bullying and cyberbullying show considerable overlap, there are two distinct characteristics of cyberbullying that should be noted. The first is that the ability to engage in cyberbullying is not dependent on physical strength, and the second is that it can be carried out under the cloak of anonymity. In combination, these two aspects considerably lower the threshold for bullying others compared with face-to-face forms of bullying. In line with these considerations, Barlett, Chamberlin, and Witkower (2017) found in a three-wave longitudinal study that participants' belief in the anonymity of cyberbullying and the irrelevance of muscularity for online bullying predicted positive attitudes towards cyberbullying which, in turn, predicted cyberbullying behaviour. These pathways remained significant when controlling for both cyberbullying and traditional bullying behaviour at the first data wave.

An international survey conducted in collaboration with the World Health Organization asked 11- to 15-year-olds in 40 countries about their experiences as perpetrators and victims of traditional face-to-face bullying (Craig et al., 2009). After presenting a definition of bullying similar to the one in Box 7.1, two questions were asked: (1) How often have you been bullied at school during the last couple of months, and (2) How often have you taken part in bullying another student/other students in the last couple of months? The response options ranged from "I have not been bullied/I have not bullied" to "Several times a week". The findings based on responses from over 200,000 participants are presented in Figure 7.1.

Across all 40 countries, 10.7% of respondents reported bullying others, 12.6% reported having been bullied, and 3.6% reported being both bullies and victims. Bullying rates were consistently higher for boys than for girls, and victimisation rates were higher for girls than for boys in most countries. A striking finding that can be gleaned from Figure 7.1 is the wide variation in reported rates of being a victim, a bully, or both between the different countries, ranging from under 10% of boys and girls in Sweden to 45% for girls and 38% for boys in Lithuania. As the questions and instructions were the same in each country, this variation cannot be attributed to differences in measurement instruments. Additional analyses would be required linking the different rates to other aspects of variation between countries, such as features of the school system, differences in other forms of aggression, or general tolerance of aggression, to understand the high variability.

A further finding apparent from Figure 7.1 is that a substantial number of respondents reported both perpetration and victimisation. An overlap in the roles of victims and perpetrators was also confirmed for cyberbullying in the meta-analysis by Kowalski (2018), who found an overall correlation between victimisation and perpetration of $r = .51$ between the two roles. These so-called "bully-victims" have been identified in many studies as a particularly problematic group (Georgiou & Stavrinides, 2008; O'Brennan, Bradshaw, & Sawyer, 2009).

Salmivalli (2010) pointed out that bullying needs to be examined in a group context, looking not only at the roles of bullies and victims but also at those of peer witnesses, who may assist or encourage the bully, intervene on behalf of the victim, or remain passive bystanders. Bullying frequently happens on a social stage, and the responses of those witnessing the bullying behaviour of the aggressor may critically affect the course of

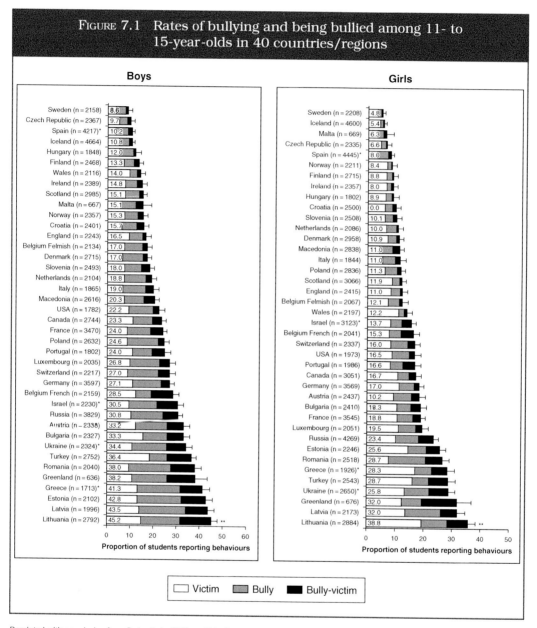

FIGURE 7.1   Rates of bullying and being bullied among 11- to 15-year-olds in 40 countries/regions

events. Research based on the "participant roles" approach has identified four different roles in addition to those of the bully and victim: assistants of bullies, reinforcers of bullies, defenders of the victim, and outsiders (Salmivalli, Lagerspetz, Björkqvist, Österman, & Kaukialnen, 1996). The higher the number of students in a classroom who condone bullying by assisting or reinforcing the bully, the more prevalent bullying behaviour was found to be. Conversely, the more students are willing to defend the victim, the lower the rates of bullying and the less adverse the effects on victims' social adjustment (Salmivalli, 2010). Unfortunately, many bystanders are reluctant to intervene on behalf of victims, despite holding negative attitudes about bullying. In an Australian study by Rigby and Johnson (2006), fewer than 10% of secondary school boys and girls said that they would "certainly" intervene if they witnessed verbal or physical bullying. Removing obstacles for defenders to come forward in support of victims is therefore an important objective for intervention efforts (see below).

Risk factors for bullying perpetration and victimisation

Beyond exploring the prevalence rates for bullying, it is important to ask what puts children and adolescents at risk of becoming victims or perpetrators of bullying. A meta-analysis integrating results from 153 individual studies provides some answers to this question by examining both personal characteristics and contextual variables associated with being a victim, a bully, or acting in both roles as a bully-victim (Cook, Williams, Guerra, Kim, & Sadek, 2010). Some risk factors were present in each of the three groups, whereas others were unique to the different roles. For example, low social problem-solving skills and internalising symptoms, such as anxiety, were individual-level risk factors for membership of each of the three groups, as were negative family environment and low peer status as contextual risk factors (see Cook et al., 2010, Table 9). Among the unique predictors, it was found that poor academic performance predicted bullying, but not victimisation or membership of the bully-victim group. Furthermore, holding negative attitudes about others was a unique risk factor for bullying, and lack of social competence was more characteristic of victims and bully-victims than of bullies. Cook et al. (2010) concluded that the group of bully-victims had the greatest number of risk factors, corroborating earlier research, and they pointed out that this group should be particularly targeted by intervention efforts. A later meta-analysis by Kljakovic and Hunt (2016) of 19 longitudinal studies with adolescents yielded consistent results. Conduct problems and social problems predicted both victimisation and perpetration, whereas school problems were a specific risk factor for perpetration and internalizing problems a specific risk factor for victimisation.

By the time they start school, children's moral development has progressed to a level where they are aware that bullying others is not an acceptable form of social behaviour (Jansen et al., 2017). Therefore, they need to find justifications for bullying to reduce its discrepancy with their moral standards. Based on Bandura's (1991) theory of moral agency, this process is called "moral disengagement", which comprises several interlocking mechanisms. One mechanism is *moral justification*, which involves the cognitive reframing of the behaviour to make it acceptable, for example because everyone in a peer group shows it. The second mechanism is *euphemistic labelling*, which downplays the harmful character of the bullying behaviour, for example by calling it a "joke". The third mechanism is *exonerating comparisons*, which minimises the seriousness of bullying behaviour by comparing it to other, more serious forms of behaviour that violate moral standards. A meta-analysis by Killer, Bussey, Hawes, and Hunt (2019) reviewed the evidence for a link between moral disengagement and involvement in the different bullying roles distinguished by the "participant roles" approach discussed above. They found positive associations between moral disengagement and both bullying perpetration and victimisation, whereas moral disengagement was negatively related to defending. Bystanding was found to be unrelated to moral disengagement.

The meta-analysis by Kowalski et al. (2014) identified a number of factors associated with a reduced likelihood of perpetration and victimisation of cyberbullying. Significant negative correlations with cyberbullying perpetration and victimisation were found for empathy, parental monitoring, perceived social support, a good school climate, and school safety. In addition, higher social intelligence and greater parental control of technology were associated with a lower likelihood of victimisation.

Consequences of bullying

Both perpetrating and experiencing bullying is associated with lasting adverse outcomes. A long-term longitudinal study by Matthews, Jennings, Lee, and Pardini (2017) followed boys from the age of ten years over a mean period of 22 years. They found that being a bully in childhood predicted a greater number of negative health behaviours, such as smoking, and higher scores on the physical aggression, verbal aggression, anger, and hostility scales of the Aggression Questionnaire (AQ; see Chapter 1). Being bullied in childhood predicted a lower socio-economic status, less perceived social support, less optimism, and more experiences of unfair treatment in adulthood. Both the bully and the victim group experienced more stressful life events as adults.

The meta-analysis by Kowalski et al. (2014) also uncovered both overlapping and specific outcomes of cyberbullying perpetration and victimisation. For both bullies and victims, elevated scores were found on measures of depression, anxiety, loneliness, and drug or alcohol use, and reduced scores were found on measures of self-esteem, life satisfaction, and academic achievement. Moreover, cyberbullying victimisation showed a unique negative association with prosocial behaviour and unique positive associations with somatic symptoms, stress, and suicidal ideation.

The link between bullying victimisation and suicide attempts was studied in 48 countries from the Global South (Africa, Asia, the Caribbean, and Latin America) by Koyanagi et al. (2019). In their sample of almost 135,000 adolescents aged between 12 and 15 years, they found that, on average, 30.4% had experienced bullying in the past 30 days, and 10.7% had attempted suicide in the past 12 months. The attempted suicide rate was three times higher among those who reported bullying victimisation.

A longitudinal study conducted in Finland by Klomek et al. (2009) examined the link between bullying and victimisation at the age of 8 years and attempted and completed suicides before the age of 25 years in a sample of more than 5,300 participants. Being a victim was associated with an increased suicidal risk: the odds that those who had been frequently bullied at age eight attempted or completed suicide before the age of 25 were 6.3 times higher for girls and 3.8 times higher for boys compared with those not bullied at age eight. This figure is adjusted for conduct disorders and depression assessed at age eight, which would be additional risk factors of suicide.

In addition to these findings, there is meta-analytic evidence that being a bully or bully-victim is associated with a heightened suicide risk (Holt et al., 2015). They considered both traditional and cyberbullying and found significantly higher rates of both suicidal ideation and suicidal behaviour in victims, bullies, and bully-victims. The odds of suicidal behaviour were about four times higher in the bully-victim group, three times higher in the victim-only and 2.5 times higher in the bully-only group, all in comparison to individuals who were neither bullies nor victims.

In combination, the studies discussed in this section provide clear evidence of the lasting negative effects of bullying. This impact has been demonstrated for both traditional and cyberbullying and for both victimization and perpetration, with a potential additive impact on the bully-victim group.

A specific research question with regard to the impact of bullying behaviour is whether engaging in bullying during childhood and/or adolescence is a risk factor for other forms of aggression in subsequent developmental periods. Basile, Espelage, Rivers, McMahon, and Simon (2009) reviewed a large body of evidence which showed that bullying shares many individual and contextual risk factors with sexual aggression, suggesting that bullies may be at greater risk of engaging in sexual aggression. Other studies found an overlap of risk factors for bullying and violence against intimate partners, arguing that both should be seen as expressions of a more general tendency to engage in aggression in social relationships (Corvo & deLara, 2010; Yahner, Dank, Zweig, & Lachman, 2015). Adopting such a broader perspective on bullying also has important implications for anti-bullying interventions. For example, interventions that address shared risk factors, such as poor problem-solving skills, may be beneficial not only with regard to bullying but also in reducing the risk of other forms of interpersonal aggression.

Interventions

Responding to the evidence on adverse effects of bullying, many interventions have been developed to prevent bullying and/or mitigate its adverse consequences. An example of a theory-based intervention is the KiVa programme developed in Finland by Salmivalli, Kärnä, and Poskiparta (2011). As the authors explain, KiVa is an acronym for the words "against bullying" in Finish and also means something that is nice, good, or friendly. The programme can be used both as a universal approach to preventing bullying and as targeted intervention when bullying has been identified as a problem. It combines lessons in which topics around bullying are discussed, such as group pressure or the effects of bullying on victims, complemented by exercises in small groups and contents provided in a virtual learning environment. Enabling students to effectively counteract bullying behaviour and support victims is also part of the programme, as is a guide for parents (www.kivaprogram.net/program).

Several rigorous meta-analyses are available to evaluate the success of these programs. Reviewing the efficacy of school-based interventions designed to reduce traditional school bullying, the meta-analysis by Gaffney, Ttofi, and Farrington (2019) included 100 studies. Their overview contains a detailed list of interventions examined in these studies that shows the broad range of available programmes, with the KiVa programme featuring prominently. Overall, they found a significant effect size for the reduction of reported bullying behaviour across the set of studies and a parallel significant effect size for a reduction in reported victimisation, amounting to a reduction in the prevalence of both outcomes of about 15–16%.

In a parallel meta-analysis of interventions directed at cyberbullying, Gaffney, Farrington, Espelage, and Ttofi (2019) included 24 studies, all with school-aged participants. Their findings indicate that cyberbullying interventions effectively reduce both perpetration and victimisation. The magnitude of the effects is similar to those for traditional bullying interventions, suggesting that across all studies, cyberbullying perpetration was reduced by approximately 10%–15% and cyberbullying victimisation by approximately 14%. It should be noted, however, that both meta-analyses evaluated the programmes as a whole without examining their different components, so it is unclear to what extent the specific parts of the programmes are necessary and successful. Such a more fine-grained analysis would be helpful for maximizing the efficacy of interventions and the cost-effectiveness of their implementation.

WORKPLACE BULLYING

workplace bullying: (also called workplace mobbing or harassment), behaviours intended to cause harm to another person at work over longer periods of time.

Aggression against weaker members of the peer group is not limited to the school setting, but also happens to people at work. *Workplace bullying*, also called workplace mobbing, or harassment, refers to behaviours intended to cause harm to another person at work over longer periods of time (Branch, Ramsay, & Barker, 2013; Samnani, 2018). As with school bullying, workplace bullying is characterised by an imbalance of power, for example a boss bullying a subordinate, or a stronger position among peers, for example a man bullying a woman of equal status in a male-dominated work group.

Workplace bullying can take different forms, and a common classification describes three major manifestations: (1) work-related bullying, such as withholding information, unreasonable deadlines, excessive monitoring and assigning an unmanageable workload, (2) person-related bullying, for example humiliation in front of colleagues or persistent criticism, and (3) physically intimidating bullying, such as shouting and threatening physical harm (Rai & Agarwal, 2018). A further form of workplace bullying that has attracted widespread attention is *sexual harassment*. Fitzgerald (1993, p. 1070) has defined sexual harassment as "any deliberate or repeated sexual behavior that is unwelcome to the recipient, as well as other sex-related behaviors that are hostile, offensive, or degrading". Such definitions of sexual harassment based on the subjective perception of the target are the most common approach in psychological studies of workplace sexual harassment (however, for alternative definitions based on objective criteria or used in a legal context, see McDonald, 2012; O'Leary-Kelly, Bowes-Sperry, Bates, & Lean, 2009).

sexual harassment: deliberate or repeated sexual behaviour that is unwelcome to the recipient, as well as other sex-related behaviours that are hostile, offensive, or degrading.

The most common way of measuring workplace bullying is through self-reports of victimisation, as exemplified by the *Revised Negative Acts Questionnaire* (NAQ-R; Einarsen, Hoel, & Notelaers, 2009). This measure contains 22 items addressing three dimensions: (a) work-related bullying (e.g., "being exposed to an unmanageable workload"), (b) person-related bullying (e.g., "being the subject of excessive teasing and sarcasm"), and (c) physically intimidating bullying (e.g., "threats of violence or physical abuse or actual abuse"). Substantial correlations were found between victimisation scores on the NAQ-R and psychosomatic complaints and intentions to leave (Einarsen et al., 2009).

Theoretical explanations of workplace bullying focus on the concepts of stressors, stress, and strain (Hershcovis & Barling, 2010). Stressors are measurable properties of the work environment, stress refers to the subjective experience and representation of these stressors by the individual, and strain describes how the individual responds to the stressors. The research reviewed in this section demonstrates how stressors, such as ill-defined roles, interact with stress, such as a person's affective negativity, to increase the risk of workplace bullying and adversely affect individual well-being and organisational functioning. Theoretical accounts of sexual harassment as a special form of workplace bullying claim that gender inequalities in society at large are reflected in gender hierarchies in organisational contexts, making sex-related aggression an easy option for asserting status and dominance (Berdahl, 2007).

Prevalence of workplace bullying

Compared with the large number of studies that have addressed bullying at school, workplace bullying has been less well researched. A meta-analysis by Nielsen, Matthiesen, and Einarsen (2010) established that on average, 15% of employees report experiences of workplace bullying. However, the rates varied substantially, not only due to differences in methodology, but also in relation to geographic regions. Lower rates were found in studies from Scandinavian countries compared with studies in other European countries and a small group of countries outside Europe. A large-scale study involving employees from 44 countries established higher prevalence rates of workplace bullying in poorer countries (van de Vliert, Einarsen, & Nielsen, 2013). A wide range of prevalence rates of experiencing adverse social behaviour at work is also documented in the Sixth European Working Conditions Survey (Eurofound, 2017). Across all 28 EU Member States, the five EU candidate countries, and Norway and Switzerland, the prevalence rate of adverse social behaviour experienced at work was just over 15%, with the lowest rate (2.5%) reported in Albania and the highest (26%) in the Netherlands. Whether the range is due to actual differences in the occurrence of workplace bullying, or reflects differences in the tolerance of these behaviours or the willingness to disclose them, cannot be decided on the basis of the survey responses.

In recent years, the prevalence of workplace bullying has been demonstrated across a wide range of occupational fields and groups, including the military (Larsen, Nye, & Fitzgerald, 2019), in hospital settings (Samsudin, Isahak, & Rampal, 2018), among teachers (Ariza-Montes, Muniz R, Leal-Rodríguez, & Leal-Millán, 2016), and in higher education institutions (Henning et al., 2017). There is some evidence that organisations with a male-dominated workforce have higher rates of workplace bullying and that bullying rates are higher at the lower as compared with the higher end of the organisational hierarchy, but more research is needed to corroborate this pattern (Nielsen & Einarsen, 2018).

In parallel to developments in school bullying, cyberbullying has been identified as a new form of workplace aggression. A study by Privitera and Campbell (2009) found that 10% of employees across a range of employment sectors reported having been bullied via electronic media over the last six months, compared with a rate of 34% for face-to-face bullying. A study by Kowalski, Toth, and Morgan (2018) found that 24% of their participants had experienced cyberbullying in adulthood, and of these, three-quarters indicated that the bully had been a co-worker. Based on their responses to a set of 20 items describing different forms of cyberbullying behaviours experienced from colleagues, 9.3% of participants in the study by Forssell (2016) were identified as victims of cyberbullying at work, defined as having experienced at least one form of cyberbullying per week in the last six weeks.

Studies of sexual harassment at work have mainly focused on women as victims (Fitzgerald & Cortina, 2018). Studies including both men and women show that victimisation rates are indeed substantially higher for women than for men (Fitzgerald & Ormerod, 1993). Confirming the gender imbalance from the perpetrator side, Perry, Schmidtke, and Kulik (1998) found that men had a significantly higher propensity than women to engage in sexually harassing behaviour. With regard to the prevalence of sexual harassment, it was estimated that one in two women will experience sexual harassment at some point in her working life (Fitzgerald, 1993). Other studies have supported this estimate. For example, O'Hare and O'Donohue (1998) found that 69% of the women they surveyed reported at least one incident of gender harassment. Schneider, Swan, and Fitzgerald (1997) collected reports from women in two organisations, a private-sector company and a university. In total, 68% of the respondents in the private company reported at least one incident of sexual harassment in the two years preceding the survey. Of these, 66% rated the experience as offensive or extremely offensive. In the university sample, 63% of the respondents reported at least one experience of sexual harassment, and 48% of these rated the experience as offensive or extremely offensive. There is also evidence that sexual harassment commonly occurs in combination with other, non-sexual forms of workplace bullying (Lim & Cortina, 2005).

Risk factors of workplace bullying

To understand who is likely to be affected by workplace bullying, both individual and organisational characteristics have been considered (for reviews, see McDonald, 2012; Rai & Agarwal, 2018). Just as some people may be more likely to engage in, or experience, bullying in the workplace, there may be certain features of the work environment that make bullying more common. A large-scale study by Smith, Singer, Hoel, and Cooper (2003) showed that the experience of bullying at school may predispose victims to later experiences of workplace bullying. Respondents who had been victimised at school were more likely to have been bullied at work in the last five years than respondents who had not been bullied at school. However, it is important to note that the relationship was inferred on the basis of retrospective reports of school bullying that may have been inaccurately recalled or distorted in the light of subsequent experiences of bullying in the workplace.

A meta-analysis of 90 victimisation studies by Bowling and Beehr (2006) found a small effect size for negative affectivity of the victim as a predictor of experiencing bullying in the workplace. Negative affectivity describes the tendency to experience distress, to be highly sensitive to negative events, and to have a pessimistic view of the self. No effects were found for victim age or gender, but Hoel, Rayner, and Cooper (1999) noted that men are mostly bullied by other men, whereas women are bullied by men as well as by women. Notelaers, Witte, and Einarsen (2010) found a significant, but small negative association between level of qualification and experience of workplace bullying, which suggests that bullying is somewhat less common at higher levels of qualification. By contrast, some studies suggest that sexual harassment is more commonly directed at higher-status women, who are seen as violating traditional female gender roles and assuming characteristics that are more desirable in men (O'Leary-Kelly, Bowes-Sperry, Bates, & Lean, 2009).

Many studies have related victimisation by workplace bullying to personality characteristics, drawing mainly on the "Big Five" personality factors (see also Chapter 4). In a meta-analysis of 101 effect sizes, a significant, but small positive association was found between workplace bullying victimisation and neuroticism, and negative associations with agreeableness, conscientiousness, and extraversion (Nielsen, Glasø, & Einarsen, 2017). However, all the studies had a correlational design, linking personality measures to reports of being bullied at the same point in time and are therefore unable to decide whether personality is the cause or the consequence of the bullying experience.

Higher effect sizes were found by Bowling and Beehr (2006) for risk factors inherent in the work environment, particularly work constraints, role conflict, and role ambiguity. Leymann (1993) suggested that power differentials within organisations play an important role. He found that 37% of all bullying incidents involved a person in a senior position who bullied a subordinate, 44% involved individuals of the same hierarchical position, and only a minority of victims were bullied by someone in a lower hierarchical position. Poor leadership quality, reflected by authoritarian management methods and communication problems, is an important organisational characteristic that allows workplace bullying to develop and persist.

Organisational characteristics also play an important role in understanding and predicting sexual harassment. Role ambiguity and job insecurity are critical stressors associated with increased levels of experiencing sexual harassment (van den Brande, Baillien, Witte, Vander Elst, & Godderis, 2016). Moreover, workplace bullying is more likely when organisations undergo change, possibly due to increased potential for conflict under conditions of uncertainty (Rai & Agarwal, 2018). In their meta-analysis, Willness, Steel, and Lee (2007) found that organisational climate was the strongest predictor of sexual harassment. Aspects of organisational climate conducive to sexual harassment are lack of sanctions for harassers and perceived risks of complaining for victims, both of which are indicators of a tolerance of sexual harassment.

A further organisational risk factor for sexual harassment is a masculine work environment that can be defined in terms of the workplace gender ratio or gendered power hierarchy with a predominance of men in more senior positions. A prime example of a masculine work environment is the military, and many studies have identified sexual harassment as a problem in this domain (Stander & Thomsen, 2016; Turchik, 2012). Another setting in which male dominance is combined with a strong power hierarchy is academia. Even though women account for a large proportion of students and relatively low-status clerical workers, men hold the majority of senior positions. Evidence of widespread sexual harassment in academic institutions has been provided by several sources (e.g., Hill & Silva, 2005; National Academies of Sciences, Engineering, and Medicine, 2018). In addition to aspects of workplace structure, gender stereotypes shared at a more general level contribute to sexual harassment. An important aspect here is the difference between men and women in terms of perceiving sexually charged comments and behaviours as inappropriate and offensive (Hunter & McClelland, 1991; Jones & Remland, 1992).

Consequences of workplace bullying

There is conclusive evidence that workplace bullying is associated with significant impairment of the victims' work-related functioning, mental health, and physical well-being, as documented in several reviews and meta-analyses. A meta-analysis of 55 studies by Hershcovis and Barling (2010) examined the effects of workplace bullying on a range of negative outcomes, distinguishing between bullying by supervisors, co-workers, and people from outside the organisation (e.g., customers). The results showed that being bullied by a supervisor was significantly more harmful than being bullied by co-workers, as indicated by higher psychological distress and intention to leave, reduced job satisfaction, and lower work performance. Being bullied by a co-worker in the workplace was more harmful than being bullied by someone from outside the workplace.

Regarding work-related outcomes, a significant association between bullying victimisation and sickness absence was established in the meta-analysis by Nielsen, Indregard, and Øverland (2016). Moreover, the meta-analysis by Yang, Caughlin, Gazica, Truxillo, and Spector (2014) found that a work climate of mistreatment was linked to reduced organisational commitment and job satisfaction and higher turnover intentions and work strain. These findings show that bullying involves costs not only for the individual members of the workforce but also for the organisation as a whole (Rai & Agarwal, 2018).

Documenting the serious impact of workplace bullying, a review by Leach, Poyser, and Butterworth (2017) found evidence of significant associations between bullying experiences and suicidal thoughts. In one of the few longitudinal studies on outcomes of workplace bullying, Nielsen, Nielsen, Notelaers, and Einarsen (2015) found that workplace bullying assessed at the first data wave predicted suicidal ideation at two subsequent data waves two and five years later. Moreover, a significant association between workplace bullying and *post-traumatic stress disorder* (PTSD) was established in the meta-analysis by Nielsen, Tangen, Idsoe, Matthiesen, and Magerøy (2015).

Just like workplace bullying in general, sexual harassment has serious consequences both for the victims and for the institution or organisation involved. Meta-analyses by Willness et al. (2007) and Chan, Lam, Chow, and Cheung (2008) identified significant negative effects of sexual harassment on a range of physical and mental health outcomes, including an increased risk of developing post-traumatic stress disorder. They also found negative effects on global job satisfaction, organisational commitment, and work group productivity. Victims of sexual harassment had higher rates of absenteeism and job turnover than non-victimised members of the workforce, indicating that the tolerance of sexual harassment is not only painful for the victims but also costly for the organisation (Sims, Drasgow, & Fitzgerald, 2005). No gender differences in the adverse consequences of sexual harassment were found by Chan et al. (2008), but age played a role as a moderator, with younger employees being more negatively affected.

post-traumatic stress disorder (PTSD): characteristic pattern of symptoms observed in survivors of traumatic experiences, such as sexual assault.

Interventions

Despite growing evidence of the negative effects of workplace bullying, there has been a shortage of interventions and their evaluation. Given the finding that bullying is more widespread in work environments with high levels of stress and problematic handling of occupational roles, an obvious intervention strategy is to reduce the stress levels within the organisation by fostering a positive organisational climate (Duffy, 2009). A review of eight intervention studies that used experimental and quasi-experimental designs with a pre-intervention and at least one post-intervention data wave, only one of which randomly assigned participants to an intervention and a control condition, was conducted by Escartín (2016). The studies were diverse in the target variables addressed by the intervention, with a primary aim of achieving a reduction in bullying prevalence at the organisation level, and additional aims, such as improving job satisfaction and reducing depressive symptoms. Five of the eight studies successfully reduced the prevalence of bullying from pre- to post-intervention, the other three yielded inconclusive results. The author highlights the need for studies using better evaluation designs to examine the efficacy of intervention efforts to reduce workplace bullying, a claim echoed by the authors of another recent review including only randomised-control trials (Gillen, Sinclair, Kernohan, Begley, & Luyben, 2017).

The first sections of this chapter on aggression as part of everyday life examined two forms of aggression in the public sphere, school bullying and workplace bullying, both of which have lasting negative effects on their victims. Although the research literature has provided some converging evidence, the majority of the findings are based on cross-sectional surveys that cannot disentangle cause–effect relationships. For example, it could be the case the negative affectivity identified to be higher in victims of bullying is a result, rather than a risk factor for experiencing workplace bullying. Similarly, role ambiguity could be the result rather than the cause of bullying in the workplace. Research on the outcomes of victimisation is also mostly cross-sectional, thus precluding a causal interpretation of the findings. For example, it may be possible that individuals are targeted as victims because of their emotional vulnerability or lower job performance, rather than developing these problems as a result of being bullied. Research using prospective designs – for example, with children who start at a new school or employees who start at a new organisation without any previous history of contact – would help to illuminate the mechanisms involved in bullying at schools and in the workplace, both at the level of the individuals involved and at the level of the social system in which they interact. Theory-based interventions are needed, and their efficacy should be examined by rigorous evaluation designs.

AGGRESSION ON THE ROADS

Another everyday context in which aggression is frequently observed is driving a car. Most motorists would admit that they become angry with other road users at least occasionally and may have behaved in an aggressive manner towards them. In terms of the situational factors promoting such responses, moving through traffic involves many frustrations. Drivers may find their progress impeded due to a high volume of traffic or through the behaviour of other motorists, they may have difficulty finding a free space when they are in a hurry to park their car, or they may feel provoked by the assertive or dangerous driving style of others. Thus, it is not surprising that frustration-related anger is often experienced in a driving context and gives rise to aggressive behaviour. In this section, we review the extensive research literature that has examined the role of personal and situational variables affecting aggressive driving. Many studies have found associations between aggressive driving and accident involvement, so understanding risk factors for aggressive driving and the underlying psychological processes has significant practical implications for improving road safety (Galovski, Malta, & Blanchard, 2006; Mann et al., 2007).

Definition and measurement of aggressive driving

aggressive driving: behaviour intended to physically, emotionally, or psychologically harm another within the driving environment.

Aggressive driving may be defined as "any behavior intended to physically, emotionally, or psychologically harm another within the driving environment" (Hennessy & Wiesenthal, 2001, p. 661). This definition is consistent with the general definition of aggression as a behaviour carried out with the intention of harming another person (see Chapter 1). It consists of a range of specific actions, which vary in terms of the severity of harm inflicted and the potential to create dangerous traffic situations. Hennessy and Wiesenthal (2002) differentiated between mild driver aggression (e.g., horn honking or hand gestures) and driver violence (e.g., fighting or deliberate contact). Aggressive driving motivated by the intention to harm needs to be distinguished from *reckless* or *assertive driving* (i.e., driving in a risky and selfish manner), which may cause harm to other drivers, but the harm is accidental rather than deliberate (Hennessy & Wiesenthal, 2002). However, other authors have suggested a broader definition of driving aggression that includes aggressive and reckless/assertive driving, defining it as "a dysfunctional pattern of social behaviors that constitutes a serious threat to public safety" (Houston, Harris, & Norman, 2003, p. 269). Most scales eliciting reports of aggressive driving are based on this broader definition, including both hostile aggression, motivated by the intent to harm, such as swearing at other drivers, and instrumental aggression, motivated by the desire to make progress, such as speeding, that constitute a threat to safety on the roads (for a summary of measures, see Van Rooy, Rotton, & Burns, 2006).

Although some authors have used aggressive driving and road rage as interchangeable and the two constructs clearly overlap, road rage more

narrowly denotes extreme acts of aggressive driving, involving assaultive behaviour with the intention of causing bodily harm and possible homicide (Ellison-Potter, Bell, & Deffenbacher, 2001). Road rage is a criminal offence and is far less common than the more general construct of aggressive driving, which includes behaviours such as honking the horn when annoyed, or swearing at other drivers. Some authors have identified road rage as a psychological disorder (Ayar, 2006).

The most common method of assessing aggressive driving is through drivers' self-reports. Several instruments have been developed that present different forms of aggressive driving behaviour and ask drivers to indicate how frequently they have engaged in each behaviour in the past (Van Rooy et al., 2006). Reports of aggressive driving obtained through self-reports have been linked to personality traits as risk factors (e.g., Lustman, Wiesenthal, & Flett, 2010), and also to reports of accident involvement as a correlate of aggressive driving (e.g., Mann et al., 2007). Moreover, several studies have used modern communication technology, such as beepers or mobile phones, to elicit state measures of anger and reports of aggressive driving while participants are actually on the road (Hennessy & Wiesenthal, 1999). Box 7.2 presents items from two instruments used to elicit self-reports of aggressive driving.

The *Driving Anger Expression Inventory* (DAX) by Deffenbacher, Lynch, Oetting, and Swaim (2002; Deffenbacher, Stephens, & Sullman, 2016) measures drivers' general propensity to engage in aggressive behaviour when they are angry while driving. It consists of four subscales, referring to (a) verbal aggression, (b) personal physical aggression, (c) using one's vehicle to express aggression, and (d) displacing aggression onto people other than the annoying motorist. A fifth subscale measures adaptive/constructive responses to anger-eliciting traffic situations. This subscale should be negatively related to the other four facets and to aggressive driving behaviour.

Comparing scores on the DAX in Danish drivers in 2008 and 2016, Møller and Haustein (2018) found that the proportion of drivers who reported expressing at least one form of anger in the past 12 months increased from 16% to 26%. The gender difference decreased in the same period. The fact that the largest increase was found among drivers in the most densely populated area around the capital city of Copenhagen is consistent with the view that frustrating driving conditions may precipitate driving anger and aggression. To measure aggressive driving in a specific situation, Hennessy and Wiesenthal's (1999) *State Behaviour Checklist* provides a brief assessment tool for contacting drivers while driving and asking them to indicate whether they engaged in aggressive driving in the previous five minutes of their journey.

A second, less frequently used approach is to study aggressive driving through behavioural observation in a driving simulator to obtain data analogous to real-life behaviour behind the wheel. Participants are exposed to different traffic situations in the virtual reality of the driving simulator to record their aggressive behaviour. An example of this method is the study

---

Box 7.2   Items measuring general and situation-specific aggressive driving behaviour

Example Items from the *Driving Anger Expression Scale* (DAX; Deffenbacher et al., 2002, Table 1)

How *often* do you *generally* react or behave in the manner described *when you are angry or furious while driving?*

Verbal aggressive expression

- I make negative comments about the other driver aloud.
- I yell questions like 'Where did you get your license?'

Personal physical aggressive expression

- I try to get out of the car and tell the other driver off.
- I try to force the other driver to the side of the road.

Use of vehicle to express anger

- I drive right up on the other driver's bumper.
- I speed up to frustrate the other driver.

Displaced aggression

- I yell at the people who are riding with me.
- I take my anger out on other people riding with me.

Adaptive/constructive responses (reverse coding)

- I try to think of positive things.
- I pay even closer attention to other's driving to avoid accidents.

Items from the *State Behaviour Checklist* (Hennessy & Wiesenthal, 1999, p. 423)

Please indicate whether you have employed the following behaviours during the last five minutes of this particular commute:

- Horn honking at other drivers out of frustration
- Purposely tailgating other drivers
- Flashing your high beams at another driver out of frustration
- Hand gestures at other drivers
- Swearing at other drivers

Adapted from Deffenbacher et al., 2002
and Hennessy & Wiesenthal, 1999.

by Bushman et al. (2017) on the effect of a weapon as a cue promoting aggressive behaviour that was discussed in Chapter 5. This approach typically yields lower correlations with risk factors or antecedents, such as state or trait anger (Nesbit, Conger, & Conger, 2007). A good example of the use of driving simulators to observe aggressive driving under controlled conditions is the study by Ellison-Potter et al. (2001). Their simulated driving task was designed as follows:

> The actual simulation task was programmed to include several potentially frustrating events (e.g., jaywalking, slow vehicles ahead, tailgating, general traffic congestion). The simulation included nine incidents of jaywalking involving 52 pedestrians, seven traffic lights, all of which were programmed to turn red when the subject approached them, and 116 other vehicles on the road. Hence, participants had the opportunity to hit pedestrians 9 times, run a red light 7 times, and hit another vehicle 116 times. Opportunities for off-road collisions were unlimited.
> (Ellison-Potter et al., 2001, p. 436)

Dependent measures were the average speed, number of red lights run, number of collisions, and number of pedestrians killed. We will turn to the findings from this experiment below.

Finally, some field experiments, conducted under naturalistic conditions, studied the impact of situational variables, such as heat, time pressure, or status of the offending car, and used horn honking as a measure of aggressive driving (for a summary, see Ellison-Potter et al., 2001). However, the validity of horn honking as a measure of aggression is questionable, as drivers may also use it as a way of communicating with other drivers that is not necessarily based on intent to harm.

Anger and aggressive driving

As shown in Chapter 2, anger is conceptualised as a critical affective state triggering aggressive behaviour, especially in response to frustration and other aversive events. Because moving through traffic can involve many frustrations, the frustration–aggression hypothesis and its extension in the cognitive neo-associationist model of aggression, both discussed in Chapter 2, offer theoretical explanations of aggressive driving behaviour. A meta-analysis by Nesbit et al. (2007) that included 28 samples found an average correlation of $r = .37$ between state anger and drivers' aggressive behaviour.

Individuals differ in their propensity to get angry (see also Chapter 4), and these individual differences are also likely to moderate responses to frustrating traffic situations, as proposed by the state-trait model of driving anger by Deffenbacher and colleagues (e.g., Deffenbacher, Deffenbacher, Lynch, & Richards, 2003). A meta-analysis that linked dispositional anger to aggressive driving found a significant effect size of moderate magnitude between general proneness to anger and aggressive driving behaviour across 33 studies (Bogdan, Măirean, & Havârneanu, 2016). Individual differences in anger proneness should be related to state anger and driving behaviour under stressful, but not under nonstressful driving conditions. Correlational evidence supports this link between trait and state driving anger under high as opposed to low frustration conditions (Deffenbacher, Lynch, Oetting, & Yingling, 2001).

In support of the state-trait model, a driving simulator study by Deffenbacher et al. (2003) found no difference between drivers who scored high and low in dispositional driving anger in low impedance situations, which involved no frustrations, but individual differences in driving anger did predict aggressive driving behaviour in high impedance situations. After they were made to drive under conditions where their progress was impeded, participants who scored high on trait driving anger reported significantly more state anger and a greater urge to be verbally and physically aggressive than did participants who scored low on trait anger. A meta-analytic review of 48 studies by Demir, Demir, and Özkan (2016) found significant overall correlations between the subscales of the DAX and aggressive driving in the expected direction, with the highest effect sizes for the verbal aggression ($r = .41$) and the use of the vehicle to express aggression ($r = .37$). A further meta-analysis by Zhang and Chan (2016) established a small, but significant association between driving anger and accident involvement across 17 studies.

Personal risk factors of aggressive driving

In addition to trait anger, several other personal characteristics have been linked to aggressive driving behaviour. Harris and Houston (2010) found significant correlations between aggressive driving and boredom susceptibility (i.e., an aversion to repetitive experiences of any kind). Boredom susceptibility is a component of sensation seeking, a personality trait characterised by the need for varied, novel, complex, and intense sensations and experiences to maintain an optimal level of arousal, associated with a high propensity towards risk taking (Zuckerman, 2007). Other studies established a link between aggressive driving and high levels of narcissism, defined as a grandiose feeling of superiority and a sense of entitlement that leads to aggression when challenged by others (see Chapter 4; Bushman, Steffgen, Kerwin, Whitlock, & Weisenberger, 2018; Lustman et al., 2010). A driving simulation study with men found that the more participants reported an obsessive passion for driving (example item: "I have difficulties controlling my urge to drive"), the more aggressively they drove as rated by independent observers (Philippe, Vallerand, Richer, Vallières, & Bergeron, 2009).

Age. Age is another personal characteristic linked to aggressive driving. Several studies suggest that aggressive driving is more common among younger than among older motorists (Vanlaar, Simpson, Mayhew, &

Robertson, 2008). There is evidence from official statistics on accident involvement and registered violations, as well as from self-reports, that aggressive driving declines with age (e.g., Åberg & Rimmö, 1998; Blockey & Hartley, 1995; Lajunen & Parker, 2001). In addition, there is evidence of an interactive effect of gender and age. Young *male* drivers have a disproportionately high risk of accident involvement and aggressive driving, and the gender gap diminishes with age. Lajunen and Parker (2001) found that age was associated with a decrease in aggressive driving behaviour among their male but not their female respondents.

Gender and gender-related self-concept. With regard to the role of gender, studies using self-reports of driving behaviour overwhelmingly suggest that men are more prone to aggressive driving (Vanlaar et al., 2008). In a study of motorists from the U.K., Finland, and the Netherlands, Parker, Lajunen, and Summala (2002) found that male drivers reacted more aggressively than did female drivers when other drivers impeded their progress or showed inconsiderate and impatient driving behaviour. Surveys show that men are more likely than women to deliberately violate traffic rules and hold attitudes about driving that may be related to aggressive and reckless driving, such as believing that men's driving skills are superior to women's (Brake, 2012; Pravossoudovitch, Martha, Cury, & Granié, 2015).

Several other studies have confirmed this gender difference (e.g., Åberg & Rimmö, 1998; Blockey & Hartley, 1995; Ellison-Potter et al., 2001; Lawton, Parker, Manstead, & Stradling, 1997). However, when aggressive driving was subdivided into mild driver aggression (e.g., horn honking out of frustration, hand gestures) and driver violence (e.g., physical confrontations, chasing other vehicles), a more differentiated picture of the role of gender differences emerged. Hennessy and Wiesenthal (2001) found that men scored higher on a measure of driving violence than did women, but no gender differences emerged with respect to mild driver aggression. A subsequent study narrowed down the higher prevalence of driving violence in men to a combination of male gender and endorsement of a vengeful attitude to driving (Hennessy & Wiesenthal, 2002).

A further body of research has examined gender-related self-concept rather than biological sex as a correlate of aggressive driving. Aggression in general and driving aggression in particular have been highlighted as central elements of the masculine gender role. The social role model (Eagly & Wood, 1999; see Chapter 4) posits that gender differences in aggression are the result of an individual's social learning experiences. They are rooted in differential gender role socialisation that rewards males for being assertive and dominant and females for being caring and submissive. Within each gender group, individuals differ in the extent to which they endorse traditional gender stereotypes of masculinity and femininity as part of their self-schemata (Bem, 1981). A subgroup of men were identified who show an exaggerated endorsement of the masculine gender role in the form of a "macho personality". The more men endorsed this macho image of masculinity, the more aggressive driving they were found to report in a study by Krahé and Fenske (2002). In a study that addressed women's gender-related self-concept, femininity was associated with lower levels of driving aggression, when trait aggression was controlled for, suggesting that femininity buffered aggressive driving (Krahé, 2005). Assessing both positive and negative facets of male and female participants' gendered self-concept, Krahé (2018) showed that negative masculinity (describing oneself with negative masculine attributes, such as "boastful") was positively related to driving anger, but that this link was eliminated for participants scoring high on positive femininity (describing the self with positive feminine attributes, such as "tender").

Contextual risk factors of aggressive driving

It has already become clear that aggressive driving is not only a function of drivers' personal characteristics, but is also critically affected by features of the driving context. Two contextual risk factors have received particular attention in research on aggressive driving: traffic congestion and anonymity. In addition, exposure to risk-glorifying media has been examined as an instigator of aggressive driving in the form of intentional violation of traffic rules.

Traffic congestion. Consistent with the proposition that frustration may increase aggression, congested traffic conditions that frustrate drivers' goal of making swift progress have been found to precipitate aggressive driving. Hennessy and Wiesenthal (1999) studied commuters whose route was either low or high in traffic volume, and contacted them via mobile phones during their journey to elicit ratings of driver stress and driving behaviours. Drivers on the high-volume traffic routes reported significantly more acute stress and more aggressive driving behaviours than did commuters on the low congestion route. Similarly, Harris and Houston (2010) reported that more tailgating occurred in heavy traffic. Hennessy, Wiesenthal, and Kohn (2000) found significantly higher levels of acute driver stress under high than under low traffic congestion conditions, and in situations of high as opposed to low time urgency, especially for drivers who were dispositionally prone to stress while driving.

Anonymity. Aggressive behaviour is generally more prevalent under conditions of anonymity (see Chapter 10), and driving a car provides such conditions. Although it is possible to identify the car, the aggressive driver's personal identity is typically concealed from others. Supporting the role of anonymity, Harris and Houston (2010) found that drivers reported more aggressive driving when they were alone in the car than when passengers were present, and an observational field study by Wiesenthal and Janovjak (1992) found that drivers in cars with tinted windows committed more deliberate violations of traffic rules. However, these correlational findings could be due to differences in the personalities of drivers who chose to drive cars with tinted windows, rather than reflecting the causal role of anonymity. By contrast, Ellison-Potter et al. (2001) used an experimental

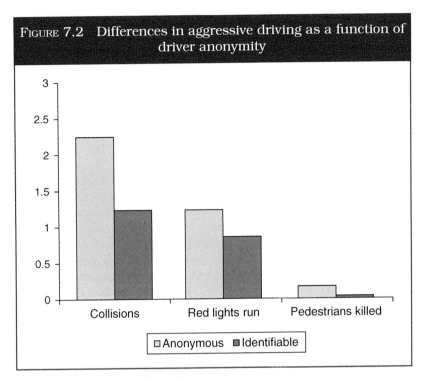

FIGURE 7.2   Differences in aggressive driving as a function of driver anonymity

Adapted from Ellison-Potter et al., 2001, Table 1.

manipulation of anonymity by telling their participants to imagine that the vehicle assigned to them in the driving simulator was an open-top convertible that would enable others to identify them personally (no anonymity), or that the vehicle was a convertible with the top closed, so that others would be able to identify the car, but not them personally (anonymity). A significant effect of the anonymity manipulation was found on all measures of aggressive driving. Participants drove faster in the anonymous condition (on average 43 miles/hour or 69 km/hour) than in the identifiable condition (on average 40 miles/hour or 64 km/hour). Moreover, they drove through more red lights, were involved in more collisions, and killed more pedestrians, as shown in Figure 7.2.

Risk-glorifying media. A final contextual factor relevant to the understanding of aggressive driving is the use of risk-glorifying media. For example, racing games in which drivers engage in speeding and other high-risk manoeuvres may contribute to more risky driving behaviour in the real world, which includes aggressive behaviour towards other drivers. A series of studies by Fischer and colleagues demonstrated that playing virtual racing games increased players' positive evaluations of risk taking, the accessibility of risk-promoting cognitions, and also risky behaviour in a driving simulator (e.g., Fischer et al., 2009; Fischer, Kubitzki, Guter, & Frey,

2007). Fischer et al. (2009) showed that the effects were evident only for racing games in which the violation of traffic rules was rewarded, and were mediated by a change in participants' self-concept in the direction of seeing themselves as reckless drivers. A meta-analysis including 11 studies found a moderate overall effect size between the use of media that glorify risky driving and risk-taking behaviour in simulated driving contexts (Fischer, Greitemeyer, Kastenmüller, Vogrincic, & Sauer, 2011).

Clarifying the psychological pathway from the use of risk-glorifying media to aggressive driving, Vingilis et al. (2016) found a positive association between playing "drive 'em up" video games and self-reported violations of traffic rules when driving on the roads, which was mediated by the extent to which participants had a self-concept as "risky drivers". "Drive' em up" games, such as *Carmageddon* or *Burnout*, involve intentionally crashing into other vehicles and killing pedestrians, and the finding that extensive engagement in these behaviours in the virtual reality of video games is linked to driving behaviour in real life is consistent with a social learning account of media influences (see Chapter 6). Also consistent with this explanation, the authors did not find a link between playing non-violent "circuit racing" games, which reward skilful, accurate driving, and aggressive driving behaviour in real life.

Interventions

Aggressive driving behaviour is a serious safety hazard on the roads. Therefore, there is a need for effective measures for preventing people from driving in a way that may harm others (and themselves). The research reviewed in this section suggests two potential avenues: (a) targeting the aggressive driver; and (b) changing the contextual conditions that precipitate aggressive driving. Given the important role of anger in eliciting aggressive driving behaviour, interventions that target aggressive drivers have focused on promoting better control of anger (for a general discussion of the anger management approach, see Chapter 12). Deffenbacher, Filetti, Lynch, Dahlen, and Oetting (2002) assigned participants who scored high on driver anger to an 8- to 9-week intervention that included three groups: one group focused on relaxation techniques, the second group received an intervention that combined relaxation exercises and cognitive techniques designed to promote cognitive appraisals of situations that would reduce anger while driving, and the third group was a non-intervention control condition. Measures of driver anger and aggressive driving behaviour were collected at baseline prior to the intervention, immediately after the intervention, and at a follow-up after four weeks. Both intervention conditions led to a significant reduction in driving anger immediately after the intervention, but the difference from the control condition was no longer significant at the 4-week follow-up. The self-reported likelihood of aggressive driving decreased significantly in both intervention groups, and was lower than in the control group immediately post-intervention. At the 4-week follow-up, only the combined cognitive training and relaxation group differed significantly from the control group. In a comprehensive review of intervention studies designed to reduce driving anger, Deffenbacher (2016) concluded that the few existing studies support the combination of cognitive interventions and relaxation techniques with elements of mindfulness techniques, such as meditation, as a further component to enhance intervention efficacy (Kazemeini, Ghanbari-e-Hashem-Abadi, & Safarzadeh, 2013).

In addition to helping anger-prone drivers to control their anger and develop non-aggressive ways of dealing with driving-related frustrations, changes in the driving context may be an effective way of reducing driver stress (Asbridge, Smart, & Mann, 2006). For example, promoting the use of public transport or introducing electronic traffic control systems may reduce congestion on the roads, thereby decreasing the experience of frustration. A study by Wiesenthal, Hennessy, and Totten (2000) explored the potential of music to buffer driver stress. They studied commuters who were using a route with either a high or a low traffic density, and randomly assigned them to either a music condition in which they were asked to listen to their favourite music during the entire journey, or a control group that was instructed not to listen to music (or any other media) during their journey. Participants were contacted by telephone twice during their journey and responded to a set of items measuring driver stress (e.g., "Trying but failing to overtake is frustrating me"). The findings from the study are presented in Figure 7.3.

A significant interaction was found between traffic congestion levels and the effects of music on driver stress. Under conditions of low congestion, driver stress was generally low, regardless of whether the participants had been listening to music or not. However, when congestion was high, participants listening to their favourite music were significantly less stressed than those in the non-music condition. These findings are consistent with the results of other research showing that pleasant music may buffer the effects of frustration on aggressive affect, cognition, and behaviour (Krahé & Bieneck, 2012; see also Chapter 12).

In summary, many studies have shown that driving through traffic is associated with a high potential for frustration. Consistent with theoretical accounts that have identified frustration as a powerful instigator of anger (see Chapter 2), frustrations encountered while driving give rise to anger, which in turn may trigger aggressive behaviour. For example, being slowed down by heavy traffic or provoked by the behaviour of other drivers instigates state anger that can lead to various forms of aggressive behaviour. Furthermore, being in the anonymity of one's car was found to lower the threshold for aggressive driving. The degree of state anger experienced in a frustrating traffic situation depends on the driver's dispositional proneness to anger. Additional personal characteristics that are related to differences in aggressive driving include age and gender, with younger motorists and men featuring more prominently among aggressive drivers. The reliance on

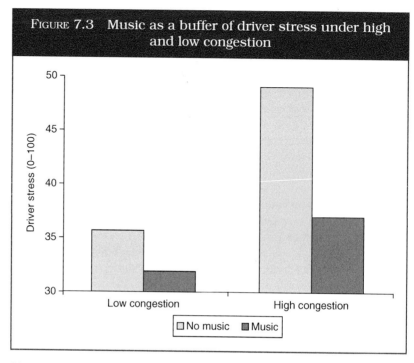

FIGURE 7.3   Music as a buffer of driver stress under high and low congestion

Adapted from Wiesenthal et al., 2000, Figure 1.

self-reports of driving anger and aggressive drivers is a limitation of many studies in this area, but there are also experimental studies that have used observations of driving behaviour in simulated conditions or in natural contexts to test causal hypotheses about risk factors for aggressive driving.

AGGRESSION IN THE SPORTS WORLD

Finally, an area in which aggression is common in everyday life is sports events, which provide a context for aggressive behaviour by performers as well as spectators (Young, 2019). As Russell (1993, p. 181) noted, "outside of wartime, sport is perhaps the only setting in which acts of interpersonal aggression are not only tolerated but enthusiastically applauded by large segments of society". Moreover, using the language of war is a common feature of the rhetoric surrounding sports events (Adubato, 2016). In this section, we review the limited body of psychological research on aggressive behaviour among performers as well as spectators who witness aggressive behaviour in the sports arena (Bartlett & Abrams, 2019; Kimble, Russo, Bergman, & Galindo, 2010; Spaaij & Schaillée, 2019). A clear example of aggressive behaviour by athletes is shown in Figure 7.4.

Aggressive behaviour in the sports context needs to be distinguished from competitive and assertive behaviour, motivated by the desire to win.

FIGURE 7.4 An example of sports aggression

Reprinted with permission, © 2019 by www.imago.com.

In line with Terry and Jackson (1985, p. 27), aggression in sport may be defined as "harm-inducing behavior bearing no direct relationship to the competitive goals of sport, and relates, therefore, to incidents of uncontrolled aggression outside the rules of sport, rather than highly competitive behavior within the rule boundaries". Two forms of aggression can be observed among competitors in sports events: *instrumental aggression*, carried out in order to promote the chances of winning, and *hostile aggression*, arising from the desire to harm another person as an expression of negative feelings (for the distinction between hostile and instrumental aggression, see Chapter 1). Although it is often difficult to distinguish between these two kinds of motivation, behaviours such as illegal tackling, tripping, or holding an opponent, would be examples of instrumental aggression, whereas behaviours such as shouting at the referee or hitting a teammate are examples of hostile aggression (Coulomb-Cabagno & Rascle, 2006).

Aggression by competitors

As with aggressive driving, predictors of aggressive behaviour in sport can be divided into two categories: personal characteristics of the actors involved, and contextual variables, such as aggression levels inherent in different sports or the outcome of contests in terms of defeat or victory (Spaaij & Schaillée, 2019). Among personal variables, several studies have identified gender as a marker of differences in the perceived legitimacy of aggressive behaviours and in the perpetration of aggressive acts. For example, male basketball players rated rule-violating behaviours as more legitimate than did female players (Duda, Olson, & Templin, 1991). In an observational study including 90 soccer games and 90 handball games in France, Coulomb-Cabagno and Rascle (2006) found that male players committed more acts of both instrumental and hostile aggression than did women across local, regional, and national levels of competition in both types of sport. In a study with male hockey players, Weinstein, Smith, and Wiesenthal (1995) showed that endorsement of a masculine gender identity was related to aggressive playing behaviour, and that more aggressive players were rated as more competent by teammates as well as coaches. With regard to personality variables, Bushman and Wells (1998) found that individual differences in high-school ice hockey players' levels of trait aggression were related to the penalties they incurred during the season for aggressive behaviour (e.g., tripping), whereas no correlation was found with penalties for non-aggressive rule breaking (e.g., delaying the game). Significant correlations were found by Maxwell (2004) between athletes' tendency of anger rumination and their self-reported aggressive behaviour (for a discussion of the construct of anger rumination, see Chapter 4).

Furthermore, several studies have found increased alcohol use among athletes in team sports. Together with the strong evidence linking alcohol use to aggression (see Chapter 5), this may explain increased levels of aggression both on and off the field, as documented in the review by Sønderlund et al. (2014). A study with over 2,000 athletes in amateur sports found that higher habitual alcohol use was significantly associated with intentional acts of violence during the sports activity in the past year and with a range of aggressive behaviours outside the sports context (O'Brien et al., 2018).

Another line of research has examined whether engagement in certain forms of sport is linked to a higher tendency to show aggressive behaviour outside the sports context (Kimble et al., 2010). For example, Endresen and Olweus (2005) found that boys engaging in power sports that involved physical fighting, such as boxing, wrestling, and martial arts, scored higher on measures of violent behaviour than did boys not practising these sports, and showed a significant increase over time not seen in the non-participating group. They explain the association by two complementary factors: the exposure to aggressive role models and the practising of physical aggression. However, a meta-analysis by Gubbels, van der Stouwe,

Spruit, and Stams (2016) found little overall evidence for an aggression-enhancing effect of martial arts, and another meta-analysis by Harwood, Lavidor, and Rassovsky (2017) even found some evidence for a reduction in youth's externalising behaviour through participation in martial arts. Further research is needed to clarify for whom and under what conditions engagement in martial arts may lead to negative or positive outcomes.

In terms of contextual risk factors, Reifman, Larrick, and Fein (1991) and Larrick, Timmerman, Carton, and Abrevaya (2011) found that the higher the temperature on the day of the match, the more aggressive acts baseball players committed against fellow players. This finding is consistent with other research on the heat hypothesis, discussed in Chapter 5. Frank and Gilovich (1988) reported a series of studies which showed that the colour of the team's outfit was linked to players' aggression, in particular the colour black. They argued that the colour black is associated with connotations of evil and badness, and should therefore serve as a cue affecting both the perceptions of others and the players' self-concept (for a discussion of the role of aggressive cues, see Chapter 5). In the first study, they established that those teams in the national football and hockey leagues who were wearing black were rated as more malevolent by participants who knew little about either sport and simply had to rate the teams based on photographs of their uniforms. The second study used archival records from 15 years of national league matches to demonstrate that teams who wore black received more penalties than their opponents, who wore uniforms of other colours. Two teams had switched from non-black to black uniforms during this period, and that change was accompanied by an increase in the number of penalties they received.

In a further experimental study, students who were knowledgeable football fans and experienced referees watched identical football scenes that were manipulated such that the players wore either black or white outfits. Across two different episodes of playing, both students and referees indicated a greater willingness to assign penalties to the teams when they were wearing black than when they were shown in white outfits, although the actions on the pitch had been exactly the same. The effect was even more pronounced among the referees than among the students. The findings for the referees are shown in Figure 7.5.

In the final experiment, Frank and Gilovich (1988) made participants wear either black or white sports shirts when choosing games in which they wanted to compete against another team. The games on offer were selected so as to differ in terms of aggressiveness (e.g., a dart gun duel or a putting contest). Participants were asked to choose five games, and the aggressiveness level of the five choices was used as a measure of aggression. Before donning the black or white shirt, each participant made a choice of games while wearing their normal clothes, and when they put on the black or white shirts, they were told that they would from then on be referred to as "the black team" or "the white team". The findings are shown in Figure 7.6.

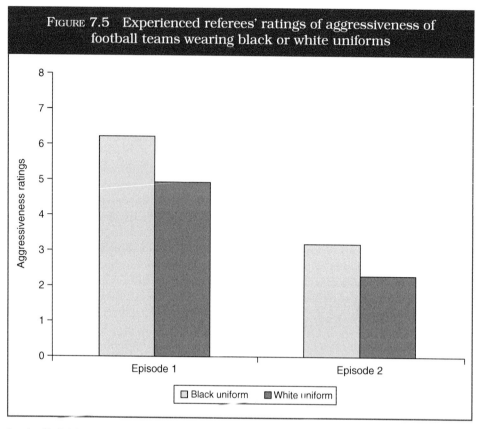

FIGURE 7.5   Experienced referees' ratings of aggressiveness of football teams wearing black or white uniforms

Based on Frank & Gilovich, 1988, p. 80.

The participants wearing black shirts and being referred to as "the black team" chose significantly more aggressive games than did the participants wearing white shirts and being called "the white team". However, the groups did not differ in the choices made under individualised conditions when they were wearing their normal clothes (for a discussion of the role of uniforms in undermining people's sense of individuality and adherence to personal norms, to create a state of de-individuation, see Chapter 10). The findings by Frank and Gilovich (1988) indicate that the colour black is an aggression-related cue that affects people's self-perceptions and the way in which their behaviour is judged by others.

Aggression by spectators

A second body of research has assessed the impact of watching sports aggression on spectators' aggressive tendencies (Spaaij, 2014). Simons and Taylor (1992) pointed out that sports which require extensive physical

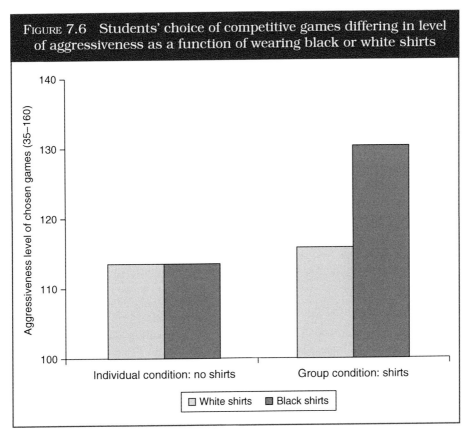

FIGURE 7.6   Students' choice of competitive games differing in level of aggressiveness as a function of wearing black or white shirts

Adapted from Frank & Gilovich, 1988, Table 4.

contact are more likely to elicit aggressive tendencies in the spectators. Arms, Russell, and Sandilands (1979) found that participants exposed to a wrestling competition (stylised aggression) or an ice hockey match (realistic aggression) subsequently showed greater hostility and punitiveness (i.e., the tendency to assign harsh sentences to individuals convicted of serious crimes) than spectators of a swimming contest (non-aggressive condition). This finding directly contradicts the notion of symbolic *catharsis*, derived from psychoanalytic theorising, which suggests that aggressive tension may be reduced by observing aggressive sports (see Chapters 2 and 12 for a discussion of the catharsis construct). Interestingly, Wann, Carlson, Holland et al. (1999) showed that individuals who engaged in, or liked to watch, aggressive sports particularly adhered to the idea that aggressive tensions may be relieved through sporting activity. Several other studies reviewed by Russell (2004) further supported the claim that the more aggression is shown by the players, the more aggression is displayed by those who are watching.

catharsis: release of aggressive tension through symbolic engagement in aggressive behaviour.

There is evidence that aggression which builds up in the context of watching a sports event may spill over into other domains. Sachs and Chu (2000) analysed police records spanning a 3-year period to examine the association between football events and the number of police calls to a domestic violence incident. They found that the number of police dispatches was higher at weekends than during the rest of the week and, more importantly, that the increase was substantially greater for weekends when there was a football event than for non-football weekends. A similar association was reported by Adubato (2016).

Contextual factors, such as the outcome of the game and alcohol use, were found to play a role in a file analysis of discipline cases at a university in the U.S. over a period of four years. Coons, Howard-Hamilton, and Waryold (1995) discovered that significantly more discipline incidents occurred during football weekends than during non-football weekends, and during home games compared with away games. Perhaps counterintuitively, the number of discipline incidents was significantly higher when the team had won than when it had lost the game. Almost half of the incidents involved the consumption of alcohol, highlighting the link between alcohol and aggressive behaviour discussed in Chapter 5. A similar finding was reported by Moore, Shepherd, Eden, and Sivarajasingam (2007) for rugby fans who were surveyed after a match that ended in a victory, a defeat, or a draw of their favoured team. Those in the victory and draw groups rated themselves as more aggressive compared with a group of fans who were surveyed before the game, but those in the defeat group did not.

Addressing changes in physiological responses, Bernhardt, Dabbs, Fielden, and Lutter (1998) conducted two studies in which they measured the testosterone levels of spectators at a baseball match (Study 1) or a televised World Cup football match (Study 2) both before and after the match. They found that testosterone levels increased from baseline among those participants who saw their favourite team win, and decreased among those who saw their favourite team lose. Given the link between testosterone levels and aggression discussed in Chapter 2, these findings can help to explain why aggression may be increased more by a victory than by a defeat of the spectator's favourite team. Over the course of two seasons, White, Katz, and Scarborough (1992) found significantly higher rates of women admitted to hospital for domestic violence injuries after victories of the local football team than after lost games. To explain their findings, the authors suggested that "viewing a hypermasculine activity in which force is used to successfully overcome others increases the likelihood that male spectators will become physically aggressive with their partners" (White et al., 1992, p. 158). However, it should be noted that the data are only correlational, showing a co-variation between wins and losses on the one hand and domestic violence incidents on the other, and therefore they do not provide evidence of a causal influence of game outcomes on fans' perpetration of domestic violence.

With regard to personal characteristics, the gender difference found for aggressive behaviour by competitors is mirrored among fans. Male adolescents rated aggressive behaviour in a range of different sport scenarios as significantly more legitimate than did their female age-matched peers (Conroy, Silva, Newcomer, Walker, & Johnson, 2001). Wann, Haynes, McLean, and Pullen (2003) found that men reported a significantly greater likelihood than did women that they would commit anonymous hostile acts of physical aggression (e.g., "trip the star player of the rival team" and even "murder the star player of the rival team"). For both genders, however, positive correlations were found between identification with their own team and willingness to commit acts of hostile aggression towards the rival team.

Fan identification has consistently been identified as a predictor of aggressive behaviour. Van Hiel, Hautman, Cornelis, and Clercq (2007) showed that the more football fans identified with their favourite team, the more physical and verbal aggression they reported showing in the context of football matches. In a field study, Wann, Carlson, and Schrader (1999) asked spectators at a college basketball match to complete a measure of how much they identified with their team prior to the match. After the match, participants indicated how many acts of instrumental verbal aggression (e.g., yelling at an official, opposing player, or coach because they thought this would help their team to win) and hostile verbal aggression (e.g., yelling at an official, opposing player, or coach because they were mad at him or her and wanted to show their anger) they had shown in the course of the match. Fans who identified strongly with their team reported significantly higher rates of both instrumental and hostile verbal aggression than did fans who identified less strongly. A subsequent study found that fans who identified strongly with their team were more likely to commit anonymous acts of physical hostile aggression against the rival team when their team had lost than after a victory (Wann et al., 2005).

Fan identification with a team not only predicts the behaviour of individuals, but is also crucially important for understanding the problem of collective spectator aggression or "hooliganism", which is notorious in the context of football matches. Several studies have found a link between trait measures of physical aggression and involvement in sports riots (for a review, see Russell, 2004). In their explanation of football hooliganism, Murphy, Williams, and Dunning (1990) have argued that this phenomenon is a form of aggression typically shown by young working-class males. They identified a subculture of aggressive masculinity, "predominantly, but not solely lower class" (p. 13), which provides the normative framework for the violent behaviour shown by football fans. Alcohol use and the level of violence on the pitch exacerbated the influence of masculinity norms on spectators' aggressive behaviour (Dunning, Murphy, & Williams, 1986). The significance of violence-condoning social norms in explaining football hooliganism was also apparent in an Italian study, in which violent fans cited "solidarity with the fan club" as their primary motive for participating in disturbances around football matches (Zani & Kirchler, 1991). The assertive nature of the game itself as well as the aggression displayed by the players in the course of the match provide additional cues that may reinforce aggressive tendencies in the spectators.

In addition to considering the individual actor, examining hooliganism as an intergroup phenomenon helps us to understand aggressive escalation in the context of football matches. Stott, Hutchison, and Drury (2001) provided a qualitative analysis that compared the behaviour of English and Scottish fans during the 1998 Football World Cup in France. They sought to understand why the English supporters were repeatedly involved in violent clashes with local youths, whereas the Scottish supporters were not. Stott et al. identified situational variables, such as perceived hostility from the outgroup and lack of police protection against illegitimate violent outgroup activities, that led English fans to close ranks and view their aggressive responses as legitimate. By contrast, Scottish fans perceived their relationship with the local youths as friendly and legitimate, and were disapproving of violent behaviour shown by members of their ingroup. The Scottish supporters cited a further reason for abstaining from aggressive behaviour, which is interesting from an intergroup perspective. One of them was quoted by Stott et al. (2001, p. 372) as saying that "No one causes trouble at Scottish games any more 'cause it makes the English look bad". This statement shows that the dynamics involved in the regulation of intergroup conflict need to be examined not just in the immediate relationships between the groups involved, but also taking into consideration the more complex issues of strategic differentiation from third parties. We shall look at other forms of intergroup aggression and discuss theoretical explanations of intergroup behaviour in more detail in Chapter 10.

To address the problem of violence associated with sports events, a variety of strategies and control mechanisms have been implemented (for a summary, see Russell, 2008). These include legal measures, such as banning identified hooligans from attending matches, or prohibiting the sale of alcohol before matches, and organisational measures, such as enforcing strategic seating arrangements for opposing fan groups and segregating rival fan clubs on their way to and from the stadium (see, for example, in the U.K. the Violent Crime Reduction Act, 2006, www.legislation.gov. uk/ukpga/2006/38/contents, and the 1989 Football Spectators Act, www. legislation.gov.uk/ukpga/1989/37/contents). In addition, measures can be directed at athletes as well as at spectators to promote anger management or induce positive affect that is incompatible with anger responses (see also Chapter 12). Finally, the strategic positioning of peaceful role models in aggressive crowds may be an effective approach, which is suggested by social learning theory (see Chapter 2), but systematic evaluations in the context of sporting events have yet to be conducted.

SUMMARY

- Aggression is a widespread feature of many domains of public life. The school, the workplace, the road, and the sports arena are environments in which aggressive encounters are common. A large body of research has examined the prevalence and potential risk factors of these forms of aggression.
- School bullying is a form of aggressive behaviour that is characterised by an imbalance of power between aggressor and victim and by occurring over a prolonged period of time. It can take the form of both physical and relational aggression, and is recognised as a problem across many countries. Cyberbullying is a new form of harassment involving the use of electronic devices that allows perpetrators to remain anonymous and reach a large audience. Some studies suggest that the experience of being bullied in school makes victims vulnerable to long-term psychological problems, including an increased risk of suicide and later experience of bullying in the workplace.
- Workplace bullying refers to behaviours intended to make another person feel miserable at work over prolonged periods. Like school bullying, it is defined by a power differential between victim and perpetrator, and it is more prevalent in environments characterised by a high level of work stress. Sexual harassment is a specific form of workplace bullying, and consists of sex-related behaviours that are unwanted by the recipient or perceived as hostile, offensive, or degrading. It is directed primarily at women and is more common in male-dominated work environments. Workplace bullying has been linked to significant impairments of victims' job satisfaction and psychological well-being, and is also costly at the organisational level in terms of high rates of absenteeism and turnover.

- Aggressive driving is a significant safety hazard on the roads. It is more common among male than female drivers, and its prevalence decreases with age. Personality variables, such as trait aggression and trait anger, are associated with aggressive driving behaviour, but situational variables, such as anonymity and frustrating traffic conditions that impede progress, are equally important. These conditions contribute to the experience of driver stress that lowers the threshold for aggressive behaviour. Therefore, strategies for reducing driver stress may also be effective in reducing aggressive driving.
- Aggression by competitors in sports events can be based on either instrumental or hostile motives. Male athletes show a greater acceptance of aggression and are also more likely to engage in aggressive behaviour on the field compared with females. Aggressive cues, such as black uniforms, have been found to increase aggressive behaviour and to affect the perception of behaviour as aggressive by third parties. The impact of observing aggression on spectators has also been widely demonstrated, and there is evidence that it may spill over into other forms of aggression, such as domestic violence. The extent to which spectators identify with their team is an important aspect of understanding fan aggression and the dynamics of aggressive confrontations between rival groups of fans.

TASKS TO DO

(1) Reflect on whether you have experienced bullying at school and/or in a work setting, as defined in this chapter. Ask a male friend and a female friend about their experience of bullying.

(2) Find out whether you are prone to aggressive driving. Indicate how often you have shown the behaviours described in the top half of Box 7.1 in the last month, using a scale ranging from 0 (*never*) to 5 (*almost every time I drove my car*), and compute your personal score by averaging across the items. To interpret your score, see if it lies below or above the midpoint of the scale.

(3) Watch the trailer for the film *Green Street Hooligans* (or *Green Street*, as it is called in the U.K.), directed by Lexi Alexander in 2005, which features violent confrontations between rival hooligan groups (www.youtube. com/watch?v=ENPMz4cY1nw). The story and screenplay were written by a former hooligan, who became an author and adviser to the British Government on how to tackle disorderly behaviour in football.

SUGGESTED READING

Fitzgerald, L. F., & Cortina, L. M. (2018). Sexual harassment in work organizations: A view from the 21st century. In C. B. Travis & J. W. White (Eds.), *APA handbook of the psychology of women* (pp. 215–234). Washington, DC: American Psychological Association.

Nielsen, M. B., & Einarsen, S. V. (2018). What we know, what we do not know, and what we should and could have known about workplace bullying: An overview of the literature and agenda for future research. *Aggression and Violent Behavior, 42*, 71–83.

Olweus, D. (2017). Cyberbullying: A critical overview. In B. J. Bushman (Ed.), *Aggression and violence: A social psychological perspective* (pp. 225–240). New York: Routledge.

Young, K. (2019). *Sport, violence and society* (2nd ed.). London: Routledge.

Chapter 8

AGGRESSION IN THE FAMILY

The ideal image of family life is one of warmth, affection, and mutual respect. At the same time, it is a sad fact that aggression is widespread in family relationships. Physical, sexual, and emotional abuse of children, intimate partner violence, and elder abuse and neglect are recognised as serious social problems worldwide. In addition, many children are forced to witness aggression and violence in their family. As Gelles (1997, p. 1) stated in the opening sentence of his book, "people are more likely to be killed, physically assaulted, hit, beat up, slapped, or spanked in their own homes by other family members than anywhere else, or by anyone else, in our society."

Drawing on the general definition of aggression as behaviour carried out with the intention to harm (see Chapter 1), aggression in the family can be defined as any form of *behaviour that is carried out with the intention to inflict harm on a family member or a close other, for example a stepchild, residing in the same household* (Barnett, Miller-Perrin, & Perrin, 2011; Gelles, 2007). *Family aggression*, also referred to as domestic or family violence, is an umbrella term that covers a range of different aggressive behaviours, such as abusing children, acting violently towards a spouse, or depriving dependent elders of proper care. Despite the diversity of manifestations, the different forms of family violence share a number of characteristics that set them apart from aggression and violence outside the family. Some of these characteristics are listed in Table 8.1.

Family aggression typically occurs behind the closed door of the home and is therefore difficult for outside observers to detect. This enables perpetrators to carry out abusive actions repeatedly and over extended periods of time with a low risk of detection. If and when third parties suspect or recognise aggression in a family, they are frequently unwilling to take action because they do not want to become involved in what is considered to be other people's private business. The desire to protect the integrity of the family is

family aggression: behaviour carried out with the intention to inflict harm on a family member or a close other, for example a stepchild, residing in the same household.

TABLE 8.1 Shared characteristics of different forms of family violence

- Exploiting and betraying a trust relationship
- Shielded from outside observation
- Involving a power differential between perpetrators and victims
- Taking place over extended periods of time
- Including both acts of commission (active harm infliction) and acts of omission (withholding proper care)
- Reluctance by victims to disclose abuse
- Transgenerational transmission
- Victim–perpetrator cycle

not limited to external observers, but is often shared by witnesses within the family and by the victims themselves. Children abused by a family member may not disclose their experience to others because they do not want to appear as troublemakers or risk being removed from the family, battered women may try to cover up their partner's violent behaviour to salvage the image of an intact family, and abused elders may fear being placed in institutional care if they speak to others about the abuse. All of these concerns act against identifying the victims and reporting the perpetrators of family violence, making it difficult to estimate true prevalence rates and to make help available to those who need it. At the same time, there is clear evidence about the long-term adverse effects of family aggression. Both experiencing and watching aggressive behaviour by family members have been found to increase the risk of violent behaviour in the victims or witnesses themselves, often creating a transgenerational cycle of violence that is difficult to break. In addition, childhood experiences of abuse put victims at risk of further victimisation in the course of adolescence and early adulthood.

This chapter provides an overview of the current state of knowledge on the prevalence, causes, and consequences of different forms of aggression between family members. The study of family aggression is a truly interdisciplinary endeavour, and the present chapter cannot do justice to the extensive literature in different fields. Several excellent sources provide comprehensive overviews (e.g., Barnett et al., 2011; Gelles, 2017; White, Koss, & Kazdin, 2011). In keeping with the social psychological perspective adopted in this volume, we concentrate on the psychological analysis of family aggression as a form of interpersonal behaviour to understand perpetrators' actions and analyse the effects on the victims.

First, we look at children as victims of family aggression and review research on physical and sexual abuse, psychological maltreatment, and the witnessing of intrafamilial aggression. In the second section, physical aggression between partners will be discussed. Reflecting the scope of the available evidence, the focus will be on aggression in heterosexual partnerships, but the problem of violence in gay and lesbian relationships will also be considered. The issue of *sexual violence* between intimate partners will be discussed in Chapter 9, where it will be considered as part of a more general analysis of the causes and consequences of sexual aggression beyond the domestic sphere. Finally, moving along the chronological life course, we examine the increasingly pressing social problems of elder abuse and neglect.

Each of the following sections will present recent research findings on the *scale* (or prevalence) of different forms of family aggression, including an examination of variables associated with an increased risk of family aggression, and on the *effects* of each form of family aggression on the victims, drawing on evidence from longitudinal studies wherever it is available. A critical issue refers to the identification of variables associated with an increased likelihood of experiencing or perpetrating aggression in the family, which may be located at the individual, interpersonal, community, and societal levels. An important conceptual point in this context is the distinction between "risk markers" and "risk factors". A risk marker is a variable that indicates higher odds of family aggression perpetration or victimisation, but is not a cause of it, such as gender or age. By contrast, a risk factor is a variable that has a causal impact on the outcome. For example witnessing violence between parents as a child may cause later perpetration of violence against an intimate partner through the social learning of conflict resolution strategies that involve physical violence. As noted consistently throughout the literature, different forms of family aggression are often related and/or can be traced back to a common set of underlying causes and facilitating conditions. Therefore, we will present theoretical explanations pertaining to the different forms of family aggression in the final section.

CHILD MALTREATMENT

Due to their status as relatively powerless members of the family system, children are particularly at risk of becoming targets of aggressive behaviour from parents, older siblings, and other adult family members. As Tedeschi and Felson (1994, p. 287) noted, "people who rarely if ever use coercion with others make an exception in case of their children." Child maltreatment occurs in several different forms, as noted by the World Health Organization (2006) and shown in Table 8.2. A report by the World Health Organization (2020) estimated that almost three in four children worldwide experience physical punishment and/or psychological maltreatment by parents or caregivers each year.

In this section, research findings will be presented on three major forms of child maltreatment: physical abuse, sexual abuse, and emotional or psychological abuse (Whitaker & Rogers-Brown, 2019). In addition, we review the growing literature on the effects of witnessing violence in the family on children's development. Child neglect, although it accounts

TABLE 8.2 Forms of child maltreatment

Physical abuse	Intentional use of physical force against a child that results in – or has a high likelihood of resulting in – harm for the child's health, survival, development or dignity. This includes hitting, beating, kicking, shaking, biting, strangling, scalding, burning, poisoning and suffocating.
Sexual abuse	Involvement of a child in sexual activity that he or she does not fully comprehend, is unable to give informed consent to, or for which the child is not developmentally prepared, or else that violates the laws or social taboos of society. Children can be sexually abused by both adults and other children who are – by virtue of their age or stage of development – in a position of responsibility, trust, or power over the victim.
Emotional/psychological abuse	Isolated incidents or a pattern of failure over time on the part of a parent or caregiver to provide a developmentally appropriate and supportive environment. Acts in this category may have a high probability of damaging the child's physical or mental health, or its physical, mental, spiritual, moral, or social development.
Neglect	Isolated incidents or a pattern of failure over time on the part of a parent or other family member to provide for the development and well-being of the child – where the parent is in a position to do so – in one or more of the following areas: • health; • education; • emotional development; • nutrition; • shelter and safe living conditions.

Based on World Health Organization, 2006.

for the majority of cases reported to child protection agencies, will not be considered in detail because it is often hard to establish whether it is based on the intent to harm required by our definition of aggressive behaviour or the result of insufficient means and resources. Because the different forms of child abuse share a number of adverse outcomes, these outcomes will be discussed together at the end of this section.

Physical abuse

As shown in Table 8.2, *physical abuse* is defined as the use of physical force intended to harm the child's health, survival, development, or dignity. One

physical abuse: the use of severe physical force intended to harm the child's health, survival, development, or dignity.

form of parental behaviour meeting this definition is corporal punishment. Corporal punishment is still practised by many parents, at least occasionally, as an accepted means of disciplining children, despite the introduction of legal bans in many countries (Zolotor & Puzia, 2010). A review of data compiled by the United Nations concluded that in the majority of countries from all parts of the world, 2 in 3 children were subjected to violent discipline by caregivers (UNICEF, 2019).

Although corporal punishment is carried out with the intention of harming the child, researchers have suggested that the term "physical abuse" should be limited to those acts of corporal punishment that result in serious injury. As suggested Gershoff (2002, p. 540), "behaviors that do not result in significant physical injury (e.g., spanking, slapping) are considered corporal punishment, whereas behaviors that risk injury (e.g., punching, kicking, burning) are considered physical abuse."

Prevalence of physical abuse. Data on the number of children who suffer physical abuse in their family come from two sources: (a) official records from child protection or law enforcement agencies and (b) parent and victim reports in surveys and research studies. The full extent of physical aggression against children is hard to establish from either source because many acts of child abuse go undetected and/or unreported. In addition, sources differ in terms of the definitions they use, and these differences affect the number of cases that fall within the boundaries of the respective categories of maltreatment. Nevertheless, the available figures are meaningful in that they can be seen as reflecting the lower boundary of the problem.

Data on severe forms of physical abuse of children are collected by child protection agencies. For example, in the U.S., the 2017 Maltreatment Report lists 123,065 cases of reported physical abuse of children, which accounts for 18.3% of all reported cases of abuse (U.S. Department of Health and Human Services, 2017). In addition to official statistics, self-reports by victims or reports by caregivers are another relevant source of information. Regarding incidence rates of corporal punishment, Finkelhor, Turner, Wormuth, Vanderminden, and Hamby (2019) found that in a large nationwide sample, 49% of parents of children aged 0 to 9 years and 23% of parents of children aged 10 to 17 years reported having spanked their child at least once in the last year. These rates, although substantial, represent a decline compared with earlier surveys, which the authors attribute to awareness-raising campaigns about the harmful effects of corporal punishment. A representative survey conducted by the National Society for the Prevention of Cruelty to Children (2017) in England revealed that 6.7% of males and 6.8% of females aged 11 to 17 years had suffered severe physical violence from a parent at least once in their lifetime. A Swedish study including a large community sample revealed that 15% of participants had been hit by a parent, but only 7% of them had disclosed the experience to the authorities (Annerbäck, Wingren, Svedin, & Gustafsson, 2010). Data from a nationally representative sample in Israel revealed reports of physical abuse victimisation in childhood of 17.1%. The rates varied substantially between ethnic groups, with almost twice as many Arab participants (27.4%) reporting physical abuse by their parents compared with Jewish participants (14.7%) (Lev-Wiesel, Eisikovits, First, Gottfried, & Mehlhausen, 2018).

The most comprehensive review of prevalence studies in physical abuse comes from Stoltenborgh, Bakermans-Kranenburg, Alink, and van IJzendoorn (2015), who included 168 prevalence rates from countries worldwide in their review of meta-analyses. Grouping their findings by continent, they found a pooled prevalence rate of 22.8% for studies from Africa, 16.7% for studies from Asia, 14.3% for studies from Australia, 22.9% for studies from Europe, and 24.0% for studies from North America. By far the highest rate of 54.8% was found in studies from South America. The majority of prevalence rates was based on self-reports, only a small number of studies relied on reports by informants, such as medical professionals and child protection workers, and these studies yielded lower rates. This discrepancy indicates once more that only a small proportion of cases is reported to the authorities, highlighting the problem of high dark figures for childhood abuse.

When compared with earlier figures, the more recent data show a decline in physical abuse rates (e.g., Annerbäck et al., 2010; Finkelhor et al., 2019; Sedlak et al., 2010), and there is some indication that legislation banning parents from using physical force against their children is having an effect (Zolotor & Puzia, 2010). However, the most recent figures clearly demonstrate that a substantial proportion of children remain exposed to physical aggression from parents and other caregivers. This has lasting negative implications for their physical, mental, and emotional well-being, as will be discussed in the final part of this section.

Risk factors for physical abuse. In the search for variables associated with an increased likelihood of physical abuse of children, researchers have looked at characteristics of the perpetrators (such as gender and personality), social circumstances (such as poverty and poor housing), and vulnerability factors in the victim (such as disability or difficult temperament) (Wolfe, 2011). As far as the sex of the abuser is concerned, some sources suggest that women are more frequently involved in physical child abuse than men (U.S. Department of Health and Human Services, 2017). A simple explanation for this difference could be that women are mostly responsible for childcare, especially with young children, and are therefore more likely to encounter problems in interacting with the child that may prompt physical aggression. In studies that controlled for differences due to childcare responsibility (e.g., by comparing women with men who were also the primary caregivers), the difference was reversed, with higher abuse rates being found for men (Featherstone, 1996). More recent incidence studies have found that biological mothers and fathers were represented equally as perpetrators of physical abuse of their children, but where children were abused by a step-parent or a parent's partner, men were over-represented as perpetrators by a wide margin (Sedlak et al., 2010). Single parents living with a new partner were found in some studies to be more likely to physically abuse their children, as were parents who had problems with alcohol and drug abuse (Barnett et al., 2011; Sedlak et al., 2010). Regarding perpetrator age, the highest prevalence rates were found in the age bracket of 25 to 34 years, with over 40% of perpetrators belonging to this group (U.S. Department of Health and Human Services, 2017). This is consistent with the finding that younger children are more likely to be victimised, as they would have parents falling into this age group. The meta-analysis by Stith et al. (2009) integrating findings from 155 studies identified parent characteristics as the strongest predictors of physical abuse. In particular, parents' perceptions of the child as a problem, parent anger and hyper-reactivity, and parent psychopathology were significantly related to the tendency to physically abuse their children in the majority of studies. High personal stress was also significantly linked to physical abuse in most of the included studies. With regard to socio-contextual variables, poverty and poor housing, living in a violence-prone neighbourhood, and poor social support were linked to a higher rate of physical abuse of children, creating higher levels of stress for parents (Barnett et al., 2011).

Among child-related factors, the risk of physical abuse was found to escalate at the age of two years, peak around the age of three to four years, and gradually decline from the age of seven years (Finkelhor et al., 2019). Following a national cohort of newborns over six months, Puls et al. (2019) found that the relative risk of being hospitalised for physical abuse was significantly higher for babies born prematurely, with a lower birth weight, or with exposure to alcohol or other drugs during pregnancy. The meta-analytic evidence by Stith et al. (2009) identified child externalising behaviour as a consistent factor associated with a greater risk of physical abuse. At the level of the family system, their analysis showed that high conflict between family members, low marital satisfaction, low family cohesion, and presence of violence between the parents were related to a higher risk of physical abuse for the children.

Sexual abuse

Sexual abuse is commonly defined as sexual contact between a child and an adult that is carried out for the sexual stimulation of the perpetrator. Because children are considered to be unable to decide whether they want to engage in sexual contacts, consent is not an issue in the definition of child sexual abuse. Sexual abuse is tied to an unequal power relationship between victims and perpetrators, whereby the perpetrators exploit their age or maturational advantage, their position of authority over the victim, or resort to the use of force or trickery (Kendall-Tackett & Marshall, 1998).

sexual abuse: sexual contact between a child and an adult that is carried out for the sexual stimulation of the perpetrator.

Beyond this broad consensus, there are substantial variations in the legal definitions of child sexual abuse across countries and the research definitions adopted across studies. These differences relate to the age limit that is used to define childhood, the minimum age difference between the victim and the perpetrator, and the nature of the sexual acts considered abusive. All of these aspects have implications for collecting and comparing data about the rates of victimisation and perpetration (Mathews & Collin-Vézina, 2019). A distinction that seems to be universally accepted in the literature is that between *contact abuse,* involving physical contact between victim and perpetrator (e.g., touching or penetration of the body), and *non-contact abuse* (e.g., exhibitionism, voyeurism, or taking photos of children for use in pornography).

Prevalence and risk factors of sexual abuse. As with physical abuse, several data sources are available for estimating the scale of child sexual abuse, each of which has its own problems. One data source consists of reports from child protection agencies. These figures only include the cases that have come to the attention of the authorities and therefore underestimate the true rate of sexual abuse. Another source is provided by large-scale victimisation surveys, which yield retrospective reports by adolescents or adults of sexual abuse in childhood.

Official agency data from the National Child Abuse and Neglect Data System (NCANDS) showed 58,114 reports of sexual abuse in 2017, accounting for 8.6% of all cases in the database (U.S. Department of Health and Human Services, 2017). In England, 37,778 sexual offences against under 16-year-olds were recorded in 2015/16, corresponding to a rate of 36.3 sexual offences per 10,000 children aged under 16 years and a 23% increase from the previous year (National Society for the Prevention of Cruelty to Children, 2017). In Germany, official crime statistics reveal that 12,321 cases of child sexual abuse were reported to the police in 2018, which corresponds to 14.9 cases per 100,000 children and represents an increase of 6.7% over the previous year (Bundeskriminalamt, 2019b). Three quarters of the victims were female. All of these figures include sexual abuse by family members, acquaintances, and strangers. Nonetheless, the data are relevant with regard to intra-familial sexual abuse, given that a large proportion of sexually abusive acts are committed by members of the child's family. It is estimated that 75–80% of sexual abusers are known to their victim, with male family members accounting for a substantial proportion of perpetrators (Kendall-Tackett & Marshall, 1998).

A second data source is provided by self-report surveys in which respondents are asked to indicate whether or not they experienced sexual abuse when they were children. The problem here is that these reports are collected retrospectively, and memories may have been affected by experiences that occurred after childhood. In addition, studies vary substantially in terms of how the critical abuse questions are phrased (Mathews & Collin-Vézina, 2019). Despite these limitations, self-report surveys are valuable because they can uncover those cases of abuse that were not reported to the authorities. The review and meta-analysis by Barth, Bermetz, Heim, Trelle, and Tonia (2013), which included 55 studies from 24 countries, yielded prevalence rates ranging from 8% to 31% for girls and from 3% to 17% for boys. Data from the review of the worldwide evidence by Stoltenborgh et al. (2015), which included 305 prevalence rates for sexual abuse, yielded prevalence rates between 11.3% (Asia) and 21.5% (Australia) for girls and between 4.1% (Asia) and 19.3% (Africa) for boys.

As the international evidence shows, sexual abuse must be seen as a pervasive threat in children's lives. No demographic or family characteristics have as yet been identified to rule out the possibility that a child will be or has been sexually abused (Finkelhor, 1994). A large research literature has investigated factors that increase children's risk of sexual abuse, summarised in two recent meta-analyses. Data from 62 studies with a total of 14,494 participants that yielded 220 effect sizes were examined by Ventus, Antfolk, and Salo (2017). Assink et al. (2019) included 72 studies from which they extracted a total of 765 potential risk factors on the perpetrator and environment side and vulnerability factors on the victim side for child sexual abuse. The two meta-analyses revealed a number of significant associations between perpetrator characteristics, family characteristics, and victim characteristics and the likelihood of sexual abuse. The vast majority of perpetrators are male, and girls are more at risk of victimisation than are boys. However, researchers agree that even though boys may experience sexual abuse at a lower rate than girls, the possibility of systematic underreporting of victimisation of boys needs to be considered. Traditional gender stereotypes portray girls as more typical victims of sexual abuse and make it harder for boys and men to identify themselves as victims, due to shame and the fear of being perceived as homosexual (Romano & De Luca, 2001).

Intrafamilial abuse tends to start at an earlier age and continue for longer than sexual abuse by perpetrators outside the family. Despite the clear gender difference in prevalence rates, Ventus et al. (2017) did not find evidence that other risk factors were moderated by gender. According to the findings by Assink et al. (2019), moderate effect sizes ($r > .20$) were found for parent history of abuse and parent overprotection, for prior sexual and nonsexual abuse of other family members, and for the child-related variables of prior sexual or other forms of abuse, chronic mental or physical illness, and poor attachment with parent. In addition, small, but significant effect sizes (r between .10 and .20) were found for growing up in a nonnuclear family or in the presence of a step-father, social isolation of the family, and low socio-economic status of the family.

Emotional abuse

Compared with the physical and sexual abuse of children, *emotional abuse* has received less attention until recently, partly because it is harder to define and to detect than abuse that leaves more visible traces. The threshold for

emotional abuse: failure to provide a developmentally appropriate, supportive environment.

deciding when parental behaviour moves from incompetent interactions to abusive behaviour is even harder to define than for physical assault (Slep et al., 2011). The World Health Organization defines emotional abuse as

> the failure to provide a developmentally appropriate, supportive environment, including the availability of a primary attachment figure, so that the child can develop a stable and full range of emotional and social competencies commensurate with her or his personal potentials and in the context of the society in which the child dwells.
>
> (World Health Organization, 1999, p. 15)

Related and partly overlapping terms used in the research literature are emotional or psychological maltreatment or psychological abuse (Barnett et al., 2011; O'Hagan, 1995). Emotional abuse can take a variety of forms: rejecting, degrading, terrorising, isolating, permitting or encouraging antisocial or delinquent behaviour, exploiting (e.g., using a child for pornography or prostitution), ignoring the child, or restricting the child's movements.

Prevalence and risk factors. In 2017, 38,653 cases of psychological maltreatment of children were reported to child protection services in the U.S., accounting for 5.7% of all incidents of child abuse (U.S. Department of Health and Human Services, 2017). However, experts agree that underreporting to official agencies is a particular problem with regard to emotional abuse because (a) it is more difficult for observers to decide what exactly constitutes emotional abuse as compared with physical or sexual abuse, and (b) emotional abuse is less likely to produce visible effects.

Statistics based on cases reported to official agencies therefore represent the lower boundaries of the problem. In England, calls to the helpline of the National Society for the Prevention of Cruelty to Children that were about emotional abuse increased by 70% from 2011/12 to 2016/17 and reached a total number of 5,878 in 2016/17 (National Society for the Prevention of Cruelty to Children, 2017).

Higher rates of psychological maltreatment were found in surveys that elicited self-reports from parents about different forms of psychological maltreatment of their children (e.g., insulting, swearing, refusing to talk). The review of 46 prevalence rates of emotional abuse by Stoltenborgh et al. (2015) showed rates of 46.7% for Africa, 41.6% for Asia, 11.3% for Australia, 29.2% for Europe, and 36.5% for North America. No studies were available from South America. A study based on a large representative sample in the U.S. found that children who experience emotional abuse are also more likely to experience other forms of abuse. For example, the odds of experiencing physical abuse was 29.6 times higher for individuals who experienced emotional abuse than for individuals who were not affected by emotional abuse (Taillieu, Brownridge, Sareen, & Afifi, 2016).

As with physical and sexual abuse, the question arises whether there are any characteristics of the children that would make them more vulnerable to psychological maltreatment. Due to the relatively low number of cases officially reported and substantiated, evidence on this issue is limited. However, there are indications that the risk of psychological maltreatment increases with the child's age and is slightly higher for girls than for boys (Miller-Perrin & Perrin, 2007). Moreover, emotional maltreatment was found to be significantly more likely in dysfunctional families (Taillieu et al., 2016). Parental aggression and hostility, neuroticism, poor relationships with fathers, and a higher level of aggression between the parents were identified as risk factors for emotional abuse in a review by Black, Smith Slep, and Heyman (2001).

Witnessing violence in the family

It has been increasingly recognised that witnessing violence between parents and other family members has adverse effects on children even if they are not directly targeted themselves. For example, 9.8% of children in the representative survey by Finkelhor, Turner, Ormrod, Hamby, and Kracke (2009) reported having witnessed a family assault in the past year. In a study of children identified as at risk for child abuse, 8–25% of mothers from four different sites reported that their child had witnessed physical aggression between them and their partner. When their children were asked, 27–46% stated that they had seen grown-ups hit each other in their home (Litrownik, Newton, Hunter, English, & Everson, 2003). Although experts agree that a large number of children are exposed to violence between their parents, establishing the exact scale of the problem is hampered by differences in the way that exposure to family aggression has

been defined and measured (for a methodological critique, see Knutson, Lawrence, Taber, Bank, & DeGarmo, 2009).

There is evidence from many studies that witnessing family aggression has adverse effects on children's mental health and psychological well-being, and the effects of exposure to interparental violence are similar to those of experiencing abuse directed at the child him- or herself (see the summary of problems by Barnett et al., 2011, p. 115). Adverse effects of being in a violent family environment can occur from birth, and there is evidence of social, emotional, and cognitive deficits, health problems, and post-traumatic stress from infancy and early childhood onwards (Lewis-O'Connor, Sharps, Humphreys, Gary, & Campbell, 2006).

The research reviewed in this section demonstrates that children experience violence within the family at a substantial rate. Studies on physical and sexual abuse, emotional abuse, and exposure to violence between parents show that many children experience violence in their family, creating a toxic environment for their development. Moreover, it is clear that these adverse experiences inflicted by people whom they trust and depend on, and which occur in the very sphere that should provide protection and security, can cause lasting harm to victims' physical, intellectual, emotional, and social development. From a social learning perspective, witnessing aggression between parents is likely to shape children's concepts and schemas about intimate relationships.

Consequences of childhood experiences of abuse

Shared consequences of different forms of abuse. Although the different forms of child maltreatment have been considered individually in this section, they often co-occur, leaving many children poly-victimised (Finkelhor, 2011). Meta-analyses and systematic reviews of the adverse consequences of childhood abuse for victims' development have shown a substantial overlap across physical, sexual, and emotional abuse as well as witnessing interparental violence. Low self-esteem, depression, and post-traumatic stress have been identified as consequences of childhood abuse across forms of abuse (Ehring et al., 2014; Gallo, Munhoz, Loret de Mola, & Murray, 2018; Hailes, Yu, Danese, & Fazel, 2019; Yoon, Cho, & Yoon, 2019; Yu, Zhao, & Liu, 2017). A meta-analysis of 68 studies with a pooled sample of over 260,000 participants by Angelakis, Gillespie, and Panagioti (2019) found a two- to threefold increase in the risk of suicide attempts and suicidal ideation in adults who experienced physical, sexual, or emotional abuse as children. Longitudinal studies also revealed significant paths from childhood abuse to illicit drug use and a number of drug-related problem behaviours, such as dropping out of school, in adolescence and young adulthood (Huang et al., 2011; Lansford et al., 2007).

A meta-analysis of the longitudinal associations between different forms of abuse and antisocial and aggressive behaviour in later life found significant associations of all types of abuse with both outcomes (Braga, Gonçalves, Basto-Pereira, & Maia, 2017). Another meta-analysis of prospective longitudinal studies confirmed this association for a broader range of violent behaviours as outcome variables. Across 18 studies, the risk of engaging in violent behaviour was 1.8 times higher in victims of childhood abuse (Fitton, Yu, & Fazel, 2018). A study by King, Kuhn, Strege, Russell, and Kolander (2019) found that physical, emotional, and sexual abuse were linked to an increased likelihood of perpetrating sexual aggression, with the strongest link emerging for childhood sexual abuse.

A specific aspect of the link between childhood experience of abuse and subsequent aggression refers to the likelihood that abused children will themselves become abusive parents or partners. The notion of an intergenerational transmission of abuse, leading to a "cycle of violence", features prominently in the literature (Maas, Herrenkohl, & Sousa, 2008). The meta-analysis by Madigan et al. (2019) of the paths from physical, sexual, and emotional abuse as well as neglect in childhood to abusive behaviour in adulthood found evidence for a transgenerational transmission within each type of abuse. For example, for physical abuse, the effect size for victims' likelihood of physically abusing their own children compared with non-victims was $d = 0.41$ across a total of 61 studies. Moreover, the meta-analysis found evidence that children who suffered one form of abuse were at an increased risk of engaging in other forms of abuse, such victims of physical abuse becoming perpetrators of sexual abuse ($d = 0.30$), emotional abuse ($d = 0.40$), and neglect ($d = 0.30$), of their own children. A further meta-analysis by Li, Zhao, and Yu (2020) found significant, but smaller positive associations with intimate partner violence perpetration for childhood experiences of physical abuse ($r = .17$), psychological abuse ($r = .13$), and sexual abuse ($r = .13$). The link was stronger for male than for female victims of childhood abuse. The review of 19 studies of the link between witnessing parental violence in childhood and engaging in intimate partner violence (IPV) in adulthood by Kimber, Adham, Gill, McTavish, and MacMillan (2018) found significant associations in 16 studies. However, the quality of the studies was considered to be low, calling for more rigorous research on witnessing parental violence as a risk factor for IPV perpetration as an adult.

It is important to note that the relative small associations found in meta-analyses and systematic reviews indicate that the relationship between childhood victimisation and adult perpetration is by no means deterministic in the sense that all abused children will grow up to be abusive. Although the risk is higher than among non-abused children, only a minority of abused children later become abusers themselves (van IJzendoorn, Bakermans-Kranenburg, Coughlan, & Reijman, 2019). Childhood abuse should be seen as a risk factor that acts in combination with other adverse conditions (Milner & Crouch, 1993). Zuravin, McMillen, DePanfilis, and Risley-Curtiss (1996) addressed the question of whether certain characteristics of the abuse experience were differentially related to the likelihood of becoming an abuser. They found that abused women who had succeeded in breaking the cycle of violence had had a better attachment relationship with their primary caregivers at the time of the abuse than those who went on to abuse their own children.

Specific consequences of different forms of abuse. In addition to the shared outcomes, there is also evidence of adverse consequences that are specific to the type of childhood abuse. Prino and Peyrot (1994) found that *physical abuse* in comparison with physical neglect (failure to provide food, clothing, supervision, medical care, etc.) was associated with distinctly different effects on the children's aggressive and prosocial behaviour. Whereas the physically abused children showed high levels of aggression, the neglected children showed high levels of withdrawal. Both abused and neglected children scored significantly lower on prosocial behaviour than the control group. The differential effects of abuse in relation to other adverse childhood experiences were also demonstrated by O'Keefe (1995) in a study of children who had witnessed violence between their parents, some of whom had also experienced physical abuse themselves. She found that physically abused children were more likely to develop aggressive behaviour problems than children who had witnessed intimate partner violence, but had not been abused themselves. However, subsequent longitudinal evidence showed that witnessing family aggression was related to a range of antisocial behaviours in the absence of physical abuse (Sousa et al., 2011). The meta-analysis by Kitzmann, Gaylord, Holt, and Kenny (2003) did not find significant differences across a range of negative outcomes between children who had witnessed physical abuse and children who had suffered abuse themselves. In addition, a high comorbidity was found for experiencing and witnessing family aggression, with heightened effects on the likelihood of later antisocial and aggressive behaviour (Wolfe, Crooks, Lee, McIntyre-Smith, & Jaffe, 2003).

Beyond the impact on aspects of mental health and psychological functioning that are shared across forms of abuse, childhood experiences of *sexual abuse* have been linked to several specific outcomes. A conceptual framework for integrating these outcomes is the *traumagenic dynamics model* proposed by Finkelhor (1987). A *traumagenic dynamic* is an experience that distorts the child's self-concept, view of the world, and affective functioning. The four distinct dynamics identified in the model are presented in Table 8.3.

traumagenic dynamic: experience that distorts the child's self-concept, view of the world, and affective functioning.

Traumatic sexualisation, betrayal, stigmatisation, and powerlessness denote four broad processes by which childhood sexual abuse undermines children's healthy development. They provide a frame of reference for the

TABLE 8.3 Consequences of childhood sexual abuse: Finkelhor's traumagenic dynamics model

Dynamic	Explanation
Traumatic sexualisation	Undermining of the child's healthy sexual development by • rewarding the child for age-inappropriate sexual behaviour • making the child use sexual behaviour for manipulation of others • making the child give distorted meaning and importance to certain parts of their anatomy • inducing misconceptions about sexual behaviour and sexual morality and • linking sexuality to feelings of anxiety and unpleasant memories.
Betrayal	• Discovery that someone on whom they depended and whom they trusted wished to cause them harm; • Encompassing both the perpetrator and other family members who fail to come to the child's support.
Stigmatisation	• Negative messages about the self communicated to the child around the experience. These messages may come from the abuser and those becoming aware of the abuse, but can also occur in the form of self-stigmatisation as victims realise that sexual abuse is regarded as deviant. • Stigmatisation varies by gender, with female victims more likely to be stigmatised as seductive and male victims more likely to be stigmatised as homosexual.
Powerlessness	• Experience that the child's wishes are repeatedly ignored and overruled by the abuser; • Experience of being unable to escape the unwanted sexual attention and avoid harm and injury.

Based on Finkelhor, 1987.

diversity of symptoms that occur in the immediate aftermath of the abuse experience as well as over extended periods of time.

Among the initial effects of sexual abuse, which occur within the first two years after the abuse, higher rates of depression, loneliness, and suicidal ideation have been identified in victim samples. Many victims show the symptomatology of post-traumatic stress disorder (PTSD) as an immediate reaction and/or as a long-term consequence of the abuse. Indeed, Kendall-Tackett, Williams, and Finkelhor (1993) concluded that PTSD is one of two core symptoms which seem to be more common in victims of sexual abuse than in other clinical groups and which carry particular diagnostic relevance (the second core symptom being sexualised behaviour; see below). As a category of the *Diagnostic and Statistical Manual of Mental Disorders, Fourth Edition (DSM-IV)* (American Psychiatric Association, 1994), PTSD is characterised by the following criteria: persistent re-experiencing of the traumatic event in the form of flashbacks and distressing dreams, a persistent state of emotional numbing and avoidance of trauma-related stimuli, and persistent symptoms of physiological arousal, such as inability to sleep and concentration problems.

A specialised literature has emerged examining the associations between *childhood sexual abuse and sexuality in adolescence and adulthood*. Given that sexual abuse involves an infringement of the victim's sexual integrity and self-determination, sexual development is particularly likely to be negatively affected by the experience of abuse. In Finkelhor's (1987) traumagenic dynamics model of the effect of childhood sexual abuse, "traumatic sexualisation" is identified as a key mechanism leading from sexual abuse to specific sexuality-related symptoms and adjustment problems. While many of the symptoms found in relation to sexual abuse can also be observed as a result of other forms of childhood traumatisation, sexualised behaviour appears to be a specific consequence of sexual abuse. Its prevalence is significantly higher among survivors of sexual abuse than in other clinical groups (Kendall-Tackett et al., 1993).

Sexuality-related problems manifest themselves in different ways depending on the victim's stage of development. In childhood, evidence of inappropriate sexual behaviour has consistently been found at a higher rate among abuse victims compared with either non-abused children or children affected by other types of clinically relevant experiences. Indeed, the majority of the behavioural symptoms listed by Barnett et al. (2011, pp. 222–223) for school-age survivors of sexual abuse are sexuality related. Their list includes sexualised behaviour, sexual preoccupation, precocious sexual knowledge, seductive behaviour, excessive masturbation, sex play with others, sexual language, genital exposure, and the sexual victimisation of others.

In adolescence, preoccupation with sexuality remains characteristic of abuse survivors. Several sources suggest that childhood sexual abuse is associated with early sexualisation, manifested in a lower age at first sexual intercourse and a higher number of sexual partners (e.g., Chandy, Blum, & Resnick, 1996; Miller, Monson, & Norton, 1995). Kendall-Tackett et al. (1993) summarised findings from two studies in which 38% of adolescents who had been abused as children were classified as promiscuous (Cahill, Llewelyn, & Pearson, 1991). A meta-analysis by Noll, Shenk, and Putnam (2009) revealed that victims of sexual assault had a significantly increased rate of adolescent pregnancy.

In late adolescence and adulthood, problems in initiating and maintaining intimate relationships are consistently reported in the literature for victims of child sexual abuse. These problems are also reflected in higher divorce rates among abuse victims compared with non-abused samples. In addition to difficulties in establishing close emotional bonds, many survivors show problems of sexual adjustment (Feiring, Simon, & Cleland, 2009). Victims of sexual abuse have been found to be more sexually anxious, to experience more sexual guilt, to have lower sexual self-esteem, and to be more likely to seek sexual therapy (Browne & Finkelhor, 1986). Furthermore, there is evidence of a link between sexual abuse in childhood and high-risk sexual behaviour, such as having multiple partners, having unprotected sex, and engaging in prostitution (Arriola, Louden, Doldren, & Fortenberry, 2005).

The majority of studies focused on female victims of childhood sexual abuse. Studies that included male victims suggest that boys and girls are similarly affected by the experience of sexual abuse (Romano & De Luca, 2001). However, two potential effects of the abuse experience specific to male victims have been considered in the literature. The first is the possibility that childhood experience of sexual abuse may be linked to the development of a homosexual orientation, mediated by the victim's uncertainty about his sexual identity. However, evidence to support this link is limited (Beitchman, Zucker, Hood, daCosta, & Akman, 1991; Browne & Finkelhor, 1986). Secondly, a meta-analysis found that male abuse victims were at higher risk of becoming perpetrators of sexual aggression, indicating a victim-to-perpetrator cycle (Seto & Lalumière, 2010). This finding is supported by longitudinal evidence showing that the experience of sexual abuse in childhood was linked to lower self-esteem in both female and male victims. Lowered sexual self-esteem was a prospective predictor of sexual aggression perpetration for males, whereas for females, it was a significant predictor of sexual victimisation reported one year later (Krahé & Berger, 2017).

The risk of *revictimisation* is a particularly worrying consequence of childhood sexual abuse. Many individual studies and several reviews have shown that both male and female victims of child sexual abuse have an increased risk of sexual victimisation in adolescence and adulthood (Aosved, Long, & Voller, 2011; Krahé, Scheinberger-Olwig, & Schütze, 2001; Messman-Moore, Walsh, & DiLillo, 2010; Murphy, Elklit, & Shevlin, 2020). A meta-analysis concluded that almost 50% of victims of childhood sexual abuse are victimised again in adulthood (Walker, Freud, Ellis, Fraine, & Wilson, 2019). To explain the pathway from child sexual abuse to later sexual victimisation, a number of studies have shown that victims of sexual abuse develop sexual behaviour patterns that put them at an increased risk of sexual victimisation. These include having more casual sexual contacts, having more sexual partners, and habitually drinking alcohol in the context of sexual encounters (e.g., Fargo, 2009; Krahé, Scheinberger-Olwig, Waizenhöfer, & Kolpin, 1999; Testa, Hoffman, & Livingston, 2010). In addition, heavy drinking and drug use, which have been identified as common problems in victims of sexual abuse, contribute to the risk of revictimisation, given the strong links between alcohol use and sexual victimisation (Testa & Livingston, 2009; see also Chapter 9). Thus, evidence from child sex abuse research and from the literature on sexual victimisation in adolescence and adulthood converges on the conclusion that the experience of childhood sexual abuse puts victims at greater risk of later sexual victimisation. Furthermore, there is evidence that rape prevention programmes directed at young adults are largely ineffective in women with a history of child sexual abuse (Blackwell, Lynn, Vanderhoff, & Gidycz, 2004).

Taken together, there is strong evidence from multiple sources that the experience of abuse has severe, often prolonged negative consequences for the affected children. However, evidence is only beginning to emerge on factors that account for individual differences in responding to the abuse, including the potential role of protective factors that might mitigate its adverse effects (Chu, Pineda, DePrince, & Freyd, 2011). The severity of the abuse, the presence of more than one form of abuse, and high levels of parental stress have been named as factors associated with poorer coping. At the same time, it is clear from the findings reviewed in this section that experience of abuse in childhood predicts negative outcomes, but the size of the effect is at best moderate. This means that a substantial proportion of victims of abuse seem to be able to be resilient, that is they come through their childhood relatively unaffected. Knowledge is still limited about the protective factors that mitigate the adverse effects of childhood abuse. Good social relationships and the presence of a supportive adult were found to buffer the adverse effects of abuse (Collishaw et al., 2007), including the effect of witnessing intimate partner violence (Fong, Hawes, & Allen, 2019). In a study by K. A. Wright, Turanovic, O'Neal, Morse, and Booth (2019), self-control was identified as the strongest protective factor that attenuated the path from childhood abuse to later violent behaviour. Social factors found to serve a protective function in these studies included being married, having a satisfying job, and having a college education. The finding concerning the critical role of self-control in particular has implications for prevention efforts by suggesting that strengthening self-control in victims of childhood abuse may enable them to break the cycle of violence as they grow up (Finkenauer et al., 2015).

PHYSICAL VIOLENCE AGAINST INTIMATE PARTNERS

Abusive interpersonal behaviours that create a toxic family environment are not limited to parent–child relationships but also occur between partners. In this section, we will focus on the problem of physical aggression in intimate relationships. Sexual aggression between intimate partners will be examined in Chapter 9 in the context of a more general discussion of sexual aggression beyond the family setting. For the purposes of the present discussion, *intimate partner violence* is defined as the perpetration or threat of an act of physical violence, by one partner towards the other, in the context of an intimate relationship. This definition is open with regard to the sex of the perpetrator and the victim, and includes both heterosexual and same-sex relationships. Intimate partner violence is recognised as a serious problem worldwide, even though the prevalence rates vary widely, not only between, but also within countries (for reviews of the international evidence, see Archer, 2006; Krahé, Bieneck, & Möller, 2005; Laskey, Bates, & Taylor, 2019).

intimate partner violence: perpetration or threat of an act of physical or sexual violence within the context of an intimate relationship.

Prevalence of physical violence against intimate partners

Three main data sources provide information on the scale of intimate partner violence (IPV): (a) crime statistics showing the proportion of violent crime committed towards an intimate partner, (b) figures from representative crime victimisation surveys, and (c) findings from research studies, as summarised by Laskey et al. (2019). These sources portray divergent pictures of the involvement of men and women as victims and perpetrators of intimate partner violence, and have fuelled an intense debate about the extent and direction of gender differences with respect to this form of aggressive behaviour (Archer, 2018).

Official crime statistics and victimisation surveys identify women as more vulnerable to intimate partner violence than men. For homicide, the most serious form of IPV, a recent international survey found that although women have a much lower probability of dying from homicide than men, 82% of all victims killed by an intimate partner in 2017 were female (United Nations Office on Drugs and Crime, 2019). For the U.S., an analysis of IPV incidents reported in the National Crime Victimization Survey from 2003 to 2012 showed that 76% of IPV acts were committed against females compared with 24% against males (Truman & Morgan, 2014). Data from the National Intimate Partner and Sexual Violence Survey collected in 2015 showed that 32.2% of heterosexual women and 28.7% of heterosexual men reported physical violence by an intimate partner experienced at some point in their lifetime, but there was a clear gender difference in the adverse impact of the IPV experience, which was reported by 28.2% of the female and 10.2% of the male respondents (Walters, Chen, & Breiding, 2013). Findings from the most recent Crime Survey for England and Wales showed that in the year from April 2018 to March 2019 2.8% of men and 5.6% of women between 16 and 74 years of age reported abuse by an intimate partner (Office for National Statistics, 2019a, Table s40a). For Germany, the official crime statistics for 2018 recorded 140,755 victims of intimate partner violence, of whom 81.3% were female (Bundeskriminalamt, 2019a).

In addition to crime statistics and victimisation surveys, a large body of research studies have investigated risk factors and consequences of IPV, many of which have used the Conflict Tactics Scales in the original (Straus, 1979) or the revised form (Straus, Hamby, Boney-McCoy, & Sugarman, 1996). In this self-report measure, participants are presented with a list of minor and severe acts of physical aggression and asked to indicate whether and how many times they have shown the behaviour in question towards an intimate partner. Parallel items are included to measure experiences of victimisation by an intimate partner. In addition, a scale measuring injuries suffered by, or inflicted on, a partner is included. The items of the *physical assault scale* and the *injury scale* of the CTS2 are shown in Box 8.1.

The physical assault scale is subdivided into five items that measure what is considered to be minor physical assault (Items 1 to 5) and seven items that measure severe physical assault (Items 6 to 12). In addition to the items presented in Box 8.1, the CTS2 contains three further scales, measuring *psychological aggression* (defined as communications intended to cause psychological pain to a partner, such as insults or verbal abuse), *sexual aggression*, and *negotiation* as a non-aggressive form of conflict resolution in relationships (Straus & Douglas, 2017). In a recent review, the CTS2 was found to have good psychometric properties for the study of IPV in community samples (Chapman & Gillespie, 2019).

A large body of evidence has shown that on the CTS women report as much as or even more physical aggression towards a partner as men. A review including 62 empirical studies found that up to two-thirds of women had used some form of physical aggression towards a heterosexual partner (Williams, Ghandour, & Kub, 2008). In a German study of young adults, all gender differences that were found on the items of the CTS2 were in the direction of women scoring higher than men on the perpetration of physical aggression by a partner, and men scoring higher than women on victimisation by physical aggression from a partner (Krahé & Berger, 2005). In a meta-analysis including 82 studies using either the original CTS or the revised CTS2 presented in Box 8.1, Archer (2000) found that women were slightly more likely than men to show physical aggression towards a partner ($d = -0.05$). A subsequent meta-analysis by Archer (2002) on the individual items of the CTS also revealed significant gender differences on seven out of nine items, but in different directions. Women were more likely than men to throw something at their partner, to slap, kick, bite, or punch them, or to hit them with an object. On the other hand, men were

Box 8.1   Items of the physical assault scale and the injury scale of the Revised Conflict Tactics Scales

Instruction: No matter how well a couple gets along, there are times when they disagree, get annoyed with the other person, want different things from each other, or just have spats or fights because they are in a bad mood, are tired, or for some other reason. Couples also have many different ways to settle their differences. This is a list of things that might happen when you have differences. Please indicate how many times you did each of the things in the past year.

How often did this happen:

1	2	3	4	5	6	B	N
Once in the past year	Twice in the past year	3–5 times in the past year	6–10 times in the past year	11–20 times in the past year	More than 20 times in the past year	Not in the past year, but happened before	This has never happened

						1	2	3	4	5	6	B	N

1. I threw something at my partner that could hurt.

2. I twisted my partner's arm or hair.

3. I pushed or shoved my partner.

4. I grabbed my partner.

5. I slapped my partner.

6. I used a knife or gun on my partner.

7. I punched or hit my partner with something that could hurt.

8. I choked my partner.

9. I slammed my partner against a wall.

10. I beat up my partner.

11. I burned or scalded my partner on purpose.

12. I kicked my partner.

13. My partner had a sprain, bruise, or small cut because of a fight with me.

14. My partner still felt physical pain the next day because of a fight we had.

1	2	3	4	5	6	B	N
Once in the past year	Twice in the past year	3–5 times in the past year	6–10 times in the past year	11–20 times in the past year	More than 20 times in the past year	Not in the past year, but happened before	This has never happened

15. My partner passed out from being hit on the head in a fight with me.

16. My partner went to a doctor because of a fight with me.

17. My partner needed to see a doctor because of a fight with me, but didn't.

18. My partner had a broken bone from a fight with me.

Note. Items 1–5 describe behaviours classified by Straus et al. as "minor physical assault", Items 6–12 represent "severe physical assault", and Items 13–18 form the "injury" scale.

Adapted from Straus et al., 1996, Appendix Part 3.

more likely than women to push, grab or shove, beat up, choke, or strangle a partner. No differences were found for using a knife or gun, and the higher rate of women who had threatened to use a knife or gun disappeared once outliers (studies with extreme values) were removed.

At the same time, there is little doubt that men's aggression towards an intimate partner leads to more dangerous consequences. The effect sizes obtained by Archer (2000) for the injury subscale revealed that men were significantly more likely to inflict injury on their partner, with an effect size of $d = 0.15$. This finding may explain why men feature more prominently as perpetrators of intimate partner violence in crime statistics. If their actions are more likely to lead to injuries, there is an increased likelihood that they will be reported to the police and find their way into official records.

Unsurprisingly, the claim derived from the CTS studies that women are at least as involved as men in the perpetration of intimate partner violence has proved highly controversial. Not only is it at odds with data from crime statistics and victimisation surveys, it also contradicts notions of femininity and masculinity that are firmly ingrained in gender stereotypes (Rudman & Glick, 2008). Critics have argued that the over-representation of women as perpetrators of intimate partner violence in studies using the CTS is distorted because this instrument records acts of violence without considering their context. In particular, it does not consider whether the behaviour shown is an act of unprovoked aggression or a response to a previous attack, so that an act of self-defence by a woman would be counted in the same way as the initial assault by her male partner. In support of this claim, a study by Lehrner and Allen (2014) found that women tended to report engaging in more acts of IPV toward an intimate partner on the CTS than in semi-structured interviews. One reason for the discrepancy was that the behaviours presented in the CTS may be endorsed even when they were shown in a playful way rather than with the intention to cause physical harm.

It is now widely acknowledged by researchers that intimate partner violence is not a unitary phenomenon, but comprises different forms, contexts, and underlying dynamics. Kelly and Johnson (2008) distinguished three types of intimate partner violence, which differ in terms of the involvement of men and women as perpetrators and victims. The first type is called *coercive controlling violence* or *intimate terrorism*, involving emotionally abusive intimidation and physical violence. It is a stable relationship feature and is more often shown by men than by women. The second type is called *violent resistance*, occurs in self-defence to a coercive controlling partner, and is more often shown by women than by men. The third and most common type, is called *situational couple violence*, arising *ad hoc* from everyday conflict situations rather than being a stable pattern in a relationship. This form of intimate violence is shown equally by men and women. If progress is to be made in understanding the role of gender in violence between heterosexual partners, greater attention needs to be paid to the specific forms and contexts in which assaults on intimate partners take place (Frieze, 2000).

The problem of intimate partner violence in same-sex relationships has received far less attention. Reviews have demonstrated substantial levels of intimate partner violence among gay and lesbian couples (Badenes-Ribera, Frias-Navarro, Bonilla-Campos, Pons-Salvador, & Monterde-i-Bort, 2015; Finneran & Stephenson, 2013). Comparing physical violence in same-sex relationship with findings from studies of heterosexual couples, the available evidence suggests that the prevalence rates are similar (for a review, see Messinger, 2011). Evidence comparing same-sex and heterosexual couples within the same study has yielded mixed results. Blosnich and Bossarte (2009) analysed data from a representative sample in the U.S. and found no differences between same-sex and heterosexual partner constellations in the rates of physical violence. By contrast, data from a representative victimisation survey, the National Violence Against Women Survey, Messinger (2011) showed that rates of victimisation of women were higher in same-sex relationships (25%) than in heterosexual relationships (21%). Men were substantially more often victimised by another man in a homosexual relationship (33%) than by a woman in a heterosexual relationship (7.5%). The National Intimate Partner and Sexual Violence Survey conducted in 2010 also yielded higher lifetime prevalence rates of women's experience of physical violence from an intimate partner for lesbian (40.4%) and bisexual (56.9%) compared with heterosexual (32.2%) respondents (Walters et al., 2013). Among men, the rates for gay (25.2%) and heterosexual (28.7%) respondents were similar, but bisexual men reported physical violence from an intimate partner at a higher rate (37.3%). The comprehensive review by Bermea, van Eeden-Moorefield, and Khaw (2018) confirmed the increased rate of IPV victimisation among bisexual women.

Overall, it has become clear that physical aggression is a major problem in intimate relationships, although the question of the gender distribution of aggressors and victims has not been resolved conclusively. The controversy surrounding the use of the Conflict Tactics Scales as a measure of intimate partner violence has highlighted the need to consider not only the aggressive acts per se, but also the context in which they occur. This includes differences in physical strength, related to differences in the potential to cause serious harm, and the proactive or reactive nature of the aggressive behaviour. In terms of the scale of intimate partner violence, a large body of evidence has been accumulated in recent years from a wide range of countries around the world. In fact, one could say that the study of intimate partner violence is the only area of aggression research for which empirical studies are available from a wide range of countries that are not typically represented in mainstream psychological research (Krahé & Berger, 2005; Krug et al., 2002; World Health Organization, 2013).

Factors associated with an increased probability of engaging in or experiencing intimate partner violence

In the search for variables associated with an increased probability of engaging in, or experiencing, violence towards intimate partners, individual, situational, and relationship variables have been examined to find out (a) who is susceptible to behaving violently towards an intimate partner and/or vulnerable to experience victimisation, (b) what situational conditions increase the likelihood of intimate partner violence, and (c) what characterises relationships that are at risk for intimate partner violence.

Among individual-level variables, particular attention has been paid to the socio-demographic and personal characteristics of men who abuse their female partners. Demographic characteristics such as lower age, education, and income were linked to higher odds of IPV perpetration in the meta-analysis by Mallory et al. (2016). The meta-analysis of risk factors for physical partner violence by Spencer, Mallory et al. (2019) that included 207 studies found significant associations of both perpetration and victimisation with several indicators of mental health. Their findings, presented in Table 8.4, show that depression, anxiety, post-traumatic stress disorder, borderline personality disorder, and antisocial personality disorder were significantly associated with both perpetration and victimisation for men and women. The strength of the association was not significantly different in the two gender groups, with one exception: the link between IPV victimisation and depression was significantly stronger for women than for men. However, the data are correlational and cannot clarify whether the associations are risk factors or outcomes of IPV perpetration and, in particular, victimisation.

Comparing a comprehensive list of 60 risk markers, that is variables associated with a higher probability of IPV perpetration, the review by Spencer, Cafferky, and Stith (2016) found that no more than three variables showed a stronger link with IPV for one gender group than the other, all in

TABLE 8.4 Mental-health correlates of intimate partner violence perpetration and victimization in men and women

Correlate	Men		Women	
	k effect sizes	**Mean r**	**k effect sizes**	**Mean r**
Depression				
Perpetration	52	.21***	27	.26***
Victimisation	25	.17***	85	.28***
Anxiety				
Perpetration	23	.14***	9	.13**
Victimisation	10	.16***	31	.21***
PTSD				
Perpetration	24	.22***	9	.17**
Victimisation	7	.31***	53	.35***
Antisocial PD				
Perpetration	29	.26***	12	.29***
Victimisation	9	.23***	8	.21**
Borderline PD				
Perpetration	17	.36***	5	.35***
Victimisation	4	.28***	3	.20***

PTSD = Posttraumatic stress disorder; PD = Personality disorder. *** $p < .001$, ** $p < .01$.
Based on Spencer, Mallory, et al., 2019, Tables 4 and 5.

the direction of a higher correlation for men: alcohol use, witnessing family aggression or experiencing physical abuse as a child, and the demand/withdrawal pattern of attachment style (Bonache, Gonzalez-Mendez, & Krahé, 2019; Velotti, Beomonte Zobel, Rogier, & Tambelli, 2018). Focusing on vulnerability factors of women's IPV victimisation, a meta-analysis of 35 prospective longitudinal studies by Yakubovich et al. (2018) found that low socio-economic status, an unplanned pregnancy, and a history of prior victimisation predicted greater odds of victimisation, whereas higher age predicted a lower likelihood of victimisation.

In addition to considering individual risk factors for intimate partner violence, several authors have proposed distinctions between different types of men who commit acts of IPV against their female partners, characterised by different risk factors and patterns of aggressive behaviour. An influential typology was developed by Holtzworth-Munroe and Stuart (1994), who distinguished between three types of male IPV perpetrators on the basis of three dimensions: severity of violence, generality of violence beyond the intimate relationship, and evidence of psychopathology.

(1) The first group consists of *family-only* batterers, whose violent behaviour is limited to members of their own family, who do not show signs of psychopathological disorders, and whose violence is generally less severe and does not extend to sexual and/or psychological abuse. This group is estimated to account for about 50% of male batterers.

(2) *Dysphoric/borderline* batterers constitute the second group. Their violence is rooted in emotional instability and psychiatric disorders. Their aggression is mainly directed towards their family, but extra-familial violence and criminal behaviour occur occasionally. About 25% of men who abuse their partners are estimated to fall into this group.

(3) *Generally violent/antisocial* batterers, who show violent behaviour both within and outside their family, and who engage in sexual and psychological aggression in addition to physical violence, form the third group. Their general tendency to engage in violent behaviour means that they are likely to have a criminal record. In addition, alcohol and substance abuse are frequently found in this group, which is estimated to account for 25% of male batterers.

A fourth group was later identified and labelled *low-level antisocial* men characterised by moderate levels on the three dimensions of severity, generality, and psychopathology (Holtzworth-Munroe, Meehan, Herron, Rehman, & Stuart, 2000).

The differentiation between these types of abusive men has been supported by several studies. A longitudinal study by Holtzworth-Munroe, Meehan, Herron, Rehman, and Stuart (2003) concluded that men who were assigned to one of these types showed behaviour consistent with the typology over a three-year period. For example, men classified as family-only batterers at the beginning of the study continued to limit any aggressive behaviour they manifested to the family context, and showed less severe aggression than did the borderline/dysphoric and generally aggressive types. Typologies such as this show that men who abuse their partners are not a homogeneous group. They come to relationships with different personal characteristics and biographical experiences, and show predictable differences in the severity and generality of their aggressive behaviour (Cameranesi, 2016).

Among the *situational variables* linked to an increased risk of violence between partners, alcohol consumption plays a major role. As we saw in Chapter 5, there is consistent evidence that aggressive behaviour becomes more likely when people are under the influence of alcohol. Alcohol exerts a disinhibiting effect by undermining people's awareness of the anti-normative character of aggression that would prevent them from lashing out if they were sober. In addition, alcohol reduces individuals' capacity for information processing, making them more responsive to salient situational cues, such as provocations, without engaging in a careful analysis of the other person's motives or intentions. Although alcohol is not necessarily a cause of intimate partner violence, it is likely to lower the threshold for aggressive behaviour in conflict situations with a partner.

Foran and O'Leary (2008) conducted a meta-analysis of 50 studies linking alcohol use and intimate partner violence. For men's violence towards a female partner, they found a significant effect size of $r = .23$. For women's violence towards a male partner, the effect size was also significant, but smaller with $r = .14$. In combination, these findings show a small effect size for the association between drinking and perpetration of intimate partner violence for both men and women. Parallel findings for a range of drugs other than alcohol were obtained in the meta-analysis by Moore et al. (2008), who found that the association with intimate partner violence was strongest for cocaine. The meta-analysis by Cafferky, Mendez, Anderson, and Stith (2018) including 285 studies confirmed the link between alcohol and drug use and IPV perpetration for both men and women,, and again the link was stronger for men.

Further evidence suggests that physical violence when the perpetrator, the victim, or both are drunk tends to be more severe and more likely to lead to serious harm. In a study by Graham, Bernards, Wilsnack, and Gmel (2011), in which data were collected from 13 countries around the world, participants were asked to think about the most severe incident of violence from a partner (if any) that they had experienced in the last two years. They were then asked to indicate the severity of the incident and to report whether they, the aggressor, or both had been drinking when the incident occurred. As predicted, incidents in which one or both partners had been drinking were rated as more severe by both men and women across all participating countries.

Variables associated with an increased risk of IPV have also been identified at the *relationship level*. The meta-analysis of risk markers of IPV victimisation by Spencer, Stith, and Cafferky (2019) concluded that the strongest predictors of victimisation were variables at the relationship level, such as low marital satisfaction, demand/withdraw relationship patterns, and perpetrator's power in the relationship. Abuse is more likely to occur in relationships based on patriarchal attitudes and role divisions in which the man dominates the relationship and has power over his female partner. This is particularly true for cultures that link male dominance to the concept of honour, in which a man's social status and reputation are defined by the extent to which he has control over his female partner (Khan, 2018; Vandello & Cohen, 2003).

Finally, research has asked whether the prevalence of IPV varies in relation to variables at the macro-level of societies and cultures. The meta-analysis by Mallory et al. (2016) examined whether the strength of a range of risk factors for IPV varied between individualist and collectivist cultures. This distinction was introduced by Hofstede (2013) to describe cultures that value autonomy and personal characteristics (individualism) from cultures that value social bonds and group memberships (collectivism). Within individualist cultures, Mallory et al. (2016) distinguished between studies from the U.S. and other countries. Younger age was a stronger risk marker for IPV perpetration in the U.S. than in studies from other individualist and from collectivist countries, witnessing parental violence and engaging in emotional abuse were stronger risk markers in collectivist countries than in individualist countries including the U.S., and relationship satisfaction was a stronger risk marker in collectivist countries and the U.S. than in other individualist countries. For the majority of risk markers, however, no significant differences between the three comparison groups were found. In another meta-analysis, Spencer, Mendez, and Stith (2019) compared the strength of risk markers of IPV perpetration between countries with high and low income inequality. They reasoned that high income inequality contributes to the disorganisation of social structures and creates stress, both of which have been linked to higher levels of violence in societies. Research studies were classified as coming from countries with high and low income inequality based on the Gini Index developed by the World Bank, https://datacatalog.worldbank.org/gini-index-world-bank-estimate-1, which ranges from zero (maximum equality) to 100 (maximum inequality). Of a total of 29 significant risk markers of physical IPV perpetration, only five differed significantly between countries with high and low income inequality: young age, emotional abuse perpetration, violence against other family members, and witnessing family aggression in childhood were more strongly related to physical IPV perpetration in countries with high income inequality, whereas experience of trauma was more strongly related to physical IPV in countries with low income inequality. Overall, the findings from the two meta-analyses, while revealing some differences at the macro-level of different countries, point to the more important role of variables at the individual and relationship level as critical risk markers and risk factors for IPV perpetration.

Consequences of physical partner violence

Intimate partner violence is costly for societies as a whole. A report by the World Health Organization highlights the economic burden of different forms of partner abuse (Waters et al., 2004). In a survey of over 3,000 women in the U.S., Rivara et al. (2007) found that annual healthcare costs were 19% higher among victims of intimate partner violence than among non-victimised women. Based on a victimisation rate of 44% in their sample, they estimated that for every 100,000 women in the healthcare system, excess healthcare costs of 19.3 million US$ are incurred each year as a result of intimate partner violence.

This section focuses on the psychological impact of partner abuse on the victim's mental health and well-being at the individual level. Intimate partner violence leads to a variety of physical consequences, including serious injuries, a higher incidence of stress-related physical illnesses, and economic effects, such as poverty resulting from leaving an abusive relationship or due to employment instability (Coker, Williams, Follingstad, & Jordan, 2011). In the 2015 National Intimate Partner and Sexual Violence Survey (NISVS), two-thirds of self-reported female victims and one third of male victims reported that the victimisation experience (across different forms of IPV) had an adverse impact on their lives (D'Inverno, Smith, Zhang, & Chen, 2019). The specific forms of adverse impact are shown in Figure 8.1. The findings also suggest that the impact of IPV is higher on women than on men, as fewer male than female victims report adverse effects. The prevalence of lifetime physical IPV victimisation in this survey was similar for women (30.6%) and men (31%), but a clear asymmetry between the gender groups appeared for the impact of victimisation.

A large research literature has demonstrated that women's experience of IPV is predictive of severe physical and mental health problems. These include a heightened risk of cardiovascular disease (E. N. Wright, Hanlon, Lozano, & Teitelman, 2019), depression (Oh, Kim, Jang, & Park, 2019), post-traumatic stress disorder, and suicidality (Golding, 1999). Evidence on male victims of intimate partner violence is more limited and less clear. The review by Randle and Graham (2011) identified several studies that showed higher rates of PTSD in victimised compared with non-victimised men, but a longitudinal study by Ehrensaft, Moffitt, and Caspi (2006) failed to corroborate this conclusion. For depression and suicidal ideation the evidence was more conclusive, showing higher rates among victimised compared with non-victimised men, paralleling the findings for female victims. Moreover, the longitudinal study by Simmons, Knight, and Menard (2015) found that IPV victimisation predicted substance abuse and depressive symptoms in male victims. Even fewer data are currently available on the effects of intimate partner abuse in LGBT samples, but what little evidence there is suggests a similar impact of IPV victimisation in these groups as in heterosexual couples (Randle & Graham, 2011). A recent longitudinal study by Reuter, Newcomb, Whitton, and Mustanski (2017) confirmed IPV victimisation as a prospective predictor of depressive symptoms in LGBT young adults.

Overall, there is strong evidence that partner abuse may lead to long-term psychological distress and impairment. To ameliorate these adverse effects, a critical first step is to stop the continuation of abuse. Becoming trapped in abusive relationships because of psychological mechanisms such as denial, self-blame, and adaptation to violence is a common fate of victims of IPV. Of those who make an attempt to break away and seek refuge in shelters for battered women, about a third eventually return to their abusive partners, and some studies suggest even higher figures (Barnett et al., 2011). Thus, empowering women to gain independence from abusive partners, both psychologically and in terms of managing their everyday lives, must be a key objective of intervention work with victims of partner abuse. Interventions to reduce violent behaviour towards partners will be discussed in Chapter 12.

ELDER ABUSE

When people think or hear about family aggression, images of abused children or battered partners come to mind as prototypical examples of this problem. Another form of family aggression is less prominent in public

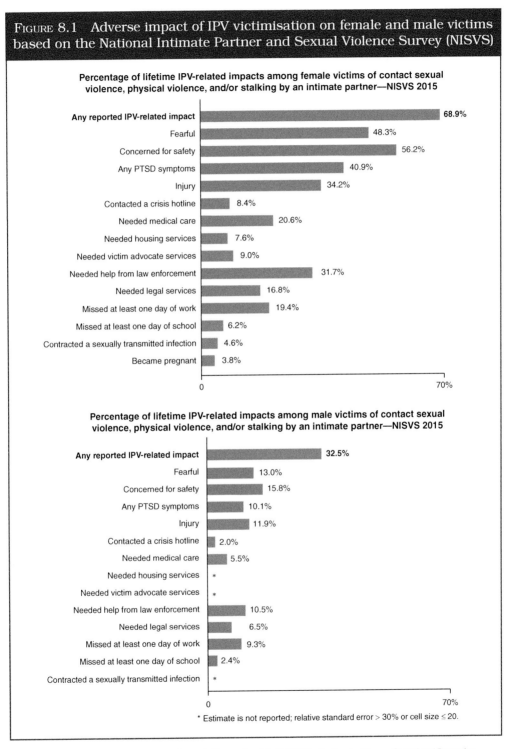

FIGURE 8.1 Adverse impact of IPV victimisation on female and male victims based on the National Intimate Partner and Sexual Violence Survey (NISVS)

Percentage of lifetime IPV-related impacts among female victims of contact sexual violence, physical violence, and/or stalking by an intimate partner—NISVS 2015

Any reported IPV-related impact	68.9%
Fearful	48.3%
Concerned for safety	56.2%
Any PTSD symptoms	40.9%
Injury	34.2%
Contacted a crisis hotline	8.4%
Needed medical care	20.6%
Needed housing services	7.6%
Needed victim advocate services	9.0%
Needed help from law enforcement	31.7%
Needed legal services	16.8%
Missed at least one day of work	19.4%
Missed at least one day of school	6.2%
Contracted a sexually transmitted infection	4.6%
Became pregnant	3.8%

Percentage of lifetime IPV-related impacts among male victims of contact sexual violence, physical violence, and/or stalking by an intimate partner—NISVS 2015

Any reported IPV-related impact	32.5%
Fearful	13.0%
Concerned for safety	15.8%
Any PTSD symptoms	10.1%
Injury	11.9%
Contacted a crisis hotline	2.0%
Needed medical care	5.5%
Needed housing services	*
Needed victim advocate services	*
Needed help from law enforcement	10.5%
Needed legal services	6.5%
Missed at least one day of work	9.3%
Missed at least one day of school	2.4%
Contracted a sexually transmitted infection	*

* Estimate is not reported; relative standard error > 30% or cell size ≤ 20.

awareness as well as in research: the abuse of elderly people. A review by the World Health Organization (2014) of legal measures introduced by countries to address the problem of violence shows that no more than 59% of the 133 countries included in the review have legislation against elder abuse, and in only 30% of the countries, this legislation is fully enforced. As the average life expectancy continues to rise worldwide, a growing number of people are becoming dependent on the care of younger relatives, most commonly their children, or of professional caregivers. Looking after dependent elders can be a highly demanding and strenuous task that may lead to abusive behaviour of the caregivers towards the elderly person in their care. In this section, we summarise some of the evidence on elder abuse in the family that has accumulated since the problem first attracted research attention in the 1980s.

Forms and prevalence of elder abuse

In order to study elder abuse, the two terms involved need to be properly defined. This obvious requirement turns out to be problematic with respect to the term "elder". Unlike children, partners, or siblings, who can be identified with relative ease, there is no clear-cut criterion as to when a person becomes an elder. As recent summaries have revealed, studies vary widely with regard to the age of entry into the category of elders (e.g., De Donder et al., 2011), ranging from 55 years or older to 75 years or older across different European studies. It is obvious that variations in defining the age range for elder abuse make it more difficult to establish prevalence rates and to compare rates across different studies. As far as the second term, "abuse", is concerned, definitions are more consistent. A review of the history of definitions of elder abuse is provided by Mysyuk, Westendorp, and Lindenberg (2013). In general, five main forms of elder abuse are distinguished in the literature (e.g., Krug et al., 2002).

(1) *Physical abuse* involves behaviour carried out with the intention of causing physical pain or injury to an elderly person, such as battering, restraining, or bruising.
(2) *Sexual abuse* denotes non-consensual sexual contact and sexual attention of any kind, from unwanted sexual touching to sexual intercourse.
(3) *Psychological* or *emotional abuse* is defined as inflicting mental pain, anguish, or distress through verbal and non-verbal behaviour, such as name calling, verbal threats, or infantilising (e.g., by using baby talk).
(4) *Financial abuse* involves the illegal and improper exploitation of the elderly person's property or assets. Since many elderly people are unable to handle their own financial affairs for physical or mental reasons, they have to trust their caregivers to do this for them.
(5) *Neglect* refers to the withholding of adequate care to meet a dependent elder's physical, medical, and psychological needs. Whereas the previous forms of elder abuse referred to acts of *commission*, neglect represents a form of elder abuse through *omission*. Refusal or failure to meet the elderly person's physical needs (e.g., regular provision of food, personal hygiene), their need for respect, or their need for financial support are forms of abuse that can be just as damaging to the victim as the active commission of abusive acts.

Prevalence rates are even more difficult to establish for elder abuse than for the other forms of family aggression considered so far. One reason is that victims are usually confined to the domestic setting, and have limited contact with people in the outside world who might be alerted to their situation. In addition, the very fact that they are dependent on the care provided by the abuser makes many victims reluctant to disclose the abuse to a third party. Furthermore, elders abused by their children may be embarrassed or even feel guilty about having brought up children who treat their parents in this way. Therefore, elder abuse is regarded as a "hidden" form of family aggression, and established prevalence rates reflect the lower limits rather than the full scale of the problem. This point is underlined by a meta-analysis of 51 studies worldwide, which found a substantially higher prevalence rate of elder abuse based on reports by third parties (e.g., healthcare workers, doctors) than on reports by elderly respondents (Ho, Wong, Chiu, & Ho, 2017). Regarding the different forms of elder abuse, the review identified emotional abuse (47.5%), followed by financial abuse (34%), neglect (32%), physical abuse (19.1%), and sexual abuse (3.1%). The analysis also identified a significantly higher prevalence of elder abuse in non-western (17.4%) compared with western countries (7.3%). A tentative explanation for this difference is offered based on a strong normative pressure towards caring for older family members in many non-western cultures, which may push relatives into the role of carers against their will. A meta-analysis focusing on reports of elder abuse experienced by women in the past year identified an overall rate of 14.1% across 28 countries and all forms of abuse (Yon, Mikton, Gassoumis, & Wilber, 2019). Psychological abuse (11.8%) was most common, followed by neglect (4.1%), financial abuse (3.8%), sexual abuse (2.2%), and physical abuse (1.9%).

More circumscribed evidence from specific world regions or countries also documents that the elderly are a risk group for family aggression (Arab-Zozani et al., 2018; De Donder et al., 2011; Lee & Lightfoot, 2014). The National Elder Mistreatment Study, conducted in the U.S. in 2008, included almost 6,000 participants aged 60 or over (Acierno et al., 2010). In this sample, 11.4% of the participants reported at least one form of abuse in the past year, with 4.6% reporting emotional abuse, 1.6% reporting physical abuse, 0.6% reporting sexual abuse, and 5.1% reporting neglect. Although the figures do not refer specifically to family members as perpetrators, additional data asking for the perpetrator of the most recent incident revealed that the majority of abusive acts were committed by a family member. For physical abuse, for example, 57% of the most recent incidents were committed by the partner or spouse, and a further 19% by children or other relatives (Acierno, Hernandez-Tejada, Muzzy, & Steve, 2009, p. 45). These data suggest that family members account for a substantial proportion of perpetrators. A review of 20 studies from 17 countries published since 2010 that focused specifically on elder abuse in the family revealed prevalence rates in the last 12 months that ranged from 2.2% and 43.7% (Schuster & Krahé, 2016). Differences in definitions of elder abuse and methodology hampered the comparison of prevalence rates across studies, calling for multi-country studies employing the same methodology in each country.

Risk markers and risk factors for elder abuse

As with other forms of family aggression, a central task for researchers has been to establish vulnerability factors that increase the risk of elder abuse victimisation, and to identify characteristics associated with an increased likelihood of becoming a perpetrator of elder abuse. In terms of risk markers for victimisation, the reviews and meta-analyses show that victims of elder abuse are more likely to be female (Amstadter et al., 2011; Ho et al., 2017), which can be explained at least partly by the higher life expectancy of women compared with men. Moreover, ill health and cognitive decline are related to a higher risk of abuse victimisation due to a greater dependency on the care of the potentially abusive family member (Fang & Yan, 2018; Mosqueda & Olsen, 2015).

On the perpetrator side, a number of variables have been linked to an increased likelihood of abusing a dependent elder, of which several overlap with risk markers of victimisation (Storey, 2020).

Gender. Men were found to be over-represented among abusers, especially in relation to the perpetration of physical abuse. This finding is due at least in part to the fact that husbands who abuse their elderly spouses account for a relatively large proportion of elder abuse cases (Biggs, Manthorpe, Tinker, Doyle, & Erens, 2009).

Physical and mental health problems and substance abuse. Abusers were found to be more likely to have a history of mental illness and psychiatric hospitalisation (Pillemer & Suitor, 1988) and report more physical health problems as well as substance-related problems (Storey, 2020).

Dependency of the abuser on the victim, both financially and emotionally (Pillemer & Suitor, 1988). It has been suggested that abuse may take place in response to the sense of powerlessness experienced by grown-up children who are dependent on their parents (Gelles, 1997). The combination of economic dependency of the caregiver and functional dependency of the elderly receiver of care creates a dynamic that makes abuse more likely (Bornstein, 2019).

Transgenerational transmission of violent behaviour. The "victim-to-perpetrator" cycle identified with regard to both child abuse and intimate partner violence has also been proposed as an explanation for elder abuse. Evidence, albeit limited, suggests that elder abuse is more frequently committed by individuals who were themselves victims of family aggression (e.g., Steinmetz, 1978).

External stress. Life stress that originates outside the family context has been linked to elder abuse. Unemployment and financial difficulties were identified as more prevalent external stressors in abusive than non-abusive carers (e.g., Bendik, 1992).

However, it is important to bear in mind that these individual risk factors may be present in many caregiving relationships, of which only few will become abusive. How different risk factors add up or interact to produce abusive behaviour, and whether there are protective factors which buffer the negative impact of risk factors has yet to be investigated.

Consequences of elder abuse

The adverse effects of abuse on elderly victims refer to different aspects of physical, psychological, and social functioning. Compared with non-abused older persons, victims of abuse have been found to have higher levels of depression, to show symptoms of learned helplessness, and to experience feelings of shame and guilt about the behaviour of their children or partner (Amstadter et al., 2011). These feelings are closely related to denial, which is another way for victims to cope with the trauma of abuse. A review of the literature on the effects of elder abuse on victims by Anetzberger (1997) identified a large number of physical, psychological, behavioural, and social effects of elder abuse, which are summarised in Table 8.5.

Although the list is not exhaustive, it demonstrates that victims of elder abuse experience serious impairments of their physical and mental health and their social relationships. A systematic review of 19 studies examining

TABLE 8.5 Consequences of elder abuse		
Psychological effects		*Behavioural effects*
Denial		Mental confusion
Resignation		Expression of anger
Fear, anxiety		Suicidal actions
Hopelessness, depression		Helplessness
Embarrassment, self-blame		Impaired coping
Phobias		
Dissociation		*Social effects*
		Fewer contacts
Physical effects		Violent actions
Sleep disturbances		Dependence
Eating problems		Withdrawal
Headaches		

Adapted from Anetzberger, 1997, Figure 2, p. 505.

health consequences of elder abuse by Yunus, Hairi, and Choo (2019) established that abused elders have a higher premature mortality rate and a higher morbidity rate, defined by a range of physical and mental health problems, in the periods covered by the prospective studies. Both female and male victims were affected, but the specific symptoms differed between gender groups.

To address the long-term outcomes of elder abuse, the second wave of the National Elder Mistreatment Study in the U.S. assessed participants again eight years after the collection of abuse reports (Acierno, Hernandez-Tejada, Anetzberger, Loew, & Muzzy, 2017). Rates of depression, generalised anxiety disorder, and post-traumatic stress disorder were significantly higher, and self-reported health significantly poorer, among victims than among non-victims. These associations remained when controlling for several other variables, such as age and income.

Overall, the research reviewed in this section has created an extensive body of evidence on the prevalence, risk factors, and outcomes of elder abuse. At the same time, several limitations have become clear that define an agenda for future research into this pressing social problem. Experts in the field have pointed out that future research into the prevalence, risk factors, and consequences of elder abuse should adopt consistent definitions and measurement approaches and conduct more longitudinal studies (Abolfathi Momtaz, Hamid, & Ibrahim, 2013; Daly, Merchant, & Jogerst, 2011; Dong, 2015). There is a lack of studies examining elder abuse in specific groups, such as LGBT elders or elders with a special vulnerability due to illness, for instance dementia, and the moderating role of cultural norms and values related to the care of elders in the family needs to be more fully recognised.

The list of adverse outcomes in Table 8.5 shows that the consequences of elder abuse are very similar to the negative effects of other forms of family aggression. Similar parallels can be observed with respect to the precipitating factors for abuse. Therefore, many of the causes and mechanisms proposed to explain one form of family aggression can also be applied to other manifestations, and several overarching explanatory concepts have been discussed in the literature. In the next section we shall discuss the main explanations for family aggression in its various facets.

EXPLAINING AGGRESSION IN THE FAMILY

As noted at the beginning of this chapter, the different forms of family aggression share a number of common characteristics (see Table 8.1). These include (1) an imbalance of power between perpetrator and victim, supported by economic factors, which enables the dominant persons to enforce their needs through the use of aggression and get away with it; (2) childhood experiences of family aggression by the abuser, promoting the use of violence as a strategy for conflict resolution that leads to the transmission of aggressive behaviour from one generation to the next; and (3) both short-term and enduring behaviour patterns of the victim, such as difficult behaviour of the child. These shared characteristics are also reflected in a common set of explanations for different forms of family aggression (Tolan, Gorman-Smith, & Henry, 2006). Explanations of family aggression can be assigned to one of four levels: (a) the macro-level of the society, or social group, in which family aggression occurs, (b) the level of family functioning, (c) the interpersonal level of interaction patterns between different family members, and (d) the individual level of the perpetrator. A summary of variables that may explain the risk of family aggression at each level is presented in Table 8.6.

Macro-level explanations

Theories in this group seek to identify variables linked to the large variation in the rates of family aggression across cultures (Heise & Kotsadam, 2015; Krahé, 2018). Moreover, they look for variables in the structure, conditions, and value systems of neighbourhoods and particular social groups (Nadan, Spilsbury, & Korbin, 2015). The extent to which violence is accepted in a culture or social group is thought to affect the prevalence of violence against family members. For example, if there is a general consensus that spanking is an accepted and effective way of disciplining children, the use of corporal punishment is seen as a legitimate child-rearing practice. Another social norm that lowers the threshold for family aggression is the view that how parents treat their children, or husbands treat their wives, is nothing but their own business and that it is inappropriate for outside observers to intervene in family conflicts. Along these lines, *cultural spillover theory* postulates that aggression in the family is higher in societies and social groups in

TABLE 8.6 A multilevel approach to understanding family violence

Level of operation	Core assumption: family violence arising out of ...	Explanatory constructs
Macro level	... cultural norms, values, and practices in a society	• Patriarchal gender relations with men dominating women • Cultural acceptance of physical punishment
Family level	... specific constellations and living conditions in a family	• Economic stress • Crowded housing • Lack of communication skills • Transgenerational transmission
Interpersonal level	... relationships and behavioural patterns between individual family members	• Low relationship satisfaction • Difficult behaviour from victim (e.g., child or elder) • Unfavourable cost–benefit analysis • Dyadic stress
Individual level	... personality, biographical experience, learning history of perpetrators ... vulnerability factors of victims	• History of victimisation • Abuser psychopathology • Insecure attachment • Social learning processes reinforcing aggressive behaviour • Misperceptions and deficits in information processing

Based on Barnett et al., 2011; Gelles, 2007; Wolfe, 2011.

which there is a broader acceptance of aggressive behaviour so that legitimate forms of violence spill over into the family context. For example, the military is a social context in which legitimate forms of violence are carried out, and studies have found elevated levels of family aggression in military samples (Rodrigues, Funderburk, Keating, & Maisto, 2015).

Using data from the International Dating Violence Study with college students from 32 countries, Lysova and Straus (2019) tested hypotheses derived from cultural spillover theory. For each country, they calculated an index of legitimate violence based on the pooled responses of participants to several items evaluating the acceptability of violence (e.g., "It is sometimes necessary to discipline a child with a good hard spanking."). This index was then related to students' responses to the physical violence and injury scales of the Conflict Tactics Scales (see Box 8.1). Consistent with cultural spillover theory, they found significant correlations between the normative acceptance of aggression and reports of overall physical IPV perpetration ($r = .35$) and severe physical IPV perpetration ($r = .58$) for the pooled scores aggregated across all participants in a country. These correlations were higher than the correlations between individual participants' approval of aggression and their IPV perpetration ($r = .14$ for the total physical violence perpetration score and $r = .15$ for the severe physical violence perpetration score). Responses to the injury scale did not vary between countries depending on the legitimisation of violence scores. Moreover, the finding of a growing body of research that IPV rates are higher in times of war and armed conflict in a society may be explained by the spillover of violence from the public into the private sphere (Clark et al., 2010; Doyle & McWilliams, 2020; Gold & Simon, 2016; Gould & Agnich, 2016).

In addition, the patriarchal structure of societies has been identified as promoting family aggression, especially in feminist accounts of men's violence against female partners (Marin & Russo, 1999). Patriarchal societies are characterised by a clear-cut power differential between men and women, with men dominating women in most areas of public and private life. Male dominance is linked to a positive evaluation of male assertiveness and aggressiveness. In societies where social institutions are dominated by men, it is hard for women to be acknowledged as victims of male violence, to secure help, and to enforce the legal prosecution of perpetrators. Although linking aggression in the family to power differentials in society would seem plausible, there is limited empirical evidence from psychology to support this notion, at least in Western cultures (Bartholomew, Cobb, & Dutton, 2015; Eckhardt, 2011). An exception is the work by Vandello and Cohen (2008), who examined differences in the acceptability of physical partner abuse in cultures that differ in their endorsement of a "culture of honour". In honour cultures, it is important for men to uphold an image of toughness, which includes their ability to make sure that their female partner behaves in a socially accepted way based on prevailing standards of female decency. If women are seen as violating the honour code by undermining men's authority or reputation, men's use of physical violence can serve to restore their threatened manhood. In addition, indirect support for the idea of patriarchal power structures as a structural variable that promotes family aggression comes from research linking masculinity to family aggression at the individual level (Moore & Stuart, 2005). Theories focussing on male dominance over women are limited in that they cannot explain aggressive behaviour by women in the context of family relationships, nor can they explain violence in same-sex relationships.

Macro-level explanations seek to explain why family aggression is more prevalent in certain societies and social groups. They cannot answer the question why domestic violence occurs in some families but not others, and is performed by some individuals and not others.

Family-level explanations

Explanations at this level treat the family as the unit of analysis and try to identify structural features of family functioning that increase the likelihood of aggression. The *family violence perspective* sees conflict as an inevitable part of family life because of the amount of time family members spend together, the closeness and reciprocity of interactions, and the norms and expectations attached to different roles (Gelles & Straus, 1979). Intra-familial stress, resulting from limited economic resources and environmental stressors, such as crowded housing conditions and poor access to childcare or other social services, has been linked to an increased risk of family aggression. Moreover, members of a family in which conflict is handled by aggressive means learn aggressive behaviour patterns through mutual reinforcement and imitation. If abusers learn that their violent actions lead to the intended consequences, and victims learn that the violence can be stopped by complying with the perpetrator's demands, interaction routines develop that reinforce aggressive behaviour. In abusive families, children learn that aggressive behaviour is rewarded in that the abusers usually achieve their objectives, and they may incorporate aggression into their own patterns of behaviour (Gelles, 2007). Aggression replaces more constructive forms of conflict resolution through negotiation, and prevents the development of appropriate communication skills.

These processes of learning through imitation and reinforcement can explain the transgenerational transmission of violence documented in the literature (Cui, Durtschi, Donnellan, Lorenz, & Conger, 2010). As noted earlier in this chapter, children who experience or witness violence at home are at greater risk of showing aggressive behaviour themselves in subsequent relationships with partners and children, because they adhere to their acquired scripts and patterns of conflict resolution by means of aggressive behaviour.

Interpersonal-level explanations

Explanations at this level consider the nature of the interactions between individual family members as precipitators of family aggression, paying special attention to the dyadic nature of aggressive interactions in the family (Bartholomew et al., 2015). Interpersonal stress resulting from relationship dissatisfaction, and reciprocal provocation (e.g., between a difficult child and a parent using harsh punishment) has been proposed as a risk factor for family aggression. From the point of view of *social exchange theory*, satisfaction with interpersonal relationships within the family is based on a cost–benefit analysis in which family members weigh their investments in the relationship (e.g., emotional commitment, time, money) against the perceived benefits (e.g., emotional rewards, material goods, social status; Gelles, 2007). If the investments are perceived as outweighing the benefits (e.g., when expectations about the partner are not fulfilled or when children place high demands on their parents' attention and care), the theory predicts that dissatisfaction will be experienced and alternative relationships will be explored. Given that marital relationships are not easily terminated and parent–child relationships are even harder if not impossible to dissolve, aggression has been explained as a response to the dissatisfaction that results from relationships in which the costs are seen as exceeding the benefits.

Individual-level explanations

A large body of research has explored the causes of family aggression at the level of the individual perpetrator. One line of explanation has focused on psychopathology to explain abusive behaviour. From this perspective, individuals who suffer from personality disorders or mental illness have a higher risk of abusing family members, particularly because they have problems controlling hostile feelings and aggressive impulses (Eckhardt, 2011). Moreover, as described above, exposure to family aggression in childhood raises the odds of engaging in abusive behaviour in adulthood. Personality characteristics such as low self-esteem, insecurity, and feelings of vulnerability have been proposed to explain why individuals behave aggressively towards family members, who are typically less powerful than themselves (for a discussion of the link between self-esteem and aggression, see Chapter 4).

As noted in Chapter 4, lack of self-control, defined as the capacity to stop, override, or alter unwanted behaviours, has been shown to be related to aggressive behaviour, which includes aggression against a family member. Self-control varies both between individuals as a trait and between situations as a state (Finkenauer et al., 2015). Exerting self-control is seen as an effortful process which is impaired by exposure to stress from outside and within the family system. As a result, the ability to override aggressive impulses is reduced. The self-control model of family aggression by Finkenauer et al. (2015) proposes that in addition to external stressors, such as poverty, frequent conflict, low marital satisfaction, harsh parenting and other negative aspects of family relations undermine the self-regulation capacities of family members, which in turn reduces their ability to control aggressive impulses. In support of this reasoning, research has shown that children exposed to family aggression show deficits in executive function, a core component of cognitive aspects of self-control, and mothers with poorer executive function respond more negatively to children's problem behaviour, leading to the escalation of conflict and violence (Deater-Deckard, 2014).

Finally, misperceptions and misguided expectations have been shown to play a role in both child abuse and partner abuse. For example, misinformed expectations about children's age-normative behaviour and abilities at different ages can lead parents to perceive their child's behaviour as unreasonable and inadequate, resulting in excessive discipline. In child sexual abuse, the abuser may misperceive the child's lack of resistance as an indication of consent. Misperceptions have also been shown to play a role in intimate partner violence. For example, Neighbors et al. (2010) found that physically abusive men significantly overestimated the rate of physical partner abuse in the population at large relative to the rates obtained in representative surveys.

The General Aggression Model (GAM) introduced in Chapter 2 has been applied to individual-level processes that give rise to aggressive behaviour against family members. The GAM conceptualises person variables, such as attitudes condoning violence, and situational influences, such as alcohol and drug use or antagonistic behaviour from a child or elder, as input variables. These factors elicit cognitive processes, such as hostile attributions, affective processes, such as anger, and arousal, undermining self-control, that pave the way for aggressive behaviour towards a partner or family member (DeWall, Anderson, & Bushman, 2011).

The explanations discussed in this section have addressed different variables associated with an increased likelihood of family aggression. Some of these highlight the specific nature of family aggression as resulting from a constellation of characteristics that distinguishes interactions in families from other types of social relationships. Other explanations refer to general theories of aggression to apply them to the family context. No single explanation can aspire, nor indeed claims, to predict precisely who will show abusive behaviour and who will not, and what social and situational conditions precipitate family aggression. Not every man who grows up in a patriarchal society turns into an abuser, nor does everyone who is exposed to external stress or aggressive role models within the family. Macro-level factors, such as cultural norms, are relatively stable and permanent. They provide the background against which aggressive behaviour is carried out. Family-level, interpersonal, and individual factors, such as distressed family relationships, external stress, and also victim-produced stress, have a more immediate impact on the unfolding of aggressive interactions. For example, children who are going through the temper-tantrum stage or elders who are losing control over their vital faculties and need full-time care may create tensions within the family and frustration in the individual carer, both increasing the likelihood of aggressive behaviour. It is the combination and interaction of these different risk factors that eventually precipitate aggressive behaviour against family members.

SUMMARY

- This chapter has reviewed the evidence on the prevalence, risk factors, and consequences of major forms of family aggression: child abuse in the form of physical, sexual, and emotional maltreatment as well as witnessing family aggression, physical aggression towards intimate partners, and abuse of elders in the family.

- Because it is shielded from outside detection and there is a general reluctance to intervene in family affairs, under-reporting is a particular problem for establishing the scale of family violence. Nonetheless, the available sources (official reports, survey data, and research studies) have identified substantial prevalence rates for each form of violence against family members.

- Many effects of family aggression on the victims are similar across different types of abuse. Post-traumatic stress disorder, depressive symptoms, and impairment of physical health are commonly identified in child and adult victims of family aggression. In addition, there is consistent evidence that early exposure to violence in the family makes individuals more vulnerable to victimisation in later life, and also puts them at greater risk of perpetrating violence in their own family.

- A controversial issue refers to gender differences in family aggression perpetration, particularly with regard to intimate partner violence. Whereas surveys and crime statistics suggest that men are more likely to show physical aggression against a female partner, data from research studies based on the Conflict Tactics Scales indicate that women are just as involved as perpetrators of intimate partner violence, if not more so. However, there is consistent evidence of a greater risk of injury to female victims. The distinction between different types of intimate partner violence, in the form of situational couple violence, controlling coercive violence, and violent resistance, may help to create a more differentiated picture of the perpetration of intimate partner violence by men and women.

- Explanations of family aggression discuss causes located at the societal level (e.g., acceptance of corporal punishment), at the level of the family system (e.g., economic stress), at the interpersonal level between family members (e.g., poor communication skills of family members, unrealistic expectations of parents about their children's behaviour), and at the level of the individual perpetrator (e.g., psychopathology, childhood experience of family aggression).

TASKS TO DO

(1) Look up the legal definition of child sexual abuse and the age of consent in your country, and find out what the latest figures are for physical and sexual abuse of children in your national crime statistics.

(2) Ask ten male and ten female students from your year to (anonymously) complete the items of the CTS2 shown in Box 8.1. Do not ask for any additional information except respondent gender. Then collect the responses in a sealed envelope and calculate the mean score on each item for the male and female participants, using the scale from 1 to 6 and calculate the overall scores for the three subscales. *Important*: Do not reveal the classification of the items as representing minor and severe physical assault to your participants. Can you replicate the finding that (a) women score higher on the physical assault scale of the CTS2 and (b) men score higher on the injury scale?

(3) Find out what resources are available in your community for female and male victims of intimate partner violence.

SUGGESTED READING

Barnett, O. W., Miller-Perrin, C. L., & Perrin, R. D. (2011). *Family violence across the lifespan* (3rd ed.). Thousand Oaks, CA: Sage.

Mosqueda, L., & Olsen, B. (2015). Elder abuse and neglect. In P. A. Lichtenberg, B. T. Mast, B. D. Carpenter, & J. L. Wetherell (Eds.), *APA handbook of clinical geropsychology: Vol. 2* (pp. 667–686). Washington, DC: American Psychological Association.

Whitaker, D. J., & Rogers-Brown, J. S. (2019). Child maltreatment and the family. In B. H. Fiese (Ed.), *APA handbook of contemporary family psychology* (pp. 471–487). Washington, DC: American Psychological Association.

Chapter 9

SEXUAL AGGRESSION

Sexual aggression is recognised as a major problem across the world, and the #metoo movement that started in 2017 in response to allegations of widespread sexual aggression in the film industry, personified by the Harvey Weinstein scandal, has raised awareness of the problem far beyond this specific context. In addition to research on childhood sexual abuse, reviewed in the previous chapter, a large and interdisciplinary body of research has studied sexual aggression in adolescence and adulthood. The majority of this work addressed sexual aggression by male perpetrators against female victims, but there is growing recognition that sexual aggression may also be committed by women towards men, as well as in same-sex relationships.

In this chapter, we discuss definitions of sexual aggression, present data on the prevalence of sexual aggression in different victim–perpetrator constellations, review current explanations of the causes of sexual aggression, ask what factors may increase a person's vulnerability to sexual victimisation, and provide findings on the effects of sexual aggression on victims' mental and physical health. The focus will be on sexual aggression in direct, face-to-face interactions, but it should be noted that online sexual harassment and stalking have also been studied as forms of sexual aggression not involving direct physical contact (Gillett, 2018; Henry & Powell, 2018; Smith et al., 2018).

In contrast to intimate partner violence (see Chapter 8), it is undisputed that sexual violence is gender-asymmetrical, with men featuring primarily as perpetrators and women as victims of sexual aggression. As will be shown, this gender imbalance is reflected both in sexual offences recorded by the police and in large-scale victimisation surveys. Nonetheless, the problem of women's sexual aggression against male victims, although far less common, entails similarly adverse consequences, as will be shown later in this chapter.

DEFINITIONS AND SCALE OF SEXUAL AGGRESSION

sexual aggression: making someone engage in sexual activities against their will through a range of coercive strategies, such as threat or use of physical force, exploitation of the inability to resist, or verbal pressure.

As a summary term, *sexual aggression* refers to a range of sexual activities, such as sexual intercourse, oral sex, kissing, and sexual touching, imposed on another person against her or his will. It involves a range of coercive strategies, such as threat or use of physical force, exploitation of the victim's inability to resist, abuse of a position of power, or verbal pressure. Sexual aggression also includes unwanted sexual attention in the form of sexual harassment, stalking, and obscene phone calls (Post, Biroscak, & Barboza, 2011; Sojo, Wood, & Genat, 2016; for a discussion of sexual harassment in the context of workplace bullying, see Chapter 7). A comprehensive definition of sexual violence is given by the World Health Organization:

> Sexual violence is defined as: any sexual act, attempt to obtain a sexual act, unwanted sexual comments or advances, or acts to traffic, or otherwise directed, against a person's sexuality using coercion, by any person regardless of their relationship to the victim, in any setting, including but not limited to home and work. Coercion can cover a whole spectrum of degrees of force. Apart from physical force, it may involve psychological intimidation, blackmail or other threats – for instance, the threat of physical harm, of being dismissed from a job or of not obtaining a job that is sought. It may also occur when the person aggressed is unable to give consent – for instance, while drunk, drugged, asleep or mentally incapable of understanding the situation.
>
> (Krug et al., 2002, p. 149)

Beyond this broad definition, specifying exactly what behaviours qualify as sexual aggression and how to distinguish between different forms of sexual aggression is not a straightforward task, and there are at least three frameworks in which definitions of sexual aggression can be located. The first is the *legal framework* that distinguishes between different forms of sexual violence in accordance with legal provisions. For example, rape is defined in many jurisdictions in terms of obtaining sexual acts involving the penetration of the body without consent, whereas sexual acts that do not involve the penetration of the body qualify as sexual assault or coercion. The second framework is provided by *research definitions* that guide conceptual and empirical work on the extent of, and risk factors for, sexual aggression. Research definitions often include forms of sexual aggression that are not considered to be criminal offences, such as verbal pressure and psychological manipulation. The third framework is the socially shared, *common-sense definition* of sexual aggression that is informed by stereotypical notions of "real rape" and plays a role in social responses to victims of sexual assault. Each set of definitions is linked to specific strategies for measuring sexual aggression, which is why we discuss definitions and data sources for the estimation of prevalence figures together in the next sections.

Legal definitions of rape and crime statistics

Legal definitions vary with regard to the type of sexual acts and coercive strategies that constitute rape, and in distinguishing between other forms of sexual aggression that are considered to be criminal offences. In this section, exemplary evidence will be provided for the U.S., England and Wales, and Germany to show how rape is defined as a criminal offence and represented in annual crime statistics recorded by the police. In all three countries, legal definitions extend to male victims and to rape in marriage. Crime statistics yield incidence rates of the number of cases reported annually to the law enforcement agencies.

For the purposes of nationwide statistics on recorded crime, the Federal Bureau of Investigation (FBI) in the U.S. defines rape as the penetration, no matter how slight, of the vagina or anus with any body part or object, or oral penetration by a sex organ of another person, without the consent of the victim. Attempts or assaults to commit rape are also included in the statistics, but statutory rape (without force) and other sex offenses are excluded (Federal Bureau of Investigation, 2019). In 2018, 139,380 cases of rape were recorded in the database, which corresponds to a rate of 42.6 cases per 100,000 inhabitants.

In England and Wales, rape is legally defined in the Sexual Offences Act of 2003 as intentional vaginal, anal, or oral penetration with the penis when the other person does not consent to the penetration and the actor does not reasonably believe that the other person consents.

This definition of rape covers both marital rape and rape of male victims, but is limited to male perpetrators. During the period from July 2018 to June 2019, 58,947 cases of rape were recorded by the police, which corresponds to a rate of 100 cases per 100.000 inhabitants (Office for National Statistics, 2019b). In Germany, the legal definition in Section 177 has recently changed from a definition based on the use of force to a definition based on lack of consent, which includes the exploitation of a victim's inability or fear to resist, for example because the offender threatens physical harm or exploits an element of surprise (www.gesetze-im-internet.de/englisch_stgb/englisch_stgb.html#p1659). Figures for 2018 show that 9,234 cases of rape were reported to the police, representing a rate of 11.2 cases per 100,000 inhabitants. Of the victims, 95.2% were female, and of the perpetrators, 99% were male (Bundeskriminalamt, 2019b).

Comparing annual incidence rates across countries is difficult because of variations in the legal definitions of rape and other sexual offences. This variability is reflected, for example, in the fifth edition of the *European Sourcebook of Crime and Criminal Justice Statistics*, which includes data from 41 countries (Aebi et al., 2014). Incidence rates of police-recorded rapes in 2011, the latest figures available for the report, showed a mean annual rate of 11.6 per 100,000 inhabitants, but the country-specific rates ranged from 0.5 per 100,000 inhabitants in Armenia to 69.4 per 100,000 in Sweden (Aebi et al., 2014, p. 72). Part of this variation is due to differences in the scope of legal definitions, but other factors, such as willingness to report, are also likely to be involved in this wide variation.

Research definitions and surveys

It is generally agreed that crime statistics reflect only a small minority of cases of sexual aggression, because sexual violence is a vastly under-reported crime, both in terms of the actual number of cases and relative to other crimes of violence (Temkin & Krahé, 2008). For example, of all respondents who reported the experience of an attempted or completed rape in the Crime Survey in England and Wales from 2014 to 2017, only 17% said they had reported it to the police (Office for National Statistics, 2018b). Of the rape experiences reported in the National Crime Victimization Survey in the U.S. in 2018, no more than 24.9% were reported to the police (U.S. Department of Justice, 2019). In the same year, the reporting rate was 62.6% for robbery and 60.5% for aggravated assault, indicating that under-reporting is a problem specific to sexual aggression.

To come closer to estimating the true scale, representative surveys elicit reports of sexual aggression from the perspective of victims irrespective of whether or not they were reported to the police. By comparing the rates detected in these studies with official crime statistics, it is possible to gauge the number of cases of rape and other forms of sexual aggression that go unreported. Moreover, victimisation surveys can examine differences in prevalence rates in relation to sexual orientation and/or gender constellations between victims and perpetrators.

Synthetising the results from population-based surveys carried out with women aged 15 years and older in a wide range of countries, the World Health Organization (2013) found that the lifetime prevalence of non-partner sexual assault was 7.2% across the 58 countries for which data were available. The life prevalence for physical and sexual assault by an intimate partner was 30% (no separate figures for sexual victimisation by an intimate partner were provided). The rates were higher in the low- and middle-income regions than in the high-income regions. However, it must be noted that the findings were aggregated across individual studies that varied in relation to the definition and assessment of sexual assault.

Regular victimisation surveys with representative samples are conducted in several countries to obtain one-year and/or lifetime prevalence data on sexual assault. In the U.S., the National Crime Victimization Survey (NCVS) provides estimates of criminal victimisation in the general popula-tion from the age of 12 years, including both heterosexual and homosexual rape. The most recent data show that the annual rate of rape or sexual-assault victimisation increased from 1.6 to 2.7 victimisations per 1,000 per-sons aged 12 years or older from 2015 to 2018 (U.S. Department of Justice, 2019). The National Intimate Partner and Sexual Violence Survey (NISVS) found that about 1 in 5 women (20.3%) surveyed in 2015 reported having experienced an attempted or completed rape (defined as unwanted pene-trative sex) at some point in their lifetime. The corresponding rate for men was 1 in 17 (2.9%) (Smith et al., 2018).

Representative victimisation surveys also examined differences in preva-lence rates in relation to sexual orientation. Analysing data from the National Violence Against Women Survey (NVAWS), which also included victimisa-tion reports from male participants, Messinger (2011) found that the rate of sexual victimisation by an intimate partner in same-sex relationships was significantly higher than in heterosexual relationships for men (3.1% vs. 0.2%), and slightly lower for women (3.5% vs. 4.5%). A review by Rothman, Exner, and Baughman (2011) of prevalence studies on sexual assault against gays, lesbians, and bisexuals found rates of adult sexual assault among gay and bisexual men ranging between 10% and 17% and rates among lesbian and bisexual women ranging between 11% and 53%.

The report of the 2013 National Intimate Partner and Sexual Violence Survey (NISVS) presented lifetime prevalence rates of sexual victimisation by sexual orientation (Walters, Chen, & Breiding, 2013). For women, the report found a far higher rape victimisation rate for bisexual (46.1%) than for heterosexual (17.4%) and lesbian (13.1%) respondents. In all three groups, the perpetrator was male in more than 85% of the cases. The rape victimisation rate for heterosexual men was 0.7%, and the numbers were too small to calculate rates for gay and bisexual respondents. However, rates for other unwanted sexual contact, such as unwanted kissing in a sexual way, fondling or grabbing sexual body parts, could be computed and were 10.8% for heterosexual, 21.1% for bisexual, and 32.3% for gay men. About three quarters of the gay and two-thirds of the bisexual victims were victimised by another man. In the heterosexual victim group, 70% of the cases involved a female perpetrator, either acting alone or with a man.

In the U.K., annual rates of sexual victimisation are provided by the Crime Survey for England and Wales (formerly: British Crime Survey). Findings covering a two-year period from March 2016 to March 2018 showed that 0.5% of female and 0.1% of male respondents reported having experienced a completed rape (non-consensual penetrative sex) (Office for National Statistics, 2018b). Among respondents surveyed between March 2016 and March 2017, 4.5% of women and 0.2% of men reported having experienced a completed rape since the age of 16. In 99% of cases, the offender was male (Office for National Statistics, 2018a).

For Germany, in a representative sample of more than 10,000 women aged between 16 and 85 years, 13% reported having had unwanted sexual experiences, defined on the basis of the legal definition of rape and sexual assault, since the age of 16 (Müller & Schröttle, 2004). A later representative survey of women aged between 21 and 40 years of age by Hellmann, Kinninger, and Kliem (2018) asked about attempted or completed unwanted sexual intercourse or similar activities through the threat or use of force and found a prevalence rate since the age of 16 of 5.4% and a five-year prevalence rate of 2.5%.

Surveys of college students. The "one-in-five" statistic for the lifetime prevalence of women's risk of sexual assault revealed by the NISVS has also been confirmed in a review of prevalence studies involving female college students (Muehlenhard, Peterson, Humphreys, & Jozkowski, 2017). In the U.S., systematic surveys on sexual aggression and victimisation among college students were pioneered by Koss, Gidycz, and Wisniewski (1987), who used the Sexual Experiences Survey (SES; see Chapter 1) to elicit women's self-reports of sexual victimisation and men's self-reports of perpetration. They found that more than 50% of female students reported some form of sexual victimisation since the age of 14. More than 25% of the male students indicated that they had forced a woman to engage in sexual acts at some point after the age of 14.

Prompted by President Obama's *White House Task Force to Protect Students from Sexual Assault* installed in 2014, large-scale surveys assessing the prevalence of sexual aggression among college students have increased. A review by Krause et al. (2019) identified 107 reports from 101 higher education institutions, which varied substantially in the way they defined and assessed sexual assault. Using a unified methodology, the AAU Campus Climate Survey commissioned by the American Association of Universities collected data at 33 universities (Cantor et al., 2019). Across the participating universities, 25.9% of female undergraduates reported having experienced nonconsensual sexual contact by force or inability to consent since starting university, with a range from 14% to 32%. The rate for male undergraduates was 6.8%. Looking at forms of sexual aggression other than attempted or completed rape, such as penetrative sex through the use of verbal pressure or non-penetrative sex using physical force or threat or exploiting the victim's inability to resist, far higher rates have been identified (Fedina, Holmes, & Backes, 2018; Muehlenhard et al., 2017).

A survey with more than 10,000 students differing in sexual orientation showed that the prevalence rate of forced sexual intercourse in the past 12 months was more than twice as high in sexual minority students (who identified as gay/lesbian, bisexual, queer, pansexual or other) than in heterosexual students (5.9 vs. 2.2%) (Eisenberg, Lust, Mathiason, & Porta, 2017). A special vulnerability for bisexual individuals or those who have sex with both men and women was also found in other studies (Coulter et al., 2017; Ford & Soto-Marquez, 2016).

Internationally, a study including convenience samples of both female and male college students in 38 sites across 18 countries established that 2.3% of women had experienced forced sex and 24.5% had experienced verbal coercion by an intimate partner in the previous year (Hines, 2007). There was considerable variation between sites, with victimisation rates for forced sex ranging from 0% to 13%. The corresponding rates for men were 2.8% and 22%, respectively, with a range for forced sex from 0% to 12%. Another study with convenience samples of university students from ten countries in the European Union also found substantial variability in the prevalence of sexual victimisation, measured across different victim–perpetrator constellations (Krahé et al., 2015). Victimisation comprised unwanted sexual touch, and attempted and completed penetrative sex through the use or threat of force, exploiting the victim's inability to resist, and the use of verbal pressure. The overall victimisation rate for women was 32.2%, and country-level figures ranged between 19.7% (Lithuania) and 45.5% (Greece). For men, the overall victimisation rate was 27.1%, with a range from 10.1% (Belgium) to 55.8% (Greece). A study with first-year students in Germany based on the same instrument and design found a victimisation rate of 35.9% for women and 19.4% for men since the age of 14 years, the age of consent in Germany (Krahé & Berger, 2013).

A smaller body of survey-based research with college students has collected prevalence data on perpetration. A review of 78 samples from studies conducted in the U.S. and Canada found an average rate of 29.3% for any form of male sexual assault perpetration and of 6.5% for rape (R. E. Anderson, Silver, Ciampaglia, Vitale, & Delahanty, 2019). In the European study by Krahé et al. (2015), perpetration reports were collected from men and women. Across all countries, 16.3% of men and 5% of women reported at least one act of sexual aggression perpetration since the age of consent, with figures ranging from 5.5% (Belgium) to 48.7% (Greece) for men and from 2.6% (Belgium) to 14.8% (Greece) for women. In the German sample studied by Krahé and Berger (2013), the perpetration rates were 13.2% for male and 7.6% for female respondents. In the two latter studies, the victimisation and perpetration rates were substantially higher among men and women for participants who had sexual contacts with both opposite-sex and same-sex partners as compared with participants who only had opposite-sex contacts, consistent with research from the U.S. discussed above.

Surveys of high-school students. It is becoming increasingly clear from large surveys of adolescents that sexual aggression and victimisation start well before college age and have substantial prevalence rates in teen dating relationships. Representative data for students in grades 9 to 12 are available from the Youth Risk Behavior Survey. In the 2017 survey, 11.3% of girls and 3.5% of boys reported having been made to engage in sexual intercourse against their will through the use of force in the past year, and a comparison of surveys showed that the rate had not changed significantly since 2007. In a separate question, youth were asked about experiencing sexual violence in a dating relationship, which was reported by 10.7% of the female and 2.8% of the male respondents (Centers for Disease Control and Prevention, 2017). Using data from the same survey, Olsen, Vivolo-Kantor, and Kann (2017) found that the rate of sexual victimisation by a dating partner was significantly higher in youth identifying as lesbian, gay, or bisexual and those not sure about their sexual identity than among heterosexual youth.

In a representative survey of adolescents aged 14 to 17 years in Germany, 22% of sexually active German girls and 30% of sexually active girls from ethnic minorities reported that a boy or man had tried to make them engage in sexual acts or sexual touch by putting pressure on them (Bundeszentrale für gesundheitliche Aufklärung, 2010). A study with Spanish adolescents presenting a broad range of coercive tactics from manipulation to the use of physical force to measure victimisation and perpetration in relationships with other youth found a victimisation rate of 46.6% for female and 48.7% for male adolescents. The perpetration rate showed a clear gender difference, with 48.1% of male and 27.6% of female participants endorsing at least one of the sexual aggression items (Fernández-Fuertes, Carcedo, Orgaz, & Fuertes, 2018).

Overall, the brief discussion of different data sources available to estimate the scale of sexual violence suggests several conclusions. First, it shows that sexual violence is, indeed, a serious societal problem, affecting a large number of individuals and showing substantial prevalence rates in general population surveys and surveys of college and high school students. Second, sexual violence is a gendered problem, in that women are more likely to be victimised than men and perpetrators are predominantly male (however, see below for a discussion of female perpetration), and there is evidence of a special vulnerability of sexual minority groups. Third, official statistics of sexual assaults reported to the police only reflect a small part of the problem, because a majority of cases never enter the criminal justice system, as established by comparing the results from victimisation surveys with official crime statistics. This last point brings us to a discussion of the potential reasons for the low reporting rates of sexual assault. As we will see in the next section, sexual assault is not only a legal category or a construct for research studies, but also a social construction that is defined by a consensus in society.

Stereotypical definitions of the "real rape"

In addition to legal definitions of sexual aggression and definitions for the purposes of surveys and research studies, there is a third and highly relevant context in which the meaning of sexual aggression is defined. This is the context of everyday discourse, reflecting people's intuitive understanding of sexual aggression, most notably rape. A large research literature has shown that the everyday definition of sexual aggression is strongly committed to the *"real rape" stereotype.* This stereotype is a generalised cognitive schema which states that in order to qualify as a "real" rape, a situation has to meet a number of specific criteria: a surprise attack in a dark or isolated place, involving the use of physical force, carried out by a stranger on an unsuspecting victim, who shows strong physical resistance. The more of these criteria are missing in a specific incident, the less likely people are to consider it as a case of "real" rape (Krahé, 2016). Moreover, the "real rape" stereotype contains beliefs about the reactions of a "real" victim after the incident, who is expected to show clear signs of distress and agitation (Klippenstine & Schuller, 2012).

Systematic analyses of rape experiences reported in victimisation surveys clearly show that the "real rape" stereotype is, indeed, a stereotype in terms of an inaccurate overgeneralisation. A consistent finding is that the majority of sexual assault victims know their perpetrators, as current or former partner, friends, or colleagues and acquaintances. For example, in a representative survey from Germany, only 7.1% of sexual assault experiences involved a perpetrator who was a stranger to the victim (Hellmann, 2014). Data from the Crime Survey in England and Wales showed that in 63% of the reported cases of sexual assault experienced since age 16, the perpetrator was a partner, ex-partner, or family member. The same survey also revealed that well over half of all reported incidents took place at either the victim's or the aggressor's home (Office for National Statistics, 2018b). Because many victims know and trust the person attacking them, many assaults come unexpectedly and may explain why there is often no physical struggle. Moreover, victims often freeze with fear and are therefore unable to put up physical resistance (Gidycz, van Wynsberghe, & Edwards, 2008).

Despite its disconfirmation by empirical data on the most common circumstances of sexual assault, the "real rape" stereotype influences the way society deals with rape victims in several critical ways. A consistent finding is the attribution of blame to victims, especially in cases that do not match the stereotype, for example because the attacker was a person known to the victim or the victim did not immediately report the incident to the police (Krahé, 2016). A common design to demonstrate the impact of the "real rape" stereotype is the "mock jury" paradigm in which participants are presented with descriptions of sexual assault incidents and asked to evaluate the perpetrator and the victim. This paradigm enables researchers to manipulate critical information, such as victim or

"real rape" stereotype: generalised cognitive schema that a "real" rape is a surprise attack in a dark or isolated place, involving the use of physical force, carried out by a stranger on an unsuspecting victim, who shows strong physical resistance.

perpetrator behaviour, while holding other aspects of the situation constant. In a recent study using this paradigm, Stuart, McKimmie, and Masser (2019) varied the prototypicality of the victim, presenting her as either emotional and upset or calm and controlled when talking about the incident, the prototypicality of the assault, presenting it as either a stranger or an acquaintance rape, and the prototypicality of the perpetrator, presenting him either as being socially awkward and becoming angry and unsympathetic during questioning or as showing the opposite behaviour. They found that the victim was perceived more negatively in the nonprototypical victim and assault condition, whereas perpetrator prototypicality did not affect participants' judgments. Legal definitions apply equally to both stranger and acquaintance rape and do not refer to victim behaviour at all, so information about the victim's emotional response to the assault and relationship to the perpetrator should not play a role in evaluating a sexual assault charge. However, such negative reactions to victims of sexual assault are common, and there is evidence that they are specific to rape as compared with other violent crimes (Bieneck & Krahé, 2011). Moreover, they proportionately reduce the responsibility attributed to the perpetrator. These social reactions are often experienced as a "second assault" by victims of rape (Temkin & Krahé, 2008; Ullman, 2010). An analysis of data extracted from Twitter showed that tweets about sexual assault that contained victim-blaming statements were retweeted more often than tweets that contained statements supportive of victims of sexual violence (Stubbs-Richardson, Rader, & Cosby, 2018). As shown by Campbell et al. (1999), victims of non-stranger rape, whose experience fell outside the "real-rape" stereotype, were particularly likely to encounter victim-blaming responses from legal or medical professionals, and had significantly higher levels of PTSD.

The "real rape" stereotype has a major impact on the documentation of the prevalence of sexual assault on the basis of surveys and crime statistics. As noted above, the reporting rate for sexual assault is low, both in absolute terms and in comparison with other violent crimes. One reason is that victims of rape may have also internalised the "real rape" stereotype and therefore do not classify an unwanted sexual experience as a sexual assault if it deviates from the stereotype. This group is called "unacknowledged rape victims" based on their endorsement of the experience of rape described in behavioural terms (see, for instance, the items of the Sexual Experiences Survey by Koss et al., 2007, shown in Chapter 1), but say "no" to the question "Have you ever been raped". A meta-analysis by Wilson and Miller (2016) found that the rate of unacknowledged victims was 60% across their 28 studies. These victims are unlikely to report their experience to the police or in surveys using broad questions and labels. Because the "real rape" stereotype completely excludes male victims, men are even less likely than women to acknowledge an unwanted sexual experience as sexual assault (Reed et al., 2020), which suggests that male victimisation rates may be even more affected by under-reporting (Depraetere, Vandeviver, Beken, & Keygnaert, 2018; Lowe & Rogers, 2017).

A second reason for not reporting a sexual assault related to the "real rape" stereotype is that victims of non-stereotypical assaults are aware that others may subscribe to the stereotype and therefore expect that they will not be believed or treated negatively by professionals in the criminal justice system (Chen & Ullman, 2010; Cohn, Zinzow, Resnick, & Kilpatrick, 2013). Several studies show that this fear may not be unfounded, as police officers, prosecutors, and judges may also be influenced by misconceptions and stereotypes about rape (Parratt & Pina, 2017). In a study with police officers in Germany, participants were asked to identify the prototypical features that characterised different rape categories, such as a typical rape, a dubious rape, or a false complaint (Krahé, 1991). When describing a "typical" rape, they selected features such as a young victim, attacked outside by a stranger who was psychologically disturbed, with severe psychological consequences. The typical features assigned to a "dubious" and a "false" rape complaint were very different. In this category, the complainant was assumed to be an older woman (above the age of 40), who was heavily drunk at the time of the alleged assault, claiming to have been assaulted by a friend or acquaintance in his or her own home, and made no attempt to resist. A later study conducted interviews with experienced police officers in England, from which three distinct victim prototypes were extracted: (a) the "real" victim, who is intelligent, well dressed, upset, vulnerable, and wants to go to court, (b) the "mad" victim, who has mental health issues and comes across as vague and irrational, and (c) the "bad" victim that is perceived as overtly sexual, cold, and unemotional (Maddox, Lee, & Barker, 2012). Further evidence shows that rape complaints that meet the definition of the "real rape" stereotype are more likely to progress through the criminal justice system and end in a conviction of the perpetrator, which further corroborates public opinion of what characterises a genuine rape complaint (Lovett & Kelly, 2009; Temkin, Gray, & Barrett, 2018; Wentz, 2019).

Taken together, the data presented in this section make it abundantly clear that the experience of sexual aggression is a reality in the lives of many women and also – although much less researched – in the lives of men. The available evidence shows that sexual assault is a gendered form of aggression, with more women than men experiencing victimisation and the vast majority of perpetrators being male (however, see the discussion on female perpetrators later in this chapter). Therefore, understanding the causes of sexual aggression is a critical task for many disciplines, not least to provide directions for the development of policies and prevention strategies (see Chapter 12).

EXPLAINING SEXUAL AGGRESSION

To understand sexual aggression as a social problem, an explanatory framework is required that considers risk factors at different levels, ranging from the societal level to the individual perpetrator. An overview of variables that affect the likelihood of men's sexual aggression is presented in Table 9.1, based on a comprehensive review of the literature in the "World Report on Violence and Health" (Krug et al., 2002).

Societal factors, such as policies related to gender equality or criminal justice responses to sexual assault, and community factors that lower

TABLE 9.1 Risk factors of male sexual aggression

Societal factors	Community factors	Relationship factors	Individual factors
• Social norms condoning sexual violence	• Poverty mediated through crisis of male identity	• Association with sexually aggressive peers	• Alcohol and drug use
• Social norms supportive of male superiority and sexual entitlement	• Lack of employment opportunities	• Violent family environment	• Coercive sexual fantasies
• Weak laws and policies against sexual violence	• Lack of institutional support from police and justice system	• Patriarchal family structures	• Rape-supportive attitudes and beliefs
• Weak laws and policies related to gender equality	• Tolerance of sexual violence in the community	• Emotionally unsupportive family environment	• Impulsive and antisocial tendencies
• High levels of violent crime	• Weak community sanctions against perpetrators of sexual violence	• Strong emphasis on family honour	• Preference for impersonal sex
			• Hostility towards women
			• History of child sexual abuse
			• Witnessing family violence

Reprinted with permission from Krug et al., 2002, p. 159, © 2002 by the World Health Organization.

the threshold for sexual violence need to be considered as a context in which relationship characteristics and individual differences come to bear. Therefore, a multi-level perspective considering these different factors is required to provide an explanation for sexual aggression. Rather than discussing all of the factors listed in Table 9.1, this section provides a summary of the current state of knowledge about the major factors associated with an increased likelihood of sexual aggression. For the purposes of this review, explanations of sexual aggression will be divided into two groups. The first group will be called "macro-level" explanations, because they locate the causes of sexual aggression in general aspects of societal functioning or in evolutionary development. The second group will be called "micro-level" explanations, because they focus on the individual perpetrator's interpersonal relationships, biographical experiences, and cognitive as well as affective processes as risk factors for sexually aggressive behaviour.

Macro-level explanations

In this section, two models of sexual aggression will be discussed which propose very different processes leading to sexual aggression: the *sociobiological approach* and the *sociocultural approach*. The sociobiological approach suggests a biological explanation of sexual aggression by placing modern-day sexual aggression within the evolutionary history of the human species. By contrast, the sociocultural approach highlights societal features as creating the breeding ground for sexual aggression and allowing it to persist. What the two approaches have in common is their emphasis on general mechanisms at the level of species and societies that promote sexual aggression.

The sociobiological approach. At the core of the sociobiological approach, also known as the evolutionary approach, is the assumption that rape is a product of differences in men's and women's evolved sexuality. The general rationale of the sociobiological explanation of human aggression was outlined in Chapter 2. It refers to the function that a particular behaviour has for the survival of members of a species and/or for the species as a whole. With regard to sexual aggression, the argument is that for some men, and under certain circumstances, rape may be an adaptive strategy that enhances the genetic fitness of the aggressor by increasing his chances of passing on his genes to future generations. A less prominent variant of the sociobiological approach is the idea that sexual aggression has evolved as a by-product of a strong male sex drive, rather than being an adaptive mechanism in its own right for enhancing reproductive fitness (Travis, 2003b).

The mainstream sociobiological argument holds that rape is a facultative mating strategy that is part of the behaviour potential of all men (McKibbin, Shackelford, Goetz, & Starratt, 2008). According to this view, rape is an option in the reproductive behaviour by which men can circumvent obstacles in gaining access to females with high mating value (indicated by youth and physical attractiveness). However, it represents a high-cost mating strategy because most societies impose sanctions on rape, such as prison sentences and social stigma, which ultimately restrict a man's reproductive opportunities even further (Apostolou, 2013). Moreover, the chances of conception from a single sexual act under force are lower than from repeated sexual contacts with a consenting partner. Therefore, sexual aggression will be used only if less risky options are not available. In line with this reasoning, evidence is quoted that rape is more prevalent among men who are at a reproductive disadvantage due to low status, lack of financial resources, or lack of physical attractiveness, which make them undesirable mating partners (Thornhill & Palmer, 2000).

To support the sociobiological model of rape, two main data sources are used: (a) findings from animal studies providing observational data on forced copulation in various species (e.g., orang-utans), as reviewed by McKibbin et al. (2008), and (b) statistical reports on the prevalence of rape perpetration and victimisation in different demographic groups. For example, the over-representation of women of reproductive age among victims and of low-status men among perpetrators is quoted in support of the sociobiological model (Shields & Shields, 1983).

However, limitations have been noted for both data sources in terms of explaining human sexual aggression. As noted by Harding (1985), the operational definition of what constitutes rape in animal behaviour is inconsistent across studies. In addition, the very use of the term rape, which implies constructs such as "without consent" or "against the female's will", to describe animal behaviour is problematic. With regard to rape in humans, relying on statistical information about rape prevalence is also problematic because as shown above, these sources represent a distorted picture of the true prevalence of sexual aggression. For example, the fact that low-status men and ethnic-minority men feature more prominently in official statistics on sexual violence than high-status or majority-group members of society may reflect the operation of social class stereotyping and ethnic bias (for detailed critiques of the sociobiological approach, see Lenington, 1985; Sunday & Tobach, 1985; Travis, 2003a). Moreover, the sociobiological explanation is confined to sexual violence against women of reproductive age, and therefore cannot easily account for several manifestations of sexual aggression: sexual assault on children, on post-menopausal women, on men, and on individuals who are genetically related to the assailant. None of these forms of sexual aggression are functional in enhancing the reproductive fitness of the aggressor, and therefore, they fall outside the scope of the sociobiological explanation of rape.

The sociocultural approach. According to this approach, the roots of sexual aggression are to be found in the fabric of a society, most notably in the social construction of gender relationships (Rennison, 2014; White & Kowalski, 1998). This perspective has been advanced in particular by

sociocultural approach: explanation of aggressive behaviour as shaped by societal and cultural norms and practices.

feminist authors, who have argued that the power differential between men and women in many societies fosters the emergence of sexual aggression (Rennison, 2014). By virtue of their greater social, material, and social power, men claim the right to seek sexual satisfaction regardless of the woman's wishes. Moreover, sexual aggression is instrumental in safeguarding and perpetuating male dominance by instilling a sense of fear and vulnerability in women.

Support for the proposition that sexual aggression is the product of power differentials between men and women that may vary between societies comes from cross-cultural research comparing Western societies with societies in which sexual aggression is far less frequent or even non-existent. For example, Sanday (1981) conducted an ethnographic study of 95 tribal societies, about half of which (47%) she identified as "rape free" (i.e., showing no or only a minimal prevalence of sexual aggression). In contrast, 18% of societies were classified as "rape prone", with a high prevalence of sexual aggression. In the remaining societies, there were reports of rape, but no frequency information was available. In the rape-prone societies, sexual aggression served a ceremonial function (e.g., as a rite of passage for adolescent males) and/or functioned as a means of domination and punishment of women. Rape-free societies were found to have low levels of aggression overall and to place a high value on the contribution of women to the reproduction and continuity of the society.

Studies linking variations in rape rates within the U.S. to women's social status, defined in terms of economic, educational, employment, and occupational indicators, yielded inconsistent findings (Martin, Vieraitis, & Britto, 2006). Whereas some studies found higher rape rates the lower the status of women compared with men, others found higher rates when women had a higher status, and yet others found no link at all. In their own analysis, which included 238 cities in the USA, Martin et al. (2006) found that the rates of police-recorded rapes were lower the higher the status of women.

A multinational study by Hines (2007) including 19 countries examined the prediction that the lower the status of women in the respective countries, the higher the rates of sexual aggression against women would be. Conversely, men's victimisation was expected to be higher in countries where women's status was high. An index of women's status in society was computed based on national-level data on women's participation in education, in the workforce, and in government. This index was related to men's and women's reports of sexual victimisation. As predicted, women's victimisation rates decreased, and men's victimisation rates increased, the higher the country-level status of women, lending support to the sociocultural model. In addition, Hines (2007) developed a country-level measure of adversarial sexual beliefs, denoting the tendency to view the relationship between men and women as hostile and manipulative and to see members of the opposite sex as adversaries. The average level of endorsement of adversarial sexual beliefs within a country was significantly correlated with sexual victimisation rates. The greater women's hostility towards men, the higher male victimisation rates, and the higher men's hostility towards women, the higher female victimisation rates.

The link between power and sexual aggression at the macro-level of societies can also be substantiated by research on the use of rape as a tactic of warfare (Houge, 2015). The analysis by Wood (2014) conceptualised sexual assault as part of a general pattern of violence used by conflict parties against both men and women of the enemy group. Research has further shown that in addition to sexual violence by armed actors, rates of sexual violence in the domestic sphere also go up during and after times of war (La Matina, 2017; Østby, 2016). The sociocultural view outlines conditions that impinge on the members of a particular society and create a platform for the development of rape-supportive attitudes and sexual scripts (see also Chapter 6). It seeks to explain how socially shared conceptions, such as rape myths and gender stereotypes of male dominance and female subordination, are fed into the socialisation experiences of individual members of the society. However, a noted limitation of the sociocultural approach is the focus on male dominance over women, which means that certain forms of sexual aggression, such as male victimisation and female perpetration, cannot be explained conclusively on this basis (Rennison, 2014).

A major source of disagreement between proponents of the sociobiological and sociocultural views on rape has been that, from the sociobiological perspective, rape is seen primarily as a result of male sexual reproduction strategies, whereas the sociocultural view sees rape primarily as a result of male power and dominance over women. However, as Vandermassen (2011) has argued, sexual and power motives for rape are not incompatible and may both be accommodated within a sociobiological framework that focuses on men's control over women. From that point of view, rape may be seen as a strategy serving men's reproductive interests under certain circumstances, a strategy that is related to a more general capacity of men to dominate others in a hierarchy of power (Buss, 1996). Other authors have argued for an integration of sociobiological thinking and psychological analyses of the individual-level risk factors for sexual aggression. A prominent example is Malamuth's (1998) "confluence model" of sexual aggression, which will be discussed below.

Individual-level explanations

Sociobiological and sociocultural explanations focus on general principles, rooted in biological mechanisms and social traditions, which facilitate sexual aggression. In order to understand why only a few members of the species or a minority of people living under certain societal conditions engage in sexual aggression, individual-level explanations are required that identify risk factors for sexual aggression in the perpetrator. Studies addressing individual-level variables have been directed primarily at identifying differences between male aggressors and non-aggressors in terms of biographical experiences, sexual behaviour patterns, as well as affective and cognitive variables, as presented in Table 9.1.

Hall and Hirschman (1991) proposed that sexually aggressive men differ from non-aggressive men with regard to four central aspects: (1) the extent to which they are physiologically aroused by sexual stimuli, (2) the way they perceive and process stimuli pertinent to sexual behaviour in general and sexual aggression in particular, (3) their ability to control their affective responses, and (4) their socialisation experiences and personality characteristics. These aspects may be used as a framework for summarising the available evidence on individual-level risk factors for sexual aggression (Lussier & Cale, 2016; Tharp et al., 2013).

Sexual arousal. Several studies have looked for differences between known sexual aggressors and non-aggressive comparison groups in terms of sexual arousal following exposure to sexually explicit stimuli (Barbaree, Lightfoot, & Prentky, 2018). Sexual arousal is commonly assessed by phallometry, which measures blood flow to the penis following exposure to sexual stimuli (Murphy et al., 2015). Two processes have been examined: *stimulus control* (i.e., whether different types of sexual stimuli – consensual vs. coercive – elicit different patterns of physiological arousal) and *response control* (i.e., whether sexual arousal can be suppressed in response to sexually aggressive stimuli). With regard to stimulus control, a meta-analysis by Hall, Shondrick, and Hirschman (1993) confirmed that sexually aggressive men show a higher level of sexual arousal to depictions of coercive as compared with consensual sexual contacts. When sexual stimuli are combined with aggressive cues (e.g., by exposing respondents to violent pornography), non-aggressive men show a *decrease* in sexual arousal compared with depictions of consensual sex, which does not occur in sexually aggressive men.

In terms of response control, sexually aggressive men were less able to deliberately suppress sexual arousal. Moreover, the incompatibility of sexual arousal and aggressive arousal, which is characteristic of non-aggressive men, was not found in sexual aggressors. Barbaree et al. (2018) propose that sexually aggressive men have a deficit in inhibiting sexual arousal in inappropriate contexts. Beyond comparing identified rapists with non-rapists, studies have examined whether the disinhibition of sexual arousal by stimuli showing nonconsenting sexual interactions can also be triggered situationally. Men in the control group in the study by Yates, Barbaree, and Marshall (1984) showed less sexual arousal to descriptions of nonconsensual compared with consensual sex. Men in the experimental group, who were angered by receiving negative feedback from an attractive female confederate, were equally aroused by the descriptions of consensual and nonconsensual sex. These results indicate that a lack of inhibition of inappropriate sexual arousal may play a role in explaining differences in men's likelihood to engage in sexual aggression.

Lack of impulse control. As noted in Chapter 4, lack of self-control and impulsivity have been identified as stable individual characteristics linked to differences in the tendency to show aggressive behaviour. Moreover, lack of self-control and disinhibition that occur situationally, for example due to alcohol intoxication, predict more aggressive behaviour (see Chapter 5). There is evidence that individual differences in impulsivity distinguish between sexually aggressive and non-aggressive men (Mouilso, Calhoun, & Rosenbloom, 2013) and prospectively predict sexual aggression perpetration (Davis, Danube, Stappenbeck, Norris, & George, 2015). The strong evidence linking alcohol consumption to sexual aggression perpetration will be discussed in a separate section below.

Cognitive processes. Cognitive processes also play an important role in differentiating sexually aggressive from non-aggressive men (for a review, see Drieschner & Lange, 1999). Sexually aggressive men were found to have greater problems than non-aggressive men in shifting attention away from sexual stimuli, as reflected in longer response latencies when they were instructed to switch to an unrelated cognitive task (Yoon & Knight, 2011). The findings of a study by Bargh, Raymond, Pryor, and Strack (1995) suggest that sexual aggressors develop a cognitive association between sex and power that is not apparent in non-aggressors. Bargh et al. (1995) conducted two reaction-time experiments in which men who scored high or low on rape proclivity (i.e., the self-reported likelihood of raping a woman if certain not to be caught and punished; Malamuth, 1981) were exposed to subliminal word primes that referred to power or sex or were neutral with regard to the two domains. Participants then had to pronounce a target word that was also sex-related, power-related, or neutral. Shorter reaction times for pronouncing a sex-related word following the presentation of a power-related prime (compared with reaction times for pronouncing neutral words following a power-related prime, or sex-related words following a neutral prime) were taken as an indication of an automatic cognitive association of power and sex. As predicted, such shorter reaction times for the power-prime/sex-target combination were found only for respondents who scored high on rape proclivity.

Another line of research examined cognitive scripts about consensual sex as risk factors of sexual aggression perpetration. The concept of aggressive scripts was introduced in Chapter 2 as part of the socio-cognitive approach to explaining aggressive behaviour. Based on both direct experience and observation, aggressive scripts contain the characteristic features of a situation in which aggressive behaviour may be shown, expectations about the behaviour of the participants involved, and beliefs about the consequences of engaging in aggressive behaviour. In a similar way, sexual scripts comprise expectations about sequences of actions and events in sexual encounters and serve as guidelines for sexual behaviour (Simon & Gagnon, 1986). Cognitive scripts for consensual sex may be considered risky in terms of predicting sexual aggression perpetration if they contain features that have been linked to increased odds of perpetration, such as seeing alcohol consumption as an integral part of a sexual encounter. Longitudinal studies including adolescents and young adults from different countries have shown that risky scripts for consensual sex predicted higher odds of sexual aggression perpetration via their impact on sexual behaviour (D'Abreu & Krahé, 2014; Krahé, Bieneck, & Scheinberger-Olwig, 2007; Schuster & Krahé, 2019b; Tomaszewska & Krahé, 2018).

Attitudes. Sexually aggressive men were found to differ from non-aggressive men on a range of attitudes related to sexual violence, acceptance of aggression in general, and gender relations. A meta-analysis by Murnen, Wright, and Kaluzny (2002) that included 38 studies found significant associations in the range of $r = .20$ to $r = .30$ between 11 different facets of a masculine gender role ideology and men's self-reported sexual aggression and likelihood to rape. A relevant construct in this context is *rape myth*

rape myth acceptance:
endorsement of stereotypical beliefs about rape that deny, downplay, or justify men's sexual violence against women.

acceptance, defined as the endorsement of stereotypical beliefs about rape that deny, downplay, or justify men's sexual violence against women (Gerger, Kley, Bohner, & Siebler, 2007). For example, rape myth acceptance is reflected in the endorsement of items such as "It is a biological necessity for men to release sexual pressure from time to time" or "Women often accuse their husbands of marital rape just to retaliate for a failed relationship" (Gerger et al., 2007). A meta-analysis by Trottier, Benbouriche, and Bonneville (2019) found a moderate correlation of $r = .23$ between rape myth acceptance and reported sexual aggression perpetration in men across a set of 28 studies. The systematic review by Yapp and Quayle (2018) found support for a significant association between rape myth acceptance and sexual aggression in all but one of the included studies. However, most of the studies were cross-sectional. The few existing longitudinal studies point to rape myth acceptance as a risk factor, not only a correlate, of sexual aggression perpetration. These studies showed that acceptance of rape myths prospectively predicted sexual aggression perpetration over a one-year period (Abbey, Wegner, Pierce, & Jacques-Tiura, 2012) and that the more men endorsed the belief that the relationship between men and women is adversarial in nature, the more likely they were to engage in sexual aggression in the next seven months (Loh, Gidycz, Lobo, & Luthra, 2005). Rape-supportive attitudes, such as agreeing with the statement "When women talk and act sexy, they are inviting rape", were significantly linked to men's sexual aggression measured eight months later (Thompson, Koss, Kingree, Goree, & Rice, 2011).

Biographical experiences and personality traits. In the search for variables that predict sexual aggression, particular attention has been paid to childhood experiences of abuse (see also Chapter 8 for a discussion of the effects of child sexual abuse on later sexual aggression). Several longitudinal studies have demonstrated that male victims of childhood sexual abuse have a higher risk of engaging in sexual aggression as adults (for a review, see Thomas & Fremouw, 2009). In addition, the meta-analysis by Seto and Lalumière (2010) found elevated rates of childhood sexual abuse among adolescent sex offenders in 29 out of 31 studies. Later studies found further evidence for a link between sexual abuse in childhood and sexual aggression perpetration in adolescence and adulthood (Casey et al., 2017;

Chapter 2: History and Theories

Theories of Aggression

	Aggression conceptualised as . . .	Main database	Empirical evidence
Biological approaches			
Ethology	. . . internal energy released by external cues: steam-boiler model	Animal studies	No support as a model for human aggression, but still popular in lay discourse
Sociobiology	. . . product of evolution through natural selection	Animal studies and correlational studies in humans	Support for correlational but not causal links
Behaviour genetics	. . . transmitted as part of genetic make-up	Twin and adoption studies	Support for the predictive value of genetic similarity
Hormonal explanations	. . . influenced by male sex hormones and cortisol	Comparisons of violent and non-violent individuals	Some empirical support
Psychological approaches			

Frustration–aggression (F–A) hypothesis	... a likely response to frustration, likelihood enhanced by aggressive cues	Experimental studies	...on important source for the F–A hypothesis Supported by empirical evidence
Cognitive neo-associationist model and excitation transfer theory	... a result of affect elicited by aversive stimulation that is interpreted as anger	Experimental studies	Supported by empirical evidence
Learning theory	... a result of reinforcement, either direct or indirect (observed)	Experimental and observational studies	Supported by empirical evidence
Social information processing models	... a result of social information processing, enactment of learned scripts	Experimental and longitudinal studies	Supported by empirical evidence
The General Aggression Model (GAM)	... a result of personal and situational input variables eliciting affective, cognitive, and physiological responses	Correlational experimental, and longitudinal studies	Integrating findings from the psychological approaches

Krahé & Berger, 2017; Peterson et al., 2018). The path from child sexual abuse to later sexual aggression is also integral to the confluence model of sexual aggression discussed below.

In terms of personality variables, the concept of psychopathy has been applied to sex offenders. *Psychopathy* is defined as a "constellation of personality traits and socially deviant behaviors, including a narcissistic, grandiose sense of self; lack of empathy, remorse or concern for others; poor impulse control; manipulative approach to interpersonal relationships; and antisocial behavior" (Abbey, Jacques-Tiura, & LeBreton, 2011, p. 451). Supporting earlier research (for a review, see Lalumière, Harris, Quinsey, & Rice, 2005), Abbey et al. found significant links between personality traits related to psychopathy and men's sexual aggression via two pathways: hostile masculinity and impersonal sex, (i.e., a dissociation of sex from emotional bonds).

psychopathy: constellation of personality traits and socially deviant behaviours, including a narcissistic sense of self, lack of empathy or remorse, poor impulse control, manipulative approach to interpersonal relationships, and antisocial behaviour.

Behavioural risk factors: Alcohol. In addition to the stable individual differences between aggressors and non-aggressors, situational factors affect the likelihood of sexual aggression. A powerful situational precipitator of sexual aggression is alcohol consumption. We saw in Chapter 5 that alcohol is generally associated with a greater likelihood of aggression, and sexual aggression is part of this general pattern. It is estimated that about half of all sexual assaults are committed by men who are under the influence of alcohol, and half of all victims of sexual aggression had been drinking at the time of the assault (Abbey, Zawacki, Buck, Clinton, & McAuslan, 2004). Moreover, sexual aggression perpetration under the influence of alcohol does not seem to be a single event. A study with over 12,000 male college students found that 87% of campus sexual assaults involving the use of alcohol were committed by serial perpetrators (Foubert, Clark-Taylor, & Wall, 2020). Both situational drinking and general habits of heavy drinking have been identified as risk factors for sexual aggression in several longitudinal studies (e.g., Abbey & McAuslan, 2004; Swartout & White, 2010).

In a diary study over two months, Testa, Brown, and Wang (2019) found a correlation between self-reported intoxication and the use of sexually coercive strategies in a sample of male college students. To test the hypothesis of a causal effect of alcohol on men's proclivity to engage in sexual aggression, experimental studies have compared intoxicated men with a non-intoxicated control group. A meta-analysis of this literature found a significant, yet relatively small effect size ($d = 0.17$), indicating that sexual aggression is more likely under alcohol intoxication (Crane, Licata, Schlauch, Testa, & Easton, 2017). As noted in Chapter 5, one of the pathways through which alcohol increases the odds of aggression is by reducing the person's information-processing capacities, creating a state of "alcohol myopia". This makes men's perceptions of women's cues of nonconsent less accurate, and increases their likelihood of misperceiving women's friendly behaviour as signalling sexual interest (Benbouriche, Testé, Guay, & Lavoie, 2019; Farris, Treat, Viken, & McFall, 2008).

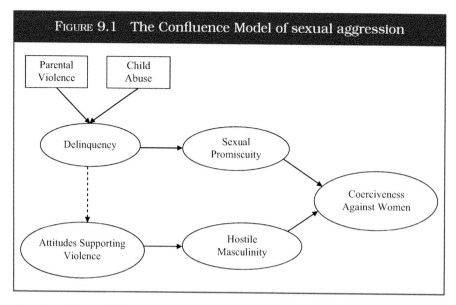

FIGURE 9.1   The Confluence Model of sexual aggression

Adapted from Malamuth, 1998, p. 233.

confluence model:
model explaining men's
sexual aggression by the two
pathways of impersonal sex
and hostile masculinity.

The confluence model of sexual aggression. A theoretical framework that integrates different risk factors for sexual aggression is the confluence model of sexual aggression by Malamuth (1998; Malamuth, Heavey, Linz, Barnes, & Acker, 1995). It was designed to analyse characteristic pathways to sexual aggression by men in the general population (Malamuth, 2018). The confluence model seeks to reconcile the sociobiological explanation of sexual aggression with the sociocultural approach and accommodates several of the risk factors discussed in this section. The original version of the confluence model is presented in Figure 9.1.

Sexual aggression is seen as driven by two independent pathways: sexual promiscuity and hostile masculinity. Sexual promiscuity is theoretically linked to the sociobiological account of sexual aggression. Seeking sexual intercourse with a large number of women is seen as an adaptive strategy for maximising reproductive success, and the willingness to engage in sexual contact without closeness or commitment is seen as lowering the threshold for sexual coercion. Hostile masculinity is theoretically rooted in the sociocultural, feminist account, which reflects cultural norms of male superiority and sees sexual aggression as a response to the threatening of male dominance by women. Hostile masculinity is conceptualised as an attitudinal variable that combines an endorsement of traditional male gender roles with negative attitudes towards women. Each of the two antecedents are predicted by different variables. Sexual promiscuity is seen as deriving from a general tendency towards delinquent behaviour, which is promoted by childhood experiences of parental violence and abuse (see also Chapter 8). Hostile masculinity is influenced by attitudes that support the use of violence, including rape myth acceptance. Either path may lead to sexual aggression independently, but the model assumes that the probability of sexual aggression is higher in men who are both promiscuous and hostile towards women.

In a large-scale study involving 3,000 men, the two paths were able to differentiate between aggressive and non-aggressive men, explaining 78% of the variance in coerciveness against women (Malamuth, Sockloskie, Koss, & Tanaka, 1991). In terms of discriminant validity, men who were sexually aggressive towards women showed elevated levels of both sexual promiscuity and hostile masculinity, whereas men who showed physical aggression towards women scored higher on hostile masculinity, but not on sexual promiscuity.

The confluence model has served as a framework for a large number of studies on risk factors for sexual aggression, and it has been expanded to include additional variables, both by the original authors and other research teams (Casey et al., 2017; Lussier & Cale, 2016; Malamuth & Hald, 2017). These extensions incorporate risk factors consistently shown to predict sexual aggression, such as alcohol use, impulsivity, dominance and low nurturance, the misperception of women's sexual intent, and the role of pornography, that may affect the strength of the model pathways to sexual aggression (Knight & Sims-Knight, 2004; Troche & Herzberg, 2017; Wegner & Abbey, 2016).

The individual-level risk factors discussed in this section could only present a glimpse of the large literature on risk factors for sexual aggression. An additional risk factor is the use of pornography, as discussed in Chapter 6, which affects the content of sexual scripts, attitudes towards women, and perceived norms about acceptable strategies for pursuing sexual interests. Furthermore, being immersed in peer groups that endorse sexual aggression and related risk factors, such as heavy drinking, is a risk factor for sexual aggression (DeKeseredy, Hall-Sanchez, & Nolan, 2018).

VULNERABILITY FACTORS FOR SEXUAL VICTIMISATION

Parallel to the search for risk factors for the perpetration of sexual aggression, research has sought to identify factors linked to an increased likelihood of experiencing sexual victimisation (for a review, see Ullman & Najdowski, 2011). We use the term vulnerability factors rather than risk factors to denote such variables to stress that they are not causal factors for the occurrence of sexual aggression, as the causal responsibility always lies with the perpetrators. Knowing what circumstances, behaviours, and personal experiences make individuals vulnerable to sexual victimisation is important for informing prevention measures and early detection of individuals who may be in danger of sexual victimisation. It may also help individuals to develop a realistic perception of potentially dangerous situations

TABLE 9.2 Factors increasing women's vulnerability to sexual victimisation

- Being married or cohabitating with a partner
- Being young
- Being poor
- Becoming more educated and economically empowered, at least where sexual violence perpetrated by an intimate partner is concerned
- Having previously been raped or sexually abused
- Having many sexual partners
- Consuming alcohol or drugs
- Being involved in sex work

Based on Krug et al., 2002, p. 157.

and behaviours and to protect themselves against sexual victimisation. Table 9.2 presents variables associated with an increased vulnerability of women to sexual assault based on the international literature analysed for the "World Report on Violence and Health" (Krug et al., 2002).

In this section, we look more closely at vulnerability factors for sexual victimisation from two broad categories: behavioural patterns and biographical experiences. For both sets of variables, remarkably consistent findings have emerged across a range of studies. Among the behavioural variables, alcohol consumption in the context of sexual encounters, the ambiguous communication of sexual intentions, and a high level of sexual activity (defined by age of onset of sexual activity and number of sexual partners) were identified as vulnerability factors for sexual victimisation. Among the biographical variables, the most widely studied variable increasing vulnerability to sexual victimisation is a childhood history of abuse.

Across a large number of studies, alcohol consumption emerged as a consistent vulnerability factor for sexual victimisation (Lorenz & Ullman, 2016; Testa & Livingston, 2009). As noted earlier, it is estimated that about half of all victims of sexual assault were drinking at the time of the assault (Abbey et al., 2004). Prospective studies that used measures of general drinking habits to predict subsequent victimisation rates found that regular drinking was linked to an increased probability of experiencing sexual victimisation (e.g., Combs-Lane & Smith, 2002; Messman-Moore, Coates, Gaffey, & Johnson, 2008). One explanation for this link is that alcohol impairs women's ability to process danger cues and assess risks (Gidycz, McNamara, & Edwards, 2006). A comprehensive review of the evidence by Melkonian and Ham (2018) examined the effects of alcohol intoxication on young women's risk recognition and responses in sexual assault situations within the framework of the social-information processing (SIP) theory of aggression (Dodge, 2011). They found that alcohol intoxication affected women's response at every stage of the model: it impaired their encoding of ambiguous cues indicating risk, the interpretation of the cues as signalling risk, the clarification of goals in terms of reducing the risk, the cognitive construction of potential responses, and the selection of a protective response in terms of an increase in passive and decrease of assertive responding. A study in ten EU countries found that general alcohol use was unrelated to the odds of sexual victimisation, but drinking alcohol in sexual situations was significantly linked to a greater likelihood of experiencing sexual victimisation (Krahé et al., 2015).

As noted in Chapter 5, alcohol effects have both a pharmacological and a psychological component. Reflecting the psychological component, alcohol-related expectancies were found to play a role in increasing the vulnerability to victimisation. Alcohol-related expectancies in relation to sexual victimisation focus on the belief that alcohol will have positive effects in sexual encounters, such as relaxation, reduction of inhibitions ("liquid courage"), and the enhancement of sexual pleasure. The more women expect alcohol to have positive effects in a sexual encounter, the higher their risk of sexual victimisation (Dir, Andrews, Wilson, Davidson, & Gilmore, 2018; Messman-Moore et al., 2008; Palmer, McMahon, Rounsaville, & Ball, 2010). Palmer et al. (2010) found that positive alcohol expectancies went hand in hand with lower use of protective strategies, suggesting that positive alcohol expectancies may prevent women from perceiving themselves at risk and taking precautions to mitigate the effects of intoxication. In addition, a woman's consumption of alcohol may indirectly increase the odds of victimisation by contributing to men's misperception of sexual intent. A woman's friendliness is more likely to be interpreted as sexual intent when she is drinking alcohol (Abbey, 2002).

The ambiguous communication of sexual intentions is another factor increasing the vulnerability to sexual victimisation. In particular, this is true for "token resistance" ("saying 'no', when you mean 'yes'"), which refers to the apparent rejection of sexual advances despite being willing to engage in sexual contacts. Muehlenhard and Hollabaugh (1988) argued that token resistance is likely to have negative consequences: it discourages honest communication, makes women appear manipulative, and encourages men to ignore women's refusals. Ambiguous messages also undermine the negotiation of consent in a sexual encounter (Beres, 2010). Several studies have shown that token resistance is widely used by women and men in sexual encounters (e.g., Loh et al., 2005). It has also been established that women who use ambiguous communication strategies are more likely to experience sexual victimisation (Krahé, 1998; Krahé, Scheinberger-Olwig, & Kolpin, 2000; Shotland & Hunter, 1995).

In terms of sexual behaviour, engaging in casual sex, such as "hook-ups" or "one-night stands", has been linked to an increased vulnerability to sexual victimisation (Flack et al., 2016). In a longitudinal study with female college students, the number of hook-up partners predicted the odds of sexual victimisation over time (Sutton, 2017). Moreover, it was found that women who start becoming sexually active at a younger age, have more sexual partners, and engage in casual sex with men were found to have a higher likelihood of experiencing unwanted sexual contacts in a number of prospective studies. In these studies, a high level of sexual activity measured at the beginning of the study was significantly associated with a higher rate of unwanted sexual experiences at a later point (Combs-Lane & Smith, 2002; Gidycz, Hanson, & Layman, 1995). High levels of sexual activity make women vulnerable because they increase the likelihood of encountering sexually aggressive men.

Drinking alcohol, the ambiguous communication of sexual intentions, and engaging in casual sex are part of the conceptualisation of risky sexual scripts, described earlier in this chapter, that have been linked to higher rates of sexual victimisation in several longitudinal studies (D'Abreu & Krahé, 2016; Krahé et al., 2007; Schuster & Krahé, 2019a; Tomaszewska & Krahé, 2018). Unlike most of the research on behavioural vulnerability factors for sexual victimisation that focused on women, this research included both men and women and largely found parallel patterns of associations in both gender groups.

Among the biographical experiences linked to sexual victimisation, childhood sexual abuse stands out as a major risk factor for subsequent revictimisation (see also Chapter 8). Across a total set of 80 studies, the most recent meta-analysis found an average revictimisation rate of 47%, indicating that almost every second victim of sexual abuse in childhood experienced re-victimisation at a later time (Walker, Freud, Ellis, Fraine, & Wilson, 2019). The majority of studies addressed the vulnerability to revictimisation in female victims of child sexual abuse, but there is limited evidence that male victims of sexual abuse also have a higher risk of sexual victimisation as adolescents and adults (Aosved, Long, & Voller, 2011; Krahé, Scheinberger-Olwig, & Schütze, 2001).

Research addressing the underlying mechanisms of the pathway from childhood or adolescent sexual victimisation to later revictimisation has emphasised the role of alcohol and high levels of sexual activity, described earlier in this chapter as risk factors for sexual victimisation (see also the discussion of Finkelhor's, 1987, traumagenic dynamics model in Chapter 8). Perhaps counterintuitively, victims of childhood sexual abuse and adolescent sexual victimisation have been shown to be more sexually active in terms of earlier onset of sexual activity and greater number of sexual partners across a wide range of studies (for a review, see Senn, Carey, & Vanable, 2008). Given the link between high levels of sexual activity and sexual victimisation described earlier, abuse victims' higher level of sexual activity may function as a mediator of the link between childhood abuse and later revictimisation. Similarly, heavy drinking was identified as a mediating variable in a longitudinal study by Testa, Hoffman, and Livingston (2010). Also in line with the traumagenics model, an indirect pathway from CSA to revictimisation via reduced sexual self-esteem in women was shown in a longitudinal study by Krahé and Berger (2017).

An integrative framework for understanding sexual revictimisation has been offered by Noll and Grych (2011). In their Read–React–Respond model, presented in Figure 9.2, they proposed that victims of

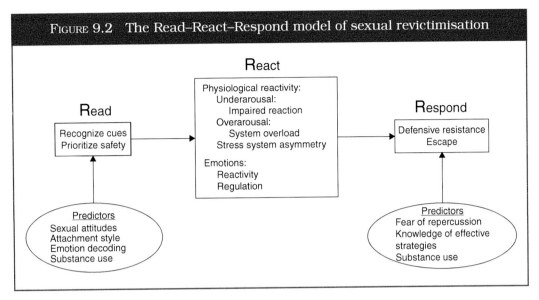

FIGURE 9.2   The Read–React–Respond model of sexual revictimisation

sexual abuse are vulnerable to revictimisation because of impairments in three essential areas of functioning. The first problem for victims of child sexual abuse is a failure to properly "Read" the situation in which an assault may occur. This mis-reading of the situation is due to a greater propensity to engage in risky sexual behaviour, a higher likelihood of alcohol or drug use, an insecure attachment style, and problems in decoding the emotional signals of others. The second phase of problematic functioning is the "React" stage, which refers to physiological and affective reactions in the face of imminent harm. Victims of sexual abuse were found to show physiological underarousal in response to threat, which is dysfunctional in terms of undermining effective resistance behaviour. Finally, in the "Respond" stage, which requires a behavioural reaction to the threat of sexual assault, a history of prior victimisation may impede effective forms of resistance or escape. Evidence from past research supports each of the three stages, but the full model has yet to be tested within a single design.

With regard to the prevention of sexual victimisation, two important messages emerge from the findings discussed in this section. First, evidence that behaviours such as high levels of sexual activity, alcohol consumption, and ambiguous communication strategies are associated with an increased vulnerability to victimisation can be incorporated into rape awareness programmes to enable women to make informed behavioural choices. Second, the evidence on revictimisation identifies victims of childhood abuse as a risk group for subsequent victimisation that should be specifically targeted by rape prevention programmes. Unfortunately, programmes that were successful for non-victimised women had little or no effect on women with a history of childhood sexual abuse or adolescent victimisation (e.g., Hanson & Gidycz, 1993). The potential and limitations of rape prevention programmes will be discussed in more detail in Chapter 12.

CONSEQUENCES OF SEXUAL VICTIMISATION

A wide range of immediate and long-term adverse effects of sexual victimisation have been identified in the research literature. In the weeks and months following the assault, many victims develop the symptomatology of post-traumatic stress disorder (PTSD; see Chapter 7 for a definition). Sexual assault has been identified as one of the strongest risk factors for PTSD in women (Klump, 2006). In fact, the finding that women in the general population show higher rates of PTSD than men has been attributed to the higher prevalence of sexual violence in this gender group (Tolin & Foa, 2008). A comprehensive review of the mental health outcomes of sexual victimisation including almost 500 effect sizes from studies conducted between 1970 and 2014 yielded strong evidence for the impact of sexual victimisation on post-traumatic stress and suicidality, as well as on other indicators of psychopathology, such as depression, disordered eating, and substance abuse (Dworkin, Menon, Bystrynski, & Allen, 2017). The higher level of psychopathology in victim samples was found not only in relation to non-victimised comparison groups, but also in comparison with victims of other traumatic events. The analysis showed that the effects were larger when the assault involved physical injury and the use of weapons, but no difference was found between victimisation experiences where the perpetrator was a stranger vs. a person known to the victim. Importantly, although more than 80% of studies were limited to female victims, comparisons showed no significant differences in the impact of sexual victimisation on women and men. In addition to the effects on mental health, many studies have demonstrated an adverse impact of sexual victimisation in the domain of sexual functioning and satisfaction, and recent studies suggest that PTSD and depressive symptoms may mediate the path from sexual victimisation to impaired sexual satisfaction and functioning (Kelley & Gidycz, 2017). Moreover, a survey of more than 20,000 women in the U.S. identified an elevated risk of a range of physical health problems (Basile, Smith, Chen, & Zwald, 2020).

Unacknowledged rape victims (i.e., those who indicated they had been forced by a man to have sexual intercourse but answered "no" to the question of whether they had ever been raped) reported more severe psychological symptoms, such as anxiety, than women who identified their experience as rape (Clements & Ogle, 2009). Another factor associated with coping problems is the tendency for victims to see the assault as their own fault, blaming it on their behaviour or on characterological faults (Janoff-Bulman, 1979). Sexual assault victims' tendency to blame themselves for the assault has been linked to higher levels of PTSD, depression, and suicidality (Sigurvinsdottir, Ullman, & Canetto, 2019). Self-blame is promoted by negative social reactions to victims who disclose an experience of sexual assault (see discussion earlier in this chapter). A meta-analytic review of the evidence on the link between social reactions and psychopathology found that negative social reactions were linked to higher levels of psychopathology in victims, whereas supportive social reactions. did not seem to have a protective effect (Dworkin, Brill, & Ullman, 2019).

WOMEN AS PERPETRATORS OF SEXUAL AGGRESSION AGAINST MEN

Evidence on the prevalence of sexual aggression clearly shows that men are significantly more likely to engage in sexual aggression compared with women. However, this does not mean that women do not show sexual aggression against men. Whether or not women's sexual aggression needs to, and should be, investigated, given the predominance of male perpetration, has been a controversial issue. A balanced argument was offered by Muehlenhard (1998), who saw the study of women's sexual aggression as important for three main reasons: to avoid research bias, to challenge gender stereotypes, and to acknowledge the reality of men's victimisation experiences. At the same time, she warned about taking a gender-neutral approach as victim and perpetrator roles are not evenly distributed between men and women.

Following a small number of earlier studies (e.g., Krahé, Waizenhöfer, & Möller, 2003; Struckman-Johnson, 1988; Struckman-Johnson, Struckman-Johnson, & Anderson, 2003), recent years have seen an increase in attention to women as perpetrators of sexual assault in relationships with men. In our brief review, we focus on findings from general population or college student samples, excluding analyses of female sexual aggression against other women (see above for prevalence data in same-sex relationships) and studies of female sex offenders in a forensic context (Blake & Gannon, 2018). A summary of the evidence showed that a substantial proportion of men are made to engage in nonconsensual sexual activities by women (Fisher & Pina, 2013). Analysing prevalence data from four large-scale victimisation surveys conducted between 2008 and 2013, Stemple, Flores, and Meyer (2017) concluded that female sexual aggression perpetration is more widespread than previously known. In one of the surveys, two-thirds of nonconsensual sexual experiences categorised as "non-rape" (i.e., being "made to penetrate" someone else, "sexual coercion", "unwanted sexual contact", and "non-contact unwanted sexual experiences") involved a female perpetrator. In another survey, female perpetrators were named in 28% of rapes reported by men. A review of 67 studies comparing male and female victimisation rates by Depraetere et al. (2018) supported this conclusion and identified 22 samples in eight studies in which higher victimisation rates were reported by men than by women.

Few studies have addressed the question of female sexual aggression perpetration by collecting perpetration reports from women. One study that collected data from male and female college students in nine countries of the EU found self-reported rates of women's sexual aggression against a man to range from 2.6% (Belgium) to 14.8% (Greece). By comparison, perpetration reports by men against a woman ranged from 5.5% (Belgium) to 48.7% (Greece) (Krahé et al., 2015). Because female-on-male sexual assaults violate traditional gender roles for both women and men, they are even less likely to be reported than male-on-female sexual aggression. Women are likely to be more reluctant than men to report perpetration (see Chapter 4 for women's sensitivity to normative constraints against aggression), and men may feel their masculinity questioned by not having been able to resist an assault by a woman (Fisher & Pina, 2013; Lowe & Rogers, 2017). The finding that men are less likely to acknowledge a nonconsensual sexual activity as a sexual assault if the perpetrator is female underlines this point (Artime, McCallum, & Peterson, 2014).

Evidence on risk factors for female sexual aggression remains scarce, but the available studies show parallels to the risk factors identified for male perpetration. Studies from several countries found a path from childhood sexual abuse to sexual aggression perpetration in women (Bouffard, Bouffard, & Miller, 2016; Hines, 2007; Krahé, Waizenhöfer et al., 2003). A high level of sexual activity was also identified as a predictor of women's use of force (P. B. Anderson, Kontos, Tanigoshi, & Struckman-Johnson, 2005). Risky sexual scripts for consensual sex predicted women's sexual aggression against men in longitudinal studies (Schuster & Krahé, 2019b; Tomaszewska & Krahé, 2018).

For vulnerability factors of men's victimisation by women, the evidence parallels the findings for women's victimisation by men. For example, alcohol consumption and engaging in casual sex were linked to male sexual victimisation in the same way as it was shown to increase the risk of sexual victimisation for women (Larimer, Lydum, Anderson, & Turner, 1999; Mellins et al., 2017). Parallel paths from risky sexual scripts to sexual victimisation via risky sexual behaviour were found in several longitudinal studies (D'Abreu & Krahé, 2016; Schuster & Krahé, 2019a; Tomaszewska & Krahé, 2018). The need and potential of applying theories of men's sexual aggression against women to the understanding of women's sexual aggression towards men has been highlighted by Turchik, Hebenstreit, and Judson (2016).

Regarding the consequences of male sexual victimisation by women, there is some evidence that men may be less adversely affected than women. In the sample studied by Struckman-Johnson (1988), 27% of the male victims said that they had felt "bad" or "very bad" about the experience, while the corresponding figure for female victims was 88%. Further studies also found that men do not report strong negative reactions following sexual coercion by a woman (Krahé, Scheinberger-Olwig, & Bieneck, 2003; Struckman-Johnson & Struckman-Johnson, 1994). However, in a study with men who were coerced by women to engage in penetrative sex, participants rated the negative emotional impact of the experience at an average score of 6.9 on a 10-point scale. Qualitative follow-up questions confirmed the distressing nature of the experience for most participants (Weare, 2018). A comprehensive review of the literature concluded that male victims may show adverse consequences similar to those identified for female victims (Peterson, Voller, Polusny, & Murdoch, 2011). Therefore, it would be premature to conclude that male victims are not strongly affected by sexual assault by women. Qualitative interviews have shown that many men are left severely traumatised by the experience of sexual victimisation (e.g., Sarrel & Masters, 1982). Measures used in quantitative studies may not be sufficiently sensitive to detect the psychological impact of men's unwanted sexual contact with women. Moreover, the possibility must be considered that men may be reluctant to acknowledge a negative impact of being sexually assaulted by a woman, which would undermine their sense of masculinity. Current evidence on the adverse effects of sexual victimisation on men rests entirely on self-reports of the extent to which they rated the experience as distressing. In order to clarify whether these responses genuinely reflect a low impact or a reluctance to acknowledge distress, self-reports need to be complemented by other indicators, such as a clinical assessment of physical and psychological symptoms.

SUMMARY

*   Legal definitions of sexual assault specify those forms of sexual aggression that constitute criminal offences (such as rape, attempted rape, and sexual coercion). Research definitions cover a wider range of coercive strategies and sexual acts, including non-criminal forms of sexual aggression, such as verbal pressure. In everyday discourse, sexual assault is defined primarily in terms of the "real-rape" stereo-type, characterising rape as an attack by a stranger who uses physical violence to force the victim to engage in sexual acts.
*   Prevalence studies demonstrate the widespread occurrence of sexual assault. Crime statistics, reflecting only cases reported to the police, seriously under-represent the true scale of sexual victimisation, as evidenced by the much higher prevalence rates obtained in victimisa-tion surveys and research studies. The majority of sexual assaults are committed by perpetrators known to the victims, such as acquaintances, dates, or intimate partners, contradicting the "real-rape" stereotype that designates stranger rape as the prototypical form of sexual assault.
*   One group of explanations of sexual aggression refers to macro-level processes, such as the evolution of sexual aggression as a strategy for enhancing male reproductive fitness or sociocultural patterns of male–female power relationships. A second group concentrates on micro-level risk factors, most notably in the individual perpetrator. Sexual aggressors have been found to differ from non-aggressors in

terms of sexual arousal patterns, rape-supportive attitudes, childhood experience of abuse, and risky patterns of sexual as well as drinking behaviour.

- Highlighting that the responsibility for sexual aggression lies with the aggressor, research has identified factors associated with an increased vulnerability to sexual victimisation. High levels of sexual activity, alcohol consumption in the context of sexual encounters, and the ambiguous communication of sexual intentions have been shown to be behavioural vulnerability factors for sexual victimisation. In addition, there is consistent evidence that childhood experiences of sexual abuse are linked to an increased risk of subsequent revictimisation.
- Sexual victimisation has a profound negative impact on victims' psychological well-being and mental health. The rate of post-traumatic stress disorder (PTSD) is high in victims of sexual assault. Victims who blame themselves for being assaulted have greater problems in coping with the assault. Moreover, responses by others to the disclosure of the assault often reflect the attribution of blame to the victim, and derogatory attitudes towards victims of rape held by laypersons, police, and legal professionals have been shown to be experienced as a "second assault".
- Women also commit sexually aggressive behaviour towards men, albeit with lower prevalence rates. Risk factors for female perpetration and male victimisation are similar to those found for male perpetrators and female victims. Even though some evidence shows that men rate their victimisation experiences as less distressing than do women, this does not necessarily mean they are less affected. For men to accept that they have been sexually victimised by a woman is a threat to their self-esteem, undermining their sense of masculinity.

TASKS TO DO

(1) Look up the legal definition of rape in your country and find out how many cases were reported in the most recent crime statistics, comparing male and female perpetrators.
(2) Ask some of your male and female friends what they consider to be a credible rape complaint and engage them in a discussion of the "real rape" stereotype.
(3) Find out what agencies there are in your area to support victims of sexual aggression, and what types of services they offer.

SUGGESTED READING

Depraetere, J., Vandeviver, C., Beken, T. V., & Keygnaert, I. (2018). Big boys don't cry: A critical interpretive synthesis of male sexual victimization. *Trauma, Violence & Abuse*, Advance online publication. doi: 10.1177/1524838018816979

Krahé, B. (2016). Societal responses to sexual violence against women: Rape myths and the "real rape" stereotype. In H. Kury, S. Redo, & E. Shea (Eds.), *Women and children as victims and offenders* (pp. 671–700). New York: Springer.

Lorenz, K., & Ullman, S. E. (2016). Alcohol and sexual assault victimization: Research findings and future directions. *Aggression and Violent Behavior, 31*, 82–94.

Malamuth, N. M., & Hald, G. M. (2017). The confluence mediational model of sexual aggression. In L. A. Craig, M. Rettenberger, A. R. Beech, T. Ward, L. E. Marshall, & W. L. Marshall (Eds.), *The Wiley handbook on the theories, assessment and treatment of sexual offending* (pp. 53–71). Chichester: Wiley Blackwell.

Chapter 10

AGGRESSION BETWEEN SOCIAL GROUPS

interpersonal aggression: aggressive behaviour between individuals rather than groups.

intergroup aggression: aggressive encounters between groups or aggression based on group membership rather than individual characteristics.

collective violence: instrumental use of violence by people who identify themselves as members of a group against another group or set of individuals, in order to achieve political, economic, or social objectives.

The forms of aggression discussed in the previous chapters were manifestations of *interpersonal aggression* involving confrontations between individuals. In the present chapter, we turn to *intergroup aggression* originating in the context of encounters between social groups (Goldstein, 2002). Groups may become involved in violent conflict because they compete for resources, such as power or material profit, which only one party can obtain. However, even in the absence of such conflicts of interest, the mere categorisation of people into groups may produce feelings of intergroup hostility resulting from the desire to promote a positive view of their own group. Intergroup aggression can be both hostile (e.g., letting off steam after the defeat of one's favoured sports team) and instrumental (e.g., attacks by political activists to achieve a particular objective).

Collective violence is another term used to denote aggression in and between social groups. In the "World Report on Violence and Health" compiled by the World Health Organization (WHO), the following definition of the term "collective violence" is offered: "the instrumental use of violence by people who identify themselves as members of a group … against another group or set of individuals, in order to achieve political, economic, or social objectives" (Krug et al., 2002, p. 215). Collective violence comprises (1) political conflicts within and between states (e.g. war, terrorism), (2) state-perpetrated violence (e.g., genocide, torture), and (3) organised violent crime (e.g., banditry, gang warfare). The WHO report identifies a range of conditions at the societal and political levels that make collective violence more likely. The main factors are summarised in Table 10.1.

At the political level, a lack of democratic participation and unequal access to power by different groups within a society increase the risk of collective violence, and inequality is also a risk factor at the societal and community level, through creating competition for material goods and

TABLE 10.1 Risk factors of collective violence	
Political factors	• Lack of democratic processes • Unequal access to political power and to natural resources of different regions, social classes, religions, or ethnic groups
Societal and community factors	• Inequality between groups in the allocation of goods and services • Fuelling of group fanaticism along ethnic, national, or religious lines • Ready availability of weapons
Demographic factors	• Rapid demographic change, particularly increases in population density and in the proportion of young people

Based on Krug et al., 2002, Chapter 8.

status. Furthermore, many of the risk and contributing factors to interpersonal violence discussed in Chapter 5, such as alcohol use, frustration, or high temperatures, can also promote aggression between social groups (Baysan, Burke, González, Hsiang, & Miguel, 2019; Hunt & Laidler, 2001). Although these risk factors may not be sufficient to explain collective violence individually, in combination they create conditions that may precipitate aggressive confrontations between groups. Collective violence may have dramatic consequences for people directly or indirectly involved in the conflict, in terms of their physical and mental health as well as their socio-economic welfare.

The risk factors shown in Table 10.1 operate at the level of society and political systems. From a social psychological perspective, it is equally important to understand what happens to individuals to make them more prone to act aggressively as members of a group. We start by looking at two general theories that seek to explain the psychological processes involved in aggressive encounters between groups. Then we move on to the situational effects of group membership on individuals' readiness to engage in aggressive behaviour when they act as part of a crowd (e.g., in rallies or riots). In the second half of the chapter we turn to more enduring processes of identification and affiliation with social groups, such as juvenile gangs, that lead to aggressive conflict with outgroups.

theory of realistic group conflict: explanation of intergroup conflict as a result of competition for resources that only one group can attain.

THEORIES OF INTERGROUP CONFLICT AND AGGRESSION

The social psychology of intergroup relations can offer two prominent theories for understanding the roots of aggression and violence between social groups: Sherif's (1958) *theory of realistic group conflict* and Tajfel's (1981) *social identity theory*. These theories address fundamental psychological processes underlying confrontations between groups, and provide

social identity theory: explains intergroup conflict as a result of social categorisation into ingroups and outgroups and the desire to favour the ingroup.

general explanations of intergroup aggression that apply to a wide variety of groups.

Theory of realistic group conflict

An obvious answer to the question of why groups get into conflict is because they often compete for goals that only one party can achieve. Aggressive clashes between rivalling sports teams from different local schools are as much a case in point as are wars between countries fought over political influence and territorial claims. Although aggression in conflicts of this kind clearly serves an instrumental function, it is typically accompanied by hostile feelings towards the opposing group. In his *theory of realistic group conflict*, Sherif (1958, 1966) explained how intergroup hostility arises from competition over scarce resources. A basic assumption of his theory is that attitudes and behaviour towards an outgroup depend on the functional relationships between the groups involved. If the relationships are cooperative, positive attitudes and behaviours are developed towards the outgroup, but if the relationships are competitive, negative attitudes and discriminating behaviour develop. These negative evaluations then become ingrained in the collective beliefs of the group and are passed on to new members, who will come to share the prejudicial attitudes and discriminating behaviour even though they may not have had any direct negative experience with the outgroup.

In a series of field experiments, Sherif and his colleagues examined these propositions under natural conditions (Sherif, Harvey, White, Hood, & Sherif, 1961). In the famous "Robbers Cave" experiment, named after the park in Oklahoma where it took place (www.stateparks.com/robbers_cave.html), they studied the behaviour of 11- to 12-year-old psychologically healthy boys, who participated in a summer camp set up by the researchers for the purposes of their studies. In the first phase of the experiment, which lasted for about a week, groups were formed consisting of previously unacquainted boys. These groups engaged in coordinated activities and quickly developed a sense of ingroup identity, calling themselves the "Rattlers" and the "Eagles". In the second phase, which lasted another week, the researchers deliberately created realistic conflicts between the two groups. This was achieved by introducing a series of competitive events in which attractive prizes could be won by the victorious group, and by creating frustrations for each group that appeared to have been caused by the other group. During this phase, the Rattlers and the Eagles developed increasingly hostile attitudes towards each other, up to the point where the Eagles burnt the Rattlers' flag (see Figure 10.1).

At the same time, ingroup solidarity became stronger, widening the psychological distance between the ingroup and the outgroup. The third stage was designed to reduce intergroup conflict by changing the functional relationships between the groups from competition to cooperation. This

FIGURE 10.1   Banner from the original Robber's Cave experiment

Reprinted with permission from the Archives of the History of American Psychology, The Center for the History of Psychology, University of Akron.

was achieved by introducing a series of "superordinate goals" that could only be reached through the joint efforts of both groups. For example, the researchers manipulated the truck that brought the provisions for a picnic so that it broke down and required the joint efforts of both groups to pull it up the hill and get it moving again to reach the picnic spot. Cooperating with the outgroup on this superordinate goal reduced intergroup hostility and promoted positive attitudes and behaviour between the Rattlers and the Eagles. Beyond observational data showing the changes in intergroup attitudes, friendship choices were obtained from the boys at the end of the second and third stages. The percentage of friends chosen from the outgroup at both points in time is shown in Figure 10.2.

In both groups, hardly anyone chose an outgroup member as a friend when there was competition between the groups, but outgroup friendship choices increased significantly following cooperation. This finding supports the assumption that realistic conflicts between groups produce hostile attitudes towards outgroup members, and also points to the role of common goals in promoting positive attitudes between groups.

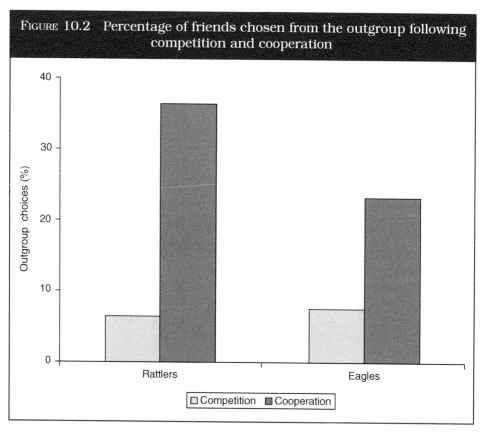

FIGURE 10.2   Percentage of friends chosen from the outgroup following competition and cooperation

Based on Sherif et al., 1961, Chapter 6, Table 1, and Chapter 7, Table 2.

However, an important qualification needs to be made regarding the effectiveness of introducing superordinate goals as a way of defusing intergroup conflict. Working together towards a common goal does little per se to relieve tensions between hostile groups. Its positive effects depend on the *success* of the joint efforts. If the groups fail to reach their superordinate goal, relationships may deteriorate even further because each group is likely to blame the other for the failure. In Sherif's controlled experiments, the successful realisation of the superordinate goal in the third stage was under the control of the researchers, so there was no risk of a boomerang effect. By contrast, in many real-life contexts, success in reaching a superordinate goal is not guaranteed, and the risks of exacerbating the conflict in the event of failure need to be carefully considered.

Striving towards superordinate goals and doing so in a cooperative way are part of the optimal conditions specified by Allport (1954) for reducing intergroup prejudice. In addition, he proposed that contact is most likely to reduce outgroup prejudice if the groups have equal status, and if intergroup contact is embedded in a supportive institutional framework. Pettigrew and Tropp (2006) conducted a meta-analysis of 515 studies and found that studies investigating intergroup contact that took place under these optimal conditions showed greater effects of contact on prejudice reduction than studies of contact that did not meet these conditions. Other research found that contact that is experienced negatively increases prejudice against the outgroup to a greater extent than positive contact can reduce it (Barlow et al., 2012). Contact with outgroup members can improve attitudes about the outgroup by weakening the preference to affiliate with similar others, a phenomenon called "homophily", which leads to segregation between groups. In a longitudinal study with adolescents in four countries (Britain, Germany, the Netherlands, and Sweden), it was shown that greater intergroup contact, defined by the number of friends with a migration background, predicted an improvement of majority members' attitudes to the outgroups over a two-year period (Wölfer & Hewstone, 2018).

As conflicts of interest are omnipresent in intergroup relations, Sherif's theorising applies to a wide range of intergroup constellations. By studying groups that were formed for his experiment and had no prior history of contact, he was able to demonstrate the causal role of introducing conflicts of interest between groups in eliciting hostility and aggression in a naturalistic context. Furthermore, he showed that intergroup attitudes improved as a result of reaching superordinate goals, pointing to a potential strategy for reducing aggression between groups. Consistent with Sherif's assumption that realistic intergroup conflict fuels aggression, a laboratory experiment by Böhm, Rusch, and Gürerk (2016) showed that group members preemptively harm members of another group by making point-allocation choices that deplete the resources of the outgroup if the outgroup has a chance to do the same to their group. In addition to the finding that having their own resources diminished by the outgroup prompts retaliation, this finding demonstrates the effect of realistic conflicts of interest in intergroup aggression.

Building on the work of Sherif, later theorising has extended the concept of realistic threat from outgroups to include symbolic threat. In real life, groups typically have a history that has given rise to a shared sense of identity based on values and traditions. Therefore, outgroups not only pose a realistic threat in terms of jeopardising a group's material interests but may also represent a symbolic threat to the identity of the group. Realistic and symbolic threat often go hand in hand, as evidenced, for example, in the so-called *refugee crisis* in Europe starting in 2015. The influx of large numbers of refugees from Africa and the Middle East into Western Europe was perceived by many members of the host societies as a threat to their material well-being due to the financial burden created. In addition, it was perceived as a threat to their cultural identity, a source of antagonism exploited by right-wing political movements in many of the host countries (Landmann, Gaschler, & Rohmann, 2019). Further demonstrating the role of symbolic threat as a trigger of aggressive behaviour, Li, Leidner, Euh, and

Choi (2016) showed that South Korean participants who were reminded of a past violent conflict with North Korea were more willing to support violent responses in a conflict with a third country, but only when the conflict with North Korea was presented as a conflict of independence between South and North Korea as two nations rather than a civil war within Korea as one nation.

Emphasising the critical role of perceived threat, *intergroup threat theory* specifies the conditions under which contact with an outgroup increases or defuses prejudice and discrimination against that group, postulating that contact that elicits threat will lead to negative attitudes and behaviours towards the outgroup (Stephan, Ybarra, & Rios, 2016). In line with this theorising, the meta-analytic review of 39 studies by Aberson (2019) supported the hypothesis that negative contact is related to higher levels of prejudice via a heightened perception of threat, and positive contact is linked to reduced prejudice via reduced perceived threat (see also Schmid, Hewstone, Küpper, Zick, & Tausch, 2014). No difference in the magnitude of the moderating effect was found between realistic and symbolic threat.

relative deprivation theory: postulates that intergroup tensions arise from the perception that one's own group is unfairly disadvantaged compared with the outgroup.

The importance of perceived rather than objective or material conflicts as a source of intergroup prejudice and hostility is also stressed by *relative deprivation theory* (Smith, Pettigrew, Pippin, & Bialosiewicz, 2012). The theory postulates that it is not the absolute deprivation of a group in terms of lack of resources that gives rises to intergroup tensions but the perception that one's own group is unfairly disadvantaged compared with the comparison outgroup. The meta-analysis by Smith et al. (2012) found small, but significant effect sizes for the association between relative deprivation and negative intergroup attitudes as well as the willingness to engage in collective action which includes violence. Experimental evidence by Greitemeyer and Sagioglou (2019) showed that even when objective resources were high, information that others were better off generated hostility that predicted aggressive behaviour.

Both intergroup threat theory and relative deprivation theory stress the subjective perception rather than the objective degree of intergroup competition for resources as the critical basis for intergroup hostility and aggression. The concept of symbolic threat suggests that intergroup tension may not even require a competitive element. Social identity theory takes this line of thinking one step further and claims that a conflict of interest, whether objective or perceived, is a sufficient, but not a necessary condition for aggression between social groups to occur.

Social identity theory

Sherif (1958, p. 351) already pointed out that individuals are inclined to assign positive attributes to their ingroup, which "tend to be praiseworthy, self-justifying, and even self-glorifying". The idea that a positive evaluation of one's ingroup may be linked to the individual members' feelings of self-worth features prominently in Tajfel's (1981) "social identity theory" (SIT), which is the second influential theoretical framework for conceptualising intergroup conflict (Ellemers & Haslam, 2012). Tajfel started from the proposition that a conflict of interest is a sufficient, but by no means necessary condition for eliciting intergroup hostility and aggression. He argued that discrimination and hostility between groups arise even in the absence of tangible conflicts of interest, merely as a result of social categorisation into ingroups and outgroups.

From the perspective of social identity theory, intergroup aggression is placed in the context of the psychological need to establish and maintain a positive identity (i.e., self-concept). In addition to a positive sense of personal identity based on their individual qualities, people seek to establish a positive identity through the social groups to which they belong (Greenaway, Cruwys, Haslam, & Jetten, 2016). For example, being a member of a national group is a source of personal pride for many people, and they are keen to stress the positive qualities of their ingroup. At the same time, they seek to minimise the positive qualities and emphasise the shortcomings of other groups, thereby achieving positive distinctiveness for their own group (Rupert Brown, 2010). Feeling close to ingroup members and distancing oneself from outgroups gives rise to *ingroup favouritism*, which is defined as preferential treatment and evaluation of ingroup members solely on the basis of their shared group membership. The meta-analysis by Postmes, Wichmann, van Valkengoed, and van der Hoef (2019) revealed a negative association between social identification with relevant groups and depression across 76 studies. The effect was stronger in studies examining identification with groups that involved social interaction, such as friends or work groups, than in studies examining identification with groups defined as social categories, such as national or gender groups.

> **ingroup favouritism:** preferential treatment and evaluation of ingroup members solely on the basis of their shared group membership.

The desire to achieve a positive social identity through seeing one's social group in a positive light is so strong that it even works in so-called "minimal groups". These are groups with no common history or face-to-face contact, to which research participants are randomly assigned. Group members have only the most superficial attribute in common, such as sharing the same group name. In a classic study, Billig and Tajfel (1973) told participants they would be assigned to either Group X or Group W based on the toss of a coin. They were then given the task of allocating money to members of Group X and Group W (without any personal gains for themselves), whereby they could allocate equal sums to members of both groups, or give members of one group more than members of the other group. The results showed a significant shift away from a fair, equal treatment of both groups towards an unfair favouring of members of their own group with whom they had nothing in common but the letter designating their group. This finding showed that social categorisation based on minimal criteria was sufficient to elicit preferential treatment of the ingroup, as suggested by social identity theory.

If group membership determined by chance is capable of eliciting ingroup favouritism (and, by implication, outgroup discrimination), the impact should be far greater in groups that share a common history and fate. The conflict between Protestants and Catholics in Northern Ireland is a case in point. As shown by Cairns, Kenworthy, Campbell, and Hewstone (2006), members of each religious group had more positive feelings for their own community than for the other community, and this pattern was particularly evident for those who identified strongly with their religious community.

Devaluing the outgroup is a stronger form of intergroup bias than merely favouring the ingroup. Outgroup derogation promotes feelings of hostility that may lower the threshold for aggressive behaviour towards outgroup members, even when there is no material conflict of interest between the groups. The minimal group experiments have shown that mere social categorisation can produce ingroup favouritism in the form of a moderate preference for members of one's own group. Hostility towards an outgroup is a much stronger feeling, and, as Roger Brown (1986) has argued, it is unlikely to be produced by minimal group distinctions alone. For hostility towards an outgroup to develop, a further condition is important, namely a sense of unfair distribution of resources that discriminates against the ingroup. This sense of unfairness is likely to arise from a combination of two psychological processes: social comparison with similar rather than dissimilar groups, and the formation of a positive social identity through stressing the positive distinctiveness of the ingroup compared with the outgroup. As Lickel, Miller, Stenstrom, Denson, and Schmader (2006) have shown, there is even a tendency for ingroup members to engage in "vicarious retribution" against outgroups (i.e., to show an aggressive response to an outgroup member after a member of their own group has been the target of aggression from another person in that outgroup). For example, if a German boy sees a member of his national group being verbally abused by a Turkish classmate, he may retaliate by yelling abuse next time he meets another Turkish boy, even though neither he nor the other boy were involved in the initial confrontation.

The link between social identity and aggression towards outgroups has been further supported by a study by Fischer, Haslam, and Smith (2010) in the U.K. In their all-female sample, they either made participants' *national* identity salient (by asking them to list three things they had in common with other British people) or they made their *gender* identity salient (by asking them to list three things they had in common with other women). Half of the participants were subsequently given a text and photos about the terrorist attacks in London on 7 July 2005, representing a threat to national identity, the other half received a text and photos referring to the oppression of women by the Taliban, posing a threat to gender identity. In response to the terrorist scenario, participants perceived a greater threat from terrorists and were more in favour of retaliatory action when their national identity was salient than when their gender identity was salient. Conversely, women whose gender identity was salient perceived a greater threat from the Taliban and greater readiness for aggression than those whose national identity had been made salient. These findings suggest that a threat to social identity is more likely to elicit aggression in contexts in which the particular identity is salient. For example, meeting a student from a university that has a rival sports team should be more likely to trigger hostility in the context of a sports event, when fan identity is salient, than in a neutral context not associated with sports rivalry between the two universities.

Social identity theory offers a broad theoretical approach for understanding hostility and aggression between groups. Seeing the ingroup in a positive light and attributing negative qualities to the outgroup creates positive distinctiveness of the ingroup that is a source of self-esteem for its members. The desire for a positive social identity is apparently so strong that even minimal criteria for defining group membership are sufficient to elicit ingroup favouritism and lay the ground for outgroup discrimination.

Individuals are members of many different groups, and the salience of different group memberships and of social vs. personal identity concerns more generally may vary depending on the context. For example, when travelling abroad, social identity defined in terms of nationality becomes salient, when interacting with professors, social identity defined in terms of student status is likely to be more salient than when interacting with one's parents. Moreover, personal identity may be generally more salient than social identity when interacting with an intimate partner, but social identity in terms of gender roles may be activated when negotiating who does the cooking and who drives the car. This diversity is reflected in *self-categorisation theory*, which has been proposed as an extension of social identity theory to explain when certain group affiliations affect individuals' responses to outgroups (J. C. Turner & Reynolds, 2012). Social identities become salient depending on how often they have been activated in the past and how well they fit with the given context. For example, individuals who strongly identify with their national group are more likely to perceive interactions with a person of different nationality as an encounter between members of two groups rather than two individual people, especially in the context of a match between their national football teams.

Although the theoretical approaches by Sherif and Tajfel focus on different underlying processes, it is clear that realistic conflicts of interest and social identity concerns often go hand in hand in intergroup conflicts. As we shall see in the following sections, this is true for intergroup relations that are relatively stable over time as well as for transient social groups that involve short-term changes in identity and social interests. As examples of intergroup violence between groups that are relatively stable over time, we examine evidence on gang violence and on hate crimes against members of minority groups, before looking at research on crowd behaviour as an example of more transient intergroup encounters.

GANG VIOLENCE

gang: an age-graded peer group that exhibits some permanence, engages in criminal activity, and has some symbolic representation of membership.

A *gang* may be defined as "an age-graded peer group that exhibits some permanence, engages in criminal activity, and has some symbolic representation of membership" (Decker & van Winkle, 1996, p. 31). Indeed, a meta-analysis by Pyrooz, Turanovic, Decker, and Wu (2016) found a robust relationship between gang membership and criminal offending, and gang membership is associated with a higher risk of violence over and above involvement in criminal behaviour (Melde & Esbensen, 2013). Gangs often adopt particular visible features, such as dress, hair style, or insignia, which serve to reinforce cohesion within the gang, present a unified group image to others, and help to achieve visible distinctiveness from other gangs. This special sense of cohesion sets gangs apart from other criminal groups, even though the degree of cohesion and identification of individual members with their gang may vary both between different gangs and within gangs over time (Papachristos, 2013). Although gang violence is by no means confined to adolescence and young adulthood, research has focused primarily on juvenile gangs, not least because membership of a juvenile gang may be the pathway into an adult criminal career. Gangs operate primarily in the neighbourhood of the gang members, including their schools, and hostility and violence between local gangs are a key element of gang activities (National Gang Intelligence Center, 2016).

A picture of the scale of gang-related violence in the U.S. and its changes over time can be gleaned from the *National Youth Gang Survey* of 2,500 U.S. law enforcement agencies that was conducted annually from 1996 to 2012. Whereas gangs were operating in 39.9% of agencies in 1996, the rate decreased to 29.6% in 2012. However, the estimated number of gangs across all agencies remained stable, with an estimated 30,800 gangs in 1996 and 30,700 in 2012 (www.nationalgangcenter.gov/Survey-Analysis/Prevalence-of-Gang-Problems).

In a nationwide survey of students aged between 12 and 18 conducted in 2007, 23% of respondents reported that gangs were active at their school (Dinkes, Kemp, & Baum, 2009, pp. 32–33). Figures for England and Wales show that in the period from March 2016 to March 2018, an estimated 28,000 children aged 10 to 15 years were members of a street gang (Office for National Statistics, 2019c). In addition to accounting for a large number of violent crimes, gang violence shows a distinctive pattern with regard to individual and situational characteristics. For example, Decker (2007) concluded that compared with other homicides, homicides committed by gangs are far more likely to involve male perpetrators, members of racial or ethnic minorities, and the use of guns, and to occur outside and with multiple participants.

According to sources from the 1990s, males outnumber females by a ratio of 20:1 as members of violent gangs (Goldstein, 1994). When girls are organised in gangs, they do not display violence at the same rate as do male gangs but are more commonly involved in auxiliary roles in boys' gangs, as girlfriends, "little sisters", and helpers in the fight against other gangs (Chesney-Lind, 1997). However, more recent research indicates that the gender imbalance has changed in recent years. A review by Sutton (2017) estimated that females make up about 30% of gang members and summarised evidence that all-female gangs are on the increase, female gang members are involved in serious acts of violence, and the age of joining a gang is lower for females than for males. The risk factors for gang membership are similar for males and females, with adverse family environments, low self-esteem, and social isolation listed among the variables. However, the motives appear to be different: males seem to be more attracted by instrumental motives, such as gaining power or escaping poverty, whereas females are more attracted by the prospect of finding affective bonds and protection. This is despite the established finding that many female gang members are subjected to physical and sexual violence by males in their gang (Molidor, 1996). The heightened risk of violent victimisation for females who are members of a gang compared with those who are not was confirmed in a study of high school students by Gover, Jennings, and Tewksbury (2009), but they also found a significantly increased risk associated with gang membership for their male participants. The evidence reviewed by Sutton (2017) further suggests members of all-female gangs are most likely to experience violent victimisation from perpetrators outside the gang, whereas females in mixed-gender gangs are more likely to be victimised by other members of their gang.

Given that involvement in violent gangs is primarily a problem involving young people, the question arises when and how gang members withdraw from these social groups. Although research in this question is scarce, the evidence reviewed by Sutton (2017) shows that both push factors, such as disillusionment and experience of violence within the gang, and pull factors, such as parenthood or employment, play a role. However, the exact impact of these factors is complex. For example, Pyrooz, McGloin, and Decker (2017) found that motherhood was generally linked to a reduction of gang-related violence in female members, whereas fatherhood only showed a parallel effect in male gang members when they lived together with their child.

Theories seeking to explain the emergence of violent gangs and the risk factors for joining them either focus on socio-structural variables in a community that facilitate the formation and activity of gangs, or they look at psychological processes underlying intergroup encounters (Wood, 2014; Wood & Alleyne, 2010). In terms of structural conditions, poor socio-economic background, which prevents legitimate forms of access to material resources and status symbols, is an important factor explaining why young people are attracted to gangs. This may also account for the high proportion of juvenile gang members from ethnic minorities, who are affected by both adverse socio-economic conditions and lack of acceptance by the dominant social group. Several studies conducted across the U.S., summarised by Decker (2007), found a concentration of gang homicides in areas characterised by poverty and social disorganisation. The term "postcode gangs" refers to the fact that gangs sometimes name themselves after the postcode of their area as a marker of territorial claims, which underlines the intergroup nature of gang violence (Whittaker et al., 2019).

In terms of the social psychological processes involved, conditions of disorganisation and marginalisation in a society or community facilitate the emergence of social norms that make violence and criminal behaviour acceptable or even imperative. These norms are passed on to new members through observational learning and peer pressure to become part of their social identity. This process is accompanied by a moral disengagement from social norms outside the gang that prohibit violent behaviour, achieved by the justification of violence, the trivialisation of its consequences, the diffusion of responsibility for any harm to reduce individual blame, and by dehumanising the persons against whom it is directed (Alleyne, Fernandes, & Pritchard, 2014). At the same time, there is evidence that gangs may also acknowledge conventional social norms, for example, by providing assistance to weaker members of the community or ensuring security during neighbourhood events (Wood & Alleyne, 2010). Gang membership may offer a positive social identity to individuals who feel marginalised in other groups, such as their family or non-deviant peers. Through rituals, insignia, and a code of loyalty, gangs create a sense of cohesion between group members (Wood, 2014). Engaging in violent or criminal activities in line with the norms of the gang is a means of gaining status and reputation for individual members.

Decker and van Winkle (1996) have offered an explanation of gang violence based on the construct of *threat*. According to their view, gangs often originate in response to perceived or genuine threats from individuals or

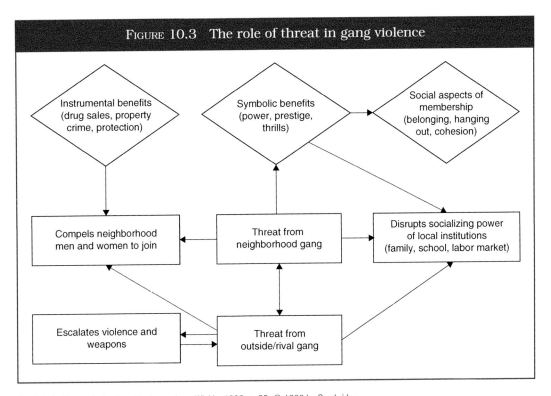

FIGURE 10.3   The role of threat in gang violence

other groups in a particular neighbourhood. This process is promoted by the failure of legal and community institutions to offer effective protection in crime-prone neighbourhoods. Threats may be, or are perceived to be, directed at gang members' physical safety, their territorial claims, and/or their personal identity. To the extent that rival gangs adopt similar perceptions of threat and try to pre-empt their opponents' attacks, gang violence has a strong potential for escalation. Furthermore, the gang's violent actions alienate its members from legitimate social institutions. This marginalisation gives rise to feelings of vulnerability, which are likely to enhance the psychological significance of gang membership for the individual and strengthen affiliation with the gang. Decker and van Winkle's (1996) model of the role of threat in gang violence is depicted in Figure 10.3.

By virtue of their ability to threaten potential opponents, neighbourhood gangs can present themselves as attractive social groups. Group membership offers both instrumental benefits (e.g., protection, or the opportunity for material profit through illegal gang actions) and symbolic benefits (e.g., sharing in the power and prestige attributed to the gang). The presence of rival gangs constitutes an additional element of threat that increases the commitment of the members to their group and sharpens intergroup boundaries. These dynamics of gang behaviour in response to external threat are reflected in the observation that the arrest and incarceration of gang members reinforces gang cohesiveness.

The analysis offered by Decker and van Winkle (1996) ties in with both the theory of realistic group conflict and social identity theory described earlier in this chapter. Rival gangs compete for material gains, such as profits from drug sales, and for symbolic status, such as dominance in their neighbourhood, and the threat of defeat inherent in the competitive nature of intergroup interactions can account for violent confrontations between them. At the same time, gangs can be seen as a means of defining a positive social identity for the individual members, both through identification with the ingroup, reflected in catchy group names and distinctive regalia, and through the derogation of outgroups.

The important role of ingroup identification in explaining gang violence has been further highlighted by Vasquez, Lickel, and Hennigan (2010), who examined gang members' readiness to engage in displaced aggression. Displaced aggression, similar to vicarious retribution discussed earlier, denotes retaliatory aggression towards an outgroup member who was not involved in the initial confrontation or who is treated with a level of violence that is disproportionate to the initial provocation (for a discussion of displaced aggression, see Chapter 2). These researchers identified group-based retribution as a source of escalation in gang-related violence, suggesting that when a gang sees itself as the target of violent actions from another gang, a strong motivation is elicited to retaliate against members of the other gang (who may not have been involved in the original incident), even in those members of the target group who were not directly affected by the initial act of violence. Vasquez et al. (2010) identified a sequence of cognitive and affective processes that underlie displaced aggression in confrontations between gangs.

(1) First, it is important that the initial provocation is perceived by the target group as an instance of intergroup aggression by virtue of the opponents' group membership, rather than an instance of interpersonal aggression between two individuals. Given that gangs typically have a history of rivalry, it is likely that any provocation between individual members will be construed as an act of intergroup aggression.
(2) Once the event is construed as an intergroup confrontation, the likelihood of engaging in aggressive action depends on group members' motivation to retaliate, which is strongly related to their identification with the ingroup. The more individuals use group membership to define a positive social identity for themselves, the more empathy they will feel for group members who become victims of an attack by the outgroup, and the greater their anger will be towards the outgroup in general, not just towards those outgroup members who were responsible for the initial attack. Identification with the ingroup can also explain why gang members feel that their need for retribution has

been satisfied even if they have not personally participated in the retaliatory action. In addition, ingroup identification entails the acceptance of ingroup norms and a readiness to respond to pressure to engage in direct or displaced aggression on behalf of the gang.

(3) Finally, one or more targets need to be chosen against whom to direct retaliative aggression. Although direct retaliation against the provocateur appears to be the most obvious choice, it may be precluded for various reasons. For example, the provocateur may be unavailable or too strong. In this case, the need for retribution can be satisfied by displacing aggression on to other outgroup targets. Vasquez et al. (2010) argued that displaced aggression is more likely the more the outgroup is seen as a cohesive entity in which members form a tightly knit community and are therefore blamed collectively for violent actions carried out by parts of their group. Subsequent research by Vasquez, Wenborne, Peers, Alleyne, and Ellis (2015) found empirical support for this prediction and showed that both ingroup identification and perceived cohesion (entativity) of the outgroup predicted gang violence, but not violence by individuals who were not members of a gang.

Based on this conceptual analysis, Vasquez et al. (2010) suggested that a potential strategy for reducing gang violence is to weaken social identification with the gang. One possibility would be to strengthen a *positive personal identity* so as to override the social identity as a gang member. This could be achieved, for example, through job programmes that enable gang members to boost their self-esteem based on personal achievements rather than affiliation with a deviant group. In support of this idea, there is some indication that dropping out of gangs is facilitated by life events associated with social participation in the mainstream of society, such as forming a stable relationship with a partner outside the gang or becoming a parent, but it only works if these changes come with the possibility of supporting a family with legal income (Moloney, MacKenzie, Hunt, & Joe-Laidler, 2009).

Taken together, the research reviewed in this section shows that gangs have a high propensity to engage in violence, much of which happens in an intergroup context as a result of rivalry with other gangs. Although structural conditions, such as poverty and social disorganisation, play an important role in explaining attraction to gangs, an analysis of the social psychological processes that operate within and between groups further adds to the understanding of gang violence. Gangs offer a means of defining a positive social identity, particularly for those who find it difficult to develop a positive personal identity based on participation in legitimate social institutions. Group identity is consolidated within the gang by shared norms and is communicated among gang members as well as to the outside world through symbolic means, such as names or dress codes. Categorical divisions between "them" and "us" promote outgroup derogation as well as the perception of the outgroup as a homogeneous entity, which facilitates displaced aggression.

HATE CRIMES

hate crimes: criminal acts toward individuals by virtue of their membership to certain social groups or categories.

In this section, we examine a form of violence in which the group membership of the *target person* motivates or triggers aggressive acts. The concept of *hate crimes* denotes criminal acts toward individuals by virtue of their membership to certain social groups or categories. In this section, we use the term in a broader sense of hate-motivated aggression, which also includes aggressive behaviour, such as verbal abuse or discriminatory behaviour, below the threshold of criminal violence against individuals based on their group membership. Groups exposed to hate-motivated aggression may be defined by many different characteristics, but the most widely studied target groups are defined by race (King, Messner, & Baller, 2009), religion (Scheitle & Hansmann, 2016), sexual orientation (Katz-Wise & Hyde, 2012), or disability (Thorneycroft & Asquith, 2015). Hate crimes occur on a large scale across the world and can be distinguished from other forms of aggression and violence by a number of characteristics. Craig (2002) has identified a set of defining features of hate crimes that are presented in Table 10.2.

Compared with acts of violence that are unrelated to the group membership of the targets, hate crimes have a symbolic function in terms of publicly identifying the target group as the object of hate. They have an instrumental function in terms of reducing the targets' social participation by making

TABLE 10.2 Characteristics distinguishing hate crimes from other forms of aggression

Targets	Hate crimes are directed specifically at members of negatively stereotyped social groups
Symbolic function	A message of hate is communicated to the community
Instrumental function	Behaviour of the disliked target groups is controlled and restricted (e.g., keeping them away from certain locations)
Presence of multiple perpetrators	Hate crimes are typically committed as group actions
Increased distress	Hate crime victims may be more traumatised than victims not targeted for their group membership
Deteriorating social relations	Hate crimes spread a climate of suspicion and fear in communities

Based on Craig, 2002.

them avoid certain places and events. They are typically perpetrated by groups of attackers and they undermine social relationships in the community by spreading suspicion and fear, and, it may be added, by reinforcing ingroup-outgroup boundaries. Craig further suggested that hate crimes are associated with greater distress for the victims than victimisation not tied to a group membership, as indicated in a study by Herek, Gillis, and Cogan (1999), but the empirical basis for this claim is as yet limited.

To establish the prevalence of hate crimes in the U.S., hate crime statistics are reported annually by the Federal Bureau of Investigation (FBI), based on the definition of hate crimes as crimes "motivated by bias against race, color, religion, national origin, sexual orientation, gender, gender identity, or disability" (Federal Bureau of Investigation, 2018). For 2018, the FBI recorded 7,036 incidents involving 8,646 victims based on a single dimension of target group membership (i.e., treating the different target groups, such as race and sexual orientation, separately and not in combination). This made it possible to break down hate crimes by target groups, showing that most hate crimes were based on targets' ethnic, racial or ancestry group membership (59.6%), followed by religious affiliation (18.7%) and sexual orientation (16.7%) (Federal Bureau of Investigation, 2018).

A much higher figure was reported for England and Wales. Between April 2018 and March 2019, 103,379 hate crime incidents were reported to the police, more than twice the figure of 42,255 cases reported in 2012 (Home Office, 2019). Of these, the majority of victims (76%) were targeted because of their race, 14% because of their sexual orientation, 8% because of their religion, and 8% because of a disability. This count exceeds 100% because of victims citing more than one group membership. To explain this large difference in the number of hate crimes recorded, it is important to take a close look at how hate crimes are defined in the two databases. In the data for England and Wales, an incident was recorded as a hate crime if it was "perceived, by the victim or any other person, to be motivated by hostility or prejudice towards someone based on a personal characteristic" (Home Office, 2019, p. 2). By contrast, a much more stringent definition is used for the FBI statistics: "Only when law enforcement investigation reveals sufficient evidence to lead a reasonable and prudent person to conclude that the offender's *actions* were motivated, in whole or in part, by his or her bias, should an incident be reported as a hate crime" (Federal Bureau of Investigation, 2011, p. 1). The FBI estimates that a total of about 250,000 hate crimes are committed annually in the U.S., of which most are never reported (Federal Bureau of Investigation, 2018). Once again, this example highlights the importance of paying close attention to the methodologies on which data on aggression are based (Herek, 2017). An informative collection of hate crime statistics in a wide range of countries is available from the website of the Office for Democratic Institutions and Human Rights (ODIHR) at http://hatecrime.osce.org/. The explanations about the databases also underline the challenges in compiling data that are comparable between different countries.

Beyond establishing the prevalence of hate crimes, it is important to understand the psychological processes that lead to acts of aggression against people on the basis of their group membership. Societal and individual factors must be considered jointly to understand hate crimes. For example, the 9/11 terrorist attacks created a general social climate of hostility against Muslims that translated into an increase in anti-Muslim attitudes at the individual level, and was accompanied by an increase in hate crimes against members of this group (Christie, 2006; see also Chapter 11). Similarly, a societal ideology of heterosexism may provide the basis for the stigmatisation of alternative sexual orientations and justify the expression of anger and hostility towards sexual minorities (Alden & Parker, 2005; Parrott & Peterson, 2008). A study from Germany showed that the number of right-wing hate crimes recorded by the police was positively correlated to the unemployment rate at the municipal level (Rees, Rees, Hellmann, & Zick, 2019). Regarding the proportion of foreigners living in a municipality, different results were obtained for West and East Germany. Whereas in West Germany, the proportion of foreigners was unrelated to right-wing hate crimes, in East Germany (the former German Democratic Republic), the hate crime rate was higher the more foreigners lived in the municipality. It is important to note that the actual number of foreigners living in East Germany was four times lower than in West Germany, which is consistent with the proposition in the contact hypothesis that fewer opportunities for contact may be linked to more negative attitudes.

At the individual level, the extent to which these socially shared ideologies are internalised defines a person's racial, religious, or sexual prejudice. *Prejudice* is generally conceptualised in social psychology as a negative evaluation of others by virtue of their membership of a certain social group or

prejudice: negative evaluation of others by virtue of their membership of a certain social group or category.

category, and it is linked to discrimination at the behavioural level (Rupert Brown, 2010). Both Sherif's theory of realistic group conflict and Tajfel's social identity theory discussed at the beginning of this chapter are relevant to understanding the roots of prejudice. The former suggests that negative attitudes towards outgroups arise from conflicts of interest between competing groups, and it would explain hate crimes against members of ethnic or racial outgroups as a result of competition for material resources and social status. The finding by Rees et al. (2019) that participants' feelings of collective deprivation of the ingroup of Germans was positively linked to endorsement of extreme right-wing attitudes is a case in point.

Social identity theory emphasises the role of ingroup favouritism and outgroup discrimination in individuals' search for a positive social identity – for example, heterosexual men's attribution of positive characteristics to their ingroup and their derogation of the outgroup of gay men. Along these lines, Herek (2000) proposed that developing hostile attitudes towards members of sexual minorities is a way of coping with the threat posed by these groups to traditional gender roles and to the masculine self-concept of heterosexual men.

Prejudicial attitudes against members of outgroups defined by race, ethnicity, or sexual orientation have been linked to discrimination against members of those groups (Jones et al., 2017; Richeson & Sommers, 2016). In a longitudinal analysis of survey data in Germany, Wagner, Christ, and Pettigrew (2008) found that ethnic prejudice prospectively predicted negative outgroup behaviour. Several studies have demonstrated significant associations between sexual prejudice and aggression towards sexual minorities (for a review, see Parrott & Peterson, 2008). However, as Baron and Richardson (1994) pointed out, there is no straightforward relationship between prejudice and aggression. Whether or not prejudiced people will respond more aggressively towards members of the rejected groups depends on the influence of mediating factors, such as fear of retaliation and anonymity. When white Americans who held strong prejudicial attitudes towards African Americans had to perform aggressive behaviour in public, they showed "reverse discrimination" (i.e., acted less aggressively towards a black than towards a white target person). By contrast, if their behaviour was recorded anonymously, they showed more aggression towards the black person (e.g., Donnerstein & Donnerstein, 1978).

Drawing on the General Aggression Model proposed by Anderson and colleagues (DeWall & Anderson, 2011) that identifies aggressive affect (anger) as a driving mechanism of aggression (see Chapter 2), Parrott and Peterson (2008) examined the role of anti-gay anger in the link between sexual prejudice and aggression. In their all-male sample, the higher participants' level of sexual prejudice, the greater was their anger about gay men and the more anti-gay aggression they reported to have shown in the past (e.g., "I have spread negative talk about someone because I suspected that he or she was gay" or "I have gotten into a physical fight with a gay person because I thought he or she had been making moves on me").

Moreover, the direct link between sexual prejudice and anti-gay aggression was no longer significant when anti-gay anger was included in the analysis, supporting the claim that men holding anti-gay prejudice tend to behave more aggressively towards this group because they are angrier with them.

It has been demonstrated that rather than behaving aggressively towards members of one particular outgroup, prejudiced people show a higher tendency to engage in aggressive behaviour in general – that is, against targets from all kinds of social outgroups. According to Bar-Tal (1990), *delegitimisation* is an important process mediating between the devaluation of outgroups and the performance of harmful actions against outgroup members. *Delegitimisation* refers to the "categorization of a group or groups into extremely negative social categories that are excluded from the realm of acceptable norms and/or values" (Bar-Tal, 1990, p. 65). If the perception of an outgroup as different and inferior is accompanied by feelings of fear, then delegitimisation is likely to occur. Its function is (a) to maximise the difference between one's own ingroup and the outgroup, and (b) to provide a justification for the exploitation or other ill treatment of the outgroup. The treatment of Jews in Nazi Germany or of black citizens under the South African apartheid regime provide extreme examples of how delegitimisation creates a basis for justifying the oppression, persecution, and killing of outgroup members (see also Bar-Tal, 1997).

Delegitimisation strategies are also reflected in the tendency to shift responsibility for aggressive behaviour from the actor to the target persons who are said to elicit, or at least deserve, the negative actions directed at them. Using a jury simulation paradigm, Plumm, Terrance, Henderson, and Ellingson (2010) showed that participants who held negative views about gay people assigned greater blame to the victim of an alleged antigay hate crime than participants who held more positive views, confirming an earlier finding by Lyons (2006). Comparing the role of prejudice in attributions of victim blame in hate crimes and non-hate crimes, Rayburn, Mendoza, and Davidson (2003) found that members of the white majority group assigned more blame to the victims of a racial, anti-Semitic, or antigay hate crime scenario than to victims of a crime unrelated to a particular outgroup membership of the victim.

An extreme form of delegitimisation is captured in the construct of *dehumanisation*, which describes the tendency to deny outgroups the quality of being humans, for example, by denying human characteristics such as "rational" or "civilised" and ascribing characteristics such as "barbaric" or "acting like animals" (Kteily & Bruneau, 2017). Examples of blatant dehumanisation in terms of denying humanness to other groups are rife in the context of war and genocide, but can also be found in the rhetoric about rejected outgroups outside these contexts. Kteily, Bruneau, Waytz, and Cotterill (2015) developed a measure to assess blatant dehumanisation that is presented in Box 10.1.

Using the "Ascent of Man" measure, Kteily et al. (2015) found that Americans saw their own group and national groups from Western Europe

delegitimisation: categorization of a group or groups into extremely negative social categories that are excluded from the realm of acceptable norms and/or values.

dehumanisation: tendency to deny outgroups the quality of being human.

Box 10.1   The "Ascent of Man" measure of dehumanisation

Instruction:

People can vary in how human like they seem. Some people seem highly evolved whereas others seem no different from lower animals. Using the image below, indicate using the sliders how evolved you consider the average member of each group to be:

Americans ●————————————————————
Arabs   ●————————————————————
Canadians ●————————————————————
Chinese   ●————————————————————
Europeans●————————————————————
Muslims   ●————————————————————

The scale ranges from 0 (*maximum dehumanization*) to 100 (*maximum humanization*) on the sliders.

Based on Kteily & Bruneau, 2015; Kteily et al., 2017.

close to the right endpoint of the sliders with scores greater than 90, but assigned a significantly lower score of 80% to Arabs and Muslims. Dehumanising these groups was related to support for military responses to terrorist acts committed by members of these outgroups that included torture and bombing an entire country in retaliation (Kteily et al., 2015). A series of studies in four European countries at the height of the refugee crisis in 2016 found clear evidence of dehumanisation of Muslim refugees, which was more pronounced in Eastern (the Czech Republic and Hungary) than in Southern (Greece, Spain) countries in Europe (Bruneau, Kteily, & Laustsen, 2018). For example, in the Czech Republic, the average score given to the ingroup of Czechs on the Ascent of Man measure was 90.4 on the scale from 0 to 100, whereas the average score given to the group of Muslim refugees was 53.0. Blatant dehumanisation scores significantly predicted support for anti-asylum policies in all four countries. The target groups are, of course, aware that they are dehumanised and likely to react with aggressive responses, which results in an escalation spiral of intergroup aggression (Kteily & Bruneau, 2017).

The research on hate-motivated aggression reviewed in this section underlines the psychological role of ingroup identification and outgroup derogation in securing a positive social identity. Outgroups become the collective targets of hostility and anger because they have characteristics, such as religious beliefs or sexual orientation, that are perceived as threatening the identity of the ingroup. The fact that many of the target groups of hate crimes represent numerical minorities with limited social power and yet attract such intense feelings of hostility further attests to the impact of psychological variables related to identity construction on this form of aggression.

CROWD BEHAVIOUR

In contrast to groups that exist permanently, such as ethnic or religious groups, or over prolonged periods of time, such as gangs, crowds are transient collectives that are formed on specific occasions. It has long been recognised that people's behaviour changes as they become members of larger groups, and everyday experience confirms this observation. For example, everyone will have witnessed members of a large party in a restaurant who talked so loudly that they entertained the entire room without being aware of the noise level they created, or people who walk through the streets in groups, stepping into the road completely oblivious of traffic. There is plenty of anecdotal evidence that people lose their inhibitions when they are in a group and engage in aggressive and antisocial behaviours, such as setting cars on fire or throwing stones, that they would never show on their own. Moreover, many acts of aggression and violence in the context of sports events are committed by crowds of rivalling fans (see Chapter 7 for research on aggression in the context of sports). In this section, we look at research on aggressive behaviour by crowds of people, asking what can explain the change in behaviour when people move from being on their own to becoming a member of a crowd.

The origins of the scientific study of crowd behaviour lie in the work of the French sociologist Le Bon (1908), who proposed three conditions that give rise to aggression in crowds: (a) anonymity, (b) diffusion of responsibility, and (c) large group size. Under these conditions, people are thought to engage in actions characterised by impulsiveness, irrationality, and regression to primitive forms of behaviour (Vilanova, Beria, Costa, & Koller, 2017). Building on Le Bon's work, Zimbardo (1969) introduced the concept of *deindividuation* to explain why ordinary people engage in behaviours as part of a group that are totally out of character for them as individuals. His *deindividuation theory* claims that individuals acting as members of a large group lose their sense of personal identity and responsibility and may show aggressive behaviour that would normally be inhibited by their internal standards. He investigated this phenomenon with dramatic results

deindividuation: loss of personal identity as a result of being in a crowd or immersed in a specific role.

in his famous "Stanford Prison Experiment" in 1971. In this experiment, he recruited a group of mentally healthy young men, randomly assigned them to the roles of prisoners or prison guards, and asked them to enact their respective roles in a mock prison established in his laboratory at Stanford University. The experiment that had been planned to last for 2 weeks had to be aborted after 6 days because the guards engaged in increasingly cruel treatment of their prisoners, and the prisoners developed symptoms of severe trauma. The study was re-created in the U.K. in a BBC programme under the supervision of social psychologists Steve Reicher and Alex Haslam in 2001, albeit with much less dramatic results (Reicher & Haslam, 2006). In their study, the guards failed to identify with their roles and the guard-prisoner hierarchy eventually collapsed. However, Zimbardo (2006) pointed out that the BBC version differed from the original Stanford prison experiment in a number of ways, not least in the degree to which the experimental setting mirrored the constraints associated with the roles of guards and prisoners in a real prison situation. For example, in the BBC study, prisoners could be promoted to guards on the basis of good behaviour, something that is not normally possible in real prisons.

Regarding the role of anonymity in explaining deindividuation, Silke (2003) analysed 500 violent assaults that occurred in Northern Ireland and compared incidents in which attackers were disguised (wearing masks, hoods, or other clothing to cover their face) with those in which the attackers' faces could be identified. He established that significantly more serious injuries were inflicted, more acts of vandalism were committed, and more people were assaulted in the incidents involving attackers who were disguised. With the advent of social media and virtual communities, new forms of deindividuation have become available to engage in aggression under the cloak of anonymity. The potential for harm of this form of behaviour is substantial, as evidenced, for example, in the growing literature on the prevalence and effects of cyberbullying (Barlett, DeWitt, Maronna, & Johnson, 2018; see also Chapter 7). A study of players of online video games found that the frequency of playing anonymous online games was significantly related to self-reported cheating in the games, and that the association between anonymous playing and cheating was mediated by how strongly players identified with the community of online game players (Chen & Wu, 2015).

To explain why members of large groups engage in aggressive behaviour that they would be unlikely to show individually, a change in attentional focus has been proposed as a key mechanism (Diener, 1980; Mullen, 1983). When people are on their own, their attention is typically focused on the self, and they monitor their own behaviour against the standard of their personal norms and values. By contrast, being part of a larger group shifts attention away from the self to the situation, reducing people's ability to regulate their behaviour in accordance with their personal norms. Instead, they pay more attention to the situational cues, particularly the aggressive behaviour of other group members. On the basis of his self-attention perspective, Mullen (1983) argued that the larger the crowd, the more difficult it is for members to retain the self-focused attention that is important for inhibiting violent behaviour. His analysis of newspaper reports of 60 lynchings in the U.S. between 1899 and 1946 confirmed this line of reasoning. Mullen (1986) demonstrated that lynch mobs were more savage in their atrocities as the size of the mob became larger relative to the number of victims. A later study used photographic records of 22 lynching events between 1890 and 1935. The number of mob members and the number of victims in each photograph were counted, and ratings were made of the level of atrocity of the victims' injuries (Leader, Mullen, & Abrams, 2007; Study 2). The results confirmed the earlier finding that the atrocities by lynch mobs became more savage as the size of the mob increased relative to the number of victims.

Explaining aggressive behaviour in large groups as resulting from a breakdown of individual inhibitions implies a view of crowd behaviour as essentially unregulated by norms that might modulate aggressive behaviour. This view of crowd behaviour as characterised by the absence of social norms has been challenged by an alternative account arguing in favour of a *shift* rather than a *loss* of normative control. *Emergent norm theory* (R. H. Turner & Killian, 1972) proposed that crowd members base their behaviour on what they perceive to be the specific norms shared among the group. This means that behaviour may become either more or less aggressive depending on the normative stance towards aggression that is associated with the group. If being in a large group involves a shift from

emergent norm theory: theory of crowd behaviour proposing that members base their behaviour on what they perceive to be the specific norms shared among the group.

individual norms to perceived group norms, it follows that group behaviour should only be more violent than individual behaviour if the group norms are seen as promoting or at least condoning aggression. This is exactly what the study by Johnson and Downing (1979) showed. They deindividuated their participants either by dressing them in the uniform of the Ku Klux Klan, a group that is strongly associated with aggressive norms, or by dressing them in the uniform of nurses, a group closely associated with prosocial values. In two further individuated conditions, participants also wore the uniforms, but with large name tags attached to make them personally identifiable ("individuated"). The intensity of shocks delivered to an alleged co-participant in a teacher–learner task was the dependent variable in the experiment (see Chapter 1 for a description of this measure). Participants were told that a shock level for each error made by the learner would be set by default, and that they could decide to increase or decrease that level. Selection of shock levels lower than the default setting therefore represented prosocial behaviour, whereas shock levels above the default setting represented aggressive behaviour. Participants in the individuated conditions believed that other group members would be able to identify the intensity of the shocks they delivered, whereas those in the deindividuated conditions believed that their shock settings would not be disclosed. Figure 10.4 presents the findings.

Participants in the Ku Klux Klan uniforms showed more aggression than those in the nurses' uniforms under both individuated and deindividuated conditions. However, as expected, the difference was greater under deindividuation, as indicated by a significant interaction between deindividuation and type of uniform. Thus, under conditions of deindividuation, participants' behaviour was affected to a greater extent by the antisocial and prosocial cues associated with the groups of Ku Klux Klan and nurses, respectively. These findings contradict the notion that deindividuation leads to a general breakdown of normative inhibitions against aggression, and support the more general proposition that it creates greater responsiveness to situational norms.

Sensitivity to group norms is also central to the explanation of crowd aggression based on social identity theory. The *social identity model of deindividuation effects (SIDE)* proposed by Reicher and colleagues stipulates that immersion in a group elicits a shift from personal identity to social identity, which increases the salience of group norms (Reicher, Spears, & Postmes, 1995; Spears, 2017). Postmes and Spears (1998) conducted a meta-analysis of 60 deindividuation studies to contrast the prediction of deindividuation theory that aggressive crowd behaviour is a function of anonymity, reducing adherence to social norms, with the prediction that aggressive behaviour is related to situational norms in favour of, or against, aggression. They found little evidence that deindividuation consistently promoted aggressive

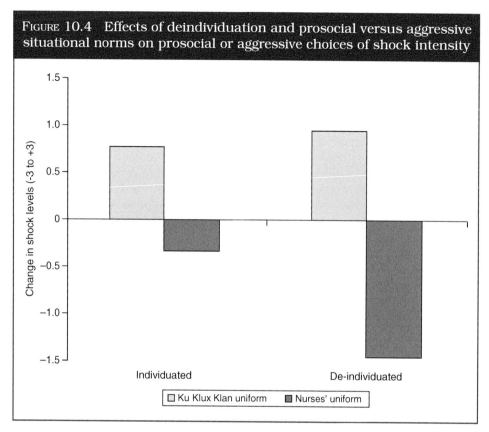

FIGURE 10.4   Effects of deindividuation and prosocial versus aggressive situational norms on prosocial or aggressive choices of shock intensity

Adapted from Johnson & Downing, 1979, Table 1.

behaviour. However, they confirmed that under deindividuation, individuals' behaviour was more affected by situational norms, resulting in more aggression in the presence of pro-aggression norms and less aggression when the perceived situational norms inhibited aggression.

Beyond laboratory settings, historical analyses of riots also disconfirm the view that crowd action is uncontrolled, disorganised, and irrational, and support the importance of shared group norms. Rioting can be defined as a form of collective violence that involves "hostile collective action by a group of about 50 or more people who physically assault persons or property or coerce someone to perform an action" (Bohstedt, 1994, p. 259). For example, Bohstedt pointed out that in early modern Europe, food riots were common in times of food shortages, due to poor harvests and crops destroyed by bad weather. These riots were restrained and organised, based on the idea of a "moral economy," and they were usually successful in bringing down food prices.

In a detailed case study of a riot in the St Paul's area of the city of Bristol in the U.K. in 1980, Reicher (1984) showed that the riot was confined to specific targets within a circumscribed geographical area, and that the rioters had developed a sense of shared identity vis-à-vis their common enemy (i.e., the police). In his sociological analysis of 341 urban riots in the U.S. during the 1960s, McPhail (1994) rejected the view that rioting is the result of structural strains particularly affecting young black males living in socially deprived ghettos. Instead, he proposed a model of rioting as a behavioural response adopted by a person to achieve a particular aim (e.g., pursuing a political goal, acting out aggressive feelings against another group). In summarising his "purposive action model," McPhail concluded that "violent actors are neither the hapless victims of structural strain nor of psychological de-individuation. Purposive actors adjust their behaviours to make their perceptions match their objectives. They bear responsibility for those violent objectives and for the violent actions in which they engage" (McPhail, 1994, p. 25). In combination, these approaches challenge Le Bon's view of crowd behaviour as characterised by impulsiveness, irrationality, and regression to primitive forms of behaviour, highlighting other psychological mechanisms, such as identity shift and attention to situational norms, in guiding the behaviour of individuals acting in a crowd.

SUMMARY

- Intergroup aggression and collective violence refer to a range of different forms of aggressive behaviour carried out by groups of individuals whose behaviour is shaped by the fact that they feel, think, or act as part of a group.
- Intergroup conflict arises out of competition when groups have incompatible goals, and it can be reduced by making groups engage in superordinate goals that require cooperation. This was argued in Sherif's theory of realistic group conflict and demonstrated in his famous Robbers Cave experiment. However, as argued by Tajfel in his social identity theory, intergroup aggression arises even in the absence of realistic conflicts as a result of social categorisations into ingroups and outgroups that enables individuals to establish a positive social identity through seeing their ingroup as more positive than the outgroup.
- Gang violence often involves extreme forms of intergroup violence, and represents a significant social problem. In addition to structural conditions, such as poverty, concerns for social identity also play a role in explaining why people, especially young people, become involved with violent gangs. Much of the violent behaviour shown by gangs is directed against rival gangs and therefore qualifies as intergroup aggression. Favouring the ingroup and derogating the outgroup in the

service of achieving a positive social identity from gang membership are potent psychological processes that fuel aggressive confrontations between gangs.

- Hate crimes are a form of intergroup aggression in which victims are targeted because of specific characteristics, such as their ethnic, racial, or religious group membership, or their sexual orientation. Hate crimes are driven by societal ideologies that marginalise or derogate the groups, which in turn gives rise to prejudicial attitudes against these groups at the individual level. Dehumanising outgroups and questioning their legitimate rights of social participation, provides a basis for justifying aggressive treatment of minority groups.
- Crowd violence and rioting are forms of collective violence that occur in specific contexts in transient social groups. Whereas earlier research on deindividuation explained aggressive crowd behaviour as the result of a breakdown of self-regulation and normative control, subsequent explanations stressed a shift from individual norms to group norms. According to this view, crowd behaviour is more aggressive than individual behaviour when the crowd endorses norms that disinhibit aggressive behaviour. Case studies of riots suggest that these forms of collective violence only superficially appear unregulated and anarchic. In fact, they are often based on a normative structure evolved within the group, such as limiting aggression to specific target groups or locations.

TASKS TO DO

(1) Look at the detailed description of the Robbers Cave experiment by Sherif et al., including original photos, on (http://psychclassics.yorku. ca/Sherif/index.htm).
(2) Visit the website of the Office for Democratic Institutions and Human Rights (ODIHR) at http://hatecrime.osce.org/ to look up the most recent hate crime statistics for your country or the country closest to where you live and compare them with one or two neighbouring countries.
(3) Watch the original video footage from Zimbardo's Stanford Prison Experiment on the official website (www.prisonexp.org). Also visit the website of the BBC Prison Study (www.bbcprisonstudy.org) and look out for differences between the two studies.

SUGGESTED READING

Ellemers, N., & Haslam, S. A. (2012). Social identity theory. In P. A. M. van Lange, A. W. Kruglanski, & E. T. Higgins (Eds.), *Handbook of theories of social psychology* (pp. 379–398). London: Sage.

Sherif, M. (1958). Superordinate goals in the reduction of intergroup conflict. *American Journal of Sociology, 63,* 349–356.

Sutton, T. E. (2017). The lives of female gang members: A review of the literature. *Aggression and Violent Behavior, 37*, 142–152.

Vilanova, F., Beria, F. M., Costa, Â. B., & Koller, S. H. (2017). Deindividuation: From Le Bon to the social identity model of deindividuation effects. *Cogent Psychology, 4*, Article ID: 1308104.

Chapter 11

TERRORISM

Terrorism is a special form of group-based aggression that poses a major threat to the safety and well-being of people around the globe. Despite the worldwide notoriety achieved by individual terrorists, such as Osama bin Laden, terrorism is for the most part an intergroup phenomenon (McCauley & Segal, 2009). Terrorism refers to violence that arises out of conflict between social groups that differ in ethnicity, religion, national or cultural identity, or political aims. It is intended to spread fear in communities (ranging from local to worldwide) in order to influence the decisions or behaviour of political agents. This chapter summarises a growing research literature on the causes, manifestations, and consequences of terrorist violence, as reflected, for example, in a collection of scholarly articles by Victoroff and Kruglanski (2009). In trying to understand the phenomenon of terrorist violence, the following discussion focuses on psychological contributions to terrorism research, acknowledging, however, that a comprehensive understanding of the problem requires a broader interdisciplinary perspective, including sociology, political science, and history (Chenoweth, English, Gofas, Kalyvas, & Lutz, 2019).

The chapter is divided into five sections. First, a working definition of terrorism is provided to identify the characteristic features of this form of aggression and to see its overlap with, and differences from, other types of group-based violence. Second, although social, political, and historical background conditions provide a basis on which terrorism develops and may be sustained, only a minority of people living under these conditions engage in terrorism. Therefore explanations are presented which seek to understand what turns individuals into terrorists and what the psychological processes are that lead them to be drawn to terrorist groups and to commit atrocious acts of violence against innocent targets. Third, we consider why it is that people accept and endorse terrorist violence, creating both the moral and practical support that is needed by terrorist groups to operate effectively. Fourth, a growing body of evidence is reviewed that has examined the impact of terrorist violence on the attitudes, behaviour, and mental health of people who experience and witness terrorist attacks, both in the countries or regions immediately affected and in the population worldwide. Finally, we ask how terrorism may be overcome and what strategies hold potential for reducing this form of intergroup aggression.

It is clearly the case that terrorist movements differ from one another in many respects, from the historical, political, and societal context in which they operate to the specific tactics they employ (Post, McGinnis, & Moody, 2014). Bearing this diversity in mind, the following discussion seeks to shed light on some common features from a social psychological point of view, trying to understand the individual and intergroup factors that may explain terrorist violence and examining its consequences.

DEFINITION AND PREVALENCE OF TERRORISM

In attempting to define terrorism, it is more useful to consider acts than to consider persons. Labelling a group of people as terrorists is ambiguous, because it is heavily dependent on the perspective and affiliation of those who make the categorisation, as reflected in the well-known saying that "one person's terrorist is another person's freedom fighter". By contrast, defining terrorism in behavioural terms is easier, because it narrows down the broad issue of what causes terrorism to the more tractable question of what makes individuals engage in terrorist acts. Although there is no consensus in the literature on how exactly to define terrorist acts (Strom & Irvin, 2007), two main features have been suggested as characteristic of these behaviours. First, terrorist acts are acts of violence that are used not only as direct means to achieve political aims, but also as instruments to achieve publicity and spread fear and intimidation. Secondly, they are directed at harming targets other than the direct opponents in the underlying political conflict, most notably targets in the civilian population.

Both criteria highlight that it is not the direct physical harm which is the primary objective of terrorist acts, but the psychological effects in terms of attracting public attention and undermining the authority of the state in ensuring the safety of its citizens. A succinct definition reflecting these criteria characterises *terrorism* as "acts of violence by non-state actors, perpetrated against civilian populations, intended to cause fear, in order to achieve a political objective" (LaFree, Morris, & Dugan, 2010, p. 624).

terrorism: acts of violence by non-state actors, perpetrated against civilian populations, intended to cause fear, in order to achieve a political objective.

In addition to describing what defines terrorist violence, it is necessary to distinguish it from other forms of violent behaviour. Strom and Irvin (2007) identified several ways in which terrorist violence differs from other forms of criminal violence.

(1) *Motivation.* Unlike the typical criminal offender whose acts of violence are motivated by personal gain, terrorist violence is motivated primarily by political or moralistic goals.

(2) *Publicity.* Whereas criminal offenders typically attempt to hide their violent acts from others, terrorists seek media attention to publicise their cause.

(3) *Organised structure.* Terrorist organisations typically operate in social networks united by a common political goal and a common enemy. Although this is also true for certain forms of organised crime, such as gang violence, Strom and Irvin (2007) pointed out that terrorist groups are much more dependent for their cohesion on the presence of a defined leader, and are more likely to break down than criminal organisations when their leader is captured or killed (see also Post, 2005).

(4) *Symbolic meaning.* Finally, as noted above, terrorist acts are intended to send out a message to a wider audience well beyond the immediate incidents and targets, something that does not typically apply to criminal violence.

As regular followers of news reports, we get the impression that terrorist violence occurs on a daily basis and with increasing frequency. Figure 11.1 presents worldwide monthly figures of the number of terrorist attacks carried out between 2012 and 2017 and the number of people killed in these attacks. Adding up the monthly figures for 2017, there were 10,900 terrorist attacks, which killed more than 26,400 people, including 8,075

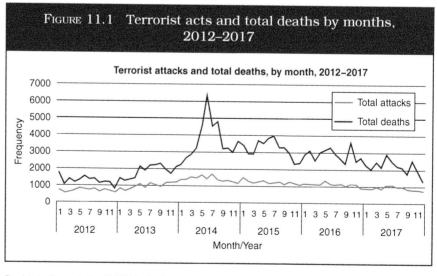

FIGURE 11.1   Terrorist acts and total deaths by months, 2012–2017

perpetrators and 18,488 victims (National Consortium for the Study of Terrorism and Responses to Terrorism, 2018). The most active and lethal terrorist groups in 2017 are presented in Table 11.1. In terms of geographic regions, two-thirds of all terrorist attacks and deaths were located in the Middle East and South Asia (National Consortium for the Study of Terrorism and Responses to Terrorism, 2018).

Although they are concentrated in certain parts of the world, terrorist acts of violence have caused a large number of deaths in Western countries, especially from the 9/11 attacks onwards (Barton, 2018). A further feature that distinguishes terrorist acts from other forms of criminal violence is that they are often carried out by individuals who are willing, or even desire, to sacrifice their own life. These so-called *suicide attacks* are defined as assaults "intended to achieve a political objective, performed outside the context of a conventional war, in which the assailant intentionally kills himself for the purpose of killing others" (Merari, Diamant, Bibi, Broshi, & Zakin, 2010, p. 89). Suicide attacks differ from non-suicidal terrorist violence in that they are embedded in a culture of martyrdom that promises special rewards to those who are willing to sacrifice their life in the service of the "good cause".

suicide attacks: assaults intended to achieve a political objective, performed outside the context of a conventional war, in which the assailant intentionally kills himself for the purpose of killing others.

TABLE 11.1 Number of attacks and number of deaths by most active terrorist groups in 2017, and change from previous year

Perpetrator group	Attacks	% Change from 2016	Total deaths	% Change from 2016
Islamic State of Iraq and the Levant (ISIL)	1321	–10%	7120	–40%
Taliban	907	–15%	4925	–3%
Al-Shabaab	573	1%	1894	20%
New People's Army (NPA)	363	111%	200	102%
Boko Haram	337	35%	1577	6%
Communist party of India - Maoist (CPI-Maoist)/Maoists	317	–12%	223	15%
Khorasan Province of the Islamic state	197	77%	1302	56%
Kurdistan workers' party (PKK)	159	–58%	190	–75%
Houthi extremists (Ansar Allah)	158	–56%	443	–50%
Sinai Province of the Islamic state	117	–20%	636	87%
Tehrik-i-Taliban Pakistan (TTP)	106	–7%	500	14%
Fulani extremists	79	–51%	344	–59%
Bangsamoro Islamic Freedom Movement (BIFM)	73	33%	53	66%
Gorkha Janmukti Morcha (GJM)	70	–	1	–
Abu Sayyaf Group (ASG)	65	–11%	72	3%
Barisan Revolusi Nasional (BRN)	62	130%	15	67%
National Liberation Army of Colombia (FLN)	61	–27%	47	31%
Communist party of Nepal - Maoist (CPN-Maoist -Chand)	61	177%	2	–
Jamaat Nusrat al-Islam wal Muslimin (JNIM)	59	–	161	–
Hizbul Mujahideen (HM)	49	188%	47	88%

PSYCHOLOGICAL PROCESSES UNDERLYING TERRORIST VIOLENCE

Our discussion will focus on the *psychological* aspects of terrorist violence that may help to explain what attracts people to terrorism, up to the point of sacrificing their own life, and what makes them willing to commit violent acts against innocent targets. However, it is clear that the historical, political, and material dimensions of intergroup conflict also play a critical role in providing the breeding ground for terrorist action (Hinde, 1997). This is highlighted, for example, in analyses of the genocide in Ruanda (Smith, 1998), as well as the long-standing conflicts between Catholics and Protestants in Northern Ireland (Cairns & Darby, 1998) or between Israelis and Palestinians in the Middle East (Fields, Elbedour, & Hein, 2002; Rouhana & Bar-Tal, 1998). As noted by Singer (1989), *systemic conditions* (e.g., material resources, allegiance bonds) at the multinational level, *dyadic conditions* in the bilateral relationship between the groups involved (e.g., trade relationship, balance of military strength), and *national conditions* within a country (e.g., economic instability) all interact to bring about terrorist violence.

To explain when and why movements directed at social change resort to violence rather than non-violent forms of political activism, several authors have transferred the frustration–aggression hypothesis, discussed in Chapter 2, from the individual to the group level. According to this view, terrorist violence can be explained as the result of perceived injustice, combined with a sense of social and political deprivation. In some cases, such as the Irish Republican Army (IRA) or the Palestine Liberation Organization (PLO), the frustrations leading to the emergence of terrorist movements are immediately traceable to a history of oppression. The actions of other terrorist groups, such as the Red Army Faction in Germany in the 1970s and 1980s, are more difficult to attribute to the blocking of specific goals. As noted by several scholars, the evidence linking terrorist violence to frustration and deprivation has been inconclusive, not least because individuals from better educated and more privileged social classes are over-represented among the members of many terrorist groups (Kruglanski & Fishman, 2009; Victoroff, 2009).

To understand why individuals associate with terrorist groups and engage in acts of violence, especially suicide attacks, an obvious hypothesis to consider is that they are mentally disturbed and suffer from some form of psychopathology. However, evidence to support this view is sparse and has largely failed to yield consistent results, leading some authors to conclude that "terrorist psychopathology is a dead issue" (Silke, 2009, p. 96) or that "the only common characteristic determined that terrorists are generally well-integrated, 'normal' individuals" (McGilloway, Ghosh, & Bhui, 2015, p. 39; Misiak et al., 2019).

Studies attempting to find evidence of psychopathology in the special group of suicide bombers are complicated by the fact that they have to rely mostly on second-hand evidence, such as interviews with relatives after the attacks were carried out. In a rare exception, Merari et al. (2010) studied 15 survivors whose suicide attacks had been foiled and compared them with a group of 14 organisers of suicide attacks and a control sample of 12 men who had been convicted of violent acts in the context of political protests. On the basis of extensive clinical assessments, Merari et al. established that 40% of the participants in the suicide group displayed suicidal tendencies, whereas none of the organisers or the control participants did so. Depressive tendencies were also found more often in the suicide group (53%) than in the organiser group (21.4%) and the control group (8.3%). At the same time, the suicide group showed significantly less ego strength (defined as the ability to cope with stress and regulate affective states) than the organisers and the control group, and were more likely to display a tense and anxiety-ridden personality style.

As Lankford (2010) pointed out, the personality characteristics and symptoms identified in suicide bombers show some overlap with the correlates of suicidality identified in the clinical literature outside the context of terrorism. However, Merari et al. (2010) did not find evidence of a history of mental illness in their sample of suicide attackers, which would be expected as a common precursor of suicide. They concluded: "Hence, although suicidality is perhaps a contributing factor in a significant minority of the terrorist martyrs, suicide bombers' motivating and background factors are different from those of ordinary people who commit suicide" (p. 100).

To elucidate these motives, Cohen (2016) conducted a content analysis of 249 personal farewell letters of Palestinian suicide bombers written in the period of the "Second Intifada" between 2000 and 2006. Farewell letters, or "last wills", have a strong tradition among Palestinian suicide bombers, and they serve both a personal function in terms of explaining their motives to relatives and friends and a social function in terms of valorising the suicide attacker as a role model for others. The author first established the most frequently mentioned words in the corpus of letters and then categorised the words into superordinate themes, considering the context in which they were used. The findings from this last step of the analysis are shown in Figure 11.2.

The analysis revealed that references to paradise and to parents were the most common themes, represented by a number of different words in the identified dictionary, whereas only a small portion of statements were related to the topic of revenge. This indicates that suicide bombers seek to present a religious rationale for their antisocial actions and a prosocial orientation in terms of minimising the pain to their parents. However, it is important to bear in mind the purpose of farewell letters, which is to justify the writers' actions and claims to martyrdom.

Beyond the search for psychopathological characteristics, attempts to establish a profile of the prototypical terrorist have not been very successful either. Neither demographic factors, such as level of education

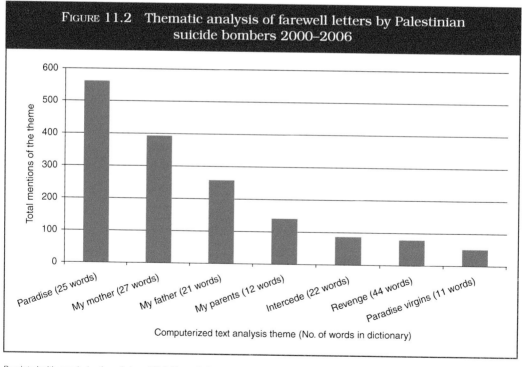

FIGURE 11.2   Thematic analysis of farewell letters by Palestinian suicide bombers 2000–2006

or economic status, nor personality traits have been found to reliably distinguish terrorists from individuals not involved in this form of violence (Kruglanski & Fishman, 2009). A consistent risk marker for terrorist violence in the past has been gender, with men being responsible for the majority of terrorist attacks. However, prominent examples, such as Ulrike Meinhof and Gudrun Ensslin in the Red Army Faction in Germany in the 1970s, showed that women were also active in leading roles in terrorist organisations. Internationally, the number of women committing terrorist acts has increased in recent years. The Global Terrorism Index 2019 noted that the number of female suicide bombers rose by 450% from 2013 to 2018, whereas the number of male suicide bombings fell by 47% in the same period (Institute for Economics & Peace, 2019). The terrorist group with the largest proportion of women among suicide bombers is Boko Haram operating in Nigeria (Markovic, 2019). In line with this development, research on the role of female terrorist has also been intensified (Bodziany & Netczuk-Gwoździewicz, 2019; Wickham, Capezza, & Stephenson, 2019). This research has shown that although women are still underrepresented in leadership positions within terrorist organisations (Jasko & LaFree, 2019), they become increasingly involved in decision-making processes (Cruise, 2016). Comparing men and women, the analysis of terrorist attacks by Brugh, Desmarais, Simons-Rudolph, and Zottola (2019) found few differences in the socio-demographic characteristics of male and female terrorists, except that female terrorists were less likely to have engaged in criminal violence prior to their involvement with terrorism. There is also evidence that women are more likely than men to be forced to join a terrorist group. An interview study with women whose bombing attacks were foiled showed that many of them were coerced into joining terrorist groups (Markovic, 2019).

The failure to establish a psychological profile of the typical terrorist is not to say that psychological processes are irrelevant for understanding terrorism. Rather than focusing on stable personality traits or demographic characteristics, it seems more promising to explore the processes by which individuals become attracted to terrorist groups. In this context, it is useful to distinguish between *attitudes* related to terrorism and manifest *behaviour* in terms of planning or carrying out acts of terrorist violence. Although, in general, the association between attitudes and behaviour is far from perfect, it is plausible to propose that developing a positive attitude towards violence and a normative belief that acts of violence are acceptable and appropriate are precursors to, or prerequisites for, engaging in terrorist behaviour. A process of radicalisation takes place when individuals (or groups) move from initially non-violent forms of protest or pursuance of political goals to the use of violence towards civilian targets. This process of radicalisation is also likely to involve an increase in anger as an emotional underpinning of terrorist behaviour, generated at least in part by frustration over the apparent failure of non-violent forms of action.

In their analysis of the developmental processes that may drive a person towards terrorist violence, Huesmann, Dubow, and Boxer (2010) began by stating that people who commit acts of violence are not "just like you and me", and that their behaviour is not normal in the human adult. The challenge, therefore, is to understand how individuals grow up to be attracted to, and willing to engage in, terrorist violence, while recognising that no single influence is likely to be able to explain these extreme forms of behaviour. Huesmann et al. applied the social-cognitive model of aggression, presented in Chapter 2, to the explanation of terrorist violence, stressing the convergence of individual predispositions and precipitating situational conditions. According to the social-cognitive model, aggressive behaviour is guided by aggressive scripts acquired through observational learning in the process of socialisation. The more prominent aggression and violence are in the social environment of a child and the more accept-able they appear to be, the more firmly they become ingrained in his or her cognitive script for dealing with conflict situations, and the more they promote a hostile world schema (i.e., the belief that the world is a vio-lent and hostile place) (for a discussion of the hostile attribution bias, see Chapter 4). Aggressive scripts include normative beliefs about the appro-priateness and legitimacy of aggression and about the situational cues that prompt an aggressive response. Emotions, such as anger or fear, play a crit-ical role in the activation, evaluation, and enactment of aggressive scripts. Not only do people select scripts that are congruent with their current emo-tional state, but they also base the decision on which script to follow in a given situation on their emotional responses. For example, an aggressive script is more likely to be activated when the person is angry, and it is more likely to be chosen for a course of action when the person feels good about it.

The script model can explain how being exposed to violence in the course of socialisation may precipitate violent behaviour through the pro-motion of aggressive scripts and hostile world schemata. However, add-itional personal dispositions need to be considered to explain why only a small number of individuals holding aggressive scripts turn to terrorist violence. Huesmann et al. (2010) identified three predisposing personal characteristics associated with an increased susceptibility to terrorist vio-lence. The first characteristic is *narcissism*, defined as a grandiose view of the self and a sense of entitlement that leads to aggression when challenged by others (see Chapter 4). As Baumeister, Smart, and Boden (1996) noted, terrorists often cultivate an attitude of moral superiority over their victims, from which they derive justification for their violent actions. Moreover, engagement in terrorism, especially suicide attacks, holds the promise of recognition by their ingroup as martyrs or heroes, which has particular appeal for narcissistic individuals. The second personal characteristic is *proneness to negative emotional states*, as captured in constructs such as irritability and trait anger (see Chapter 4), which lowers the threshold for the activation of aggressive scripts. The third characteristic is *low arousal* in response to depictions of violence, which enables the person to engage in violent behaviour without remorse and concern for the victims. As noted in Chapter 2, under-reactivity, indicated by low levels of resting cortisol, has been identified as a precursor to aggressive behaviour. In addition, being exposed to violence in the process of socialisation may lead to reduced reactivity to violence through a process of desensitisation. If these individual predisposing factors meet with a social context in which violence is common and even encouraged – for example, by a charismatic leader – violent behaviour becomes more likely. Although this conceptual framework has not yet been applied systematically to the study of terrorist violence, there is support from studies on exposure to high levels of violence in the community (e.g., Guerra, Huesmann, & Spindler, 2003) and from a longitudinal study in Northern Ireland showing that exposure to terrorism in childhood was a predictor of terrorist activities in adulthood (Fields, 1979). In addition, a study with relatives of suicide bombers in Indonesia found normative support for their violent actions from the immediate family members, especially among those who had strong anti-western sentiments (King, Noor, & Taylor, 2011).

In addition to variables associated with an increased risk of involvement in terrorist violence, researchers have looked for protective factors that may mitigate the risk. The review by Lösel, King, Bender, and Jugl (2018) identified 21 studies that addressed protective factors against radicalisation of adolescents and young adults as a precursor to engagement in terrorist violence, half of which considered attitudes supporting violence and the other half considered violent behaviour as outcome variables. Their analysis showed several factors that overlapped with protective factors against youth violence involvement in general, such as good self-control, positive parenting behaviour, and association with non-violent peers. However, the majority of studies were cross-sectional and therefore cannot address any causal impact of these factors in mitigating risk factors of terrorist radicalisation.

Beyond the acquisition of aggressive scripts and normative beliefs condoning the killing of civilian targets, the question arises of the motivations that drive people to perform terrorist acts. Researchers have identified a diversity of motives underlying terrorists' activities, which can be broadly subsumed under three different headings: (a) *ideological reasons* (e.g., the aim of promoting particular religious and political beliefs), (b) *personal causes* (e.g. a desire for revenge, and (c) a sense of *social duty* (e.g. protecting one's country against enemies) (for a summary, see Kruglanski, Chen, Dechesne, Fishman, & Orehek, 2009).

In an attempt to integrate these different motives, Kruglanski et al. (2009; Webber & Kruglanski, 2018) proposed an overarching motivation, namely the *search for significance*, as the driving force behind terrorists' activities. Focusing on suicide bombers, they argued that sacrificing one's life in the service of a common cause provides a means of achieving personal significance beyond death by becoming a martyr and living on in the collective memory of one's group. According to an influential social psychological approach termed *terror management theory* (TMT), the terror invoked by the knowledge of mortality induces people to identify more strongly with their cultural norms and world views as a way of becoming part of a lasting collective identity that transcends their own physical existence (Greenberg & Arndt, 2012). Being reminded of their mortality induces fear and anxiety, which makes individuals respond favourably to people who share their world view, and to react with hostility towards those who threaten it (Juhl & Routledge, 2016; see Burke, Martens, & Faucher, 2010, for a meta-analysis of mortality salience effects). Alerting people to their mortality is a strong cue to insignificance, and the prospect of achieving immortality through an act of martyrdom, coupled with the promise of paradise in some religiously motivated terrorist movements, decreases death anxiety by reducing the threat of insignificance. Furthermore, the quest for significance can explain why feelings of relative deprivation, the sense of being denied their fair share of resources such as wealth or status, may lead people to engage in terrorist activities (see also Chapter 10). Being deprived of something one feels entitled to is a clear indication of personal insignificance, eliciting the need to restore significance by other, potentially violent means.

Whether individuals seek to restore the feeling of significance by engaging in violent action depends on the availability of a narrative that presents violence as a means for gaining significance. Religious or political ideologies may provide such narratives, for example by offering rewards for those who sacrifice their lives for the good cause of the group or presenting violence as a means of redressing injustices. Individuals who embrace these ideologies are likely to affiliate with others who share these views, drawing them into networks that promote and reinforce violent action.

The fact that terrorist violence is to a large extent an intergroup phenomenon points to social identity theory (SIT) as a framework for understanding engagement in terrorist violence (Schwartz, Dunkel, & Waterman, 2009). This theory, described in detail in Chapter 10, proposes that individuals seek to achieve a positive social identity by assigning positive qualities to the groups to which they belong and derogating outgroups. Although SIT argues that even categorisation based on minimally important criteria is enough to elicit ingroup favouritism and outgroup derogation, hostility against outgroups is stronger the more they are seen as a threat, for example, to territorial claims or cultural values. Under conditions of intergroup conflict, differences between ingroup and outgroups are highlighted, presenting the ingroup as superior and leading to categorical distinctions between "them" and "us". The fact that single incidents highlighting intergroup boundaries can have dramatic effects on people's willingness to join terrorist groups underlines this point. For example, when the British Army killed 26 unarmed civil rights protesters in Northern Ireland in 1972 in what came to be known as the "Bloody Sunday", the number of new recruits into the IRA showed a sharp increase. Defining outgroups as "inferior", "evil", or even dehumanising them serves an important function in disabling inhibitions against violence directed towards outgroup targets, such as innocent civilians, as discussed in relation to hate crimes in Chapter 10.

PATHWAYS INTO TERRORISM: THE "STAIRCASE MODEL"

Societal-level variables cannot explain why out of all the people living under the same adverse conditions, only very few end up becoming terrorists. Similarly, individual-level variables cannot explain why out of all the people to whom particular individual characteristics apply, only very few engage in terrorist violence. Given the widespread nature of social and political injustice that affects large numbers of people without turning them into terrorists, individual and intergroup characteristics must be considered in conjunction to explain how these conditions at the macro level of society are channelled into terrorist activities. Friedland (1988, p. 111) presented an interactionist model, arguing that terrorism is a joint function of both situational and individual factors. The origin, in most instances, is a widespread social protest movement. Confrontations, often violent, with authorities and failure to elicit an acceptable response lead to disillusion and deterioration of the movement. Remnants of the movement form small, clandestine groups that maintain little external contact and a fierce ingroup loyalty and cohesion. These circumstances enhance the status of violent individuals within the groups, elevate them to leadership positions, and allow them to establish terrorism as the groups' preferred mode of operation.

Moghaddam (2005) used the metaphor of a staircase to conceptualise the interplay of societal, intergroup, and individual variables, and to describe the stages through which people are drawn into terrorism. The staircase becomes narrower on each floor, and only very few people eventually climb to the top. Moghaddam's *staircase model* is depicted in Figure 11.3.

The *ground floor* is occupied by all members of society who evaluate their living conditions in terms of fairness and justice. Those who perceive their conditions to be fair and just remain on the ground floor, while those who see them as unjust move on to the first floor. On the *first floor*, they evaluate the options for improving their conditions. Those who conclude that there are options for them as individuals to improve their position and influence decision makers through non-violent participation leave the staircase to terrorism at this level and pursue alternative paths. Those who are dissatisfied with the available options for redressing injustices move on to the second floor.

On the *second floor*, feelings of anger and frustration about not being able to improve their situation predominate, activating the search for a target – an "enemy" – to blame for their misfortune (Claassen, 2016). This enemy

staircase model: describes the pathway to terrorism as a succession of steps explaining why out of large numbers of disaffected people in a society only very few end up committing terrorist acts.

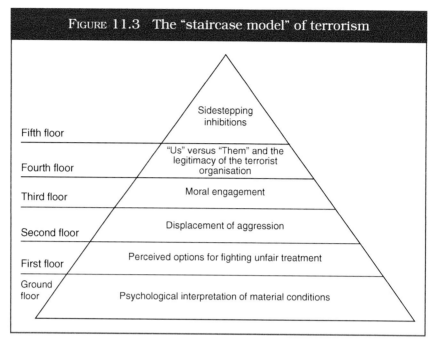

FIGURE 11.3   The "staircase model" of terrorism

Fifth floor — Sidestepping inhibitions

Fourth floor — "Us" versus "Them" and the legitimacy of the terrorist organisation

Third floor — Moral engagement

Second floor — Displacement of aggression

First floor — Perceived options for fighting unfair treatment

Ground floor — Psychological interpretation of material conditions

Based on Moghaddam, 2005.

can be either a direct opponent, such as a central government denying autonomy to an ethnic group or region, or a third party towards whom aggression is shifted, such as reflected in the widespread anti-Americanism in the Middle East. People on this level, who believe that there is an enemy towards whom they can direct their aggressive tendencies, will then climb up to the next floor.

By the time they arrive on the *third floor*, individuals have developed a certain readiness towards violence that can now be exploited by terrorist organisations through offering a sense of "moral engagement" to their potential new recruits. Increasingly, social media platforms are used to recruit and radicalise potential members on this level (Awan, 2017). Violent actions against the alleged enemy are presented as morally acceptable or even imperative, and recruits are offered a new and appealing social identity as members of a highly selective ingroup of fighters for freedom and justice. Those for whom this offer is attractive climb up to the next floor.

On the *fourth floor*, categorical thinking in terms of "us" and "them" is promoted by isolating new recruits from their families and friends, imposing strict secrecy, and emphasising the legitimacy of the terrorist organisation. There is virtually no chance for people who have climbed up to this floor to withdraw and exit alive. Therefore, they have no choice but to move up to the *fifth floor*, which involves carrying out the terrorist act. In order to operate effectively on this floor, inhibitions against killing innocent people must be overcome, and this is achieved by two well-established psychological mechanisms: *categorisation*, stressing the differentiation between ingroup and outgroup, and *distancing*, which exaggerates the differences between the ingroup and the targets that are seen as the enemy.

The staircase metaphor is useful for conceptualising the process by which a small number of individuals from large groups of disaffected people living under adverse conditions end up committing acts of violence against innocent targets. At the same time, it provides some promising ideas about the prevention of terrorism. Moghaddam (2005) pointed out that it is not enough to try to identify the individuals prepared to carry out terrorist acts before they get a chance to do so, because that would only make room for new people to step forward. Instead, terrorism can only be ended by reforming the conditions on the ground floor so that they are no longer perceived as unjust and hopeless by large parts of the population.

WHY DO PEOPLE SUPPORT TERRORISM?

Terrorist organisations require support from a wider constituency to recruit their members and to sustain their sense of legitimacy. Without this support, they would be unable to survive, and therefore they are sensitive to public responses to their activities and willing to abandon strategies that alienate those who sympathise with them. A case in point is the "proxy bomb" campaign in Northern Ireland in the early 1990s, in which the IRA forced Catholic civilians who worked for the British army (i.e., the enemy) to drive car bombs into British military sites and blow themselves up. The use of proxy bombs was stopped when it caused "a tide of public revulsion" (Bloom & Horgan, 2008, p. 599). But why do people support terrorist violence even if it entails a risk of harm to themselves by triggering violence in retaliation from the attacked party? For example, survey data from the Palestinian Center for Policy and Survey Research showed that 69% of Palestinians interviewed supported the suicide bombing in Tel Aviv in April 2006 that killed 11 civilians (Gill, 2007, p. 150).

How can we explain this support for terrorist attacks on Israel despite the high risk of being targeted by Israeli retaliation? Several social psychological theories may prove useful for understanding public support for terrorist violence. The *theory of realistic group conflict* and its extension to symbolic conflict or threat, described in Chapter 10, suggests that violence is considered justified against outgroups that present a material or symbolic threat to the well-being and values of the ingroup. In line with this reasoning, Sidanius, Kteily, Levin, Pratto, and Obaidi (2016) showed that Lebanese participants' support for violence by fundamentalist groups against American targets was positively related to their perception of a clash of values between the Arab world and the U.S.

Social identity theory (SIT), beyond helping to explain why people are prepared to engage in terrorist violence against an outgroup, also offers an explanation of why people support terrorism. According to SIT, a positive evaluation of terrorist acts committed by members of the ingroup towards targets of a disliked outgroup helps members of that ingroup to achieve a positive social identity. In line with this reasoning, Levin, Henry, Pratto, and Sidanius (2009) showed, in a study with Lebanese students at the American University of Beirut, that the stronger the participants' Arab identification, the more they supported the 9/11 attack on the World Trade Center.

A strong ingroup identification also affects attributions of the causes of behaviour shown by members of the ingroup versus the outgroup. As demonstrated by research on the "group-serving bias" (Bond, Hewstone, Wan, & Chiu, 1985), negative behaviour by ingroup members is likely to be attributed to external or uncontrollable factors, whereas negative behaviour by outgroup members is attributed to internal factors. Moreover, negative behaviour by a member of the ingroup is seen as atypical of the group as a whole (the so-called "black sheep" effect), whereas negative behaviour by an outgroup member is generalised to the group as a whole. This "intergroup attribution bias" (Hewstone, 1990) may explain why people make external attributions for terrorist acts by ingroup members with whom they share religious, political, or ethnic affiliations. They see terrorist violence by ingroup members as caused by external forces, such as wrongdoing by the outgroup, and also as uncharacteristic of the ingroup as a whole, whereas they attribute behaviour by members of the outgroup to negative qualities that are typical of the outgroup in general. A series of studies by Doosje, Zebel, Scheermeijer, and Mathyi (2007) conducted in the Netherlands found support for the intergroup attribution bias in explaining terrorist violence. They compared Islamic and non-Islamic participants' attributions for the murder of the Dutch film-maker Theo van Gogh by an Islamic terrorist in 2004. Non-Islamic participants attributed more responsibility to the assailant and also to the Islamic world in general than did Islamic participants. Non-Islamic participants also perceived the assailant as a more typical member of the Islamic world than did Islamic participants, and this tendency was stronger the more they identified with being Dutch (i.e., their own national ingroup).

Research by Tarrant, Branscombe, Warner, and Weston (2012) has shown that people are more accepting of violence when it is perpetrated by an ingroup rather than an outgroup member. Participants in two studies conducted with British and American students received an alleged newspaper report on a suspected terrorist who had been tortured by a member of the security forces. They were asked to rate how morally justified the torture was and how much empathy they felt for the target. When the torturer was presented as belonging to the ingroup (a member of the British security services for British participants and a member of the U.S. security services for American participants), they found torturing the suspect more morally justified and reported less empathy for the target than if the torturer was presented as belonging to the security services of the respective other country.

Terror management theory (TMT), introduced earlier as an explanation for suicide bombers' willingness to give up their lives, is another useful approach for explaining public support for terrorist violence. The theory stipulates that the existential terror associated with the knowledge of one's mortality activates the desire to achieve a symbolic sense of immortality through the endorsement of consensually shared cultural values. Seeing oneself as part of a system of values that is passed on through the generations can provide an anxiety-buffering function, counteracting the fear of death (Pyszczynski et al., 2009). Two implications follow from this line of reasoning. First, the higher the level of awareness of one's mortality (e.g., because of attacks by a political enemy), the greater the need for affiliation with the value system of one's own cultural group. Secondly, the more that value system is questioned and threatened by outside forces, the greater the willingness to defend it. In combination, these two mechanisms suggest that the more terrorist violence is framed as a way of defending the cultural values of the ingroup against an enemy, the more support it should attract from the terrorists' community. Research by Pyszczynski et al. (2009) with Islamic students in Iran confirmed this prediction. In the first study, participants were asked to evaluate a fellow student who allegedly either supported martyrdom attacks against the U.S. or opposed such attacks, and to indicate their willingness to consider joining the martyrdom cause. Before reading about the fellow student's attitudes, those in the mortality salience condition were asked "to describe the emotions that the thought of your own death arouses in you" and to "jot down, as specifically as you can, what will happen to you as you physically die" (Pyszczynski et al., 2009, p. 285). A control condition was included in which participants were given the same instructions with regard to dental pain rather than their own death. The findings are presented in Figure 11.4.

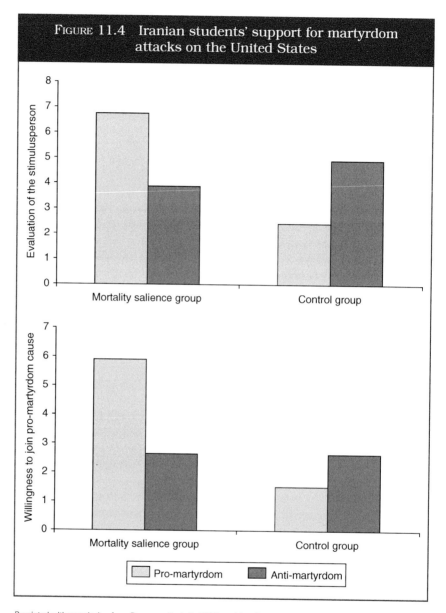

FIGURE 11.4   Iranian students' support for martyrdom attacks on the United States

As expected, support for terrorist violence, indicated by a positive evaluation of the person holding pro-martyrdom views and by their own willingness to consider joining the martyrdom cause, was significantly higher after participants had thought about their own death (the mortality salience condition) than in the control condition. Mortality salience did not significantly affect the evaluation of the person holding an anti-martyrdom attitude or their own willingness to consider joining the anti-martyrdom cause. These findings are in line with the proposition that reminders of death make people more susceptible to threats to their world view and more willing to support actions designed to defend it. This tendency is reinforced by a rhetoric, adopted by many terrorist movements, which designates the groups that are seen as the source of the threat as evil, and the fight against them as a holy cause.

EFFECTS OF TERRORISM ON ATTITUDES, BEHAVIOUR, AND MENTAL HEALTH

Terrorist violence is designed to spread fear and intimidation among civilian populations, and there is no doubt that it is successful in achieving this goal. In this section, we look at the effects of terrorist violence on three areas of psychological functioning and well-being. First, we examine the effects of terrorist violence on attitudes towards the ethnic, religious, or political groups to which terrorists belong, and towards threats to the social order more generally. Next, we ask what kind of behavioural responses people adopt to adjust to the terrorist threat. Finally, we look at the impact of terrorist violence on mental health, particularly in terms of the development of post-traumatic stress disorder.

Changes in attitude

Several studies have shown that terrorist attacks lead to a deterioration in attitudes towards the group to which the terrorists belong and, in addition, to a general increase in prejudicial attitudes towards outgroups. A quasi-experimental study conducted in Spain demonstrated that attitudes towards Arabs became more negative after the Islamic terrorist attack in Madrid in 2004. In addition, there was a rise in anti-Semitism as well as in authoritarianism, and endorsement of conservative values and a decrease in support for liberal values (Echebarria-Echabe & Fernández-Guede, 2006). American research by Carnagey and Anderson (2007) demonstrated that attitudes towards war became more positive immediately after the attacks of 9/11, and remained elevated a year later. An experimental study conducted in the Netherlands confirmed that exposure to news about terrorist attacks carried out by Muslims increased anti-Muslim prejudice among non-Muslims, just as exposure to news about terrorism by non-Muslims increased prejudicial attitudes against them among Muslims (Das, Bushman, Bezemer, Kerkhof, & Vermeulen, 2009). The effect was mediated by an increase in death-related thoughts after reading the news items, lending support to the prediction of terror management theory that awareness of one's mortality increases ingroup affiliation. Not only does mortality salience increase support for terrorist violence, as shown in the study by Pyszczynski et al. (2009) described above, it also increases support for violent retaliation. In a companion study by the same authors, American students showed more support for the use of extreme military force against individuals and countries posing a threat to the U.S. after a mortality reminder than in a control condition. However, this effect was moderated by participants' conservative as opposed to liberal political attitudes. Only those with a conservative political orientation (associated with greater affinity to the use of military force in general) responded to the mortality salience manipulation with a greater endorsement of the use of violence. A more recent study by Vail, Courtney, and Arndt (2019) found that participants who were reminded of their mortality showed more support for a statement expressing strong anti-Islamic prejudice than participants in a control condition. However, the effect was eliminated when participants were exposed to a prime highlighting the value of tolerance prior to the mortality salience induction.

Thus, terror management theory offers an explanation in terms of highlighting cultural value systems of why people accept violent action against outgroups, which can help to explain public support for both terrorist violence and violent retaliation. Unfortunately, acts of terrorist violence as well as violent retaliation, killing innocent targets on both sides, themselves work as reminders of mortality, in a way creating a natural mortality salience manipulation that serves to escalate support for violence on all sides of the conflict. In a quasi-experimental study, Lindén, Björklund, and Bäckström (2018) found that support for torture in a Swedish sample was significantly higher immediately after the terrorist attacks in Paris and Brussels in 2017, when they were highly salient in the media, than at a later time when the topic had become less prominent in media reports. Comparing attitudes towards Muslims in British participants before and after the London bombings of 2005, Abrams, van de Vyver, Houston, and Vasiljevic (2017) observed a significant increase in anti-Muslim attitudes after the attacks, which was mediated by increased perceptions of threats to safety and symbolic threats to cultural customs.

Studying the same terrorist event, a quasi-experiment conducted in Germany by Fischer, Greitemeyer, Kastenmüller, Frey, and Osswald (2007) tested the proposition that terrorist violence presents a threat to social order that makes people less tolerant towards any behaviours threatening the social order, even if they are completely unrelated to terrorism. They asked participants to suggest an appropriate criminal punishment for a car thief either one day after the London bombings (representing high salience of terrorist threat), or four weeks after the attack (representing lower salience of terrorist threat). As predicted, the participants assigned a significantly higher fine to the car thief one day after the attack than four weeks after the attack (an average of 8,503 vs. 5,996 euros). The finding was replicated in two further studies in the same series that experimentally induced high terror salience by means of articles highlighting the risk of an imminent attack or photographs referring to terrorist attacks.

In addition to changes in the direction of more negative attitudes toward the outgroups from which terrorist attacks originate, several studies have examined how attitudes toward democracy change after a terrorist attack. Based on the need to affirm one's cultural values, suggested by Social Identity Theory as well as Terror Management Theory, one would expect that participation in democratic political processes should increase after a terrorist attack. However, the evidence available to date is inconsistent. An analysis of three waves of panel data in Tunisia, where major terrorist attacks happened in 2015, found that attitudes toward introducing democracy in the country became less favourable after the attacks (Andersen & Brym, 2017). By contrast, a study conducted in Spain revealed that intentions to participate in democratic elections increased following terrorist acts of violence (Balcells & Torrats-Espinosa, 2018). To complicate matters further, a study on voting intentions after the attacks in Paris in 2015 showed that feelings of anger elicited by the attacks predicted stronger voting intentions for the right-wing Front National party, whereas feelings of fear predicted stronger intentions to vote against the Front National (Vasilopoulos, Marcus, Valentino, & Foucault, 2019). The conditions under which terrorist attacks reduce or increase the desire to strengthen democratic institutions clearly need further investigation.

Changes in behaviour

A small body of research has examined the proposition that exposure to terrorist violence increases aggressive behaviour. This proposition draws on a wider research literature showing that exposure to violence other than terrorism (e.g., family violence) is a risk factor for aggressive behaviour (see Chapter 8). Research conducted in regions in which terrorist attacks are common provides some support for this hypothesis. A four-wave longitudinal study conducted with Israeli and Palestinian youths showed that exposure to ethnic-political violence in the first three waves predicted engaging in severe physical violence and joining violent demonstrations at the fourth wave (Dubow et al., 2019). Even-Chen and Itzhaky (2007) compared adolescents from parts of Israel with high vs. low levels of exposure to terrorism, and obtained self-reports of their sense of personal danger as well as changes in their behaviour following terrorist attacks. They found that exposure to terrorism predicted higher levels of interpersonal aggression, even when controlling for exposure to violence in the family and in the community. However, an interesting finding emerged when hope about the future was considered as an additional variable. Only in the group who scored low on hope for the future was a sense of danger related to higher levels of violence, whereas for those who scored high on hope for the future the correlation was non-significant. A study from Northern Ireland found that exposure to sectarian aggression by the religious outgroup of Protestants or Catholics, respectively, predicted adolescents' sectarian aggression against that outgroup over a one-year period. The link was stronger the higher the identification with the religious ingroup (Merrilees et al., 2013). Exposure to sectarian antisocial behaviour by the outgroup also predicted a higher level of aggressive behaviour outside the intergroup context. On this measure, however, the link was stronger the less participants identified with their religious ingroup.

In addition, there is evidence that terrorist violence also has a wider impact on personality dispositions related to aggression. A longitudinal study by Carnagey and Anderson (2007) using the Aggression Questionnaire (see Chapter 1) found an increase in college students' self-reported physical and verbal aggression as well as in anger and hostility from pre-9/11 levels to the post-9/11 measurement a year after the terrorist attacks.

Changes in behaviour following terrorist violence may not only be observed with respect to the tendency to engage in aggressive behaviour but have been shown across a wide range of domains of everyday activities. The largest research literature is available on responses by citizens in the U.S. following the attacks of 9/11. For example, in a survey by Torabi and Seo (2004), 29.2% of participants reported that their behaviour "had changed as a result of 9/11". The different areas in which behavioural changes were reported are depicted in Figure 11.5.

As shown in Figure 11.5, changes in mode of transportation were among the most frequently reported behavioural adaptations following 9/11 in the Torabi and Seo (2004) survey. Similarly, in a survey of Londoners in the wake of the bombings of 7 July 2005, 32.5% of respondents indicated that they intended to travel less on underground transport, trains, and buses in or into central London (Rubin, Brewin, Greenberg, Simpson, & Wessley, 2005). When the same participants were interviewed again seven months later, 19% of them still said that they intended to use public transport less than before the attacks (Rubin et al., 2005).

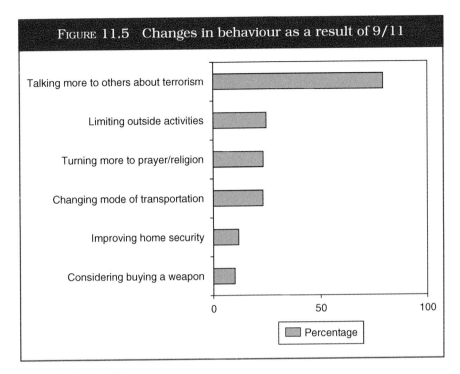

FIGURE 11.5   Changes in behaviour as a result of 9/11

Based on Torabi & Seo, 2004.

However, other studies suggest that changes in everyday, routine behaviours after a terrorist attack may only be short-lived. A multi-wave poll asking about changes in behaviour after the 9/11 attack found that six months after the attack, 54% of respondents reported that they had changed their behaviour, whereas the figure had dropped to 33% two years after the attack (McArdle, Rosoff, & John, 2012). In a French study measuring behaviour change in response to the Charlie Hebdo attack in Paris in 2015, only about 10–15% of participants recruited in Paris said they changed a range of everyday behavioural routines one week, one month, or two months after the attack (Pelletier & Drozda-Senkowska, 2016).

Two studies by Gigerenzer (2004, 2006) examined the consequences of behavioural adaptations to the threat of terrorism based on an analysis of terrorism as a "dread risk" – that is, an event that has a low probability of occurring but a high risk of harm. Gigerenzer pointed out that terrorist violence not only causes direct effects, most notably injuries and loss of life, but also has indirect effects, such as job losses in the tourism industry, which are not under the immediate control of the terrorist agents. Examining a particular type of indirect effect resulting from the 9/11 terrorist attacks, namely people's fear of flying and avoidance of plane journeys, Gigerenzer investigated whether the shift from air travel to car journeys would be reflected in the rate of fatal road traffic accidents.

Calculating the mean number of fatal road traffic accidents in the U.S. between 1996 and 2000 and comparing them with the figures for 2001, he found significantly higher rates in the months following 9/11 (i.e., October to December 2001). Extrapolating from the figures for the same period in the preceding years, he calculated that an additional 353 people were killed in road traffic accidents in the three months after 9/11, outnumbering the toll of 246 passengers and crew who died on board the planes crashed by the 9/11 terrorists. When the period of examination was extended to the full 12 months following the 9/11 attacks, and data on the average number of road miles travelled were included, the increase in fatalities was confirmed and linked to an increase in road traffic during the same period (Gigerenzer, 2006).

Effects on mental health

Beyond affecting attitudes and behaviour, terrorist attacks may severely undermine mental health and psychological well-being, both in individuals directly exposed to the attacks and in the population at large. One way of addressing this issue is through large-scale surveys in which samples from the general population are questioned about psychological symptoms, such as depression and anxiety, typically based on standard diagnostic criteria, such as the *Diagnostic and Statistical Manual of Mental Disorders, Fourth Edition (DSM-IV)* (American Psychiatric Association, 1994). For example, DeLisi et al. (2003) interviewed a sample of 1,009 people living or working in New York between 3 and 6 months after the 9/11 attack. They used a validated measure of psychological trauma that addressed the frequency and severity of 17 symptoms, such as painful memories, avoidance of feelings, and sleep problems. More than half of the people surveyed (56.3%) had at least one severe symptom or two or more mild or moderate symptoms.

A substantial body of literature, reviewed by Fischer and Ai (2008), examined the traumatic effects of terrorist violence as conceptualised in the symptomatology of post-traumatic stress disorder (PTSD). As noted in Chapter 8, PTSD is defined in the DSM-IV by three main criteria, all of which must persist for more than one month: (a) re-experiencing of the traumatic event, (b) avoidance of stimuli associated with the trauma and numbing of general responsiveness, and (c) symptoms of increased arousal. Several studies conducted in the first few months after the 9/11 attacks found elevated rates of PTSD in general population samples. In the study by Schlenger et al. (2002), which included more than 2,000 adults in New York and Washington, DC, the prevalence rate of PTSD was 11.2%, a figure that was higher than the national average of 4.2%. However, findings about the persistence of symptoms beyond the first few weeks after the attack are inconclusive. Several studies suggest that the elevated rates of PTSD in general population samples returned to baseline levels within a few months after the attacks (e.g., Galea et al., 2003; Silver, Holman,

McIntosh, Poulin, & Gil-Rivas, 2002). On the other hand, a review of 20 longitudinal and treatment studies with individuals who were directly exposed to the 9/11 attacks showed that PTSD rates in rescue workers and firefighters were in the region of 8% to12% and even showed an increase over time (Lowell et al., 2018). The rates in volunteer helpers without professional experiences in dealing with major attacks were much higher, ranging between 20% and 30%.

Research conducted in parts of the world where terrorist violence is a constant threat, such as the Middle East, has also shown increased levels of PTSD. A study by Besser, Neria, and Haynes (2009) conducted in Israel compared a group who had been exposed to ongoing terrorist violence with a group who had not been exposed to terrorist threat. They found significantly higher levels of perceived stress and a significantly higher association between perceived stress and PTSD in the exposed sample. A review of the evidence on PTSD in young children affected by terrorist violence concluded that the highest rates of PTSD, ranging from 21% to 44%, were found in studies with children exposed to the ongoing Israeli–Palestinian conflict (Slone & Mann, 2016). A meta-analysis from the same region found significant effects of children's exposure to political violence on behavioural, post-traumatic, and psychological symptoms (Slone, Lavi, Ozer, & Pollak, 2017).

The problem with much of this research literature is that it is unclear whether the experience of terrorism is *causally* related to PTSD, because the data were collected after the event. In one of the few studies that were able to relate symptoms to measures obtained prior to a terrorist attack, Rosen, Tiet, Cavella, Finney, and Lee (2005) found that patients diagnosed with PTSD prior to 9/11 did not show a deterioration of their symptoms when studied again post 9/11. However, this finding does not address the question of whether the rate of PTSD increased in populations that did not show signs of the disorder prior to 9/11.

In addition to the expected negative effects of terrorist violence on mental health and well-being, the experience of collective trauma may also entail positive aspects, as captured in the construct of "post-traumatic growth". *Post-traumatic growth* refers to the experience of positive change that occurs as a result of struggling with highly challenging life crises (Tedeschi & Calhoun, 2004). In an interview study with caregivers of young people who survived the terrorist attack on the Norwegian island of Utøya in 2011, Glad, Kilmer, Dyb, and Hafstad (2019) found that about two-thirds of caregivers reported that they had seen positive changes in personal development (e.g., greater maturity) and interpersonal relations (e.g., stronger family bonds) in the survivors in the two-and-a-half years after the attack.

It is intuitively plausible that post-traumatic growth could be a protective factor against developing PTSD, so that the more people saw the trauma as allowing personal growth, the better they would cope, reflected in lower susceptibility to PTSD. However, the evidence on this issue is not clear, as many studies have found positive correlations between post-traumatic

post-traumatic growth: experience of positive change that occurs as a result of the struggle with highly challenging life crises.

growth and PTSD (Shakespeare-Finch & Lurie-Beck, 2014). For example, Hobfoll et al. (2008) found in a sample of Israeli Jews directly exposed to terrorist violence that those who reported a high level of post-traumatic growth, defined in terms of an increase in social resources, were at greater risk of developing PTSD symptoms. However, no such link was found for Israeli Arabs directly exposed to violence. A study by Levi and Bachar (2019) found that narcissism moderated the link between PTSD and post-traumatic growth: trauma survivors low on narcissism showed no association between PTSD and post-traumatic growth, but a positive association was found for survivors scoring high on narcissism (see Chapter 4 for a discussion of narcissism). The authors explain this finding with the greater tendency toward self-deception by narcissistic individuals, who deceive themselves into thinking that they are invulnerable to negative experiences caused by exposure to trauma and deny being affected by symptoms of PTSD.

Again, cross-sectional studies such as this one are unable to address the possibility that people who are more adversely affected by exposure to terrorism are more motivated to seek post-traumatic growth, rather than post-traumatic growth being maladaptive in the sense of increasing the risk of PTSD. A longitudinal analysis, again conducted in Israel, disentangled the temporal ordering of PTSD and post-traumatic growth, showing that greater PTSD predicted higher post-traumatic growth over time, whereas the path from post-traumatic growth to PTSD over time was not significant (Hall, Saltzman, Canetti, & Hobfoll, 2015). This finding supports the view of post-traumatic growth as an attempt to cope with post-traumatic stress (Hobfoll et al., 2007). The findings of a longitudinal study by Updegraff, Silver, and Holman (2008) showed that *searching* for meaning shortly after the 9/11 attacks was linked to higher levels of PTSD a year later, whereas a sense of *finding* meaning was linked to a reduction in symptoms. It may well be that people's beliefs about personal growth as a result of exposure to trauma change in the course of the coping process. Perhaps they move from "wishful thinking", as a way of seeking comfort in the initial stages when post-traumatic stress levels are high, to a more constructive re-examination of core beliefs and values that may attenuate the negative impact of the trauma (Tedeschi, Calhoun, & Cann, 2007).

PSYCHOLOGICAL STRATEGIES FOR PREVENTING TERRORIST VIOLENCE

Finding effective ways of responding to terrorist violence is a global challenge, and as reflected in reports of new acts of terrorism coming in almost daily, it has so far had limited success. For example, an analysis comparing acts by Islamic terrorists in the U.S. before and after President Trump imposed an immigration ban on individuals from seven predominantly Muslim countries in January 2017 showed that acts of terrorism were higher from one week to five months after the introduction of the ban than they had been before the ban (Hodwitz & Tracy, 2019). Beyond this example, no attempt will be made in this section to discuss the strategies adopted at the political and military level – for example, by engaging in violent retaliation as a means of deterrence, or by reducing opportunities for attacks by reinforcing air travel security (see, for example, Victoroff & Kruglanski, 2009, Section VIII). Instead we shall briefly examine approaches at the individual and intergroup levels that exemplify a social psychological perspective on preventing terrorist violence.

Many of the processes that explain an increased readiness for aggression can also be applied to the aim of reducing support for, and commitment to, terrorist violence. Terror management theory is a case in point. As discussed earlier, this theory proposes that terrorist threat functions as a reminder of mortality that increases commitment to prevailing cultural value systems and world views in an attempt to cope with the existential fear of death. This reasoning suggests that if the prevailing world view proclaims values which promote peace and compassion, mortality salience should decrease support for terrorist violence. A study by Rothschild, Abdollahi, and Pyszczynski (2009) provided support for this prediction. They found that reading a passage from the Koran which emphasised compassion reduced the endorsement of aggressive attitudes against the West in a sample of Shiite Muslims.

The staircase model discussed earlier as an explanation of radicalisation may also inform a better understanding of effective strategies for deradicalisation. *Deradicalisation* is the process of rejecting the ideology underpinning the membership in a terrorist group (Doosje et al., 2016). It can be triggered by changes in personal circumstances at the "ground floor" level, such as marriage or parenthood, by disappointment with the lack of effectiveness of terrorist acts, and/or conflict within the group. On the first floor, providing nonviolent options for redressing unfair treatment may be a viable strategy. For example, Moghaddam (2006) has outlined ways of establishing a "contextualised democracy" that builds upon existing cultural traditions. Other research has shown that terrorist attacks are less likely to be carried out by members of countries with a higher level of gender equality, which reduces unfair treatment and creates anti-discrimination norms both within the family and societies at large (Saiya, Zaihra, & Fidler, 2017).

There is also some evidence that deradicalisation may be helped by promoting perspective-taking and empathy with members of outgroups against which terrorist acts are directed (Hasson et al., 2019; Pelletier & Drozda-Senkowska, 2020). These findings point to the role of social identity construction as a factor involved in both radicalisation and deradicalisation. As noted above, engaging in violence to express feelings of hatred towards outgroups and to protect the ingroup against material or symbolic harm is a way of maintaining a positive social identity. Experiencing violent retaliation from the target group serves to strengthen ingroup solidarity and increases the willingness to commit further attacks. From this perspective,

deradicalisation: process of rejecting the ideology underpinning the membership in a terrorist group.

trying to undermine the identity construction that gives rise to terrorism may be a way forward, for example by the weakening of intergroup boundaries that separate "them" and "us" through cooperative contact between the conflicting groups (Staub, 2007).

Finally, it is important to offer more attractive social identities than that of being a terrorist by alternative strategies for achieving significance and providing mainstream forms of social participation that make individuals less susceptible to terrorist ideologies (Kruglanski et al., 2014; Milla, Hudiyana, & Arifin, 2019). None of these tasks will be easy or sufficient in themselves to prevent terrorist violence. However, they may help to shape an agenda for reducing the global threat of terrorism in the long term, and stop potential terrorists on their way up the staircase that leads to extreme forms of violence.

SUMMARY

- Terrorism is defined as the commitment of acts of violence by non-state actors, perpetrated against civilian populations, intended to cause fear, in order to achieve a political objective.
- There is little evidence that terrorists suffer from psychopathological disorders. Instead, psychological analyses have proposed that the learning of aggressive scripts through exposure to violence, the search for significance as a motivational basis, and the striving for a positive social identity are critical psychological processes that draw individuals towards terrorist groups. The "staircase model" was developed to explain why out of the large number of people who are disenchanted with their personal or social circumstances, only a small minority eventually engage in terrorist violence.
- *Social identity theory*, stressing the influence of ingroup solidarity and outgroup derogation, and *terror management theory*, focussing on the impact of terrorist violence as a mortality salience cue that instigates the need to affirm one's cultural values, offer explanations of why people support terrorist violence.
- Terrorist attacks elicit changes in attitudes, behaviour, and mental health in the targeted communities and beyond. Attitudes towards the ethnic, religious, or political groups to which terrorists belong become more negative, and support for war and military action increases. At the behavioural level, exposure to terrorist violence has been linked to increased aggression as well as to changes in behaviour that may lead to alternative risks, such as changes in transportation behaviour associated with increases in road traffic fatalities. However, the latter changes are short-lived, as people are quick to return to their daily routines.
- In terms of the effects on mental health, there is evidence of post-traumatic stress responses even in people not directly exposed to terrorist violence, although it is not clear how persistent the effects are.

Research on post-traumatic growth points to a potentially constructive way of coping with terrorist violence, but the links between post-traumatic growth and post-traumatic stress responses are not yet clear.

- Social psychological theories of intergroup behaviour suggest strategies for reducing the likelihood of terrorist violence by capitalising on the activation of non-violent world views to reduce support for terrorism under conditions of mortality salience, and by weakening intergroup boundaries as well as offering alternative, non-violent social identities to people who might otherwise be attracted to terrorist groups.

TASKS TO DO

(1) Visit the website of START, the National Consortium for the Study of Terrorism and Responses to Terrorism, to find out more about their work (www.start.umd.edu/start/research/investigators/investigator.asp?id=24).

(2) On the START website, look at the Global Terrorism Database, which contains a systematic collection of more than 190,000 incidents of terrorism and search for the list of incidents in your country (www.start.umd.edu/gtd).

(3) Visit the websites of two leading journals that specialise in the subject of terrorism to see the range of research topics addressed in this field: *Studies in Conflict and Terrorism*, started in 1977 (www.tandfonline.com/loi/uter20) and *Behavioral Sciences of Terrorism and Political Aggression*, started in 2009 (www.tandfonline.com/toc/rirt20/current). Pick and read one article from the most recent issues that you find most interesting to discuss with your friends.

SUGGESTED READING

Cohen, S. J. (2016). Mapping the minds of suicide bombers using linguistic methods: The corpus of Palestinian suicide bombers' farewell letters (CoPSBFL). *Studies in Conflict & Terrorism, 39,* 749–780.

Huesmann, L. R., Dubow, E. F., & Boxer, P. (2010). How to grow a terrorist without really trying: The psychological development of terrorism from childhood to adulthood. In D. Antonius, A. D. Brown, T. K. Walters, J. M. Ramirez, & S. J. Sinclair (Eds.), *Interdisciplinary analyses of terrorism and political aggression* (pp. 1–21). Newcastle upon Tyne, U.K.: Cambridge Scholars Publishing.

Moghaddam, F. M. (2005). The staircase to terrorism. *American Psychologist, 60,* 161–169.

Victoroff, J., & Kruglanski, A. W. (Eds) (2009). *Psychology of terrorism.* New York: Psychology Press.

Chapter 12

PREVENTING AND REDUCING AGGRESSIVE BEHAVIOUR

The research discussed so far has made it abundantly clear that aggressive behaviour is rife in many areas of social life and brings misery and long-term suffering to large numbers of people. In addition, the economic costs of aggression and violence for health services, the labour market, and the criminal justice system are immense. Therefore, exploring effective ways to prevent and reduce aggressive behaviour is a pressing task. The research brought together in this volume has accumulated a large body of knowledge that can be used to design strategies for prevention grounded in theory and based on empirical evidence. This chapter offers a selective overview of approaches designed to tackle the task of reducing aggression and violence. To systematise the large literature, it may be helpful to distinguish between general approaches and specific approaches. *General approaches* seek to influence processes involved in many different forms of aggressive behaviour, such as promoting self-regulation or reducing realistic intergroup conflict by achieving a more equitable distribution of scarce resources. *Specific approaches* are custom-tailored to address particular forms of aggressive behaviour, such as sexual abuse of children or bullying in the workplace. Within each of the two categories, a further broad distinction can be made between measures that target the *individual* person and measures that are implemented at the *societal* level. Table 12.1 illustrates these classifications.

In the first part of this chapter, we examine general strategies for reducing aggression that are implemented at the societal level or directed at the individual person. In addition to strategies that have been shown to be successful in reducing aggression, we also take a critical look at approaches that, despite their common-sense appeal and popularity in everyday discourse, have been demonstrated to be ineffective or even counterproductive. In the second part of the chapter, examples of prevention and intervention efforts to tackle specific forms of aggression, such as gang violence, family

Scope	Level of implementation	
	Individual	Society/Community
General	Anger management	Capital punishment
	Eliciting incompatible responses	Gun control
	Modelling and reinforcement	Alcohol restrictions
Domain-specific		
Gang violence	Training effective refusal skills	Imposing curfews
Child abuse	Promoting parenting skills	Mandatory reporting
Sexual violence	Rape prevention classes	Restricting opportunities

TABLE 12.1 Approaches to prevention: illustrative examples

aggression, and sexual aggression, will be discussed. This part complements the discussion of prevention approaches in the earlier chapters, for example in relation to the use of violent media (Chapter 6), bullying, workplace aggression, and aggressive driving (Chapter 7), and terrorism (Chapter 11).

GENERAL STRATEGIES FOR PREVENTING AND REDUCING AGGRESSION

Theories of aggression specify the mechanisms by which aggressive behaviour is elicited and maintained, both in the course of individual development and in the immediate situation (see Chapter 2). By implication, these theories also provide a basis for developing strategies to prevent and modify aggressive behaviour (Meier & Wilkowski, 2013). For example, the theoretical assumption and empirical evidence that aggression is the result of angry arousal suggest that aggressive behaviour may be reduced by promoting anger control. Explaining aggression as a response to the observation of aggressive behavioural models suggests that keeping children and adolescents away from violent media content may be effective in reducing aggression. In the present section, general prevention strategies such as these are discussed that are applicable to many manifestations of aggressive behaviours. We begin by looking at strategies implemented at the societal level, and then move on to measures targeting the individual to ask what the evidence has to say about the effectiveness.

Societal-level approaches

Every society is under an obligation to offer its members the best possible protection against aggression and violence. Evidence that levels of aggression and violence vary between societies to the extent that they endorse peace-promoting norms and values and support nonviolent forms of bringing about social change is discussed by Anwar, Fry, and Grigaityté (2017). Despite the fact that aggressive behaviour must ultimately be changed at the level of the individual aggressor, societal norms and practices can have a profound effect on the scale of aggression displayed by individual members. The issue of alcohol as a risk factor for aggressive behaviour is a case in point (see also Chapter 5). In a study conducted in Australia, Menéndez, Kypri, and Weatherburn (2017) compared rates of violence in two entertainment areas of Sydney five years before and five years after the introduction of legislation containing various measures to restrict the sale of alcohol. Moreover, they examined changes in adjacent areas to test the possibility that a decrease in the targeted areas might be offset by an increase in violence in neighbouring parts of the city. The critical dependent measure was the count of police-recorded incidents of non-domestic violence. The rate of violent incidents was reduced by 27% across the two areas where the legislation came into force, and no evidence was found for an increase in violence rates in adjacent parts of the city. However, as the authors note, other factors may have contributed to this outcome, for example the fact that the legislation was introduced following fatal attacks that had received widespread publicity. As a result, fewer people may have visited the area in the period following the tightening of the law. This example illustrates both the potential for society-level measures to reduce aggression and violence and the challenges involved in evaluating their causal effects.

A general approach towards prevention at the societal level is to reduce opportunities for carrying out aggressive behaviours through influencing the social and physical environment to make it harder for aggressors to carry out their intentions to harm (Goldstein, 1994). Examples of measures implemented at the societal or community level to reduce opportunities for aggression are presented in Table 12.2. For example, tightening security controls at airports worldwide was introduced in the wake of the 9/11 attacks to stop terrorists from carrying weapons and explosives on board planes. In the U.K., one measure designed to reduce aggressive

TABLE 12.2 Examples of societal measures for reducing opportunities for aggressive behaviour

- Airport security controls
- Alcohol bans in public
- Designated women's spaces in public car parks
- Dispersal zones for curbing antisocial behaviour
- Gun control measures
- Restraining orders for stalkers or violent partners
- Neighbourhood watch schemes
- Strategic seating areas separating fan groups at sports events
- Surveillance cameras in public places

and antisocial behaviour at the community level is the implementation of legislation that gives police officers the right to disperse groups who they reasonably believe have intimated, harassed, alarmed, or distressed any members of the public through their presence or behaviour (Antisocial Behaviour Act 2003, Section 30).

As indicated by the Australian example of legislation to control access to alcohol, a central way in which societies seek to prevent and control aggressive behaviour is by means of legal regulations. The law is used to enforce adherence to social norms, not only by punishing individual lawbreakers but also by deterring future perpetrators from committing acts of aggression. The World Health Organization conducted a worldwide review of legal measures designed to reduce different forms of violence and found that there was substantial variation in how responsive countries were in recognising the need for legal regulations, as illustrated in Figure 12.1 (World Health Organization, 2014, p. 39).

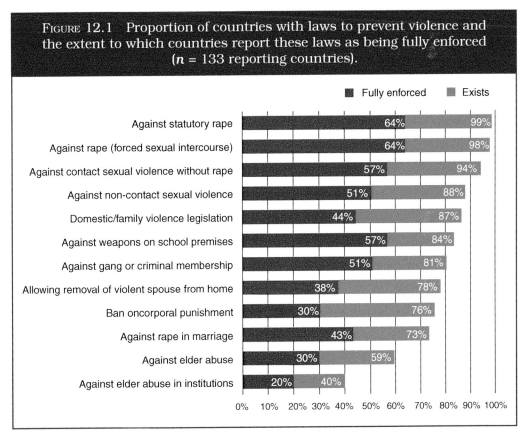

FIGURE 12.1 Proportion of countries with laws to prevent violence and the extent to which countries report these laws as being fully enforced (*n* = 133 reporting countries).

The report distinguishes between the existence of legal regulations and their full enforcement., and the figure shows that for most forms of violence, only about half of the countries that have passed relevant laws fully enforce them. Two legal measures designed to achieve a general effect on reducing aggression and violence will be discussed briefly to illustrate the potential and limitations of this approach: capital punishment and gun control legislation. Legal regulations addressing specific forms of aggression, such as corporal punishment of children or intimate partner violence, will be discussed later in this chapter.

Capital punishment. Whether or not legal sanctions have a deterrent effect on violence can be assessed with respect to the effectiveness of capital punishment. *Deterrence theory* assumes that "preventing crime requires the development of a system of punishment that will teach the lesson that 'crime does not pay' " (Bailey & Peterson, 1999, p. 258). It presupposes that criminal acts are preceded by a rational decision-making process in which the potential offender weighs the presumed benefits of the criminal act against the cost of punishment. With few exceptions, studies that have examined the deterrent effect of capital punishment on homicides are limited to the U.S. as the only Western nation still carrying out the death penalty. The number of death penalties executed in the U.S. decreased continuously over the last 20 years, from 279 in 1999 to 34 in 2019 (www.deathpenaltyinfo.org). No solid data and research are currently available from countries with the highest rates of death penalty executions, such as China and Iran, but a comprehensive report on the state of capital punishment worldwide is provided by Amnesty International (2019).

Two main strategies have been employed to assess the deterrence potential of capital punishment: comparing homicide rates between U.S. states with and without capital punishment, and comparing homicide rates before and after the abolition of capital punishment within a state (for reviews, see Bailey & Peterson, 1999; Land, Teske, & Zheng, 2009). Findings from both paradigms have disconfirmed the deterrence hypothesis by failing to provide evidence of lower homicide rates in states with capital punishment and increases in states that have abolished capital punishment. However, as noted by Land et al. (2009), any inferences are fragile, given the small number of executions in many of the jurisdictions. Focusing on Texas as a state with a comparatively high execution rate, these authors found a small short-term dip in the number of homicides following executions, but this was followed by an increase in the subsequent months. A later review by Chalfin, Haviland, and Raphael (2013) also concluded that the empirical basis for evaluating the deterrence hypothesis of capital punishment is weak. Major problems lie in the correlational nature of data looking for the covariation of death penalty executions and murder rates over time, which

deterrence theory: theory that preventing crime requires the development of a system of punishment that will teach the lesson that "crime does not pay".

may be driven by a range of third variables or open to the reverse inter-pretation that an increase in murder rates leads to a stricter stance toward executing death penalties.

Further disconfirmation of the deterrence hypothesis comes from findings showing that neither the certainty nor the speed with which the death penalty was imposed was related to homicide rates (V. L. Wright, 2010). Even when enforced swiftly and with high certainty, capital punishment failed to act as a deterrent against future crimes. This was true for different types of murder, including police killings and homicides committed by female perpetrators. Critics have also proposed that rather than acting as a deterrent to homicide, the death penalty may have a brutalising effect, increasing homicide rates, by suggesting that it is appropriate to kill others against whom one has a grievance. There is some support for the brutalisation hypothesis in the evidence reviewed by Land et al. (2009).

Bailey and Peterson (1999, p. 274) concluded "that policy makers would do well to consider means *other* than capital punishment to sig-nificantly reduce the rate of homicide in the United States." More recent evidence reviewed above has confirmed this conclusion. The findings also send a clear message to those countries that have abolished capital pun-ishment but in which public opinion regularly calls for its re-introduction following high-profile murder cases.

Gun-control legislation. As we saw in Chapter 5, there is consistent evi-dence for a link between gun ownership rates and rates of violent crime. Therefore, reducing ownership rates and restricting access to firearms may be considered as potentially effective strategies for preventing firearm-related deaths and injuries. Whether or not reducing access to firearms would bring down homicide rates has been a controversial issue, as illustrated, for example, by Michael Moore's well-known film *Bowling for Columbine* (2002). It has been argued that restricting access to firearms might not only be ineffective, but could in fact increase violence by limiting citizens' right and ability to defend themselves. Isolating the effects of gun-control legislation from the complex network of variables associated with the role of firearms, particularly in American society, is a difficult task. Worldwide reviews have shown substantial positive correlations between rates of gun ownership and violent crime. For example, a study that included 26 high-income countries yielded a substantial correlation in the region of $r = .70$ between rates of gun ownership and rates of homicide, indicating that about 50% of the variance in homicide rates can be attributed to variations in the prevalence of firearms (Hemenway & Miller, 2000).

However, such correlational analyses suffer from the problem that gun ownership rates could be the consequence rather than the cause of homicide, and both firearm prevalence and homicide could be driven by other variables, such as cultural norms about violence, so that they do not necessarily

suggest that reducing the availability of firearms would bring down homicide rates. Vigdor and Mercy (2006) examined changes in intimate partner homicide in different U.S. states contingent upon the introduction of legal regulations restricting access to firearms for perpetrators of intimate partner violence. They found that intimate partner homicides, especially those with female victims, decreased after states had passed such laws. Another study found that intimate partner homicide rates were 50% lower in states that require a waiting period of up to a week before a firearm is issued, which may allow the aggressors to "cool off" in the interim (Roberts, 2009). However, other studies failed to find a decrease in homicide rates after the introduction of tighter gun control laws (Gilmour, Wattanakamolkul, & Sugai, 2018; Kleck, 2019; Langmann, 2012). Looking at specific gun control measures, introducing a waiting period between application and provision of a firearm was found to be significantly associated with a decrease in gun-related homicides (Luca, Malhotra, & Poliquin, 2017), whereas introducing a ban on the buying and carrying of guns by young people aged 18 to 20 years was found to be unrelated to homicide rates (Kleck, 2019). In addition to implementing tighter regulations for buying and carrying a gun, several countries have introduced so-called gun buyback policies that encourage owners to return their guns. Isolating the effect of this particular measure on homicide rates is difficult, but there is some evidence that it may be linked to a reduction in violent crime (Bartos, McCleary, Mazerolle, & Luengen, 2020).

Overall, studies have presented an inconclusive picture on the effectiveness of tightening gun control legislation as a strategy for reducing gun-related violence. One problem with these studies is that a large number of weapons are not registered (Karp, 2018), undermining the reliable estimation of rates of gun ownership. Moreover, the evidence is almost exclusively quasi-experimental, comparing rates before and after the introduction of legal measures or rates between countries differing in gun control laws. This means that a host of additional factors may have differed between time-points as well as countries that may be related to gun ownership rates, homicide rates, or both. The same challenges apply to other societal-level measures for preventing aggression, requiring sophisticated evaluation designs that include proper control for possible covariates.

Measures directed at the individual

Ultimately, aggressive behaviour is performed by individual actors. Therefore, a central objective is to influence the individual person so as to reduce the likelihood that he or she will show aggressive behaviour, both as a habitual pattern of behaviour over time and in a specific situation. As discussed in Chapter 2, psychological theories conceptualise aggressive behaviour as the result of an individual's learning history in the course of socialisation and the interplay of affective, physiological, and cognitive processes in a specific situation. Thus, influencing these processes seems like a promising approach for reducing the likelihood of aggressive behaviour.

Punishment and observational learning. There is ample evidence that aggression is a form of learned behaviour shaped by direct reinforcement and observational learning (see Chapter 2). Therefore, it follows that aggression can also potentially be reduced using the same mechanisms, by introducing punishment to reduce the likelihood of aggressive behaviour and providing non-aggressive role models to promote non-aggressive responses and the acquisition of non-aggressive scripts. The principle of reinforcement suggests that aggression should decrease and eventually be extinguished if it is followed by negative consequences, such as *punishment*. Indeed, punishment is widely used to deter people from engaging in aggressive behaviour. However, learning theory tells us that the effectiveness of punishment in stopping people from acting aggressively is dependent on several critical preconditions (Berkowitz, 1993):

(1) The anticipated punishment must be seen as adverse, so that the desire to avoid it is sufficiently strong.
(2) It must have a high probability of being imposed, which implies that the odds of being detected must be high.
(3) It must be imposed swiftly after the aggressive behaviour for the connection to be made between the aggressive behaviour and the negative consequence.

(4) Affective arousal must not be so high that it prevents actors from engaging in a rational calculation of the costs of an aggressive behaviour in terms of the likely punishment.
(5) The person has to see alternative behavioural options in the given context.

If these conditions are met, punishment may be an effective strategy for stopping people from behaving aggressively on future occasions. However, the probability that these necessary conditions will co-occur in a given situation is relatively low, which limits the scope of punishment as a strategy for controlling aggression at the individual level. In addition to this practical limitation, a more fundamental criticism of punishment must be raised. Punitive responses, particularly in the form of verbal and corporal punishment, may in themselves instigate aggression by functioning as aggressive cues or norms. They may reinforce aggressive scripts by presenting aggressive behaviour as an acceptable way of regulating interpersonal and intergroup conflict. This has been shown by a large number of studies showing that harsh parental discipline is associated with higher levels of aggressive behaviour in children (Del Hoyo-Bilbao, Gámez-Guadix, & Calvete, 2018; Wang & Liu, 2018; see also Chapters 3 and 8). A multicultural study with two data waves confirmed the significant association between corporal punishment and child aggression (Alampay et al., 2017). Imposing negative consequences to reduce aggression needs to be embedded within a more general approach towards social-emotional learning in which the primary aim is to reward desirable rather than to punish undesirable behaviour (Jones, Brown, & Aber, 2011).

A second approach based on learning principles is *observational learning*, as discussed in Chapter 2 with reference to Bandura's well-known Bobo-Doll studies. Exposure to non-violent role models is directed at the acquisition of new behavioural repertoires by which aggressive response patterns can be replaced in a more lasting way. Longitudinal evidence has demonstrated that low physical punishment and inter-parental aggression as elements of positive family interactions at eight years of age predicted lower levels of criminal violence at 48 years (Dubow, Huesmann, Boxer, & Smith, 2016). Regarding exposure to models in the media, the meta-analysis by Coyne et al. (2018) found a significant, albeit small negative association between watching prosocial media contents and aggressive behaviour.

Both punishment and observational learning principles suggest that promoting the use of non-aggressive discipline strategies by parents is a viable strategy for reducing children's aggressive behaviour. This objective is an integral part of *parent management trainings* designed to teach parents to interact with their children in a way that avoids negative and reinforces positive social behaviour (Heinrichs, Kliem, & Hahlweg, 2014). Parent management trainings were shown in a wide range of studies to be successful in terms of changing children's antisocial behaviour patterns (e.g., Pearl, 2009).

Anger control. At the level of affective processes, anger has been identified as a critical antecedent of aggressive behaviour, and evidence for the link between deficits in anger regulation and aggressive behaviour was discussed for children (Chapter 3) and adults (Chapter 4). This research suggests that promoting the ability to control their anger (e.g., in response to a provocation) should reduce individuals' readiness to show an aggressive response. Anger management trainings aim to achieve just that. They are primarily directed at individuals with a history of poor anger control, but may also be used in the general population to promote anger regulation skills. The focus of *anger management trainings* is on conveying to the aggressive individual "an understandable model of anger and its relationship to triggering events, thoughts, and violent behaviour itself" (Howells, 1989, p. 166).

anger management trainings: convey to aggressive individuals an understandable model of anger and its relationship to triggering events, thoughts, and aggressive behaviour.

Anger management approaches draw heavily on the principles of cognitive-behavioural therapy, in particular Meichenbaum's (1975) *"stress inoculation training"*, which was adapted to anger management by Novaco (1975). The central features of the anger-related stress inoculation training, as summarised by Beck and Fernandez (1998), are presented in Table 12.3. In the course of the training, participants first learn to

> ### TABLE 12.3 The "stress inoculation training" approach to anger management
>
> *Phase 1*   • Identification of situational triggers which precipitate the onset of the anger response.
>   • Rehearsal of self-statements intended to reframe the situation and facilitate healthy responses (e.g., "I can handle this. It isn't important enough to blow up over this").
>
> *Phase 2*   • Acquisition of relaxation skills.
>   • Coupling cognitive self-statements with relaxation after exposure to anger triggers, with clients attempting to mentally and physically soothe themselves.
>
> *Phase 3*   • Exposure to trigger utilising imagery or role play.
>   • Practising cognitive and relaxation techniques until the mental and physical responses can be achieved automatically and on cue.
>
> Based on Beck & Fernandez, 1998, p. 64.

identify the cues that arouse their anger and to reduce their angry affect by interpreting the situation in a de-escalating way. Next, they are trained to use relaxation techniques to calm themselves, which are then combined with the cognitive strategies for self-appeasement. The two strategies are rehearsed through role playing and practised repeatedly so that they can be activated on cue in anger-eliciting situations.

A meta-analysis of anger management studies based on the stress inoculation approach was conducted by Beck and Fernandez (1998). Their analysis included a total of 50 studies, the majority of which used self-reported anger as the dependent variable. The remaining studies used behavioural observation of aggression as the criterion. In total, 40 studies compared differences in anger or aggressive behaviour between an anger management group and a control group, and ten studies explored intra-individual changes in the critical variable (anger or aggression) from a pre-test to a post-test subsequent to the anger management training. The meta-analysis yielded a large effect size across the set of studies (average weighted $d = 0.70$), suggesting that anger management is an effective strategy for reducing anger-based aggression. A review of 42 studies conducted between 2000 and 2017 revealed a significant reduction in anger following an anger management intervention in all but one of the studies (Fernandez, Malvaso, Day, & Guharajan, 2018). A meta-analysis of school-based anger management interventions with children including 60 studies found a significant, yet smaller effect in terms of a reduction in anger ($d = -0.33$) and aggression ($d = -0.34$) (Candelaria, Fedewa, & Ahn, 2012). A meta-analysis of anger management interventions with violent offenders showed a reduction in violent recidivism of 28% in the intervention groups across 14 studies (Henwood, Chou, & Browne, 2015).

Anger management training is often used as part of a broader package of strategies of cognitive behavioural interventions. For example, it is one element of an approach called aggression replacement training (ART) where it is combined with the training of social skills for handling interpersonal conflict and with the promotion of moral reasoning in terms of strengthening participants' sense of fairness and respect for others. Recent reviews suggest that this approach may be effective in reducing aggressive behaviour, although a number of methodological problems of the available evaluation studies were noted (Brännström, Kaunitz, Andershed, South, & Smedslund, 2016; Ensafdaran, Krahé, Njad, & Arshadi, 2019). In addition, improving anger management has been part of interventions based on inducing mindfulness, which are designed to teach participants to focus their attention, be non-judgemental and accepting, and be present in the moment. There is evidence that mindfulness interventions may reduce aggressive behaviour both in community and offender samples, but similar concerns regarding the methodological strength of the evidence base have been raised as for the ART studies (Fix & Fix, 2013; Murray, Amann, & Thom, 2018).

Whereas anger management interventions are specifically designed to enable individuals to control their angry affect, a more general approach is to promote individuals' self-control beyond anger management. In a study by Denson, Capper, Oaten, Friese, and Schofield (2011), participants in the intervention condition underwent two weeks of self-control training that involved a physical regulation task when engaging in everyday activities (e.g. using their non-dominant hand when brushing their teeth or carrying items). In a subsequent experimental session, those in the training condition were less likely to respond aggressively to a provocation and reported less anger towards the provocateur than untrained participants in the control condition.

A critical limitation of anger management interventions is that they can only work with individuals who are aware of the fact that their aggressive behaviour results from a failure to control their aggressive impulses, and who are motivated to change their inadequate handling of these impulses (Deffenbacher, 2011). Unfortunately, these requirements are rarely met in those high-risk groups who experience the greatest problems with anger control.

Eliciting incompatible responses. Whereas anger management interventions are designed to promote a person's ability to control anger in the longer term, evidence suggests that it is also possible to counteract anger-based aggressive behaviour situationally. This is done by eliciting affective states and cognitions that are incompatible with anger, and thereby buffer the effects of aggression-eliciting stimuli on angry affect and anger-related cognitions (Tyson, 1998). For example, Krahé and Bieneck (2012) showed that participants who listened to music rated as pleasant in a pilot study (e.g. Grieg's *Peer Gynt Suite*) while receiving a provocation subsequently reported less anger than did participants who listened to music rated as aversive (a mix of Hardcore and Techno) or those in a no-music control condition. Addressing the buffering role of music in a real-life context, Wiesenthal, Hennessy, and Totten (2000) assigned a sample of commuters to listen to self-selected music while driving to work, or to a no-music group. Depending on the level of traffic congestion on the route to work, participants were classified as experiencing low vs. high traffic congestion, representing different stress levels. Self-reported driver stress was the dependent variable. Under low traffic congestion conditions, listening to music made no difference, but under high congestion conditions, participants in the music group reported significantly lower levels of stress than did those in the no-music condition (for a discussion of research on the link between driver stress and aggressive driving, see Chapter 7).

Music is just one way to elicit positive affective states that are incompatible with anger. A study by Krahé, Lutz, and Sylla (2018) found that participants who were angered by negative feedback were more relaxed, less angry and showed less aggressive behaviour in terms of negative evaluations of a confederate if they received the feedback while leaning back in a deckchair as compared with sitting upright on an office chair. Research by DeWall, Lambert, Pond, Kashdan, and Fincham (2012) showed that gratitude, defined as a moral emotion, buffered the anger-eliciting effect of a provocation on aggressive behaviour. Both feeling relaxed and feeling grateful are states that are incompatible with anger. By the same logic, handling objects that induce positive mood, such as a cuddly toy, may instigate affective states that are incompatible with anger and promote prosocial behaviour (Tai, Zheng, & Narayanan, 2011).

Affective states do not have to be positive to be incompatible with anger and buffer its impact on aggressive behaviour. Inducing sadness can also eliminate the effect of a frustration on anger and aggressive behaviour (Lutz & Krahé, 2018). Pond et al. (2012) argued that whereas anger and aggression are approach oriented, disgust is avoidance oriented, eliciting withdrawal behaviour. Therefore, the urge to withdraw should interfere with aggression that requires approach, so that people who are sensitive to the experience of disgust should be less inclined to show aggressive behaviour. Supporting this line of reasoning, they showed in a series of studies that high disgust sensitivity was linked to less aggressive behaviour across different measures of aggression. The buffering effect of sadness may be explained in the same fashion.

Eliciting incompatible responses to suppress aggression can also work via the cognitive route. In another study by Krahé and Bieneck (2012), participants who were listening to pleasant music while receiving a

provocation in the form of a negative essay evaluation (for the essay evaluation paradigm, see Chapter 1), took significantly longer to recognise
aggressive words in a lexical decision task than did provoked participants
who were listening to aversive music or no music at all. A study by Bremner,
Koole, and Bushman (2011) showed that priming religious thoughts
decreased anger following a negative feedback in the essay-evaluation paradigm. After receiving a provocation, their participants were either asked
to pray for a sick fellow student or just to think about her. Those who
had engaged in praying subsequently reported less anger than did those
who had merely thought about the sick student. A second study found a
buffering effect of praying on aggressive behaviour measured by the noise
blast paradigm.

Greitemeyer and Osswald (2009) asked participants to play either a prosocial video game (*Lemmings*) or a neutral game (*Tetris*) before administering
a word completion task as a measure of aggressive cognitions. Participants
who had played the prosocial game produced significantly fewer aggressive
word completions than did those who had played the neutral game. In a
subsequent set of studies, Greitemeyer (2011) showed a parallel effect for
music with prosocial as opposed to neutral lyrics. Furthermore, participants
reported lower state hostility and showed less relational and physical
aggression after listening to music with prosocial as compared with neutral
lyrics.

Overall, there is some promise from the empirical evidence that eliciting
affective and cognitive states that are incompatible with the experience of

anger may be an effective situational strategy for reducing aggressive behaviour. The findings have potential for translating them into real-life settings, such as playing pleasant music in public places. However, designing a rigorous evaluation of such measures outside the laboratory is likely to be challenging.

Catharsis. The term "catharsis" refers to the idea in Greek tragedy that watching the unfolding and resolution of tragic conflict on stage leads to a purification or "cleansing" of the emotions of pity and fear in the audience, and brings about spiritual renewal or release from tension. It has been borrowed in aggression research to describe the idea that symbolic engagement in aggressive thoughts or actions may reduce the need to engage in aggressive behaviour with the potential to harm. As we saw in Chapter 2, Freud (1920) used the concept of catharsis to argue that the venting of hostile feelings can lead to a discharge of aggressive impulses that reduces the likelihood of aggressive behaviour. Similarly, the idea that aggressive urges can be channelled into harmless forms of expression is part of Lorenz's (1966) steam-boiler model of aggression, also described in Chapter 2. The idea that bottling up one's angry feelings carries the risk of uncontrolled outbursts of aggression and that aggressive tensions can be released through sports activities, sarcastic humour, or killing opponents in a video game, is deeply engrained in everyday beliefs about aggression. This is reflected, for instance, in the popularity of "rage rooms" or "anger rooms" that have been opened in many parts of the world to offer people the chance to act out their aggressive impulses by smashing and destroying objects (Brigida, 2016).

However, anger rooms are more likely to fill the bank accounts of their owners than to make their customers more peaceful and agreeable. Both theoretical considerations and empirical findings suggest that engaging in aggressive behaviour in this seemingly innocuous way is not only ineffective but even counterproductive for reducing aggression. There is plenty of evidence that the imaginary performance of aggressive behaviour (e.g., in pretend play or when watching media violence) is more likely to enhance aggression than to reduce it (e.g., Bushman, 2002). Several theoretical explanations can account for this finding (see Chapter 2). Social learning theory would say that thinking about the positive effects of aggression has a reinforcing quality, and script theory would argue that engaging in mental simulations of aggressive behaviour rehearses aggressive scripts. Furthermore, symbolic acts of aggression can be regarded as aggressive cues that prime hostile thoughts and feelings, and thereby pave the way for aggressive behaviour. It is clear from a number of studies that aggressive fantasising is positively linked to aggressive behaviour (e.g., Guerra, Huesmann, & Spindler, 2003).

Focusing on the arousal component of catharsis, Verona and Sullivan (2008) conducted a study in which they made participants engage in aggressive behaviour by delivering unpleasant air blasts to a confederate, and recorded the participants' heart rate before and after they engaged in aggressive behaviour. They found that those participants who showed the greatest reduction in heart rate after performing the aggressive behaviour – that is those who could be said to have experienced most catharsis – were most aggressive in the next phase of the experiment. This finding indicates that the reduction in arousal experienced after an aggressive act makes people more rather than less aggressive in a subsequent situation. Results by Bresin and Gordon (2013) yielded similar results in a more realistic context by showing that individuals in a diary study who reported lower levels of anger after reacting with an aggressive as compared with a distracting response were more likely to show aggressive behaviour when they felt angry on following days.

Several approaches for preventing aggression by targeting the individual have been discussed in this section. Support was shown for changing aggressive behaviour through observational learning, improving anger control, and eliciting responses that are incompatible with aggression in reducing aggressive behaviour. The evidence suggests a more critical view of punishment, because it only works under certain conditions and it sends out the message that coercion is an acceptable strategy. Finally, little systematic evidence is available to support the idea that the imaginary or symbolic expression of aggression can serve to inhibit aggression. Instead, feeling good about aggressive behaviour increases the chances of future aggression, in line with social learning and social-cognitive theories of aggression.

APPROACHES DIRECTED AT SPECIFIC FORMS OF AGGRESSION AND VIOLENCE

In addition to strategies designed to reduce aggression and violence across a wide range of domains, custom-tailored approaches have been developed to address specific forms of aggression. To illustrate these approaches, this section offers a brief review of strategies directed at three types of aggression: gang violence, aggression in the family, and sexual aggression.

Tackling gang violence

As noted in Chapter 10, a characteristic feature of gangs is the strong sense of cohesion, which is demonstrated within the group and to the outside world through shared symbols, rituals, and codes of conduct. Cohesion is defined by the strength of group members' attachment to the group as well as the number of close ties they have with other members, and it varies between groups. Successful interventions need to recognise the internal structure of the group as a starting point from which change may be achieved. For example, interventions to disrupt group communication may be more effective if they target individuals who are well-connected within their group or those who are more immersed in violent networks. This section briefly describes an approach for preventing young people from joining gangs. Prevention and intervention measures implemented at the level of police and criminal justice responses to reduce gang violence are beyond the scope of this discussion (see Braga & Weisburd, 2012; Valasik, Reid, West, & Gravel, 2018).

Many negative effects of involvement in violent juvenile gangs on future development and life chances have been documented in the literature, including a higher risk of child maltreatment (Augustyn, Thornberry, & Krohn, 2014; Connolly & Jackson, 2019; see also Chapter 10). Therefore, programmes are needed to stop young people from joining violent gangs. Gang resistance programmes depend on knowledge about risk factors that make gang membership attractive and likely, especially in neighbourhoods characterised by high levels of crime and social deprivation. Studies identified risk factors at the interpersonal level of violence in peer and family relations, and the individual level of attitudes, antisocial tendencies and exposure to critical life events (Gilman, Hill, Hawkins, Howell, & Kosterman, 2014; Hennigan, Kolnick, Vindel, & Maxson, 2015).

An example of a school-based approach for the prevention of gang membership and delinquency is the Gang Resistance Education and Training (G.R.E.A.T.) programme (Esbensen et al., 2011). It was chosen as an example because it is rooted in psychological theories of gang-related aggression and was subjected to two rounds of evaluations using state-of-the-art methods. G.R.E.A.T. is a school-based intervention delivered by law enforcement personnel that consists of a curriculum of 13 lessons, presented in Table 12.4. It is clear from the modules listed in Table 12.4 that G.R.E.A.T. is a programme targeting the individual. In addition to providing background information about the problem of gang-related violence, the programme aims to promote social skills that enable adolescents to resist peer pressure to join gangs, and to find non-aggressive ways of dealing with interpersonal conflict.

Two large-scale evaluations were conducted to assess the effectiveness of the programme. The first round of evaluation of the initial curriculum included longitudinal comparisons of programme groups and control groups over a four-year period. It yielded some intended effects, such as more negative views about gangs, but failed to demonstrate lower levels of violence, delinquency, or gang membership (Esbensen, Osgood, Taylor, Peterson, & Freng, 2001). The curriculum presented in Table 12.4 is the result of a thorough revision of the programme based on the evaluation results. In addition to improving the contents and teaching methods of the school-based intervention, the main change was to incorporate it in a wider approach that includes a summer programme and a family-based training component. An evaluation of the revised programme using a randomised controlled trial yielded more positive findings, as reported by Esbensen et al. (2011). Compared with the non-intervention control groups, participants

TABLE 12.4 Curriculum of the G.R.E.A.T. programme for preventing gang membership

1. *Welcome to G.R.E.A.T.*: An introductory lesson designed to provide students with basic knowledge about the connection between gangs, violence, drug abuse, and crime.

2. *What's the Real Deal?*: Designed to help students learn ways to analyze information sources and develop realistic beliefs about gangs and violence.

3. *It's About Us*: A lesson to help students learn about their communities (e.g., family, school, residential area) and their responsibilities.

4. *Where Do We Go From Here?*: Designed to help students learn ways of developing realistic and achievable goals.

5. *Decisions, Decisions, Decisions*: A lesson to help students develop decision-making skills.

6. *Do You Hear What I Am Saying?*: Designed to help students develop effective verbal and nonverbal communication skills.

7. *Walk in Someone Else's Shoes*: A lesson to help students develop active listening and empathy skills, with a particular emphasis on understanding victims of crime and violence.

8. *Say It Like You Mean It*: Designed to help students develop effective refusal skills.

9. *Getting Along Without Going Along*: A lesson to reinforce and practice the refusal skills learned in Lesson 8.

10. *Keeping Your Cool*: A lesson to help students understand signs of anger and ways to manage the emotion.

11. *Keeping It Together*: Designed to help students use the anger management skills learned in Lesson 10 and apply them to interpersonal situations where conflicts and violence are possible.

12. *Working It Out*: A lesson to help students develop effective conflict-resolution techniques.

13. *Looking Back*: Designed to conclude the G.R.E.A.T. program with an emphasis on the importance of conflict resolution skills as a way to avoid gangs and violence; students also present their projects aimed at improving their schools.

Reprinted with permission from Esbensen et al., 2011, p. 70; © 2011 by Sage Publications.

in the programme groups showed less positive attitudes about gangs, more frequent use of refusal skills, greater resistance to peer pressure, and lower rates of gang membership at the follow-up assessment one year after the intervention. In fact, participants in the intervention groups were less than half as likely to identify themselves as members of a gang as those in the control groups. A subsequent evaluation covering a four-year follow-up period still found that the odds of joining a gang in the intervention group were reduced by 24% (Esbensen, Osgood, Peterson, Taylor, & Carson, 2013).

The complexity of designing and evaluating school-based interventions is further illustrated by another project, incidentally also called GREAT (for "Guiding Responsibility and Expectations in Adolescents Today and Tomorrow"), that included the risk of violence perpetration and the risk of violent victimisation as target variables (Simon et al., 2009). An evaluation was conducted that addressed these target variables in schools where the programme was implemented for unselected groups of students (the "universal" condition), in schools where it was implemented as a family-based intervention for students with an increased risk of aggression (the "selected" condition), and in schools that used a combination of both approaches. The three groups were compared with a no-intervention control group. Over a two-year period, no positive programme effects on aggression were found in the intervention groups. In fact the decrease in aggression that occurred in the control group over time was not seen in either the universal or the selected intervention groups. There was little evidence of a decrease in victimisation in the intervention groups compared with the control group, and the combined intervention was no more effective than the universal and selected conditions on their own.

Taken together, the two studies reported here illustrate that changing aggressive behaviour by means of theory-based interventions is a difficult task that may even carry the risk of counterproductive outcomes, such as apparently interfering with the decline in aggression shown by the no-intervention group. At the same time, the two examples lend themselves as prototypical designs for the implementation of theory-based interventions using state-of-the-art methods of programme development and evaluation.

Preventing aggression in the family

The experience of family aggression may lead to a wide range of negative consequences that affect the victim's future development in many ways (see Chapter 8). Therefore, finding effective ways of preventing aggression against children, partners, and elders is a primary concern of practitioners and policy makers, and researchers can provide a basis for achieving this goal. Just as theories of family aggression were classified as pertaining to the macro level, the micro level, or the individual level in Chapter 8, prevention strategies designed can be located at these levels.

Societal-level interventions. Changing the societal conditions that allow family violence to occur requires, first and foremost, establishing a consensus that violence is unacceptable. Gelles (1997, p. 166) noted that "we need to cancel the hitting license in society", and Schwartz and DeKeseredy (2008) stressed the widespread peer support for violence as a major factor in explaining violence against women. Challenging the societal acceptance of aggression involves measures directly related to domestic violence, such as creating an awareness that corporal punishment is not an adequate child-rearing technique. It also includes wider issues, such as restricting the availability of firearms and challenging media presentations of violence as masculine, entertaining, and ultimately rewarding (see Chapter 6). It further requires the removal of the traditional gender gap in the distribution of power, both within relationships and in society at large. To the extent that social structures become more egalitarian (e.g., by providing equal pay and job opportunities), women will gain a stronger position in society, and patriarchal attitudes will become less influential.

One specific way in which family violence can be tackled at the societal level is by means of the legal system. Legal regulations have been introduced to enhance the protection of victims and improve the detection of domestic violence. For example, many countries now have the instrument of imposing *restraining orders* on individuals who have used or threatened to use violence against an intimate partner. This instrument prohibits abusers from getting close to the persons they threaten to attack, and enforces legal sanctions on those who violate the order. Other legal regulations are designed to increase the likelihood of criminal prosecution of domestic violence offenders in the form of *warrantless arrests* or *mandatory arrest* policies in cases of domestic violence. In their review of criminal justice responses to violence, Goodman and Epstein (2011) describe these efforts as highly successful. Evaluations of success are mostly based on official records, indicating increases in the number of arrests and criminal prosecutions in domestic violence incidents. At the same time, there have also been critical voices. For example, critics have argued that restraining orders may serve to escalate rather than de-escalate domestic conflicts because they create frustration, and that mandatory arrest policies have increased the number of victims arrested alongside the aggressor (e.g., Hovmand, Ford, Flom, & Kyriakakis, 2009). The file analysis by Muller, Desmarais, and Hamel (2009) showed that temporary restraining orders in cases of low-level intimate partner aggression were more likely to be granted to female than to male applicants, leading those authors to ask whether men are discriminated against as targets of aggression by female partners. However, this imbalance may also reflect the fact that men's aggression towards intimate partners is more likely to lead to injuries than is women's aggression, as discussed in Chapter 8.

With regard to the protection of children from experiencing aggression in the family, banning physical punishment by law is an example of macro-level efforts to prevent family violence. Finland was the second country in the world after Sweden to introduce legislation to criminalise the physical punishment of children. Reviewing the rates of corporal punishment reported by participants born before and after this change in the law, Österman, Björkqvist, and Wahlbeck (2014) found a significantly lower prevalence rate of physical punishment in the younger cohort. However, as noted as a limitation with other quasi-experimental studies reviewed in this chapter, it is not possible to attribute the difference conclusively to the legal ban on physical punishment because other variables related to a reduction in physical punishment may also have changed in the period covered by the study.

Whereas criminalising corporal punishment is a measure of primary prevention, seeking to reduce the prevalence in the population as a whole, introducing *mandatory reporting* of suspected cases of abuse as a legal tool for addressing family violence is a measure of secondary prevention, seeking to discover a greater number of cases and reduce the recurrence of violence against family members (Liu & Vaughn, 2019). Mandatory reporting laws put professionals, such as social workers, medical staff, and mental health professionals, under a legal obligation to report suspected cases of abuse. The introduction of mandatory reporting of childhood abuse as well as elder abuse has led to a substantial increase in the number of recorded cases of alleged abuse (Levesque, 2011; Palusci, Vandervort, & Lewis, 2016). However, a large proportion of cases are later dropped as unsubstantiated, raising the question of unintended side effects associated with this measure (e.g., Morton & Oravecz, 2009). If mandatory reporting is to expose cases of abuse that would otherwise have gone unrecognised while at the same time keeping the number of false alarms low, it is essential that the professionals mandated to report abuse are sufficiently well educated about the different forms of abuse to read the warning signs, and to avoid raising false alarms (Liu & Vaughn, 2019).

The third approach for dealing with domestic violence at the societal level consists of improving *protective services* that offer support to the victims. Measures include the provision of sheltered accommodation for women and children who have suffered domestic violence, regular visits by social workers to families identified as "at risk" to pre-empt the development of abusive situations, provisions for placing abused children and elders into high-quality care, and providing treatment programmes for the perpetrators of abuse (Barnett, Miller-Perrin, & Perrin, 2011). Beyond offering safe places, shelters can also provide effective interventions to improve victims' mental health (Jonker, Sijbrandij, van Luijtelaar, Cuijpers, & Wolf, 2015). The demand for shelters for victims of family violence cannot be met by the number of available places, as experts from a wide range of countries agree. For Europe, Article 23 of the so-called Istanbul Convention on Violence against Women recommends safe accommodation in specialised women's shelters, available in every region, with one family place per 10,000 members of the population (Council of Europe, 2011).

Evaluating the effectiveness of such macro-level responses to family violence is difficult, not least because the criteria for success are hard to define. For example, it is almost impossible to establish whether the introduction of restraining orders causes rates of intimate partner homicide to decline, given the many factors that affect the incidence of such assaults. Similarly, it is hard to decide whether mandatory reporting leads to an increased rate of detection of genuine child abuse cases that outweighs the increase in the number of false alarms. In the case of intimate partner violence, it has been argued that mandatory reporting laws may undermine the autonomy of victims and reduce the likelihood of help-seeking (Lippy, Jumarali, Nnawulezi, Williams, & Burk, 2019).

Family-level measures. Measures directed at preventing abuse or ameliorating its consequences by influencing the micro system of the family focus on changing dysfunctional interaction patterns (Staggs & Schewe, 2011). The first step in this approach is the development of instruments for identifying families at risk for child abuse. One such measure is the Parenting Stress Index (PSI) (Abidin, 1995). The short form of the PSI consists of two subscales: "personal distress", captured by items such as "I feel trapped in parenting responsibilities", and "childrearing stress", including items such as "My child does not like me or want to be close" (Haskett, Ahern, Ward, & Allaire, 2006). The higher parents scored on these scales, the less sensitivity to their children's needs they displayed as observed in standardised parent–child interactions. Another widely used measure is the Child Abuse Potential Inventory (CAPI) (Milner & Wimberley, 1980), which measures three parental risk factors for child abuse: rigidity, unhappiness, and problems with child and self. Milner and Wimberley (1980) showed that scores on the CAPI were able to discriminate between abusive and non-abusive parents.

Once families have been identified as at risk for abuse, *behavioural family interventions* can set in as strategies of secondary prevention for preventing the recurrence of abuse (Turner & Sanders, 2006). Parenting programmes, such as the Triple P Positive Parenting Programme (Sanders, Cann, & Markie-Dadds, 2003) seek to improve the quality of the parent–child relationship and promote positive parenting behaviour. Thomas and Zimmer-Gembeck (2011) evaluated a parent–child interaction training in families with a history of child maltreatment. Recognising the dynamic interaction of parent and child behaviour, the training was aimed at both parents (promoting self-confidence in their parenting skills and changing attributions about their child's problem behaviour) and children (reducing their externalising behaviour). Critical variables of parent and child behaviour were measured before the start of the intervention and 12 weeks after the end of the intervention. Parents in the intervention group were observed to show an increase in positive behaviours towards their children, and reported a significant decrease in their child's externalising behaviour from pre-test to post-intervention, whereas no change was observed in the waiting-list control group. A meta-analysis of 37 studies evaluating the efficacy of parenting programmes in reducing child maltreatment found an effect size of $d = 0.30$ (Chen & Chan, 2016). Significant effects were also found on some risk factors for maltreatment, such as attitudes about corporal punishment, parenting stress, and relationship between parents, but not on parental depression. Another meta-analysis of 14 studies found a modest, but significant reduction in the recurrence of physical abuse of 11% in trained vs. untrained parents (Vlahovicova, Melendez-Torres, Leijten, Knerr, & Gardner, 2017). However, the reviews also reveal a substantial variation in the methodological rigour of the available studies, so the overall findings should be interpreted with that limitation in mind (Euser, Alink, Stoltenborgh, Bakermans-Kranenburg, & van IJzendoorn, 2015).

Individual-level interventions. At this level, the focus of interventions is on the individual person who commits aggressive acts towards a family member. Many interventions are directed at men who physically or sexually assault their female partners, and participation is often mandated by a court. Several approaches have been developed and evaluated in the literature (Babcock, Green, & Robie, 2004). The first is the psycho-educational approach designed to increase men's understanding of the detrimental effects of violence and to challenge role perceptions of male power or dominance. The second approach draws on cognitive-behavioural therapy to help abusers to "unlearn" violent behaviour through improving their communication skills and anger management.

The rate of recidivism by participants of intervention programmes is the main criterion by which intervention success is evaluated, and the current evidence regarding this outcome is inconclusive. For example, the review of 17 studies by Karakurt, Koç, Çetinsaya, Ayluçtarhan, and Bolen (2019) found that self-reported rates of violence against a partner dropped from pre- to post-intervention, but the three studies that conducted randomised control trials to compare the intervention group to a control group did not yield significant differences. Moreover, a meta-analytic review by Arias, Arce, and Vilariño (2013) found that recidivism rates assessed by reports of the couples involved were significantly higher than rates taken from official crime records, highlighting the impact of methodological decisions on the conclusions reached about programme effectiveness. The authors suggest that official records may be lower because victims may be afraid to report partner violence for fear of further victimisation. A further meta-analysis of educational and skill-based interventions to address relationship violence in young people aged 12 to 25 years found no evidence of intervention effects in terms of changing attitudes, behaviour, and relationship skills (Fellmeth, Heffernan, Nurse, Habibula, & Sethi, 2013).

In addition to treating aggressors, interventions can be directed at potential victims of family violence to enable them to better protect themselves from the risk of aggression. This approach is exemplified by programmes directed at the prevention of childhood sexual abuse (CSA), both within and outside the family. Educational programmes have been designed to empower children to resist sexual exploitation (e.g., by teaching them to enforce their right to privacy, to be assertive in rejecting unwanted touch, and to seek support from other adults (Del Campo & Fávero, 2019; Rudolph & Zimmer-Gembeck, 2018). The outcome measures in most of the evaluation studies are changes at the level of social skills and cognitive variables, such as knowledge about sexual abuse, perception of risk, self-protection, and willingness to disclose abuse experiences. Although they found substantial variation in programme success in their review of 24 studies evaluating school-based interventions, Topping and Barron (2009) concluded that participation in sexual abuse prevention programmes leads to moderate increases in the targeted knowledge and skills variables, at least immediately after the intervention. A study by Krahé and Knappert (2009) that evaluated a theatre play for elementary-school children found positive intervention effects that were sustained over a period of 30 weeks. Meta-analytic reviews have found little evidence that the programmes have detrimental side-effects, such as frightening or upsetting children (Walsh, Zwi, Woolfenden, & Shlonsky, 2015). However, it must be noted there is virtually no evidence on the efficacy of CSA prevention programmes in reducing the number of children who become victims of sexual abuse.

Whereas the sexual abuse prevention programmes are primary interventions designed to prevent victimisation in unselected samples of children, other reviews focused on interventions targeting victims of intimate partner aggression. Such programmes are tertiary interventions designed to offer therapy to ameliorate the consequences of the victimisation experience and to empower victims to seek effective help and resist revictimisation. While a systematic review of 57 studies showed such interventions to be successful overall, the efficacy varied depending on different outcomes (Trabold, McMahon, Alsobrooks, Whitney, & Mittal, 2018).

Preventing sexual aggression

Given the widespread occurrence of sexual aggression from adolescence onward and the lasting negative effects it has on the victims (see Chapter 9), it is clear that the development of measures for preventing sexual aggression is a key challenge for researchers and policy makers alike. Approaches aimed at reducing the risk of sexual aggression can be broadly located at the societal and the individual level. This section presents some illustrative examples from both categories.

Societal measures designed to reduce sexual aggression. As with other society-level approaches, the law provides an instrument for preventing and reducing sexual aggression. Major legal changes implemented in many countries in the last decades are the introduction of marital rape as a criminal offence and the broadening of legal definitions to conclude male victims. For example, in the U.S., marital rape has been a criminal offence in all states since 1993, and Germany followed in 1997. As shown in Figure 12.1 earlier in this chapter, 73% of 133 countries included in a WHO report have laws against rape in marriage. However, the same figure also shows that these laws are fully enforced in only 43% of countries, amounting to a substantial justice gap in the legal protection against marital rape (Randall & Venkatesh, 2015). Whether or not making it a criminal offence reduces the prevalence of marital rape is hard to establish. Based on findings from victim surveys, it has been found that only a small proportion of sexual assaults is reported to the police and included in official crime statistics. Among this small proportion, the majority of reported cases are assaults by strangers, which correspond to the "real rape" stereotype described in Chapter 9 (Temkin & Krahé, 2008).

Based on research findings that about one in four women studying at higher education institutions in the U.S. is likely to experience sexual violence (Muehlenhard, Peterson, Humphreys, & Jozkowski, 2017), legal measures known as Title IX have been tightened to reduce the rate of sexual assault among college students. Title IX is part of the Education Amendments Act of 1972 and states: "No person in the United States shall, on the basis of sex, be excluded from participation in, be denied the benefits of, or be subjected to discrimination under any education program or activity receiving Federal financial assistance." Universities are obliged to take immediate and effective steps to end sexual harassment and sexual violence (National Sexual Violence Resource Center, 2011). To meet this obligation, procedures for reporting, investigating, and adjudicating complaints of sexual aggression have been implemented at universities and colleges nationwide (Graham et al., 2017), and there is evidence that more comprehensive policies are linked to lower prevalence rates of campus sexual assault (DeLong et al., 2018).

Other measures at the societal or community level seek to influence established risk factors by changing the social context that allows sexual violence to occur (for a discussion of society-level risk factors, see Chapter 9). Drawing on research on the links between alcohol use and sexual aggression, enforcing stricter observation of age limits on the sale of alcohol could be a possible measure for reducing the likelihood of sexual aggression. For example, a study of 524 colleges and universities found that sexual assault rates were significantly higher in institutions that allowed students to possess alcohol on campus than in institutions where this was not allowed (Stotzer & MacCartney, 2016). Similarly, as we saw in Chapter 6, there is considerable evidence that exposure to violent pornography is linked to a higher risk of engaging in sexually aggressive behaviour. This suggests that restricting access to violent pornography, especially for an underage audience, could contribute to the prevention of sexual aggression. Although such measures have been adopted as part of youth protection legislation and policies (e.g., Hingson, 2010), there is a shortage of rigorous evaluations of their effectiveness in reducing the rate of sexual aggression.

A further societal response to the problem of rape and other sexual offences is to address the low conviction rates in the criminal prosecution by implementing changes in the treatment of rape victims by the police and the medical system (see also Chapter 9). Although these measures are directed in the first instance at survivors of sexual assault, they are also intended to have a wider effect on increasing reporting rates by removing the expectation of secondary victimisation by police and medical staff as a barrier to reporting. In the U.K., specialised Sexual Assault Referral Centres (SARCs) were introduced to better meet the needs of victims and improve the chances of criminal prosecution, and further recommendations for change were made in an independent report to the government (Stern, 2010). In the U.S., initiatives have been developed to ensure that sexual assault victims are examined by specialised teams, such as sexual assault nurse examiners (the SANE programme) to secure vital evidence to increase the number of cases progressing through the criminal justice system (Campbell et al., 2014).

Individual-level approaches to the prevention of sexual aggression. Targeting the individual, primary rape prevention programmes have been directed at potential perpetrators, victims, and bystanders. Interventions targeting men are called "rape education programmes" and interventions targeting women are called "risk reduction programmes". Findings from evaluation studies suggest that these programmes are best implemented in single-sex groups (Gidycz, Orchowski, & Berkowitz, 2011). A third group of interventions are designed to promote the willingness of bystanders to intervene in situations that entail the risk of a sexual assault. Many studies have been conducted over the last two decades to address the effectiveness of rape prevention programmes, especially for reducing sexual assault among college students (see DeGue et al., 2014, for a review).

Rape education programmes are designed to reduce the acceptance of rape myths, highlight the importance of consent, and alter the perceived social norms that sexual aggression is common and accepted among same-age peers. They are directed primarily at men, and participation is mandatory for students entering university in many places. Programme duration is usually short, ranging from a single session to a total of 3–4 sessions. An overview of the key components of rape education programmes directed at men as provided by Orchowski et al. (2018) is presented in Figure 12.2. The key constructs targeted are the promotion of empathy, the teaching of skills, such as negotiating consent, and the correction of misperceptions about sexual assault. The immediate effects of the intervention are changes in psychological risk factors for sexual aggression perpetration, such as adherence to traditional gender roles and rape-supportive attitudes, and promoting skills for intervening as bystanders. The ultimate criterion of success is the reduction of sexual aggression perpetration in the groups that received the training.

In terms of *reducing rape myth acceptance*, defined as beliefs about sexual aggression that serve to deny, downplay, or justify sexually aggressive behaviour that men commit against women (Gerger, Kley, Bohner, & Siebler, 2007), a meta-analysis by Flores and Hartlaub (1998) found evidence for short-term reductions in rape myth acceptance, and later studies have confirmed this finding (e.g., Langhinrichsen-Rohling, Foubert, Brasfield, Hill, & Shelley-Tremblay, 2011; Peterson et al., 2018). Some studies have shown that the effects of the programmes are stronger for participants with high initial levels of rape myth acceptance (Pacifici, Stoolmiller, & Nelson, 2001). However, the results are less encouraging with regard to the sustainability of intervention effects (Anderson & Whiston, 2005; Schewe, 2002). Rape myth acceptance is typically measured immediately before and after

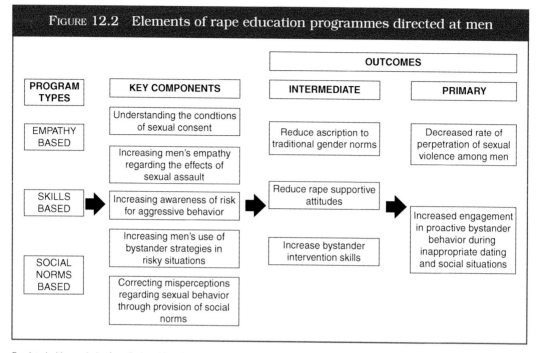

FIGURE 12.2   Elements of rape education programmes directed at men

participation in the intervention, with some studies including follow-ups of up to two months post-intervention. The reviews concluded that the effects tended to disappear within a few weeks post-intervention, with attitudes returning to pre-intervention levels.

In addition to challenging the belief in rape myths, prevention programmes have been directed at *changing social norms about sexual violence.* Several studies have shown that men are susceptible to normative information about the acceptance and perpetration of sexual aggression among their peers. For example, Edwards and Vogel (2015) found that men's exposure to messages indicating that most young men accepted sexual violence in certain situations reported a greater likelihood of engaging in sexual aggression compared with men exposed to anti-rape messages. The "social norms approach" seeks to counter the rape-supportive normative environment by engaging men as social justice allies, both in terms of challenging misperceptions and in promoting active intervention to stop other men from engaging in sexual aggression (Fabiano, Perkins, Berkowitz, Linkenbach, & Stark, 2003). A study by Zounlome and Wong (2019) presented male students with the information that a high percentage of men in general (general norms; e.g., "89.1% of men agree that verbal resistance shows a lack of legitimate agreement to sexual activity") or of students at their own university (local norms) rejected sexual assault and rape-supportive beliefs. Men in both norms conditions indicated a lower likelihood to engage in sexual aggression than did men in a control condition, who were presented with general statistics about their university unrelated to sexual aggression. The effect was stronger for men with a prior history of sexual aggression. Overall, the existing evidence suggests that brief interventions directed at men may be successful in reducing rape-supportive attitudes. However, meta-analytic reviews on the ability of rape prevention programmes to reduce men's perpetration of sexual aggression have found little evidence of their effectiveness in reducing sexual aggression perpetration (DeGue et al., 2014; L. A. Wright, Zounlome, & Whiston, 2018).

A second line of intervention research has examined the effectiveness of *risk reduction programmes* directed at women. The core elements of these programmes as summarised by Orchowski et al. (2018) are presented in Figure 12.3. The main outcome variable is the reduction in the likelihood of sexual victimisation, but further aims are added to reduce the fear of sexual assault and strengthen coping skills in the event of an assault.

Broadly speaking, rape resistance programmes address two main aspects: (a) increasing women's awareness and understanding of the factors that increase the vulnerability to sexual aggression, and (b) enabling them to engage in more effective resistance when faced with a situation in which a sexual assault may be imminent. For example, understanding that most sexual assaults are committed by someone known to the victim may increase women's sensitivity to warning signs in interactions with dates, acquaintances, and partners. Based on evidence on the critical role of alcohol in impairing the recognition of risk cues and predicting sexual victimisation (Melkonian & Ham, 2018), interventions have targeted a reduction of women's alcohol consumption and were found to be effective in reducing victimisation rates in women with problematic drinking behaviour (Gilmore, Lewis, & George, 2015). Moreover, self-defence trainings for women have been shown to reduce the risk of assault (McCaughey & Cermele, 2017; Senn et al., 2015).

An example of a rape resistance programme is the Enhanced Assess, Acknowledge, Act (EAAA) programme, which combines the promotion of risk awareness (Assess; e.g., the role of alcohol), risk assessment (Acknowledge, e.g., the identification of warning signs), and protective action (Act, knowledge about effective resistance strategies). EAAA also contains a module on Sex and Relationships in which participants apply the knowledge gained in the first three modules to their own intimate and sexual relationships (Senn et al., 2013). In an evaluation of programme effectiveness over a follow-up period of 24 months, Senn et al. (2017) found that programme participants had a higher confidence in their ability to defend themselves in a sexual attack, had a better knowledge of effective resistance strategies, rejected rape myths and victim blaming to a greater extent, and were less likely to experience attempted rape compared with a control group. The

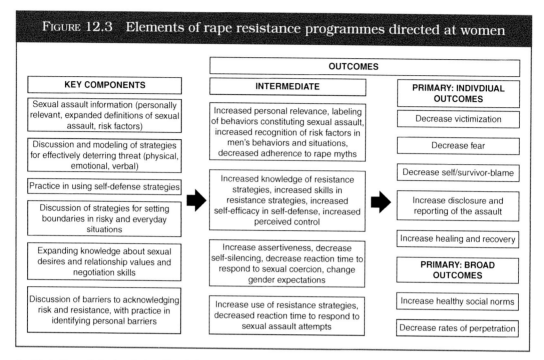

FIGURE 12.3   Elements of rape resistance programmes directed at women

Reprinted with permission from Orchowski et al., 2018, p. 2, © 2018 by Sage Publications.

likelihood of experiencing a completed rape was reduced up to 18 months post-intervention but was no longer significantly lower after 24 months.

In addition to the education of potential perpetrators and empowerment of potential victims, promoting *bystander intervention* has also been explored as an effective way of pre-empting sexual aggression. The elements of bystander interventions are summarised by Orchowski et al. (2018), as presented in Figure 12.4. Bystander intervention approaches seek to increase individuals' ability to detect situations involving a risk of sexual assault for others and their willingness to step in. Research in the field of prosocial behaviour has identified obstacles that prevent bystanders from helping people in need, such as a diffusion of responsibility, the failure to correctly interpret the situation (pluralistic ignorance), and the fear of negative responses from others in case of taking action (Latané & Darley, 1970). Thus, these obstacles need to be addressed in programmes to promote bystander intervention. Several recent reviews have concluded that existing interventions are effective in increasing participants' willingness to intervene (Evans, Burroughs, & Knowlden, 2019; Kettrey & Marx, 2019; Mujal, Taylor, Fry, Gochez-Kerr, & Weaver, 2019). However, there is no conclusive evidence so far that bystander intervention programmes are able to reduce the prevalence of sexual assault perpetration (Kettrey & Marx, 2019).

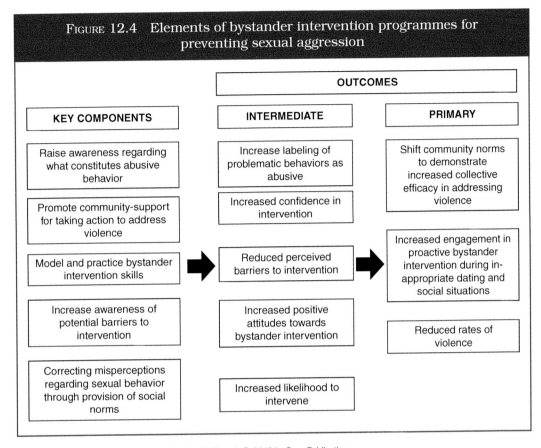

FIGURE 12.4   Elements of bystander intervention programmes for preventing sexual aggression

To conclude, research on effective strategies for reducing sexual assault has intensified in recent years, especially with regard to the prevalence on college campuses. There is no standard curriculum for rape prevention efforts, and the effectiveness varies between programmes (DeGue et al., 2014). Programmes targeting potential perpetrators, victims, and bystanders have largely been conducted in separate strands despite overlapping goals and components, which has led Orchowski et al. (2018) to call for a better integrated, comprehensive approach to sexual assault prevention. In addition to examining changes in attitudes, such as rape myth acceptance, and behaviours, such as alcohol consumption, an increasing number of studies has examined a reduction in prevalence rates as the key outcome. Although there is still a shortage of rigorously designed evaluation studies, the knowledge base on what works and what doesn't to reduce the scale of sexual violence is growing steadily.

WICKED PROBLEMS AND WISE INTERVENTIONS

The research reviewed in this chapter has illustrated the challenges of finding effective ways to reduce the pervasiveness of aggression in many domains of life. Some firmly entrenched beliefs about effective control mechanisms, such as the deterrent function of punishment or the positive effects of a "cathartic" release of aggressive feelings, need to be revised on the basis of this research. New courses of action have been developed that address aggressive behaviour at the societal, interpersonal, and individual levels, but these are still awaiting more extensive evaluations. In the words of Kazdin (2011), aggression and violence can be seen as "wicked problems" that are characterised by a number of problematic features, listed in Table 12.5. Taken together, these features illustrate why it is so difficult to find successful ways of reducing aggression. They also point to a tension between seeking broad solutions that pertain to many forms of aggression, and specialised responses that are geared towards more narrowly defined forms of aggression. Specialisation runs the risk of producing fragmented lines of research that fail to acknowledge the common

TABLE 12.5 Characteristics of aggression and violence as "wicked problems"

- Multiple stakeholders have divergent views about what the problem "really" is.
- Aggression and violence do not result from any single cause but from a set of interrelated causes that influence each other.
- Aggression and violence are not isolated problems but embedded in other critical social issues.
- There is no single solution that will eliminate the problem.
- Action needs to be taken on the basis of insufficient evidence.
- The problem is not likely to be ever completely resolved.

Based on Kazdin, 2011.

roots and consequences of different forms of aggression, whereas broader approaches may lose sight of the unique causes and outcomes of particular forms of aggression. Therefore, general strategies for intervention need to be combined with domain-specific approaches for preventing particular forms of aggression.

Moreover, a closer bond needs to be forged between basic research, directed at identifying causes of aggression and violence, and applied research, seeking to reduce aggressive behaviour as a major social problem. Such a bond could provide a basis for strategies that Walton and Wilson (2018) call "psychologically wise interventions". The starting point for wise interventions is the proposition that social experiences as well as perceptions of the self are open to interpretation, and that these interpretations hold a key to understanding affect, thinking, and behaviour. The hostile attribution bias, discussed in Chapters 3 and 4, is a good example supporting this proposition, because it refers to a particular style of interpreting ambiguous social behaviour as motivated hostile intentions. Therefore, interventions that help people to change their interpretations of specific experiences or views of themselves so as to alter their construction of meaning may bring about changes in their behaviour that lead to more adaptive interpretations and increase their psychological well-being. The idea that "wise interventions" promote such a cycle of person–situation interactions as described by Walton and Wilson (2018) is illustrated in Figure 12.5. Interventions are designed to promote the alteration of meanings, placed in the middle box of the table, to create a change in behaviour that may lead to more adaptive behaviour, an improvement of situation conditions, and a more positive style of thinking.

The constructs in Figure 12.5 can be easily referred to the domain of aggression, in fact they can be accommodated in the General Aggression Model (GAM) presented in Chapter 2. Like in the GAM, person variables (negative behaviour) and negative situations or social contexts shape

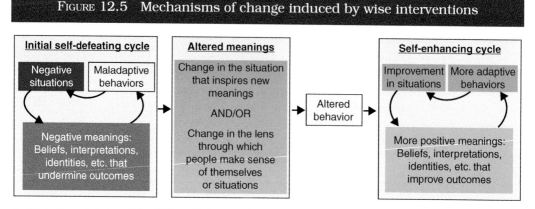

FIGURE 12.5   Mechanisms of change induced by wise interventions

individuals' cognitions that guide their behaviour, and interventions that inspire a change in these cognitions and behaviours may lead to more positive outcomes. Applying this proposition to altering negative perceptions of outgroups, research has shown that an intervention promoting the general belief that groups may change led Israeli Jews and Palestinians to hold less negative evaluations of the respective outgroup and show a greater willingness to make concessions for the sake of peace (Halperin, Russell, Trzesniewski, Gross, & Dweck, 2011). In a later study, the effect of this type of intervention was shown to last over a six-month period of intense conflict between the two groups (Goldenberg et al., 2018). These examples show the potential of using established knowledge about basic principles of cognition and behaviour change to develop strategies that can be applied to the reduction of intergroup conflict.

Previous chapters have shown that the causes of aggression and violence lie at different levels from the individual person to the interpersonal encounter of two or more individuals and from the micro-system of social groups to the macro level of society. Accordingly, approaches designed to prevent and reduce aggressive behaviour need to reflect this multi-level causality. First, it is critical to reduce the odds of aggression and violence universally (i.e., in societies as a whole) by promoting individual development and well-being, strengthening interpersonal skills for non-violent conflict resolution, and creating a social consensus that aggression and violence are unacceptable. However, it is equally important to develop measures that are specifically directed at persons and situations with an increased risk for aggression and violence. Finally, measures are required targeting those individuals and groups that already have a history of aggression and violence and therefore have a special indication for interventions, not least to protect their victims from further experiences of aggression.

SUMMARY

- Compared with the wealth of research into the causes of, and precipitating factors for, aggressive behaviour, evidence on how to prevent and reduce it is more limited. Measures designed to reduce the scale of aggression and violence may be classified into two groups: general strategies for preventing aggression in its variety of manifestations, and specific strategies custom-tailored to reduce particular forms of aggression.

- At the societal level, reducing the opportunity for crime (e.g., by restricting access to firearms) and using capital punishment to deter violent offenders were discussed as general measures. Evidence on the effects of capital punishment on homicide rates provides little support for the deterrence hypothesis. By contrast, measures limiting the availability and use of firearms have been shown to reduce the fatal effects of violent attacks. However, the evidence is mostly correlational and does not provide evidence of the causal effects of such measures.

- Approaches directed at changing the general propensity towards aggressive behaviour in the individual can build on the principles of reinforcement and observational learning. Trying to reduce aggressive behaviour through punishment is of limited value because it requires several preconditions that rarely co-occur in a given context. Instead, reinforcing positive social behaviour and providing non-aggressive behavioural models are more promising avenues for prevention. These aspects are captured in parent management trainings designed to teach parents constructive forms of discipline and conflict resolution.

- Contrary to popular wisdom, catharsis (i.e., acting out aggressive impulses in a symbolic or innocuous way) is largely counterproductive in reducing aggression. It generally leads to an increase rather than a decrease in aggressive responses. Instead, eliciting responses that are incompatible with angry arousal and aggressive cognitions (e.g., through prosocial behaviour or using pleasant music to buffer stress and anger) is a way of reducing aggression by influencing affective and cognitive antecedents of aggressive behaviour.

- Anger management and observational learning can also be used to modify aggressive behaviour. Rather than suppressing aggression, they replace aggressive responses with more adequate ways of dealing with frustration and provocation.

- As an example of tailored interventions directed at specific forms of aggression, school-based programmes have been developed for tackling gang violence. Their aim is to stop young people from joining violent gangs by promoting social skills that enable adolescents to resist peer pressure to join gangs and to find non-aggressive ways of dealing with interpersonal conflict.

- Strategies for the prevention of family violence are located at three levels. At the societal level, legal instruments can be used for protecting potential victims and for improving the detection of abuse. At the family level, interventions for improving communication skills among family members are promising measures for breaking up inadequate patterns of conflict resolution. Finally, at the individual level, programmes directed at abusive partners with the aim of teaching them anger management skills and alternative strategies for resolving conflicts with children and partners were of limited success. In addition, preventive measures directed at the potential victims of domestic violence seek to empower them to successfully defend their physical, sexual, and emotional integrity.

- Strategies for preventing sexual assault at the societal level, such as improving the treatment of rape victims by the police and the medical system, and increasing reporting rates, are designed to create a social climate in which the seriousness of sexual assault is recognised and victims are treated with sympathy and respect. Individual-level measures are directed at changing men's rape-supportive attitudes and challenging misconceptions about the acceptability of sexual aggression. Risk reduction interventions that target women seek to raise their awareness about risky behaviours and situations and to promote effective rape-resistance strategies. Finally, strengthening bystanders' ability and willingness to intervene when they perceive someone else in danger of being sexually assaulted have yielded some promising results.

TASKS TO DO

(1) Find out what the policy is in your country, state, or city about carrying and drinking alcohol in public.
(2) Visit the website of the G.R.E.A.T. programme to prevent gang involvement: www.great-online.org/GREAT-Home, and find out whether similar schemes exist in your community.
(3) Conduct an Internet search using the key words "rape prevention" and the name of your country to find out about initiatives available in your country or local area.

SUGGESTED READING

Esbensen, F. A., Peterson, D., Taylor, T. J., Freng, A., Osgood, D. W., Carson, D., & Matsuda, K. N. (2011). Evaluation and evolution of the Gang Resistance Education and Training (G.R.E.A.T.) program. *Journal of School Violence, 10*, 53–70.
Meier, B. P., & Wilkowski, B. M. (2013). Reducing the tendency to aggress: Insights from social and personality psychology. *Social and Personality Psychology Compass, 7*, 343–354.

Orchowski, L. M., Edwards, K. M., Hollander, J. A., Banyard, V. L., Senn, C. Y., & Gidycz, C. A. (2018). Integrating sexual assault resistance, bystander, and men's social norms strategies to prevent sexual violence on college campuses: A call to action. *Trauma, Violence & Abuse*, Advance online publication.

Vlahovicova, K., Melendez-Torres, G. J., Leijten, P., Knerr, W., & Gardner, F. (2017). Parenting programs for the prevention of child physical abuse recurrence: A systematic review and meta-analysis. *Clinical Child and Family Psychology Review, 20*, 351–365.

Chapter 13

OUTLOOK AND CONCLUSION

The present volume has brought together research on aggressive behaviour from different fields, selected and examined through the lens of a social psychologist. This perspective is rooted in the conceptualisation of aggression as a form of social behaviour between individuals and groups. In line with Kurt Lewin's (1936) famous formula of behaviour as a function of the person and the situation, it is based on the proposition that aggressive behaviour needs to be understood as an interaction of the person and the environment. Aggression and violence are the products not only of cognitions, emotions, and actions of individual persons, acting alone or in groups, but also of the environment in which they live and the specific situations in which they find themselves. The two sources of aggressive behaviour do not simply add up but mutually influence each other in complex ways. Only by considering the person and the situation in interaction can we answer the question why one person's aggressive behaviour varies between different situations and why different persons vary in the aggressive behaviour they show in one and the same situation (for a discussion of the interactionist perspective see Krahé, 1992; 2020).

The large body of recent research presented in this volume clearly indicates that aggression research is alive and well in (social) psychology. This conclusion, which would be seen as an unreservedly positive development in most other fields of study, has a distressing side to it in the case of aggression. It highlights the urgent need to find answers to the questions of causation and prevention of aggression and violence, which bring immeasurable suffering to victims and their families and place a heavy burden on societies as a whole. Therefore, gaining a better understanding of the processes that lead individuals and groups to engage in aggressive, often lethal actions against each other, and then using this understanding to develop strategies for their prevention and control, remains one of the greatest challenges for both basic and applied research in psychology.

It must be noted that a comprehensive understanding of the forms, origins, and prevention of aggression and violence needs a multidisciplinary approach that goes well beyond the field of psychology but was outside the scope of this book and the expertise of its author. We need the historical perspective to remind us that views about aggression and violence are shaped by specific historical circumstances and intellectual traditions and have been construed and handled differently over the centuries, for example with respect to defining childhood abuse or marital rape. We need the criminological perspective to describe how legal definitions of different forms of violence have changed and how the criminal justice system can deal with the challenges of prosecuting and sanctioning new forms of aggressive behaviour, such as hate speech and cyberbullying. We need political scientists to explain the causes of protracted intergroup conflicts in different world regions and their potential for breeding terrorist violence, and sociologists to inform us about the role of macro-level risk factors for aggression, such as social inequality or material deprivation. We need the expertise of geneticists and neuroscientists to explain the biological basis of differences in aggressive behaviour, both in terms of stable individual characteristics and with regard to situational reactions. And we need a greater input from research in anthropology and ethnology to study aggression and violence in a cross-cultural perspective. This list is far from complete, but it highlights the need to invest more effort and resources into the development of an interdisciplinary agenda for the study of aggression and violence.

However, intensifying academic research is only one part of the challenge facing societies. We need a civic debate on how much aggression we want to tolerate in our societies, what forms of behaviour intended to harm others we consider serious or negligible, and to what extent we see the need for action. The #metoo campaign serves as an example of how certain topics that have long been on the agenda of scientific research gain attention and spark intense public debate when prominent single cases come to light. The "March for your lives" campaign for stricter gun control legislation in the wake of the school shooting in Parkland, Florida, in which 17 people were killed in 2018, is another example, as is the "Black lives matter" campaign that has placed the problem of race-related police violence on the worldwide agenda following the killing of George Floyd by police in Minneapolis in 2020. Campaigns like these have clear messages for change, and our research can contribute sound theorising and empirical evidence on useful (but also on counterproductive) approaches for achieving these goals.

At the same time, these examples illustrate that initiatives to prevent aggression and violence are located in a context of divergent attitudes, values, and interests, and a broad consensus that action is needed and in what direction is hard, if not impossible to achieve. Therefore, not all the findings and conclusions generated by the research presented in this volume will be gladly accepted outside the academic debate. This is true, for example, for evidence identifying the use of violent media as a risk factor for aggression, and for evidence on the effects of tightening gun-control legislation on reducing violent crime, neither of which has been, or will be, translated into policy responses without strong opposition from the respective interest groups in the media and gun lobbies. In addition to accumulating knowledge about the scale, causes, and consequences of aggression, psychological aggression research is therefore faced with the challenge of spreading this knowledge beyond the scientific community to inform both policy makers and public opinion.

To conclude, the new edition of this textbook has aimed to offer an up-to-date and critical coverage of the current state of social psychological knowledge on aggression and violence. It has demonstrated the wide-ranging and high-quality research activities in this field, not least reflected in the large number of rigorous experiments, longitudinal studies, and meta-analytic reviews that have been published since the last edition. These developments show that we are making steady progress in identifying the scale of aggressive and violent behaviour and in understanding the causes, and consequences of these forms of harmful social behaviour. The next step is to intensify our efforts to translate this knowledge into effective strategies for prevention and intervention that are tested using state-of the art evaluation designs. Although we are still a long way from providing a conclusive answer to the question of why aggression and violence occur and what can be done to make the world a more peaceful place for the interactions of individuals as well as social groups, the evidence covered in this textbook has shown that we continue to make good progress.

GLOSSARY

adoption studies study design whereby the similarity between children and their biological parents is compared to the similarity with their adoptive parents to compare shared genes against shared environment.

aggression any form of behaviour intended to harm or injure another living being who is motivated to avoid such treatment.

Aggression Questionnaire (AQ) self-report instrument to measure stable individual differences in trait aggressiveness.

aggressive cues situational cues with an aggressive meaning that increase the accessibility of aggressive cognitions.

aggressive driving behaviour intended to physically, emotionally, or psychologically harm another within the driving environment.

aggressive scripts cognitive representations of when and how to show aggressive behaviour.

alcohol myopia alcohol-caused reduction of attentional capacities that hampers a comprehensive appraisal of situational cues.

anger a syndrome of relatively specific feelings, cognitions, and physiological reactions linked associatively with an urge to injure some target.

anger management trainings convey to aggressive individuals an understandable model of anger and its relationship to triggering events, thoughts, and aggressive behaviour.

anger rumination perseverative thinking about a personally meaningful anger-inducing event.

antisocial behaviour behaviour that violates social norms about appropriate conduct.

behaviour genetics field of study devoted to the genetic basis of social behaviour.

"Big Five" personality factors basic dimensions of individual differences, consisting of openness to experience, conscientiousness, extraversion, agreeableness, and neuroticism.

Bobo doll paradigm using a large inflatable doll (Bobo) to show that adults' aggressive behaviour towards the doll leads to imitation by children who observed their behaviour.

bullying (also known as *mobbing*) denotes aggressive behaviour directed at victims who cannot easily defend themselves, commonly in schools and at the workplace.

catharsis release of aggressive tension through symbolic engagement in aggressive behaviour.

cognitive neo-associationist model explains aggressive behaviour as the result of negative affect that is subjected to cognitive processing and activates a network of aggression-related thoughts and feelings.

collective violence instrumental use of violence by people who identify themselves as members of a group against another group or set of individuals, in order to achieve political, economic, or social objectives.

competitive reaction time task (CRTT) measure of aggressive behaviour in the lab in which participants assign aversive stimuli to an alleged opponent if they are faster in responding to a signal detection task.

concomitant heat approach method for testing the heat hypothesis by manipulating room temperature and observing covariations between temperature and aggressive behaviour.

Conflict Tactics Scales (CTS) instrument for measuring intimate partner violence by collecting self-reports of perpetration and/or victimization.

confluence model model explaining men's sexual aggression by the two pathways of impersonal sex and hostile masculinity.

cyberbullying involves the use of modern technology, such as computers, mobile phones or other electronic devices, to inflict intentional harm on others.

dehumanisation tendency to deny outgroups the quality of being human.

deindividuation loss of personal identity as a result of being in a crowd or immersed in a specific role.

delegitimisation categorization of a group or groups into extremely negative social categories that are excluded from the realm of acceptable norms and/or values.

deradicalisation process of rejecting the ideology underpinning the membership in a terrorist group.

desensitisation process whereby the ability of a stimulus to elicit arousal becomes weaker with each consecutive presentation.

deterrence theory theory that preventing crime requires the development of a system of punishment that will teach the lesson that "crime does not pay".

direct aggression aggressive behaviour directed immediately at the target, such as hitting or shouting abuse.

direct reinforcement experience of positive consequences of aggressive behaviour (e.g., status gain among peers) that increases the probability of future aggressive acts.

disinhibition weakening the inhibitions against showing aggressive behaviour, e.g., by repeated exposure to violence in the media.

displaced aggression tendency to react to frustration with an aggressive response directed not at the original source of the frustration but at an unrelated, more easily accessible target.

dual hormone hypothesis postulates that it is the combination of high testosterone and low cortisol that promotes aggressive behaviour.

emergent norm theory theory of crowd behaviour proposing that members base their behaviour on what they perceive to be the specific norms shared among the group.

emotional abuse failure to provide a developmentally appropriate, supportive environment.

epigenetics field of study showing that adverse experiences may change a person's genes related to aggressive behaviour.

essay evaluation paradigm measure of aggressive behaviour in the lab whereby participants assign negative feedback on an alleged co-participant's essay.

excitation transfer theory transfer of neutral physiological arousal onto arousal resulting from frustration, thus augmenting negative affect and increasing the strength of an aggressive response.

executive function cognitive activities that govern goal-directed action and planning of behaviour, and enable adaptive responses to novel, complex, or ambiguous situations.

family aggression behaviour carried out with the intention to inflict harm on a family member or a close other, for example a stepchild, residing in the same household.

field experiment manipulating conditions in everyday situations to observe the effects of the manipulation on the likelihood of aggressive behaviour.

firearm availability easy access to firearms as a risk factor for violence.

frustration external interference with the goal-directed behaviour of the person.

frustration–aggression hypothesis assumes that frustration – that is, blockage of a goal-directed activity – increases the likelihood of aggressive behaviour.

gang an age-graded peer group that exhibits some permanence, engages in criminal activity, and has some symbolic representation of membership.

General Aggression Model (GAM) integrative theoretical framework explaining how personal and situational input variables lead to aggressive behaviour via cognitive appraisal, negative affect, and physiological arousal.

geographic regions approach method for testing the heat hypothesis by comparing violence rates in cooler and hotter climates.

hate crimes criminal acts toward individuals by virtue of their membership to certain social groups or categories.

heat hypothesis hypothesis that aggression increases with higher temperatures.

hormones higher levels of testosterone and lower levels of cortisol have been linked to aggression, but they need to be considered in combination with environmental influences.

hostile aggression aggressive behaviour motivated by the desire to express anger and hostile feelings.

hostile attribution bias/hostile attributional style tendency to attribute hostile intentions to a person who has caused harm when it is unclear whether or not the harm was caused accidentally or on purpose.

hot sauce paradigm measure of aggressive behaviour in the lab whereby participants assign a certain quantity of aversively hot sauce to an alleged co-participant who does not like spicy food.

I^3 theory theory that explains aggression by the interplay of three factors: instigation, impellance, and inhibition.

Implicit association test (IAT) reaction-time measure to assess the speed with which a person can activate aggressive cognitions.

indirect aggression aggression delivered behind the target person's back by damaging their social relationships, for example through spreading rumours.

ingroup favouritism preferential treatment and evaluation of ingroup members solely on the basis of their shared group membership.

instrumental aggression aggressive behaviour performed to reach a particular goal, as a means to an end.

intergroup aggression aggressive encounters between groups or aggression based on group membership rather than individual characteristics.

interpersonal aggression aggressive behaviour between individuals rather than groups.

intimate partner violence perpetration or threat of an act of physical or sexual violence within the context of an intimate relationship.

irritability habitual tendency to react impulsively, controversially, or rudely at the slightest provocation or disagreement.

media violence media (movies, video games, music videos, etc.) showing or describing behaviour intended to cause harm, especially severe physical harm, to media characters.

media violence–aggression link hypothesis that exposure to violent media contents makes users more aggressive.

meta-analysis quantitative review integrating the findings from individual studies into a common metric of effect size.

narcissism personality trait denoting a grandiose view of the self and strong sense of entitlement.

naturalistic observation recording the natural occurrence of aggressive behaviour in everyday situations.

observational learning learning aggressive behaviour by observing and imitating the aggressive behaviour of others.

official records data collected for purposes other than research providing information about aggressive and violent behaviour (e.g., crime statistics, newspaper reports).

ostracism ignoring people or excluding them from social interactions.

peer nominations method for measuring aggressive behaviour by asking other people (e.g., classmates) to rate the aggressiveness of an individual.

perspective taking ability to orient oneself non-egocentrically to the perspective of another person.

physical abuse the use of severe physical force intended to harm the child's health, survival, development, or dignity.

physical aggression behaviour intended to cause physical harm to another person.

pornography media material used or intended to increase sexual arousal.

post-traumatic growth experience of positive change that occurs as a result of the struggle with highly challenging life crises.

post-traumatic stress disorder (PTSD) characteristic pattern of symptoms observed in survivors of traumatic experiences, such as sexual assault.

prejudice negative evaluation of others by virtue of their membership of a certain social group or category.

proactive aggression also called unprovoked aggression; aggressive behaviour shown without a prior provocation.

projective techniques measures of aggressive dispositions in which participants project their aggressive thoughts, feelings, and behavioural intention onto ambiguous stimulus material.

provocation anger-eliciting interpersonal encounter.

psychopathy constellation of personality traits and socially deviant behaviours, including a narcissistic sense of self, lack of empathy or remorse, poor impulse control, manipulative approach to interpersonal

relationships, and antisocial behaviour.

rape myth acceptance endorsement of stereotypical beliefs about rape that deny, downplay, or justify men's sexual violence against women.

reactive aggression also called retaliative aggression; aggressive behaviour shown in response to a provocation.

"real rape" stereotype generalised cognitive schema that a "real" rape is a surprise attack in a dark or isolated place, involving the use of physical force, carried out by a stranger on an unsuspecting victim, who shows strong physical resistance.

relational aggression behaviour intended to harm the target person through damaging their social relationships.

relative deprivation theory postulates that intergroup tensions arise from the perception that one's own group is unfairly disadvantaged compared with the outgroup.

self-control capacity to stop, override, or alter unwanted behaviours.

sexual abuse sexual contact between a child and an adult that is carried out for the sexual stimulation of the perpetrator.

sexual aggression making someone engage in sexual activities against their will through a range of coercive strategies, such as threat or use of physical force, exploitation of the inability to resist, or verbal pressure.

Sexual Experiences Survey (SES) self-report measure to assess the perpetration of, and victimization by, sexual aggression.

sexual harassment deliberate or repeated sexual behaviour that is unwelcome to the recipient, as well as other sex-related behaviours that are hostile, offensive, or degrading.

sexual scripts cognitive representations of sequences of actions and events in sexual encounters, serving as guidelines for sexual behaviour.

sociobiology discipline devoted to the study of the evolutionary basis of social behaviour.

sociocultural approach explanation of aggressive behaviour as shaped by societal and cultural norms and practices.

social identity approach explains intergroup conflict as a result of social categorisation into ingroups and outgroups and the desire to favour the ingroup.

social information processing (SIP) approach theory about social–cognitive processes that pave the way to aggressive behaviour

staircase model describes the pathway to terrorism as a succession of steps explaining why out of large numbers of disaffected people in a society only very few end up committing terrorist acts.

State-Trait-Anger Expression Inventory (STAXI) measure of individual differences in anger expression (state and trait scales).

steam-boiler model part of Konrad Lorenz's theory of aggression, assuming that aggressive energy is produced continuously within the organism and will burst out spontaneously unless released by an external stimulus.

suicide attacks assaults intended to achieve a political objective, performed outside the context of a conventional war, in which the assailant intentionally kills himself for the purpose of killing others.

Tangram help/hurt task measure of aggressive behaviour in the lab whereby participants assign easy (help) or difficult (hurt) Tangram puzzles to a co-participant. Tangram puzzles consist of a set of polygonal pieces that need to be put together without overlap.

teacher–learner paradigm measure of aggressive behaviour in the lab whereby participants in the role of teachers assign aversive stimuli to an alleged learner.

terrorism acts of violence by non-state actors, perpetrated against civilian populations, intended to cause fear, in order to achieve a political objective.

terror management theory terror invoked by the knowledge of mortality induces people to identify more strongly with their cultural norms and world views as a way of becoming part of a lasting collective identity that transcends their own physical existence.

theory of mind ability to form a mental representation of the internal states of other people.

theory of realistic group conflict explanation of intergroup conflict as a result of competition for resources that only one group can attain.

time periods approach method for testing the heat hypothesis by comparing violence rates in the same region during cooler and hotter periods.

trait aggressiveness denotes stable differences between individuals in the likelihood and intensity of aggressive behaviour.

traumagenic dynamic experience that distorts the child's self-concept, view of the world, and affective functioning.

twin studies study design comparing identical and fraternal twins in how similar they are in their aggressive behaviour.

verbal aggression use of verbal means, such as insults, to cause harm to another person.

violence behaviours carried out with the intention to cause serious harm that involve the use or threat of physical force.

weapons effect finding that individuals who were previously angered showed more aggressive behaviour in the presence of weapons than in the presence of neutral objects.

workplace bullying (also called workplace mobbing or harassment) behaviours intended to cause harm to another person at work over longer periods of time.

References

Abbey, A. (2002). Alcohol-related sexual assault: A common problem among college students. *Journal of Studies on Alcohol, Suppl. 14*, 118–128.

Abbey, A., Jacques-Tiura, A. J., & LeBreton, J. M. (2011). Risk factors for sexual aggression in young men: An expansion of the confluence model. *Aggressive Behavior, 37*, 450–464. doi: 10.1002/ab.20399

Abbey, A., & McAuslan, P. (2004). A longitudinal examination of male college students' perpetration of sexual assault. *Journal of Consulting and Clinical Psychology, 72*, 747–756. doi: 10.1037/0022-006X.72.5.747

Abbey, A., Wegner, R., Pierce, J., & Jacques-Tiura, A. J. (2012). Patterns of sexual aggression in a community sample of young men: Risk factors associated with persistence, desistance, and initiation over a 1-year interval. *Psychology of Violence, 2*, 1–15. doi: 10.1037/a0026346

Abbey, A., Zawacki, T., Buck, P. O., Clinton, A. M., & McAuslan, P. (2004). Sexual assault and alcohol consumption: What do we know about their relationship and what types of research are still needed? *Aggression and Violent Behavior, 9*, 271–303. doi: 10.1016/S1359-1789(03)00011-9

Åberg, L., & Rimmö, P.-A. (1998). Dimensions of aberrant driver behaviour. *Ergonomics, 41*, 39–56. doi: 10.1080/001401398187314

Aberson, C. L. (2019). Indirect effects of threat on the contact–prejudice relationship. *Social Psychology, 50*, 105–126. doi: 10.1027/1864-9335/a000364

Abidin, R. R. (1995). *Parenting Stress Index (PSI) manual* (3rd ed.). Charlottesville, VA: Pediatric Psychology Press.

Abolfathi Momtaz, Y., Hamid, T. A., & Ibrahim, R. (2013). Theories and measures of elder abuse. *Psychogeriatrics, 13*, 182–188. doi: 10.1111/psyg.12009

Abrams, D., van de Vyver, J., Houston, D. M., & Vasiljevic, M. (2017). Does terror defeat contact? Intergroup contact and prejudice toward Muslims before and after the London bombings. *Peace and Conflict: Journal of Peace Psychology, 23*, 260–268. doi: 10.1037/pac0000167

Acierno, R., Hernandez, M. A., Amstadter, A. B., Resnick, H. S., Steve, K., Muzzy, W., & Kilpatrick, D. G. (2010). Prevalence and correlates of emotional, physical, sexual, and financial abuse and potential neglect in the United States: The National Elder Mistreatment Study. *American Journal of Public Health, 100*, 292–297. doi: 10.2105/AJPH.2009.163089

Acierno, R., Hernandez-Tejada, M. A., Anetzberger, G. J., Loew, D., & Muzzy, W. (2017). The National Elder Mistreatment Study: An 8-year longitudinal study of outcomes. *Journal of Elder Abuse & Neglect, 29*, 254–269. doi: 10.1080/08946566.2017.1365031

Acierno, R., Hernandez-Tejada, M. A., Muzzy, W., & Steve, K. (2009). *Final report: The National Elder Mistreatment Study*. Washington, DC: U.S. Department of Justice. Retrieved from www.ncjrs.gov/pdffiles1/nij/grants/226456.pdf

Adams, T. M. (2006). The words have changed but the ideology remains the same: Misogynistic lyrics in rap music. *Journal of Black Studies, 36*, 938–957. doi: 10.1177/0021934704274072

Adubato, B. (2016). The promise of violence. *Journal of Sport and Social Issues, 40*, 22–37. doi: 10.1177/0193723515594209

Aebi, M. F., Akdeniz, G., Barclay, G., Campistol, C., Caneppele, S., Gruszczyńska, B., ... Þórisdóttir, R. (2014). *European sourcebook of crime and criminal justice statistics 2014*. Retrieved from www.heuni.fi/material/attachments/heuni/reports/qrMWoCVTF/HEUNI_report_80_European_Sourcebook.pdf

Ainsworth, S. E., & Maner, J. K. (2014). Assailing the competition: Sexual selection, proximate mating motives, and aggressive behavior in men. *Personality and Social Psychology Bulletin, 40*, 1648–1658. doi: 10.1177/0146167214554590

Alampay, L. P., Godwin, J., Lansford, J. E., Bombi, A. S., Bornstein, M. H., Chang, L., ... Bacchini, D. (2017). Severity and justness do not moderate the relation between corporal punishment and negative child outcomes: A multicultural and longitudinal study. *International Journal of Behavioral Development, 41*, 491–502. doi: 10.1177/0165025417697852

Alden, H. L., & Parker, K. F. (2005). Gender role ideology, homophobia and hate crime: Linking attitudes to macro-level anti-gay and lesbian hate crimes. *Deviant Behavior, 26*, 321–343. doi: 10.1080/016396290931614

Alink, L. R. A., Mesman, J., van Zeijl, J., Stolk, M. N., Juffer, F., Koot, H. M., ... van IJzendoorn, M. H. (2006). The early childhood aggression curve: Development of physical aggression in 10- to 50-month-old children. *Child Development, 77*, 954–966. doi: 10.1111/j.1467-8624.2006.00912.x

Allen, M., D'Alessio, D., & Brezgel, K. (1995). A meta-analysis summarizing the effects of pornography II: Aggression after exposure. *Human Communication Research, 22*, 258–283. doi: 10.1111/j.1468-2958.1995.tb00368.x

Alleyne, E., Fernandes, I., & Pritchard, E. (2014). Denying humanness to victims: How gang members justify violent behavior. *Group Processes & Intergroup Relations*, 750–762. doi: 10.1177/1368430214536064

Allport, G. H. (1954). *The nature of prejudice*. Reading, MA: Addison-Wesley.

American Psychiatric Association (1994). *Diagnostic and statistical manual of mental disorders*. Retrieved from www.psychnet-uk.com/dsm_iv/post-traumatic_stress_disorder.htm

Amnesty International (2019). *Death sentences and executions world-wide 2018*. Retrieved from www.amnesty.org/download/Documents/ACT5098702019ENGLISH.PDF

Amstadter, A. B., Cisler, J. M., McCauley, J. L., Hernandez, M. A., Muzzy, W., & Acierno, R. (2011). Do incident and perpetrator characteristics of elder mistreatment differ by gender of the victim? Results from the National Elder Mistreatment Study. *Journal of Elder Abuse & Neglect*, *23*, 43–57. doi: 10.1080/08946566.2011.534707

Andersen, R., & Brym, R. (2017). How terrorism affects attitudes toward democracy: Tunisia in 2015. *Canadian Review of Sociology*, *54*, 519–529. doi: 10.1111/cars.12175

Anderson, C. A. (1989). Temperature and aggression: Ubiquitous effects of heat on occurrence of human violence. *Psychological Bulletin*, *106*, 74–96. doi: 10.1037/0033-2909.106.1.74

Anderson, C. A. (1997). Effects of violent movies and trait hostility on hostile feelings and aggressive thoughts. *Aggressive Behavior*, *23*, 161–178. doi: 10.1002/(SICI)1098-2337(1997)23:3<161::AID-AB2>3.0.CO;2-P

Anderson, C. A. (2001). Heat and violence. *Current Directions in Psychological Science*, *10*, 33–38.

Anderson, C. A., & Anderson, K. B. (1998). Temperature and aggression: Paradox, controversy, and a (fairly) clear picture. In R. G. Geen & E. I. Donnerstein (Eds.), *Human aggression: Theories, research, and implications for social policy* (pp. 247–298). San Diego, CA: Academic Press.

Anderson, C. A., Anderson, K. B., Dorr, N., DeNeve, K. M., & Flanagan, M. (2000). Temperature and aggression. In M. P. Zanna (Ed.), *Advances in experimental social psychology* (Vol. 32, pp. 63–133). San Diego, CA: Academic Press.

Anderson, C. A., Benjamin, A. J., & Bartholow, B. D. (1998). Does the gun pull the trigger? Automatic priming effects of weapon pictures and weapon names. *Psychological Science*, *9*, 308–314. doi: 10.1111/1467-9280.00061

Anderson, C. A., & Bushman, B. J. (1997). External validity of 'trivial' experiments: The case of laboratory aggression. *Review of General Psychology*, 19–41.

Anderson, C. A., & Bushman, B. J. (2018). Media violence and the General Aggression Model. *Journal of Social Issues*, *74*, 386–413. doi: 10.1111/josi.12275

Anderson, C. A., Bushman, B. J., & Groom, R. W. (1997). Hot years and serious and deadly assault: Empirical tests of the heat hypothesis.

Journal of Personality and Social Psychology, 73, 1213–1223. doi: 10.1037/0022-3514.73.6.1213

Anderson, C. A., & Carnagey, N. L. (2004). Violent evil and the general aggression model. In A. Miller (Ed.), *The social psychology of good and evil* (pp. 168–192). New York: Guilford Press.

Anderson, C. A., & Carnagey, N. L. (2009). Causal effects of violent sports video games on aggression: Is it competitiveness or violent content? *Journal of Experimental Social Psychology, 45*, 731–739. doi: 10.1037/t00691-000;

Anderson, C. A., & Dill, K. E. (2000). Video games and aggressive thoughts, feelings, and behavior in the laboratory and in life. *Journal of Personality and Social Psychology, 78*, 772–790. doi: 10.1037//0022-3514.78.4.772

Anderson, C. A., & Murphy, C. R. (2003). Violent video games and aggressive behavior in young women. *Aggressive Behavior, 29*, 423–429. doi: 10.1002/ab.10042

Anderson, C. A., Shibuya, A., Ihori, N., Swing, E. L., Bushman, B. J., Sakamoto, A., ... Saleem, M. (2010). Violent video game effects on aggression, empathy, and prosocial behavior in Eastern and Western countries: A meta-analytic review. *Psychological Bulletin, 136*, 151–173. doi: 10.1037/a0018251

Anderson, C. A., Suzuki, K., Swing, E. L., Groves, C. L., Gentile, D. A., Prot, S., ... Petrescu, P. (2017). Media violence and other aggression risk factors in seven nations. *Personality and Social Psychology Bulletin, 43*, 986–998. doi: 10.1177/0146167217703064

Anderson, L. A., & Whiston, S. C. (2005). Sexual assault education programs: A meta-analytic examination of their effectiveness. *Psychology of Women Quarterly, 29*, 374–388. doi: 10.1111/j.1471-6402.2005.00237.x

Anderson, P. B., Kontos, A. P., Tanigoshi, H., & Struckman-Johnson, C. (2005). An examination of sexual strategies used by urban Southern and rural Midwestern university women. *Journal of Sex Research, 42*, 335–341. doi: 10.1080/00224490509552289

Anderson, R. E., Silver, K. E., Ciampaglia, A. M., Vitale, A. M., & Delahanty, D. L. (2019). *The frequency of sexual perpetration in college men: A systematic review of reported prevalence rates from 2000–2017*. Retrieved from commons. und.edu/psych-fac/11/?utm_source=commons.und.edu%2Fpsych-fac%2F11&utm_medium=PDF&utm_campaign=PDFCoverPages

Anetzberger, G. J. (1997). Elderly adult survivors of family violence. *Violence Against Women, 3*, 499–514.

Angelakis, I., Gillespie, E. L., & Panagioti, M. (2019). Childhood maltreatment and adult suicidality: A comprehensive systematic review with meta-analysis. *Psychological Medicine, 49*, 1057–1078. doi: 10.1017/S0033291718003823

Anglemyer, A., Horvath, T., & Rutherford, G. (2014). The accessibility of firearms and risk for suicide and homicide victimization among household members: A systematic review and meta-analysis. *Annals of Internal Medicine, 160*, 101–110. doi: 10.7326/M13-1301

Annerbäck, E.-M., Wingren, G., Svedin, C. G., & Gustafsson, P. A. (2010). Prevalence and characteristics of child physical abuse in Sweden: Findings from a population-based youth survey. *Acta Paediatrica, 99,* 1229–1236.

Antoniadou, N., & Kokkinos, C. M. (2015). Cyber and school bullying: Same or different phenomena? *Aggression and Violent Behavior, 25,* 363–372. doi: 10.1016/j.avb.2015.09.013

Anwar, F., Fry, D. P., & Grigaityté, I. (2017). Reducing aggression and violence. In B. J. Bushman (Ed.), *Aggression and violence: A social psychological perspective* (pp. 307–320). New York: Routledge.

Aosved, A. C., Long, P. J., & Voller, E. K. (2011). Sexual revictimization and adjustment in college men. *Psychology of Men & Masculinity, 12,* 285–296. doi: 10.1037/a0020828

Apostolou, M. (2013). The evolution of rape: The fitness benefits and costs of a forced-sex mating strategy in an evolutionary context. *Aggression and Violent Behavior, 18,* 484–490. doi: 10.1016/j.avb.2013.06.006

Arab-Zozani, M., Mostafazadeh, N., Arab-Zozani, Z., Ghoddoosi-Nejad, D., Hassanipour, S., & Soares, J. J. F. (2018). The prevalence of elder abuse and neglect in Iran: A systematic review and meta-analysis. *Journal of Elder Abuse & Neglect, 30,* 408–423. doi: 10.1080/08946566.2018.1523765

Archer, J. (1988). *The behavioural biology of aggression.* Cambridge, U.K.: Cambridge University Press.

Archer, J. (1991). The influence of testosterone on human aggression. *British Journal of Psychology, 82,* 1–28.

Archer, J. (1995). What can ethology offer the psychological study of human aggression? *Aggressive Behavior, 21,* 243–255. doi: 10.1002/1098-2337(1995)21:4<243::AID-AB2480210402>3.0.CO;2-6

Archer, J. (2000). Sex differences in aggression between heterosexual partners: A meta-analytic review. *Psychological Bulletin, 126,* 651–680.

Archer, J. (2002). Sex differences in physically aggressive acts between heterosexual partners: A meta-analytic review. *Aggression and Violent Behavior, 7,* 313–351. doi: 10.1016/S1359-1789(01)00061-1

Archer, J. (2004). Sex differences in aggression in real-world settings: A meta-analytic review. *Review of General Psychology, 8,* 291–322. doi: 10.1037/1089-2680.8.4.291

Archer, J. (2006). Cross-cultural differences in physical aggression between partners: A social-role analysis. *Personality and Social Psychology Review, 10,* 133–153. doi: 10.1207/s15327957pspr1002_3

Archer, J. (2009). The nature of human aggression. *International Journal of Law and Psychiatry, 32,* 202–208. doi: 10.1016/j.ijlp.2009.04.001

Archer, J. (2018). Violence to partners: Gender asymmetry revisited. In J. L. Ireland, P. Birch, & C. A. Ireland (Eds.), *The Routledge international handbook of human aggression* (pp. 155–169). London: Routledge.

Archer, J. (2019). The reality and evolutionary significance of human psychological sex differences. *Biological Reviews of the Cambridge Philosophical Society, 94,* 1381–1415. doi: 10.1111/brv.12507

Archer, J., Birring, S. S., & Wu, F. C. W. (1998). The association between testosterone and aggression among young men: Empirical findings and a meta-analysis. *Aggressive Behavior, 24,* 411–420. doi: 10.1002/(SICI)1098-2337(1998)24:6<411::AID-AB2>3.0.CO;2-9

Archer, J., & Browne, K. D. (1989). Concepts and approaches to the study of aggression. In J. Archer & K. D. Browne (Eds.), *Human aggression: Naturalistic approaches* (pp. 3–24). London: Routledge.

Archer, J., & Carré, J. (2017). Testosterone and aggression. In B. J. Bushman (Ed.), *Aggression and violence: A social psychological perspective* (pp. 90–104). New York: Routledge.

Archer, J., & Côté, S. M. (2005). Sex differences in aggressive behavior: A developmental and evolutionary perspective. In R. E. Tremblay, W. W. Hartup, & J. Archer (Eds.), *Developmental origins of aggression* (pp. 425–443). New York: Guilford Press.

Archer, J., & Coyne, S. M. (2005). An integrated review of indirect, relational, and social aggression. *Personality and Social Psychology Review, 9,* 212–230. doi: 10.1207/s15327957pspr0903_2

Archer, J., Fernández-Fuertes, A. A., & Thanzami, V. L. (2010). Does cost-benefit analysis or self-control predict involvement in two forms of aggression? *Aggressive Behavior, 36,* 292–304. doi: 10.1002/ab.20358

Archer, J., Graham-Kevan, N., & Davies, M. (2005). Testosterone and aggression: A reanalysis of Book, Starzyk, and Quinsey's (2001) study. *Aggression and Violent Behavior, 10,* 241–261. doi: 10.1016/j.avb.2004.01.001

Archer, J., Holloway, R., & McLoughlin, K. (1995). Self-reported physical aggression among young men. *Aggressive Behavior, 21,* 325–342. doi: 10.1002/1098-2337(1995)21:5<325::AID-AB2480210503>3.0.CO;2-R

Archer, J., & Thanzami, V. L. (2007). The relation between physical aggression, size and strength, among a sample of young Indian men. *Personality and Individual Differences, 43,* 627–633. doi: 10.1016/j.paid.2007.01.005

Arendt, F. (2018). Reporting on suicide between 1819 and 1944: Suicide rates, the press, and possible long-term Werther effects in Austria. *Crisis, 39,* 344–352. doi: 10.1027/0227-5910/a000507

Arias, E., Arce, R., & Vilariño, M. (2013). Batterer intervention programmes: A meta-analytic review of effectiveness. *Psychosocial Intervention, 22,* 153–160. doi: 10.5093/in2013a18

Ariel, B., Lawes, D., Weinborn, C., Henry, R., Chen, K., & Sabo Brants, H. (2019). The "less-than-lethal weapons effect"—Introducing TASERs to routine police operations in England and Wales: A randomized controlled trial. *Criminal Justice and Behavior, 46,* 280–300. doi: 10.1177/0093854818812918

Ariza-Montes, A., Muniz R, N. M., Leal-Rodríguez, A. L., & Leal-Millán, A. G. (2016). Workplace bullying among teachers: An analysis from the Job Demands-Resources (JD-R) Model perspective. *Journal of*

Occupational and Environmental Medicine, 58, 818–827. doi: 10.1097/JOM.0000000000000804

Arms, R. L., Russell, G. W., & Sandilands, M. L. (1979). Effects on the hostility of spectators of viewing aggressive sports. *Social Psychology Quarterly, 42,* 275–279. doi: 10.2307/3033771

Arriola, K. R.J., Louden, T., Doldren, M. A., & Fortenberry, R. M. (2005). A meta-analysis of the relationship of child sexual abuse to HIV risk behavior among women. *Child Abuse & Neglect, 29,* 725–746. doi: 10.1016/j.chiabu.2004.10.014

Artime, T. M., McCallum, E. B., & Peterson, Z. D. (2014). Men's acknowledgment of their sexual victimization experiences. *Psychology of Men & Masculinities, 15,* 313–323. doi: 10.1037/a0033376

Asbridge, M., Smart, R. G., & Mann, R. E. (2006). Can we prevent road rage? *Trauma, Violence, & Abuse, 7,* 109–121. doi: 10.1177/1524838006286689

Ashton, M. C., & Lee, K. (2005). Honesty-humility, the big five, and the five-factor model. *Journal of Personality, 73,* 1321–1353. doi: 10.1111/j.1467-6494.2005.00351.x

Assink, M., van der Put, C. E., Meeuwsen, M. W. C. M., Jong, N. M. de, Oort, F. J., Stams, G. J. J. M., & Hoeve, M. (2019). Risk factors for child sexual abuse victimization: A meta-analytic review. *Psychological Bulletin, 145,* 459–489. doi: 10.1037/bul0000188

Augustyn, M. B., Thornberry, T. P., & Krohn, M. D. (2014). Gang membership and pathways to maladaptive parenting. *Journal of Research on Adolescence, 24,* 252–267. doi: 10.1111/jora.12110

Averill, J. R., Malmstrom, E. J., Koriat, A., & Lazarus, R. S. (1972). Habituation to complex emotional stimuli. *Journal of Abnormal Psychology, 80,* 20–28. doi: 10.1037/h0033309

Awan, I. (2017). Cyber-extremism: Isis and the power of social media. *Society, 54,* 138–149. doi: 10.1007/s12115-017-0114-0

Ayar, A. A. (2006). Road rage: Recognizing a psychological disorder. *Journal of Psychiatry & Law, 34,* 123–150.

Ayduk, Ö., Gyurak, A., & Luerssen, A. (2008). Individual differences in the rejection–aggression link in the hot sauce paradigm: The case of rejection sensitivity. *Journal of Experimental Social Psychology, 44,* 775–782. doi: 10.1016/j.jesp.2007.07.004

Babcock, J. C., Green, C. E., & Robie, C. (2004). Does batterers' treatment work? A meta-analytic review of domestic violence treatment. *Clinical Psychology Review, 23,* 1023–1053. doi: 10.1016/j.cpr.2002.07.001

Badenes-Ribera, L., Frias-Navarro, D., Bonilla-Campos, A., Pons-Salvador, G., & Monterde-i-Bort, H. (2015). Intimate partner violence in self-identified lesbians: A meta-analysis of its prevalence. *Sexuality Research and Social Policy, 12,* 47–59. doi: 10.1007/s13178-014-0164-7

Bailey, W. C., & Peterson, R. D. (1999). Capital punishment, homicide, and deterrence: An assessment of the evidence and extension to female homicide. In M. D. Smith & M. A. Zahn (Eds.), *Homicide: A sourcebook of social research* (pp. 257–276). Thousand Oaks, CA: Sage.

Balcells, L., & Torrats-Espinosa, G. (2018). Using a natural experiment to estimate the electoral consequences of terrorist attacks. *Proceedings of the National Academy of Sciences of the United States of America, 115,* 10624–10629. doi: 10.1073/pnas.1800302115

Bandura, A. (1983). Psychological mechanisms of aggression. In R. G. Geen & E. I. Donnerstein (Eds.), *Aggression: Theoretical and empirical reviews* (pp. 1–40). New York: Academic Press.

Bandura, A. (1991). Social cognitive theory of moral thought and action. In W. M. Kurtines (Ed.), *Handbook of moral behavior and development* (Vol. 1, pp. 45–103). Hillsdale NJ: Lawrence Erlbaum.

Bandura, A., Ross, D., & Ross, S. A. (1961). Transmission of aggression through imitation of aggressive models. *The Journal of Abnormal and Social Psychology, 63,* 575–582. doi: 10.1037/h0045925

Bandura, A., Ross, D., & Ross, S. A. (1963). Vicarious reinforcement and imitative learning. *The Journal of Abnormal and Social Psychology, 67,* 601–607. doi: 10.1037/h0045550

Barbaree, H. E., Lightfoot, E., & Prentky, R. A. (2018). The development of sexual aggression. In J. L. Ireland, P. Birch, & C. A. Ireland (Eds.), *The Routledge international handbook of human aggression* (pp. 251–266). London: Routledge.

Bargh, J. A., Raymond, P., Pryor, J. B., & Strack, F. (1995). Attractiveness of the underling: An automatic power → sex association and its consequences for sexual harassment and aggression. *Journal of Personality and Social Psychology, 68,* 768–781. doi: 10.1037/0022-3514.68.5.768

Barker, E. D., Séguin, J. R., White, H. R., Bates, M. E., Lacourse, É., Carbonneau, R., & Tremblay, R. E. (2007). Developmental trajectories of male physical violence and theft. *Archives of General Psychiatry, 64,* 592–599. doi: 10.1001/archpsyc.64.5.592

Barlett, C. P., Anderson, C. A., & Swing, E. L. (2009). Video game effects – Confirmed, suspected, and speculative: A review of the evidence. *Simulation & Gaming, 40,* 377–403. doi: 10.1177/1046878108327539

Barlett, C. P., Branch, O., Rodeheffer, C., & Harris, R. (2009). How long do the short-term violent video game effects last? *Aggressive Behavior, 35,* 225–236. doi: 10.1002/ab.20301

Barlett, C. P., Chamberlin, K., & Witkower, Z. (2017). Predicting cyberbullying perpetration in emerging adults: A theoretical test of the Barlett Gentile Cyberbullying Model. *Aggressive Behavior, 43,* 147–154. doi: 10.1002/ab.21670

Barlett, C. P., & Coyne, S. M. (2014). A meta-analysis of sex differences in cyber-bullying behavior: The moderating role of age. *Aggressive Behavior, 40,* 474–488. doi: 10.1002/ab.21555

Barlett, C. P., DeWitt, C. C., Madison, C. S., Heath, J. B., Maronna, B., & Kirkpatrick, S. M. (2020). Hot temperatures and even hotter tempers: Sociological mediators in the relationship between global climate change and homicide. *Psychology of Violence, 10,* 1–7. doi: 10.1037/vio0000235

Barlett, C. P., DeWitt, C. C., Maronna, B., & Johnson, K. (2018). Social media use as a tool to facilitate or reduce cyberbullying perpetration: A review focusing on anonymous and nonanonymous social media platforms. *Violence and Gender, 5*, 147–152. doi: 10.1089/vio.2017.0057

Barlett, C. P., Harris, R., & Baldassaro, R. (2007). Longer you play, the more hostile you feel: Examination of first person shooter video games and aggression during video game play. *Aggressive Behavior, 33*, 486–497. doi: 10.1002/ab.20227

Barlett, C. P., Harris, R., & Bruey, C. (2008). The effect of the amount of blood in a violent video game on aggression, hostility, and arousal. *Journal of Experimental Social Psychology, 44*, 539–546. doi: 10.1016/j.jesp.2007.10.003

Barlow, F. K., Paolini, S., Pedersen, A., Hornsey, M. J., Radke, H. R. M., Harwood, J., ... Sibley, C. G. (2012). The contact caveat: Negative contact predicts increased prejudice more than positive contact predicts reduced prejudice. *Personality and Social Psychology Bulletin, 38*, 1629–1643. doi: 10.1177/0146167212457953

Barnett, O. W., Miller-Perrin, C. L., & Perrin, R. D. (2011). *Family violence across the lifespan: An introduction* (3rd ed.). Thousand Oaks, CA: Sage.

Barnwell, S. S., Borders, A., & Earleywine, M. (2006). Alcohol-aggression expectancies and dispositional aggression moderate the relationship between alcohol consumption and alcohol-related violence. *Aggressive Behavior, 32*, 517–527. doi: 10.1002/ab.20152

Baron, R. A. (1976). The reduction of human aggression: A field study of the influence of incompatible reactions. *Journal of Applied Social Psychology, 6*, 260–274. doi: 10.1111/j.1559-1816.1976.tb01330.x

Baron, R. A., & Bell, P. A. (1976). Aggression and heat: The influence of ambient temperature, negative affect, and a cooling drink on physical aggression. *Journal of Personality and Social Psychology, 33*, 245–255. doi: 10.1037/0022-3514.33.3.245

Baron, R. A., & Richardson, D. S. (1994). *Human aggression* (2nd ed.). New York: Plenum Press.

Bar-Tal, D. (1990). Causes and consequences of delegitimization: Models of conflict and ethnocentrism. *Journal of Social Issues, 46*, 65–81. doi: 10.1111/j.1540-4560.1990.tb00272.x

Bar-Tal, D. (1997). The monopolization of patriotism. In D. Bar-Tal & E. Staub (Eds.), *Patriotism: In the lives of individuals and nations* (pp. 246–270). Chicago, IL: Nelson-Hall.

Barth, J., Bermetz, L., Heim, E., Trelle, S., & Tonia, T. (2013). The current prevalence of child sexual abuse worldwide: A systematic review and meta-analysis. *International Journal of Public Health, 58*, 469–483. doi: 10.1007/s00038-012-0426-1

Bartholomew, K., Cobb, R. J., & Dutton, D. G. (2015). Established and emerging perspectives on violence in intimate relationships. In M. Mikulincer (Ed.), *APA handbook of personality and social psychology, Vol. 1, Attitudes and social cognition* (pp. 605–630). Washington, DC: American Psychological Association.

Bartholow, B. D. (2017). The aggressive brain. In B. J. Bushman (Ed.), *Aggression and violence: A social psychological perspective* (pp. 47–60). New York: Routledge.

Bartholow, B. D., & Anderson, C. A. (2002). Effects of violent video games on aggressive behavior: Potential sex differences. *Journal of Experimental Social Psychology, 38*, 283–290. doi: 10.1006/jesp.2001.1502

Bartholow, B. D., Bushman, B. J., & Sestir, M. A. (2006). Chronic violent video game exposure and desensitization to violence: Behavioral and event-related brain potential data. *Journal of Experimental Social Psychology, 42*, 532–539. doi: 10.1016/j.jesp.2005.08.006

Bartholow, B. D., Sestir, M. A., & Davis, E. B. (2005). Correlates and consequences of exposure to video game violence: Hostile personality, empathy, and aggressive behavior. *Personality and Social Psychology Bulletin, 31*, 1573–1586. doi: 10.1177/0146167205277205

Bartlett, M. L., & Abrams, M. (2019). Anger and aggression in sport. In M. H. Anshel, T. A. Petrie, & J. A. Steinfeldt (Eds.), *APA handbooks in psychology series. APA handbook of sport and exercise psychology* (pp. 509–528). Washington, DC: American Psychological Association.

Barton, G. (2018). Jihadi-Salafi terrorism and violent extremism in the era of al_Qaeda and the Islamic State. In J. L. Ireland, P. Birch, & C. A. Ireland (Eds.), *The Routledge international handbook of human aggression* (pp. 376–387). London: Routledge.

Bartos, B. J., McCleary, R., Mazerolle, L., & Luengen, K. (2020). Controlling gun violence: Assessing the impact of Australia's gun buyback program using a synthetic control group experiment. *Prevention Science, 21*, 131–136. doi: 10.1007/s11121-019-01064-8

Basile, K. C., Espelage, D. L., Rivers, I., McMahon, P. M., & Simon, T. R. (2009). The theoretical and empirical links between bullying behavior and male sexual violence perpetration. *Aggression and Violent Behavior, 14*, 336–347. doi: 10.1016/j.avb.2009.06.001

Basile, K. C., Smith, S. G., Chen, J., & Zwald, M. (2020). Chronic diseases, health conditions, and other impacts associated with rape victimization of U.S. Women. *Journal of Interpersonal Violence*, Advance online publication. doi: 10.1177/0886260519900335

Baumeister, R. F., & Boden, J. M. (1998). Aggression and the self: High self-esteem, low self-control, and ego-threat. In R. G. Geen & E. I. Donnerstein (Eds.), *Human aggression: Theories, research, and implications for social policy* (pp. 111–137). San Diego, CA: Academic Press.

Baumeister, R. F., Bushman, B. J., & Campbell, W. K. (2000). Self-esteem, narcissism, and aggression: Does violence result from low self-esteem or from threatened egotism? *Current Directions in Psychological Science, 9*, 26–29. doi: 10.1111/1467-8721.00053

Baumeister, R. F., Smart, L., & Boden, J. M. (1996). Relation of threatened egotism to violence and aggression: The dark side of high self-esteem. *Psychological Review, 103*, 5–33. doi: 10.1037/0033-295X.103.1.5

Baysan, C., Burke, M., González, F., Hsiang, S., & Miguel, E. (2019). Non-economic factors in violence: Evidence from organized crime, suicides and climate in Mexico. *Journal of Economic Behavior & Organization, 168,* 434–452. doi: 10.1016/j.jebo.2019.10.021

Beck, R., & Fernandez, E. (1998). Cognitive-behavioral therapy in the treatment of anger: A meta-analysis. *Cognitive Therapy and Research, 22,* 63–74. doi: 10.1023/A:1018763902991

Bedrosian, T. A., & Nelson, R. J. (2018). The biology of human aggression. In J. L. Ireland, P. Birch, & C. A. Ireland (Eds.), *The Routledge international handbook of human aggression* (pp. 43–53). London: Routledge.

Bègue, L., & Subra, B. (2008). Alcohol and aggression: Perspectives on controlled and uncontrolled social information processing. *Social and Personality Psychology Compass, 2,* 511–538. doi: 10.1111/j.1751-9004.2007.00051.x

Beitchman, J. H., Zucker, K. J., Hood, J. E., daCosta, G. A., & Akman, D. (1991). A review of the short-term effects of child sexual abuse. *Child Abuse & Neglect, 15,* 537–556. doi: 10.1016/0145-2134(91)90038-F

Bem, S. L. (1981). Gender schema theory: A cognitive account of sex typing. *Psychological Review, 88,* 354–364. doi: 10.1037/0033-295X.88.4.354

Benbouriche, M., Testé, B., Guay, J.-P., & Lavoie, M. E. (2019). The role of rape-supportive attitudes, alcohol, and sexual arousal in sexual (mis) perception: An experimental study. *Journal of Sex Research, 56,* 766–777. doi: 10.1080/00224499.2018.1496221

Bendik, M. F. (1992). Reaching the breaking point: Dangers of mistreatment in elder caregiving situations. *Journal of Elder Abuse and Neglect, 4,* 39–59.

Benjamin, A. J., Kepes, S., & Bushman, B. J. (2018). Effects of weapons on aggressive thoughts, angry feelings, hostile appraisals, and aggressive behavior: A meta-analytic review of the weapons effect literature. *Personality and Social Psychology Review, 22,* 347–377. doi: 10.1177/1088868317725419

Benton, D. (1992). Hormones and human aggression. In K. Björkqvist & P. Niemelä (Eds.), *Of mice and women: Aspects of female aggression* (pp. 37–48). San Diego, CA: Academic Press.

Berdahl, J. L. (2007). Harassment based on sex: Protecting social status in the context of gender hierarchy. *Academy of Management Review, 32,* 641–658. doi: 10.5465/AMR.2007.24351879

Beres, M. (2010). Sexual miscommunication? Untangling assumptions about sexual communication between casual sex partners. *Culture, Health & Sexuality, 12,* 1–14. doi: 10.1080/13691050903075226

Berkowitz, L. (1962). *Aggression: A social psychological analysis.* New York: McGraw-Hill.

Berkowitz, L. (1989). Frustration-aggression hypothesis: Examination and reformulation. *Psychological Bulletin, 106,* 59–73. doi: 10.1037/0033-2909.106.1.59

Berkowitz, L. (1993). *Aggression: Its causes, consequences, and control.* New York: McGraw-Hill.

Berkowitz, L. (1997). On the determinants and regulation of impulsive aggression. In S. Feshbach & J. Zagrodzka (Eds.), *Aggression: Biological, developmental, and social perspectives* (pp. 187–211). New York: Plenum Press.

Berkowitz, L. (1998). Affective aggression: The role of stress, pain, and negative affect. In R. G. Geen & E. I. Donnerstein (Eds.), *Human aggression: Theories, research, and implications for social policy* (pp. 49–72). San Diego, CA: Academic Press.

Berkowitz, L. (2008). On the consideration of automatic as well as controlled psychological processes in aggression. *Aggressive Behavior, 34,* 117–129. doi: 10.1002/ab.20244

Berkowitz, L., & Harmon-Jones, E. (2004). Toward an understanding of the determinants of anger. *Emotion, 4,* 107–130. doi: 10.1037/1528-3542.4.2.107

Berkowitz, L., & LePage, A. (1967). Weapons as aggression-eliciting stimuli. *Journal of Personality and Social Psychology, 7,* 202–207. doi: 10.1037/h0025008

Bermea, A. M., van Eeden-Moorefield, B., & Khaw, L. (2018). A systematic review of research on intimate partner violence among bisexual women. *Journal of Bisexuality, 18,* 399–424. doi: 10.1080/15299716.2018.1482485

Bernhardt, P. C., Dabbs, J. M. J., Fielden, J. A., & Lutter, C. D. (1998). Testosterone changes during vicarious experiences of winning and losing among fans at sporting events. *Physiology & Behavior, 65,* 59–62. doi: 10.1016/S0031-9384(98)00147-4

Besser, A., Neria, Y., & Haynes, M. (2009). Adult attachment, perceived stress, and PTSD among civilians exposed to ongoing terrorist attacks in Southern Israel. *Personality and Individual Differences, 47,* 851–857. doi: 10.1016/j.paid.2009.07.003

Bettencourt, B. A., & Kernahan, C. (1997). A meta-analysis of aggression in the presence of violent cues: Effects of gender differences and aversive provocation. *Aggressive Behavior, 23,* 447–456. doi: 10.1002/(SICI)1098-2337(1997)23:6<447::AID-AB4>3.0.CO;2-D

Bettencourt, B. A., & Miller, N. E. (1996). Gender differences in aggression as a function of provocation: A meta-analysis. *Psychological Bulletin, 119,* 422–447. doi: 10.1037/0033-2909.119.3.422

Bettencourt, B. A., Talley, A., Benjamin, A. J., & Valentine, J. (2006). Personality and aggressive behavior under provoking and neutral conditions: A meta-analytic review. *Psychological Bulletin, 132,* 751–777. doi: 10.1037/0033-2909.132.5.751

Beyer, F., Buades-Rotger, M., Claes, M., & Krämer, U. M. (2017). Hit or run: Exploring aggressive and avoidant reactions to interpersonal provocation using a novel Fight-or-Escape Paradigm (FOE). *Frontiers in Behavioral Neuroscience, 11,* 190. doi: 10.3389/fnbeh.2017.00190

Bieneck, S., & Krahé, B. (2011). Blaming the victim and exonerating the perpetrator in cases of rape and robbery: Is there a double standard? *Journal of Interpersonal Violence, 26,* 1785–1797. doi: 10.1177/0886260510372945

Biggs, S., Manthorpe, J., Tinker, A., Doyle, M., & Erens, B. (2009). Mistreatment of older people in the United Kingdom: Findings from the First National Prevalence Study. *Journal of Elder Abuse & Neglect, 21,* 1–14. doi: 10.1080/08946560802571870

Bijvank, M. N., Konijn, E. A., Bushman, B. J., & Roelofsma, P. H. (2009). Age and violent-content labels make video games forbidden fruits for youth. *Pediatrics, 123,* 870–876. doi: 10.1542/peds.2008-0601

Billig, M., & Tajfel, H. (1973). Social categorization and similarity in intergroup behaviour. *European Journal of Social Psychology, 3,* 27–52. doi: 10.1002/ejsp.2420030103

Birkley, E. L., & Eckhardt, C. I. (2019). Effects of instigation, anger, and emotion regulation on intimate partner aggression: Examination of "perfect storm" theory. *Psychology of Violence, 9,* 186–195. doi: 10.1037/vio0000190

Björkqvist, K., Lagerspetz, K., & Österman, K. (1992). *The Direct and Indirect Aggression Scales.* Vasa, FI: Abo Akademi University, Department of Social Sciences.

Black, D. A., Smith Slep, A. M., & Heyman, R. E. (2001). Risk factors for child psychological abuse. *Aggression and Violent Behavior, 6,* 189–201. doi: 10.1016/S1359-1789(00)00022-7

Blackhart, G. C., Nelson, B. C., Knowles, M. L., & Baumeister, R. F. (2009). Rejection elicits emotional reactions but neither causes immediate distress nor lowers self-esteem: A meta-analytic review of 192 studies on social exclusion. *Personality and Social Psychology Review, 13,* 269–309. doi: 10.1177/1088868309346065

Blackwell, L. M., Lynn, S. J., Vanderhoff, H., & Gidycz, C. A. (2004). Sexual assault revictimization: Toward effective risk-reduction programs. In L. J. Koenig, L. S. Doll, A. O'Leary, & W. Pequegnat (Eds.), *From child sexual abuse to adult sexual risk: Trauma, revictimization, and intervention* (pp. 269–295). Washington, DC: American Psychological Association.

Blake, E., & Gannon, T. A. (2018). Females who sexually offend. In J. L. Ireland, P. Birch, & C. A. Ireland (Eds.), *The Routledge international handbook of human aggression* (pp. 278–290). London: Routledge.

Bleakley, A., Jamieson, P. E., & Romer, D. (2012). Trends of sexual and violent content by gender in top-grossing U.S. Films, 1950–2006. *The Journal of Adolescent Health, 51,* 73–79. doi: 10.1016/j.jadohealth.2012.02.006

Blockey, P. N., & Hartley, L. R. (1995). Aberrant driving behaviour: Errors and violations. *Ergonomics, 38,* 1759–1771. doi: 10.1080/00140139508925225

Bloom, M., & Horgan, J. (2008). Missing their mark: The IRA's proxy bomb campaign. *Social Research, 75,* 579–614.

Blosnich, J. R., & Bossarte, R. M. (2009). Comparisons of intimate partner violence among partners in same-sex and opposite-sex relationships in the United States. *American Journal of Public Health, 99,* 2182–2184. doi: 10.2105/AJPH.2008.139535

Bluemke, M., Friedrich, M., & Zumbach, J. (2010). The influence of violent and nonviolent computer games on implicit measures of aggressiveness. *Aggressive Behavior, 36,* 1–13. doi: 10.1002/ab.20329

Bodziany, M., & Netczuk-Gwoździewicz, M. (2019). Feminization of terror: Psychological analysis of the role of women in terrorist structures. *Studies in Conflict & Terrorism*, 1–18. doi: 10.1080/1057610X.2018.1531542

Bogdan, S. R., Măirean, C., & Havârneanu, C. E. (2016). A meta-analysis of the association between anger and aggressive driving. *Transportation Research Part F: Traffic Psychology and Behaviour, 42*, 350–364. doi: 10.1016/j.trf.2016.05.009

Böhm, R., Rusch, H., & Gürerk, Ö. (2016). What makes people go to war? Defensive intentions motivate retaliatory and preemptive intergroup aggression. *Evolution and Human Behavior, 37*, 29–34. doi: 10.1016/j.evolhumbehav.2015.06.005

Bohstedt, J. (1994). The dynamics of riots: Escalation and diffusion/contagion. In M. Potegal & J. F. Knutson (Eds.), *The dynamics of aggression: Biological and social processes in dyads and groups* (pp. 257–306). Hillsdale, NJ: Lawrence Erlbaum.

Bonache, H., Gonzalez-Mendez, R., & Krahé, B. (2019). Adult attachment styles, destructive conflict resolution, and the experience of intimate partner violence. *Journal of Interpersonal Violence, 34*, 287–309. doi: 10.1177/0886260516640776

Bond, M. H., Hewstone, M., Wan, K.-C., & Chiu, C.-K. (1985). Group-serving attributions across intergroup contexts: Cultural differences in the explanation of sex-typed behaviours. *European Journal of Social Psychology, 15*, 435–451. doi: 10.1002/ejsp.2420150406

Bondü, R., & Krahé, B. (2015). Links of justice and rejection sensitivity with aggression in childhood and adolescence. *Aggressive Behavior, 41*, 353–368. doi: 10.1002/ab.21556

Book, A., Visser, Volk, A., Holden, R. R., & D'Agatac, M. T. (2019). Ice and fire: Two paths to provoked aggression. *Personality and Individual Differences, 138*, 247–251. doi: 10.1016/j.paid.2018.10.010

Borah, T. J., Murray, A. L., Eisner, M., & Jugl, I. (2018). Developing and validating an experience sampling measure of aggression: The Aggression-ES Scale. *Journal of Interpersonal Violence*, Advance online publication. doi: 10.1177/0886260518812068

Borders, A., Barnwell, S. S., & Earleywine, M. (2007). Alcohol-aggression expectancies and dispositional rumination moderate the effect of alcohol consumption on alcohol-related aggression and hostility. *Aggressive Behavior, 33*, 327–338. doi: 10.1002/ab.20187

Borders, A., & Giancola, P. R. (2011). Trait and state hostile rumination facilitate alcohol-related aggression. *Journal of Studies on Alcohol and Drugs, 72*, 545–554. doi: 10.15288/jsad.2011.72.545

Bornstein, R. F. (2019). Synergistic dependencies in partner and elder abuse. *The American Psychologist, 74*, 713–724. doi: 10.1037/amp0000456

Bösche, W. (2010). Violent video games prime both aggressive and positive cognitions. *Journal of Media Psychology, 22*, 139–146. doi: 10.1027/1864-1105/a000019

Bouffard, J. A., Bouffard, L. A., & Miller, H. A. (2016). Examining the correlates of women's use of sexual coercion: Proposing an explanatory model. *Journal of Interpersonal Violence, 31,* 2360–2382. doi: 10.1177/0886260515575609

Bowling, N. A., & Beehr, T. A. (2006). Workplace harassment from the victim's perspective: A theoretical model and meta-analysis. *Journal of Applied Psychology, 91,* 998–1012. doi: 10.1037/0021-9010.91.5.998

Braga, A. A., & Weisburd, D. (2012). The effects of focused deterrence strategies on crime. *Journal of Research in Crime and Delinquency, 49,* 323–358. doi: 10.1177/0022427811419368

Braga, T., Gonçalves, L. C., Basto-Pereira, M., & Maia, Â. (2017). Unraveling the link between maltreatment and juvenile antisocial behavior: A meta-analysis of prospective longitudinal studies. *Aggression and Violent Behavior, 33,* 37–50. doi: 10.1016/j.avb.2017.01.006

Braithwaite, S. R., Coulson, G., Keddington, K., & Fincham, F. D. (2015). The influence of pornography on sexual scripts and hooking up among emerging adults in college. *Archives of Sexual Behavior, 44,* 111–123. doi: 10.1007/s10508-014-0351-x

Brake (2012). Men vs. women: Direct Line & Brake Reports on Safe Driving 2009–7 2012. REPORT SEVEN. Retrieved from www.brake.org.uk/assets/docs/dl_reports/DL-MvW-Report-2012.pdf

Branch, S., Ramsay, S., & Barker, M. (2013). Workplace bullying, mobbing and general harassment: A review. *International Journal of Management Reviews, 15,* 280–299. doi: 10.1111/j.1468-2370.2012.00339.x

Brännström, L., Kaunitz, C., Andershed, A.-K., South, S., & Smedslund, G. (2016). Aggression replacement training (ART) for reducing antisocial behavior in adolescents and adults: A systematic review. *Aggression and Violent Behavior, 27,* 30–41. doi: 10.1016/j.avb.2016.02.006

Bremner, R. H., Koole, S. L., & Bushman, B. J. (2011). "Pray for those who mistreat you": Effects of prayer on anger and aggression. *Personality and Social Psychology Bulletin, 37,* 830–837. doi: 10.1177/0146167211402215

Bresin, K. (2019). Impulsivity and aggression: A meta-analysis using the UPPS model of impulsivity. *Aggression and Violent Behavior, 48,* 124–140. doi: 10.1016/j.avb.2019.08.003

Bresin, K., & Gordon, K. H. (2013). Aggression as affect regulation: Extending catharsis theory to evaluate aggression and experiential anger in the laboratory and daily life. *Journal of Social and Clinical Psychology, 32,* 400–423. doi: 10.1521/jscp.2013.32.4.400

Bridges, A. J., Wosnitzer, R., Scharrer, E., Sun, C., & Liberman, R. (2010). Aggression and sexual behavior in best-selling pornography videos: A content analysis update. *Violence Against Women, 16,* 1065–1085. doi: 10.1177/1077801210382866

Brigida, A. C. (2016). *A look inside 'rage rooms,' Where you de-stress by smashing things.* Retrieved from www.vice.com/en_asia/article/4xyqbm/a-look-inside-rage-rooms-where-you-de-stress-by-smashing-things-en-id

Broidy, L. M., Nagin, D. S., Tremblay, R. E., Bates, J. E., Brame, B., Dodge, K. A., … Vitaro, F. (2003). Developmental trajectories of childhood disruptive behaviors and adolescent delinquency: A six-site, cross-national

study. *Developmental Psychology, 39*, 222–245. doi: 10.1037/0012-1649.
39.2.222

Brosowski, T., Wachs, S., Scheithauer, H., & Vazsonyi, A. T. (2018). Bullying perpetration and victimization: A test of traditional and cyber-behaviors as latent constructs. *Journal of Interpersonal Violence*, Advance online publication. doi: 10.1177/0886260518807212

Brown, G. R. (2000). Can studying non-human primates inform us about human rape? A zoologist's perspective. *Psychology, Evolution & Gender, 2*, 321–324. doi: 10.1080/14616660010024625

Brown, R. [Roger] (1986). *Social psychology* (2nd ed.). New York: Free Press.

Brown, R. [Rupert] (2010). *Prejudice: Its social psychology* (2nd ed.). Malden, MA: Wiley Blackwell.

Browne, A., & Finkelhor, D. (1986). Impact of child sexual abuse: A review of the research. *Psychological Bulletin, 99*, 66–77. doi: 10.1037/0033-2909.99.1.66

Browne, K. D., & Hamilton-Giachritsis, C. (2005). The influence of violent media on children and adolescents: A public-health approach. *The Lancet, 365*(9460), 702–710. doi: 10.1016/S0140-6736(05)17952-5

Brugh, C. S., Desmarais, S. L., Simons-Rudolph, J., & Zottola, S. A. (2019). Gender in the jihad: Characteristics and outcomes among women and men involved in jihadism-inspired terrorism. *Journal of Threat Assessment and Management, 6*, 76–92. doi: 10.1037/tam0000123

Bruneau, E., Kteily, N., & Laustsen, L. (2018). The unique effects of blatant dehumanization on attitudes and behavior towards Muslim refugees during the European 'refugee crisis' across four countries. *European Journal of Social Psychology, 48*, 645–662. doi: 10.1002/ejsp.2357

Bryant, F. B., & Smith, B. D. (2001). Refining the architecture of aggression: A measurement model for the Buss-Perry Aggression Questionnaire. *Journal of Research in Personality, 35*, 138–167. doi: 10.1006/jrpe.2000.2302

Bundeskriminalamt (2017). *Polizeiliche Kriminalstatistik 2017 (Bd. 4)*. Wiesbaden: Bundeskriminalamt. Retrieved from: https://www.bka.de/SharedDocs/Downloads/DE/Publikationen/PolizeilicheKriminalstatistik/2017/pks2017Jahrbuch4Einzelne.pdf?__blob=publicationFile&v=8

Bundeskriminalamt (2019a). *Partnerschaftsgewalt: Kriminalstatistische Auswertung - Berichtsjahr 2018*. Retrieved from www.bka.de/SharedDocs/Downloads/DE/Publikationen/JahresberichteUndLagebilder/Partnerschaftsgewalt/Partnerschaftsgewalt_2018.html

Bundeskriminalamt (Ed.) (2019b). *PKS 2018 – Jahrbuch Band 4 Einzelne Straftaten/-gruppen und ausgewählte Formen der Kriminalität: Bundesrepublik Deutschland*. Retrieved from www.bka.de/SharedDocs/Downloads/DE/Publikationen/PolizeilicheKriminalstatistik/2018/pks2018Jahrbuch4Einzelne.pdf?__blob=publicationFile&v=7

Bundeszentrale für gesundheitliche Aufklärung (2010). *Jugendsexualität 2010*. Retrieved from service.bzga.de/pdf.php?id=50d94e7e90a5bc55df165f7d07dcaba9

Burke, B. L., Martens, A., & Faucher, E. H. (2010). Two decades of terror management theory: A meta-analysis of mortality salience research.

Personality & Social Psychology Review, 14, 155–195. doi: 10.1177/1088868309352321

Burke, M., Hsiang, S. M., & Miguel, E. (2015). Climate and conflict. *Annual Review of Economics, 7*, 577–617. doi: 10.1146/annurev-economics-080614-115430

Burks, V. S., Laird, R. D., Dodge, K. A., Pettit, G. S., & Bates, J. E. (1999). Knowledge structures, social information processing, and children's aggressive behavior. *Social Development, 8*, 220–236.

Burt, S. A. (2009). Are there meaningful etiological differences within antisocial behavior? Results of a meta-analysis. *Clinical Psychology Review, 29*, 163–178. doi: 10.1016/j.cpr.2008.12.004

Busching, R., & Krahé, B. (2013). Charging neutral cues with aggressive meaning through violent video game play. *Societies, 3*, 445–456. doi: 10.3390/soc3040445

Busching, R., & Krahé, B. (2015). The girls set the tone: Gendered classroom norms and the development of aggression in adolescence. *Personality and Social Psychology Bulletin, 41*, 659–676. doi: 10.1177/0146167215573212

Busching, R., & Krahé, B. (2018). The contagious effect of deviant behavior in adolescence. *Social Psychological and Personality Science, 9*, 815–824. doi: 10.1177/1948550617725151

Bushman, B. J. (1993). Human aggression while under the influence of alcohol and other drugs: An integrative research review. *Current Directions in Psychological Science, 2*, 148–152. doi: 10.1111/1467-8721.ep10768961

Bushman, B. J. (1995). Moderating role of trait aggressiveness in the effects of violent media on aggression. *Journal of Personality and Social Psychology, 69*, 950–960. doi: 10.1037/0022-3514.69.5.950

Bushman, B. J. (1997). Effects of alcohol on human aggression: Validity of proposed explanations. In M. Galanter (Ed.), *Recent developments in alcoholism: Alcohol and violence: Epidemiology, neurobiology, psychology, family issues* (pp. 227–243). New York: Plenum Press.

Bushman, B. J. (1998). Priming effects of media violence on the accessibility of aggressive constructs in memory. *Personality and Social Psychology Bulletin, 24*, 537–545. doi: 10.1177/0146167298245009

Bushman, B. J. (2002). Does venting anger feed or extinguish the flame? Catharsis, rumination, distraction, anger and aggressive responding. *Personality and Social Psychology Bulletin, 28*, 724–731. doi: 10.1177/0146167202289002

Bushman, B. J. (2016). Violent media and hostile appraisals: A meta-analytic review. *Aggressive Behavior, 42*, 605–613. doi: 10.1002/ab.21655

Bushman, B. J. (Ed.) (2017). *Aggression and violence: A social psychological perspective*. New York: Routledge.

Bushman, B. J., & Anderson, C. A. (1998). Methodology in the study of aggression: Integrating experimental and nonexperimental findings. In R. G. Geen & E. I. Donnerstein (Eds.), *Human aggression: Theories, research, and implications for social policy* (pp. 23–48). San Diego, CA: Academic Press.

Bushman, B. J., & Anderson, C. A. (2001). Is it time to pull the plug on hostile versus instrumental aggression dichotomy? *Psychological Review, 108,* 273–279. doi: 10.1037/0033-295X.108.1.273

Bushman, B. J., & Anderson, C. A. (2002). Violent video games and hostile expectations: A test of the general aggression model. *Personality and Social Psychology Bulletin, 28,* 1679–1686. doi: 10.1177/014616702237649

Bushman, B. J., Baumeister, R. F., Thomaes, S., Ryu, E., Begeer, S., & West, S. G. (2009). Looking again, and harder, for a link between low self-esteem and aggression. *Journal of Personality, 77,* 427–446. doi: 10.1111/j.1467-6494.2008.00553.x

Bushman, B. J., Bonacci, A. M., Pedersen, W. C., Vasquez, E. A., & Miller, N. E. (2005). Chewing on it can chew you up: Effects of rumination on triggered displaced aggression. *Journal of Personality and Social Psychology, 88,* 969–983. doi: 10.1037/0022-3514.88.6.969

Bushman, B. J., & Cantor, J. (2003). Media ratings for violence and sex: Implications for policymakers and parents. *American Psychologist, 58,* 130–141. doi: 10.1037/0003-066X.58.2.130

Bushman, B. J., & Cooper, H. M. (1990). Effects of alcohol on human aggression: An intergrative research review. *Psychological Bulletin, 107,* 341–354. doi: 10.1037/0033-2909.107.3.341

Bushman, B. J., & Huesmann, L. R. (2006). Short-term and long-term effects of violent media on aggression in children and adults. *Archives of Pediatrics and Adolescent Medicine, 160,* 348–352.

Bushman, B. J., Kerwin, T., Whitlock, T., & Weisenberger, J. M. (2017). The weapons effect on wheels: Motorists drive more aggressively when there is a gun in the vehicle. *Journal of Experimental Social Psychology, 73,* 82–85. doi: 10.1016/j.jesp.2017.06.007

Bushman, B. J., Ridge, R. D., Das, E., Key, C. W., & Busath, G. L. (2007). When God sanctions killing: Effect of scriptural violence on aggression. *Psychological Science, 18,* 204–207. doi: 10.1111/j.1467-9280.2007.01873.x

Bushman, B. J., Steffgen, G., Kerwin, T., Whitlock, T., & Weisenberger, J. M. (2018). "Don't you know I own the road?" The link between narcissism and aggressive driving. *Transportation Research Part F: Traffic Psychology and Behaviour, 52,* 14–20. doi: 10.1016/j.trf.2017.10.008

Bushman, B. J., & Wells, G. L. (1998). Trait aggressiveness and hockey penalties: Predicting hot tempers on the ice. *Journal of Applied Psychology, 83,* 969–974.

Buss, A. H. (1961). *The psychology of aggression.* New York: Wiley.

Buss, A. H., & Durkee, A. (1957). An inventory for assessing different kinds of hostility. *Journal of Consulting Psychology, 21,* 343–349. doi: 10.1037/h0046900

Buss, A. H., & Perry, M. (1992). The Aggression Questionnaire. *Journal of Personality and Social Psychology, 63,* 452–459. doi: 10.1037/0022-3514.63.3.452

Buss, A. H., & Warren, W. L. (2000). *The Aggression Questionnaire manual.* Los Angeles, CA: Western Psychological Services.

Buss, D. M. (1996). Sexual conflict: Evolutionary insights into feminism and the "battle of the sexes". In D. M. Buss & N. M. Malamuth (Eds.), *Sex, power, conflict: Evolutionary and feminist perspectives* (pp. 296–318). New York: Oxford University Press.

Buss, D. M., & Shackelford, T. K. (1997). Human aggression in evolutionary psychological perspective. *Clinical Psychology Review, 17*, 605–619. doi: 10.1016/S0272-7358(97)00037-8

Byrne, S. (2009). Media literacy interventions: What makes them boom or boomerang? *Communication Education, 58*, 1–14. doi: 10.1080/03634520802226444

Cafferky, B., Mendez, M., Anderson, J. R., & Stith, S. M. (2018). Substance use and intimate partner violence: A meta-analytic review. *Psychology of Violence, 8*, 110–131. doi: 10.1037/vio0000074

Cahill, C., Llewelyn, S. P., & Pearson, C. (1991). Long-term effects of sexual abuse which occurred in childhood: A review. *British Journal of Clinical Psychology, 30*, 117–130. doi: 10.1111/j.2044-8260.1991.tb00927.x

Cairns, E., & Darby, J. (1998). The conflict in Northern Ireland: Causes, consequences, and controls. *American Psychologist, 53*, 754–760. doi: 10.1037/0003-066X.53.7.754

Cairns, E., Kenworthy, J., Campbell, A., & Hewstone, M. (2006). The role of in-group identification, religious group membership and intergroup conflict in moderating in-group and out-group affect. *British Journal of Social Psychology, 45*, 701–716. doi: 10.1348/014466605X69850

Cameranesi, M. (2016). Battering typologies, attachment insecurity, and personality disorders: A comprehensive literature review. *Aggression and Violent Behavior, 28*, 29–46. doi: 10.1016/j.avb.2016.03.005

Campbell, A. (2006). Sex differences in direct aggression: What are the psychological mediators? *Aggression and Violent Behavior, 11*, 237–264. doi: 10.1016/j.avb.2005.09.002

Campbell, A. (2013). The evolutionary psychology of women's aggression. *Philosophical Transactions of the Royal Society of London. Series B, Biological Sciences, 368*(1631), 20130078. doi: 10.1098/rstb.2013.0078

Campbell, R., Bybee, D., Townsend, S. M., Shaw, J., Karim, N., & Markowitz, J. (2014). The impact of sexual assault nurse examiner programs on criminal justice case outcomes: A multisite replication study. *Violence Against Women, 20*, 607–625. doi: 10.1177/1077801214536286

Campbell, R., Sefl, T., Barnes, H. E., Ahrens, C. E., Wasco, S. M., & Zaragoza-Diesfeld, Y. (1999). Community services for rape survivors: Enhancing psychological well-being or increasing trauma? *Journal of Consulting and Clinical Psychology, 67*, 847–858. doi: 10.1037/0022-006X.67.6.847

Candelaria, A. M., Fedewa, A. L., & Ahn, S. (2012). The effects of anger management on children's social and emotional outcomes: A meta-analysis. *School Psychology International, 33*, 596–614. doi: 10.1177/0143034312454360

Cantor, D., Fisher, B., Chibnall, S., Harps, S., Townsend, R., Thomas, G., ... Madden, K. (2019). *AAU Campus Climate Survey* (2019). Retrieved from https://www.aau.edu/sites/default/files/AAU-Files/Key-Issues/Campus-Safety/Revised%20Aggregate%20report%20%20and%20appendices%201-7_(01-16-2020_FINAL).pdf

Caprara, G. V., Cinnani, V., D'Imperio, G., Passerini, S., Rezi, P., & Travaglia, G. (1985). Indicators of impulsive aggression: Present status of research on irritability and emotional susceptibility scales. *Personality and Individual Differences, 6*, 665–674. doi: 10.1016/0191-8869(85)90077-7

Caprara, G. V., Perugini, M., & Barbaranelli, C. (1994). Studies of individual differences in aggression. In M. Potegal & J. F. Knutson (Eds.), *The dynamics of aggression: Biological and social processes in dyads and groups* (pp. 123–153). Hillsdale, NJ: Lawrence Erlbaum.

Card, N. A., Stucky, B. D., Sawalani, G. M., & Little, T. D. (2008). Direct and indirect aggression during childhood and adolescence: A meta-analytic review of gender differences, intercorrelations, and relations to maladjustment. *Child Development, 79*, 1185–1229. doi: 10.1111/j.1467-8624.2008.01184.x

Carlson, M., Marcus-Newhall, A., & Miller, N. E. (1989). Evidence for a general construct of aggression. *Personality and Social Psychology Bulletin, 15*, 377–389. doi: 10.1177/0146167289153008

Carlson, M., Marcus-Newhall, A., & Miller, N. E. (1990). Effects of situational aggression cues: A quantitative review. *Journal of Personality and Social Psychology, 58*, 622–633. doi: 10.1037/0022-3514.58.4.622

Carnagey, N. L., & Anderson, C. A. (2005). The effects of reward and punishment in violent video games on aggressive affect, cognition, and behavior. *Psychological Science, 16*, 882–889. doi: 10.1111/j.1467-9280.2005.01632.x

Carnagey, N. L., & Anderson, C. A. (2007). Changes in attitudes towards war and violence after September 11, 2001. *Aggressive Behavior, 33*, 118–129. doi: 10.1002/ab.20173

Carnagey, N. L., Anderson, C. A., & Bushman, B. J. (2007). The effect of video game violence on physiological desensitization to real-life violence. *Journal of Experimental Social Psychology, 43*, 489–496. doi: 10.1016/j.jesp.2006.05.003

Casey, E. A., Masters, N. T., Beadnell, B., Hoppe, M. J., Morrison, D. M., & Wells, E. A. (2017). Predicting sexual assault perpetration among heterosexually active young men. *Violence Against Women, 23*, 3–27. doi: 10.1177/1077801216634467

Caspi, A., Elder, G. H., & Bem, D. J. (1987). Moving against the world: Life-course patterns of explosive children. *Developmental Psychology, 23*, 308–313. doi: 10.1037/0012-1649.23.2.308

Centers for Disease Control and Prevention (2017). *Youth Risk Behavior Survey: Data summary and trends report 2007–2017*. Retrieved from www.cdc.gov/healthyyouth/data/yrbs/pdf/trendsreport.pdf

Chalfin, A., Haviland, A. M., & Raphael, S. (2013). What do panel studies tell us about a deterrent effect of capital punishment? A critique of the literature. *Journal of Quantitative Criminology, 29*, 5–43. doi: 10.1007/s10940-012-9168-8

Chan, D. K.-S., Lam, C. B., Chow, S. Y., & Cheung, S. F. (2008). Examining the job-related, psychological, and physical outcomes of workplace sexual harassment: A meta-analytic review. *Psychology of Women Quarterly, 32*, 362–376. doi: 10.1111/j.1471-6402.2008.00451.x

Chandy, J. M., Blum, R. W., & Resnick, M. D. (1996). Female adolescents with a history of sexual abuse: Risk outcome and protective factors. *Journal of Interpersonal Violence, 11*, 503–518. doi: 10.1177/088626096011004004

Chang, L.-Y., Wang, M.-Y., & Tsai, P.-S. (2016). Neighborhood disadvantage and physical aggression in children and adolescents: A systematic review and meta-analysis of multilevel studies. *Aggressive Behavior, 42*, 441–454. doi: 10.1002/ab.21641

Chapman, H., & Gillespie, S. M. (2019). The Revised Conflict Tactics Scales (CTS2): A review of the properties, reliability, and validity of the CTS2 as a measure of partner abuse in community and clinical samples. *Aggression and Violent Behavior, 44*, 27–35. doi: 10.1016/j.avb.2018.10.006

Chen, M., & Chan, K. L. (2016). Effects of parenting programs on child maltreatment prevention: A meta-analysis. *Trauma, Violence & Abuse, 17*, 88–104. doi: 10.1177/1524838014566718

Chen, V. H. H., & Wu, Y. (2015). Group identification as a mediator of the effect of players' anonymity on cheating in online games. *Behaviour & Information Technology, 34*, 658–667. doi: 10.1080/0144929X.2013.843721

Chen, Y., & Ullman, S. E. (2010). Women's reporting of sexual and physical assaults to police in the National Violence Against Women Survey. *Violence Against Women, 16*, 262–279. doi: 10.1177/1077801209360861

Chenoweth, E., English, R., Gofas, A., Kalyvas, S. N., & Lutz, B. J. (Eds.) (2019). *The Oxford handbook of terrorism.* Oxford: Oxford University Press.

Chesney-Lind, M. (1997). *The female offender: Girls, women, and crime.* Thousand Oaks, CA: Sage.

Chester, D. S. (2019). Beyond the aggregate score: Using multilevel modeling to examine trajectories of laboratory-measured aggression. *Aggressive Behavior, 45*, 498-506. doi: 10.1002/ab.21837

Christie, D. J. (2006). 9/11 Aftershocks: An analysis of conditions ripe for hate crimes. In P. R. Kimmel & C. E. Stout (Eds.), *Collateral damage: The psychological consequences of America's war on terrorism* (pp. 19–44). Westport, CT: Praeger Publishers/Greenwood Publishing Group.

Claassen, C. (2016). Group entitlement, anger and participation in intergroup violence. *British Journal of Political Science, 46*, 127–148. doi: 10.1017/S000712341400012X

Clark, C. J., Everson-Rose, S. A., Suglia, S. F., Btoush, R., Alonso, A., & Haj-Yahia, M. M. (2010). Association between exposure to political violence and intimate-partner violence in the occupied Palestinian territory: A cross-sectional study. *The Lancet, 375*(9711), 310–316. doi: 10.1016/S0140-6736(09)61827-4

Clements, C. M., & Ogle, R. L. (2009). Does acknowledgment as an assault victim impact postassault psychological symptoms and coping? *Journal of Interpersonal Violence, 24,* 1595–1614. doi: 10.1177/0886260509331486

Cohen, D., Nisbett, R. E., Bowdle, B. F., & Schwarz, N. (1996). Insult, aggression, and the southern culture of honor: An "experimental ethnography". *Journal of Personality and Social Psychology, 70,* 945–960. doi: 10.1037/0022-3514.70.5.945

Cohen, J. (1988). *Statistical power analysis for the behavioral sciences* (2nd ed.). Hillsdale, NJ: Lawrence Erlbaum.

Cohen, L. E., & Felson, M. (1979). Social change and crime rate trends: A routine activity approach. *American Sociological Review, 44,* 588–608. doi: 10.2307/2094589

Cohen, S. J. (2016). Mapping the minds of suicide bombers using linguistic methods: The corpus of Palestinian suicide bombers' farewell letters (CoPSBFL). *Studies in Conflict & Terrorism, 39,* 749–780. doi: 10.1080/1057610X.2016.1141005

Cohn, A. M., Zinzow, H. M., Resnick, H. S., & Kilpatrick, D. G. (2013). Correlates of reasons for not reporting rape to police: Results from a national telephone household probability sample of women with forcible or drug-or-alcohol facilitated/incapacitated rape. *Journal of Interpersonal Violence, 28,* 455–473. doi: 10.1177/0886260512455515

Coker, A. L., Williams, C. M., Follingstad, D. R., & Jordan, C. E. (2011). Psychological, reproductive and maternal health, behavioral, and economic impact of intimate partner violence. In J. W. White, M. P. Koss, & A. E. Kazdin (Eds.), *Violence against women and children* (pp. 265–284). Washington, DC: American Psychological Association.

Collishaw, S., Pickles, A., Messer, J., Rutter, M., Shearer, C., & Maughan, B. (2007). Resilience to adult psychopathology following childhood maltreatment: Evidence from a community sample. *Child Abuse & Neglect, 31,* 211–229. doi: 10.1016/j.chiabu.2007.02.004

Combs-Lane, A. M., & Smith, D. W. (2002). Risk of sexual victimization in college women: The role of behavioral intentions and risk-taking behaviors. *Journal of Interpersonal Violence, 17,* 165–183. doi: 10.1177/0886260502017002004

Connolly, E. J., & Jackson, D. B. (2019). Adolescent gang membership and adverse behavioral, mental health, and physical health outcomes in young adulthood: A within-family analysis. *Criminal Justice and Behavior, 46,* 1566–1586. doi: 10.1177/0093854819871076

Conroy, D. E., Silva, J. M., Newcomer, R. R., Walker, B. W., & Johnson, M. S. (2001). Personal and participatory socializers of the perceived legitimacy of aggressive behavior in sport. *Aggressive Behavior, 27,* 405–418. doi: 10.1002/ab.1026

Cook, C. R., Williams, K. R., Guerra, N. G., Kim, T. E., & Sadek, S. (2010). Predictors of bullying and victimization in childhood and adolescence: A meta-analytic investigation. *School Psychology Quarterly, 25,* 65–83. doi: 10.1037/a0020149

Coons, C. J., Howard-Hamilton, M., & Waryold, D. (1995). College sports and fan aggression: Implications for residence hall discipline. *Journal of College Student Development, 36*, 587–593.

Corvo, K., & deLara, E. (2010). Towards an integrated theory of relational violence: Is bullying a risk factor for domestic violence? *Aggression and Violent Behavior, 15*, 181–190. doi: 10.1016/j.avb.2009.12.001

Coulomb-Cabagno, G., & Rascle, O. (2006). Team sports players' observed aggression as a function of gender, competitive level, and sport type. *Journal of Applied Social Psychology, 36*, 1980–2000. doi: 10.1111/j.0021-9029.2006.00090.x

Coulter, R. W. S., Mair, C., Miller, E., Blosnich, J. R., Matthews, D. D., & McCauley, H. L. (2017). Prevalence of past-year sexual assault victimization among undergraduate students: Exploring differences by and intersections of gender identity, sexual identity, and race/ethnicity. *Prevention Science, 18*, 726–736. doi: 10.1007/s11121-017-0762-8

Council of Europe (2011). *Explanatory report to the Council of Europe Convention on preventing and combating violence against women and domestic violence*: Council of Europe Treaty Series – No. 210. Retrieved from rm.coe.int/16800d383a

Coyne, S. M., Padilla-Walker, L. M., Holmgren, H. G., Davis, E. J., Collier, K. M., Memmott-Elison, M. K., & Hawkins, A. J. (2018). A meta-analysis of prosocial media on prosocial behavior, aggression, and empathic concern: A multidimensional approach. *Developmental Psychology, 54*, 331–347. doi: 10.1037/dev0000412

Coyne, S. M., Robinson, S. L., & Nelson, D. A. (2010). Does reality backbite? Physical, verbal, and relational aggression in reality television programs. *Journal of Broadcasting & Electronic Media, 54*, 282–298. doi: 10.1080/08838151003737931

Coyne, S. M., Warburton, W. A., Essig, L. W., & Stockdale, L. A. (2018). Violent video games, externalizing behavior, and prosocial behavior: A five-year longitudinal study during adolescence. *Developmental Psychology, 54*, 1868–1880. doi: 10.1037/dev0000574

Coyne, S. M., & Whitehead, E. (2008). Indirect aggression in animated Disney films. *Journal of Communication, 58*, 382–395. doi: 10.1111/j.1460-2466.2008.00390.x

Craig, K. M. (2002). Examining hate-motivated aggression: A review of the social psychological literature on hate crimes as a distinct form of aggression. *Aggression and Violent Behavior, 7*, 85–101. doi: 10.1016/S1359-1789(00)00039-2

Craig, W., Harel-Fisch, Y., Fogel-Grinvald, H., Dostaler, S., Hetland, J., Simons-Morton, B., ... Pickett, W. (2009). A cross-national profile of bullying and victimization among adolescents in 40 countries. *Industrial Journal of Public Health, 54*, 216–224. doi: 10.1007/s00038-009-5413-9

Crane, C. A., Godleski, S. A., Przybyla, S. M., Schlauch, R. C., & Testa, M. (2016). The proximal effects of acute alcohol consumption on male-to-female aggression: A meta-analytic review of the experimental literature. *Trauma, Violence, & Abuse, 17*, 520–531. doi: 10.1177/1524838015584374

Crane, C. A., Licata, M. L., Schlauch, R. C., Testa, M., & Easton, C. J. (2017). The proximal effects of acute alcohol use on female aggression: A meta-analytic review of the experimental literature. *Psychology of Addictive Behaviors, 31*, 21–26. doi: 10.1037/adb0000244

Crane, C. A., Schlauch, R. C., Testa, M., & Easton, C. J. (2018). Provocation and target gender as moderators of the relationship between acute alcohol use and female perpetrated aggression. *Aggression and Violent Behavior, 40*, 39–43. doi: 10.1016/j.avb.2018.03.001

Crick, N. R., Casas, J. F., & Mosher, M. (1997). Relational and overt aggression in preschool. *Developmental Psychology, 33*, 579–588. doi: 10.1037/0012-1649.33.4.579

Crick, N. R., & Grotpeter, J. K. (1995). Relational aggression, gender, and social-psychological adjustment. *Child Development, 66*, 710–722. doi: 10.1111/1467-8624.ep9506152720

Crick, N. R., Ostrov, J. M., & Kawabata, Y. (2007). Relational aggression and gender: An overview. In D. J. Flannery, A. T. Vazsonyi, & I. D. Waldman (Eds.), *The Cambridge handbook of violent behavior and aggression* (pp. 245–259). New York: Cambridge University Press.

Cross, C. P., & Campbell, A. (2011). Women's aggression. *Aggression and Violent Behavior, 16*, 390–398. doi: 10.1016/j.avb.2011.02.012

Cruise, R. S. (2016). Enough with the stereotypes: Representations of women in terrorist organizations. *Social Science Quarterly, 97*, 33–43. doi: 10.1111/ssqu.12250

Cui, M., Durtschi, J. A., Donnellan, M. B., Lorenz, F. O., & Conger, R. D. (2010). Intergenerational transmission of relationship aggression: A prospective longitudinal study. *Journal of Family Psychology, 24*, 688–697. doi: 10.1037/a0021675

Cukier, W., Eagen, S. A., & Decat, G. (2017). Gun violence. In B. J. Bushman (Ed.), *Aggression and violence: A social psychological perspective* (pp. 169–183). New York: Routledge.

D'Inverno, A. S., Smith, S. G., Zhang, X., & Chen, J. (2019). *The impact of intimate partner violence: A 2015 NISVS Research-in-Brief*. Retrieved from www.cdc.gov/violenceprevention/pdf/nisvs/nisvs-impactbrief-508.pdf

D'Abreu, L. C. F., & Krahé, B. (2014). Predicting sexual aggression in male college students in Brazil. *Psychology of Men & Masculinity, 15*, 152–162. doi: 10.1037/a0032789

D'Abreu, L. C. F., & Krahé, B. (2016). Vulnerability to sexual victimization in female and male college students in Brazil: Cross-sectional and prospective evidence. *Archives of Sexual Behavior, 45*, 1101–1115. doi: 10.1007/s10508-014-0451-7

Daly, J. M., Merchant, M. L., & Jogerst, G. J. (2011). Elder abuse research: A systematic review. *Journal of Elder Abuse & Neglect, 23*, 348–365. doi: 10.1080/08946566.2011.608048

Daly, M., & Wilson, M. (1994). Evolutionary psychology of male violence. In J. Archer (Ed.), *Male violence* (pp. 253–288). London: Routledge.

Darwin, C. (1859). *On the origin of species.* London: Murray.

Das, E., Bushman, B. J., Bezemer, M. D., Kerkhof, P., & Vermeulen, I. E. (2009). How terrorism news reports increase prejudice against outgroups: A terror management account. *Journal of Experimental Social Psychology, 45,* 453–459. doi: 10.1016/j.jesp.2008.12.001

Davis, K. C. (2010). The influence of alcohol expectancies and intoxication on men's aggressive unprotected sexual intentions. *Experimental and Clinical Psychopharmacology, 18,* 418–428. doi: 10.1037/a0020510

Davis, K. C., Danube, C. L., Stappenbeck, C. A., Norris, J., & George, W. H. (2015). Background predictors and event-specific characteristics of sexual aggression incidents: The roles of alcohol and other factors. *Violence Against Women, 21,* 997–1017. doi: 10.1177/1077801215589379

De Donder, L. de, Luoma, M.-L., Penhale, B., Lang, G., Santos, A. J., Tamutiene, I., ... Verté, D. (2011). European map of prevalence rates of elder abuse and its impact for future research. *European Journal of Ageing, 8,* 129–143. doi: 10.1007/s10433-011-0187-3

Deater-Deckard, K. (2014). Family matters: Intergenerational and interpersonal processes of executive function and attentive behavior. *Current Directions in Psychological Science, 23,* 230–236. doi: 10.1177/0963721414531597

DeBoer, S. F. (2017). Animal models: Implications for human behavior. In B. J. Bushman (Ed.), *Aggression and violence: A social psychological perspective* (pp. 22–43). New York: Routledge.

Decker, S. H. (2007). Youth gangs and violent behavior. In D. J. Flannery, A. T. Vazsonyi, & I. D. Waldman (Eds.), *The Cambridge handbook of violent behavior and aggression* (pp. 388–401). New York: Cambridge University Press.

Decker, S. H., & van Winkle, B. (1996). *Life in the gang: Family, friends and violence.* New York: Cambridge University Press.

Deffenbacher, J. L. (2011). Cognitive-behavioral conceptualization and treatment of anger. *Cognitive and Behavioral Practice, 18,* 212–221. doi: 10.1016/j.cbpra.2009.12.004

Deffenbacher, J. L. (2016). A review of interventions for the reduction of driving anger. *Transportation Research Part F: Traffic Psychology and Behaviour, 42,* 411–421. doi: 10.1016/j.trf.2015.10.024

Deffenbacher, J. L., Deffenbacher, D. M., Lynch, R. S., & Richards, T. L. (2003). Anger, aggression, and risky behavior: A comparison of high and low anger drivers. *Behaviour Research and Therapy, 41,* 701–718. doi: 10.1016/S0005-7967(02)00046-3

Deffenbacher, J. L., Filetti, L. B., Lynch, R. S., Dahlen, E. R., & Oetting, E. R. (2002). Cognitive-behavioral treatment of high anger drivers. *Behaviour Research and Therapy, 40,* 895–910. doi: 10.1016/S0005-7967(01)00067-5

Deffenbacher, J. L., Lynch, R. S., Oetting, E. R., & Swaim, R. C. (2002). The Driving Anger Expression Inventory: A measure of how people express their anger on the road. *Behaviour Research and Therapy, 40,* 717–737. doi: 10.1016/S0005-7967(01)00063-8

Deffenbacher, J. L., Lynch, R. S., Oetting, E. R., & Yingling, D. A. (2001). Driving anger: Correlates and a test of state-trait theory. *Personality and Individual Differences, 31,* 1321–1331. doi: 10.1016/S0191-8869(00)00226-9

Deffenbacher, J. L., Stephens, A. N., & Sullman, M. J. M. (2016). Driving anger as a psychological construct: Twenty years of research using the Driving Anger Scale. *Transportation Research Part F: Traffic Psychology and Behaviour, 42,* 236–247. doi: 10.1016/j.trf.2015.10.021

DeGue, S., Valle, L. A., Holt, M. K., Massetti, G. M., Matjasko, J. L., & Tharp, A. T. (2014). A systematic review of primary prevention strategies for sexual violence perpetration. *Aggression and Violent Behavior, 19,* 346–362. doi: 10.1016/j.avb.2014.05.004

DeKeseredy, W. S., Hall-Sanchez, A., & Nolan, J. (2018). College campus sexual assault: The contribution of peers' proabuse informational support and attachments to abusive peers. *Violence Against Women, 24,* 922–935. doi: 10.1177/1077801217724920

Del Campo, A., & Fávero, M. (2020). Effectiveness of programs for the prevention of child sexual abuse. *European Psychologist, 25,* 1–15. doi: 10.1027/1016-9040/a000379

Del Hoyo-Bilbao, J., Gámez-Guadix, M., & Calvete, E. (2018). Corporal punishment by parents and child-to-parent aggression in Spanish adolescents. *Anales De Psicología, 34,* 108–116. doi: 10.6018/analesps.34.1.259601

DeLisi, L. E., Maurizio, A., Yost, M., Papparozzi, C. F., Fulchino, C., Katz, C. L., … Stevens, P. (2003). A survey of New Yorkers after the Sept. 11, 2001, terrorist attacks. *American Journal of Psychiatry, 160,* 780–783. doi: 10.1176/appi.ajp.160.4.780

DeLong, S. M., Graham, L. M., Magee, E. P., Treves-Kagan, S., Gray, C. L., McClay, A. M., … Martin, S. L. (2018). Starting the conversation: Are campus sexual assault policies related to the prevalence of campus sexual assault? *Journal of Interpersonal Violence, 33,* 3315–3343. doi: 10.1177/0886260518798352

Demir, B., Demir, S., & Özkan, T. (2016). A contextual model of driving anger: A meta-analysis. *Transportation Research Part F: Traffic Psychology and Behaviour, 42,* 332–349. doi: 10.1016/j.trf.2016.09.020

Denson, T. F. (2013). The multiple systems model of angry rumination. *Personality and Social Psychology Review, 17,* 103–123. doi: 10.1177/1088868312467086

Denson, T. F., Capper, M. M., Oaten, M., Friese, M., & Schofield, T. P. (2011). Self-control training decreases aggression in response to provocation in aggressive individuals. *Journal of Research in Personality, 45,* 252–256. doi: 10.1016/j.jrp.2011.02.001

Denson, T. F., O'Dean, S. M., Blake, K. R., & Beames, J. R. (2018). Aggression in women: Behavior, brain and hormones. *Frontiers in Behavioral Neuroscience, 12,* 81. doi: 10.3389/fnbeh.2018.00081

Denson, T. F., Pedersen, W. C., Friese, M., Hahm, A., & Roberts, L. (2011). Understanding impulsive aggression: Angry rumination and reduced self-control capacity are mechanisms underlying the provocation-aggression relationship. *Personality and Social Psychology Bulletin, 37,* 850–862. doi: 10.1177/0146167211401420

Denson, T. F., Pedersen, W. C., & Miller, N. E. (2006). The Displaced Aggression Questionnaire. *Journal of Personality and Social Psychology, 90,* 1032–1051. doi: 10.1037/0022-3514.90.6.1032

Depraetere, J., Vandeviver, C., Beken, T. V., & Keygnaert, I. (2018). Big boys don't cry: A critical interpretive synthesis of male sexual victimization. *Trauma, Violence & Abuse,* 1524838018816979. doi: 10.1177/1524838018816979

Derksen, D. G., Hunsche, M. C., Giroux, M. E., Connolly, D. A., & Bernstein, D. M. (2018). A systematic review of theory of mind's precursors and functions. *Zeitschrift für Psychologie, 226,* 87–97. doi: 10.1027/2151-2604/a000325

Deselms, J. L., & Altman, J. D. (2003). Immediate and prolonged effects of videogame violence. *Journal of Applied Social Psychology, 33,* 1553–1563. doi: 10.1111/j.1559-1816.2003.tb01962.x

DeWall, C. N., & Anderson, C. A. (2011). The General Aggression Model. In P. R. Shaver & M. Mikulincer (Eds.), *Human aggression and violence: Causes, manifestations, and consequences* (pp. 15–33). Washington, DC: American Psychological Association.

DeWall, C. N., Anderson, C. A., & Bushman, B. J. (2011). The General Aggression Model: Theoretical extensions to violence. *Psychology of Violence, 1,* 245–258. doi: 10.1037/a0023842

DeWall, C. N., Bushman, B. J., Giancola, P. R., & Webster, G. D. (2010). The big, the bad, and the boozed-up: Weight moderates the effect of alcohol on aggression. *Journal of Experimental Social Psychology, 46,* 619–623. doi: 10.1016/j.jesp.2010.02.008

DeWall, C. N., Lambert, N. M., Pond, R. S., Kashdan, T. B., & Fincham, F. D. (2012). A grateful heart is a nonviolent heart. *Social Psychological and Personality Science, 3,* 232–240. doi: 10.1177/1948550611416675

DeWall, C. N., Twenge, J. M., Gitter, S. A., & Baumeister, R. F. (2009). It's the thought that counts: The role of hostile cognition in shaping aggressive responses to social exclusion. *Journal of Personality and Social Psychology, 96,* 45–59. doi: 10.1037/a0013196

Diener, E. (1980). Deindividuation: The absence of self-awareness and self-regulation in group members. In P. B. Paulus (Ed.), *Psychology of group influence* (pp. 209–242). Hillsdale, NJ: Lawrence Erlbaum.

DiLalla, L. F., & Gottesman, I. I. (1991). Biological and genetic contributors to violence: Widom's untold tale. *Psychological Bulletin, 109,* 125–129. doi: 10.1037/0033-2909.109.1.125

Dill, K. E., Anderson, C. A., Anderson, K. B., & Deuser, W. E. (1997). Effects of aggressive personality on social expectations and social perceptions. *Journal of Research in Personality, 31,* 272–292. doi: 10.1006/jrpe.1997.2183

Dinić, B. M., & Smederevac, S. (2019). Effects of HEXACO traits and experimental provocation on aggression. *Zeitschrift für Psychologie, 227*, 225–229. doi: 10.1027/2151-2604/a000381

Dinkes, R., Kemp, J., & Baum, K. (2009). *Indicators of school crime and safety: 2009.* Washington, DC: National Center for Education Statistics, Institute of Education Sciences, U.S. Department of Education, and Bureau of Justice Statistics, Office of Justice Programs, U.S. Department of Justice. Retrieved from http://nces.ed.gov/pubs2010/2010012.pdf

Dir, A. L., Andrews, A. R., Wilson, S. M., Davidson, T. M., & Gilmore, A. (2018). The role of sex-related alcohol expectancies in alcohol-involved consensual and nonconsensual sex among women of Asian/Pacific Islander and women of European race/ethnicity. *Journal of Sex Research, 55*, 850–862. doi: 10.1080/00224499.2017.1366411

Dishion, T. J. (2015). A developmental model of aggression and violence: Microsocial and macrosocial dynamics within an ecological framework. In M. Lewis & K. D. Rudolph (Eds.), *Handbook of developmental psychopathology* (pp. 449–465). New York: Springer.

Dodge, K. A. (2006). Translational science in action: Hostile attributional style and the development of aggressive behavior problems. *Development and Psychopathology, 18*, 791–814. doi: 10.1017/S0954579406060391

Dodge, K. A. (2011). Social information processing patterns as mediators of the interaction between genetic factors and life experiences in the development of aggressive behavior. In P. R. Shaver & M. Mikulincer (Eds.), *Human aggression and violence: Causes, manifestations, and consequences* (pp. 165–185). Washington, DC: American Psychological Association.

Dollard, J., Doob, L. W., Miller, N. E., Mowrer, O. H., & Sears, R. R. (1939). *Frustration and aggression.* New Haven, CT: Yale University Press.

Dong, X. Q. (2015). Elder abuse: Systematic review and implications for practice. *Journal of the American Geriatrics Society, 63*, 1214–1238. doi: 10.1111/jgs.13454

Donnerstein, E. I. (1984). Pornography: Its effect on violence against women. In N. M. Malamuth & E. I. Donnerstein (Eds.), *Pornography and sexual aggression* (pp. 53–81). Orlando, FL: Academic Press.

Donnerstein, E. I., & Wilson, D. W. (1976). Effects of noise and perceived control on ongoing and subsequent aggressive behavior. *Journal of Personality and Social Psychology, 34*, 774–781. doi: 10.1037/0022-3514.34.5.774

Donnerstein, M., & Donnerstein, E. I. (1978). Direct and vicarious censure in the control of interracial aggression. *Journal of Personality, 46*, 162–175. doi: 10.1111/1467-6494.ep7380380

Doosje, B., Moghaddam, F. M., Kruglanski, A. W., Wolf, A. de, Mann, L., & Feddes, A. R. (2016). Terrorism, radicalization and de-radicalization. *Current Opinion in Psychology, 11*, 79–84. doi: 10.1016/j.copsyc.2016.06.008

Doosje, B., Zebel, S., Scheermeijer, M., & Mathyi, P. (2007). Attributions of responsibility for terrorist attacks: The role of group membership and identification. *International Journal of Conflict and Violence, 1*, 127–141.

Doyle, J. L., & McWilliams, M. (2020). What difference does peace make? Intimate partner violence and violent conflict in Northern Ireland. *Violence Against Women*, Advance online publication. doi: 10.1177/1077801219832902

Drieschner, K., & Lange, A. (1999). A review of cognitive factors in the etiology of rape. *Clinical Psychology Review, 19*, 57–77. doi: 10.1016/S0272-7358(98)00016-6

Dubow, E. F., Huesmann, L. R., Boxer, P., & Smith, C. (2016). Childhood and adolescent risk and protective factors for violence in adulthood. *Journal of Criminal Justice, 45*, 26–31. doi: 10.1016/j.jcrimjus.2016.02.005

Dubow, E. F., Huesmann, L. R., Boxer, P., Smith, C., Landau, S., Dvir Gvirsman, S., & Shikaki, K. (2019). Serious violent behavior and anti-social outcomes as consequences of exposure to ethnic-political conflict and violence among Israeli and Palestinian youth. *Aggressive Behavior, 45*, 287–299. doi: 10.1002/ab.21818

Duda, J. L., Olson, L. K., & Templin, T. J. (1991). The relationship of task and ego orientation to sportsmanship attitudes and the perceived legitimacy of injurious acts. *Research Quarterly for Exercise and Sport, 62*, 79–87. doi: 10.1080/02701367.1991

Duffy, M. (2009). Preventing workplace mobbing and bullying with effective organizational consultation, policies, and legislation. *Consulting Psychology Journal: Practice and Research, 61*, 242–262. doi: 10.1037/a0016578

Duke, A. A., Bègue, L., Bell, R., & Eisenlohr-Moul, T. (2013). Revisiting the serotonin-aggression relation in humans: A meta-analysis. *Psychological Bulletin, 139*, 1148–1172. doi: 10.1037/a0031544

Duke, A. A., Smith, K. M. Z., Oberleitner, L. M. S., Westphal, A., & McKee, S. A. (2018). Alcohol, drugs, and violence: A meta-meta-analysis. *Psychology of Violence, 8*, 238–249. doi: 10.1037/vio0000106

Dunning, E., Murphy, P., & Williams, J. (1986). Spectator violence at football matches: Towards a sociological explanation. *British Journal of Sociology, 37*, 21–244. doi: 10.2307/590355

Dworkin, E. R., Brill, C. D., & Ullman, S. E. (2019). Social reactions to disclosure of interpersonal violence and psychopathology: A systematic review and meta-analysis. *Clinical Psychology Review, 72*, 101750. doi: 10.1016/j.cpr.2019.101750

Dworkin, E. R., Menon, S. V., Bystrynski, J., & Allen, N. E. (2017). Sexual assault victimization and psychopathology: A review and meta-analysis. *Clinical Psychology Review, 56*, 65–81. doi: 10.1016/j.cpr.2017.06.002

Eagly, A. H. (1987). *Sex differences in social behavior: A social-role interpretation*. Hillsdale, NJ: Lawrence Erlbaum.

Eagly, A. H., & Steffen, V. J. (1986). Gender and aggressive behavior: A meta-analytic review of the social psychological literature. *Psychological Bulletin, 100*, 309–330. doi: 10.1037/0033-2909.100.3.309

Eagly, A. H., & Wood, W. (1999). The origins of sex differences in human behavior: Evolved dispositions versus social roles. *American Psychologist, 54*, 408–423. doi: 10.1037/0003-066X.54.6.408

Eastin, M. S. (2006). Video game violence and the female game player: Self- and opponent gender effects on presence and aggressive thoughts. *Human Communication Research, 32,* 351–372. doi: 10.1111/ j.1468-2958.2006.00279.x

Eatough, E., Shockley, K., & Yu, P. (2016). A review of ambulatory health data collection methods for employee experience sampling research. *Applied Psychology, 65,* 322–354. doi: 10.1111/apps.12068

Echebarria-Echabe, A., & Fernández-Guede, E. (2006). Effects of terrorism on attitudes and ideological orientation. *European Journal of Social Psychology, 36,* 259–265. doi: 10.1002/ejsp.294

Eckhardt, C. I. (2011). Intimate partner violence: Cognitive, affective, and relational factors. In J. P. Forgas, A. W. Kruglanski, & K. D. Williams (Eds.), *The psychology of social conflict and aggression* (pp. 167–184). New York: Psychology Press.

Eckhardt, C. I., Norlander, B., & Deffenbacher, J. L. (2004). The assessment of anger and hostility: A critical review. *Aggression and Violent Behavior, 9,* 17–43. doi: 10.1016/S1359-1789(02)00116-7

Edguer, N., & Janisse, M. P. (1994). Type A behaviour and aggression: Provocation, conflict and cardiovascular responsivity in the Buss teacher-learner paradigm. *Personality and Individual Differences, 17,* 377–393. doi: 10.1016/0191-8869(94)90285-2

Edwards, S. R., & Vogel, D. L. (2015). Young men's likelihood ratings to be sexually aggressive as a function of norms and perceived sexual interest. *Psychology of Men & Masculinities, 16,* 88–96. doi: 10.1037/a0035439

Ehrensaft, M., Moffitt, T. E., & Caspi, A. (2006). Is domestic violence followed by an increased risk of psychiatric disorders among women but not among men? A longitudinal cohort study. *American Journal of Psychiatry, 163,* 885–892. doi: 10.1176/appi.ajp.163.5.885

Ehring, T., Welboren, R., Morina, N., Wicherts, J. M., Freitag, J., & Emmelkamp, P. M. G. (2014). Meta-analysis of psychological treatments for posttraumatic stress disorder in adult survivors of childhood abuse. *Clinical Psychology Review, 34,* 645–657. doi: 10.1016/j. cpr.2014.10.004

Einarsen, S., Hoel, H., & Notelaers, G. (2009). Measuring exposure to bullying and harassment at work: Validity, factor structure and psychometric properties of the Negative Acts Questionnaire-Revised. *Work & Stress, 23,* 24–44. doi: 10.1080/02678370902815673

Eisenberg, M. E., Lust, K., Mathiason, M. A., & Porta, C. M. (2017). Sexual assault, sexual orientation, and reporting among college students. *Journal of Interpersonal Violence,* Advance online publication. doi: 10.1177/ 0886260517726414

Eisenberger, N. I., Lieberman, M. D., & Williams, K. D. (2003). Does rejection hurt? An fMRI study of social exclusion. *Science, 302*(5643), 290– 292. doi: 10.1126/science.1089134

Ekstein, R. (1949). A biographical comment on Freud's dual instinct theory. *American Imago, 6,* 211–216.

Ellemers, N., & Haslam, S. A. (2012). Social identity theory. In P. A. M. van Lange, A. W. Kruglanski, & E. T. Higgins (Eds.), *Handbook of theories of social psychology* (pp. 379–398). London: Sage.

Ellison-Potter, P., Bell, P. A., & Deffenbacher, J. L. (2001). The effects of trait driving anger, anonymity, and aggressive stimuli on aggressive driving behavior. *Journal of Applied Social Psychology, 31,* 431–443. doi: 10.1111/j.1559-1816.2001.tb00204.x

Elson, M., Mohseni, M. R., Breuer, J., Scharkow, M., & Quandt, T. (2014). Press CRTT to measure aggressive behavior: The unstandardized use of the competitive reaction time task in aggression research. *Psychological Assessment, 26,* 419–432. doi: 10.1037/a0035569

Endresen, I. M., & Olweus, D. (2005). Participation in power sports and antisocial involvement in preadolescent and adolescent boys. *Journal of Child Psychology and Psychiatry, 46,* 468–478. doi: 10.1111/j.1469-7610.2005.00414.x

Ensafdaran, F., Krahé, B., Njad, S. B., & Arshadi, N. (2019). Efficacy of different versions of Aggression Replacement Training (ART): A review. *Aggression and Violent Behavior,* Advance online publication. doi: 10.1016/j.avb.2019.02.006

Erdley, C. A., & Asher, S. R. (1998). Linkages between children's beliefs about the legitimacy of aggression and their behavior. *Social Development, 7,* 321–339. doi: 10.1111/1467-9507.00070

Eron, L. D. (1987). The development of aggressive behavior from the perspective of a developing behaviorism. *American Psychologist, 42,* 435–442. doi: 10.1037/0003-066X.42.5.435

Esbensen, F. A., Osgood, D. W., Peterson, D., Taylor, T. J., & Carson, D. C. (2013). Short- and long-term outcome results from a multisite evaluation of the G.R.E.A.T. Program. *Criminology & Public Policy, 12,* 375–411. doi: 10.1111/1745-9133.12048

Esbensen, F. A., Osgood, D. W., Taylor, T. J., Peterson, D., & Freng, A. (2001). How great is G.R.E.A.T.? Results from a quasi-experimental design. *Criminology & Public Policy, 1,* 87–118. doi: 10.1111/j.1745-9133.2001.tb00078.x

Esbensen, F. A., Peterson, D., Taylor, T. J., Freng, A., Osgood, D. W., Carson, D. C., & Matsuda, K. N. (2011). Evaluation and evolution of the Gang Resistance Education and Training (G.R.E.A.T.) program. *Journal of School Violence, 10,* 53–70. doi: 10.1080/15388220.2010.519374

Escartín, J. (2016). Insights into workplace bullying: Psychosocial drivers and effective interventions. *Psychology Research and Behavior Management, 9,* 157–169. doi: 10.2147/PRBM.S91211

Eurofound (2017). Bullying and sexual harassment at the workplace, in public spaces, and in political life in the EU: Sixth European Working Conditions Survey. Retrieved from www.eurofound.europa.eu/publications/report/2016/working-conditions/sixth-european-working-conditions-survey-overview-report

Euser, S., Alink, L. R. A., Stoltenborgh, M., Bakermans-Kranenburg, M. J., & van IJzendoorn, M. H. (2015). A gloomy picture: A meta-analysis of randomized controlled trials reveals disappointing effectiveness of programs aiming at preventing child maltreatment. *BMC Public Health, 15*, 1068. doi: 10.1186/s12889-015-2387-9

Evans, G. W. (2019). Projected behavioral impacts of global climate change. *Annual Review of Psychology, 70*, 449–474. doi: 10.1146/annurev-psych-010418-103023

Evans, J. L., Burroughs, M. E., & Knowlden, A. P. (2019). Examining the efficacy of bystander sexual violence interventions for first- year college students: A systematic review. *Aggression and Violent Behavior, 48*, 72–82. doi: 10.1016/j.avb.2019.08.016

Even-Chen, M. S., & Itzhaky, H. (2007). Exposure to terrorism and violent behavior among adolescents in Israel. *Journal of Community Psychology, 35*, 43–55. doi: 10.1002/jcop.20133

Fabiano, P. M., Perkins, H. W., Berkowitz, A. D., Linkenbach, J., & Stark, C. (2003). Engaging men as social justice allies in ending violence against women: Evidence for a social norms approach. *Journal of American College Health, 52*, 105–112. doi: 10.1080/07448480309595732

Fang, B., & Yan, E. (2018). Abuse of older persons with dementia: A review of the literature. *Trauma, Violence & Abuse, 19*, 127–147. doi: 10.1177/1524838016650185

Fargo, J. D. (2009). Pathways to adult sexual revictimization: Direct and indirect behavioral risk factors across the lifespan. *Journal of Interpersonal Violence, 24*, 1771–1791. doi: 10.1177/0886260508325489

Farrington, D. P., Ttofi, M. M., & Coid, J. W. (2009). Development of adolescence-limited, late-onset, and persistent offenders from age 8 to age 48. *Aggressive Behavior, 35*, 150–163. doi: 10.1002/ab.20296

Farris, C., Treat, T. A., Viken, R. J., & McFall, R. M. (2008). Sexual coercion and the misperception of sexual intent. *Clinical Psychology Review, 28*, 48–66. doi: 10.1016/j.cpr.2007.03.002

Featherstone, B. (1996). Victims or villains? Women who physically abuse their children. In B. Fawcett, B. Featherstone, J. Hearn, & C. Toft (Eds.), *Violence and gender relations: Theories and interventions* (pp. 178–189). London: Sage.

Federal Bureau of Investigation (2011). *Hate crime statistics 2009.* Retrieved from www2.fbi.gov/ucr/hc2009/documents/methodology.pdf

Federal Bureau of Investigation (2018). *Hate crime statistics 2018.* Retrieved from www.justice.gov/hatecrimes/hate-crime-statistics

Federal Bureau of Investigation (2019). 2018 Crime in the United States. Retrieved from ucr.fbi.gov/crime-in-the-u.s/2018/crime-in-the-u.s.-2018/topic-pages/rape

Fedina, L., Holmes, J. L., & Backes, B. (2018). Campus sexual assault: A systematic review of prevalence research from 2000 to 2015. *Trauma, Violence & Abuse, 19*, 76–93. doi: 10.1177/1524838016631129

Feiring, C., Simon, V. A., & Cleland, C. M. (2009). Childhood sexual abuse, stigmatization, internalizing symptoms, and the development of sexual difficulties and dating aggression. *Journal of Consulting and Clinical Psychology, 77*, 127–137. doi: 10.1037/a0013475

Fellmeth, G. L. T., Heffernan, C., Nurse, J., Habibula, S., & Sethi, D. (2013). Educational and skills-based interventions for preventing relationship and dating violence in adolescents and young adults. *The Cochrane Database of Systematic Reviews*, CD004534. doi: 10.1002/14651858. CD004534.pub3

Ferguson, C. J. (2010). Blazing angels or resident evil? Can violent video games be a force for good? *Review of General Psychology, 14*, 68–81. doi: 10.1037/a0018941

Ferguson, C. J., & Beaver, K. M. (2009). Natural born killers: The genetic origins of extreme violence. *Aggression and Violent Behavior, 14*, 286–294. doi: 10.1016/j.avb.2009.03.005

Ferguson, C. J., & Hartley, R. D. (2009). The pleasure is momentary … the expense damnable? The influence of pornography on rape and sexual assault. *Aggression and Violent Behavior, 14*, 323–329. doi: 10.1016/ j.avb.2009.04.008

Ferguson, C. J., & Rueda, S. M. (2009). Examining the validity of the modified Taylor competitive reaction time test of aggression. *Journal of Experimental Criminology, 5*, 121–137. doi: 10.1007/s11292-009-9069-5

Fernandez, E., Malvaso, C., Day, A., & Guharajan, D. (2018). 21st century cognitive behavioural therapy for anger: A systematic review of research design, methodology and outcome. *Behavioural and Cognitive Psychotherapy, 46*, 385–404. doi: 10.1017/S1352465818000048

Fernández-Fuertes, A. A., Carcedo, R. J., Orgaz, B., & Fuertes, A. (2018). Sexual coercion perpetration and victimization: Gender similarities and differences in adolescence. *Journal of Interpersonal Violence, 33*, 2467–2485. doi: 10.1177/0886260518774306

Ferriday, C., Vartanian, O., & Mandel, D. R. (2011). Public but not private ego threat triggers aggression in narcissists. *European Journal of Social Psychology, 41*, 564–568. doi: 10.1002/ejsp.801

Fields, R. M. (1979). Child terror victims and adult terrorists. *Journal of Psychohistory, 7*, 71–75.

Fields, R. M., Elbedour, S., & Hein, F. A. (2002). The Palestinian suicide bomber. In C. E. Stout (Ed.), *The psychology of terrorism* (pp. 193–223). Westport, CT: Praeger.

Finkel, E. J. (2014). The I³ model: Metatheory, theory, and evidence. In M. P. Zanna (Ed.), *Advances in experimental social psychology* (Vol. 49, pp. 1–104). San Diego, CA: Academic Press.

Finkel, E. J., & Hall, A. N. (2018). The I³ Model: A metatheoretical framework for understanding aggression. *Current Opinion in Psychology, 19*, 125–130. doi: 10.1016/j.copsyc.2017.03.013

Finkelhor, D. (1987). The trauma of child sexual abuse: Two models. *Journal of Interpersonal Violence, 2*, 348–366. doi: 10.1177/088626058700200402

Finkelhor, D. (1994). The international epidemiology of child sexual abuse. *Child Abuse & Neglect, 18*, 409–417. doi: 10.1016/0145-2134(94)90026-4

Finkelhor, D. (2011). Prevalence of child victimization, abuse, crime, and violence exposure. In J. W. White, M. P. Koss, & A. E. Kazdin (Eds.), *Violence against women and children* (pp. 9–29). Washington, DC: American Psychological Association.

Finkelhor, D., Turner, H., Ormrod, R., Hamby, S. L., & Kracke, K. (2009). *Children's exposure to violence: A comprehensive national survey.* Washington, DC: U.S. Department of Justice. Retrieved from www.ncjrs.gov/pdffiles1/ojjdp/227744.pdf

Finkelhor, D., Turner, H., Wormuth, B. K., Vanderminden, J., & Hamby, S. L. (2019). Corporal punishment: Current rates from a national survey. *Journal of Child and Family Studies, 28*, 1991–1997. doi: 10.1007/s10826-019-01426-4

Finkenauer, C., Buyukcan-Tetik, A., Baumeister, R. F., Schoemaker, K., Bartels, M., & Vohs, K. D. (2015). Out of control: Identifying the role of self-control strength in family violence. *Current Directions in Psychological Science, 24*, 261–266. doi: 10.1177/0963721415570730

Finneran, C., & Stephenson, R. (2013). Intimate partner violence among men who have sex with men: A systematic review. *Trauma, Violence & Abuse, 14*, 168–185. doi: 10.1177/1524838012470034

Fischer, P., & Ai, A. L. (2008). International terrorism and mental health: Recent research and future directions. *Journal of Interpersonal Violence, 23*, 339–361. doi: 10.1177/0886260507312292

Fischer, P., & Greitemeyer, T. (2006). Music and aggression: The impact of sexual-aggressive song lyrics on aggression-related thoughts, emotions, and behavior toward the same and the opposite sex. *Personality and Social Psychology Bulletin, 32*, 1165–1176. doi: 10.1177/0146167206288670

Fischer, P., Greitemeyer, T., Kastenmüller, A., Frey, D., & Osswald, S. (2007). Terror salience and punishment: Does terror salience induce threat to social order? *Journal of Experimental Social Psychology, 43*, 964–971. doi: 10.1016/j.jesp.2006.10.004

Fischer, P., Greitemeyer, T., Kastenmüller, A., Vogrincic, C., & Sauer, A. (2011). The effects of risk-glorifying media exposure on risk-positive cognitions, emotions, and behaviors: A meta-analytic review. *Psychological Bulletin, 137*, 367–390. doi: 10.1037/a0022267

Fischer, P., Greitemeyer, T., Morton, T., Kastenmüller, A., Postmes, T., Frey, D., ... Odenwalder, J. (2009). The racing-game effect: Why do video racing games increase risk-taking inclinations? *Personality and Social Psychology Bulletin, 35*, 1395–1409. doi: 10.1177/0146167209339628

Fischer, P., Haslam, S. A., & Smith, L. (2010). "If you wrong us, shall we not revenge?" Social identity salience moderates support for retaliation in response to collective threat. *Group Dynamics: Theory, Research, and Practice, 14*, 143–150. doi: 10.1037/a0017970

Fischer, P., Kastenmüller, A., & Greitemeyer, T. (2010). Media violence and the self: The impact of personalized gaming characters in aggressive video games on aggressive behavior. *Journal of Experimental Social Psychology, 46,* 192–195. doi: 10.1016/j.jesp.2009.06.010

Fischer, P., Kubitzki, J., Guter, S., & Frey, D. (2007). Virtual driving and risk taking: Do racing games increase risk-taking cognitions, affect, and behaviors? *Journal of Experimental Psychology: Applied, 13,* 22–31. doi: 10.1037/1076-898X.13.1.22

Fisher, N. L., & Pina, A. (2013). An overview of the literature on female-perpetrated adult male sexual victimization. *Aggression and Violent Behavior, 18,* 54–61. doi: 10.1016/j.avb.2012.10.001

Fite, P. J., Raine, A., Stouthamer-Loeber, M., Loeber, R., & Pardini, D. A. (2010). Reactive and proactive aggression in adolescent males: Examining differential outcomes 10 years later in early adulthood. *Criminal Justice and Behavior, 37,* 141–157. doi: 10.1177/0093854809353051

Fitton, L., Yu, R., & Fazel, S. (2018). Childhood maltreatment and violent outcomes: A systematic review and meta-analysis of prospective studies. *Trauma, Violence & Abuse,* Advance online publication. doi: 10.1177/1524838018795269

Fitzgerald, L. F. (1993). Sexual harassment: Violence against women in the workplace. *American Psychologist, 48,* 1070–1076. doi: 10.1037/0003-066X.48.10.1070

Fitzgerald, L. F., & Cortina, L. M. (2018). Sexual harassment in work organizations: A view from the 21st century. In C. B. Travis & J. W. White (Eds.), *APA handbook of the psychology of women* (pp. 215–234). Washington, DC: American Psychological Association.

Fitzgerald, L. F., & Ormerod, A. J. (1993). Breaking the silence: The sexual harassment of women in the academia and the workplace. In F. Denmark & M. A. Paludi (Eds.), *Psychology of women: A handbook of issues and theories* (pp. 553–581). Westport, CT: Greenwood Press.

Fix, R. L., & Fix, S. T. (2013). The effects of mindfulness-based treatments for aggression: A critical review. *Aggression and Violent Behavior, 18,* 219–227. doi: 10.1016/j.avb.2012.11.009

Flack, W. F., Hansen, B. E., Hopper, A. B., Bryant, L. A., Lang, K. W., Massa, A. A., & Whalen, J. E. (2016). Some types of hookups may be riskier than others for campus sexual assault. *Psychological Trauma: Theory, Research, Practice and Policy, 8,* 413–420. doi: 10.1037/tra0000090

Flores, S. A., & Hartlaub, M. G. (1998). Reducing rape-myth acceptance in male college students: A meta-analysis of intervention studies. *Journal of College Student Development, 39,* 438–448.

Fong, V. C., Hawes, D., & Allen, J. L. (2019). A systematic review of risk and protective factors for externalizing problems in children exposed to intimate partner violence. *Trauma, Violence & Abuse, 20,* 149–167. doi: 10.1177/1524838017692383

Fontaine, R. G., & Dodge, K. A. (2009). Social information processing and aggressive behavior: A transactional perspective. In A. Sameroff (Ed.), *The transactional model of development: How children and contexts shape each other* (pp. 117–135). Washington, DC: American Psychological Association.

Foran, H. M., & O'Leary, K. D. (2008). Alcohol and intimate partner violence: A meta-analytic review. *Clinical Psychology Review, 28,* 1222–1234. doi: 10.1016/j.cpr.2008.05.001

Ford, J., & Soto-Marquez, J. G. (2016). Sexual assault victimization among straight, gay/lesbian, and bisexual college students. *Violence and Gender, 3,* 107–115. doi: 10.1089/vio.2015.0030

Forgays, D. G., Forgays, D. K., & Spielberger, C. D. (1997). Factor structure of the State-Trait Anger Expression Inventory. *Journal of Personality Assessment, 69,* 497–507. doi: 10.1207/s15327752jpa6903_5

Forrest, S., Eatough, V., & Shevlin, M. (2005). Measuring adult indirect aggression: The development and psychometric assessment of the Indirect Aggression Scales. *Aggressive Behavior, 31,* 84–97. doi: 10.1002/ab.20074

Forssell, R. (2016). Exploring cyberbullying and face-to-face bullying in working life – Prevalence, targets and expressions. *Computers in Human Behavior, 58,* 454–460. doi: 10.1016/j.chb.2016.01.003

Foubert, J. D., Clark-Taylor, A., & Wall, A. F. (2020). Is campus rape primarily a serial or one-time problem? Evidence from a multicampus study. *Violence Against Women, 26,* 296–311. doi: 10.1177/1077801219833820

Fox, J. A., & Fridel, E. E. (2017). Gender differences in patterns and trends in U.S. homicide, 1976–2015. *Violence and Gender, 4,* 37–43. doi: 10.1089/vio.2017.0016

Frank, M. G., & Gilovich, T. (1988). The dark side of self-and social perception: black uniforms and aggression in professional sports. *Journal of Personality and Social Psychology, 54,* 74–85. doi: 10.1037/0022-3514.54.1.74

Freud, S. (1920). *Beyond the pleasure principle.* New York: Bantam Books.

Friedland, N. (1988). Political terrorism: A social psychological perspective. In W. Stroebe, A. W. Kruglanski, D. Bar-Tal, & M. Hewstone (Eds.), *The social psychology of intergroup conflict: Theory, research and applications* (pp. 103–114). Berlin: Springer.

Frieze, I. H. (2000). Violence in close relationships—development of a research area: Comment on Archer (2000). *Psychological Bulletin, 126,* 681–684. doi: 10.1037/0033-2909.126.5.681

Funk, J. B., Baldacci, H. B., Pasold, T., & Baumgardner, J. (2004). Violence exposure in real-life, video games, television, movies, and the internet: Is there desensitization? *Journal of Adolescence, 27,* 23–39. doi: 10.1016/j.adolescence.2003.10.005

Funk, J. B., Buchman, D. D., Jenks, J., & Bechtoldt, H. (2003). Playing violent video games, desensitization, and moral evaluation in children. *Journal of Applied Developmental Psychology, 24,* 413–436. doi: 10.1016/S0193-3973(03)00073-X

Funk, J. B., Flores, G., Buchman, D. D., & Germann, J. N. (1999). Rating electronic games: Violence is in the eye of the beholder. *Youth & Society, 30*, 283–312. doi: 10.1177/0044118X99030003002

Gaffney, H., Farrington, D. P., Espelage, D. L., & Ttofi, M. M. (2019). Are cyberbullying intervention and prevention programs effective? A systematic and meta-analytical review. *Aggression and Violent Behavior, 45*, 134–153. doi: 10.1016/j.avb.2018.07.002

Gaffney, H., Ttofi, M. M., & Farrington, D. P. (2019). Evaluating the effectiveness of school-bullying prevention programs: An updated meta-analytical review. *Aggression and Violent Behavior, 45*, 111–133. doi: 10.1016/j.avb.2018.07.001

Galea, S., Vlahov, D., Resnik, H., Ahern, J., Susser, E., Gold, J., ... Kilpatrick, D. G. (2003). Trends of probable post-traumatic stress disorder in New York City after the September 11 terrorist attack. *American Journal of Epidemiology, 158*, 514–524. doi: 10.1093/aje/kwg187

Gallo, E. A. G., Munhoz, T. N., Loret de Mola, C., & Murray, J. (2018). Gender differences in the effects of childhood maltreatment on adult depression and anxiety: A systematic review and meta-analysis. *Child Abuse & Neglect, 79*, 107–114. doi: 10.1016/j.chiabu.2018.01.003

Galovski, T. E., Malta, L. S., & Blanchard, E. B. (2006). *Road rage: Assessment and treatment of the angry, aggressive driver.* Washington, DC: American Psychological Association.

Geen, R. G. (1995). Violence. In A. S. R. Manstead (Ed.), *Blackwell dictionary of social psychology* (p. 669). Oxford: Blackwell.

Geen, R. G. (1998). Aggression and antisocial behavior. In D. T. Gilbert, S. T. Fiske, & G. Lindzey (Eds.), *The handbook of social psychology* (4th ed., pp. 317–356). New York: McGraw-Hill.

Geen, R. G., & McCown, E. J. (1984). Effects of noise and attack on aggression and physiological arousal. *Motivation and Emotion, 8*, 231–241. doi: 10.1007/BF00991891

Geen, R. G., & O'Neal, E. C. (1969). Activation of cue-elicited aggression by general arousal. *Journal of Personality and Social Psychology, 11*, 289–292. doi: 10.1037/h0026885

Gelles, R. J. (1997). *Intimate violence in families* (3rd ed.). Thousand Oaks, CA: Sage.

Gelles, R. J. (2007). Family violence. In D. J. Flannery, A. T. Vazsonyi, & I. D. Waldman (Eds.), *The Cambridge handbook of violent behavior and aggression* (pp. 403–417). New York: Cambridge University Press.

Gelles, R. J. (2017). *Intimate violence and abuse in families* (4th ed.). New York: Oxford University Press.

Gelles, R. J., & Straus, M. A. (1979). Determinants of violence in the family: Toward a theoretical integration. In W. Burr, R. Hill, F. I. Nye, & Reiss, I. L. (Eds.), *Contemporary theories about the family.* (pp. 549–581). New York: Free Press.

Geneva Declaration on Armed Violence and Development (2015). *Global burden of armed violence 2015: Every body counts.* Retrieved from www.genevadeclaration.org/fileadmin/docs/GBAV3/GBAV3_ExecSummary_pp1-10.pdf

Gentile, D. A. (2010). Are motion picture ratings reliable and valid? *Journal of Adolescent Health, 47*, 423–424. doi: 10.1016/j.jadohealth.2010.08.016

Gentile, D. A. (2013). Catharsis and media violence: A conceptual analysis. *Societies, 3*, 491–510. doi: 10.3390/soc3040491

Gentile, D. A., & Anderson, C. A. (2006). Violent video games: The effects on youth, and public policy implications. In N. Dowd & D. G. Singer (Eds.), *Handbook of children, cultre and violence* (pp. 225–246). Thousand Oaks, CA: Sage.

Gentile, D. A., Anderson, C. A., Yukawa, S., Ihori, N., Saleem, M., Ming, L. K., ... Sakamoto, A. (2009). The effects of prosocial video games on prosocial behaviors: International evidence from correlational, longitudinal, and experimental studies. *Personality and Social Psychology Bulletin, 35*, 752–763. doi: 10.1177/0146167209333045

Gentile, D. A., & Gentile, J. R. (2008). Violent video games as exemplary teachers: A conceptual analysis. *Journal of Youth and Adolescence, 37*, 127–141. doi: 10.1007/s10964-007-9206-2

Gentile, D. A., Lynch, P. J., Linder, J. R., & Walsh, D. A. (2004). The effects of violent video game habits on adolescent hostility, aggressive behaviors, and school performance. *Journal of Adolescence, 27*, 5–22. doi: 10.1016/j.adolescence.2003.10.002

Georgiev, A. V., Klimczuk, A. C. E., Traficonte, D. M., & Maestripieri, D. (2013). When violence pays: A cost-benefit analysis of aggressive behavior in animals and humans. *Evolutionary Psychology, 11*, 678–699. doi: 10.1177/147470491301100313

Georgiou, S. N., & Stavrinides, P. (2008). Bullies, victims and bully-victims: Psychosocial profiles and attribution styles. *School Psychology International, 29*, 574–589. doi: 10.1177/0143034308099202

Gerger, H., Kley, H., Bohner, G., & Siebler, F. (2007). The acceptance of modern myths about sexual aggression scale: Development and validation in German and English. *Aggressive Behavior, 33*, 422–440. doi: 10.1002/ab.20195

Gershoff, E. T. (2002). Corporal punishment by parents and associated child behaviors and experiences: A meta-analytic and theoretical review. *Psychological Bulletin, 128*, 539–579. doi: 10.1037/0033-2909.128.4.539

Giancola, P. R. (2002a). The influence of trait anger on the alcohol-aggression relation in men and women. *Alcoholism: Clinical and Experimental Research, 26*, 1350–1358. doi: 10.1097/00000374-200209000-00007

Giancola, P. R. (2002b). Irritability, acute alcohol consumption and aggressive behavior in men and women. *Drug and Alcohol Dependence, 68*, 263–274. doi: 10.1016/S0376-8716(02)00221-1

Giancola, P. R., & Chermack, S. T. (1998). Construct validity of laboratory aggression paradigms. *Aggression and Violent Behavior, 3*, 237–253. doi: 10.1016/S1359-1789(97)00004-9

Giancola, P. R., & Corman, M. D. (2007). Alcohol and aggression: A test of the attention-allocation model. *Psychological Science, 18,* 649–655. doi: 10.1111/j.1467-9280.2007.01953.x

Giancola, P. R., Josephs, R. A., Parrott, D. J., & Duke, A. A. (2010). Alcohol myopia revisited: Clarifying aggression and other acts of disinhibition through a distorted lens. *Perspectives on Psychological Science, 5,* 265–278. doi: 10.1177/1745691610369467

Giancola, P. R., & Parrott, D. J. (2008). Further evidence for the validity of the Taylor Aggression Paradigm. *Aggressive Behavior, 34,* 214–229. doi: 10.1002/ab.20235

Giancola, P. R., Reagin, C. M., van Weenen, R. V., & Zeichner, A. (1998). Alcohol-induced stimulation and sedation: Relation to physical aggression. *The Journal of General Psychology, 125,* 297–304. doi: 10.1080/00221309809595339

Gidycz, C. A., Hanson, K. A., & Layman, M. J. (1995). A prospective analysis of the relationships among sexual assault experiences. *Psychology of Women Quarterly, 19,* 5–29. doi: 10.1111/j.1471-6402.1995.tb00276.x

Gidycz, C. A., McNamara, J. R., & Edwards, K. M. (2006). Women's risk perception and sexual victimization: A review of the literature. *Aggression and Violent Behavior, 11,* 441–456. doi: 10.1016/j.avb.2006.01.004

Gidycz, C. A., Orchowski, L. M., & Berkowitz, A. D. (2011). Preventing sexual aggression among college men: An evaluation of a social norms and bystander intervention program. *Violence Against Women, 17,* 720–742. doi: 10.1177/1077801211409727

Gidycz, C. A., van Wynsberghe, A., & Edwards, K. M. (2008). Prediction of women's utilization of resistance strategies in a sexual assault situation: A prospective study. *Journal of Interpersonal Violence, 23,* 571–588. doi: 10.1177/0886260507313531

Gigerenzer, G. (2004). Dread risk, September 11, and fatal traffic accidents. *Psychological Science, 15,* 286–287. doi: 10.1111/j.0956-7976.2004.00668.x

Gigerenzer, G. (2006). Out of the frying pan into the fire: Behavioral reactions to terrorist attacks. *Risk Analysis: An International Journal, 26,* 347–351. doi: 10.1111/j.1539-6924.2006.00753.x

Gilbert, F., & Daffern, M. (2011). Illuminating the relationship between personality disorder and violence: Contributions of the General Aggression Model. *Psychology of Violence, 1,* 230–244. doi: 10.1037/a0024089

Gill, P. (2007). A multi-dimensional approach to suicide bombing. *International Journal of Conflict and Violence, 1,* 142–159.

Gillen, P. A., Sinclair, M., Kernohan, W. G., Begley, C. M., & Luyben, A. G. (2017). Interventions for prevention of bullying in the workplace. *The Cochrane Database of Systematic Reviews, 1,* CD009778. doi: 10.1002/14651858.CD009778.pub2

Gillett, R. (2018). Intimate intrusions online: Studying the normalisation of abuse in dating apps. *Women's Studies International Forum, 69,* 212–219. doi: 10.1016/j.wsif.2018.04.005

Gilman, A., Hill, K. G., Hawkins, J. D., Howell, J. C., & Kosterman, R. (2014). The developmental dynamics of joining a gang in adolescence: Patterns and predictors of gang membership. *Journal of Research on Adolescence, 24*, 204–219. doi: 10.1111/jora.12121

Gilmore, A., Lewis, M. A., & George, W. H. (2015). A randomized controlled trial targeting alcohol use and sexual assault risk among college women at high risk for victimization. *Behaviour Research and Therapy, 74*, 38–49. doi: 10.1016/j.brat.2015.08.007

Gilmour, S., Wattanakamolkul, K., & Sugai, M. K. (2018). The effect of the Australian National Firearms Agreement on suicide and homicide mortality, 1978–2015. *American Journal of Public Health, 108*, 1511–1516. doi: 10.2105/AJPH.2018.304640

Giumetti, G. W., & Markey, P. M. (2007). Violent video games and anger as predictors of aggression. *Journal of Research in Personality, 41*, 1234–1243. doi: 10.1016/j.jrp.2007.02.005

Glad, K. A., Kilmer, R. P., Dyb, G., & Hafstad, G. S. (2019). Caregiver-reported Positive Changes in Young Survivors of a Terrorist attack. *Journal of Child and Family Studies, 28*, 704–719. doi: 10.1007/s10826-018-1298-7

Glass, G. V., McGaw, B., & Smith, M. L. (1981). *Meta-analysis in social research*. Beverly Hills, CA: Sage.

Godleski, S. A., Kamper, K. E., Ostrov, J. M., Hart, E. J., & Blakely-McClure, S. J. (2015). Peer victimization and peer rejection during early childhood. *Journal of Clinical Child and Adolescent Psychology, 44*, 380–392. doi: 10.1080/15374416.2014.940622

Gold, L. H., & Simon, R. I. (Eds.) (2016). *Gun violence and mental illness*. Arlington, VA: American Psychiatric Association Publishing.

Goldenberg, A., Cohen-Chen, S., Goyer, J. P., Dweck, C. S., Gross, J. J., & Halperin, E. (2018). Testing the impact and durability of a group malleability intervention in the context of the Israeli-Palestinian conflict. *Proceedings of the National Academy of Sciences of the United States of America, 115*, 696–701. doi: 10.1073/pnas.1706800115

Golding, J. M. (1999). Intimate partner violence as a risk factor for mental disorders: A meta-analysis. *Journal of Family Violence, 14*, 99–132. doi: 10.1023/A:1022079418229

Goldstein, A. P. (1994a). Delinquent gangs. In L. R. Huesmann (Ed.), *Aggressive behavior: Current perspectives* (pp. 255–273). New York: Plenum Press.

Goldstein, A. P. (1994b). *The ecology of aggression*. New York: Plenum Press.

Goldstein, A. P. (2002). *The psychology of group aggression*. Chichester, U.K.: Wiley.

Gollwitzer, M., Banse, R., Eisenbach, K., & Naumann, A. (2007). Effectiveness of the Vienna Social Competence Training on explicit and implicit aggression: Evidence from an Aggressiveness-IAT. *European Journal of Psychological Assessment, 23*, 150–156. doi: 10.1027/1015-5759.23.3.150

Goodman, L. A., & Epstein, D. (2011). The justice system response to domestic violence. In M. P. Koss, J. W. White, & A. E. Kazdin (Eds.),

Violence against women and children (pp. 215–235). Washington, DC: American Psychological Association.

Gottfredson, M. R. (2007). Self-control theory and criminal violence. In D. J. Flannery, A. T. Vazsonyi, & I. D. Waldman (Eds.), *The Cambridge handbook of violent behavior and aggression* (pp. 533–544). New York: Cambridge University Press.

Gould, L. A., & Agnich, L. E. (2016). Exploring the relationship between gender violence and state failure: A cross-national comparison. *Violence Against Women, 22,* 1343–1370. doi: 10.1177/1077801215624790

Gover, A. R., Jennings, W. G., & Tewksbury, R. (2009). Adolescent male and female gang members' experiences with violent victimization, dating violence, and sexual assault. *American Journal of Criminal Justice, 34,* 103–115. doi: 10.1007/s12103-008-9053-z

Graham, K., Bernards, S., Wilsnack, S. C., & Gmel, G. (2011). Alcohol may not cause partner violence but it seems to make it worse: A cross national comparison of the relationship between alcohol and severity of partner violence. *Journal of Interpersonal Violence, 26,* 1503–1523. doi: 10.1177/0886260510370596

Graham, K., & Wells, S. (2001). Aggression among young adults in the social context of the bar. *Addiction Research & Theory, 9,* 193–219. doi: 10.3109/16066350109141750

Graham, L. M., Treves-Kagan, S., Magee, E. P., DeLong, S. M., Ashley, O. S., Macy, R. J., … Bowling, J. M. (2017). Sexual assault policies and consent definitions: A nationally representative investigation of U.S. colleges and universities. *Journal of School Violence, 16,* 243–258. doi: 10.1080/15388220.2017.1318572

Green, J., & Plant, M. A. (2007). Bad bars: A review of risk factors. *Journal of Substance Use, 12,* 157–189. doi: 10.1080/14659890701374703

Greenaway, K. H., Cruwys, T., Haslam, S. A., & Jetten, J. (2016). Social identities promote well-being because they satisfy global psychological needs. *European Journal of Social Psychology, 46,* 294–307. doi: 10.1002/ejsp.2169

Greenberg, J., & Arndt, J. (2012). Terror management theory. In P. van Lange, A. W. Kruglanski, & E. T. Higgins (Eds.), *Handbook of theories of social psychology* (Vol. 1, 398-415). London: Sage.

Greenwald, A. G., McGhee, D. E., & Schwartz, J. L. (1998). Measuring individual differences in implicit cognition: The implicit association test. *Journal of Personality and Social Psychology, 74,* 1464–1480. doi: 10.1037/0022-3514.74.6.1464

Greitemeyer, T. (2011). Exposure to music with prosocial lyrics reduces aggression: First evidence and test of the underlying mechanism. *Journal of Experimental Social Psychology, 47,* 28–36. doi: 10.1016/j.jesp.2010.08.005

Greitemeyer, T. (2018). The spreading impact of playing violent video games on aggression. *Computers in Human Behavior, 80,* 216–219. doi: 10.1016/j.chb.2017.11.022

Greitemeyer, T. (2019). The contagious impact of playing violent video games on aggression: Longitudinal evidence. *Aggressive Behavior, 45*, 635–642. doi: 10.1002/ab.21857

Greitemeyer, T., & Mügge, D. O. (2014). Video games do affect social outcomes: A meta-analytic review of the effects of violent and prosocial video game play. *Personality and Social Psychology Bulletin, 40*, 578–589. doi: 10.1177/0146167213520459

Greitemeyer, T., & Osswald, S. (2009). Prosocial video games reduce aggressive cognitions. *Journal of Experimental Social Psychology, 45*, 896–900. doi: 10.1016/j.jesp.2009.04.005

Greitemeyer, T., & Sagioglou, C. (2019). The experience of deprivation: Does relative more than absolute status predict hostility? *The British Journal of Social Psychology, 58*, 515–533. doi: 10.1111/bjso.12288

Grimm, P., Kirste, K., & Weiß, J. (2005). *Gewalt zwischen Fakten und Fiktionen: Eine Untersuchung von Gewaltdarstellungen im Fernsehen unter besonderer Berücksichtigung ihres Realitäts- und Fiktionalitätsgrades*. Berlin: Vistas.

Groves, C. L. (2017). Aversive events and aggression. In B. J. Bushman (Ed.), *Aggression and violence: A social psychological perspective* (pp. 139–154). New York: Routledge.

Gubbels, J., van der Stouwe, T., Spruit, A., & Stams, G. J. J. M. (2016). Martial arts participation and externalizing behavior in juveniles: A meta-analytic review. *Aggression and Violent Behavior, 28*, 73–81. doi: 10.1016/j.avb.2016.03.011

Guerra, N. G., Huesmann, L. R., & Spindler, A. (2003). Community violence exposure, social cognition, and aggression among urban elementary school children. *Child Development, 74*, 1561–1576. doi: 10.1111/1467-8624.00623

Hailes, H. P., Yu, R., Danese, A., & Fazel, S. (2019). Long-term outcomes of childhood sexual abuse: an umbrella review. *The Lancet Psychiatry, 6*, 830–839. doi: 10.1016/S2215-0366(19)30286-X

Halbrook, Y. J., O'Donnell, A. T., & Msetfi, R. M. (2019). When and how video games can be good: A review of the positive effects of video games on well-being. *Perspectives on Psychological Science, 14*, 1096–1104. doi: 10.1177/1745691619863807

Hald, G. M., Malamuth, N. M., & Yuen, C. (2010). Pornography and attitudes supporting violence against women: Revisiting the relationship in nonexperimental studies. *Aggressive Behavior, 36*, 14–20. doi: 10.1002/ab.20328

Hald, G. M., Seaman, C., & Linz, D. G. (2014). Sexuality and pornography. In D. L. Tolman, M. Diamond, J. A. Bauermeister, W. H. George, J. G. Pfaus, & L. M. Ward (Eds.), *APA handbook of sexuality and psychology* (pp. 3–35). Washington, DC: American Psychological Association.

Hale, W. W., VanderValk, I., Akse, J., & Meeus, W. (2008). The interplay of early adolescents' depressive symptoms, aggression and perceived parental rejection: A four-year community study. *Journal of Youth and Adolescence, 37,* 928–940. doi: 10.1007/s10964-008-9280-0

Hall, B. J., Saltzman, L. Y., Canetti, D., & Hobfoll, S. E. (2015). A longitudinal investigation of the relationship between posttraumatic stress symptoms and posttraumatic growth in a cohort of Israeli Jews and Palestinians during ongoing violence. *PloS One, 10,* e0124782. doi: 10.1371/journal.pone.0124782

Hall, G. C. N., & Hirschman, R. (1991). Toward a theory of sexual aggression: A quadripartite model. *Journal of Consulting & Clinical Psychology, 59,* 662–669. doi: 10.1037/0022-006X.59.5.662

Hall, G. C. N., Shondrick, D. D., & Hirschman, R. (1993). The role of sexual arousal in sexually aggressive behavior: A meta-analysis. *Journal of Consulting and Clinical Psychology, 61,* 1091–1095. doi: 10.1037/0022-006X.61.6.1091

Halligan, S. L., & Philips, K. J. (2010). Are you thinking what I'm thinking? Peer group similarities in adolescent hostile attribution tendencies. *Developmental Psychology, 46,* 1385–1388. doi: 10.1037/a0020383

Halperin, E., Russell, A. G., Trzesniewski, K. H., Gross, J. J., & Dweck, C. S. (2011). Promoting the Middle East peace process by changing beliefs about group malleability. *Science, 333*(6050), 1767–1769. doi: 10.1126/science.1202925

Halpern, C. T., Udry, J. R., Campbell, B., & Suchindran, C. (1993). Relationships between aggression and pubertal increases in testosterone: A panel analysis of adolescent males. *Biodemography and Social Biology, 40,* 8–24. doi: 10.1080/19485565.1993.9988832

Haninger, K., & Thompson, K. M. (2004). Content and ratings of teen-rated video games. *JAMA: Journal of the American Medical Association, 291,* 856–865. doi: 10.1001/jama.291.7.856

Hanson, K. A., & Gidycz, C. A. (1993). Evaluation of a sexual assault prevention program. *Journal of Consulting and Clinical Psychology, 61,* 1046–1052. doi: 10.1037/0022-006X.61.6.1046

Harding, C. F. (1985). Sociobiological hypotheses about rape: A critical look at the data behind the hypotheses. In S. R. Sunday & E. Tobach (Eds.), *Violence against women: A critique of the sociobiology of rape* (pp. 23–85). New York: Gordian Press.

Harris, M. B. (1974). Mediators between frustration and aggression in a field experiment. *Journal of Experimental Social Psychology, 10,* 561–571. doi: 10.1016/0022-1031(74)90079-1

Harris, P. B., & Houston, J. M. (2010). Recklessness in context: Individual and situational correlates to aggressive driving. *Environment and Behavior, 42,* 44–60. doi: 10.1177/0013916508325234

Hart, W., Richardson, K., & Breeden, C. J. (2019). An interactive model of narcissism, self-esteem, and provocation extent on aggression. *Personality and Individual Differences, 145,* 112–118. doi: 10.1016/j.paid.2019.03.032

Hartmann, T., Krakowiak, K. M., & Tsay-Vogel, M. (2014). How violent video games communicate violence: A literature review and content analysis of moral disengagement factors. *Communication Monographs, 81*, 310–332. doi: 10.1080/03637751.2014.922206

Harwood, A., Lavidor, M., & Rassovsky, Y. (2017). Reducing aggression with martial arts: A meta-analysis of child and youth studies. *Aggression and Violent Behavior, 34*, 96–101. doi: 10.1016/j.avb.2017.03.001

Haskett, M. E., Ahern, L. S., Ward, C. S., & Allaire, J. C. (2006). Factor structure and validity of the Parenting Stress Index-Short Form. *Journal of Clinical Child and Adolescent Psychology, 35*, 302–312. doi: 10.1207/ s15374424jccp3502_14

Hasson, Y., Schori-Eyal, N., Landau, D., Hasler, B. S., Levy, J., Friedman, D., & Halperin, E. (2019). The enemy's gaze: Immersive virtual environments enhance peace promoting attitudes and emotions in violent intergroup conflicts. *PloS One, 14*(9), e0222342. doi: 10.1371/journal. pone.0222342

Hawes, S. W., Perlman, S. B., Byrd, A. L., Raine, A., Loeber, R., & Pardini, D. A. (2016). Chronic anger as a precursor to adult antisocial personality features: The moderating influence of cognitive control. *Journal of Abnormal Psychology, 125*, 64–74. doi: 10.1037/abn0000129

Hay, D. F. (2007). The gradual emergence of sex differences in aggression: Alternative hypotheses. *Psychological Medicine, 37*, 1527– 1537. doi: 10.1017/S0033291707000165

Hay, D. F. (2017). The early development of human aggression. *Child Development Perspectives, 11*, 102–106. doi: 10.1111/cdep.12220

Hay, D. F., Johansen, M. K., Daly, P., Hashmi, S., Robinson, C., Collishaw, S., & Van Goozen, S. M. H. (2018). Seven-year-olds' aggressive choices in a computer game can be predicted in infancy. *Developmental Science, 21*, e12576. doi: 10.1111/desc.12576

Hay, D. F., Perra, O., Hudson, K., Waters, C. S., Mundy, L., Phillips, R., ... Van Goozen, S. M. H. (2010). Identifying early signs of aggression: Psychometric properties of the Cardiff Infant Contentiousness Scale. *Aggressive Behavior, 36*, 351–357. doi: 10.1002/ab.20363

Heinrichs, N., Kliem, S., & Hahlweg, K. (2014). Four-year follow-up of a randomized controlled trial of Triple P group for parent and child outcomes. *Prevention Science, 15*, 233–245. doi: 10.1007/ s11121-012-0358-2

Heise, L. L., & Kotsadam, A. (2015). Cross-national and multilevel correlates of partner violence: an analysis of data from population-based surveys. *The Lancet Global Health, 3*(6), e332–e340. doi: 10.1016/ S2214-109X(15)00013-3

Hellmann, D. F. (2014). *Repräsentativbefragung zu Viktimisierungserfahrungen in Deutschland*: Forschungsbericht No. 122. Retrieved from kfn.de/wp-content/uploads/Forschungsberichte/FB_122.pdf

Hellmann, D. F., Kinninger, M. W., & Kliem, S. (2018). Sexual violence against women in Germany: Prevalence and risk markers. *International Journal of Environmental Research and Public Health, 15*(8). doi: 10.3390/ ijerph15081613

Hemenway, D., & Miller, M. (2000). Firearm availability and homicide rates across 26 high-income countries. *Journal of Trauma, Injury, Infection, and Critical Care, 49*, 985–988. doi: 10.1097/00005373-200012000-00001

Hennessy, D. A. (2017). The role of anger rumination in the frustration-aggression link. In J. F. A. Cruz & R. M. C. Sofia (Eds.), *Anger and anxiety: Predictors, coping strategies, and health effects* (pp. 201–215). New York: Nova Science.

Hennessy, D. A., & Wiesenthal, D. L. (1999). Traffic congestion, driver stress, and driver aggression. *Aggressive Behavior, 25*, 409–423. doi: 10.1002/(SICI)1098-2337(1999)25:6<409::AID-AB2>3.0.CO;2-0

Hennessy, D. A., & Wiesenthal, D. L. (2001). Gender, driver aggression, and driver violence: An applied evaluation. *Sex Roles, 44*, 661–676. doi: 10.1023/A:1012246213617

Hennessy, D. A., & Wiesenthal, D. L. (2002). Aggression, violence, and vengeance among male and female drivers. *Transportation Quarterly, 56*, 65–75.

Hennessy, D. A., Wiesenthal, D. L., & Kohn, P. M. (2000). The influence of traffic congestion, daily hassles, and trait stress susceptibility on state driver stress: An interactive perspective. *Journal of Applied Biobehavioral Research, 5*, 162–179. doi: 10.1111/j.1751-9861.2000.tb00072.x

Hennigan, K., Kolnick, K. A., Vindel, F., & Maxson, C. L. (2015). Targeting youth at risk for gang involvement: Validation of a gang risk assessment to support individualized secondary prevention. *Children and Youth Services Review, 56*, 86–96. doi: 10.1016/j.childyouth.2015.07.002

Henning, M. A., Zhou, C., Adams, P., Moir, F., Hobson, J., Hallett, C., & Webster, C. S. (2017). Workplace harassment among staff in higher education: a systematic review. *Asia Pacific Education Review, 18*, 521–539. doi: 10.1007/s12564-017-9499-0

Henry, N., & Powell, A. (2018). Technology-facilitated sexual violence: A literature review of empirical research. *Trauma, Violence & Abuse, 19*, 195–208. doi: 10.1177/1524838016650189

Henwood, K. S., Chou, S., & Browne, K. D. (2015). A systematic review and meta-analysis on the effectiveness of CBT informed anger management. *Aggression and Violent Behavior, 25*, 280–292. doi: 10.1016/j.avb.2015.09.011

Herek, G. M. (2000). The psychology of sexual prejudice. *Current Directions in Psychological Science, 9*, 19–22. doi: 10.1111/1467-8721.00051

Herek, G. M. (2017). Documenting hate crimes in the United States: Some considerations on data sources. *Psychology of Sexual Orientation and Gender Diversity, 4*, 143–151. doi: 10.1037/sgd0000227

Herek, G. M., Gillis, J. R., & Cogan, J. C. (1999). Psychological sequelae of hate-crime victimization among lesbian, gay, and bisexual adults. *Journal of Consulting and Clinical Psychology, 67*, 945–951. doi: 10.1037/0022-006X.67.6.945

Hershcovis, S. M., & Barling, J. (2010). Towards a multi-foci approach to workplace aggression: A meta-analytic review of outcomes from different perpetrators. *Journal of Organizational Behavior, 31*(1), 24–44. doi: 10.1002/job.621

Herzberg, P. Y. (2003). Faktorstruktur, Gütekriterien und Konstruktvalidität der deutschen Übersetzung des Aggressionsfragebogens von Buss und Perry. *Zeitschrift für Differentielle und Diagnostische Psychologie, 24*, 311–323. doi: 10.1024/0170-1789.24.4.311

Hewstone, M. (1990). The 'ultimate attribution error'? A review of the literature on intergroup causal attribution. *European Journal of Social Psychology, 20*, 311–335. doi: 10.1002/ejsp.2420200404

Hill, C., & Silva, E. (2005). *Drawing the line: Sexual harassment on campus.* Washington, DC: American Association of University Women. Retrieved from http://files.eric.ed.gov/fulltext/ED489850.pdf

Hinde, R. A. (1997). Is war a consequence of human aggression? In S. Feshbach & J. Zagrodzka (Eds.), *Aggression: Biological, developmental, and social perspectives* (pp. 177–183). New York: Plenum Press.

Hines, D. A. (2007). Predictors of sexual coercion against women and men: A multilevel, multinational study of university students. *Archives of Sexual Behavior, 36*, 403–422. doi: 10.1007/s10508-006-9141-4

Hingson, R. W. (2010). Magnitude and prevention of college drinking and related problems. *Alcohol Research & Health, 33*, 45–54.

Hittner, J. B. (2005). How robust is the Werther effect? A re-examination of the suggestion-imitation model of suicide. *Mortality, 10*, 193–200. doi: 10.1080/13576270500178112

Ho, C. S., Wong, S. Y., Chiu, M. M., & Ho, R. C. (2017). Global prevalence of elder abuse: A meta-analysis and meta-regression. *East Asian Archives of Psychiatry, 27*, 43–55.

Hobfoll, S. E., Canetti-Nisim, D., Johnson, R. J., Palmieri, P. A., Varley, J. D., & Galea, S. (2008). The association of exposure, risk, and resiliency factors with PTSD among Jews and Arabs exposed to repeated acts of terrorism in Israel. *Journal of Traumatic Stress, 21*, 9–21. doi: 10.1002/jts.20307

Hobfoll, S. E., Hall, B. J., Canetti-Nisim, D., Galea, S., Johnson, R. J., & Palmieri, P. A. (2007). Refining our understanding of traumatic growth in the face of terrorism: Moving from meaning cognitions to doing what is meaningful. *Applied Psychology, 56*, 345–366. doi: 10.1111/j.1464-0597.2007.00292.x

Hodwitz, O., & Tracy, H. (2019). President Trump's Travel Ban: Inciting or deterring terrorism? *Behavioral Sciences of Terrorism and Political Aggression, 12*, 1–15. doi: 10.1080/19434472.2019.1701525

Hoeffler, A. (2017). What are the costs of violence? *Politics, Philosophy & Economics, 16*, 422–445. doi: 10.1177/1470594X17714270

Hoel, H., Rayner, C., & Cooper, C. L. (1999). Workplace bullying. In C. L. Cooper & I. T. Robertson (Eds.), *International review of industrial and organizational psychology* (pp. 195–230). New York: Wiley.

Hofstede, G. (2013). *Culture's consequences: Comparing values, behaviors, institutions, and organizations across nations* (2nd ed.). Thousand Oaks, CA: Sage.

Holl, A. K., Kirsch, F., Rohlf, H., Krahé, B., & Elsner, B. (2018). Longitudinal reciprocity between theory of mind and aggression in middle childhood. *International Journal of Behavioral Development, 42,* 257–266. doi: 10.1177/0165025417727875

Holt, M. K., Vivolo-Kantor, A., Polanin, J. R., Holland, K. M., DeGue, S., Matjasko, J. L., ... Reid, G. (2015). Bullying and suicidal ideation and behaviors: A meta-analysis. *Pediatrics, 135,* e496–509. doi: 10.1542/peds.2014-1864

Holtzworth-Munroe, A., Meehan, J. C., Herron, K., Rehman, U., & Stuart, G. L. (2000). Testing the Holtzworth-Munroe and Stuart (1994) batterer typology. *Journal of Consulting and Clinical Psychology, 68,* 1000–1019. doi: 10.1037/0022-006X.68.6.1000

Holtzworth-Munroe, A., Meehan, J. C., Herron, K., Rehman, U., & Stuart, G. L. (2003). Do subtypes of maritally violent men continue to differ over time? *Journal of Consulting and Clinical Psychology, 71,* 728–740. doi: 10.1037/0022-006X.71.4.728

Holtzworth-Munroe, A., & Stuart, G. L. (1994). Typologies of male batterers: Three subtypes and the differences among them. *Psychological Bulletin, 116,* 476–497. doi: 10.1037/0033-2909.116.3.476

Home Office (2019). *Hate crime, England and Wales, 2018/19.* Retrieved from www.gov.uk/government/statistics/hate-crime-england-and-wales-2018-to-2019

Houge, A. B. (2015). Sexualized war violence. Knowledge construction and knowledge gaps. *Aggression and Violent Behavior, 25,* 79–87. doi: 10.1016/j.avb.2015.07.009

Houston, J. M., Harris, P. B., & Norman, M. (2003). The aggressive driving behavior scale: Developing a self-report measure of unsafe driving practices. *North American Journal of Psychology, 5,* 269–278.

Hovmand, P. S., Ford, D. N., Flom, I., & Kyriakakis, S. (2009). Victims arrested for domestic violence: Unintended consequences of arrest policies. *System Dynamics Review, 25,* 161–181. doi: 10.1002/sdr.418

Howells, K. (1989). Anger-management methods in relation to the prevention of violent behaviour. In J. Archer & K. D. Browne (Eds.), *Human aggression: Naturalistic approaches* (pp. 153–181). London: Routledge.

Höynck, T., Mößle, T., Kleimann, M., Pfeiffer, C., & Rehbein, F. (2007). *Jugendmedienschutz bei gewalthaltigen Computerspielen: Eine Analyse der USK-Alterseinstufungen.* Forschungsbericht Nr. 101. Hannover: Kriminologisches Forschungsinstitut Niedersachsen. Retrieved from https://kfn.de/wp-content/uploads/Forschungsberichte/FB_101.pdf.

Hsiang, S. M., Meng, K. C., & Cane, M. A. (2011). Civil conflicts are associated with the global climate. *Nature, 476*(7361), 438–441. doi: 10.1038/nature10311

Huang, S., Trapido, E., Fleming, L., Arheart, K., Crandall, L., French, M., ... Prado, G. (2011). The long-term effects of childhood maltreatment experiences on subsequent illicit drug use and drug-related problems in young adulthood. *Addictive Behaviors, 36,* 95–102. doi: 10.1016/j.addbeh.2010.09.001

Hubbard, J. A., McAuliffe, M. D., Morrow, M. T., & Romano, L. J. (2010). Reactive and proactive aggression in childhood and adolescence: Precursors, outcomes, processes, experiences, and measurement. *Journal of Personality, 78,* 95–118. doi: 10.1111/j.1467-6494.2009.00610.x

Hubbard, J. A., Smithmyer, C. M., Ramsden, S. R., Parker, E. H., Flanagan, K. D., Dearing, K. F., … Simons, R. F. (2002). Observational, physiological, and self-report measures of children's anger: Relations to reactive versus proactive aggression. *Child Development, 73,* 1101–1118. doi: 10.1111/1467-8624.00460

Huesmann, L. R. (1998). The role of social information processing and cognitive schema in the acquisition and maintenance of habitual aggressive behavior. In R. G. Geen & E. I. Donnerstein (Eds.), *Human aggression: Theories, research, and implications for social policy* (pp. 73–109). San Diego, CA: Academic Press.

Huesmann, L. R. (2010). Nailing the coffin shut on doubts that violent video games stimulate aggression: Comment on Anderson et al. (2010). *Psychological Bulletin, 136,* 179–181. doi: 10.1037/a0018567

Huesmann, L. R. (2017). An integrative theoretical understanding of aggression. In B. J. Bushman (Ed.), *Aggression and violence: A social psychological perspective* (pp. 3–21). New York: Routledge.

Huesmann, L. R., Dubow, E. F., & Boxer, P. (2009). Continuity of aggression from childhood to early adulthood as a predictor of life outcomes: Implications for the adolescent-limited and life-course-persistent models. *Aggressive Behavior, 35,* 136–149. doi: 10.1002/ab.20300

Huesmann, L. R., Dubow, E. F., & Boxer, P. (2010). How to grow a terrorist without really trying: The psychological development of terrorism from childhood to adulthood. In D. Antonius, A. D. Brown, T. K. Walters, J. M. Ramirez, & S. J. Sinclair (Eds.), *Interdisciplinary analyses of terrorism and political aggression* (pp. 1–21). Newcastle upon Tyne, U.K.: Cambridge Scholars Publishing.

Huesmann, L. R., & Guerra, N. G. (1997). Children's normative beliefs about aggression and aggressive behavior. *Journal of Personality and Social Psychology, 72,* 408–419. doi: 10.1037/0022-3514.72.2.408

Huesmann, L. R., & Kirwil, L. (2007). Why observing violence increases the risk of violent behavior by the observer. In D. J. Flannery, A. T. Vazsonyi, & I. D. Waldman (Eds.), *The Cambridge handbook of violent behavior and aggression* (pp. 545–570). New York: Cambridge University Press.

Huesmann, L. R., Moise-Titus, J., Podolski, C.-L., & Eron, L. D. (2003). Longitudinal relations between children's exposure to TV violence and their aggressive and violent behavior in young adulthood: 1977–1992. *Developmental Psychology, 39,* 201–221. doi: 10.1037/0012-1649.39.2.201

Hull, J. G., Levenson, R. W., Young, R. D., & Sher, K. J. (1983). Self-awareness-reducing effects of alcohol consumption. *Journal of Personality and Social Psychology, 44,* 461–473. doi: 10.1037/0022-3514.44.3.461

Hunt, G. P., & Laidler, K. J. (2001). Alcohol and violence in the lives of gang members. *Alcohol Research & Health, 25,* 66–71.

Hunter, C., & McClelland, K. (1991). Honoring accounts for sexual harassment: A factorial survey analysis. *Sex Roles, 24,* 725–751. doi: 10.1007/BF00288209

Hyatt, C. S., Chester, D. S., Zeichner, A., & Miller, J. D. (2020). Analytic flexibility in laboratory aggression paradigms: Relations with personality traits vary (slightly) by operationalization of aggression. *Aggressive Behavior, 45,* 377–388. doi: 10.1002/ab.21830

Hyatt, C. S., Zeichner, A., & Miller, J. D. (2019). Laboratory aggression and personality traits: A meta-analytic review. *Psychology of Violence, 9,* 675–689. doi: 10.1037/vio0000236

Hyde, J. S. (1984). How large are gender differences in aggression? A developmental meta-analysis. *Developmental Psychology, 20,* 722–736. doi: 10.1037/0012-1649.20.4.722

Institute for Economics & Peace (2019). *Global Terrorism Index 2019: Measuring the impact of terrorism.* Retrieved from http://visionofhumanity.org/reports

Ireland, J. L., Birch, P., & Ireland, C. A. (Eds.) (2018). *The Routledge international handbook of human aggression.* London: Routledge.

Ito, T. A., Miller, N. E., & Pollock, V. E. (1996). Alcohol and aggression: A meta-analysis on the moderating effects of inhibitory cues, triggering events, and self-focused attention. *Psychological Bulletin, 120,* 60–82. doi: 10.1037/0033-2909.120.1.60

Jabr, M. M., Denke, G., Rawls, E., & Lamm, C. (2018). The roles of selective attention and desensitization in the association between video game-play and aggression: An ERP investigation. *Neuropsychologia, 112,* 50–57. doi: 10.1016/j.neuropsychologia.2018.02.026

Jaffe, D. S., & Straus, M. A. (1982). Aggression: Instinct, drive, behavior. *Psychoanalytic Inquiry, 2,* 77–94. doi: 10.1080/07351698209533436

Janoff-Bulman, R. (1979). Characterological versus behavioral self-blame: Inquiries into depression and rape. *Journal of Personality and Social Psychology, 37,* 1798–1809. doi: 10.1037/0022-3514.37.10.1798

Jansen, P. W., Zwirs, B., Verlinden, M., Mieloo, C. L., Jaddoe, V. W. V., Hofman, A., … Tiemeier, H. (2017). Observed and parent-reported conscience in childhood: Relations with bullying involvement in early primary school. *Social Development, 26,* 965–980. doi: 10.1111/sode.12233

Jasko, K., & LaFree, G. (2020). Who is more violent in extremist groups? A comparison of leaders and followers. *Aggressive Behavior, 46,* 141–150. doi: 10.1002/ab.21865

Johnson, R. D., & Downing, L. L. (1979). Deindividuation and valence of cues: Effects on prosocial and antisocial behavior. *Journal of Personality and Social Psychology, 37,* 1532–1538. doi: 10.1037/0022-3514.37.9.1532

Jolliffe, D., Farrington, D. P., Piquero, A. R., MacLeod, J. F., & van de Weijer, S. (2017). Prevalence of life-course-persistent, adolescence-limited, and late-onset offenders: A systematic review of prospective longitudinal studies. *Aggression and Violent Behavior, 33,* 4–14. doi: 10.1016/j.avb.2017.01.002

Jones, J. W. (1978). Adverse emotional reactions of nonsmokers to secondary cigarette smoke. *Environmental Psychology & Nonverbal Behavior, 3,* 125–127.

Jones, K. P., Sabat, I. E., King, E. B., Ahmad, A., McCausland, T. C., & Chen, T. (2017). Isms and schisms: A meta-analysis of the prejudice-discrimination relationship across racism, sexism, and ageism. *Journal of Organizational Behavior, 38,* 1076–1110. doi: 10.1002/job.2187

Jones, R. T., Browne, K. D., & Chou, S. (2017). A critique of the revised Conflict Tactics Scales-2 (CTS-2). *Aggression and Violent Behavior, 37,* 83–90. doi: 10.1016/j.avb.2017.08.005

Jones, S. E., Miller, J. D., & Lynam, D. R. (2011). Personality, antisocial behavior, and aggression: A meta-analytic review. *Journal of Criminal Justice, 39,* 329–337. doi: 10.1016/j.jcrimjus.2011.03.004

Jones, S. M., Brown, J. L., & Aber, J. L. (2011). Two-year impacts of a universal school-based social-emotional and literacy intervention: An experiment in translational developmental research. *Child Development, 82,* 533–554. doi: 10.1111/j.1467-8624.2010.01560.x

Jones, T. S., & Remland, M. S. (1992). Sources of variability in perceptions of and responses to sexual harassment. *Sex Roles, 27,* 121–142. doi: 10.1007/BF00290013

Jonker, I. E., Sijbrandij, M., van Luijtelaar, M. J. A., Cuijpers, P., & Wolf, J. R. L. M. (2015). The effectiveness of interventions during and after residence in women's shelters: A meta-analysis. *European Journal of Public Health, 25,* 15–19. doi: 10.1093/eurpub/cku092

Juhl, J., & Routledge, C. (2016). Putting the terror in terror management theory. *Current Directions in Psychological Science, 25,* 99–103. doi: 10.1177/0963721415625218

Jung, J., Busching, R., & Krahé, B. (2019). Catching aggression from one's peers: A longitudinal and multilevel analysis. *Social and Personality Psychology Compass, 13,* e12433. doi: 10.1111/spc3.12433

Jung, J., Krahé, B., Bondü, R., Esser, G., & Wyschkon, A. (2018). Dynamic progression of antisocial behavior in childhood and adolescence: A three-wave longitudinal study from Germany. *Applied Developmental Science, 22,* 74–88. doi: 10.1080/10888691.2016.1219228

Kalmoe, N. P. (2015). Trait aggression in two representative U.S. Surveys: Testing the generalizability of college samples. *Aggressive Behavior, 41,* 171–188. doi: 10.1002/ab.21547

Karakurt, G., Koç, E., Çetinsaya, E. E., Ayluçtarhan, Z., & Bolen, S. (2019). Meta-analysis and systematic review for the treatment of perpetrators of intimate partner violence. *Neuroscience and Biobehavioral Reviews, 105,* 220–230. doi: 10.1016/j.neubiorev.2019.08.006

Karp, A. (2018). *Estimating global civilian-held firearms numbers.* Retrieved from www.smallarmssurvey.org/fileadmin/docs/T-Briefing-Papers/SAS-BP-Civilian-Firearms-Numbers.pdf

Karr, J. E., Areshenkoff, C. N., Rast, P., Hofer, S. M., Iverson, G. L., & Garcia-Barrera, M. A. (2018). The unity and diversity of executive functions: A systematic review and re-analysis of latent variable studies. *Psychological Bulletin, 144*, 1147–1185. doi: 10.1037/bul0000160

Katz-Wise, S. L., & Hyde, J. S. (2012). Victimization experiences of lesbian, gay, and bisexual individuals: A meta-analysis. *Journal of Sex Research, 49*, 142–167. doi: 10.1080/00224499.2011.637247

Kazdin, A. E. (2011). Conceptualizing the challenge of reducing interpersonal violence. *Psychology of Violence, 1*, 166–187. doi: 10.1037/a0022990

Kazemeini, T., Ghanbari-e-Hashem-Abadi, B., & Safarzadeh, A. (2013). Mindfulness based cognitive group therapy vs cognitive behavioral group therapy as a treatment for driving anger and aggression in Iranian taxi drivers. *Psychology, 4*, 638–644. doi: 10.4236/psych.2013.48091

Keenan, K., Wroblewski, K., Hipwell, A., Loeber, R., & Stouthamer-Loeber, M. (2010). Age of onset, symptom threshold, and expansion of the nosology of conduct disorder for girls. *Journal of Abnormal Psychology, 119*, 689–698. doi: 10.1037/a0019346

Kelley, E. L., & Gidycz, C. A. (2017). Mediators of the relationship between sexual assault and sexual functioning difficulties among college women. *Psychology of Violence, 7*, 574–582. doi: 10.1037/vio0000073

Kelly, J. B., & Johnson, M. P. (2008). Differentiation among types of intimate partner violence: Research update and implications for interventions. *Family Court Review, 46*, 476–499. doi: 10.1111/j.1744-1617.2008.00215.x

Kendall-Tackett, K. A., & Marshall, R. (1998). Sexual victimization of children: Incest and child sexual abuse. In R. K. Bergen (Ed.), *Issues in intimate violence* (pp. 47–63). Thousand Oaks, CA: Sage.

Kendall-Tackett, K. A., Williams, L. M., & Finkelhor, D. (1993). Impact of sexual abuse on children: A review and synthesis of recent empirical studies. *Psychological Bulletin, 113*, 164–180. doi: 10.1037/0033-2909.113.1.164

Kettrey, H. H., & Marx, R. A. (2019). The effects of bystander programs on the prevention of sexual assault across the college years: A systematic review and meta-analysis. *Journal of Youth and Adolescence, 48*, 212–227. doi: 10.1007/s10964-018-0927-1

Khan, R. (2018). Attitudes towards 'honor' violence and killings in collectivist cultures. In J. L. Ireland, P. Birch, & C. A. Ireland (Eds.), *The Routledge international handbook of human aggression* (pp. 216–226). London: Routledge.

Killer, B., Bussey, K., Hawes, D., & Hunt, C. (2019). A meta-analysis of the relationship between moral disengagement and bullying roles in youth. *Aggressive Behavior, 45*, 450–462. doi: 10.1002/ab.21833

Kimber, M., Adham, S., Gill, S., McTavish, J., & MacMillan, H. L. (2018). The association between child exposure to intimate partner violence (IPV) and perpetration of IPV in adulthood-A systematic review. *Child Abuse & Neglect, 76*, 273–286. doi: 10.1016/j.chiabu.2017.11.007

Kimble, N. B., Russo, S. A., Bergman, B. G., & Galindo, V. H. (2010). Revealing an empirical understanding of aggression and violent behavior in athletics. *Aggression and Violent Behavior, 15,* 446–462. doi: 10.1016/j.avb.2010.08.001

King, A. R., Kuhn, S. K., Strege, C., Russell, T. D., & Kolander, T. (2019). Revisiting the link between childhood sexual abuse and adult sexual aggression. *Child Abuse & Neglect, 94,* 104022. doi: 10.1016/j.chiabu.2019.104022

King, A. R., & Russell, T. D. (2019). Lifetime acts of violence assessment (LAVA) predictors of laboratory aggression. *Aggressive Behavior, 45,* 477–488. doi: 10.1002/ab.21835

King, M., Noor, H., & Taylor, D. M. (2011). Normative support for terrorism: The attitudes and beliefs of immediate relatives of Jema'ah Islamiyah members. *Studies in Conflict & Terrorism, 34,* 402–417. doi: 10.1080/1057610X.2011.561471

King, R. D., Messner, S. F., & Baller, R. D. (2009). Contemporary hate crimes, law enforcement, and the legacy of racial violence. *American Sociological Review, 74,* 291–315. doi: 10.1177/000312240907400207

Kingston, L., & Prior, M. (1995). The development of patterns of stable, transient, and school-age onset aggressive behavior in young children. *Journal of the American Academy of Child & Adolescent Psychiatry, 34,* 348–358. doi: 10.1097/00004583-199503000-00021

Kirsch, F., Busching, R., Rohlf, H., & Krahé, B. (2019). Using behavioral observation for the longitudinal study of anger regulation in middle childhood. *Applied Developmental Science, 25,* 105–118. doi: 10.1080/10888691.2017.1325325

Kitzmann, K. M., Gaylord, N. K., Holt, A. R., & Kenny, E. D. (2003). Child witnesses to domestic violence: A meta-analytic review. *Journal of Consulting and Clinical Psychology, 71,* 339–352. doi: 10.1037/0022-006X.71.2.339

Kivisto, A. J., & Swan, S. A. (2013). Rorschach measures of aggression: A laboratory-based validity study. *Journal of Personality Assessment, 95,* 38–45. doi: 10.1080/00223891.2012.713882

Klasios, J. (2019). Aggression among men: An integrated evolutionary explanation. *Aggression and Violent Behavior, 47,* 29–45. doi: 10.1016/j.avb.2019.02.015

Kleck, G. (2019). Regulating guns among young adults. *American Journal of Criminal Justice, 44,* 689–704. doi: 10.1007/s12103-019-09476-6

Klein Tuente, S., Bogaerts, S., & Veling, W. (2019). Hostile attribution bias and aggression in adults - a systematic review. *Aggression and Violent Behavior, 46,* 66–81. doi: 10.1016/j.avb.2019.01.009

Klinesmith, J., Kasser, T., & McAndrew, F. T. (2006). Guns, testosterone, and aggression: An experimental test of a mediational hypothesis. *Psychological Science, 17,* 568–571. doi: 10.1111/j.1467-9280.2006.01745.x

Klippenstine, M. A., & Schuller, R. (2012). Perceptions of sexual assault: expectancies regarding the emotional response of a rape victim over time. *Psychology, Crime & Law, 18*, 79–94. doi: 10.1080/1068316X.2011.589389

Kljakovic, M., & Hunt, C. (2016). A meta-analysis of predictors of bullying and victimisation in adolescence. *Journal of Adolescence, 49*, 134–145. doi: 10.1016/j.adolescence.2016.03.002

Klomek, A. B., Sourander, A., Niemelä, S., Kumpulainen, K., Piha, J., Tamminen, T., ... Gould, M. S. (2009). Childhood bullying behaviors as a risk for suicide attempts and completed suicides: A population-based birth cohort study. *Journal of the American Academy of Child & Adolescent Psychiatry, 48*, 254–261. doi: 10.1097/CHI.0b013e318196b91f

Klump, M. C. (2006). Posttraumatic stress disorder and sexual assault in women. *Journal of College Student Psychotherapy, 21*, 67–83. doi: 10.1300/J035v21n02_07

Knight, G. P., Fabes, R. A., & Higgins, D. A. (1996). Concerns about drawing causal inferences from meta-analyses: An example in the study of gender differences in aggression. *Psychological Bulletin, 119*, 410–421. doi: 10.1037/0033-2909.119.3.410

Knight, N. M., Dahlen, E. R., Bullock-Yowell, E., & Madson, M. B. (2018). The HEXACO model of personality and Dark Triad in relational aggression. *Personality and Individual Differences, 122*, 109–114. doi: 10.1016/j.paid.2017.10.016

Knight, R. A., & Sims-Knight, J. E. (2004). Testing an etiological model for male juvenile sexual offending against females. *Journal of Child Sexual Abuse, 13*, 33–55. doi: 10.1300/J070v13n03_03

Knopov, A., Sherman, R. J., Raifman, J. R., Larson, E., & Siegel, M. (2019). Household gun ownership and youth suicide rates at the state level, 2005-2015. *American Journal of Preventive Medicine, 56*, 335–342. doi: 10.1016/j.amepre.2018.10.027

Knutson, J. F., Lawrence, E., Taber, S. M., Bank, L., & DeGarmo, D. S. (2009). Assessing children's exposure to intimate partner violence. *Clinical Child and Family Psychology Review, 12*, 157–173. doi: 10.1007/s10567-009-0048-1

Kokko, K., Pulkkinen, L., Huesmann, L. R., Dubow, E. F., & Boxer, P. (2009). Intensity of aggression in childhood as a predictor of different forms of adult aggression: A two-country (Finland and the United States) analysis. *Journal of Research on Adolescence, 19*, 9–34. doi: 10.1111/j.1532-7795.2009.00579.x

Koss, M. P., Abbey, A., Campbell, R., Cook, S. L., Norris, J., Testa, M., ... White, J. W. (2007). Revising the SES: A collaborative process to improve assessment of sexual aggression and victimization. *Psychology of Women Quarterly, 31*, 357–370. doi: 10.1111/j.1471-6402.2007.00385.x

Koss, M. P., Abbey, A., Campbell, R., Cook, S. L., Norris, J., Testa, M., ... White, J. W. (2008). Revising the SES: A collaborative process to improve assessment of sexual aggression and victimization: Erratum. *Psychology of Women Quarterly, 32*, 493. doi: 10.1111/j.1471-6402.2008.00468.x

Koss, M. P., Gidycz, C. A., & Wisniewski, N. (1987). The scope of rape: Incidence and prevalence of sexual aggression and victimization in a national sample of higher education students. *Journal of Consulting and Clinical Psychology, 55,* 162–170. doi: 10.1037/0022-006X.55.2.162

Koss, M. P., & Oros, C. J. (1982). Sexual Experiences Survey: A research instrument investigating sexual aggression and victimization. *Journal of Consulting and Clinical Psychology, 50,* 455–457. doi: 10.1037/0022-006X.50.3.455

Kowalski, R. M. (2018). Cyberbullying. In J. L. Ireland, P. Birch, & C. A. Ireland (Eds.), *The Routledge international handbook of human aggression* (pp. 131–142). London: Routledge.

Kowalski, R. M., Giumetti, G. W., Schroeder, A. N., & Lattanner, M. R. (2014). Bullying in the digital age: A critical review and meta-analysis of cyberbullying research among youth. *Psychological Bulletin, 140,* 1073–1137. doi: 10.1037/a0035618

Kowalski, R. M., Toth, A., & Morgan, M. (2018). Bullying and cyberbullying in adulthood and the workplace. *The Journal of Social Psychology, 158,* 64–81. doi: 10.1080/00224545.2017.1302402

Koyanagi, A., Oh, H., Carvalho, A. F., Smith, L., Haro, J. M., Vancampfort, D., ... DeVylder, J. E. (2019). Bullying victimization and suicide attempt among adolescents aged 12–15 years from 48 countries. *Journal of the American Academy of Child and Adolescent Psychiatry, 58,* 907–918. doi: 10.1016/j.jaac.2018.10.018

Krafka, C., & Penrod, S. (1997). Women's reactions to sexually aggressive mass media depictions. *Violence Against Women, 3,* 149–181. doi: 10.1177/1077801297003002004

Krahé, B. (1991). Police officers' definitions of rape: A prototype study. *Journal of Community & Applied Social Psychology, 1,* 223–244. doi: 10.1002/casp.2450010305

Krahé, B. (1992). *Personality and social psychology: Towards a synthesis.* London: Sage.

Krahé, B. (1998). Sexual aggression among adolescents: Prevalence and predictors in a German sample. *Psychology of Women Quarterly, 22,* 537–554. doi: 10.1111/%28ISSN%291471-6402

Krahé, B. (2005). Predictors of women's aggressive driving behavior. *Aggressive Behavior, 31,* 537–546. doi: 10.1002/ab.20070

Krahé, B. (2016). Societal responses to sexual violence against women: Rape myths and the "real rape" stereotype. In H. Kury, S. Redo, & E. Shea (Eds.), *Women and children as victims and offenders* (pp. 671–700). New York: Springer.

Krahé, B. (2018a). Gendered self-concept and the aggressive expression of driving anger: Positive femininity buffers negative masculinity. *Sex Roles, 79,* 98–108. doi: 10.1007/s11199-017-0853-9

Krahé, B. (2018b). Men's violence against female partners: The role of culture. In T. K. Shackelford & V. A. Weekes-Shackelford (Eds.), *Encyclopedia of evolutionary psychological science* (Vol. 10, pp. 1–8). New York: Springer.

Krahé, B. (2020). Risk factors for the development of aggressive behavior from middle childhood to adolescence: The interaction of person and environment. *Current Directions in Psychological Science, 29*, 333–339. doi: 10.1177/0963721420917721

Krahé, B., & Berger, A. (2005). Sex differences in relationship aggression among young adults in Germany. *Sex Roles, 52*, 829–838. doi: 10.1007/s11199-005-4202-z

Krahé, B., & Berger, A. (2013). Men and women as perpetrators and victims of sexual aggression in heterosexual and same-sex encounters: A study of first-year college students in Germany. *Aggressive Behavior, 39*, 391–404. doi: 10.1002/ab.21482

Krahé, B., & Berger, A. (2017). Gendered pathways from child sexual abuse to sexual aggression victimization and perpetration in adolescence and young adulthood. *Child Abuse & Neglect, 63*, 261–272. doi: 10.1016/j.chiabu.2016.10.004

Krahé, B., Berger, A., Vanwesenbeeck, I., Bianchi, G., Chliaoutakis, J., Fernández-Fuertes, A. A., ... Zygadło, A. (2015). Prevalence and correlates of young people's sexual aggression perpetration and victimisation in 10 European countries: A multi-level analysis. *Culture, Health & Sexuality, 17*, 682–699. doi: 10.1080/13691058.2014.989265

Krahé, B., & Bieneck, S. (2012). The effect of music-induced mood on aggressive affect, cognition, and behavior. *Journal of Applied Social Psychology, 42*, 271–290. doi: 10.1111/j.1559-1816.2011.00887.x

Krahé, B., Bieneck, S., & Möller, I. (2005). Understanding gender and intimate partner violence from an international perspective. *Sex Roles, 52*, 807–827. doi: 10.1007/s11199-005-4201-0

Krahé, B., Bieneck, S., & Scheinberger-Olwig, R. (2007). The role of sexual scripts in sexual aggression and victimization. *Archives of Sexual Behavior, 36*, 687–701. doi: 10.1007/s10508-006-9131-6

Krahé, B., Bondü, R., Höse, A., & Esser, G. (2015). Child aggression as a source and a consequence of parenting stress: A three-wave longitudinal study. *Journal of Research on Adolescence, 25*, 328–339. doi: 10.1111/jora.12115

Krahé, B., & Busching, R. (2015). Breaking the vicious cycle of media violence use and aggression: A test of intervention effects over 30 months. *Psychology of Violence, 5*, 217–226. doi: 10.1037/a0036627

Krahé, B., Busching, R., & Möller, I. (2012). Media violence use and aggression among German adolescents: Associations and trajectories of change in a three-wave longitudinal study. *Psychology of Popular Media Culture, 1*, 152–166. doi: 10.1037/a0028663

Krahé, B., & Fenske, I. (2002). Predicting aggressive driving behavior: The role of macho personality, age, and power of car. *Aggressive Behavior, 28*, 21–29. doi: 10.1002/ab.90003

Krahé, B., Haas, S. de, Vanwesenbeeck, I., Bianchi, G., Chliaoutakis, J., Fuertes, A., ... Zygadło, A. (2016). Interpreting survey questions about sexual aggression in cross-cultural research: A qualitative study with young adults from nine European countries. *Sexuality & Culture, 20*, 1–23. doi: 10.1007/s12119-015-9321-2

Krahé, B., & Knappert, L. (2009). A group-randomized evaluation of a theatre-based sexual abuse prevention programme for primary school children in Germany. *Journal of Community & Applied Social Psychology, 19*, 321–329. doi: 10.1002/casp.1009

Krahé, B., Lutz, J., & Sylla, I. (2018). Lean back and relax: Reclined seating position buffers the effect of frustration on anger and aggression. *European Journal of Social Psychology, 48*, 718–723. doi: 10.1002/ejsp.2363

Krahé, B., & Möller, I. (2011). Links between self-reported media violence exposure and teacher ratings of aggression and prosocial behavior among German adolescents. *Journal of Adolescence, 34*, 279–287. doi: 10.1016/j.adolescence.2010.05.003

Krahé, B., Möller, I., Huesmann, L. R., Kirwil, L., Felber, J., & Berger, A. (2011). Desensitization to media violence: Links with habitual media violence exposure, aggressive cognitions, and aggressive behavior. *Journal of Personality and Social Psychology, 100*, 630–646. doi: 10.1037/a0021711

Krahé, B., Scheinberger-Olwig, R., & Bieneck, S. (2003). Men's reports of nonconsensual sexual interactions with women: Prevalence and impact. *Archives of Sexual Behavior, 32*, 165–175. doi: 10.1023/A:1022456626538

Krahé, B., Scheinberger-Olwig, R., & Kolpin, S. (2000). Ambiguous communication of sexual intentions as a risk marker of sexual aggression. *Sex Roles, 42*, 313–337.

Krahé, B., Scheinberger-Olwig, R., & Schütze, S. (2001). Risk factors of sexual aggression and victimization among homosexual men. *Journal of Applied Social Psychology, 31*, 1385–1408. doi: 10.1111/j.1559-1816.2001.tb02679.x

Krahé, B., Scheinberger-Olwig, R., Waizenhöfer, E., & Kolpin, S. (1999). Childhood sexual abuse and revictimization in adolescence. *Child Abuse and Neglect, 23*, 383–394. doi: 10.1016/S0145-2134(99)00002-2

Krahé, B., Waizenhöfer, E., & Möller, I. (2003). Women's sexual aggression against men: Prevalence and predictors. *Sex Roles, 49*, 219–232. doi: 10.1023/A:1024648106477

Krause, K. H., Woofter, R., Haardörfer, R., Windle, M., Sales, J. M., & Yount, K. M. (2019). Measuring campus sexual assault and culture: A systematic review of campus climate surveys. *Psychology of Violence, 9*, 611–622. doi: 10.1037/vio0000209

Kretschmar, J. M., & Flannery, D. J. (2007). Substance use and violent behavior. In D. J. Flannery, A. T. Vazsonyi, & I. D. Waldman (Eds.), *The Cambridge handbook of violent behavior and aggression* (pp. 647–663). New York: Cambridge University Press.

Krug, E. G., Dahlberg, L. L., Mercy, J. A., Zwi, A. B., & Lozano, R. (2002). *World report on violence and health*. Geneva: World Health Organization. Retrieved from http://whqlibdoc.who.int/hq/2002/9241545615.pdf

Kruglanski, A. W., Chen, X., Dechesne, M., Fishman, S., & Orehek, E. (2009). Fully committed: Suicide bombers' motivation and the quest

for personal significance. *Political Psychology, 30,* 331–357. doi: 10.1111/
j.1467-9221.2009.00698.x

Kruglanski, A. W., & Fishman, S. (2009). The psychology of terrorism:
'Syndrome' versus 'tool' perspectives. In J. Victoroff, & A. W. Kruglanski
(Eds.), *Psychology of terrorism: Classic and contemporary insights* (pp. 35–
53). New York: Psychology Press.

Kruglanski, A. W., Gelfand, M. J., Bélanger, J. J., Sheveland, A., Hetiarachchi,
M., & Gunaratna, R. (2014). The psychology of radicalization and
deradicalization: How significance quest impacts violent extremism.
Political Psychology, 35, 69–93. doi: 10.1111/pops.12163

Kteily, N., & Bruneau, E. (2017). Darker demons of our nature: The need
to (re)focus attention on blatant forms of dehumanization. *Current
Directions in Psychological Science, 26,* 487–494. doi: 10.1177/096372141
7708230

Kteily, N., Bruneau, E., Waytz, A., & Cotterill, S. (2015). The ascent of
man: Theoretical and empirical evidence for blatant dehumanization.
Journal of Personality and Social Psychology, 109, 901–931. doi: 10.1037/
pspp0000048

La Matina, G. (2017). *Domestic violence and childhood exposure to armed conflict: Attitudes and experiences.* Retrieved from www.hicn.org/wordpress/
wp-content/uploads/2012/06/HiCN-WP255.pdf

Labella, M. H., & Masten, A. S. (2017). Family influences on aggression and
violence. In B. J. Bushman (Ed.), *Aggression and violence: A social psychological perspective* (pp. 74–89). New York: Routledge.

LaFree, G., Morris, N. A., & Dugan, L. (2010). Cross-national patterns of
terrorism: Comparing trajectories for total, attributed and fatal attacks,
1970–2006. *British Journal of Criminology, 50,* 622–649. doi: 10.1093/
bjc/azp066

Lahm, K. F. (2008). Inmate-on-inmate assault: A multilevel examination of
prison violence. *Criminal Justice and Behavior, 35,* 120–137. doi: 10.1177/
0093854807308730

Lajunen, T., & Parker, D. (2001). Are aggressive people aggressive drivers?
A study of the relationship between self-reported general aggressiveness,
driver anger and aggressive driving. *Accident Analysis and Prevention, 33,*
243–255. doi: 10.1016/S0001-4575(00)00039-7

Lalumière, M. L., Harris, G. T., Quinsey, V. L., & Rice, M. E. (2005).
Antisociality and mating effort. In M. L. Lalumière, G. T. Harris, V. L.
Quinsey, & M. E. Rice (Eds.), *The causes of rape: Understanding indi-
vidual differences in male propensity for sexual aggression* (pp. 61–103).
Washington, DC: American Psychological Association.

Lamarche, V. M., & Seery, M. D. (2019). Come on, give it to me baby: Self-
esteem, narcissism, and endorsing sexual coercion following social rejection. *Personality and Individual Differences, 149,* 315–325. doi: 10.1016/
j.paid.2019.05.060

Lambe, S., Hamilton-Giachritsis, C., Garner, E., & Walker, J. (2018). The role
of Narcissism in aggression and violence: A systematic review. *Trauma,
Violence & Abuse, 19,* 209–230. doi: 10.1177/1524838016650190

Lampe, K. G., Mulder, E. A., Colins, O. F., & Vermeiren, R. R.J.M. (2017). The inter-rater reliability of observing aggression: A systematic literature review. *Aggression and Violent Behavior, 37*, 12–25. doi: 10.1016/j.avb.2017.08.001

Land, K. C., Teske, R. H., & Zheng, H. (2009). The short-term effects of executions on homicides: Deterrence, displacement, or both. *Criminology, 47*, 1009–1043. doi: 10.1111/j.1745-9125.2009.00168.x

Landmann, H., Gaschler, R., & Rohmann, A. (2019). What is threatening about refugees? Identifying different types of threat and their association with emotional responses and attitudes towards refugee migration. *European Journal of Social Psychology, 49*, 1401–1420. doi: 10.1002/ejsp.2593

Langhinrichsen-Rohling, J., Foubert, J. D., Brasfield, H. M., Hill, B., & Shelley-Tremblay, S. (2011). The Men's Program: Does it impact college men's self-reported bystander efficacy and willingness to intervene? *Violence Against Women, 17*, 743–759. doi: 10.1177/1077801211409728

Langley, T., O'Neal, E. C., Craig, K. M., & Yost, E. A. (1992). Aggression-consistent, -inconsistent, and -irrelevant priming effects on selective exposure to media violence. *Aggressive Behavior, 18*, 349–356. doi: 10.1002/1098-2337(1992)18:5<349::AID-AB2480180504>3.0.CO;2-A

Langmann, C. (2012). Canadian firearms legislation and effects on homicide 1974 to 2008. *Journal of Interpersonal Violence, 27*, 2303–2321. doi: 10.1177/0886260511433515

Lankford, A. (2010). Do suicide terrorists exhibit clinically suicidal risk factors? A review of initial evidence and call for future research. *Aggression and Violent Behavior, 15*, 334–340. doi: 10.1016/j.avb.2010.06.001

Lansford, J. E., Malone, P. S., Dodge, K. A., Pettit, G. S., & Bates, J. E. (2010). Developmental cascades of peer rejection, social information processing biases, and aggression during middle childhood. *Development and Psychopathology, 22*, 593–602. doi: 10.1017/S0954579410000301

Lansford, J. E., Miller-Johnson, S., Berlin, L. J., Dodge, K. A., Bates, J. E., & Pettit, G. S. (2007). Early physical abuse and later violent delinquency: A prospective longitudinal study. *Child Maltreatment, 12*, 233–245. doi: 10.1177/1077559507301841

Larimer, M. E., Lydum, A. R., Anderson, B. K., & Turner, A. P. (1999). Male and female recipients of unwanted sexual contact in a college student sample: Prevalence rates, alcohol use, and depression symptoms. *Sex Roles, 40*, 295–308. doi: 10.1023/A:1018807223378

Larrick, R. P., Timmerman, T. A., Carton, A. M., & Abrevaya, J. (2011). Temper, temperature, and temptation: Heat-related retaliation in baseball. *Psychological Science, 22*, 423–428. doi: 10.1177/0956797611399292

Larsen, S. E., Nye, C. D., & Fitzgerald, L. F. (2019). Sexual harassment expanded: An examination of the relationships among sexual harassment, sex discrimination, and aggression in the workplace. *Military Psychology, 31*, 35–44. doi: 10.1080/08995605.2018.1526526

Larson, M., Vaughn, M. G., Salas-Wright, C. P., & DeLisi, M. (2015). Narcissism, low self-control, and violence among a nationally representative sample. *Criminal Justice and Behavior, 42,* 644–661. doi: 10.1177/0093854814553097

Laskey, P., Bates, E. A., & Taylor, J. C. (2019). A systematic literature review of intimate partner violence victimisation: An inclusive review across gender and sexuality. *Aggression and Violent Behavior, 47,* 1–11. doi: 10.1016/j.avb.2019.02.014

Latané, B., & Darley, J. M. (1970). *The unresponsive bystander: Why doesn't he help?* New York: Appleton Century Crofts.

Lawrence, C., & Andrews, K. (2004). The influence of perceived prison crowding on male inmates' perception of aggressive events. *Aggressive Behavior, 30,* 273–283. doi: 10.1002/ab.20024

Lawton, R., Parker, D., Manstead, A. S. R., & Stradling, S. G. (1997). The role of affect in predicting social behaviors: The case of road traffic violations. *Journal of Applied Social Psychology, 27,* 1258–1276. doi: 10.1111/j.1559-1816.1997.tb01805.x

Leach, L. S., Poyser, C., & Butterworth, P. (2017). Workplace bullying and the association with suicidal ideation/thoughts and behaviour: A systematic review. *Occupational and Environmental Medicine, 74,* 72–79. doi: 10.1136/oemed-2016-103726

Leader, T., Mullen, B., & Abrams, D. (2007). Without mercy: The immediate impact of group size on lynch mob atrocity. *Personality and Social Psychology Bulletin, 33,* 1340–1352. doi: 10.1177/0146167207303951

Leander, N. P., & Chartrand, T. L. (2017). On thwarted goals and displaced aggression: A compensatory competence model. *Journal of Experimental Social Psychology, 72,* 88–100. doi: 10.1016/j.jesp.2017.04.010

Leander, N. P., Stroebe, W., Kreienkamp, J., Agostini, M., Gordijn, E., & Kruglanski, A. W. (2019). Mass shootings and the salience of guns as means of compensation for thwarted goals. *Journal of Personality and Social Psychology, 116,* 704–723. doi: 10.1037/pspa0000150

Leary, M. R., Kowalski, R. M., Smith, L., & Phillips, S. (2003). Teasing, rejection, and violence: Case studies of the school shootings. *Aggressive Behavior, 29,* 202–214. doi: 10.1002/ab.10061

Leary, M. R., Tambor, E. S., Terdal, S. K., & Downs, D. L. (1995). Self-esteem as an interpersonal monitor: The sociometer hypothesis. *Journal of Personality and Social Psychology, 68,* 518–530. doi: 10.1037/0022-3514.68.3.518

Le Bon, G. (1908). *The crowd: A study of the popular mind.* London: Fisher Unwin.

Lee, H. Y., & Lightfoot, E. (2014). The culture-embedded social problem of elder mistreatment: A review of international literature on Asian elders. *Journal of Aggression, Maltreatment & Trauma, 23,* 5–19. doi: 10.1080/10926771.2014.864743

Lehrner, A., & Allen, N. E. (2014). Construct validity of the Conflict Tactics Scales: A mixed-method investigation of women's intimate partner violence. *Psychology of Violence, 4,* 477–490. doi: 10.1037/a0037404

Leibman, M. (1970). The effects of sex and race norms on personal space. *Environment and Behavior, 2*, 208–246. doi: 10.1177/001391657000200205

Lemerise, E. A., & Arsenio, W. F. (2000). An integrated model of emotion processes and cognition in social information processing. *Child Development, 71*, 107–118. doi: 10.1111/1467-8624.00124

Lemmer, G., Gollwitzer, M., & Banse, R. (2015). On the psychometric properties of the aggressiveness-IAT for children and adolescents. *Aggressive Behavior, 41*, 84–95. doi: 10.1002/ab.21575

Lenhart, A., Kahne, J., Middaugh, E., Macgill, A. R., Evans, C., & Vitak, J. (2008). *Teens, video games, and civics.* Retrieved from http://pewinternet.org/~/media//Files/Reports/2008/PIP_Teens_Games_and_Civics_Report_FINAL.pdf.pdf

Lenhart, A., & Macgill, A. R. (2008). *Over half of American adults play video games, and four out of five young adults play.* Retrieved from www.pewinternet.org/~/media//Files/Reports/2008/PIP_Adult_gaming_memo.pdf.pdf

Lenington, S. (1985). Sociobiological theory and the violent abuse of women. In S. R. Sunday & E. Tobach (Eds.), *Violence against women: A critique of the sociobiology of rape* (pp. 13–22). New York: Gordian Press.

Lennings, B. H. I., & Warburton, W. A. (2011). The effect of auditory versus visual violent media exposure on aggressive behaviour: The role of song lyrics, video clips and musical tone. *Journal of Experimental Social Psychology, 47*, 794–799. doi: 10.1016/j.jesp.2011.02.006

Leonard, K. E. (1989). The impact of explicit aggressive and implicit nonaggressive cues on aggression in intoxicated and sober males. *Personality and Social Psychology Bulletin, 15*, 390–400. doi: 10.1177/0146167289153009

Leonard, K. E., Collins, R. L., & Quigley, B. M. (2003). Alcohol consumption and the occurrence and severity of aggression: An event-based analysis of male to male barroom violence. *Aggressive Behavior, 29*, 346–365. doi: 10.1002/ab.10075

Leonard, K. E., & Roberts, L. J. (1998). The effects of alcohol on the marital interactions of aggressive and nonaggressive husbands and their wives. *Journal of Abnormal Psychology, 107*, 602–615. doi: 10.1037/0021-843X.107.4.602

Leone, R. M., & Parrott, D. J. (2018). Hegemonic masculinity and aggression. In J. L. Ireland, P. Birch, & C. A. Ireland (Eds.), *The Routledge international handbook of human aggression* (pp. 31–42). London: Routledge.

Levesque, R. J. R. (2011). Justice responses to child abuse and maltreatment. In M. P. Koss, J. W. White, & A. E. Kazdin (Eds.), *Violence against women and children* (pp. 47–69). Washington, DC: American Psychological Association.

Levi, E., & Bachar, E. (2019). The moderating role of narcissism on the relationship between posttraumatic growth and PTSD symptoms.

Personality and Individual Differences, 138, 292–297. doi: 10.1016/j.paid.2018.10.022

Levin, S., Henry, P. J., Pratto, F., & Sidanius, J. (2009). Social dominance and social identity in Lebanon: Implications for support of violence against the West. In J. Victoroff & A. W. Kruglanski (Eds.), *Psychology of terrorism: Classic and contemporary insights* (pp. 253–267). New York: Psychology Press.

Lev-Wiesel, R., Eisikovits, Z., First, M., Gottfried, R., & Mehlhausen, D. (2018). Prevalence of child maltreatment in Israel: A national epidemiological study. *Journal of Child & Adolescent Trauma, 11*, 141–150. doi: 10.1007/s40653-016-0118-8

Lewin, K. (1936). *Principles of topological psychology.* New York: McGraw-Hill.

Lewis-O'Connor, A., Sharps, P., Humphreys, J., Gary, F. A., & Campbell, J. (2006). Children exposed to intimate partner violence. In M. M. Feerick & G. B. Silverman (Eds.), *Children exposed to violence* (pp. 3–28). Baltimore, MD: Paul H Brookes Publishing.

Leymann, H. (1993). *Mobbing: Psychoterror am Arbeitsplatz und wie man sich dagegen wehren kann.* Reinbek: Rowohlt.

Li, J.-B., Dou, K., Situ, Q.-M., Salcuni, S., Wang, Y.-J., & Friese, M. (2019). Anger rumination partly accounts for the association between trait self-control and aggression. *Journal of Research in Personality, 81*, 207–223. doi: 10.1016/j.jrp.2019.06.011

Li, J.-B., Nie, Y.-G., Boardley, I. D., Dou, K., & Situ, Q.-M. (2015). When do normative beliefs about aggression predict aggressive behavior? An application of I^3 theory. *Aggressive Behavior, 41*, 544–555. doi: 10.1002/ab.21594

Li, M., Leidner, B., Euh, H., & Choi, H.-S. (2016). The contagion of interstate violence: Reminders of historical interstate (but not intrastate) violence increase support for future violence against unrelated third-party states. *Personality and Social Psychology Bulletin, 42*, 1003–1024. doi: 10.1177/0146167216649609

Li, S., Zhao, F., & Yu, G. (2020). A meta-analysis of childhood maltreatment and intimate partner violence perpetration. *Aggression and Violent Behavior, 50.* doi: 10.1016/j.avb.2019.101362

Lickel, B., Miller, N. E., Stenstrom, D. M., Denson, T. F., & Schmader, T. (2006). Vicarious retribution: The role of collective blame in intergroup aggression. *Personality & Social Psychology Review, 10*, 372–390. doi: 10.1207/s15327957pspr1004_6

Lieberman, J. D., Solomon, S., Greenberg, J., & McGregor, H. A. (1999). A hot new way to measure aggression: Hot sauce allocation. *Aggressive Behavior, 25*, 331–348. doi: 10.1002/(SICI)1098-2337(1999)25:5<331::AID-AB2>3.0.CO;2-1

Lievaart, M., Franken, I. H. A., & Hovens, J. E. (2016). Anger assessment in clinical and nonclinical populations: Further validation of the State-Trait Anger Expression Inventory-2. *Journal of Clinical Psychology, 72*, 263–278. doi: 10.1002/jclp.22253

Lightdale, J. R., & Prentice, D. A. (1994). Rethinking sex differences in aggression: Aggressive behavior in the absence of social roles. *Personality and Social Psychology Bulletin, 20*, 34–44. doi: 10.1177/0146167294201003

Lim, S., & Cortina, L. M. (2005). Interpersonal mistreatment in the workplace: The interface and impact of general incivility and sexual harassment. *Journal of Applied Psychology, 90*, 483–496. doi: 10.1037/0021-9010.90.3.483

Lindén, M., Björklund, F., & Bäckström, M. (2018). How a terror attack affects right-wing authoritarianism, social dominance orientation, and their relationship to torture attitudes. *Scandinavian Journal of Psychology, 59*, 547–552. doi: 10.1111/sjop.12463

Linz, D. G., Donnerstein, E. I., & Adams, S. M. (1989). Physiological desensitization and judgments about female victims of violence. *Human Communication Research, 15*, 509–522. doi: 10.1111/j.1468-2958.1989.tb00197.x

Lippy, C., Jumarali, S. N., Nnawulezi, N. A., Williams, E. P., & Burk, C. (2019). The impact of mandatory reporting laws on survivors of intimate partner violence: Intersectionality, help-seeking and the need for change. *Journal of Family Violence, 2*, 284. doi: 10.1007/s10896-019-00103-w

Litrownik, A. J., Newton, R., Hunter, W. M., English, D., & Everson, M. D. (2003). Exposure to family violence in young at-risk children: A longitudinal look at the effects of victimization and witnessed physical and psychological aggression. *Journal of Family Violence, 18*, 59–73. doi: 10.1023/A:1021405515323

Liu, B. C. C., & Vaughn, M. S. (2019). Legal and policy issues from the United States and internationally about mandatory reporting of child abuse. *International Journal of Law and Psychiatry, 64*, 219–229. doi: 10.1016/j.ijlp.2019.03.007

Loeber, R., & Hay, D. F. (1997). Key issues in the development of aggression and violence from childhood to early adulthood. *Annual Review of Psychology, 48*, 371–410. doi: 10.1146/annurev.psych.48.1.371

Loeber, R., & Stouthamer-Loeber, M. (1998). Development of juvenile aggression and violence: Some common misconceptions and controversies. *American Psychologist, 53*, 242–259. doi: 10.1037/0003-066X.53.2.242

Loh, C., Gidycz, C. A., Lobo, T. R., & Luthra, R. (2005). A prospective analysis of sexual assault perpetration: Risk factors related to perpetrator characteristics. *Journal of Interpersonal Violence, 20*, 1325–1348. doi: 10.1177/0886260505278528

Lore, R. K., & Schultz, L. A. (1993). Control of human aggression: A comparative perspective. *American Psychologist, 48*, 16–25. doi: 10.1037/0003-066X.48.1.16

Lorenz, K. [Katherine], & Ullman, S. E. (2016). Alcohol and sexual assault victimization: Research findings and future directions. *Aggression and Violent Behavior, 31*, 82–94. doi: 10.1016/j.avb.2016.08.001

Lorenz, K. [Konrad] (1966). *On aggression*. London: Methuen & Co.

Lösel, F., King, S., Bender, D., & Jugl, I. (2018). Protective factors against extremism and violent radicalization: A systematic review of research. *International Journal of Developmental Science, 12*, 89–102. doi: 10.3233/DEV-170241

Lovett, J., & Kelly, L. (2009). *Different systems – similar outcomes? Tracking attrition in reported rape cases across Europe.* Retrieved from www.researchgate.net/publication/228847968_Different_systems_similar_outcomes_Tracking_attrition_in_reported_rape_cases_in_eleven_countries

Lowe, M., & Rogers, P. (2017). The scope of male rape: A selective review of research, policy and practice. *Aggression and Violent Behavior, 35*, 38–43. doi: 10.1016/j.avb.2017.06.007

Lowell, A., Suarez-Jimenez, B., Helpman, L., Zhu, X., Durosky, A., Hilburn, A., ... Neria, Y. (2018). 9/11-related PTSD among highly exposed populations: A systematic review 15 years after the attack. *Psychological Medicine, 48*, 537–553. doi: 10.1017/S0033291717002033

Lubek, I. (1995). Aggression research: A critical-historical, multi-level approach. *Theory & Psychology, 5*, 99–129. doi: 10.1177/0959354395051005

Luca, M., Malhotra, D., & Poliquin, C. (2017). Handgun waiting periods reduce gun deaths. *Proceedings of the National Academy of Sciences of the United States of America, 114*, 12162–12165. doi: 10.1073/pnas.1619896114

Lussier, P., & Cale, J. (2016). Understanding the origins and the development of rape and sexual aggression against women: Four generations of research and theorizing. *Aggression and Violent Behavior, 31*, 66–81. doi: 10.1016/j.avb.2016.07.008

Lustman, M., Wiesenthal, D. L., & Flett, G. L. (2010). Narcissism and aggressive driving: Is an inflated view of the self a road hazard? *Journal of Applied Social Psychology, 40*, 1423–1449. doi: 10.1111/j.1559-1816.2010.00624.x

Lutz, J. (2016). The validity of crowdsourcing data in studying anger and aggressive behavior. *Social Psychology, 47*, 38–51. doi: 10.1027/1864-9335/a000256

Lutz, J., & Krahé, B. (2018). Inducing sadness reduces anger-driven aggressive behavior: A situational approach to aggression control. *Psychology of Violence, 8*, 358–366. doi: 10.1037/vio0000167

Lyons, C. J. (2006). Stigma or sympathy? Attributions of fault to hate crime victims and offenders. *Social Psychology Quarterly, 69*, 39–59. doi: 10.1177/019027250606900104

Lysova, A., & Straus, M. A. (2019). Intimate Partner Violence: A multinational test of cultural spillover theory. *Journal of Interpersonal Violence,* Advance online publication. doi: 10.1177/0886260519839421

Maas, C., Herrenkohl, T. I., & Sousa, C. (2008). Review of research on child maltreatment and violence in youth. *Trauma, Violence, & Abuse, 9*, 56–67. doi: 10.1177/1524838007311105

McArdle, S. C., Rosoff, H., & John, R. S. (2012). The dynamics of evolving beliefs, concerns emotions, and behavioral avoidance following 9/11: A longitudinal analysis of representative archival samples. *Risk Analysis, 32*, 744–761. doi: 10.1111/j.1539-6924.2012.01814.x

McBurnett, K., Lahey, B. B., Rathouz, P. J., & Loeber, R. (2000). Low salivary cortisol and persistent aggression in boys referred for disruptive behavior. *Archives of General Psychiatry, 57*, 38–43. doi: 10.1001/archpsyc.57.1.38

McCaughey, M., & Cermele, J. (2017). Changing the hidden curriculum of campus rape prevention and education: Women's self-defense as a key protective factor for a public health model of prevention. *Trauma, Violence & Abuse, 18*, 287–302. doi: 10.1177/1524838015611674

McCauley, C. R., & Segal, M. E. (2009). Social psychology of terrorist groups. In J. Victoroff & A. W. Kruglanski (Eds.), *Psychology of terrorism: Classic and contemporary insights* (pp. 331–346). New York: Psychology Press.

McDonald, P. (2012). Workplace sexual harassment 30 years on: A review of the literature. *International Journal of Management Reviews, 14*, 1–17. doi: 10.1111/j.1468-2370.2011.00300.x

McGilloway, A., Ghosh, P., & Bhui, K. (2015). A systematic review of pathways to and processes associated with radicalization and extremism amongst Muslims in Western societies. *International Review of Psychiatry, 27*, 39–50. doi: 10.3109/09540261.2014.992008

McGregor, H. A., Lieberman, J. D., Greenberg, J., Solomon, S., Arndt, J., Simon, L., & Pyszczynski, T. (1998). Terror management and aggression: Evidence that mortality salience motivates aggression against worldview-threatening others. *Journal of Personality and Social Psychology, 74*, 590–605. doi: 10.1037/0022-3514.74.3.590

McKay, M. T., Perry, J. L., & Harvey, S. A. (2016). The factorial validity and reliability of three versions of the Aggression Questionnaire using confirmatory factor analysis and Exploratory Structural Equation Modelling. *Personality and Individual Differences, 90*, 12–15. doi: 10.1016/j.paid.2015.10.028

McKibbin, W. F., Shackelford, T. K., Goetz, A. T., & Starratt, V. G. (2008). Why do men rape? An evolutionary psychological perspective. *Review of General Psychology, 12*, 86–97. doi: 10.1037/1089-2680.12.1.86

McPhail, C. (1994). The dark side of purpose: Individual and collective violence in riots. *Sociological Quarterly, 35*, 1–32.

Maddox, L., Lee, D., & Barker, C. (2012). The impact of psychological consequences of rape on rape case attrition: The police perspective. *Journal of Police and Criminal Psychology, 27*, 33–44. doi: 10.1007/s11896-011-9092-0

Madigan, S., Cyr, C., Eirich, R., Fearon, R. M. P., Ly, A., Rash, C., … Alink, L. R. A. (2019). Testing the cycle of maltreatment hypothesis: Meta-analytic evidence of the intergenerational transmission of child maltreatment. *Development and Psychopathology, 31*, 23–51. doi: 10.1017/S0954579418001700

Malamuth, N. M. (1981). Rape proclivity among males. *Journal of Social Issues, 37*, 138–157. doi: 10.1111/j.1540-4560.1981.tb01075.x

Malamuth, N. M. (1998). The confluence model as an organizing framework for research on sexually aggressive men: Risk moderators, imagined aggression, and pornography consumption. In R. G. Geen & E. I. Donnerstein (Eds.), *Human aggression: Theories, research, and implications for social policy* (pp. 229–245). San Diego, CA: Academic Press.

Malamuth, N. M. (2018). "Adding fuel to the fire"? Does exposure to non-consenting adult or to child pornography increase risk of sexual aggression? *Aggression and Violent Behavior, 41*, 74–89. doi: 10.1016/j.avb.2018.02.013

Malamuth, N. M., & Hald, G. M. (2017). The confluence mediational model of sexual aggression. In L. A. Craig, M. Rettenberger, A. R. Beech, T. Ward, L. E. Marshall, & W. L. Marshall (Eds.), *The Wiley handbook on the theories, assessment and treatment of sexual offending* (pp. 53–71). Chichester, U.K.: Wiley Blackwell.

Malamuth, N. M., Heavey, C. L., Linz, D. G., Barnes, G., & Acker, M. (1995). Using the confluence model of sexual aggression to predict men's conflict with women: A 10-year follow-up study. *Journal of Personality & Social Psychology, 69*, 353–369.

Malamuth, N. M., & Heilmann, M. F. (1998). Evolutionary psychology and sexual aggression. In C. B. Crawford & D. L. Krebs (Eds.), *Handbook of evolutionary psychology: Ideas, issues, and applications* (pp. 515–542). Mahwah, NJ: Lawrence Erlbaum.

Malamuth, N. M., Sockloskie, R. J., Koss, M. P., & Tanaka, J. S. (1991). Characteristics of aggressors against women: Testing a model using a national sample of college students. *Journal of Consulting and Clinical Psychology, 59*, 670–681. doi: 10.1037/0022-006X.59.5.670

Mallory, A. B., Dharnidharka, P., Deitz, S. L., Barros-Gomes, P., Cafferky, B., Stith, S. M., & Van, K. (2016). A meta-analysis of cross cultural risk markers for intimate partner violence. *Aggression and Violent Behavior, 31*, 116–126. doi: 10.1016/j.avb.2016.08.004

Mann, R. E., Zhao, J., Stoduto, G., Adlaf, E. M., Smart, R. G., & Donovan, J. E. (2007). Road rage and collision involvement. *American Journal of Health Behavior, 31*, 384–391. doi: 10.5993/AJHB.31.4.5

Marcus-Newhall, A., Pedersen, W. C., Carlson, M., & Miller, N. E. (2000). Displaced aggression is alive and well: A meta-analytic review. *Journal of Personality and Social Psychology, 78*, 670–689. doi: 10.1037/0022-3514.78.4.670

Marin, A., & Russo, N. F. (1999). Feminist perspectives on male violence against women: Critiquing O'Neil and Harway's Model. In M. Harway & J. M. O'Neil (Eds.), *What causes men's violence against women?* (pp. 18–35). Thousand Oaks, CA: Sage.

Markovic, V. (2019). Suicide squad: Boko Haram's use of the female suicide bomber. *Women & Criminal Justice, 29*, 283–302. doi: 10.1080/08974454.2019.1629153

Marshall, E. A., Miller, H. A., & Bouffard, J. A. (2017). Crossing the threshold from porn use to porn problem: Frequency and modality of porn use as predictors of sexually coercive behaviors. *Journal of Interpersonal Violence*, Advance online publication. doi: 10.1177/0886260517743549

Martin, K., Vieraitis, L. M., & Britto, S. (2006). Gender equality and women's absolute Status: A test of the feminist models of rape. *Violence Against Women, 12*, 321–339. doi: 10.1177/1077801206286311

Martinelli, A., Ackermann, K., Bernhard, A., Freitag, C. M., & Schwenck, C. (2018). Hostile attribution bias and aggression in children and adolescents: A systematic literature review on the influence of aggression subtype and gender. *Aggression and Violent Behavior, 39*, 25–32. doi: 10.1016/j.avb.2018.01.005

Martino, S. C., Ellickson, P. L., Klein, D. J., McCaffrey, D., & Edelen, M. O. (2008). Multiple trajectories of physical aggression among adolescent boys and girls. *Aggressive Behavior, 34*, 61–75. doi: 10.1002/ab.20215

Martins, N., & Weaver, A. (2019). The role of media exposure on relational aggression: A meta-analysis. *Aggression and Violent Behavior, 47*, 90–99. doi: 10.1016/j.avb.2019.03.001

Mathews, B., & Collin-Vézina, D. (2019). Child sexual abuse: Toward a conceptual model and definition. *Trauma, Violence & Abuse, 20*, 131–148. doi: 10.1177/1524838017738726

Mathur, M. B., & VanderWeele, T. J. (2019). Finding common ground in meta-analysis "wars" on violent video games. *Perspectives on Psychological Science, 14*, 705–708. doi: 10.1177/1745691619850104

Mattaini, M. A., McGowan, B. G., & Williams, G. (1996). Child maltreatment. In M. A. Mattaini & B. A. Thyer (Eds.), *Finding solutions to social problems: Behavioral strategies for change* (pp. 223–266). Washington, DC: American Psychological Association.

Matthews, K. A., Jennings, J. R., Lee, L., & Pardini, D. A. (2017). Bullying and being bullied in childhood are associated with different psychosocial risk factors for poor physical health in men. *Psychological Science, 28*, 808–821. doi: 10.1177/0956797617697700

Maxwell, J.P. (2004). Anger rumination: An antecedent of athlete aggression? *Psychology of Sport and Exercise, 5*, 279–289. doi: 10.1016/S1469-0292(03)00007-4

Medienpädagogischer Forschungsverbund Südwest (2017). *JIM-Studie 2017: Jugend, Information, (Multi-) Media*. Stuttgart: MPFS. Retrieved from www.mpfs.de/studien/jim-studie/2017/

Meichenbaum, D. H. (1975). *Stress inoculation training*. New York: Pergamon Press.

Meier, B. P., & Hinsz, V. B. (2004). A comparison of human aggression committed by groups and individuals: An interindividual-intergroup discontinuity. *Journal of Experimental Social Psychology, 40*, 551–559. doi: 10.1016/j.jesp.2003.11.002

Meier, B. P., & Wilkowski, B. M. (2013). Reducing the tendency to aggress: Insights from social and personality psychology. *Social and Personality Psychology Compass, 7*, 343–354. doi: 10.1111/spc3.12029

Melde, C., & Esbensen, F. A. (2013). Gangs and violence: Disentangling the impact of gang membership on the level and nature of offending. *Journal of Quantitative Criminology, 29*, 143–166. doi: 10.1007/s10940-012-9164-z

Melkonian, A. J., & Ham, L. S. (2018). The effects of alcohol intoxication on young adult women's identification of risk for sexual assault: A systematic review. *Psychology of Addictive Behaviors, 32*, 162–172. doi: 10.1037/adb0000349

Mellins, C. A., Walsh, K., Sarvet, A. L., Wall, M., Gilbert, L., Santelli, J. S., ... Hirsch, J. S. (2017). Sexual assault incidents among college undergraduates: Prevalence and factors associated with risk. *PloS One, 12*, e0186471. doi: 10.1371/journal.pone.0186471

Menéndez, P., Kypri, K., & Weatherburn, D. (2017). The effect of liquor licensing restrictions on assault: A quasi-experimental study in Sydney, Australia. *Addiction, 112*, 261–268. doi: 10.1111/add.13621

Merari, A., Diamant, I., Bibi, A., Broshi, Y., & Zakin, G. (2010). Personality characteristics of "self martyrs"/"suicide bombers" and organizers of suicide attacks. *Terrorism and Political Violence, 22*, 87–101. doi: 10.1080/09546550903409312

Merrilees, C. E., Cairns, E., Taylor, L. K., Goeke-Morey, M. C., Shirlow, P., & Cummings, E. M. (2013). Social identity and youth aggressive and delinquent behaviors in a context of political violence. *Political Psychology, 34*. doi: 10.1111/pops.12030

Messinger, A. M. (2011). Invisible victims: Same-sex IPV in the national violence against women survey. *Journal of Interpersonal Violence, 26*, 2228–2243. doi: 10.1177/0886260510383023

Messman-Moore, T. L., Coates, A. A., Gaffey, K. J., & Johnson, C. F. (2008). Sexuality, substance use, and susceptibility to victimization: Risk for rape and sexual coercion in a prospective study of college women. *Journal of Interpersonal Violence, 23*, 1730–1746. doi: 10.1177/0886260508314336

Messman-Moore, T. L., Walsh, K., & DiLillo, D. (2010). Emotion dysregulation and risky sexual behavior in revictimization. *Child Abuse & Neglect, 34*, 967–976. doi: 10.1016/j.chiabu.2010.06.004

Miles, D. R., & Carey, G. (1997). Genetic and environmental architecture on human aggression. *Journal of Personality and Social Psychology, 72*, 207–217. doi: 10.1037/0022-3514.72.1.207

Miles-Novelo, A., & Anderson, C. A. (2019). Climate change and psychology: Effects of rapid global warming on violence and aggression. *Current Climate Change Reports, 5*, 36–46. doi: 10.1007/s40641-019-00121-2

Milgram, S. (1974). *Obedience to authority*. New York: Harper & Row.

Milla, M. N., Hudiyana, J., & Arifin, H. H. (2019). Attitude toward rehabilitation as a key predictor for adopting alternative identities in deradicalization programs: An investigation of terrorist detainees' profiles. *Asian Journal of Social Psychology, 48*, 389. doi: 10.1111/ajsp.12380

Miller, B. C., Monson, B. H., & Norton, M. C. (1995). The effects of forced sexual intercourse on white female adolescents. *Child Abuse & Neglect, 19*, 1289–1301. doi: 10.1016/0145-2134(95)00081-I

Miller, L. (2014). Rape: Sex crime, act of violence, or naturalistic adaptation? *Aggression and Violent Behavior, 19*, 67–81. doi: 10.1016/j.avb.2013.11.004

Miller, M., Barber, C., & Azrael, D. (2016). Firearms and suicide in the United States. In L. H. Gold & R. I. Simon (Eds.), *Gun violence and mental illness* (pp. 31–48). Arlington, VA: American Psychiatric Association.

Miller, N. E. (1941). The frustration-aggression hypothesis. *Psychological Review, 48*, 337–342. doi: 10.1037/h0055861

Miller, N. E., Pedersen, W. C., Earleywine, M., & Pollock, V. E. (2003). A theoretical model of triggered displaced aggression. *Personality and Social Psychology Review, 7*, 75–97. doi: 10.1207/S15327957PSPR0701_5

Miller, P. A., & Eisenberg, N. (1988). The relation of empathy to aggressive and externalizing/antisocial behavior. *Psychological Bulletin, 103*, 324–344. doi: 10.1037/0033-2909.103.3.324

Miller-Perrin, C. L., & Perrin, R. D. (2007). *Child maltreatment: An introduction* (2nd ed.). Thousand Oaks, CA: Sage.

Milner, J. S., & Crouch, J. L. (1993). Child physical abuse: Theory and research. In R. L. Hampton (Ed.), *Family violence: Prevention and treatment* (pp. 33–65). Newbury Park, CA: Sage.

Milner, J. S., & Wimberley, A. C. (1980). Prediction and explanation of child abuse. *Journal of Clinical Psychology, 36*, 875–884. doi: 10.1002/1097-4679(198010)36:4<875::AID-JCLP2270360407>3.0.CO;2-1

Misiak, B., Samochowiec, J., Bhui, K., Schouler-Ocak, M., Demunter, H., Kuey, L., ... Dom, G. (2019). A systematic review on the relationship between mental health, radicalization and mass violence. *European Psychiatry, 56*, 51–59. doi: 10.1016/j.eurpsy.2018.11.005

Modecki, K. L., Minchin, J., Harbaugh, A. G., Guerra, N. G., & Runions, K. C. (2014). Bullying prevalence across contexts: A meta-analysis measuring cyber and traditional bullying. *The Journal of Adolescent Health, 55*, 602–611. doi: 10.1016/j.jadohealth.2014.06.007

Moffitt, T. E. (1993). Adolescence-limited and life-course-persistent antisocial behavior: A developmental taxonomy. *Psychological Review, 100*, 674–701. doi: 10.1037/0033-295X.100.4.674

Moffitt, T. E. (2007). A review of research on the taxonomy of life-course persistent versus adolescence-limited antisocial behavior. In D. J. Flannery, A. T. Vazsonyi, & I. D. Waldman (Eds.), *The Cambridge handbook of violent behavior and aggression* (pp. 49–74). New York: Cambridge University Press.

Moffitt, T. E., Caspi, A., Harrington, H., & Milne, B. J. (2002). Males on the life-course-persistent and adolescence-limited antisocial pathways: Follow-up at age 26 years. *Development and Psychopathology, 14*, 179–207. doi: 10.1017/S0954579402001104

Moghaddam, F. M. (2005). The staircase to terrorism. *American Psychologist, 60*, 161–169. doi: 10.1037/0003-066X.60.2.161

Moghaddam, F. M. (2006). *From the terrorists' point of view: What they experience and why they come to destroy*. Westport, CT: Praeger Security International.

Molidor, C. E. (1996). Female gang members: A profile of aggression and victimization. *Social Work, 41,* 251–257.

Möller, I., & Krahé, B. (2009). Exposure to violent video games and aggression in German adolescents: A longitudinal analysis. *Aggressive Behavior, 35,* 75–89. doi: 10.1002/ab.20290

Möller, I., Krahé, B., Busching, R., & Krause, C. (2012). Efficacy of an intervention to reduce the use of media violence and aggression: An experimental evaluation with adolescents in Germany. *Journal of Youth and Adolescence, 41,* 105–120. doi: 10.1007/s10964-011-9654-6

Møller, M., & Haustein, S. (2018). Road anger expression: Changes over time and attributed reasons. *Accident; Analysis and Prevention, 119,* 29–36. doi: 10.1016/j.aap.2018.06.013

Moloney, M., MacKenzie, K., Hunt, G., & Joe-Laidler, K. (2009). The path and promise of fatherhood for gang members. *British Journal of Criminology, 49,* 305–325. doi: 10.1093/bjc/azp003

Montoya, E. R., Terburg, D., Bos, P. A., & van Honk, J. (2012). Testosterone, cortisol, and serotonin as key regulators of social aggression: A review and theoretical perspective. *Motivation and Emotion, 36,* 65–73. doi: 10.1007/s11031-011-9264-3

Moore, S. C., Shepherd, J. P., Eden, S., & Sivarajasingam, V. (2007). The effect of rugby match outcome on spectator aggression and intention to drink alcohol. *Criminal Behaviour and Mental Health, 17,* 118–127. doi: 10.1002/cbm.647

Moore, T. M., & Stuart, G. L. (2005). A review of the literature on masculinity and partner violence. *Psychology of Men & Masculinity, 6,* 46–61. doi: 10.1037/1524-9220.6.1.46

Moore, T. M., Stuart, G. L., Meehan, J. C., Rhatigan, D., Hellmuth, J. C., & Keen, S. M. (2008). Drug abuse and aggression between intimate partners: A meta-analytic review. *Clinical Psychology Review, 28,* 247–274. doi: 10.1016/j.cpr.2007.05.003

Morton, G. M., & Oravecz, L. M. (2009). The mandatory reporting of abuse: Problem creation through problem solution? *Journal of Feminist Family Therapy: An International Forum, 21,* 177–197. doi: 10.1080/08952830903079052

Mosher, D. L., & Sirkin, M. (1984). Measuring a macho personality constellation. *Journal of Research in Personality, 18,* 150–163. doi: 10.1016/0092-6566(84)90026-6

Mosqueda, L., & Olsen, B. (2015). Elder abuse and neglect. In P. A. Lichtenberg, B. T. Mast, B. D. Carpenter, & J. L. Wetherell (Eds.), *APA handbook of clinical geropsychology* (Vol. 2, pp. 667–686). Washington, DC: American Psychological Association.

Mouilso, E. R., Calhoun, K. S., & Rosenbloom, T. G. (2013). Impulsivity and sexual assault in college men. *Violence and Victims, 28,* 429–442. doi: 10.1891/0886-6708.vv-d-12-00025

Mrug, S., Madan, A., Cook, E. W., & Wright, R. A. (2015). Emotional and physiological desensitization to real-life and movie violence. *Journal of Youth and Adolescence, 44,* 1092–1108. doi: 10.1007/s10964-014-0202-z

Muehlenhard, C. L. (1998). The importance and danger of studying sexually aggressive women. In P. B. Anderson & C. Struckman-Johnson (Eds.), *Sexually aggressive women: Current perspectives and controversies* (pp. 19–48). New York: Guilford Press.

Muehlenhard, C. L., & Hollabaugh, L. C. (1988). Do women sometimes say no when they mean yes? The prevalence and correlates of women's token resistance to sex. *Journal of Personality and Social Psychology, 54,* 872–879. doi: 10.1037/0022-3514.54.5.872

Muehlenhard, C. L., Peterson, Z. D., Humphreys, T. P., & Jozkowski, K. N. (2017). Evaluating the one-in-five statistic: Women's risk of sexual assault while in college. *Journal of Sex Research, 54,* 549–576. doi: 10.1080/00224499.2017.1295014

Mujal, G. N., Taylor, M. E., Fry, J. L., Gochez-Kerr, T. H., & Weaver, N. L. (2019). A systematic review of bystander interventions for the prevention of sexual violence. *Trauma, Violence & Abuse,* 1524838019849587. doi: 10.1177/1524838019849587

Mullen, B. (1983). Operationalizing the effect of the group on the individual: A self-attention perspective. *Journal of Experimental Social Psychology, 19,* 295–322. doi: 10.1016/0022-1031(83)90025-2

Mullen, B. (1986). Atrocity as a function of lynch mob composition: A self-attention perspective. *Personality and Social Psychology Bulletin, 12,* 187–197. doi: 10.1177/0146167286122005

Muller, H. J., Desmarais, S. L., & Hamel, J. M. (2009). Do judicial responses to restraining order requests discriminate against male victims of domestic violence? *Journal of Family Violence, 24,* 625–637. doi: 10.1007/s10896-009-9261-4

Müller, U., & Schröttle, M. (2004). *Health, well-being and personal safety of women in Germany. A representative study of violence against women in Germany.* Retrieved from www.bmfsfj.de/blob/jump/93906/frauenstudie-englisch-gewalt-gegen-frauen-data.pdf

Mullin, C. R., & Linz, D. G. (1995). Desensitization and resensitization to violence against women: Effects of exposure to sexually violent films on judgments of domestic violence victims. *Journal of Personality and Social Psychology, 69,* 449–459. doi: 10.1037/0022-3514.69.3.449

Muris, P., Merckelbach, H., Otgaar, H., & Meijer, E. (2017). The malevolent side of human nature. *Perspectives on Psychological Science, 12,* 183–204. doi: 10.1177/1745691616666070

Murnen, S. K., Wright, C., & Kaluzny, G. (2002). If 'boys will be boys,' then girls will be victims? A meta-analytic review of the research that relates masculine ideology to sexual aggression. *Sex Roles, 46,* 359–375. doi: 10.1037/t00748-000;

Murphy, L., Ranger, R., Fedoroff, J. P., Stewart, H., Dwyer, R. G., & Burke, W. (2015). Standardization of penile plethysmography testing in assessment of problematic sexual interests. *The Journal of Sexual Medicine, 12,* 1853–1861. doi: 10.1111/jsm.12979

Murphy, P., Williams, J., & Dunning, E. (1990). *Football on trial: Spectator violence and development in the football world.* London: Routledge.

Murphy, S., Elklit, A., & Shevlin, M. (2020). Child maltreatment typologies and intimate partner violence: Findings from a Danish national study of young adults. *Journal of Interpersonal Violence, 35*, 755–770. doi: 10.1177/0886260517689889

Murray, R., Amann, R., & Thom, K. (2018). Mindfulness-based interventions for youth in the criminal justice system: a review of the research-based literature. *Psychiatry, Psychology and Law, 25*, 829–838. doi: 10.1080/13218719.2018.1478338

Mysuyk, Y., Westendorp, R. G. J., & Lindenberg, J. (2013). Added value of elder abuse definitions: A review. *Ageing Research Reviews, 12*, 50–57. doi: 10.1016/j.arr.2012.04.001

Nadan, Y., Spilsbury, J. C., & Korbin, J. E. (2015). Culture and context in understanding child maltreatment: Contributions of intersectionality and neighborhood-based research. *Child Abuse & Neglect, 41*, 40–48. doi: 10.1016/j.chiabu.2014.10.021

Nakano, K. (2001). Psychometric evaluation on the Japanese adaptation of the Aggression Questionnaire. *Behaviour Research and Therapy, 39*, 853–858. doi: 10.1016/S0005-7967(00)00057-7

Nalkur, P. G., Jamieson, P. E., & Romer, D. (2010). The effectiveness of the Motion Picture Association of America's rating system in screening explicit violence and sex in top-ranked movies from 1950 to 2006. *Journal of Adolescent Health, 47*, 440–447. doi: 10.1016/j.jadohealth.2010.01.019

Narvaes, R., & Martins de Almeida, R. M. (2014). Aggressive behavior and three neurotransmitters: dopamine, GABA, and serotonin: A review of the last 10 years. *Psychology & Neuroscience, 7*, 601–607. doi: 10.3922/j.psns.2014.4.20

National Academies of Sciences, Engineering, and Medicine (2018). *Sexual harassment of women: Climate, culture, and consequences in academic sciences, engineering, and medicine.* Washington, DC: The National Academies Press.

National Consortium for the Study of Terrorism and Responses to Terrorism (2018). *Global terrorism in 2017: Background report.* Retrieved from www.start.umd.edu/pubs/START_GTD_Overview2017_July2018.pdf

National Gang Intelligence Center (2016). *National gang report 2015.* Retrieved from www.fbi.gov/file-repository/stats-services-publications-national-gang-report-2015.pdf/view

National Sexual Violence Resource Center (2011). *Dear Colleague Letter: Sexual Violence.* Retrieved from obamawhitehouse.archives.gov/sites/default/files/dear_colleague_sexual_violence.pdf

National Society for the Prevention of Cruelty to Children (2017). *How safe are our children.* Retrieved from bettercarenetwork.org/sites/default/files/how-safe-children-2017-report_0.pdf

Neighbors, C., Walker, D. D., Mbilinyi, L. F., O'Rourke, A., Edleson, J. L., Zegree, J., & Roffman, R. A. (2010). Normative misperceptions of abuse among perpetrators of intimate partner violence. *Violence Against Women, 16*, 370–386. doi: 10.1177/1077801210363608

Nesbit, S. M., Conger, J. C., & Conger, A. J. (2007). A quantitative review of the relationship between anger and aggressive driving. *Aggression and Violent Behavior, 12*, 156–176. doi: 10.1016/j.avb.2006.09.003

Niederkrotenthaler, T., Till, B., Kapusta, N. D., Voracek, M., Dervic, K., & Sonneck, G. (2009). Copycat effects after media reports on suicide: A population-based ecologic study. *Social Science & Medicine, 69*, 1085–1090. doi: 10.1016/j.socscimed.2009.07.041

Nielsen, M. B., & Einarsen, S. (2018). What we know, what we do not know, and what we should and could have known about workplace bullying: An overview of the literature and agenda for future research. *Aggression and Violent Behavior, 42*, 71–83. doi: 10.1016/j.avb.2018.06.007

Nielsen, M. B., Glasø, L., & Einarsen, S. (2017). Exposure to workplace harassment and the Five Factor Model of personality: A meta-analysis. *Personality and Individual Differences, 104*, 195–206. doi: 10.1016/j.paid.2016.08.015

Nielsen, M. B., Indregard, A.-M. R., & Øverland, S. (2016). Workplace bullying and sickness absence: A systematic review and meta-analysis of the research literature. *Scandinavian Journal of Work, Environment & Health, 42*, 359–370. doi: 10.5271/sjweh.3579

Nielsen, M. B., Matthiesen, S. B., & Einarsen, S. (2010). The impact of methodological moderators on prevalence rates of workplace bullying. A meta-analysis. *Journal of Occupational and Organizational Psychology, 83*, 955–979. doi: 10.1348/096317909X481256

Nielsen, M. B., Nielsen, G. H., Notelaers, G., & Einarsen, S. (2015). Workplace bullying and suicidal ideation: A 3-wave longitudinal Norwegian study. *American Journal of Public Health, 105*, e23–8. doi: 10.2105/AJPH.2015.302855

Nielsen, M. B., Tangen, T., Idsoe, T., Matthiesen, S. B., & Magerøy, N. (2015). Post-traumatic stress disorder as a consequence of bullying at work and at school. A literature review and meta-analysis. *Aggression and Violent Behavior, 21*, 17–24. doi: 10.1016/j.avb.2015.01.001

Nisbett, R. E. (1993). Violence and U.S. regional culture. *American Psychologist, 48*, 441–449. doi: 10.1037/0003-066X.48.4.441

Nivette, A., Sutherland, A., Eisner, M., & Murray, J. (2019). Sex differences in adolescent physical aggression: Evidence from sixty-three low-and middle-income countries. *Aggressive Behavior, 45*, 82–92. doi: 10.1002/ab.21799

Noll, J. G., & Grych, J. H. (2011). Read-react-respond: An integrative model for understanding sexual revictimization. *Psychology of Violence, 1*, 202–215. doi: 10.1037/a0023962

Noll, J. G., Shenk, C. E., & Putnam, K. T. (2009). Childhood sexual abuse and adolescent pregnancy: A meta-analytic update. *Journal of Pediatric Psychology, 34*, 366–378. doi: 10.1093/jpepsy/jsn098

Notelaers, G., Witte, H. de, & Einarsen, S. (2010). A job characteristics approach to explain workplace bullying. *European Journal of Work and Organizational Psychology, 19*, 487–504. doi: 10.1080/13594320903007620

Novaco, R. W. (1975). *Anger control: The development and evaluation of an experimental treatment*. Oxford: Lexington.

O'Brennan, L. M., Bradshaw, C. P., & Sawyer, A. L. (2009). Examining developmental differences in the social-emotional problems among frequent bullies, victims, and bully/victims. *Psychology in the Schools, 46*, 100–115. doi: 10.1002/pits.20357

O'Brien, K. S., Forrest, W., Greenlees, I., Rhind, D., Jowett, S., Pinsky, I., ... Iqbal, M. (2018). Alcohol consumption, masculinity, and alcohol-related violence and anti-social behaviour in sportspeople. *Journal of Science and Medicine in Sport, 21*, 335–341. doi: 10.1016/j.jsams.2017.06.019

Office for National Statistics (2018a). *Sexual offences in England and Wales: Year ending March 2017*. Retrieved from www.ons.gov.uk/peoplepopulationandcommunity/crimeandjustice/articles/sexualoffenc esinenglandandwales/yearendingmarch2017/pdf

Office for National Statistics (2018b). *Sexual offending: Victimisation and the path through the criminal justice system*. Retrieved from www.ons.gov.uk/peoplepopulationandcommunity/crimeandjustice/articles/sexualoffe ndingvictimisationandthepaththroughthecriminaljusticesystem/2018-12-13/pdf

Office for National Statistics (2019a). *Crime in England and Wales: Annual supplementary tables*. Retrieved from www.ons.gov.uk/file?uri=%2fpeople populationandcommunity%2fcrimeandjustice%2fdatasets%2fcrimein englandandwalesannualsupplementarytables%2fmarch2019/annualsu pplementarytablesyemar1911.xlsx

Office for National Statistics (2019b). *Crime in England and Wales: Year ending June 2019*. Retrieved from www.ons.gov.uk/peoplepopulationandcommunity/crimeandjustice/bulletins/crimeinenglandandwales/yearendingjune2019

Office for National Statistics (2019c). *Crime Survey for England and Wales (CSEW) estimates of gang membership and knife carrying among 10 to 15 year old children, England and Wales: years ending March 2016 and March 2018*. Retrieved from www.ons.gov.uk/peoplepopulationandcommunity/crimeandjustice/adhocs/009653crimesurveyforenglandandwalescsewes timatesofgangmembershipandknifecarryingamong10to15yearoldchildr enenglandandwalesyearsendingmarch2016andmarch2018

Ogilvie, J. M., Stewart, A.L., Chan, R. C. K., & Shum, D. H. K. (2011). Neuropsychological measures of executive function and antisocial behavior: A meta-analysis. *Criminology, 49*, 1063–1107. doi: 10.1111/j.1745-9125.2011.00252.x

Oh, S. S., Kim, W., Jang, S.-I., & Park, E.-C. (2019). The association between intimate partner violence onset and gender-specific depression: A longitudinal study of a nationally representative sample. *Journal of Affective Disorders, 250*, 79–84. doi: 10.1016/j.jad.2019.02.065

O'Hagan, K. P. (1995). Emotional and psychological abuse: Problems of definition. *Child Abuse & Neglect, 19*, 449–461. doi: 10.1016/0145-2134(95)00006-T

O'Hare, E. O., & O'Donohue, W. (1998). Risk factors relating to sexual harassment: An examination of four models. *Archives of Sexual Behavior*, 561–580. doi: 10.1023/a:1018769016832

O'Keefe, M. (1995). Predictors of child abuse in maritally violent families. *Journal of Interpersonal Violence*, *10*, 3–25. doi: 10.1177/088626095010001001

O'Leary-Kelly, A. M., Bowes-Sperry, L., Bates, C. A., & Lean, E. R. (2009). Sexual harassment at work: A decade (plus) of progress. *Journal of Management*, *35*, 503–536. doi: 10.1177/0149206308330555

Olsen, E. O.'M., Vivolo-Kantor, A., & Kann, L. (2017). Physical and sexual teen dating violence victimization and sexual identity among U.S. High school students, 2015. *Journal of Interpersonal Violence*, Advance online publication. doi: 10.1177/0886260517708757

Olweus, D. (1979). Stability of aggressive reaction patterns in males: A review. *Psychological Bulletin*, *86*, 852–875. doi: 10.1037/0033-2909.86.4.852

Olweus, D. (2012). Cyberbullying: An overrated phenomenon? *European Journal of Developmental Psychology*, *9*, 520–538. doi: 10.1080/17405629.2012.682358

Olweus, D. (2017). Cyberbullying: A critical overview. In B. J. Bushman (Ed.), *Aggression and violence: A social psychological perspective* (pp. 225–240). New York: Routledge.

Orchowski, L. M., Edwards, K. M., Hollander, J. A., Banyard, V., Senn, C. Y., & Gidycz, C. A. (2018). Integrating sexual assault resistance, bystander, and men's social norms strategies to prevent sexual violence on college campuses: A call to action. *Trauma, Violence & Abuse*, 1524838018789153. doi: 10.1177/1524838018789153

Orobio de Castro, B., Veerman, J. W., Koops, W., Bosch, J. D., & Monshouwer, H. J. (2002). Hostile attribution of intent and aggressive behavior: A meta-analysis. *Child Development*, *73*, 916–934. doi: 10.1111/1467-8624.00447

Østby, G. (2016). *Violence begets violence: Armed conflict and domestic sexual violence in Sub-Saharan Africa*. Retrieved from www.hicn.org/wordpress/wp-content/uploads/2012/06/HiCN-WP-233.pdf

Österman, K., Björkqvist, K., & Wahlbeck, K. (2014). Twenty-eight years after the complete ban on the physical punishment of children in Finland: Trends and psychosocial concomitants. *Aggressive Behavior*, *40*, 568–581. doi: 10.1002/ab.21537

Ostrov, J. M., & Keating, C. F. (2004). Gender differences in preschool aggression during free play and structured interactions: An observational study. *Social Development*, *13*, 255–277. doi: 10.1111/j.1467-9507.2004.000266.x

Ostrowsky, M. K. (2010). Are violent people more likely to have low self-esteem or high self-esteem? *Aggression and Violent Behavior*, *15*, 69–75. doi: 10.1016/j.avb.2009.08.004

Pacifici, C., Stoolmiller, M., & Nelson, C. (2001). Evaluating a prevention program for teenagers on sexual coercion: A differential effectiveness approach. *Journal of Consulting and Clinical Psychology, 69*, 552–559. doi: 10.1037/0022-006X.69.3.552

Paik, H., & Comstock, G. (1994). The effects of television violence on anti-social behavior: A meta-analysis. *Communication Research, 21*, 516–546. doi: 10.1177/009365094021004004

Palmer, R. S., McMahon, T. J., Rounsaville, B. J., & Ball, S. A. (2010). Coercive sexual experiences, protective behavioral strategies, alcohol expectancies and consumption among male and female college students. *Journal of Interpersonal Violence, 25*, 1563–1578. doi: 10.1177/0886260509354581

Palumbo, S., Mariotti, V., Iofrida, C., & Pellegrini, S. (2018). Genes and aggressive behavior: Epigenetic mechanisms underlying individual susceptibility to aversive environments. *Frontiers in Behavioral Neuroscience, 12*, 427. doi: 10.3389/fnbeh.2018.00117

Palusci, V. J., Vandervort, F. E., & Lewis, J. M. (2016). Does changing mandated reporting laws improve child maltreatment reporting in large U.S. counties? *Children and Youth Services Review, 66*, 170–179. doi: 10.1016/j.childyouth.2016.05.002

Papachristos, A. V. (2013). The importance of cohesion for gang research, policy, and practice. *Criminology & Public Policy, 12*, 49–58. doi: 10.1111/1745-9133.12006

Parker, D., Lajunen, T., & Summala, H. (2002). Anger and aggression among drivers in three European countries. *Accident Analysis & Prevention, 34*, 229–235. doi: 10.1016/S0001-4575(01)00018-5

Parker, R. N., & Auerhahn, K. (1999). Drugs, alcohol, and homicide. In M. D. Smith & M. A. Zahn (Eds.), *Homicide: A sourcebook of social research* (pp. 176–191). Thousand Oaks, CA: Sage.

Parratt, K. A., & Pina, A. (2017). From "real rape" to real justice: A systematic review of police officers' rape myth beliefs. *Aggression and Violent Behavior, 34*, 68–83. doi: 10.1016/j.avb.2017.03.005

Parrott, D. J., & Eckhardt, C. I. (2017). Effects of alcohol and other drugs. In B. J. Bushman (Ed.), *Aggression and violence: A social psychological perspective* (pp. 199–222). New York: Routledge.

Parrott, D. J., & Giancola, P. R. (2004). A further examination of the relation between trait anger and alcohol-related aggression: The role of anger control. *Alcoholism: Clinical and Experimental Research, 28*, 855–864. doi: 10.1097/01.ALC.0000128226.92708.21

Parrott, D. J., & Giancola, P. R. (2007). Addressing "The criterion problem" in the assessment of aggressive behavior: Development of a new taxonomic system. *Aggression and Violent Behavior, 12*, 280–299. doi: 10.1016/j.avb.2006.08.002

Parrott, D. J., Miller, C. A., & Hudepohl, A. D. (2015). Immediate and short-term reactions to participation in laboratory aggression research. *Psychology of Violence, 5*, 209–216. doi: 10.1037/a0035922

Parrott, D. J., & Peterson, J. L. (2008). What motivates hate crimes based on sexual orientation? Mediating effects of anger on antigay aggression. *Aggressive Behavior, 34*, 306–318. doi: 10.1002/ab.20239

Patterson, G. R., DeBaryshe, B. D., & Ramsey, E. (1989). A developmental perspective on antisocial behavior. *American Psychologist, 44*, 329–335. doi: 10.1037/0003-066X.44.2.329

Patterson, M. L., Mullens, S., & Romano, J. (1971). Compensatory reactions to spatial intrusion. *Sociometry, 34*, 114–121. doi: 10.2307/2786354

Pearl, E. S. (2009). Parent management training for reducing oppositional and aggressive behavior in preschoolers. *Aggression and Violent Behavior, 14*, 295–305. doi: 10.1016/j.avb.2009.03.007

Pedersen, W. C., Gonzales, C., & Miller, N. E. (2000). The moderating effect of trivial triggering provocation on displaced aggression. *Journal of Personality and Social Psychology, 78*, 913–927. doi: 10.1037/0022-3514.78.5.913

Peled, M., & Moretti, M. M. (2010). Ruminating on rumination: Are rumination on anger and sadness differentially related to aggression and depressed mood? *Journal of Psychopathology and Behavioral Assessment, 32*, 108–117. doi: 10.1007/s10862-009-9136-2

Pellegrini, A. D., & Long, J. D. (2003). A sexual selection theory longitudinal analysis of sexual segregation and integration in early adolescence. *Journal of Experimental Child Psychology, 85*, 257–278. doi: 10.1016/S0022-0965(03)00060-2

Pelletier, P., & Drozda-Senkowska, E. (2016). The Charlie Hebdo terror attack in Paris: Follow-up of French citizens' terrorist threat perception and its aftermath. *International Review of Social Psychology, 29*, 85. doi: 10.5334/irsp.51

Pelletier, P., & Drozda-Senkowska, E. (2020). Virtual reality as a tool for deradicalizing the terrorist mind: Conceptual and methodological insights from intergroup conflict resolution and perspective-taking research. *Peace and Conflict: Journal of Peace Psychology*, Advance online publication. doi: 10.1037/pac0000442

Pepler, D. J. (2018). The development of aggression in childhood and adolescence. In J. L. Ireland, P. Birch, & C. A. Ireland (Eds.), *The Routledge international handbook of human aggression* (pp. 3–18). London: Routledge.

Perry, E. L., Schmidtke, J. M., & Kulik, C. T. (1998). Propensity to sexually harass: An exploration of gender differences. *Sex Roles, 38*, 443–460. doi: 10.1023/A:1018761922759

Peter, J., & Valkenburg, P. M. (2016). Adolescents and pornography: A review of 20 years of research. *Journal of Sex Research, 53*, 509–531. doi: 10.1080/00224499.2016.1143441

Petersen, I. T., Bates, J. E., Dodge, K. A., Lansford, J. E., & Pettit, G. S. (2015). Describing and predicting developmental profiles of externalizing problems from childhood to adulthood. *Development and Psychopathology, 27*, 791–818. doi: 10.1017/S0954579414000789

Peterson, K., Sharps, P., Banyard, V., Powers, R. A., Kaukinen, C., Gross, D., ... Campbell, J. (2018). An evaluation of two dating violence prevention programs on a college campus. *Journal of Interpersonal Violence, 33*, 3630–3655. doi: 10.1177/0886260516636069

Peterson, Z. D., Janssen, E., Goodrich, D., Fortenberry, J. D., Hensel, D. J., & Heiman, J. R. (2018). Child sexual abuse and negative affect as shared risk factors for sexual aggression and sexual HIV risk behavior in heterosexual men. *Archives of Sexual Behavior, 47*, 465–480. doi: 10.1007/s10508-017-1079-1

Peterson, Z. D., Voller, E. K., Polusny, M. A., & Murdoch, M. (2011). Prevalence and consequences of adult sexual assault of men: Review of empirical findings and state of the literature. *Clinical Psychology Review, 31*, 1–24. doi: 10.1016/j.cpr.2010.08.006

Pettigrew, T. F., & Tropp, L. R. (2006). A meta-analytic test of intergroup contact theory. *Journal of Personality and Social Psychology, 90*, 751–783. doi: 10.1037/0022-3514.90.5.751

Pew Research Center (2017). *America's complex relationship with guns.* Retrieved from www.pewsocialtrends.org/2017/06/22/americas-complex-relationship-with-guns/

Phil, R. O., & Sutton, R. (2009). Drugs and aggression readily mix; so what now? *Substance Use & Misuse, 44*, 1188–1203. doi: 10.1080/10826080902959884

Philippe, F. L., Vallerand, R. J., Richer, I., Vallières, É., & Bergeron, J. (2009). Passion for driving and aggressive driving behavior: A look at their relationship. *Journal of Applied Social Psychology, 39*, 3020–3043. doi: 10.1111/j.1559-1816.2009.00559.x

Pillemer, K., & Suitor, J. J. (1988). Elder abuse. In V. B. Van Hasselt (Ed.), *Handbook of family violence* (pp. 247–270). New York: Plenum Press.

Plante, C., Anderson, C. A., Allen, J. J., Groves, C., & & Gentile, D. A. (2020). *Video games: Mayhem or moral panic? FAQs and a moderate approach to media violence research.* Ames, IA: Zengen LLC Publishing.

Plumm, K. M., Terrance, C. A., Henderson, V. R., & Ellingson, H. (2010). Victim blame in a hate crime motivated by sexual orientation. *Journal of Homosexuality, 57*, 267–286. doi: 10.1080/00918360903489101

Polman, H., Orobio de Castro, B., & van Aken, M. A. G. (2008). Experimental study of the differential effects of playing versus watching violent video games on children's aggressive behavior. *Aggressive Behavior, 34*, 256–264. doi: 10.1002/ab.20245

Poltavski, D., van Eck, R., Winger, A. T., & Honts, C. (2018). Using a polygraph system for evaluation of the social desirability response bias in self-report measures of aggression. *Applied Psychophysiology and Biofeedback, 43*, 309–318. doi: 10.1007/s10484-018-9414-4

Pond, R. S., DeWall, C. N., Lambert, N. M., Deckman, T., Bonser, I. M., & Fincham, F. D. (2012). Repulsed by violence: Disgust sensitivity buffers trait, behavioral, and daily aggression. *Journal of Personality and Social Psychology, 102*, 175–188. doi: 10.1037/a0024296

Portnoy, J., & Farrington, D. P. (2015). Resting heart rate and antisocial behavior: An updated systematic review and meta-analysis. *Aggression and Violent Behavior, 22*, 33–45. doi: 10.1016/j.avb.2015.02.004

Post, J. M. (2005). When hatred is bred in the bone: Psycho-cultural foundations of contemporary terrorism. *Political Psychology, 26,* 615–636. doi: 10.1111/j.1467-9221.2005.00434.x

Post, J. M., McGinnis, C., & Moody, K. (2014). The changing face of terrorism in the 21st century: The communications revolution and the virtual community of hatred. *Behavioral Sciences & the Law, 32,* 306–334. doi: 10.1002/bsl.2123

Post, L. A., Biroscak, B. J., & Barboza, G. (2011). Prevalence of sexual violence. In J. W. White, M. P. Koss, & A. E. Kazdin (Eds.), *Violence against women and children* (pp. 101–123). Washington, DC: American Psychological Association.

Postmes, T., & Spears, R. (1998). Deindividuation and antinormative behavior: A meta-analysis. *Psychological Bulletin, 123,* 238–259. doi: 10.1037/0033-2909.123.3.238

Postmes, T., Wichmann, L. J., van Valkengoed, A. M., & van der Hoef, H. (2019). Social identification and depression: A meta-analysis. *European Journal of Social Psychology, 49,* 110–126. doi: 10.1002/ejsp.2508

Pouwels, J. L., Lansu, T. A. M., & Cillessen, A. H. N. (2016). Participant roles of bullying in adolescence: Status characteristics, social behavior, and assignment criteria. *Aggressive Behavior, 42,* 239–253. doi: 10.1002/ab.21614

Pravossoudovitch, K., Martha, C., Cury, F., & Granié, M.-A. (2015). Sex and age differences in the endorsement of sex stereotypes associated with driving. *The Spanish Journal of Psychology, 18,* e100. doi: 10.1017/sjp.2015.94

Prescott, A. T., Sargent, J. D., & Hull, J. G. (2018). Metaanalysis of the relationship between violent video game play and physical aggression over time. *Proceedings of the National Academy of Sciences of the United States of America, 115,* 9882–9888. doi: 10.1073/pnas.1611617114

Price, J., Patterson, R., Regnerus, M., & Walley, J. (2016). How much more XXX is generation X consuming? Evidence of changing attitudes and behaviors related to pornography since 1973. *Journal of Sex Research, 53,* 12–20. doi: 10.1080/00224499.2014.1003773

Prino, C. T., & Peyrot, M. (1994). The effect of child physical abuse and neglect on aggressive, withdrawn, and prosocial behavior. *Child Abuse & Neglect, 18,* 871–884. doi: 10.1016/0145-2134(94)90066-3

Privitera, C., & Campbell, M. A. (2009). Cyberbullying: The new face of workplace bullying? *CyberPsychology & Behavior, 12,* 395–400. doi: 10.1089/cpb.2009.0025

Probst, F., Golle, J., Lory, V., & Lobmaier, J. S. (2018). Reactive aggression tracks within-participant changes in women's salivary testosterone. *Aggressive Behavior, 44,* 362–371. doi: 10.1002/ab.21757

Puhalla, A. A., Kulper, D. A., Fahlgren, M. K., & McCloskey, M. S. (2019). The relationship between resting heart rate variability, hostility, and in vivo aggression among young adults. *Journal of Aggression, Maltreatment & Trauma, 97,* 1–17. doi: 10.1080/10926771.2018.1558324

Puls, H. T., Anderst, J. D., Bettenhausen, J. L., Clark, N., Krager, M., Markham, J. L., & Hall, M. (2019). Newborn risk factors for subsequent physical abuse hospitalizations. *Pediatrics, 143.* doi: 10.1542/peds.2018-2108

Pyrooz, D. C., McGloin, J. M., & Decker, S. H. (2017). Parenthood as a turning point in the life course for male and female gang members: A study of within-individual changes in gang membership and criminal behavior. *Criminology, 55,* 869–899. doi: 10.1111/1745-9125.12162

Pyrooz, D. C., Turanovic, J. J., Decker, S. H., & Wu, J. (2016). Taking stock of the relationship between gang membership and offending. *Criminal Justice and Behavior, 43,* 365–397. doi: 10.1177/0093854815605528

Pyszczynski, T., Abdollahi, A., Solomon, S., Greenberg, J., Cohen, F., & Weise, D. (2009). Mortality salience, martyrdom, and military might: The great Satan versus the axis of evil. In J. Victoroff & A. W. Kruglanski (Eds.), *Psychology of terrorism: Classic and contemporary insights* (pp. 281–297). New York: Psychology Press.

Quigley, B. M., Levitt, A., Derrick, J. L., Testa, M., Houston, R. J., & Leonard, K. E. (2018). Alcohol, self-regulation and partner physical aggression: Actor-partner effects over a three-year time frame. *Frontiers in Behavioral Neuroscience, 12,* 130. doi: 10.3389/fnbeh.2018.00130

Rai, A., & Agarwal, U. A. (2018). A review of literature on mediators and moderators of workplace bullying. *Management Research Review, 41,* 822–859. doi: 10.1108/MRR-05-2016-0111

Raine, A. (1996). Autonomic nervous system activity and violence. In D. M. Stoff & R. B. Cairns (Eds.), *Aggression and violence: Genetic, neurobiological, and biosocial perspectives* (pp. 145–168). Mahwah, NJ: Lawrence Erlbaum.

Raine, A., Dodge, K. A., Loeber, R., Gatzke-Kopp, L., Lynam, D. R., Reynolds, C., ... Liu, J. (2006). The Reactive-Proactive Aggression Questionnaire: Differential correlates of reactive and proactive aggression in adolescent boys. *Aggressive Behavior, 32,* 159–171. doi: 10.1002/ab.20115

Randall, M., & Venkatesh, V. (2015). The right to no: The crime of marital rape, women's human rights, and international law. *Brooklyn Journal of International Law, 41.* Retrieved from brooklynworks.brooklaw.edu/bjil/vol41/iss1/3

Randle, A. A., & Graham, C. A. (2011). A review of the evidence on the effects of intimate partner violence on men. *Psychology of Men & Masculinity, 12,* 97–111. doi: 10.1037/a0021944

Raskin, R., & Terry, H. (1988). A principal-components analysis of the Narcissistic Personality Inventory and further evidence of its construct validity. *Journal of Personality and Social Psychology, 54,* 890–902. doi: 10.1037/0022-3514.54.5.890

Rasmussen, K. (2016). Entitled vengeance: A meta-analysis relating narcissism to provoked aggression. *Aggressive Behavior, 42,* 362–379. doi: 10.1002/ab.21632

Ratan, R., Beyea, D., Li, B. J., & Graciano, L. (2019). Avatar characteristics induce users' behavioral conformity with small-to-medium effect sizes: A meta-analysis of the Proteus effect. *Media Psychology, 11,* 1–25. doi: 10.1080/15213269.2019.1623698

Rathert, J., Fite, P. J., Gaertner, A. E., & Vitulano, M. (2011). Associations between effortful control, psychological control and proactive and reactive aggression. *Child Psychiatry and Human Development, 42,* 609–621. doi: 10.1007/s10578-011-0236-3

Rayburn, N. R., Mendoza, M., & Davidson, G. C. (2003). Bystanders' perceptions of perpetrators and victims of hate crime: An investigation using the person perception paradigm. *Journal of Interpersonal Violence, 18,* 1055–1074. doi: 10.1177/0886260503254513

Reed, R. A., Pamlanye, J. T., Truex, H. R., Murphy-Neilson, M. C., Kunaniec, K. P., Newins, A. R., & Wilson, L. C. (2020). Higher rates of unacknowledged rape among men: The role of rape myth acceptance. *Psychology of Men & Masculinities, 21,* 162–167. doi: 10.1037/men0000230

Rees, J. H., Rees, Y. P. M., Hellmann, J. H., & Zick, A. (2019). Climate of hate: Similar correlates of far right electoral support and right-wing hate crimes in Germany. *Frontiers in Psychology, 10,* 2328. doi: 10.3389/fpsyg.2019.02328

Regoeczi, W. C. (2008). Crowding in context: An examination of the differential responses of men and women to high-density living environments. *Journal of Health and Social Behavior, 49,* 254–268. doi: 10.1177/002214650804900302

Rehbein, F., Kleimann, M., & Mößle, T. (2009). *Computerspielabhängigkeit im Kindes- und Jugendalter.* KFN-Forschungsbericht No 108. Hannover: Kriminologisches Forschungsinstitut Niedersachsen. Retrieved from www.kfn.de/versions/kfn/assets/fb108.pdf

Rehm, J., Steinleitner, M., & Lilli, W. (1987). Wearing uniforms and aggression: A field experiment. *European Journal of Social Psychology, 17,* 357–360. doi: 10.1002/ejsp.2420170310

Reicher, S. D. (1984). The St. Paul's riot: An explanation of the limits of crowd action in terms of a social identity model. *European Journal of Social Psychology, 14,* 1–21. doi: 10.1002/ejsp.2420140102

Reicher, S. D., & Haslam, S. A. (2006). Rethinking the psychology of tyranny: The BBC prison study. *British Journal of Social Psychology, 45,* 1–40. doi: 10.1348/014466605X48998

Reicher, S. D., Spears, R., & Postmes, T. (1995). A social identity model of deindividuation phenomena. *European Review of Social Psychology, 6,* 161–198. doi: 10.1080/14792779443000049

Reidy, D. E., Foster, J. D., & Zeichner, A. (2010). Narcissism and unprovoked aggression. *Aggressive Behavior, 36,* 414–422. doi: 10.1002/ab.20356

Reidy, D. E., Shirk, S. D., Sloan, C. A., & Zeichner, A. (2009). Men who aggress against women: Effects of feminine gender role violation on physical aggression in hypermasculine men. *Psychology of Men & Masculinity, 10,* 1–12. doi: 10.1037/a0014794

Reidy, D. E., Zeichner, A., Foster, J. D., & Martinez, M. A. (2008). Effects of narcissistic entitlement and exploitativeness on human physical aggression. *Personality and Individual Differences, 44*, 865–875. doi: 10.1016/j.paid.2007.10.015

Reifman, A. S., Larrick, R. P., & Fein, S. (1991). Temper and temperature on the diamond: The heat-aggression relationship in major league baseball. *Personality and Social Psychology Bulletin, 17*, 580–585.

Ren, D., Wesselmann, E. D., & Williams, K. D. (2018). Hurt people hurt people: Ostracism and aggression. *Current Opinion in Psychology, 19*, 34–38. doi: 10.1016/j.copsyc.2017.03.026

Rennison, C. M. (2014). Feminist theory in the context of sexual violence. In G. Bruinsma & D. Weisburd (Eds.), *Encyclopedia of criminology and criminal justice* (Vol. 5, pp. 1617–1627). New York: Springer.

Reuter, T. R., Newcomb, M. E., Whitton, S. W., & Mustanski, B. (2017). Intimate partner violence victimization in LGBT young adults: Demographic differences and associations with health behaviors. *Psychology of Violence, 7*, 101–109. doi: 10.1037/vio0000031

Rhee, S. H., & Waldman, I. D. (2002). Genetic and environmental influences on antisocial behavior: A meta-analysis of twin and adoption studies. *Psychological Bulletin, 128*, 490–529. doi: 10.1037/0033-2909.128.3.490

Richardson, D. S. (2014). Everyday aggression takes many forms. *Current Directions in Psychological Science, 23*, 220–224. doi: 10.1177/0963721414530143

Richardson, D. S., & Green, L. R. (2003). Defining direct and indirect aggression: The Richardson Conflict Response Questionnaire. *International Review of Social Psychology, 16*, 11–23.

Richardson, D. S., Green, L. R., & Lago, T. (1998). The relationship between perspective-taking and nonaggressive responding in the face of an attack. *Journal of Personality, 66*, 235–256. doi: 10.1111/1467-6494.00011

Richardson, D. S., & Hammock, G. S. (2007). Social context of human aggression: Are we paying too much attention to gender? *Aggression and Violent Behavior, 12*, 417–426. doi: 10.1016/j.avb.2006.11.001

Richardson, D. S., Hammock, G. S., Smith, S. M., Gardner, W., & Signo, M. (1994). Empathy as a cognitive inhibitor of interpersonal aggression. *Aggressive Behavior, 20*, 275–289. doi: 10.1002/1098-2337(1994)20:4<275::AID-AB2480200402>3.0.CO;2-4

Richeson, J. A., & Sommers, S. R. (2016). Toward a social psychology of race and race relations for the twenty-first century. *Annual Review of Psychology, 67*, 439–463. doi: 10.1146/annurev-psych-010213-115115

Richetin, J., & Richardson, D. S. (2008). Automatic processes and individual differences in aggressive behavior. *Aggression and Violent Behavior, 13*, 423–430. doi: 10.1016/j.avb.2008.06.005

Richetin, J., Richardson, D. S., & Mason, G. D. (2010). Predictive validity of IAT aggressiveness in the context of provocation. *Social Psychology, 41*, 27–34. doi: 10.1027/1864-9335/a000005

Riddle, K., Potter, W. J., Metzger, M. J., Nabi, R. L., & Linz, D. G. (2011). Beyond cultivation: Exploring the effects of frequency, recency, and vivid autobiographical memories for violent media. *Media Psychology*, *14*, 168–191. doi: 10.1080/15213269.2011.573464

Rigby, K., & Johnson, B. (2006). Expressed readiness of Australian school-children to act as bystanders in support of children who are being bullied. *Educational Psychology*, *26*, 425–440. doi: 10.1080/01443410500342047

Ritter, D., & Eslea, M. (2005). Hot sauce, toy guns, and graffiti: A critical account of current laboratory aggression paradigms. *Aggressive Behavior*, *31*, 407–419. doi: 10.1002/ab.20066

Rivara, F. P., Anderson, M. L., Fishman, P., Bonomi, A. E., Reid, R. J., Carrell, D., & Thompson, R. S. (2007). Healthcare utilization and costs for women with a history of intimate partner violence. *American Journal of Preventive Medicine*, *32*, 89–96. doi: 10.1016/j.amepre.2006.10.001

Rivenbark, J. G., Odgers, C. L., Caspi, A., Harrington, H., Hogan, S., Houts, R. M., ... Moffitt, T. E. (2018). The high societal costs of childhood conduct problems: Evidence from administrative records up to age 38 in a longitudinal birth cohort. *Journal of Child Psychology and Psychiatry, and Allied Disciplines*, *59*, 703–710. doi: 10.1111/jcpp.12850

Roberts, D. W. (2009). Intimate partner homicide: Relationships to alcohol and firearms. *Journal of Contemporary Criminal Justice*, *25*, 67–88. doi: 10.1177/1043986208329771

Robinson, T. N., Wilde, M. L., Navracruz, L. C., Haydel, K. F., & Varady, A. (2001). Effects of reducing children's television and video game use on aggressive behavior. *Archives of Pediatrics and Adolescent Medicine*, *155*, 17–23.

Rodenhizer, K. A. E., & Edwards, K. M. (2019). The impacts of sexual media exposure on adolescent and emerging adults' dating and sexual violence attitudes and behaviors: A critical review of the literature. *Trauma, Violence & Abuse*, *20*, 439–452. doi: 10.1177/1524838017717745

Rodrigues, A. E., Funderburk, J. S., Keating, N. L., & Maisto, S. A. (2015). A methodological review of intimate partner violence in the military: Where do we go from here? *Trauma, Violence & Abuse*, *16*, 231–240. doi: 10.1177/1524838014526066

Rohlf, H., Busching, R., & Krahé, B. (2017). Longitudinal links between maladaptive anger regulation, peer problems, and aggression in middle childhood. *Merrill-Palmer Quarterly*, *63*, 282–309. doi: 10.13110/merrpalmquar1982.63.2.0282

Rohlf, H., Holl, A. K., Kirsch, F., Krahé, B., & Elsner, B. (2018). Longitudinal links between executive function, anger, and aggression in middle childhood. *Frontiers in Behavioral Neuroscience*, *12*, 27. doi: 10.3389/fnbeh.2018.00027

Rohlf, H., & Krahé, B. (2015). Assessing anger regulation in middle childhood: Development and validation of a behavioral observation measure. *Frontiers in Psychology*, *6*, 453. doi: 10.3389/fpsyg.2015.00453

Rohlf, H., Krahé, B., & Busching, R. (2016). The socializing effect of classroom aggression on the development of aggression and social rejection: A two-wave multilevel analysis. *Journal of School Psychology, 58,* 57–72. doi: 10.1016/j.jsp.2016.05.002

Roisman, G. I., Monahan, K. C., Campbell, S. B., Steinberg, L., & Cauffman, E. (2010). Is adolescence-onset antisocial behavior developmentally normative? *Development and Psychopathology, 22,* 295–311. doi: 10.1017/S0954579410000076

Romano, E., & De Luca, R. V. (2001). Male sexual abuse: A review of effects, abuse characteristics, and links with later psychological functioning. *Aggression and Violent Behavior, 6,* 55–78. doi: 10.1016/S1359-1789(99)00011-7

Rosen, C., Tiet, Q., Cavella, S., Finney, J., & Lee, T. (2005). Chronic PTSD patients' functioning before and after the September 11 attacks. *Journal of Traumatic Stress, 18,* 781–784. doi: 10.1002/jts.20086

Rosenkoetter, L. I., Rosenkoetter, S. E., & Acock, A. C. (2009). Television violence: An intervention to reduce its impact on children. *Journal of Applied Developmental Psychology, 30,* 381–397. doi: 10.1016/j.appdev.2008.12.019

Rosenkoetter, L. I., Rosenkoetter, S. E., Ozretich, R. A., & Acock, A. C. (2004). Mitigating the harmful effects of television violence. *Journal of Applied Developmental Psychology, 25,* 25–47.

Rosenthal, R. (1990). Media violence, antisocial behavior, and the social consequences of small effects. In R. Surette (Ed.), *The media and criminal justice policy: Recent research and social effects* (pp. 53–61). Springfield, IL: Charles C Thomas, Publisher.

Rosenzweig, S. (1945). The picture-association method and its application in a study of reactions to frustration. *Journal of Personality, 14,* 3–23. doi: 10.1111/j.1467-6494.1945.tb01036.x

Rosenzweig, S. (1976). Aggressive behavior and the Rosenzweig Picture-Frustration (P-F) Study. *Journal of Clinical Psychology, 32,* 885–891. doi: 10.1002/1097-4679(197610)32:4<885::AID-JCLP2270320434>3.0.CO;2-R

Rosenzweig, S., Fleming, E. E., & Rosenzweig, L. (1948). The children's form of the Rosenzweig Picture-Frustration Study. *The Journal of Psychology, 26,* 141–191. doi: 10.1080/00223980.1948.9917400

Rosenzweig, S., Ludwig, D. J., & Adelman, S. (1975). Retest reliability of the Rosenzweig Picture-Frustration Study and similar semiprojective techniques. *Journal of Personality Assessment, 39,* 3–12. doi: 10.1207/s15327752jpa3901_1

Rothman, E. F., Exner, D., & Baughman, A. L. (2011). The prevalence of sexual assault against people who identify as gay, lesbian, or bisexual in the United States: A systematic review. *Trauma, Violence, & Abuse, 12,* 55–66. doi: 10.1177/1524838010390707

Rothschild, Z. K., Abdollahi, A., & Pyszczynski, T. (2009). Does peace have a prayer? The effect of mortality salience, compassionate values, and religious fundamentalism on hostility toward out-groups. *Journal of Experimental Social Psychology, 45,* 816–827. doi: 10.1016/j.jesp.2009.05.016

Rotton, J., Frey, J., Barry, T., Milligan, M., & Fitzpatrick, M. (1979). The air pollution experience and physical aggression. *Journal of Applied Social Psychology, 9,* 397–412. doi: 10.1111/j.1559-1816.1979.tb02714.x

Rouhana, N. N., & Bar-Tal, D. (1998). Psychological dynamics of intractable ethnonational conflicts: The Israeli-Palestinian case. *American Psychologist, 53,* 761–770. doi: 10.1037/0003-066X.53.7.761

Rubin, G. J., Brewin, C. R., Greenberg, N., Simpson, J., & Wessley, S. (2005). Psychological and behavioural reactions to the bombings in London on 7 July 2005: Cross sectional survey of a representative sample of Londoners. *British Medical Journal, 331*(7517), 606-0. doi: 10.1136/bmj.38583.728484.3A

Rudman, L. A., & Glick, P. (2008). *The social psychology of gender: How power and intimacy shape gender relations.* New York: Guilford Press.

Rudolph, J., & Zimmer-Gembeck, M. J. (2018). Reviewing the focus: A summary and critique of child-focused sexual abuse prevention. *Trauma, Violence, & Abuse, 19,* 543–554. doi: 10.1177/1524838016675478

Russell, G. W. (1993). *The social psychology of sport.* New York: Springer.

Russell, G. W. (2004). Sport riots: A social-psychological review. *Aggression and Violent Behavior, 9,* 353–378. doi: 10.1016/S1359-1789(03) 00031-4

Russell, G. W. (2008). *Aggression in the sports world: A social psychological perspective.* New York: Oxford University Press.

Sachs, C. J., & Chu, L. D. (2000). The association between professional football games and domestic violence in Los Angeles County. *Journal of Interpersonal Violence, 15,* 1192–1201. doi: 10.1177/08862600001 5011006

Saiya, N., Zaihra, T., & Fidler, J. (2017). Testing the Hillary doctrine. *Political Research Quarterly, 70,* 421–432. doi: 10.1177/1065912917698046

Saleem, M., Anderson, C. A., & Barlett, C. P. (2015). Assessing helping and hurting behaviors through the Tangram help/hurt task. *Personality and Social Psychology Bulletin, 41,* 1345–1362. doi: 10.1177/0146167215 594348

Saleem, M., Barlett, C. P., Anderson, C. A., & Hawkins, I. (2017). Helping and hurting others: Person and situation effects on aggressive and prosocial behavior as assessed by the Tangram task. *Aggressive Behavior, 43,* 133–146. doi: 10.1002/ab.21669

Salguero, J. M., García-Sancho, E., Ramos-Cejudo, J., & Kannis-Dymand, L. (2020). Individual differences in anger and displaced aggression: The role of metacognitive beliefs and anger rumination. *Aggressive Behavior, 46,* 162–169. doi: 10.1002/ab.21878

Salmivalli, C. (2010). Bullying and the peer group: A review. *Aggression and Violent Behavior, 15,* 112–120. doi: 10.1016/j.avb.2009.08.007

Salmivalli, C., Kärnä, A., & Poskiparta, E. (2011). Counteracting bullying in Finland: The KiVa program and its effects on different forms of being bullied. *International Journal of Behavioral Development, 35,* 405–411. doi: 10.1177/0165025411407457

Salmivalli, C., Lagerspetz, K., Björkqvist, K., Österman, K., & Kaukialnen, A. (1996). Bullying as a group process: Participant roles and their relations to social status within the group. *Aggressive Behavior, 22,* 1–15. doi: 10.1002/(SICI)1098-2337(1996)22:1<1::AID-AB1>3.0.CO;2-T

Samnani, A. K. (2018). Aggression in the workplace. In J. L. Ireland, P. Birch, & C. A. Ireland (Eds.), *The Routledge international handbook of human aggression* (pp. 121–130). London: Routledge.

Samsudin, E. Z., Isahak, M., & Rampal, S. (2018). The prevalence, risk factors and outcomes of workplace bullying among junior doctors: a systematic review. *European Journal of Work and Organizational Psychology, 3*, 1–19. doi: 10.1080/1359432X.2018.1502171

Sanday, P. R. (1981). The socio-cultural context of rape: A cross-cultural study. *Journal of Social Issues, 37*, 5–27. doi: 10.1111/j.1540-4560.1981.tb01068.x

Sanders, M. R., Cann, W., & Markie-Dadds, C. (2003). The Triple P-Positive Parenting Programme: A universal population-level approach to the prevention of child abuse. *Child Abuse Review, 12*, 155–171. doi: 10.1002/car.798

Santisteban, C., Alvarado, J. M., & Recio, P. (2007). Evaluation of a Spanish version of the Buss and Perry aggression questionnaire: Some personal and situational factors related to the aggression scores of young subjects. *Personality and Individual Differences, 42*, 1453–1465. doi: 10.1016/j.paid.2006.10.019

Santos, D., Briñol, P., Petty, R. E., Gandarillas, B., & Mateos, R. (2019). Trait aggressiveness predicting aggressive behavior: The moderating role of meta-cognitive certainty. *Aggressive Behavior, 45*, 255–264. doi: 10.1002/ab.21815

Sarrel, P. M., & Masters, W. H. (1982). Sexual molestation of men by women. *Archives of Sexual Behavior, 11*, 117–131. doi: 10.1007/BF01541979

Schachter, S. (1964). The interaction of cognitive and physiological determinants of emotional state. In L. Berkowitz (Ed.), *Advances in experimental social psychology* (Vol. 1, pp. 49–80). New York: Academic Press.

Schank, R. C., & Abelson, R. P. (1977). *Scripts, plans, goals and understanding: An inquiry into human knowledge structures.* Oxford: Lawrence Erlbaum.

Scheithauer, H., Haag, N., Mahlke, J., & Ittel, A. (2008). Gender and age differences in the development of relational/indirect aggression: First results of a meta-analysis. *European Journal of Developmental Science, 2*, 176–189.

Scheitle, C. P., & Hansmann, M. (2016). Religion-related hate crimes: Data, trends, and limitations. *Journal for the Scientific Study of Religion, 55*, 859–873. doi: 10.1111/jssr.12299

Schewe, P. A. (2002). Guidelines for developing rape prevention and risk reduction interventions. In P. A. Schewe (Ed.), *Preventing violence in relationships: Interventions across the life span* (pp. 107–136). Washington, DC: American Psychological Association.

Schlenger, W. E., Caddell, J. M., Ebert, L., Jordan, B. Kathleen, Rourke, K. M., Wilson, D., ... Kulka, R. A. (2002). Psychological reactions to terrorist attacks: Findings from the National Study of Americans' Reactions to September 11. *JAMA: Journal of the American Medical Association, 288*, 581–588. doi: 10.1037/t00789-000

Schmid, K., Hewstone, M., Küpper, B., Zick, A., & Tausch, N. (2014). Reducing aggressive intergroup action tendencies: Effects of intergroup contact via perceived intergroup threat. *Aggressive Behavior, 40*, 250–262. doi: 10.1002/ab.21516

Schneider, K. T., Swan, S., & Fitzgerald, L. F. (1997). Job-related and psychological effects of sexual harassment in the workplace: Empirical evidence from two organizations. *Journal of Applied Psychology, 82*, 401–415. doi: 10.1037/0021-9010.82.3.401

Schuster, I., & Krahé, B. (2016). Abuse of elders living at home: A review of recent prevalence studies. *International Journal of Behavioral Science, 11*, 93–108.

Schuster, I., & Krahé, B. (2019a). Predicting sexual victimization among college students in Chile and Turkey: A cross-cultural analysis. *Archives of Sexual Behavior, 48*, 2565–2580. doi: 10.1007/s10508-018-1335-z

Schuster, I., & Krahé, B. (2019b). Predictors of sexual aggression perpetration among male and female college students: Cross-cultural evidence from Chile and Turkey. *Sexual Abuse, 31*, 318–343. doi: 10.1177/1079063218793632

Schwartz, M. D., & DeKeseredy, W. S. (2008). Interpersonal violence against women: The role of men. *Journal of Contemporary Criminal Justice, 24*, 178–185. doi: 10.1177/1043986208315483

Schwartz, S. J., Dunkel, C. S., & Waterman, A. S. (2009). Terrorism: An identity theory perspective. *Studies in Conflict & Terrorism, 32*, 537–559. doi: 10.1080/10576100902888453

Sedlak, A. J., Mettenburg, J., Basena, M., Petta, I., McPherson, K., Greene, A., & Li, S. (2010). *The fourth national incidence study on child abuse and neglect (NIS-4): Report to Congress, Executive Summary.* Washington, DC: U.S. Department of Health and Human Services. Retrieved from www.acf.hhs.gov/programs/opre/abuse_neglect/natl_incid/nis4_report_congress_full_pdf_jan2010.pdf

Senn, C. Y., Eliasziw, M., Barata, P. C., Thurston, W. E., Newby-Clark, I. R., Radtke, H. L., & Hobden, K. L. (2013). Sexual assault resistance education for university women: Study protocol for a randomized controlled trial (SARE trial). *BMC Women's Health, 13*, 25. doi: 10.1186/1472-6874-13-25

Senn, C. Y., Eliasziw, M., Barata, P. C., Thurston, W. E., Newby-Clark, I. R., Radtke, H. L., & Hobden, K. L. (2015). Efficacy of a sexual assault resistance program for university women. *The New England Journal of Medicine, 372*, 2326–2335. doi: 10.1056/NEJMsa1411131

Senn, C. Y., Eliasziw, M., Hobden, K. L., Newby-Clark, I. R., Barata, P. C., Radtke, H. L., & Thurston, W. E. (2017). Secondary and 2-year outcomes of a sexual assault resistance program for university women. *Psychology of Women Quarterly, 41*, 147–162. doi: 10.1177/0361684317690119

Senn, T. E., Carey, M. P., & Vanable, P. A. (2008). Childhood and adolescent sexual abuse and subsequent sexual risk behavior: Evidence from controlled studies, methodological critique, and suggestions for research. *Clinical Psychology Review, 28*, 711–735. doi: 10.1016/j.cpr.2007.10.002

Seto, M. C., & Lalumière, M. L. (2010). What is so special about male adolescent sexual offending? A review and test of explanations through meta-analysis. *Psychological Bulletin, 136*, 526–575. doi: 10.1037/a0019700

Shakespeare-Finch, J., & Lurie-Beck, J. (2014). A meta-analytic clarification of the relationship between posttraumatic growth and symptoms of posttraumatic distress disorder. *Journal of Anxiety Disorders, 28*, 223–229. doi: 10.1016/j.janxdis.2013.10.005

Sherif, M. (1958). Superordinate goals in the reduction of intergroup conflict. *American Journal of Sociology, 63*, 349–356. doi: 10.1086/222258

Sherif, M. (1966). *In common predicament: Social psychology in intergroup conflict and cooperation.* Boston, MA: Houghton Mifflin.

Sherif, M., Harvey, O. J., White, B. J., Hood, W. R., & Sherif, C. W. (1961). *Intergroup conflict and cooperation: The Robbers Cave experiment.* Norman, OK: University of Oklahoma Book Exchange.

Sherrill, A. M., Magliano, J. P., Rosenbaum, A., Bell, K. M., & Wallace, P. S. (2016). Trait aggressiveness and aggressive behavior in the context of provocation and inhibition. *Journal of Aggression, Maltreatment & Trauma, 25*, 487–502. doi: 10.1080/10926771.2015.1121192

Shibuya, A., Sakamoto, A., Ihori, N., & Yukawa, S. (2007). The effects of the presence and contexts of video game violence on children: A longitudinal study in Japan. *Simulation & Gaming, 39*, 528–539. doi: 10.1177/1046878107306670

Shields, W. M., & Shields, L. M. (1983). Forcible rape: An evolutionary perspective. *Ethology and Sociobiology, 4*, 115–136. doi: 10.1016/0162-3095(83)90026-2

Shoal, G. D., Giancola, P. R., & Kirillova, G. P. (2003). Salivary cortisol, personality, and aggressive behavior in adolescent boys: A 5-year longitudinal study. *Journal of the American Academy of Child & Adolescent Psychiatry, 42*, 1101–1107. doi: 10.1097/01.CHI.0000070246.24125.6D

Shor, E. (2019). Age, aggression, and pleasure in popular online pornographic videos. *Violence Against Women, 25*, 1018–1036. doi: 10.1177/1077801218804101

Shor, E., & Seida, K. (2019). "Harder and harder"? Is mainstream pornography becoming increasingly violent and do Viewers prefer violent content? *Journal of Sex Research, 56*, 16–28. doi: 10.1080/00224499.2018.1451476

Shotland, R. L., & Hunter, B. A. (1995). Women's "token resistant" and compliant sexual behaviors are related to uncertain sexual intentions and rape. *Personality and Social Psychology Bulletin, 21*, 226–236. doi: 10.1177/0146167295213004

Shrum, L. J. (1996). Psychological processes underlying cultivation effects: Further tests of construct accessibility. *Human Communication Research, 22*, 482–509. doi: 10.1111/j.1468-2958.1996.tb00376.x

Sidanius, J., Kteily, N., Levin, S., Pratto, F., & Obaidi, M. (2016). Support for asymmetric violence among Arab populations: The clash of cultures, social identity, or counterdominance? *Group Processes & Intergroup Relations, 19,* 343–359. doi: 10.1177/1368430215577224

Siegel, M., Negussie, Y., Vanture, S., Pleskunas, J., Ross, C. S., & King, C. (2014). The relationship between gun ownership and stranger and nonstranger firearm homicide rates in the United States, 1981–2010. *American Journal of Public Health, 104,* 1912–1919. doi: 10.2105/AJPH.2014.302042

Sigurvinsdottir, R., Ullman, S. E., & Canetto, S. S. (2020). Self-blame, psychological distress, and suicidality among African American female sexual assault survivors. *Traumatology, 26,* 1–10. doi: 10.1037/trm0000195

Silke, A. (2003). Deindividuation, anonymity, and violence: Findings from Northern Ireland. *The Journal of Social Psychology, 143,* 493–499. doi: 10.1080/00224540309598458

Silke, A. (2009). Cheshire-cat logic: The recurring theme of terrorist abnormality in psychological research. In J. Victoroff & A. W. Kruglanski (Eds.), *Psychology of terrorism: Classic and contemporary insights* (pp. 95–107). New York: Psychology Press.

Silver, R. C., Holman, E. A., McIntosh, D. N., Poulin, M., & Gil-Rivas, V. (2002). Nationwide longitudinal study of psychological responses to September 11. *Journal of the American Medical Association, 288,* 1235–1244. doi: 10.1001/jama.288.10.1235

Simmons, S. B., Knight, K. E., & Menard, S. (2015). Consequences of intimate partner violence on substance use and depression for women and men. *Journal of Family Violence, 30,* 351–361. doi: 10.1007/s10896-015-9691-0

Simon, T. R., Ikeda, R. M., Smith, E. P., Reese, L.'R. E., Rabiner, D. L., Miller, S., … Allison, K. W. (2009). The ecological effects of universal and selective violence prevention programs for middle school students: A randomized trial. *Journal of Consulting and Clinical Psychology, 77,* 526–542. doi: 10.1037/a0014395

Simon, W., & Gagnon, J. H. (1986). Sexual scripts: Permanence and change. *Archives of Sexual Behavior, 15,* 97–120. doi: 10.1007/BF01542219

Simons, Y., & Taylor, J. (1992). A psychosocial model of fan violence in sports. *International Journal of Sport Psychology, 23,* 207–226.

Sims, C. S., Drasgow, F., & Fitzgerald, L. F. (2005). The effects of sexual harassment on turnover in the military: Time-dependent modeling. *Journal of Applied Psychology, 90,* 1141–1152. doi: 10.1037/0021-9010.90.6.1141

Singer, J. D. (1989). The political origins of international war: A multifactorial review. In J. Groebel & R. A. Hinde (Eds.), *Aggression and war: Their biological and social bases* (pp. 202–220). New York: Cambridge University Press.

Slater, M. D., Henry, K. L., Swaim, R. C., & Anderson, L. L. (2003). Violent media content and aggressiveness in adolescents: A downward spiral model. *Communication Research, 30,* 713–736. doi: 10.1177/0093650203258281

Slep, A. M. S., Heyman, R. E., Snarr, J. D., Foster, R. E., Linkh, D. J., & Whitworth, J. D. (2011). Child emotional aggression and abuse: Definitions and prevalence. *Child Abuse & Neglect, 35*, 783–796. doi: 10.1016/j.chiabu.2011.07.002

Slone, M., Lavi, I., Ozer, E. J., & Pollak, A. (2017). The Israeli-Palestinian conflict: Meta-analysis of exposure and outcome relations for children of the region. *Children and Youth Services Review, 74*, 50–61. doi: 10.1016/j.childyouth.2017.01.019

Slone, M., & Mann, S. (2016). Effects of war, terrorism and armed conflict on young children: A systematic review. *Child Psychiatry and Human Development, 47*, 950–965. doi: 10.1007/s10578-016-0626-7

Slotter, E. B., & Finkel, E. J. (2011). I³ Theory: Instigating, impelling, and inhibiting factors in aggression. In P. R. Shaver & M. Mikulincer (Eds.), *Human aggression and violence: Causes, manifestations, and consequences* (pp. 35–52). Washington, DC: American Psychological Association.

Smeijers, D., Benbouriche, M., & Garofalo, C. (2020). The association between emotion, social information processing, and aggressive behavior. *European Psychologist*, 1–11. doi: 10.1027/1016-9040/a000395

Smith, D. N. (1998). The psychocultural roots of genocide: Legitimacy and crisis in Rwanda. *American Psychologist, 53*, 743–753. doi: 10.1037/0003-066X.53.7.743

Smith, H. J., Pettigrew, T. F., Pippin, G. M., & Bialosiewicz, S. (2012). Relative deprivation: A theoretical and meta-analytic review. *Personality and Social Psychology Review, 16*, 203–232. doi: 10.1177/1088868311430825

Smith, P. K. (2016). Bullying: Definition, types, causes, consequences and intervention. *Social and Personality Psychology Compass, 10*, 519–532. doi: 10.1111/spc3.12266

Smith, P. K., Singer, M., Hoel, H., & Cooper, C. L. (2003). Victimization in the school and the workplace: Are there any links? *British Journal of Psychology, 94*, 175–188. doi: 10.1348/000712603321661868

Smith, S. G., Zhang, X., Basile, K. C., Merrick, M. T., Wang, J., Kresnow, M., & Chen, J. (2018). *The National Intimate Partner and Sexual Violence Survey (NISVS): 2015 Data Brief – Updated Release.* Retrieved from www.cdc.gov/violenceprevention/pdf/2015data-brief508.pdf

Smith, S. L., & Boyson, A. R. (2002). Violence in music videos: Examining the prevalence and context of physical aggression. *Journal of Communication, 52*, 61–83. doi: 10.1111/j.1460-2466.2002.tb02533.x

Sojo, V. E., Wood, R. E., & Genat, A. E. (2016). Harmful workplace experiences and women's occupational well-being. *Psychology of Women Quarterly, 40*, 10–40. doi: 10.1177/0361684315599346

Sønderlund, A. L., O'Brien, K. S., Kremer, P., Rowland, B., Groot, F. de, Staiger, P., ... Miller, P. G. (2014). The association between sports participation, alcohol use and aggression and violence: A systematic review. *Journal of Science and Medicine in Sport, 17*, 2–7. doi: 10.1016/j.jsams.2013.03.011

Sousa, C., Herrenkohl, T. I., Moylan, C. A., Tajima, E. A., Klika, J. B., Herrenkohl, R. C., & Russo, M. J. (2011). Longitudinal study on the effects of child abuse and children's exposure to domestic violence, parent-child attachments, and antisocial behavior in adolescence. *Journal of Interpersonal Violence, 26*, 111–136. doi: 10.1177/0886260510362883

Soyer, R. B., Rovenpor, J. L., Kopelman, R. E., Mullins, L. S., & Watson, P. J. (2001). Further assessment of the construct validity of four measures of narcissism: Replication and extension. *Journal of Psychology, 135*, 245–258. doi: 10.1080/00223980109603695

Spaaij, R. (2014). Sports crowd violence: An interdisciplinary synthesis. *Aggression and Violent Behavior, 19*, 146–155. doi: 10.1016/j.avb.2014.02.002

Spaaij, R., & Schaillée, H. (2019). Unsanctioned aggression and violence in amateur sport: A multidisciplinary synthesis. *Aggression and Violent Behavior, 44*, 36–46. doi: 10.1016/j.avb.2018.11.007

Sparks, G. G., & Sparks, C. W. (2002). Effects of media violence. In J. Bryant & D. Zillmann (Eds.), *Media effects: Advances in theory and research* (2nd ed., pp. 269–285). Mahwah, NJ: Lawrence Erlbaum.

Spears, R. (2017). Deindividuation. In S. G. Harkins, K. D. Williams, J. Burger, & R. Spears (Eds.), *The Oxford handbook of social influence* (pp. 279–297). Oxford: Oxford University Press.

Spencer, C., Cafferky, B., & Stith, S. M. (2016). Gender differences in risk markers for perpetration of physical partner violence: Results from a meta-analytic review. *Journal of Family Violence, 31*, 981–984. doi: 10.1007/s10896-016-9860-9

Spencer, C., Mallory, A. B., Cafferky, B., Kimmes, J. G., Beck, A. R., & Stith, S. M. (2019). Mental health factors and intimate partner violence perpetration and victimization: A meta-analysis. *Psychology of Violence, 9*, 1–17. doi: 10.1037/vio0000156

Spencer, C., Mendez, M., & Stith, S. M. (2019). The role of income inequality on factors associated with male physical intimate partner violence perpetration: A meta-analysis. *Aggression and Violent Behavior, 48*, 116–123. doi: 10.1016/j.avb.2019.08.010

Spencer, C., Stith, S. M., & Cafferky, B. (2019). Risk markers for physical intimate partner violence victimization: A meta-analysis. *Aggression and Violent Behavior, 44*, 8–17. doi: 10.1016/j.avb.2018.10.009

Spielberger, C. D. (1996). *Manual for the State-Trait Anger Expression Inventory (STAXI)*. Odessa, FL: Psychological Assessment Resources.

Stadler, C., Rohrmann, S., Steuber, S., & Poustka, F. (2006). Effects of provocation on emotions and aggression: An experimental study with aggressive children. *Swiss Journal of Psychology, 65*, 117–124. doi: 10.1024/1421-0185.65.2.117

Staggs, S. L., & Schewe, P. A. (2011). Primary prevention of domestic violence. In M. P. Koss, J. W. White, & A. E. Kazdin (Eds.), *Violence against women and children* (pp. 237–257). Washington, DC: American Psychological Association.

Stander, V. A., & Thomsen, C. J. (2016). Sexual harassment and assault in the U.S. Military: A review of policy and research trends. *Military Medicine, 181*(1 Suppl), 20–27. doi: 10.7205/MILMED-D-15-00336

Staub, E. (2007). Preventing violence and terrorism and promoting positive relations between Dutch and Muslim communities in Amsterdam. *Peace and Conflict: Journal of Peace Psychology, 13*, 333–360. doi: 10.1080/10781910701471397

Steele, C. M., & Josephs, R. A. (1990). Alcohol myopia: Its prized and dangerous effects. *American Psychologist, 45*, 921–933. doi: 10.1037/0003-066X.45.8.921

Steinmetz, S. K. (1978). Battered parents. *Society, 15*, 54–55. doi: 10.1007/BF02701616

Stemple, L., Flores, A., & Meyer, I. H. (2017). Sexual victimization perpetrated by women: Federal data reveal surprising prevalence. *Aggression and Violent Behavior, 34*, 302–311. doi: 10.1016/j.avb.2016.09.007

Stephan, W. G., Ybarra, O., & Rios, K. (2016). Intergroup threat theory. In T. D. Nelson (Ed.), *Handbook of prejudice, stereotyping, and discrimination* (2nd ed., pp. 255–278). New York: Psychology Press.

Stern, V. (2010). *The Stern review: A report by Baroness Vivien Stern CBE of an independent review into how rape complaints are handled by public authorities in England and Wales.* Retrieved from http://webarchive.nationalarchives.gov.uk/20110608160754/http:/www.equalities.gov.uk/PDF/Stern_Review_acc_FINAL.pdf

Stith, S. M., Liu, T., Davies, L. C., Boykin, E. L., Alder, M. C., Harris, J. M., ... Dees, J. E. M. E. G. (2009). Risk factors in child maltreatment: A meta-analytic review of the literature. *Aggression and Violent Behavior, 14*, 13–29. doi: 10.1016/j.avb.2006.03.006

Stoltenborgh, M., Bakermans-Kranenburg, M. J., Alink, L. R. A., & van IJzendoorn, M. H. (2015). The prevalence of child maltreatment across the globe: Review of a series of meta-analyses. *Child Abuse Review, 24*, 37–50. doi: 10.1002/car.2353

Storey, J. E. (2020). Risk factors for elder abuse and neglect: A review of the literature. *Aggression and Violent Behavior, 50*. doi: 10.1016/j.avb.2019.101339

Stott, C., Hutchison, P., & Drury, J. (2001). "Hooligans" abroad? Inter-group dynamics, social identity and participation in collective "disorder" at the 1998 World Cup finals. *British Journal of Social Psychology, 40*, 359–384. doi: 10.1348/014466601164876

Stotzer, R. L., & MacCartney, D. (2016). The role of institutional factors on on-campus reported rape prevalence. *Journal of Interpersonal Violence, 31*, 2687–2707. doi: 10.1177/0886260515580367

Straus, M. A. (1979). Measuring intrafamily conflict and violence: The Conflict Tactics (CT) Scales. *Journal of Marriage and the Family, 41*, 75–88. doi: 10.2307/351733

Straus, M. A., & Douglas, E. M. (2017). Eight new developments, uses, and clarifications of the Conflict Tactics Scales. *Journal of Family Issues, 38*, 1953–1973. doi: 10.1177/0192513X17729720

Straus, M. A., Hamby, S. L., Boney-McCoy, S., & Sugarman, D. B. (1996). The revised Conflict Tactics Scales (CTS2): Development and preliminary psychometric data. *Journal of Family Issues, 17*, 283–316. doi: 10.1177/019251396017003001

Straus, M. A., Hamby, S. L., Finkelhor, D., Moore, D. W., & Runyan, D. (1998). Identification of child maltreatment with the Parent–Child Conflict Tactics Scales: Development and psychometric data for a national sample of American parents. *Child Abuse & Neglect, 22*, 249–270. doi: 10.1016/S0145-2134(97)00174-9

Stroebe, W. (2013). Firearm possession and violent death: A critical review. *Aggression and Violent Behavior, 18*, 709–721. doi: 10.1016/j.avb.2013.07.025

Stroebe, W. (2016). Firearm availability and violent death: The need for a culture change in attitudes toward guns. *Analyses of Social Issues and Public Policy, 16*, 7–35. doi: 10.1111/asap.12100

Strom, K. J., & Irvin, C. (2007). Terrorism as a form of violence. In D. J. Flannery, A. T. Vazsonyi, & I. D. Waldman (Eds.), *The Cambridge handbook of violent behavior and aggression* (pp. 583–601). New York: Cambridge University Press.

Struckman-Johnson, C. (1988). Forced sex on dates: It happens to men, too. *Journal of Sex Research, 24*, 234–241. doi: 10.1080/00224498809551418

Struckman-Johnson, C., & Struckman-Johnson, D. (1994). Men pressured and forced into sexual experience. *Archives of Sexual Behavior, 23*, 93–114. doi: 10.1007/BF01541620

Struckman-Johnson, C., Struckman-Johnson, D., & Anderson, P. B. (2003). Tactics of sexual coercion: When men and women won't take no for an answer. *Journal of Sex Research, 40*, 76–86. doi: 10.1080/00224490309552168

Stuart, S. M., McKimmie, B. M., & Masser, B. M. (2019). Rape perpetrators on trial: The effect of sexual assault-related schemas on attributions of blame. *Journal of Interpersonal Violence, 34*, 310–336. doi: 10.1177/0886260516640777

Stubbs-Richardson, M., Rader, N. E., & Cosby, A. G. (2018). Tweeting rape culture: Examining portrayals of victim blaming in discussions of sexual assault cases on Twitter. *Feminism & Psychology, 28*, 90–108. doi: 10.1177/0959353517715874

Sturmey, P. (Ed.) (2017). *The Wiley handbook of violence and aggression (3 vols.)*. Chichester, U.K.: Wiley Blackwell.

Subra, B., Muller, D., Bègue, L., Bushman, B. J., & Delmas, F. (2010). Automatic effects of alcohol and aggressive cues on aggressive thoughts and behaviors. *Personality and Social Psychology Bulletin, 36*, 1052–1057. doi: 10.1177/0146167210374725

Subramani, O. S., Parrott, D. J., Latzman, R. D., & Washburn, D. A. (2019). Breaking the link: Distraction from emotional cues reduces the association between trait disinhibition and reactive physical aggression. *Aggressive Behavior, 45*, 151–160. doi: 10.1002/ab.21804

Sunday, S. R., & Tobach, E. (Eds.) (1985). *Violence against women: A critique of the sociobiology of rape.* New York: Gordian Press.

Sutton, T. E. (2017). The lives of female gang members: A review of the literature. *Aggression and Violent Behavior, 37,* 142–152. doi: 10.1016/j.avb.2017.10.001

Swartout, K. M., & White, J. W. (2010). The relationship between drug use and sexual aggression in men across time. *Journal of Interpersonal Violence, 25,* 1716–1735. doi: 10.1177/0886260509354586

Tafrate, R. C., Kassinove, H., & Dundin, L. (2002). Anger episodes in high- and low-trait-anger community adults. *Journal of Clinical Psychology, 58,* 1573–1590. doi: 10.1002/jclp.10076

Tai, K., Zheng, X., & Narayanan, J. (2011). Touching a teddy bear mitigates negative effects of social exclusion to increase prosocial behavior. *Social Psychological and Personality Science, 2,* 618–626. doi: 10.1177/1948550611404707

Taillieu, T. L., Brownridge, D. A., Sareen, J., & Afifi, T. O. (2016). Childhood emotional maltreatment and mental disorders: Results from a nationally representative adult sample from the United States. *Child Abuse & Neglect, 59,* 1–12. doi: 10.1016/j.chiabu.2016.07.005

Tajfel, H. (1981). *Human groups and social categories: Studies in social psychology.* Cambridge, U.K.: Cambridge University Press.

Takarangi, M. K. T., Polaschek, D. L. L., Hignett, A., & Garry, M. (2008). Chronic and temporary aggression causes hostile false memories for ambiguous information. *Applied Cognitive Psychology, 22,* 39–49. doi: 10.1002/acp.1327

Tarrant, M., Branscombe, N. R., Warner, R. H., & Weston, D. (2012). Social identity and perceptions of torture: It's moral when we do it. *Journal of Experimental Social Psychology, 48,* 513–518. doi: 10.1016/j.jesp.2011.10.017

Taylor, L. D., Davis-Kean, P., & Malanchuk, O. (2007). Self-esteem, academic self-concept, and aggression at school. *Aggressive Behavior, 33,* 130–136. doi: 10.1002/ab.20174

Taylor, S. P. (1967). Aggressive behavior and physiological arousal as a function of provocation and the tendency to inhibit aggression. *Journal of Personality, 35,* 297–310. doi: 10.1111/j.1467-6494.1967.tb01430.x

Tedeschi, J. T., & Felson, R. B. (1994). *Violence, aggression, and coercive actions.* Washington, DC: American Psychological Association. doi: 10.1037/10160-000

Tedeschi, J. T., & Quigley, B. M. (1996). Limitations of laboratory paradigms for studying aggression. *Aggression and Violent Behavior, 1,* 163–177. doi: 10.1016/1359-1789(95)00014-3

Tedeschi, R. G., & Calhoun, L. G. (2004). Posttraumatic growth: Conceptual foundations and empirical evidence. *Psychological Inquiry, 15,* 1–18. doi: 10.1207/s15327965pli1501_01

Tedeschi, R. G., Calhoun, L. G., & Cann, A. (2007). Evaluating resource gain: Understanding and misunderstanding posttraumatic growth. *Applied Psychology, 56,* 396–406. doi: 10.1111/j.1464-0597.2007.00299.x

Temcheff, C. E., Serbin, L. A., Martin-Storey, A., Stack, D. M., Hodgins, S., Ledingham, J., & Schwartzman, A. E. (2008). Continuity and pathways from aggression in childhood to family violence in adulthood: A 30-year longitudinal study. *Journal of Family Violence, 23*, 231–242. doi: 10.1007/s10896-007-9147-2

Temkin, J., Gray, J. M., & Barrett, J. (2018). Different functions of rape myth use in court: Findings from a trial observation study. *Feminist Criminology, 13*, 205–226. doi: 10.1177/1557085116661627

Temkin, J., & Krahé, B. (2008). *Sexual assault and the justice gap: A question of attitude.* Oxford: Hart Publishing.

Teng, Z., Liu, Y., & Guo, C. (2015). A meta-analysis of the relationship between self-esteem and aggression among Chinese students. *Aggression and Violent Behavior, 21*, 45–54. doi: 10.1016/j.avb.2015.01.005

Terburg, D., Morgan, B., & van Honk, J. (2009). The testosterone-cortisol ratio: A hormonal marker for proneness to social aggression. *International Journal of Law and Psychiatry, 32*, 216–223. doi: 10.1016/j.ijlp.2009.04.008

Terry, P. C., & Jackson, J. J. (1985). The determinants and control of violence in sport. *Quest, 37*, 27–37. doi: 10.1080/00336297.1985.10483817

Testa, M., Brown, W. C., & Wang, W. (2019). Do men use more sexually aggressive tactics when intoxicated? A within-person examination of naturally occurring episodes of sex. *Psychology of Violence, 9*, 546–554. doi: 10.1037/vio0000186

Testa, M., Hoffman, J. H., & Livingston, J. A. (2010). Alcohol and sexual risk behaviors as mediators of the sexual victimization–revictimization relationship. *Journal of Consulting and Clinical Psychology, 78*, 249–259. doi: 10.1037/a0018914

Testa, M., & Livingston, J. A. (2009). Alcohol consumption and women's vulnerability to sexual victimization: Can reducing women's drinking prevent rape? *Substance Use & Misuse, 44*, 1349–1376. doi: 10.1080/10826080902961468

Teymoori, A., Côté, S. M., Jones, B. L., Nagin, D. S., Boivin, M., Vitaro, F., ... Tremblay, R. E. (2018). Risk factors associated with boys' and girls' developmental trajectories of physical aggression from early childhood through early adolescence. *JAMA Network Open, 1*, e186364. doi: 10.1001/jamanetworkopen.2018.6364

Tharp, A. T., DeGue, S., Valle, L. A., Brookmeyer, K. A., Massetti, G. M., & Matjasko, J. L. (2013). A systematic qualitative review of risk and protective factors for sexual violence perpetration. *Trauma, Violence & Abuse, 14*, 133–167. doi: 10.1177/1524838012470031

Thomaes, S., Bushman, B. J., Orobio de Castro, B., Cohen, G. L., & Denissen, J. J. A. (2009). Reducing narcissistic aggression by buttressing self-esteem: An experimental field study. *Psychological Science, 20*, 1536–1542. doi: 10.1111/j.1467-9280.2009.02478.x

Thomas, H. J., Connor, J. P., & Scott, J. (2015). Integrating traditional bullying and cyberbullying: Challenges of definition and measurement in adolescents – A review. *Educational Psychology Review, 27,* 135–152. doi: 10.1007/s10648-014-9261-7

Thomas, R., & Zimmer-Gembeck, M. J. (2011). Accumulating evidence for parent-child interaction therapy in the prevention of child maltreatment. *Child Development, 82,* 177–192. doi: 10.1111/j.1467-8624.2010.01548.x

Thomas, T. A., & Fremouw, W. (2009). Moderating factors of the sexual "victim to offender cycle" in males. *Aggression and Violent Behavior, 14,* 382–387. doi: 10.1016/j.avb.2009.06.006

Thompson, M. P., Koss, M. P., Kingree, J. B., Goree, J., & Rice, J. (2011). A prospective mediational model of sexual aggression among college men. *Journal of Interpersonal Violence, 26,* 2716–2734. doi: 10.1177/0886260510388285

Thorneycroft, R., & Asquith, N. L. (2015). The dark figure of disablist violence. *The Howard Journal of Criminal Justice, 54,* 489–507. doi: 10.1111/hojo.12147

Thornhill, R., & Palmer, C. T. (2000). *A natural history of rape: Biological bases of sexual coercion.* Cambridge, MA: MIT Press.

Thornhill, R., & Thornhill, N. W. (1991). Coercive sexuality of men: Is there psychological adaptation to rape? In E. Grauerholz & M. A. Koralewski (Eds.), *Sexual coercion: A sourcebook on its nature, causes, and prevention* (pp. 91–107). Lexington, MA: Lexington Books/D. C. Heath & Co.

Todorov, A., & Bargh, J. A. (2002). Automatic sources of aggression. *Aggression and Violent Behavior, 7,* 53–68. doi: 10.1016/S1359-1789(00)00036-7

Tolan, P. H., Gorman-Smith, D., & Henry, D. B. (2006). Family violence. *Annual Review of Psychology, 57,* 557–583. doi: 10.1146/annurev. psych.57.102904.190110

Tolin, D. F., & Foa, E. B. (2008). Sex differences in trauma and posttraumatic stress disorder: A quantitative review of 25 years of research. *Psychological Trauma: Theory, Research, Practice, and Policy, S,* 37–85. doi: 10.1037/1942-9681.S.1.37

Tomaszewska, P., & Krahé, B. (2018). Predictors of sexual aggression victimization and perpetration among Polish university students: A longitudinal study. *Archives of Sexual Behavior, 47,* 493–505. doi: 10.1007/s10508-016-0823-2

Toohey, M. J., & DiGiuseppe, R. (2017). Defining and measuring irritability: Construct clarification and differentiation. *Clinical Psychology Review, 53,* 93–108. doi: 10.1016/j.cpr.2017.01.009

Topping, K. J., & Barron, I. G. (2009). School-based child sexual abuse prevention programs: A review of effectiveness. *Review of Educational Research, 79,* 431–463. doi: 10.3102/0034654308325582

Torabi, M. R., & Seo, D. C. (2004). National study of behavioral and life changes since September 11. *Health Education & Behavior, 31,* 179–192. doi: 10.1177/1090198103259183

Trabold, N., McMahon, J., Alsobrooks, S., Whitney, S., & Mittal, M. (2018). A systematic review of intimate partner violence interventions: State of the field and implications for practitioners. *Trauma, Violence & Abuse,* 1524838018767934. doi: 10.1177/1524838018767934

Travis, C. B. (Ed.) (2003a). *Evolution, gender, and rape.* Cambridge, MA: MIT Press.

Travis, C. B. (2003b). Theory and data on rape and evolution. In C. B. Travis (Ed.), *Evolution, gender, and rape* (pp. 207–220). Cambridge, MA: MIT Press.

Tremblay, R. E., Japel, C., Perusse, D., Mcduff, P., Boivin, M., Zoccolillo, M., & Montplaisir, J. (1999). The search for the age of 'onset' of physical aggression: Rousseau and Bandura revisited. *Criminal Behaviour and Mental Health, 9,* 8–23. doi: 10.1002/cbm.288

Tremblay, R. E., Vitaro, F., & Côté, S. M. (2018). Developmental origins of chronic physical aggression: A bio-psycho-social model for the next generation of preventive interventions. *Annual Review of Psychology, 69,* 383–407. doi: 10.1146/annurev-psych-010416-044030

Troche, S. J., & Herzberg, P. Y. (2017). On the role of dominance and nurturance in the confluence model: A person-centered approach to the prediction of sexual aggression. *Aggressive Behavior, 43,* 251–262. doi: 10.1002/ab.21685

Trottier, D., Benbouriche, M., & Bonneville, V. (2019). A meta-analysis on the association between rape myth acceptance and sexual coercion perpetration. *Journal of Sex Research,* 1–8. doi: 10.1080/00224499.2019.1704677

Truman, J. L., & Morgan, R. M. (2014). *Nonfatal domestic violence, 2003-2012.* Retrieved from www.bjs.gov/content/pub/pdf/ndv0312.pdf

Turchik, J. A. (2012). Sexual victimization among male college students: Assault severity, sexual functioning, and health risk behaviors. *Psychology of Men & Masculinity, 13,* 243–255. doi: 10.1037/a0024605

Turchik, J. A., Hebenstreit, C. L., & Judson, S. S. (2016). An examination of the gender inclusiveness of current theories of sexual violence in adulthood: Recognizing male victims, female perpetrators, and same-sex violence. *Trauma, Violence & Abuse, 17,* 133–148. doi: 10.1177/1524838014566721

Turkmen, M. (2016). Violence in animated feature films: Implications for children. *Educational Process, 5,* 22–37. doi: 10.12973/edupij.2016.51.2

Turner, J. C., & Reynolds, K. J. (2012). Self-categorization theory. In P. A. M. van Lange, A. W. Kruglanski, & E. T. Higgins (Eds.), *Handbook of theories of social psychology* (pp. 399–417). London: Sage.

Turner, K. M.T., & Sanders, M. R. (2006). Dissemination of evidence-based parenting and family support strategies: Learning from the Triple P-Positive Parenting Program system approach. *Aggression and Violent Behavior, 11,* 176–193. doi: 10.1016/j.avb.2005.07.005

Turner, R. H., & Killian, L. M. (1972). *Collective behavior* (2nd ed.). Englewood Cliffs, NJ: Prentice Hall.

Twenge, J. M., Baumeister, R. F., Tice, D. M., & Stucke, T. S. (2001). If you can't join them, beat them: Effects of social exclusion on aggressive behavior. *Journal of Personality and Social Psychology, 81,* 1058–1069. doi: 10.1037/0022-3514.81.6.1058

Twenge, J. M., & Campbell, W. K. (2003). 'Isn't it fun to get the respect that we're going to deserve?' Narcissism, social rejection, and aggression. *Personality and Social Psychology Bulletin, 29,* 261–272. doi: 10.1177/0146167202239051

Twenge, J. M., Konrath, S., Foster, J. D., Campbell, W. K., & Bushman, B. J. (2008). Egos inflating over time: A cross-temporal meta-analysis of the Narcissistic Personality Inventory. *Journal of Personality, 76,* 875–902. doi: 10.1111/j.1467-6494.2008.00507.x

Tyson, P. D. (1998). Physiological arousal, reactive aggression, and the induction of an incompatible relaxation response. *Aggression and Violent Behavior, 3,* 143–158. doi: 10.1016/S1359-1789(97)00002-5

U.S. Department of Health and Human Services (2017). *Child maltreatment 2017.* Retrieved from www.acf.hhs.gov/sites/default/files/cb/cm2017.pdf

U.S. Department of Justice (2018). *Crime in the United States 2018: About Crime in the U.S. (CIUS).* Retrieved from ucr.fbi.gov/crime-in-the-u.s/2018/crime-in-the-u.s.-2018/tables/table-42

U.S. Department of Justice (2019). *Criminal victimization, 2018.* Retrieved from www.bjs.gov/content/pub/pdf/cv18.pdf.

Uhlmann, E., & Swanson, J. (2004). Exposure to violent video games increases automatic aggressiveness. *Journal of Adolescence, 27,* 41–52. doi: 10.1016/j.adolescence.2003.10.004

Ullman, S. E. (2010). *Talking about sexual assault: Society's response to survivors.* Washington, DC: American Psychological Association.

Ullman, S. E., & Najdowski, C. J. (2011). Prospective changes in attributions of self-blame and social reactions to women's disclosures of adult sexual assault. *Journal of Interpersonal Violence, 26,* 1934–1962. doi: 10.1177/0886260510372940

UNICEF (2019). *Violent discipline.* Retrieved from data.unicef.org/topic/child-protection/violence/violent-discipline/

United Nations Office on Drugs and Crime (2019a). *Global study on homicide: Homicide trends, patterns and criminal justice response* (Vol. 2). Vienna: UNODC. Retrieved from www.unodc.org/documents/data-and-analysis/gsh/Booklet2.pdf

United Nations Office on Drugs and Crime (2019b). *Global study on homicide: Homicide trends, patterns and criminal justice response* (Vol. 1). Vienna: UNODC. Retrieved from www.unodc.org/documents/data-and-analysis/gsh/Booklet1.pdf

Updegraff, J. A., Silver, R. C., & Holman, E. A. (2008). Searching for and finding meaning in collective trauma: Results from a national longitudinal study of the 9/11 terrorist attacks. *Journal of Personality and Social Psychology, 95,* 709–722. doi: 10.1037/0022-3514.95.3.709

Uskul, A. K., & Over, H. (2017). Culture, social interdependence, and ostracism. *Current Directions in Psychological Science, 26,* 371–376. doi: 10.1177/0963721417699300

Vail, K. E., Courtney, E., & Arndt, J. (2019). The influence of existential threat and tolerance salience on anti-Islamic attitudes in American politics. *Political Psychology, 40*(5), 1143–1162. doi: 10.1111/pops.12579

Vaillancourt, T. (2005). Indirect aggression among humans: Social construct or evolutionary adaptation? In R. E. Tremblay, W. W. Hartup, & J. Archer (Eds.), *Developmental origins of aggression* (pp. 158–177). New York: Guilford Press.

Valasik, M., Reid, S. E., West, J. S., & Gravel, J. (2018). Group process and gang delinquency intervention. In J. L. Ireland, P. Birch, & C. A. Ireland (Eds.), *The Routledge international handbook of human aggression* (pp. 411–423). London: Routledge.

Van de Vliert, E., Einarsen, S., & Nielsen, M. B. (2013). Are national levels of employee harassment cultural covariations of climato-economic conditions? *Work & Stress, 27,* 106–122. doi: 10.1080/02678373.2013.760901

Van den Brande, W., Baillien, E., Witte, H. de, Vander Elst, T., & Godderis, L. (2016). The role of work stressors, coping strategies and coping resources in the process of workplace bullying: A systematic review and development of a comprehensive model. *Aggression and Violent Behavior, 29,* 61–71. doi: 10.1016/j.avb.2016.06.004

Van Goozen, S. M. H. (2005). Hormones and the developmental origins of aggression. In R. E. Tremblay, W. W. Hartup, & J. Archer (Eds.), *Developmental origins of aggression* (pp. 281–306). New York: Guilford Press.

Van Goozen, S. M. H. (2015). The role of early emotion impairments in the development of persistent antisocial behavior. *Child Development Perspectives, 9,* 206–210. doi: 10.1111/cdep.12134

Van Goozen, S. M. H., Fairchild, G., Snoek, H., & Harold, G. T. (2007). The evidence for a neurobiological model of childhood antisocial behavior. *Psychological Bulletin, 133,* 149–182. doi: 10.1037/0033-2909.133.1.149

Van Hiel, A., Hautman, L., Cornelis, I., & Clercq, B. de (2007). Football hooliganism: Comparing self-awareness and social identity theory explanations. *Journal of Community & Applied Social Psychology, 17,* 169–186. doi: 10.1002/casp.902

Van IJzendoorn, M. H., Bakermans-Kranenburg, M. J., Coughlan, B., & Reijman, S. (2020). Annual research review: Umbrella synthesis of meta-analyses on child maltreatment antecedents and interventions: Differential susceptibility perspective on risk and resilience. *Journal of Child Psychology and Psychiatry, and Allied Disciplines, 61,* 272-290. doi: 10.1111/jcpp.13147

Van Lange, P., Rinderu, M. I., & Bushman, B. J. (2018). CLASH: Climate (change) and cultural evolution of intergroup conflict. *Group Processes & Intergroup Relations, 21,* 457–471. doi: 10.1177/1368430217735579

Van Rooy, D. L., Rotton, J., & Burns, T. M. (2006). Convergent, discriminant, and predictive validity of aggressive driving inventories: They drive as they live. *Aggressive Behavior, 32,* 89–98. doi: 10.1002/ab.20113

Van Vugt, M. (2011). The male warrior hypothesis. In J. P. Forgas, A. W. Kruglanski, & K. D. Williams (Eds.), *The psychology of social conflict and aggression* (pp. 233–248). New York: Psychology Press.

Vandello, J. A., & Cohen, D. (2003). Male honor and female fidelity: Implicit cultural scripts that perpetuate domestic violence. *Journal of Personality and Social Psychology, 84,* 997–1010. doi: 10.1037/0022-3514.84.5.997

Vandello, J. A., & Cohen, D. (2008). Culture, gender, and men's intimate partner violence. *Social and Personality Psychology Compass, 2,* 652–667. doi: 10.1111/j.1751-9004.2008.00080.x

Vandenbosch, L., & van Oosten, J. M. F. (2017). The relationship between online pornography and the sexual objectification of women: The attenuating role of porn literacy education. *Journal of Communication, 67,* 1015–1036. doi: 10.1111/jcom.12341

Vandenbosch, L., & van Oosten, J. M. F. (2018). Explaining the relationship between sexually explicit Internet material and casual sex: A two-step mediation model. *Archives of Sexual Behavior, 47,* 1465–1480. doi: 10.1007/s10508-017-1145-8

Vandermassen, G. (2011). Evolution and rape: A feminist Darwinian perspective. *Sex Roles, 64,* 732–747. doi: 10.1007/s11199-010-9895-y

Vanlaar, W., Simpson, H., Mayhew, D., & Robertson, R. (2008). Aggressive driving: A survey of attitudes, opinions and behaviors. *Journal of Safety Research, 39,* 375–381. doi: 10.1016/j.jsr.2008.05.005

Vasilopoulos, P., Marcus, G. E., Valentino, N. A., & Foucault, M. (2019). Fear, anger, and voting for the far right: Evidence from the November 13, 2015 Paris terror attacks. *Political Psychology, 40,* 679–704. doi: 10.1111/pops.12513

Vasquez, E. A., Denson, T. F., Pedersen, W. C., Stenstrom, D. M., & Miller, N. E. (2005). The moderating effect of trigger intensity on triggered displaced aggression. *Journal of Experimental Social Psychology, 41,* 61–67. doi: 10.1016/j.jesp.2004.05.007

Vasquez, E. A., Lickel, B., & Hennigan, K. (2010). Gangs, displaced, and group-based aggression. *Aggression and Violent Behavior, 15,* 130–140. doi: 10.1016/j.avb.2009.08.001

Vasquez, E. A., Wenborne, L., Peers, M., Alleyne, E., & Ellis, K. (2015). Any of them will do: In-group identification, out-group entitativity, and gang membership as predictors of group-based retribution. *Aggressive Behavior, 41,* 242–252. doi: 10.1002/ab.21581

Vazsonyi, A. T., & Javakhishvili, M. (2019). The role of infant socialization and self-control in understanding reactive-overt and relational aggression: A 15-year study. *Aggression and Violent Behavior,* Advance online publication. doi: 10.1016/j.avb.2019.07.011

Veenstra, L., Bushman, B. J., & Koole, S. L. (2018). The facts on the furious: A brief review of the psychology of trait anger. *Current Opinion in Psychology, 19*, 98–103. doi: 10.1016/j.copsyc.2017.03.014

Velotti, P., Beomonte Zobel, S., Rogier, G., & Tambelli, R. (2018). Exploring relationships: A systematic review on intimate partner violence and attachment. *Frontiers in Psychology, 9*, 1166. doi: 10.3389/fpsyg.2018.01166

Ventus, D., Antfolk, J., & Salo, B. (2017). The associations between abuse characteristics in child sexual abuse: A meta-analysis. *Journal of Sexual Aggression, 23*, 167–180. doi: 10.1080/13552600.2017.1318963

Verheijen, G. P., Burk, W. J., Stoltz, S. E. M. J., van den Berg, Y. H. M., & Cillessen, A. H. N. (2018). Friendly fire: Longitudinal effects of exposure to violent video games on aggressive behavior in adolescent friendship dyads. *Aggressive Behavior, 44*, 257–267. doi: 10.1002/ab.21748

Verona, E., & Sullivan, E. A. (2008). Emotional catharsis and aggression revisited: Heart rate reduction following aggressive responding. *Emotion, 8*, 331–340. doi: 10.1037/1528-3542.8.3.331

Victoroff, J. (2009). The mind of the terrorist: A review and critique of psychological approaches. In J. Victoroff & A. W. Kruglanski (Eds.), *Psychology of terrorism: Classic and contemporary insights* (pp. 55–86). New York: Psychology Press.

Victoroff, J., & Kruglanski, A. W. (Eds.) (2009). *Psychology of terrorism: Classic and contemporary insights*. New York: Psychology Press.

Vigdor, E. R., & Mercy, J. A. (2006). Do laws restricting access to firearms by domestic violence offenders prevent intimate partner homicide? *Evaluation Review, 30*, 313–346. doi: 10.1177/0193841X06287307

Vilanova, F., Beria, F. M., Costa, Â. B., & Koller, S. H. (2017). Deindividuation: From Le Bon to the social identity model of deindividuation effects. *Cogent Psychology, 4*, 825. doi: 10.1080/23311908.2017.1308104

Vingilis, E., Yıldırım-Yenier, Z., Fischer, P., Wiesenthal, D. L., Wickens, C. M., Mann, R. E., & Seeley, J. (2016). Self-concept as a risky driver: Mediating the relationship between racing video games and on-road driving violations in a community-based sample. *Transportation Research Part F: Traffic Psychology and Behaviour, 43*, 15–23. doi: 10.1016/j.trf.2016.09.021

Vize, C. E., Miller, J. D., & Lynam, D. R. (2018). FFM facets and their relations with different forms of antisocial behavior: An expanded meta-analysis. *Journal of Criminal Justice, 57*, 67–75. doi: 10.1016/j.jcrimjus.2018.04.004

Vlahovicova, K., Melendez-Torres, G. J., Leijten, P., Knerr, W., & Gardner, F. (2017). Parenting programs for the prevention of child physical abuse recurrence: A systematic review and meta-analysis. *Clinical Child and Family Psychology Review, 20*, 351–365. doi: 10.1007/s10567-017-0232-7

Vrij, A., Van der Steen, J., & Koppelaar, L. (1994). Aggression of police officers as a function of temperature: An experiment with the fire arms training system. *Journal of Community & Applied Social Psychology, 4,* 365–370. doi: 10.1002/casp.2450040505

Wagner, U., Christ, O., & Pettigrew, T. F. (2008). Prejudice and group-related behavior in Germany. *Journal of Social Issues, 64,* 403–416. doi: 10.1111/j.1540-4560.2008.00568.x

Walker, H. E., Freud, J. S., Ellis, R. A., Fraine, S. M., & Wilson, L. C. (2019). The prevalence of sexual revictimization: A meta-analytic review. *Trauma, Violence & Abuse, 20,* 67-80. doi: 10.1177/1524838017692364

Walker, J., & Bright, J. A. (2009). False inflated self-esteem and violence: A systematic review and cognitive model. *Journal of Forensic Psychiatry & Psychology, 20,* 1–32. doi: 10.1080/14789940701656808

Walsh, D. A., & Gentile, D. A. (2001). A validity test of movie, television and video-game ratings. *Pediatrics, 107,* 1302–1308.

Walsh, K., Zwi, K., Woolfenden, S., & Shlonsky, A. (2015). School-based education programmes for the prevention of child sexual abuse. *The Cochrane Database of Systematic Reviews, 4,* CD004380. doi: 10.1002/14651858.CD004380.pub3

Walters, M. L., Chen, J., & Breiding, M. J. (2013). *The National Intimate Partner and Sexual Violence Survey (NISVS): 2010 Findings on victimization by sexual orientation.* Retrieved from www.cdc.gov/violenceprevention/pdf/nisvs_report2010-a.pdf

Waltes, R., Chiocchetti, A. G., & Freitag, C. M. (2016). The neurobiological basis of human aggression: A review on genetic and epigenetic mechanisms. *American Journal of Medical Genetics. Part B, Neuropsychiatric Genetics, 171,* 650–675. doi: 10.1002/ajmg.b.32388

Walton, G. M., & Wilson, T. D. (2018). Wise interventions: Psychological remedies for social and personal problems. *Psychological Review, 125,* 617–655. doi: 10.1037/rev0000115

Wang, M., & Liu, L. (2018). Reciprocal relations between harsh discipline and children's externalizing behavior in China: A 5-year longitudinal study. *Child Development, 89,* 174–187. doi: 10.1111/cdev.12724

Wann, D. L., Carlson, J. D., Holland, L. C., Jacob, B. E., Owens, D. A., & Wells, D. D. (1999). Beliefs in symbolic catharsis: The importance of involvement with aggressive sports. *Social Behavior & Personality, 27,* 155–164. doi: 10.2224/sbp.1999.27.2.155

Wann, D. L., Carlson, J. D., & Schrader, M. P. (1999). The impact of team identification on the hostile and instrumental verbal aggression of sport spectators. *Journal of Social Behavior & Personality, 14,* 279–286.

Wann, D. L., Culver, Z., Akanda, R., Daglar, M., Divitiis, C. de, & Smith, A. (2005). The effects of team identification and game outcome on willingness to consider anonymous acts of hostile aggression. *Journal of Sport Behavior, 28,* 282–294.

Wann, D. L., Haynes, G., McLean, B., & Pullen, P. (2003). Sport team identification and willingness to consider anonymous acts of hostile aggression. *Aggressive Behavior, 29,* 406–413. doi: 10.1002/ab.10046

Warburton, W. A., & Bushman, B. J. (2019). The competitive reaction time task: The development and scientific utility of a flexible laboratory aggression paradigm. *Aggressive Behavior, 45,* 389–396. doi: 10.1002/ab.21829

Warburton, W. A., Williams, K. D., & Cairns, D. R. (2006). When ostracism leads to aggression: The moderating effects of control deprivation. *Journal of Experimental Social Psychology, 42,* 213–220. doi: 10.1016/j.jesp.2005.03.005

Waters, H., Hyder, A., Rajkotia, Y., Basu, S., Rehwinkel, J. A., & Butchart, A. (Eds.) (2004). *The economic dimensions of interpersonal violence.* Geneva, CH: World Health Organization. Retrieved from http://whqlibdoc.who.int/publications/2004/9241591609.pdf

Watkins, L. E., DiLillo, D., & Maldonado, R. C. (2015). The interactive effects of emotion regulation and alcohol intoxication on lab-based intimate partner aggression. *Psychology of Addictive Behaviors, 29,* 653–663. doi: 10.1037/adb0000074

Weare, S. (2018). "I feel permanently traumatized by it": Physical and emotional impacts reported by men forced to penetrate women in the United Kingdom. *Journal of Interpersonal Violence,* Advance online publication. doi: 10.1177/0886260518820815

Webber, D., & Kruglanski, A. W. (2017). The psychology of terrorism. In B. J. Bushman (Ed.), *Aggression and violence: A social psychological perspective* (pp. 290–303). New York: Routledge.

Webster, G. D., DeWall, C. N., Pond, R. S., Deckman, T., Jonason, P. K., Le, B. M., ... Bator, R. J. (2015). The Brief Aggression Questionnaire: Structure, validity, reliability, and generalizability. *Journal of Personality Assessment, 97,* 638–649. doi: 10.1080/00223891.2015.1044093

Wegner, R., & Abbey, A. (2016). Individual differences in men's misperception of women's sexual intent: Application and extension of the confluence model. *Personality and Individual Differences, 94,* 16–20. doi: 10.1016/j.paid.2015.12.027

Wehby, J. H., & Symons, F. J. (1996). Revisiting conceptual issues in the measurement of aggressive behavior. *Behavioral Disorders, 22,* 29–35.

Weinstein, M. D., Smith, M. D., & Wiesenthal, D. L. (1995). Masculinity and hockey violence. *Sex Roles, 33,* 831–847. doi: 10.1007/BF01544782

Wellman, H. M., Cross, D., & Watson, J. (2001). Meta-analysis of theory-of-mind development: The truth about false belief. *Child Development, 72,* 655–684. doi: 10.1111/1467-8624.00304

Wells, S., Mihic, L., Tremblay, P. F., Graham, K., & Demers, A. (2008). Where, with whom, and how much alcohol is consumed on drinking events involving aggression? Event-level associations in a Canadian national survey of university students. *Alcoholism: Clinical and Experimental Research, 32,* 522–533. doi: 10.1111/j.1530-0277.2007.00596.x

Wentz, E. A. (2019). Funneled through or filtered out: An examination of police and prosecutorial decision-making in adult sexual assault cases. *Violence Against Women*, 1077801219890419. doi: 10.1177/1077801219890419

Wesselmann, E. D., Butler, F. A., Williams, K. D., & Pickett, C. L. (2010). Adding injury to insult: Unexpected rejection leads to more aggressive responses. *Aggressive Behavior, 36*, 232–237. doi: 10.1002/ab.20347

Wesselmann, E. D., Ren, D., & Williams, K. D. (2017). Ostracism and aggression. In B. J. Bushman (Ed.), *Aggression and violence: A social psychological perspective* (pp. 155–168). New York: Routledge.

Whitaker, D. J., & Rogers-Brown, J. S. (2019). Child maltreatment and the family. In B. H. Fiese (Ed.), *APA handbook of contemporary family psychology* (pp. 471–487). Washington, DC: American Psychological Association.

White, G. F., Katz, J., & Scarborough, K. E. (1992). The impact of professional football games upon violent assaults on women. *Violence & Victims, 7*, 157–171.

White, J. W., Koss, M. P., & Kazdin, A. E. (Eds.) (2011). *Violence against women and children* (Vol. 1: Mapping the terrain). Washington, DC: American Psychological Association.

White, J. W., & Kowalski, R. M. (1998). Male violence toward women: An integrated perspective. In R. G. Geen & E. I. Donnerstein (Eds.), *Human aggression: Theories, research, and implications for social policy* (pp. 203–228). San Diego, CA: Academic Press.

Whittaker, A., Densley, J., Cheston, L., Tyrell, T., Higgins, M., Felix-Baptiste, C., & Havard, T. (2020). Reluctant gangsters revisited: The evolution of gangs from postcodes to profits. *European Journal on Criminal Policy and Research, 26*, 1–22. doi: 10.1007/s10610-019-09408-4

Wickham, B. M., Capezza, N. M., & Stephenson, V. L. (2019). Misperceptions and motivations of the female terrorist: A psychological perspective. *Journal of Aggression, Maltreatment & Trauma, 9*, 1–16. doi: 10.1080/10926771.2019.1685041

Widman, L., & McNulty, J. K. (2010). Sexual narcissism and the perpetration of sexual aggression. *Archives of Sexual Behavior, 39*, 926–939. doi: 10.1007/s10508-008-9461-7

Wiesenthal, D. L., Hennessy, D. A., & Totten, B. (2000). The influence of music on driver stress. *Journal of Applied Social Psychology, 30*, 1709–1719. doi: 10.1111/j.1559-1816.2000.tb02463.x

Wiesenthal, D. L., & Janovjak, D. P. (1992). *Deindividuation and automobile driving behaviour*. Toronto: LaMarsh Research Programme.

Wilkowski, B. M., & Robinson, M. D. (2008). The cognitive basis of trait anger and reactive aggression: An integrative analysis. *Personality and Social Psychology Review, 12*, 3–21. doi: 10.1177/1088868307309874

Williams, J. R., Ghandour, R. M., & Kub, J. E. (2008). Female perpetration of violence in heterosexual intimate relationships: Adolescence through adulthood. *Trauma, Violence, & Abuse, 9*, 227–249. doi: 10.1177/1524838008324418

Williams, K. D. [Kevin D.] (2010). The effects of homophily, identification, and violent video games on players. *Mass Communication and Society, 14*, 3–24. doi: 10.1080/15205430903359701

Williams, K. D. (1997). Social ostracism. In R. M. Kowalski (Ed.), *Aversive interpersonal behaviors* (pp. 133–170). New York: Plenum Press.

Williams, K. D. (2007a). Ostracism. *Annual Review of Psychology, 58,* 425–452. doi: 10.1146/annurev.psych.58.110405.085641

Williams, K. D. (2007b). Ostracism: The kiss of social death. *Social and Personality Psychology Compass, 1,* 236–247. doi: 10.1111/j.1751-9004.2007.00004.x

Williams, K. D., Cheung, C. K. T., & Choi, W. (2000). Cyberostracism: Effects of being ignored over the Internet. *Journal of Personality and Social Psychology, 79,* 748–762. doi: 10.1037//0022-3514.79.5.748

Williams, K. D., Warburton, W. A. (2003). Ostracism: A form of indirect aggression that can result in aggression. *Revue Internationale De Psychologie Sociale, 16,* 101–126.

Williams, S. T., Conger, K. J., & Blozis, S. A. (2007). The development of interpersonal aggression during adolescence: The importance of parents, siblings, and family economics. *Child Development, 78,* 1526–1542. doi: 10.1111/j.1467-8624.2007.01081.x

Willis, M., Canan, S. N., Jozkowski, K. N., & Bridges, A. J. (2019). Sexual consent communication in best-selling pornography films: A content analysis. *Journal of Sex Research,* 1–12. doi: 10.1080/00224499.2019.1655522

Willness, C. R., Steel, P., & Lee, K. (2007). A meta-analysis of the antecedents and consequences of workplace sexual harassment. *Personnel Psychology, 60,* 127–162. doi: 10.1111/j.1744-6570.2007.00067.x

Wilson, B. J., Smith, S. L., Potter, W. J., Kunkel, D., Linz, D. G., Colvin, C. M., & Donnerstein, E. I. (2002). Violence in children's television programming: Assessing the risks. *Journal of Communication, 52,* 5–35. doi: 10.1111/j.1460-2466.2002.tb02531.x

Wilson, L. C., & Miller, K. E. (2016). Meta-analysis of the prevalence of unacknowledged rape. *Trauma, Violence & Abuse, 17,* 149–159. doi: 10.1177/1524838015576391

Wolfe, D. A. (2011). Risk factors for child abuse perpetration. In J. W. White, M. P. Koss, & A. E. Kazdin (Eds.), *Violence against women and children* (pp. 31–53). Washington, DC: American Psychological Association. doi: 10.1037/12307-002

Wolfe, D. A., Crooks, C. V., Lee, V., McIntyre-Smith, A., & Jaffe, P. G. (2003). The effects of children's exposure to domestic violence: A meta-analysis and critique. *Clinical Child and Family Psychology Review, 6,* 171–187. doi: 10.1023/A:1024910416164

Wölfer, R., & Hewstone, M. (2015). Intra- versus intersex aggression: Testing theories of sex differences using aggression networks. *Psychological Science, 26,* 1285–1294. doi: 10.1177/0956797615586979

Wölfer, R., & Hewstone, M. (2018). What buffers ethnic homophily? Explaining the development of outgroup contact in adolescence. *Developmental Psychology, 54,* 1507–1518. doi: 10.1037/dev0000547

Wood, E. J. (2014). Conflict-related sexual violence and the policy implications of recent research. *International Review of the Red Cross, 96*(894), 457–478. doi: 10.1017/S1816383115000077

Wood, J. (2014). Understanding gang membership: The significance of group processes. *Group Processes & Intergroup Relations, 17,* 710–729. doi: 10.1177/1368430214550344

Wood, J., & Alleyne, E. (2010). Street gang theory and research: Where are we now and where do we go from here? *Aggression and Violent Behavior, 15,* 100–111. doi: 10.1016/j.avb.2009.08.005

World Health Organization (1999). *Report of the Consultation on Child Abuse Prevention 29–31 March 1999.* Retrieved from apps.who.int/iris/handle/10665/65900

World Health Organization (2004). *Young people's health in context.* Retrieved from www.euro.who.int/__data/assets/pdf_file/0008/110231/e82923.pdf?ua=1

World Health Organization (2006). *Preventing child maltreatment: A guide to taking action and generating evidence.* Retrieved from whqlibdoc.who.int/publications/2006/9241594365_eng.pdf

World Health Organization (2013). *Global and regional estimates of violence against women.* Retrieved from www.who.int/reproductivehealth/publications/violence/9789241564625/en/

World Health Organization (2014). *Global status report on violence prevention.* Retrieved from www.who.int/violence_injury_prevention/violence/status_report/2014/en/

World Health Organization (2020). *Global status report on preventing violence against children.* Retrieved from https://www.who.int/publications-detail-redirect/9789240004191

Worth, K. A., Chambers, J. G., Nassau, D. H., Rakhra, B. K., & Sargent, J. D. (2008). Exposure of US adolescents to extremely violent movies. *Pediatrics, 122,* 306–312. doi: 10.1542/peds.2007-1096

Wright, E. N., Hanlon, A., Lozano, A., & Teitelman, A. M. (2019). The impact of intimate partner violence, depressive symptoms, alcohol dependence, and perceived stress on 30-year cardiovascular disease risk among young adult women: A multiple mediation analysis. *Preventive Medicine, 121,* 47–54. doi: 10.1016/j.ypmed.2019.01.016

Wright, K. A., Turanovic, J. J., O'Neal, E. N., Morse, S. J., & Booth, E. T. (2019). The cycle of violence revisited: Childhood victimization, resilience, and future violence. *Journal of Interpersonal Violence, 34,* 1261–1286. doi: 10.1177/0886260516651090

Wright, L. A., Zounlome, N. O. O., & Whiston, S. C. (2018). The effectiveness of male-targeted sexual assault prevention programs: A meta-analysis. *Trauma, Violence & Abuse,* Advance online publication. doi: 10.1177/1524838018801330

Wright, P. J. (2011). Mass media effects on youth sexual behavior: Assessing the claim for causality. *Annals of the International Communication Association, 35,* 343–385. doi: 10.1080/23808985.2011.11679121

Wright, P. J., & Bae, S. (2018). Pornography and male socialization. In Y. E. Wong & S. R. Wester (Eds.), *APA handbook of men and masculinities* (pp. 551–568). Washington, DC: American Psychological Association.

Wright, P. J., Sun, C., Steffen, N. J., & Tokunaga, R. S. (2015). Pornography, alcohol, and male sexual dominance. *Communication Monographs, 82,* 252–270. doi: 10.1080/03637751.2014.981558

Wright, P. J., Tokunaga, R. S., & Kraus, A. (2016). A meta-analysis of pornography consumption and actual acts of sexual aggression in general population studies. *Journal of Communication, 66,* 183–205. doi: 10.1111/jcom.12201

Wright, V. L. (2010). Celerity, capital punishment, and murder: Do quicker executions deter criminal homicides? *Dissertation Abstracts International Section a: Humanities and Social Sciences, 70.*

Yahner, J., Dank, M., Zweig, J. M., & Lachman, P. (2015). The co-occurrence of physical and cyber dating violence and bullying among teens. *Journal of Interpersonal Violence, 30,* 1079–1089. doi: 10.1177/08862605 14540324

Yakubovich, A. R., Stöckl, H., Murray, J., Melendez-Torres, G. J., Steinert, J. I., Glavin, C. E. Y., & Humphreys, D. K. (2018). Risk and protective factors for intimate partner violence against women: Systematic review and meta-analyses of prospective-longitudinal studies. *American Journal of Public Health, 108,* e1–e11. doi: 10.2105/AJPH.2018.304428

Yang, G. S., Huesmann, L. R., & Bushman, B. J. (2014). Effects of playing a violent video game as male versus female avatar on subsequent aggression in male and female players. *Aggressive Behavior, 40,* 537–541. doi: 10.1002/ab.21551

Yang, L.-Q., Caughlin, D. E., Gazica, M. W., Truxillo, D. M., & Spector, P. E. (2014). Workplace mistreatment climate and potential employee and organizational outcomes: A meta-analytic review from the target's perspective. *Journal of Occupational Health Psychology, 19,* 315–335. doi: 10.1037/a0036905

Yao, M. Z., Mahood, C., & Linz, D. G. (2010). Sexual priming, gender stereotyping, and likelihood to sexually harass: Examining the cognitive effects of playing a sexually-explicit video game. *Sex Roles, 62,* 77–88. doi: 10.1007/s11199-009-9695-4

Yapp, E. J., & Quayle, E. (2018). A systematic review of the association between rape myth acceptance and male-on-female sexual violence. *Aggression and Violent Behavior, 41,* 1–19. doi: 10.1016/j.avb.2018.05.002

Yates, E., Barbaree, H. E., & Marshall, W. L. (1984). Anger and deviant sexual arousal. *Behavior Therapy, 15,* 287–294. doi: 10.1016/S0005-7894(84)80031-3

Yon, Y., Mikton, C., Gassoumis, Z. D., & Wilber, K. H. (2019). The prevalence of self-reported elder abuse among older women in community settings: A systematic review and meta-analysis. *Trauma, Violence & Abuse, 20,* 245–259. doi: 10.1177/1524838017697308

Yoon, J., & Knight, R. A. (2011). Sexual material perception in sexually coercive men: Disattending deficit and its covariates. *Sexual Abuse, 23,* 275–291. doi: 10.1177/1079063210391104

Yoon, M., Cho, S., & Yoon, D. (2019). Child maltreatment and depressive symptomatology among adolescents in out-of-home care: The mediating role of self-esteem. *Children and Youth Services Review, 101*, 255–260. doi: 10.1016/j.childyouth.2019.04.015

Young, K. (2019). *Sport, violence and society*. London: Routledge.

Younger, J. C., & Doob, A. N. (1978). Attribution and aggression: The misattribution of anger. *Journal of Research in Personality, 12*, 164–171. doi: 10.1016/0092-6566(78)90092-2

Yu, Z., Zhao, A., & Liu, A. (2017). Childhood maltreatment and depression: A meta-analysis. *Acta Psychologica Sinica, 49*, 40. doi: 10.3724/SP.J.1041.2017.00040

Yunus, R. M., Hairi, N. N., & Choo, W. Y. (2019). Consequences of elder abuse and neglect: A systematic review of observational studies. *Trauma, Violence & Abuse, 20*, 197–213. doi: 10.1177/1524838017692798

Zadro, L. (2011). Silent rage: When being ostracized leads to aggression. In J. P. Forgas, A. W. Kruglanski, & K. D. Williams (Eds.), *The psychology of social conflict and aggression* (pp. 201–216). New York: Psychology Press.

Zadro, L., Williams, K. D., & Richardson, R. (2004). How low can you go? Ostracism by a computer is sufficient to lower self-reported levels of belonging, control, self-esteem, and meaningful existence. *Journal of Experimental Social Psychology, 40*, 560–567. doi: 10.1016/j.jesp.2003.11.006

Zani, B., & Kirchler, E. (1991). When violence overshadows the spirit of sporting competition: Italian football fans and their clubs. *Journal of Community & Applied Social Psychology, 1*, 5–21. doi: 10.1002/casp.2450010103

Zhang, Q., Cao, Y., Gao, J., Yang, X., Rost, D. H., Cheng, G., ... Espelage, D. L. (2019). Effects of cartoon violence on aggressive thoughts and aggressive behaviors. *Aggressive Behavior, 45*, 489–497. doi: 10.1002/ab.21836

Zhang, T., & Chan, A. H. S. (2016). The association between driving anger and driving outcomes: A meta-analysis of evidence from the past twenty years. *Accident; Analysis and Prevention, 90*, 50–62. doi: 10.1016/j.aap.2016.02.009

Zillmann, D. (1979). *Hostility and aggression*. Hillsdale, NJ: Lawrence Erlbaum.

Zillmann, D. (1998). *Connections between sexuality and aggression* (2nd ed.). Mahwah, NJ: Lawrence Erlbaum.

Zillmann, D., Baron, R. A., & Tamborini, R. (1981). Social costs of smoking: Effects of tobacco smoke on hostile behavior. *Journal of Applied Social Psychology, 11*, 548–561. doi: 10.1111/j.1559-1816.1981.tb00842.x

Zillmann, D., & Bryant, J. (1974). Effect of residual excitation on the emotional response to provocation and delayed aggressive behavior. *Journal of Personality and Social Psychology, 30*, 782–791. doi: 10.1037/h0037541

Zimbardo, P. G. (1969). The human choice: Individuation, reason, and order versus deindividuation, impulse, and chaos. In W. T. Arnold & D.

Levine (Eds.), *Nebraska symposium on Motiviation* (Vol. 17, pp. 237–307). Lincoln, NB: University of Nebraska Press.

Zimbardo, P. G. (2006). On rethinking the psychology of tyranny: The BBC prison study. *British Journal of Social Psychology, 45*, 47–53. doi: 10.1348/014466605X81720

Zolotor, A. J., & Puzia, M. E. (2010). Bans against corporal punishment: A systematic review of the laws, changes in attitudes and behaviours. *Child Abuse Review, 19*, 229–247. doi: 10.1002/car.1131

Zounlome, N. O. O., & Wong, Y. J. (2019). Addressing male-targeted university sexual aggression: An experimental evaluation of a social norms approach. *Psychology of Men & Masculinities, 20*, 528–540. doi: 10.1037/men0000181

Zuckerman, M. (2007). *Sensation seeking and risky behavior*. Washington, DC: American Psychological Association.

Zuravin, S., McMillen, C., DePanfilis, D., & Risley-Curtiss, C. (1996). The intergenerational cycle of child maltreatment: Continuity versus discontinuity. *Journal of Interpersonal Violence, 11*, 315–334. doi: 10.1177/088626096011003001

INDEX